Leadership

Leadership

Understanding the Dynamics of Power and Influence in Organizations

Robert P. Vecchio
Editor

University of Notre Dame Press
Notre Dame, Indiana

Manufactured in the United States of America

Library of Congress Cataloging-in-Publication Data

Vecchio, Robert P.
    Leadership : understanding the dynamics of power and influence in
organizations / Robert P. Vecchio.
      p.   cm.
    Includes bibliographical references.
    ISBN 0-268-01316-0 (pbk. :alk. paper)
    1. Leadership. 2. Executive ability. I. Title.
HD57.7.V43   1997
658.4'092—dc21
                                          97-20806
                                           CIP

Contents

IV.   Models of Leadership

V.   Alternative Views of Leadership

VI.   Emerging Issues

Preface

At the present time, employees in both large and small organizations are experiencing tremendous personal and professional pressures which are a product of the changing context in which organizations operate today. Chief among these changes are growing globalization, down-sizing of organizations, the introduction of participative work-team structures, increasing diversity in the work force, and greater legal constraints. In order to cope with these forces, supervisors and administrators need a deeper understanding of how to marshal and manage human resources.

In response to these challenges, leadership training is frequently cited as an area warranting greater investment. Today, more and more universities are offering leadership classes—often as electives within colleges of business administration or departments of psychology and sociology. Leadership courses are also found in continuing education programs, such as those in executive development and management training. Despite growing recognition of this area within the curriculum, there is still a shortage of strong (i.e., academically grounded) college-level texts in this area. *Leadership*, an anthology of key writings by renowned contributors, is designed to meet the need for a text that encompasses the major theories in the field. Materials have been selected from journals and periodicals widely recognized for publishing in the areas of general management and leadership.

This book is aimed at upper-level undergraduate and graduate-level students in leadership and management, and would be appropriate for executive MBA courses. Portions of the text may also be useful for continuing education training programs of short duration (one to three days), with a reliance on assigned readings for participants. Departments of psychology, political science, sociology, public administration, nursing, safety, and education will also find it relevant. By going beyond a general introduction, *Leadership* fills a need at the university level for a text on leadership with an academic, critical focus which is rich with high quality writing and innovative, yet practical, material.

Leadership is divided into six sections. Part I provides an overview of the subject with readings that examine what leaders actually do, as well as the many myths surrounding the notion of leadership. Part II focuses on the fundamentals of leadership by taking a close look at the specific tactics people use to get their own way. These readings analyze the political games people play and the two-way nature of leader-subordinate influence. Part III considers problems that can arise from leadership gone wrong—when power and influence are abused. The major, formal models of leadership that have been offered over the years are reviewed in Part IV. These articles include newer variations of the leadership-trait model, as well as behavioral and situational views. Part V looks at contemporary views of leadership, emphasizing reliance on maturity of subordinates for success. This area includes leadership in the context of self-directed work teams, the notion of the leader as servant, and examples of leaders who are recognized for having empowered others or for providing moral leadership. The final section, Part VI, overviews the roles of societal and organizational cultures as they pertain to leadership. This section also considers experiences of women and minorities in managerial roles and the problems inherent in situations where extreme emotions are present in the workplace.

Each of the six sections opens with a selection of interesting quotes on leadership. These quotes are drawn from a variety of business, popular, historical, and academic sources. They are intended to raise issues that are of relevance to the theme of each section, and may help serve as discussion starters.

I am grateful to Jeff Gainey of the Notre Dame Press for his enthusiastic support of this text. His strong belief in the value of this book helped to make it a reality. I am, as ever, indebted to the support of my staff assistants, Donna J. Frahn and Jacqueline Marnocha, and my wife Betty for their help in the preparation of the final manuscript, and also to the support of Dean Carolyn Woo of the College of Business Administration.

Acknowledgments

The author and publisher are grateful to the following for permission to reprint:

The Free Press, publishers of Bass & Stogdill's *Handbook of Leadership*, for "Concepts of Leadership," (1990): 3–15.

Harvard Business School Press, publishers of *Harvard Business Review*, for "What Leaders Really Do," (May–June 1990): 103–105, 107, 111.

Harvard Business School Press, publishers of *Harvard Business Review*, for "The Manager's Job: Folklore and Fact," (July–August 1975): 49–61.

Academy of Management, publishers of *Academy of Management Review*, for "The Ambiguity of Leadership," (January 1977): 104–112.

Harcourt Brace & Company, publishers of *Organizational Behavior*, Third Edition, for "Power, Politics, and Influence," Chapter 9, (1995): 298–322.

Harvard Business School Press, publishers of *Harvard Business Review*, for "Managing Your Boss," (January–February 1980): 92–100.

Faulkner & Gray, Inc., publishers of *Journal of Business Strategies*, for "Effective Followership: Leadership Turned Upside Down," reprinted from vol. 4, 1(1987): 39–47.

American Psychological Association, publishers of *Journal of Applied Psychology*, for "Intraorganizational Influence Tactics: Explorations in Getting One's Way," reprinted from vol. 65, 4 (1980): 440–452.

Academy of Management, publishers of *Academy of Management Review*, for "A Social Influence Interpretation of Worker Motivation," reprinted from vol. 7, 2(1982): 177–186.

Sussex Publishers, Inc., publishers of *Psychology Today*, for "Groupthink," (November 1971): 43, 44, 46, 74–76.

JAI Press, Inc., publishers of *Leadership Quarterly*, for "Leadership and Expectations: Pygmalion Effects and Other Self-Fulfilling Prophecies in Organizations," reprinted from vol. 3, 4 (1992): 271–305.

Plenum Publishing Corporation, publishers of *Human Relations*, for "Narcissism and Leadership: An Object Relations Perspective," reprinted from vol. 38, 6 (1985): 583–601.

American Management Association, publishers of *Organizational Dynamics*, for "The Dark Side of Leadership," (1990): 44–55.

American Management Association, publishers of *Organizational Dynamics*, for "Leaders Who Self-Destruct: The Causes and Cures," (1989): 5–17.

Academy of Management, publishers of *Academy of Management Journal*, for "On the Folly of Rewarding A, While Hoping for B," reprinted from vol. 18, 4 (December 1975): 769–775, 779–783.

University of Washington, publishers of *Journal of Contemporary Business*, for "Path-Goal Theory of Leadership," reprinted from vol. 4, 3 (Autumn 1974): 81–97.

Indiana University, Graduate School of Business, publishers of *Business Horizons*, for "Are You *In* or *Out* with Your Boss?" (November–December 1986): 76–78.

American Management Association, publishers of *Organizational Dynamics*, for "Can Leaders Learn to Lead?" (1975): 17–28.

JAI Press, Inc., publishers of *Journal of Management*, for "Managerial Intelligence: Why IQ Isn't Enough," reprinted from vol. 23, Issue 3 (1997): 475–493.

American Management Association, publishers of *Organizational Dynamics*, for "From Transactional to Transformational Leadership: Learning to Share the Vision," (1990): 19–31.

American Psychological Association, publishers of *Journal of Applied Psychology*, for "Situational Leadership Theory: An Examination of a Prescriptive Theory," reprinted from vol. 72, (1987): 444–451.

JAI Press, Inc., publishers of *Leadership Quarterly*, for "The Contingency Model of Leadership Effectiveness: Its Levels of Analysis," reprinted from vol. 6, 2 (1995): 147–167.

American Management Association, publishers of *Organizational Dynamics*, for "Substitutes for Leadership: Effective Alternatives to Ineffective Leadership," (1990): 21–38.

Plenum Publishing Corporation, publishers of *Human Relations*, for "Leadership for Self-Managing Work Teams: A Typology and Integrative Model," reprinted from vol. 48, 7 (1995): 747–770.

American Management Association, publishers of *Organizational Dynamics*, for "SuperLeadership: Beyond the Myth of Heroic Leadership," (1991): 18–35.

Paulist Press, publishers of *Servant Leadership*, for "The Servant as Leader," (1977): 7–17.

The New Yorker for "A Man of Transactions," (December 1993): 83–88.

Academy of Management, publishers of *Academy of Management Executive*, for "Cultural Constraints in Management Theories," reprinted from vol. 7, 1 (1993): 81–93.

Pittsburgh State University, publishers of *Journal of Managerial Issues*, for "Organizational Culture and Strategic Leadership: Issues in the Management of Strategic Change," reprinted from vol. 5, 1 (Spring 1993): 53–70.

American Psychological Association, publishers of *American Psychologist*, for "Women and Minorities in Management," reprinted from vol. 45, 2 (1990): 200–208,

JAI Press, Inc., publishers of *Research in Personnel and Human Resources Management*, for "It's Not Easy Being Green: Jealousy and Envy in the Workplace," reprinted from vol. 13, (1995): 202–207, 213–216, 220–244.

PART I

Introduction and Overview

By working faithfully eight hours a day, you may eventually get to be a boss
and work twelve hours a day.

> Robert Frost

Management is the art of getting other people to do all the work.

> Anonymous

If I were truly lucky, I wouldn't have this job.

> Ronald Reagan

Boy, the things I do for England.

> Prince Charles (on sampling snake meat)

Leadership is always a fascinating topic. Although the subject goes
in and out of vogue, it never ceases to draw the attention of both academic and business audiences. Perhaps this fascination stems from our
admiration of the ability of others to reach their goals and to be influential, or out of our desire to be more effective in obtaining desired results
ourselves. Academic areas that consider leadership to be a topic within
their domain include business, politics, communication, sociology, and
psychology. This breadth of interest reveals the allure of leadership. In
this volume, we will examine a number of perennial questions. For
example, is leadership a reality or is it merely a social construction that
observers attribute to perceived and interpreted events? Does leadership
make a difference in a group's performance, or is the actual outcome more
powerfully determined by the interaction of members and the force of
contextual dynamics?

Part of our interest in leadership derives from our expectation that
people who are nominal heads (such as managers and administrators)

1

should display leadership. In addition, we are concerned with our own abilities to successfully project strong leadership qualities over and above mere administrative competence. Individual interest in social dominance predates recorded history; however, only in the past century has serious attention been devoted to the study of leadership as a social phenomenon.

The first section opens with Bernie Bass's consideration of the origins of leadership concepts, from the most primitive to contemporary definitions of the construct. Professor Bass looks at various theories of leadership, the questions which they raise and attempt to answer. Next, John Kotter of Harvard University examines the differences between management and leadership, and suggests that most organizations are overmanaged but underled. Henry Mintzberg, in a classic discussion of the manager's job, distinguishes between the folklore of a manager's presumed activities and the factual reality of a fragmented, reactive set of activities. Jeffrey Pfeffer of Stanford University then addresses the difficulty of defining and measuring leadership and the study of leaders as symbols.

Concepts of Leadership

Bernard M. Bass

Leadership is one of the world's oldest preoccupations. The understanding of leadership has figured strongly in the quest for knowledge. Purposeful stories have been told through the generations about leaders' competencies, ambitions, and shortcomings; leaders' rights and privileges; and the leaders' duties and obligations.

THE BEGINNINGS

Leaders as prophets, priests, chiefs, and kings served as symbols, representatives, and models for their people in the Old and New Testaments, in the Upanishads, in the Greek and Latin classics, and in the Icelandic sagas. In the *Iliad*, higher, transcendental goals are emphasized: "He serves me most, who serves his country best" (Book X, line 201). The *Odyssey* advises leaders to maintain their social distance: "The leader, mingling with the vulgar host, is in the common mass of matter lost" (Book III, line 297). The subject of leadership was not limited to the classics of Western literature. It was of as much interest to Asoka and Confucius as to Plato and Aristotle.

Myths and legends about great leaders were important in the development of civilized societies. Stories about the exploits of individual heroes (and occasionally heroines) are central to the Babylonian *Gilgamesh, Beowolf*, the *Chanson de Roland*, the Icelandic sagas, and the Ramayana (now they would be called cases). All societies have created myths to provide plausible and acceptable explanations for the dominance of their leaders and the submission of their subordinates (Paige, 1977). The greater the socioeconomic injustice in the society, the more distorted the realities of leadership—its powers, morality and effectiveness—in the mythology.

The study of leadership rivals in age the emergence of civilization, which shaped its leaders as much as it was shaped by them. From its infancy, the study of history has been the study of leaders—what they did and why they did it. Over the centuries, the effort to formulate principles

3

of leadership spread from the study of history and the philosophy associated with it to all the developing social sciences. In modern psycho-history, there is still a search for generalizations about leadership, built on the in-depth analysis of the development, motivation, and competencies of world leaders, living and dead.

In 2300 B.C. in the Instruction of Ptahhotep, three qualities were attributed to the Pharoah. "Authoritative utterness is in thy mouth, perception is in thy heart, and thy tongue is the shrine of justice" (Lichtheim, 1973). The Chinese classics, written as early as the sixth century B.C., are filled with hortatory advice to the country's leaders about their responsibilities to the people. Confucius urged leaders to set a moral example and to manipulate rewards and punishments for teaching what was right and good. Taoism emphasized the need for the leader to work himself out of his job by making the people believe that successes were due to their efforts.

Greek concepts of leadership were exemplified by the heroes in Homer's *Iliad*. Ajax symbolized inspirational leadership and law and order. Other qualities that the Greeks admired and thought were needed (and sometimes wanting) in heroic leaders were (1) justice and judgment (Agamemnon), (2) wisdom and counsel (Nestor), (3) shrewdness and cunning (Odysseus), and (4) valor and activism (Achilles) (see Sarachek, 1968). (Shrewdness and cunning are not regarded as highly in contemporary society as they once were.) Later, Greek philosophers, such as Plato in the *Republic*, looked at the requirements for the ideal leader of the ideal state (the philosopher king). The leader was to be the most important element of good government, educated to rule with order and reason. In *Politics*, Aristotle was disturbed by the lack of virtue among those who wanted to be leaders. He pointed to the need to educate youths for such leadership. Plutarch, although he was involved with prosocial ideals about leadership, compared the traits and behavior of actual Greek and Roman leaders to support his point of view in *The Parallel Lives* (Kellerman, 1987).

A scholarly highlight of the Renaissance was Machiavelli's (1513/1962) *The Prince*. Machiavelli's thesis that "there is nothing more difficult to take in hand, more perilous to conduct, or more uncertain in its success, than to take the lead in the introduction of a new order of things" is still a germane description of the risks of leadership and the resistance to it. Machiavelli was the ultimate pragmatist. He believed that leaders needed steadiness, firmness, and concern for the maintenance of authority, power, and order in government. It was best if these objectives could be accomplished by gaining the esteem of the populace, but if they could not, then craft, deceit, threat, treachery, and violence were required (Kellerman, 1987). Machiavelli is still widely quoted as a guide to an effective leadership of sorts, which was the basis for a modern line of investigation with the Mach scale (Christie & Geis, 1970). A 1987 survey of 117 college presidents reported that they still found *The Prince* highly relevant.

In the same way, a fundamental principle at West Point today can be traced back to Hegel's (1830/1971) *Philosophy of Mind* which argued that by first serving as a follower, a leader subsequently can best understand his followers. Hegel thought that this understanding is a paramount requirement for effective leadership.

Universality

Leadership is a universal phenomenon in humans and in many species of animals.

Animal Origins

Leadership predates the emergence of humankind. Allee (1945, 1949, 1951) maintained that all vertebrates that live in groups exhibit social organization and leadership. High-ranking males feed more freely than do other members of the group and tend to have more ready access to females. In some cases, high status involves guard duty and protection of the herd.

Pecking Order

Individual animals dominate or submit their local spaces to others in the well-known pecking order. In one of the early experiments on animal social relations, Murchison (1935) placed roosters at opposite ends of a narrow runway and measured the distance that each advanced toward the other. As a result of successive pairings, he was able to determine a strict hierarchy of dominance. Rooster A invariably dominated all the remaining subjects. At the bottom of the hierarchy was the rooster who yielded to all the others.

Douglis (1948) removed hens from their home flocks and placed them in other flocks for short periods. The hen's pecking order in each flock was observed. It was found that a hen can become an assimilated member in at least five different flocks and have a different status in each. The hen can recognize and react to the status or esteem of as many as 27 individuals. Highly dominant hens become assimilated within three days, but hens that were not dominant required three to six weeks to become assimilated. Once established, a hierarchy tended to maintain itself.

Dominance Effects in Primates

Miller and Murphy (1956) and Warren and Maroney (1969) tested pairs of monkeys who were competing for food in an area and observed strict dominance hierarchies. Subordinate animals were more successful in obtaining low-preference, rather than middle- or high-preference, foods. Bernstein (1964) noted that when the dominant male was removed from a group of monkeys, the activities of other males increased. After the dominant male returned, he resumed his dominant status and the activities of other males decreased.

Carpenter (1963) studied societies of monkeys and apes. His general findings suggested that the leader tended to control the group's movement in its search for food and shelter, regulate intragroup status, defend the group, and maintain its integrity in its contacts with other organized groupings. When the dominant male was removed from the group, the territory covered by the group was markedly reduced. Thus, the leader enlarged the freedom of the group's movement. But the dominant male tended to be avoided by low-ranking males. In some bands, the one or two males that were next in rank stood by the leader to ward off intruders and were permitted to groom him on occasion.

Again, Mason (1964) reported that leaders among groups of monkeys and apes appeared to have the primary function of initiating progressions and determining the line of march. The dominant males quelled intragroup fights, protected the females and young, were attractive to all members, were sought out by females, and influenced the size of the group's territorial range.

Zajonc (1969) interpreted the fact that fighting disappears almost entirely in primate groups after a hierarchy of dominance has been established as evidence that such groups develop norms. The norms are learned by group members, are stable but can be changed, and are complied with by the majority of members. Koford (1963) observed that the relative dominance of two bands of monkeys that meet at an eating place is usually determined by the relative dominance of the leaders of the bands. Once the dominance of a band has been established, it is observed by the other group, even in the absence of the other leader. Experimentation and observation in natural settings suggest that groups of animals develop strongly differentiated status hierarchies that their members recognize and observe. In primate groups, leaders obtain privileges that tend to bolster their dominance. Their presence is an advantage to the group in gaining possession of a desired territory and in expanding the area of free movement for the group. However, whether these findings and similar results reported for packs of wolves and hyenas, elephant matriarchies, bands of gorillas, and pods of whales are relevant to understanding the human condition remains controversial.

Humans

Parenthood, a condition that unarguably cuts across cultural lines, makes for ready-made patterns of leadership. Nevertheless, the patterns of behavior that are regarded as acceptable in leaders differ from time to time and from one culture to another. Citing various anthropological reports on primitive groups in Australia, Fiji, New Guinea, the Congo, and elsewhere, H. L. Smith and Krueger (1933) concluded that leadership occurs among all people, regardless of culture, be they isolated Indian villagers, nomads of the Eurasian steppes, or Polynesian fisherfolk. Lewis (1974) concluded, from a more recent anthropological review, that even when a society does not have institutionalized chiefs, rules, or elected officials, there are always leaders who initiate action and play central roles in the group's decision making. No societies are known that do not have leadership in some aspects of their social life, although many may lack a single overall leader to make and enforce decisions.

Leaders, such as Abraham, Moses, David, Solomon, and the Macabees, were singled out in the Old Testament for a detailed exposition of their behavior and relations with God and their people. God was the supreme leader of his Chosen People who clarified, instructed, and directed what was to be done through the words of his Prophets and arranged for rewards for compliance and punishment for disobedience to the laws and rules He had handed down to Moses. In Islam, the ideal caliphate leadership was based on religious law (Rabi, 1967).

In *The Parallel Lives*, Plutarch (1932), in about A.D. 100, tried to show the similarities between 50 Greek and Roman leaders. Latin authors, such as Caesar, Cicero, and Seneca to name just a few, wrote extensively on the subject of leadership and administration. Their influence was considerable on the medieval and Renaissance periods, which looked back to the classics for guidance. Their influence on Thomas Jefferson and James Madison has an impact on the design of the U.S. government as we know it, as did such Renaissance scholars as Montesquieu in his *The Spirit of Laws* (1748).

Military writings about leadership stretch from the Chinese classics to the present. Napoleon listed 115 qualities that are essentials for a military leader. Meyer (1980) called for a renaissance in the concern for military leadership, in contrast to the focus on the "over-management" of logistics. Resources must be managed by the military leader but are no substitute for effective leadership.

The Importance of Leaders and Leadership

Napoleon expressed his feelings about the importance of leadership in his quip that he would rather have an army of rabbits led by a lion than an army of lions led by a rabbit. Surveys of job satisfaction from the 1920s onward illustrated the importance of leadership.[1] They uniformly reported that employees' favorable attitudes toward their supervisors contributed to the employees' satisfaction. In turn, employees' favorable attitudes toward their supervisors were usually found to be related to the productivity of the work group (see, for example, Lawshe & Nagle, 1953). Since then, countless surveys can be cited to support the contention that leaders make a difference in their subordinates' satisfaction and performance. Leaders also can make the difference in whether their organizations succeed or fail.

The usual efforts to estimate the number of leaders in the United States use census data on proprietors and officials. But Gardner (1988) noted that although owners, managers, and officials are in the posi-

[1] Bergen (1939), Houser (1927), Kornhauser and Sharp (1932), and Viteles (1953).

tion to do so, they do not necessarily act as leaders. Cleveland (1985) estimated the number of opinion leaders in the United States and how they grew in number between 1955 and 1985. In 1955, he estimated that there were 555,000 opinion leaders, whereas in 1971, he guessed that at least 1 million Americans could be classified as opinion leaders. He considered seven out of ten public executives to be opinion leaders— policymakers in public, philanthropic, voluntary, and large-scale "private" enterprises—in 1971. By 1985 he estimated the number to have multiplied to 1 out of every 200 Americans.

> As Cleveland (1985, p. 4) stated: There are some 83,000 government units in the United States, and about 175,000 corporations each doing more than $1 million worth of business a year. The galloping rate of growth of complexity means that a growth curve of the requirement for leaders (if anyone were clever enough to construct such an index) would show a steeper climb than any other growth rate in our political economy.

Is Leadership a Figment of the Imagination?

Some critics argue that all the effects of leadership are in the eyes of their beholders. Followers attribute effects that are due to historical, economic, or social forces to leadership, as in romantic fiction (Meindl & Ehrlich, 1987; Meindl, Ehrlich, & Dukerich, 1985). Other critics, such as Pandey (1976), regard leadership as a useless concept for understanding social influence. For Calder (1977), the objective contributions of the "leader" to outcomes may be more interesting than true. The extreme position taken by some attribution theorists is that organizational outcomes are determined primarily by other factors, but leaders are credited with what happened after the fact.

Organizational leaders who are perceived to be exerting leadership on organizational performance are merely the subjects of misperceptions, some critics contend. That is, organizational outcomes are objectively determined by environmental and organizational factors in which leadership, at best, can play only a minor role. For instance, M. C. Brown (1982, p. 1) concluded that "once other factors influencing effectiveness are accounted for, it is likely that leadership will have little bearing on organizational performance."

Pfeffer (1977) took a similar but not as extreme position: Leadership is a sense-making heuristic to account for organizational performance and is important primarily for its symbolic role in organizations. Leaders are selected or self-selected to fulfil the fate of the organization and are highly constrained by organization and external factors. Therefore, they can have only limited impact on organizational outcomes compared to external factors. Leaders are able only to react to contingencies, to facilitate the adjustment of the organization in its context, and to alter that environment to some limited extent. Also they have no control over many factors that affect organizational performance and they typically have unilateral control over few resources.

Despite these constraints, management and leadership seem to have a substantial effect on some organizational outcomes. Thus, when Lieberson and O'Connor (1972) examined the effects of top management on the success of 167 firms over a 20-year period, they found that the effects depended on which outcomes were considered. Managers had the greatest effect on profit margins but the least effect on sales; they also were of less consequence in capital-intensive industries. In the same way, Salancik and Pfeffer (1977) showed that the mayors of 30 U.S. cities had considerable influence only on those budgetary issues, such as libraries and parks, that were not in the domain of important special-interest groups, such as the police, fire fighters, and highway maintenance personnel. In all, Pfeffer concluded that since people want to achieve the feeling that they are in control of their environment, they find it useful to attribute outcomes of their group and organizational performance to leaders, rather than to the complex internal and external environmental forces that actually are most important. Meindl and Ehrlich (1987) showed that if performance outcomes of firms were attributed to the leadership of the top management, rather than to the employees, market conditions, or the government, the judges gave better evaluations of the outcomes. Meindl and Ehrlich attributed this finding to the judges' assumption that leaders have a reliable and potent impact on outcomes.

Even when the true causes of outcomes were logically not determinable, Meindl, Ehrlich, and Dukerich (1985) showed that there was a tendency to view leadership as the likely cause of the outcomes. This study and the one by Meindl and Ehrich (1987) were thought to demonstrate that leadership is more of a romantic notion than a phenomenon that truly affects group and organizational outcomes.

Then there is evidence that would-be followers, subordinates, and groups of employees are so constrained by technology, rules, job requirements, and organizational policies that there is little discretionary room for a superior or leader to make much of a difference in how things get done (Katz & Kahn, 1966). Furthermore, subordinates may have much more effect on the behavior of their superiors than vice versa (Goodstadt & Kipnis, 1970).

Miner (1975, p. 200) was ready to abandon the concept of leadership, stating that "the concept of leadership itself has outlived its usefulness. Hence, I suggest that we abandon leadership in favor of some other, more fruitful way of cutting up the theoretical pie." In 1982, Miner recanted this statement but still maintained that the concept has limited usefulness because so much of the empirical research has been on emergent leadership in small groups, rather than within more complex organizations. For Miner, the fragile, distressed leadership that arises in the small, temporary group to develop, maintain, and enforce the norms of the group may have little relevance for leadership in the impersonal "task system" of the traditional organization.

Leaders Do Make a Difference

Despite the skepticism about the reality and importance of leadership, all social and political movements require leaders to begin them. As Tucker (1981, p. 87) put it, "in the beginning is the leadership act. A 'leaderless movement' is naturally out of the question." This does not mean that formal, institutionalized leadership is required. In fact, no leader in an institutional form appeared in the numerous peasant revolts from the sixteenth to nineteenth centuries in Southern Germany. The same was true for journeymen's strikes during the eighteenth century. Leadership remained informal and egalitarian. Only in the middle of the nineteenth century did definite leaders, such as Ferdinand Lasalle, emerge. Lasalle placed himself at the head of the German workers' movement and worked out its explicit ideology, along with the myth that he founded the movement (Groh, 1986). This behavior is consistent with most cases of institutional development: Leaders determine the direction they will take. The historical records of the early British Royal Society of the seventeenth century illustrate that its secretaries were responsible for who joined the society and what kinds of science were sponsored (Mulligan & Mulligan, 1981).

Indeed, leadership is often regarded as the single most critical factor in the success or failure of institutions. For instance, T. H. Allen (1981) argued that the school principal's leadership is the most important factor in determining a school's climate and the students' success. Sylvia and Hutchison (1985) concluded that the motivation of 167 Oklahoma teachers depended considerably on their perceptions of the quality of their relationships with their superiors. And Smith, Carson, and Alexander (1984) found that among the 50 Methodist ministers they studied, some were more effective leaders than were others. The effectiveness of these ministers was evidenced by the differential impact that their ministries had on church attendance, membership, property values, and contributions to the church.

In the business and industrial sector, Maccoby (1979, p. 313) concluded, from his observations of the manager as a game-playing politician, that the need of firms to survive and prosper in a world of increasing competition, of technological advances, of changing governmental regulations, of changing worker attitudes, requires "a higher level of leadership than ever before." When an organization must be changed to reflect changes in technology, the environment, and the completion of programs, its leadership is critical in orchestrating the process (Burke, Richley, & DeAngelis, 1985). Mintzberg and Waters (1982) examined the evolution of a retail firm over a 60-year period and found that a senior executive could successfully reorient the firm by intervening to change previous strategies and organizational structures. In the same way, Day and Lord (1986) noted that when confounding errors are controlled in studies of the effects of executive succession, differences in executive leaders can explain as much as 45 percent of their organizations' performance. Agreeing with Chandler (1962), they stated that historical analyses of changes of leadership over significant periods have shown that leadership has a profound influence on an organization. Concurrent correlational analyses of a sample of executives and their organizations at the same point in time reach similar conclusions, although the effects are not as strong.

In a review of experiments in the United States on the productivity of workers between 1971 and 1981, Katzell and Guzzo (1983) concluded that supervisory methods seemed particularly effective in increasing output. In Sweden, Westerlund (1952) observed that the high-quality performance of supervisors improved the attitudes and performance of telephone operators. Also in Sweden, Ekvall and Arvonen (1984) found that leadership styles accounted for 65 percent of the variance in organizational climate in the 25 units they studied. Virany and Tushman (1986) stated that the senior managers of better-performing minicomputer firms were systematically different from those of firms that performed poorly. The senior management in the better firms had had previous experience in the electronic industry and was more likely to include the founder of the firm who still served as chief executive officer. Although most attention has been paid to industrial leaders as developers and builders, Hansen (1974) pointed out that the success with which a firm, such as the Ford Motor Company, closed a plant without much human dislocation depended on effective leadership.

Leadership has been considered a critical factor in military successes since records have been kept; that is, better-led forces repeatedly have been victorious over poorly led forces. Thus, not unexpectedly, morale and cohesion among Israeli and U.S. enlisted soldiers correlated with measures of the soldiers' confidence in their company, division, and battalion commanders (Gal & Manning, 1987).

Personnel of the Mississippi Cooperative Extension reported that they felt less job stress if they saw their supervisors displaying more leadership in structuring the work to be done and showing concern for the subordinates' needs (Graham, 1982). In a study of 204 innovations in state programs, Cheek (1987) found that the governors came up with 55 percent of the innovations and the agencies with only 36 percent.

Studies by Tucker (1981), Hargrove and Nelson (1984), and Hargrove (1987) concluded that the style and performance of a U.S. president makes a big difference in what happens to legislation, policy, and programs. Successful presidents are more sensitive to the inherent politics of policy-making. They define and publicize the policy dilemmas facing the country and earn widespread public and Congressional support for their positions. They construct their policy agendas with the felt needs of the country in mind and create political support for their agendas; they also realize that timing is important (Tucker, 1981). But like Jimmy Carter, they can fail if they push for what they deem to be right but what is not politically feasible and if they favor comprehensive integrated solutions rather than incremental steps (Hargrove, 1987). Presidents can make decisions that are not implemented because they or their assistants do not follow them up. For example, as part of the agreement to resolve the Cuban missile crisis, President Kennedy ordered the removal of U.S. missiles from Turkey on the border of the Soviet Union. Six months later, he was astonished to learn that the missiles were still in place (Manchester, 1988). Although presidents spend relatively little time trying to make major reorientations in policy, they have an important impact on the smaller substantive decisions that affect the larger overall strategies (Neustadt, 1980). History may be drastically altered by a sudden change in presidents. Before leaving Washington, D.C., for his fateful trip to Texas in November 1963, Kennedy signed the first order for a phased withdrawal from Vietnam. On assuming office after Kennedy's assassination, Lyndon Johnson rescinded the order. The war continued for another decade.

According to Richard Nixon's "Silent Majority" speech in 1969, presidents may have to take an unpopular stand, but when they do, they can strengthen acceptance by explaining their reasons, soliciting support, and winning approval (Safire, 1975). Presidents also provide symbolic support for the development of norms, values, and beliefs that contribute to subsequent national and organizational development (Sayles, 1979). As Gardner (1988) noted, for a society to function, its people must share beliefs and values regarding the standards of acceptable behavior. Leaders can revitalize those shared beliefs and help keep the values fresh. "They have a role in creating the state of mind that is the society" (Gardner, 1988, p. 18). They conceive and articulate goals that move people from their own interests to unite for higher ends.

Often, the effects of leadership are indirect. For example, Katzell (1987) showed through a path analysis that although supervisors' direct influence on their subordinates was modest, they exerted indirect influence and increased the employees' morale by providing rewards, relating rewards to performance, and treating employees equitably; the increased morale, in turn, improved the employees' performance.

Jongbloed and Frost (1985) modified Pfeffer's (1977) reasoning to argue that leaders still have an important general role to play. What leaders really manage in organizations are the employees' interpretations or understanding of what goes on in the organizations. The leaders manage meanings and, therefore, exert a strong impact on organizational outcomes. Jongbloed and Frost showed how the laboratory director in one Canadian hospital, compared to another in a second hospital with the same formal assignments and the same absence of control of issues, successfully lobbied for the importance of pathology and convinced the hospital administrators to allocate more funds for operations and budget than were allocated in the second hospital.

The importance of leadership is attested by academic and lay interest in leadership as a subject for development, training, and education (Campbell, 1977).[2] Although U.S. college presidents believe that our educational institutions are reluctant to incorporate leadership education into their curricula (Cronin, 1984), the college landscape is not bleak. Gregory's (1986) survey of all known U.S. degree-granting institutions of higher learning uncovered 53 that offered an academic course on leadership, 70 that made it possible to major or concentrate in the subject, 181 that incorporated the study of leadership in an academic course or a student-affairs program, and 81 that offered the subject in continuing education or professional programs.[3]

Leadership as a Subject of Inquiry

The importance of leadership is also demonstrated by its place in social science research. According to Mitchell (1979) and DeMeuse (1986), leadership has been one of the frequent subjects of empirical research, concentrating on the antecedents of leaders' behavior and the factors that contribute to its effectiveness. Leadership is a featured topic in almost every textbook on organizational behavior. The scholarly books on leadership number in the hundreds, and articles, reports, and essays number in the thousands.

Several different schools of thought have prevailed simultaneously since leadership first was studied. The early sociological theorists

[2] Recognition of the importance to the nation of leadership and its development for all types of organizations is witnessed by the Alliance for Leadership Development, which includes the following members: American Leadership Forum of Houston; Association of American Colleges of Washington, D.C.; Association of Governing Boards of Universities and Colleges; Center for Creative Leadership of Greensboro, N.C.; Coro Foundation of St. Louis; International Leadership Center of Dallas; National Association of Secondary School Principals of Reston, Va.; and the National Executive Service Corps of New York. The Alliance's programs include the promotion of research on and teaching of leadership, related conferences and publications, a clearinghouse of information on leadership programs at universities and secondary schools, leadership development programs in the community, and development programs for corporate executives.

[3] Details about these can be found in Clark, Freeman, and Britt (1987).

tended to explain leadership in terms of either the person or the environment. Later researchers tended to view leadership as an aspect of role differentiation or as an outgrowth of social interaction processes. Recently, the naïve theories of leadership we hold have been considered most important in explaining what is going on. But this is as it should be. Theory and empirical research should move forward together, each stimulating, supporting, and modifying the other. Neither can stand alone. An elegant theory without prospects of elegant data gathering makes for a sketchy theory. Early in a line of investigation, crude data and theory may be useful. Later, as understanding develops and practice improves, more stringent standards are required (Bass, 1974).

Assumptions

An almost insurmountable problem is the question of the extent to which we pour old wine into new bottles when proposing "new" theories. For instance, Julius Caesar's descriptions of his leadership style in the Gallic Wars in the first century B.C. are clear, succinct endorsements of the need for what Blake and Mouton (1964) conceived as "9-9" style—a style that Fleishman (1953) described in terms of high initiation and consideration and that in the year 2500 some new theorist will give a new name. When does a field advance? Are we beyond Caesar's understanding of how to lead infantry shock troops?

THE MEANING OF LEADERSHIP

The word leadership is a sophisticated, modern concept. In earlier times, words meaning "head of state," "military commander," "princeps," "proconsul," "chief," or "king" were common in most societies; these words differentiated the ruler from other members of society. A preoccupation with leadership, as opposed to headship based on inheritance, usurpation, or appointment, occurred predominantly in countries with an Anglo-Saxon heritage. Although the *Oxford English Dictionary* (1933) noted the appearance of the word "leader" in the English language as early as the year 1300, the word "leadership" did not appear until the first half of the nineteenth century in writings about the political influence and control of British Parliament. And the word did not appear in the most other modern languages until recent times.

Defining Leadership

There are almost as many different definitions of leadership as there are persons who have attempted to define the concept.[4] Moreover, as Pfeffer (1977) noted, many of the definitions are ambiguous. Furthermore, the distinction between leadership and other social-influence processes is often blurred (Bavelas, 1960; Hollander & Julian, 1969). The many dimensions into which leadership has been cast and their overlapping meanings have added to the confusion. Therefore, the meaning of leadership may depend on the kind of institution in which it is found (Spitzberg, 1986). Nevertheless, there is sufficient similarity among definitions to permit a rough scheme of classification. Leadership has been conceived as the focus of group processes, as a matter of personality, as a matter of inducing compliance, as the exercise of influence, as particular behaviors, as a form of persuasion, as a power relation, as an instrument to achieve goals, as an effect of interaction, as a differentiated role, as initiation of structure, and as many combinations of these definitions.

WORKS CITED

Allee, W. C. 1945. Social biology of subhuman groups. *Sociometry*, 8, 21–29.

———. 1951. *Cooperation among animals, with human implications*. New York: Schuman.

———. Emerson, A. E., Park, O., Park, T., & Schmidt, K. P. 1949. *Principles of animal ecology*. Philadelphia: Saunders.

Allen, T. H. 1981. Situational management roles: A conceptual model. *Dissertation Abstracts International*, 42 (2A) 465.

Allport, F. H. 1924. *Social psychology*. Boston: Hougton Mifflin.

Babikan, K. 1981. The leader-entrepreneur in the public sector. In F. I. Khuri, ed., *Leadership and Development in Arab Society*. Beirut: American University of Beirut, Center for Arab and Middle East Studies.

Bass, B. M. 1960. *Leadership, psychology, and organizational behavior*. New York: Harper.

———. 1974. The substance and the shadow. *American Psychologist*, 29, 870–886.

Bavelas, A. 1960. Leadership: Man and function. *Administrative Science Quarterly*, 4, 491–498.

---

[4] Different definitions and conceptions of leadership have been reviewed briefly by Morris and Seeman (1950), Shartle (1951a, 1951b, 1956), L. F. Carter (1953), C. A. Gibb (1954, 1969), Bass (1960), Stogdill (1975), and Schriesheim and Kerr (1977).

Bennis, W. G. 1970. *American bureaucracy*. Chicago: Aldine.

Bernard, L. L. 1926. *An introduction to social psychology*. New York: Holt.

———. 1927. Leadership and propaganda. In J. Davis & H. E. Barnes, *An introduction to sociology*. New York: Heath.

Bernstein, I. S. 1964. Group social patterns as influenced by removal and later reintroduction of the dominant male Rhesus. *Psychological Reports*, 14, 3–10.

Bingham, W. V. 1927. Leadership. In H. C. Metcalf, *The psychological foundations of management*. New York: Shaw.

Blackmar, F. W. 1911. Leadership in reform. *American Journal of Sociology*, 16, 626–644.

Blake, R. R., Mouton, J. S., Barnes, L. B., & Greiner, L. E. 1964. Breakthrough in organization development. *Harvard Business Review*, 42, 133–155.

Bowden, A. O. 1926. A study of the personality of student leaders in the United States. *Journal of Abnormal and Social Psychology*, 21, 149–160.

Brown, J. F. 1936. *Psychology and the social order*. New York: McGraw-Hill.

Brown, M. C. 1982. Administrative succession and organizational performance: The succession effect. *Administrative Science Quarterly*, 27, 1–16.

Bundel, C. M. 1930. Is leadership losing its importance? *Infantry Journal*, 36, 339–349.

Burke, W., Richley, E. A., & DeAngelis, L. 1985. Changing leadership and planning processes at the Lewis Research Center, National Aeronautics and Space Administration. *Human Resource Management*, 24(1), 81–90.

Burns, J. M. 1978. *Leadership*. New York: Harper & Row.

Calder, B. J. 1977. An attribution theory of leadership. In B. M. Staw and G. R. Salancik, eds., *New directions in organizational behavior*. Chicago: St. Clair.

Campbell, J. P. 1977. The cutting edge of leadership: An overview. In J. G. Hunt and L. L. Larson, eds. *Leadership: The cutting edge*. Carbondale: Southern Illinois University Press.

Carpenter, C. R. 1963. Societies of monkeys and apes. In C. H. Southwich, ed., *Primate social behavior*. Princeton, N.J.: Van Nostrand.

Carter, L. F. 1953. Leadership and small group behavior. In M. Sherif & M. O. Wilson, eds., *Group relations at the crossroads*. New York: Harper.

Cartwright, D. 1965. Influence, leadership, control. In J. G. March, ed., *Handbook of organizations*. Chicago: Rand McNally.

Chandler, A. D., Jr. 1962. Strategy and structure: *Chapters in the history of the industrial enterprises*. Cambridge, Mass.: M.I.T. Press.

Chapin, F. S. 1924b. Leadership and group activity. *Journal of Applied Sociology*, 8, 141–145.

Cheek, S. K. 1987. *Recent state initiatives: The governor as policy leader: The governor as chief administrator*. Paper, Academy of Management, New Orleans.

Christie, R., & Geis, F. L. 1970. *Studies in Machiavellianism*. New York: Academic Press.

Clark, M. B., Freeman, F. H., & Britt, S. K. 1987. *Leadership education '87: A source book*. Greensboro, N.C.: Center for Creative Leadership.

Cleeton, G. U., & Mason, C. W. 1934. *Executive ability-its discovery and development*. Yellow Springs, Ohio: Antioch Press.

Cleveland, H. 1985. *The knowledge executive: Leadership in an information society*. New York: Dutton.

Cooley, C. H. 1902. *Human nature and the social order*. New York: Scribners.

Copeland, N. 1942. *Psychology and the soldier*. Harrisburg, Pa.: Military Service Publishing.

Cronin, T. E. 1984. Thinking and learning about leadership. *Presidential Studies Quarterly*, 14(1), 22–34.

Day, D. V., & Lord, R. G. 1986. Executive leadership and organizational performance: Suggestions for a new theory and methodology. Paper, Academy of Management, Chicago. Also 1988. *Journal of Management*, 14, 453–464.

DeMeuse, K. P. 1986. A compendium of frequently used measures in industrial/organizational psychology. *The Industrial-Organizational Psychologist*, 23(2), 53–59.

Douglis, M. B. 1948. Social factors influencing the hierarchies of small flocks of the domestic hen; Interactions between resident and part-time members of organized flocks. *Physiological Zoology*, 21, 147–182.

Dyer, W. G., & Dyer, J. H. 1984. The M*A*S*H generation: Implications for future organizational values. *Organizational Dynamics*, 13(1), 66–79.

Ekvall, G., & Arvonen, J. 1984. *Leadership styles and organizational climate for creativity: Some findings in one company* (Report 1). Stockholm: Ferreted.

Ferris, G. O., & Rowland, K. M. 1981. Leadership, job perceptions, and influence: A conceptual integration. *Human Relations*, 34, 1069–1077.

Fiedler, F. E. 1967. *A theory of leadership effectiveness*. New York: McGraw-Hill.

Fleishman, E. A. 1953. The measurement of leadership attitudes in industry. *Journal of Applied Psychology*. 37, 153–158.

French, J. R. P. 1956. A formal theory of social power. *Psychological Review*, 63, 181–194.

Gal, R., & Manning, F. J. 1987. Morale and its components: A cross national comparison. *Journal of Applied Social Psychology*, 17, 369–391.

Gardner, J. W. 1988. *The task of motivating* (Leadership Paper No. 9). Washington, D.C.: Independent Sector.

Gerth, H., & Mills, C. W. 1953. *Character and social structure*. New York: Harcourt, Brace.

Gibb, J. R. 1954. *Factors producing defensive behavior within groups.* (Annual Tech. Report). Boulder: University of Colorado, Human Relations Lab.

———. 1969. Leadership. In G. Lindzey & E. Aronson, eds., *The handbook of social psychology,* 2d ed., vol. 4. Reading, Mass.: Addison-Wesley.

Graham, F. C. 1982. Job stress in Mississippi cooperative extension services county personnel as related to age, gender, district, tenure, position and perceived leadership behavior of immediate supervisors. *Dissertation Abstracts International*, 43(7A), 2180.

Goodstadt, B. E., & Kipnis, D. 1970. Situational influences on the use of power. *Journal of Applied Psychology*, 54, 201–207.

Gregory, R. A. 1986. *Leadership education in institutions of higher education: An assessment.* Greensboro, N.C.: Center for Creative Leadership.

Groh, D. 1986. The dilemma of unwanted leadership in social movements: The German example before 1914. G.F. Graumann & S. Moscovici, eds., *Changing conception of leadership.* New York: Springer-Verlag.

Haiman, F. S. 1951. Group leadership and democratic action. Boston: Hougton Mifflin.

Hansen, P. 1974. *Sex differences in supervision.* Paper, American Psychological Association, New Orleans.

Hargrove, E. C. 1987. Jimmy Carter as President. Paper, Conference on the Presidency, Princeton University, Princeton, N.J.

———, & Nelson, M. 1984. *Presidents, politics, and policy.* Baltimore: John Hopkins University Press.

Hemphill, J. K. 1949. The leader and his group. *Journal of Educational Research,* 28, 225–229, 245–246.

Hollander, E. P., & Julian, J. W. 1969. Contemporary trends in the analysis of leadership processes. *Psychological Bulletin,* 71, 387–397.

Iliad of Homer. 1720/1943. A. Pope, trans. New York: Heritage Press.

Jacobs, T. O., & Jaques, E. 1987. Leadership in complex systems. In J. Zeidner, ed., *Human productivity enhancement.* New York: Praeger.

Janda, K. F. 1960. Towards the explication of the concept of leadership in terms of the concept of power. *Human Relations,* 13, 345–363.

Jongbloed, L., & Frost, P. J. 1985. Pfeffer's model of management: An expansion and modification. *Journal of Management,* 11, 97–110.

Katz, D., & Kahn, R. L. 1966, 1978. *The social psychology of organizations.* New York: Wiley.

Katzell, R. 1987. *How leadership works.* Paper, Conference on Military Leadership: Traditions and Future Trends, United States Naval Academy, Annapolis, Md.

Katzell, R. A., & Guzzo, R. A. 1983. Psychological approaches to productivity improvement. *American Psychologist,* 38, 468–472.

Kellerman, B. 1987. *The politics of leadership in America: Implications for higher education in the late 20th century.* Paper, Invitational Interdisciplinary Colloquium on Leadership in Higher Education, National Center for Post-secondary Governance and Finance, Teachers College, Columbia University, New York.

Koford, C. B. 1963. Group relations in an island colony of Rhesus monkeys. In C. H. Southwick, ed., *Primate social behavior.* Princeton, N.J.: Van Nostrand.

Koontz, H., & O'Donnell, C. 1955. *Principles of management.* New York: McGraw-Hill.

Knickerbocker, I. 1948. Leadership: A conception and some implications. *Journal of Social Issues,* 4, 23–40.

Krech, D., & Crutchfield, R. S. 1948. *Theory and problems of social psychology.* New York: McGraw-Hill.

Larson, A. 1968. *Eisenhower: The president nobody knew.* New York: Popular Library.

Lawshe, C. H., & Nagle, B. F. 1953. Productivity and attitude toward supervisor. *Journal of Applied Psychology*, 37, 159–162.

Lewis, H. S. 1974. Leaders and followers: Some anthropological perspectives. *Addison-Wesley Module in Anthropology No. 50 Reading*, Mass.: Addison-Wesley.

Lichtheim, M. 1973. *Ancient Egyptian literature, Vol. 1: The old and middle kingdoms*. Los Angeles: University of California Press.

Lieberson, S., & O'Connor, J. F. 1972. Leadership and organizational performance: A study of large corporations. *American Sociological Review*, 37, 117–130.

Lippmann, W. 1922. *Public opinion*. New York: Harcourt, Brace.

Maccoby, M. 1979. Leadership needs of the 1980's. *Current Issues in Higher Education*, 2, 17–23.

Manchester, W. 1988. Manchester on leadership. *Modern Maturity*, 31(5), 40–46, 108–111.

Mason, W. A. 1964. Sociability and social organization in monkeys and apes. In L. Berkowitz, ed., *Advances in experimental social psychology*. New York: Academic Press.

Meindl, J. R., Ehrlich, S. B., & Dukerich, J. M. 1985. The romance of leadership. *Administrative Science Quarterly*, 30, 78–102.

Meindl, J. R., & Ehrlich, S. B. 1987. The romance of leadership and the evaluation of organizational performance. *Academy of Management Journal*, 30, 90–109.

Merton, R. K. 1969. The social nature of leadership. *American Journal of Nursing*, 69, 2614–2618.

Meyer, E. C. 1980. Leadership: A return to the basics. *Military Review*, 60(7), 4–9.

Miller, J. A. 1973. *Structuring/destructuring: Leadership in open systems*. (Tech. Rep. No. 64). Rochester, NY: University of Rochester, Management Research Center.

Miller, R. E., & Murphy, J. V. 1956. Social interactions of Rhesus monkeys: I. Food-getting dominance as a dependent variable. *Journal of Social Psychology*, 44, 249–255.

Miner, J. B. 1975. The uncertain future of the leadership concept: An overview. In J. G. Hunt & L. L. Larson, eds., *Leadership frontiers*. Kent, Ohio: Kent State University Press.

Mintzberg, H., & Waters, J. A. 1982. Tracking strategy in an entrepreneurial firm. *Academy of Management Journal*, 25, 465–499.

Mitchell, T. R. 1979. Organizational behavior. *Annual Review of Psychology*, 30, 243–281.

Moore, B. V. 1927. The May conference on leadership. *Personnel Journal*, 6, 124–128.

Morris, R. T., & Seeman, M. 1950. The problem of leadership: An interdisciplinary approach. *American Journal of Sociology*, 56, 149–155.

Mulligan, L., & Mulligan, G. 1981. Reconstructing restoration science: Styles of leadership and social composition of the early royal society. *Social Studies of Science*, 11, 327–364.

Murchison, C. 1935. The experimental measurement of a social hierarchy in Gallus Domesticus. *Journal of General Psychology*, 12, 3–39.

Mumford, E. 1906/1907. Origins of leadership. *American Journal of Sociology*, 12, 216–240, 367–397, 500–531.

Munson, E. L. 1921. *The management of men*. New York: Holt.

Nash, J. B. 1929. Leadership. *Phi Delta Kappan*, 12, 24–25.

Neustadt, R. E. 1960. *Presidential power*. New York: Wiley.

———. 1980. *Presidential power: The politics of leadership from FDR to Carter*. New York: Wiley.

Odier, C. 1948. Valeur et valence du chef. *Schweizerisches Archiv fur Neurologisches Psychiatrie*, 61, 408–410.

Osborn, R. N., Hunt, J. G., & Jauch, L. R. 1980. *Organization theory: An integrated approach*. New York: Wiley.

Oxford English Dictionary. 1933. London: Oxford University Press.

Paige, G. G. 1977. *The scientific study of political leadership*. New York: Free Press.

Pandey, J. 1976. Effects of leadership style, personality characteristics and methods of leader selection on members' leaders' behavior. *European Journal of Social Psychology*, 6, 475–489.

Pfeffer, J. 1977. The ambiguity of leadership. *Academy of Management Review*, 2, 104–112.

Phillips, T. R. 1939. Leader and led. *Journal of the Coast Artillery*, 82, 45–58.

Plutarch. 1932. *Lives of the noble Grecians and Romans*. New York: Modern Library.

Rabi, M. M. 1967. *The political theory of Ibn Khaldun*. Leiden: Brill.

Raven, B. H., & French, J. R. P. 1958a. Group support, legitimate power, and social influence. *Journal of Personality*, 26, 400–409.

———. 1958b. Legitimate power, coercive power, and observability in social influence. *Sociometry*, 21, 83–97.

Redl, F. 1942. Group emotion and leadership. *Psychiatric*, 5, 573–596.

Safire, W. 1975. *Before the fall: An inside view of the pre-Watergate White House*. New York: Doubleday.

Salancik, G. R., & Pfeffer, J. 1977. Constraints on administrative discretion: The limited influence of mayors on city budgets. *Urban Affairs Quarterly*, 12, 475–498.

Sarachek, B. 1968. Greek concepts of leadership. *Academy of Management Journal*, 11, 39–48.

Sayles, L. 1979. *Leadership: What effective managers really do . . . and how they do it*. New York: McGraw-Hill.

Schenk, C. 1928. Leadership. *Infantry Journal*, 33, 111–122.

Schreisheim, C. A., & Kerr, S. 1977. Theories and measures of leadership. In J. G. Hunt & L. L. Larson, eds., *Leadership: The cutting edge*. Carbondale: Southern Illinois University Press.

Shartel, C. L. 1951a. Leader behavior in jobs. *Occupations*, 30, 164–166.

———. 1951b. Studies in naval leadership. In H. Guetzkow, ed., *Groups, leadership, and men*. Pittsburgh, Pa.: Carnegie Press.

———. 1956. *Executive performance and leadership*. Englewood Cliffs, N.J.: Prentice-Hall.

Smith, H. L., & Krueger, L. M. 1933. *A brief summary of literature on leadership.* Bloomington: Indiana University, School of Education Bulletin.

Smith, J. E., Carson, K. P., & Alexander, R. A. 1984. Leadership: It can make a difference. *Academy of Management Journal*, 27, 765–776.

Smith, M. 1934. Personality dominance and leadership. *Sociology and Social Research*, 19, 18–25.

Smith, M. 1948. Control interaction. *Journal of Social Psychology*, 28, 263–273.

Spitzberg, I. J., Jr. 1986. *Questioning leadership.* Unpublished manuscript.

Stark, S. 1970. Toward a psychology of charisma: III. Intuitional empathy, Vorbilder, Fuehrers, transcendence-striving, and inner creation. *Psychological Reports*, 26, 683–696.

Stogdill, R. 1950. Leadership, membership and organization. *Psychological Bulletin*, 47, 1–14.

Stogdill, R. M. 1975. The evolution of leadership theory. *Proceedings of the Academy of Management.* New Orleans, 4–6.

Sylvia, D., & Hutchinson, T. 1985. What makes Ms. Johnson teach? A study of teacher motivation. *Human Relations*, 38, 841–856.

Tannenbaum, R., Weschler, I. R., & Massarik, F. 1961. *Leadership and organization.* New York: McGraw-Hill.

Tead, O. 1929. The technique of creative leadership. In human nature and management. New York: McGraw-Hill.

———. 1935. *The art of leadership.* New York: McGraw-Hill.

Truman, H. S. 1958. *Memoirs.* New York: Doubleday.

Tucker, R. C. 1981. *Politics as leadership.* Columbia: University of Missouri Press.

Virany, B., & Tushman, M. L. 1986. *Executive succession: The changing characteristics of top management teams.* Paper, Academy of Management, Chicago.

Warren, J. M., & Maroney, R. J. 1969. Competitive social interaction between monkeys. In R.B.I. Zajonc, ed., *Animal social psychology.* New York: Wiley.

Warriner, C. K. 1955. Leadership in the small group. *American Journal of Sociology*, 60, 361–369.

Weiss, W. 1958. The relationship between judgments of communicator's position and extent of opinion change. *Journal of Abnormal and Social Psychology*, 56, 380–384.

Westerlund, G. 1952. *Behavior in a work situation with functional supervision and with group leaders.* Stockholm: Nordisk Rotogravyr.

Zajonc, R. B. 1969. *Animal social psychology*: A reader of experimental studies. New York: Wiley.

What Leaders Really Do

John P. Kotter

Leadership is different from management, but not for the reasons most people think. Leadership isn't mystical and mysterious. It has nothing to do with having "charisma" or other exotic personality traits. It is not the province of a chosen few. Nor is leadership necessarily better than management or a replacement for it.

Rather, leadership and management are two distinctive and complementary systems of action. Each has its own function and characteristic activities. Both are necessary for success in an increasingly complex and volatile business environment.

Most U.S. corporations today are overmanaged and underled. They need to develop their capacity to exercise leadership. Successful corporations don't wait for leaders to come along. They actively seek out people with leadership potential and expose them to career experiences designed to develop that potential. Indeed, with careful selection, nurturing, and encouragement, dozens of people can play important leadership roles in a business organization.

But while improving their ability to lead, companies should remember that strong leadership with weak management is no better, and is sometimes actually worse, than the reverse. The real challenge is to combine strong leadership and strong management and use each to balance the other.

Of course, not everyone can be good at both leading and managing. Some people have the capacity to become excellent managers but not strong leaders. Others have great leadership potential but, for a variety of reasons, have great difficulty becoming strong managers. Smart companies value both kinds of people and work hard to make them a part of the team.

But when it comes to preparing people for executive jobs, such companies rightly ignore the recent literature that says people cannot manage *and* lead. They try to develop leader-managers. Once companies understand the fundamental difference between leadership and management, they can begin to groom their top people to provide both.

24

THE DIFFERENCE BETWEEN MANAGEMENT
AND LEADERSHIP

Management is about coping with complexity. Its practices and procedures are largely a response to one of the most significant developments of the twentieth century: the emergence of large organizations. Without good management, complex enterprises tend to become chaotic in ways that threaten their very existence. Good management brings a degree of order and consistency to key dimensions like the quality and profitability of products.

Leadership, by contrast, is about coping with change. Part of the reason it has become so important in recent years is that the business world has become more competitive and more volatile. Faster technological change, greater international competition, the deregulation of markets, overcapacity in capital-intensive industries, an unstable oil cartel, raiders with junk bonds, and the changing demographics of the work force are among the many factors that have contributed to this shift. The net result is that doing what was done yesterday, or doing it 5% better, is no longer a formula for success. Major changes are more and more necessary to survive and compete effectively in this new environment. More change always demands more leadership.

Consider a simple military analogy: a peacetime army can usually survive with good administration and management up and down the hierarchy, coupled with good leadership concentrated at the very top. A wartime army, however, needs competent leadership at all levels. No one yet has figured out how to manage people effectively into battle; they must be *led*.

These different functions—coping with complexity and coping with change—shape the characteristic activities of management and leadership. Each system of action involves deciding what needs to be done, creating networks of people and relationships that can accomplish an agenda, and then trying to ensure that those people actually do the job. But each accomplishes these three tasks in different ways.

Companies manage complexity first by *planning and budgeting*—setting targets or goals for the future (typically for the next month or year), establishing detailed steps for achieving those targets, and then allocating resources to accomplish those plans. By contrast, leading an organization to constructive change begins by *setting a direction*—

developing a vision of the future (often the distant future) along with strategies for producing the changes needed to achieve that vision.

Management develops the capacity to achieve its plan by *organizing and staffing*—creating an organizational structure and set of jobs for accomplishing plan requirements, staffing the jobs with qualified individuals, communicating the plan to those people, delegating responsibility for carrying out the plan, and devising systems to monitor implementation. The equivalent leadership activity, however, is *aligning people*. This means communicating the new direction to those who can create coalitions that understand the vision and are committed to its achievement.

Finally, management ensures plan accomplishment by *controlling and problem solving*—monitoring results versus the plan in some detail, both formally and informally, by means of reports, meetings, and other tools; identifying deviations; and then planning and organizing to solve the problems. But for leadership, achieving a vision requires *motivating and inspiring*—keeping people moving in the right direction, despite major obstacles to change, by appealing to basic but often untapped human needs, values, and emotions.

A closer examination of each of these activities will help clarify the skills leaders need.

SETTING A DIRECTION VS. PLANNING AND BUDGETING

Since the function of leadership is to produce change, setting the direction of that change is fundamental to leadership.

Setting direction is never the same as planning or even long-term planning, although people often confuse the two. Planning is a management process, deductive in nature and designed to produce orderly results, not change. Setting a direction is more inductive. Leaders gather a broad range of data and look for patterns, relationships, and linkages that help explain things. What's more, the direction-setting aspect of leadership does not produce plans; it creates vision and strategies. These describe a business, technology, or corporate culture in terms of what it should become over the long term and articulate a feasible way of achieving this goal.

Most discussions of vision have a tendency to degenerate into the mystical. The implication is that a vision is something mysterious that mere mortals, even talented ones, could never hope to have. But developing good business direction isn't magic. It is a tough, sometimes exhausting process of gathering and analyzing information. People who articulate such visions aren't magicians but broad-based strategic thinkers who are willing to take risks.

Nor do visions and strategies have to be brilliantly innovative; in fact, some of the best are not. Effective business visions regularly have an almost mundane quality, usually consisting of ideas that are already well known. The particular combination or patterning of the ideas may be new, but sometimes even that is not the case.

For example, when CEO Jan Carlzon articulated his vision to make Scandinavian Airline Systems (SAS) the best airline in the world for the frequent business traveler, he was not saying anything that everyone in the airline industry didn't already know. Business travelers fly more consistently than other market segments and are generally willing to pay higher fares. Thus focusing on business customers offers an airline the possibility of high margins, steady business, and considerable growth. But in an industry known more for bureaucracy than vision, no company had ever put these simple ideas together and dedicated itself to implementing them. SAS did, and it worked.

What's crucial about a vision is not its originality but how well it serves the interests of important constituencies—customers, stockholders, employees—and how easily it can be translated into a realistic competitive strategy. Bad visions tend to ignore the legitimate needs and rights of important constituencies—favoring, say, employees over customers or stockholders. Or they are strategically unsound. When a company that has never been better than a weak competitor in an industry suddenly starts talking about becoming number one, that is a pipe dream, not a vision.

One of the most frequent mistakes that over-managed and underled corporations make is to embrace "long-term planning" as a panacea for their lack of direction and inability to adapt to an increasingly competitive and dynamic business environment. But such an approach misinterprets the nature of direction setting and can never work.

Long-term planning is always time consuming. Whenever something unexpected happens, plans have to be redone. In a dynamic business environment, the unexpected often becomes the norm, and long-term planning can become an extraordinarily burdensome activity. This is why most successful corporations limit the time frame of their planning activities. Indeed, some even consider "long-term planning" a contradiction in terms.

In a company without direction, even short-term planning can become a black hole capable of absorbing an infinite amount of time and energy. With no vision and strategy to provide constraints around the planning process or to guide it, every eventuality deserves a plan. Under these circumstances, contingency planning can go on forever, draining time and attention from far more essential activities, yet without ever providing the clear sense of direction that a company desperately needs. After awhile, managers inevitably become cynical about all this, and the planning process can degenerate into a highly politicized game.

Planning works best not as a substitute for direction setting but as a complement to it. A competent planning process serves as a useful reality check on direction-setting activities. Likewise, a competent direction-setting process provides a focus in which planning can then be realistically carried out. It helps clarify what kind of planning is essential and what kind is irrelevant.

ALIGNING PEOPLE VS. ORGANIZING AND STAFFING

A central feature of modern organizations is interdependence, where no one has complete autonomy, where most employees are tied to many others by their work, technology, management systems, and hierarchy. These linkages present a special challenge when organizations attempt to change. Unless many individuals line up and move together in the same direction, people will tend to fall all over one another. To executives who are overeducated in management and undereducated in leadership, the idea of getting people moving in the same direction appears to be an organizational problem. What executives need to do, however, is not organize people but align them.

Managers "organize" to create human systems that can implement plans as precisely and efficiently as possible. Typically, this requires a number of potentially complex decisions. A company must choose a structure of jobs and reporting relationships, staff it with individuals suited to the jobs, provide training for those who need it, communicate plans to the work force, and decide how much authority to delegate and to whom. Economic incentives also need to be constructed to accomplish the plan, as well as systems to monitor its implementation. These organizational judgments are much like architectural decisions. It's a question of fit within a particular context.

Aligning is different. It is more of a communications challenge than a design problem. First, aligning invariably involves talking to many more individuals than organizing does. The target population can involve not only a manager's subordinates but also bosses, peers, staff in other parts of the organization, as well as suppliers, governmental officials, or even customers. Anyone who can help implement the vision and strategies or who can block implementation is relevant.

Trying to get people to comprehend a vision of an alternative future is also a communications challenge of a completely different magnitude from organizing them to fulfill a short-term plan. It's much like the difference between a football quarterback attempting to describe to his team the next two or three plays versus his trying to explain to them a totally new approach to the game to be used in the second half of the season.

Whether delivered with many words or a few carefully chosen symbols, such messages are not necessarily accepted just because they are understood. Another big challenge in leadership efforts is credibility—getting people to believe the message. Many things contribute to credibility: the track record of the person delivering the message, the content of the message itself, the communicator's reputation for integrity and trustworthiness, and the consistency between words and deeds.

Finally, aligning leads to empowerment in a way that organizing rarely does. One of the reasons some organizations have difficulty adjusting to rapid changes in markets or technology is that so many people in those companies feel relatively powerless. They have learned from experience that even if they correctly perceive important external changes and then initiate appropriate actions, they are vulnerable to someone higher up who does not like what they have done. Reprimands can take many different forms: "That's against policy" or "We can't afford it" or "Shut up and do as you're told."

Alignment helps overcome this problem by empowering people in at least two ways. First, when a clear sense of direction has been communicated throughout an organization, lower level employees can initiate actions without the same degree of vulnerability. As long as their behavior is consistent with the vision, superiors will have more difficulty reprimanding them. Second, because everyone is aiming at the same target, the probability is less that one person's initiative will be stalled when it comes into conflict with someone else's.

MOTIVATING PEOPLE VS. CONTROLLING
AND PROBLEM SOLVING

Since change is the function of leadership, being able to generate highly energized behavior is important for coping with the inevitable barriers to change. Just as direction setting identifies an appropriate path for movement and just as effective alignment gets people moving down that path, successful motivation ensures that they will have the energy to overcome obstacles.

According to the logic of management, control mechanisms compare system behavior with the plan and take action when a deviation is detected. In a well-managed factory, for example, this means the planning process establishes sensible quality targets, the organizing process builds an organization that can achieve those targets, and a control process makes sure that quality lapses are spotted immediately, not in 30 or 60 days, and corrected.

For some of the same reasons that control is so central to management, highly motivated or inspired behavior is almost irrelevant. Managerial processes must be as close as possible to fail-safe and risk-free. That means they cannot be dependent on the unusual or hard to obtain. The whole purpose of systems and structures is to help normal people who behave in normal ways to complete routine jobs successfully, day after day. It's not exciting or glamorous. But that's management.

Leadership is different. Achieving grand visions always requires an occasional burst of energy. Motivation and inspiration energize people, not by pushing them in the right direction as control mechanisms do but by satisfying basic human needs for achievement, a sense of belonging, recognition, self-esteem, a feeling of control over one's life, and the ability to live up to one's ideals. Such feelings touch us deeply and elicit a powerful response.

Good leaders motivate people in a variety of ways. First, they always articulate the organization's vision in a manner that stresses the values of the audience they are addressing. This makes the work important to those individuals. Leaders also regularly involve people in deciding how to achieve the organization's vision (or the part most relevant to a particular individual). This gives people a sense of control. Another important motivational technique is to support employee efforts to realize the vision by providing coaching, feedback, and role modeling, thereby helping people grow professionally and enhancing their self-esteem. Finally, good leaders recognize and reward success, which not only gives people a sense of accomplishment but also makes them feel like they belong to an organization that cares about them. When all this is done, the work itself becomes intrinsically motivating.

The more that change characterizes the business environment, the more that leaders must motivate people to provide leadership as well. When this works, it tends to reproduce leadership across the entire organization, with people occupying multiple leadership roles throughout the hierarchy. This is highly valuable, because coping with change in any complex business demands initiatives from a multitude of people. Nothing less will work.

Of course, leadership from many sources does not necessarily converge. To the contrary, it can easily conflict. For multiple leadership roles to work together, people's actions must be carefully coordinated by mechanisms that differ from those coordinating traditional management roles.

Strong networks of informal relationships—the kind found in companies with healthy cultures—help coordinate leadership activities in much the same way that formal structure coordinates managerial activities. The key difference is that informal networks can deal with the greater demands for coordination associated with nonroutine activities and change. The multitude of communication channels and the trust among the individuals connected by those channels allow for an ongoing process of accommodation and adaptation. When conflicts arise among roles, those same relationships help resolve the conflicts. Perhaps most important, this process of dialogue and accommodation can produce visions that are linked and compatible instead of remote and competitive. All this requires a great deal more communication than is needed to coordinate managerial roles, but unlike formal structure, strong informal networks can handle it.

Of course, informal relations of some sort exist in all corporations. But too often these networks are either very weak—some people are well connected but most are not—or they are highly fragmented—a strong network exists inside the marketing group and inside R&D but not across the two departments. Such networks do not support multiple leadership initiatives well. In fact, extensive informal networks are so important that if they do not exist, creating them has to be the focus of activity early in a major leadership initiative.

CREATING A CULTURE OF LEADERSHIP

Despite the increasing importance of leadership to business success, the on-the-job experiences of most people actually seem to undermine the development of attributes needed for leadership. Nevertheless, some companies have consistently demonstrated an ability to develop people into outstanding leader-managers. Recruiting people with leadership potential is only the first step. Equally important is managing their career patterns. Individuals who are effective in large leadership roles often share a number of career experiences.

Perhaps the most typical and most important is significant challenge early in a career. Leaders almost always have had opportunities during their twenties and thirties to actually try to lead, to take a risk, and to learn from both triumphs and failures. Such learning seems essential in developing a wide range of leadership skills and perspectives. It also teaches people something about both the difficulty of leadership and its potential for producing change.

Later in their careers, something equally important happens that has to do with broadening. People who provide effective leadership in important jobs always have a chance, before they get into those jobs, to grow beyond the narrow base that characterizes most managerial careers. This is usually the result of lateral career moves or of early pro-motions to unusually broad job assignments. Sometimes other vehicles help, like special task-force assignments or a lengthy general manage-ment course. Whatever the case, the breadth of knowledge developed in this way seems to be helpful in all aspects of leadership. So does the net-work of relationships that is often acquired both inside and outside the company. When enough people get opportunities like this, the relation-ships that are built also help create the strong informal networks needed to support multiple leadership initiatives.

Corporations that do a better-than-average job of developing leaders put an emphasis on creating challenging opportunities for relatively young employees. In many businesses, decentralization is the key. By definition, it pushes responsibility lower in an organization and in the process creates more challenging jobs at lower levels. Johnson & Johnson, 3M, Hewlett-Packard, General Electric, and many other well-known companies have used that approach quite successfully. Some of those same companies also create as many small units as possible so there are a lot of challenging lower-level general management jobs available.

Sometimes these businesses develop additional challenging opportunities by stressing growth through new products or services. Over the years, 3M has had a policy that at least 25% of its revenue should come from products introduced within the last five years. That encourages small new ventures, which in turn offer hundreds of opportunities to test and stretch young people with leadership potential.

Such practices can, almost by themselves, prepare people for small- and medium-sized leadership jobs. But developing people for important leadership positions requires more work on the part of senior executives, often over a long period of time. That work begins with efforts to spot people with great leadership potential early in their careers and to identify what will be needed to stretch and develop them.

Again, there is nothing magic about this process. The methods successful companies use are surprisingly straightforward. They go out of their way to make young employees and people at lower levels in their organizations visible to senior management. Senior managers then judge for themselves who has potential and what the development needs of those people are. Executives also discuss their tentative conclusions among themselves to draw more accurate judgments.

Armed with a clear sense of who has considerable leadership potential and what skills they need to develop, executives in these companies then spend time planning for that development. Sometimes that is done as part of a formal succession planning or high-potential development process; often it is more informal. In either case, the key ingredient appears to be an intelligent assessment of what feasible development opportunities fit each candidate's needs.

To encourage managers to participate in these activities, well-led businesses tend to recognize and reward people who successfully develop leaders. This is rarely done as part of a formal compensation or bonus formula, simply because it is so difficult to measure such achievements with precision. But it does become a factor in decisions about promotion, especially to the most senior levels, and that seems to make a big difference. When told that future promotions will depend to some degree on their ability to nurture leaders, even people who say that leadership cannot be developed somehow find ways to do it.

Such strategies help create a corporate culture where people value strong leadership and strive to create it. Just as we need more people to provide leadership in the complex organizations that dominate our world today, we also need more people to develop the cultures that will create that leadership. Institutionalizing a leadership-centered culture is the ultimate act of leadership.

The Manager's Job: Folklore and Fact

Henry Mintzberg

If you ask managers what they do, they will most likely tell you that they plan, organize, coordinate, and control. Then watch what they do. Don't be surprised if you can't relate what you see to these words.

When a manager is told that a factory has just burned down and then advises the caller to see whether temporary arrangements can be made to supply customers through a foreign subsidiary, is that manager planning, organizing, coordinating, or controlling? How about when he or she presents a gold watch to a retiring employee? Or attends a conference to meet people in the trade and returns with an interesting new product idea for employees to consider?

These four words, which have dominated management vocabulary since the French industrialist Henri Fayol first introduced them in 1916, tell us little about what managers actually do. At best, they indicate some vague objectives managers have when they work.

The field of management, so devoted to progress and change, has for more than half a century not seriously addressed *the* basic question: What do managers do? Without a proper answer, how can we teach management? How can we design planning or information systems for managers? How can we improve the practice of management at all?

Our ignorance of the nature of managerial work shows up in various ways in the modern organization—in boasts by successful managers who never spent a single day in a management training program; in the turnover of corporate planners who never quite understood what it was the manager wanted; in the computer consoles gathering dust in the back room because the managers never used the fancy on-line MIS some analyst thought they needed. Perhaps most important, our ignorance shows up in the inability of our large public organizations to come to grips with some of their most serious policy problems.

Somehow, in the rush to automate production, to use management science in the functional areas of marketing and finance, and to apply the skills of the behavioral scientist to the problem of worker motivation, the manager—the person in charge of the organization or one of its subunits—has been forgotten.

I intend to break the reader away from Fayol's words and introduce a more supportable and useful description of managerial work. This description derives from my review and synthesis of research on how various managers have spent their time.

In some studies, managers were observed intensively; in a number of others, they kept detailed diaries; in a few studies, their records were analyzed. All kinds of managers were studied—foremen, factory supervisors, staff managers, field sales managers, hospital administrators, presidents of companies and nations, and even street gang leaders. These "managers" worked in the United States, Canada, Sweden, and Great Britain.

A synthesis of these findings paints an interesting picture, one as different from Fayol's classical view as a cubist abstract is from a Renaissance painting. In a sense, this picture will be obvious to anyone who has ever spent a day in a manager's office, either in front of the desk or behind it. Yet, at the same time, this picture throws into doubt much of the folklore that we have accepted about the manager's work.

FOLKLORE AND FACTS ABOUT MANAGERIAL WORK

There are four myths about the manager's job that do not bear up under careful scrutiny of the facts.

Folklore: The manager is a reflective, systematic planner. The evidence on this issue is overwhelming, but not a shred of it supports this statement.

Fact: Study after study has shown that managers work at an unrelenting pace, that their activities are characterized by brevity, variety, and discontinuity, and that they are strongly oriented to action and dislike reflective activities. Consider this evidence:

Half of the activities engaged in by the five chief executives of my study lasted less than nine minutes, and only 10% exceeded one hour.[1] A study of 56 U.S. foremen found that they averaged 583 activities per eight-hour shift, an average of 1 every 48 seconds.[2] The work pace for both chief executives and foremen was unrelenting. The chief executives met a steady stream of callers and mail from the moment they arrived in the morning until they left in the evening. Coffee breaks and lunches were inevitably work related, and ever-present subordinates seemed to usurp any free moment.

A diary study of 160 British middle and top managers found that they worked without interruption for a half hour or more only about once every two days.[3]

Of the verbal contacts the chief executives in my study engaged in, 93% were arranged on an ad hoc basis. Only 1% of the executives' time was spent in open-ended observational tours. Only 1 out of 368 verbal contacts was unrelated to a specific issue and could therefore be called general planning. Another researcher found that "in *not one single case* did a manager report obtaining important external information from a general conversation or other undirected personal communication."[4]

Is this the planner that the classical view describes? Hardly. The manager is simply responding to the pressures of the job. I found that my chief executives terminated many of their own activities, often leaving meetings before the end, and interrupted their desk work to call in subordinates. One president not only placed his desk so that he could look down a long hallway but also left his door open when he was alone—an invitation for subordinates to come in and interrupt him.

Clearly, these managers wanted to encourage the flow of current information. But more significantly, they seemed to be conditioned by their own work loads. They appreciated the opportunity cost of their own time, and they were continually aware of their ever-present obligations—mail to be answered, callers to attend to, and so on. It seems that a manager is always plagued by the possibilities of what might be done and what must be done.

When managers must plan, they seem to do so implicitly in the context of daily actions, not in some abstract process reserved for two weeks in the organization's mountain retreat. The plans of the chief executives I studied seemed to exist only in their heads—as flexible, but often specific, intentions. The traditional literature notwithstanding, the job of managing does not breed reflective planners; managers respond to stimuli, they are conditioned by their jobs to prefer live to delayed action.

Folklore: The effective manager has no regular duties to perform. Managers are constantly being told to spend more time planning and delegating and less time seeing customers and engaging in negotiations.

These are not, after all, the true tasks of the manager. To use the popular analogy, the good manager, like the good conductor, carefully orchestrates everything in advance, then sits back, responding occasionally to an unforeseeable exception. But here again the pleasant abstraction just does not seem to hold up.

Fact: Managerial work involves performing a number of regular duties, including ritual and ceremony, negotiations, and processing of soft information that links the organization with its environment. Consider some evidence from the research:

A study of the work of the presidents of small companies found that they engaged in routine activities because their companies could not afford staff specialists and were so thin on operating personnel that a single absence often required the president to substitute.[5]

One study of field sales managers and another of chief executives suggest that it is a natural part of both jobs to see important customers, assuming the managers wish to keep those customers.[6]

Someone, only half in jest, once described the manager as the person who sees visitors so that other people can get their work done. In my study, I found that certain ceremonial duties—meeting visiting dignitaries, giving out gold watches, presiding at Christmas dinners—were an intrinsic part of the chief executive's job.

Studies of managers' information flow suggest that managers play a key role in securing "soft" external information (much of it available only to them because of their status) and in passing it along to their subordinates.

Folklore: The senior manager needs aggregated information, which a formal management information system best provides. Not too long ago, the words *total information system* were everywhere in the management literature. In keeping with the classical view of the manager as that individual perched on the apex of a regulated, hierarchical system, the literature's manager was to receive all important information from a giant, comprehensive MIS.

But lately, these giant MIS systems are not working—managers are simply not using them. The enthusiasm has waned. A look at how managers actually process information makes it clear why.

Fact: Managers strongly favor verbal media, telephone calls and meetings, over documents. Consider the following:

In two British studies, managers spent an average of 66% and 80% of their time in verbal (oral) communication.[7] In my study of five American chief executives, the figure was 78%.

These five chief executives treated mail processing as a burden to be dispensed with. One came in Saturday morning to process 142 pieces of mail in just over three hours, to "get rid of all the stuff." This same manager looked at the first piece of "hard" mail he had received all week, a standard cost report, and put it aside with the comment, "I never look at this."

These same five chief executives responded immediately to 2 of the 40 routine reports they received during the five weeks of my study and to 4 items in the 104 periodicals. They skimmed most of these periodicals in seconds, almost ritualistically. In all, these chief executives of good-sized organizations initiated on their own—that is, not in response to something else—a grand total of 25 pieces of mail during the 25 days I observed them.

An analysis of the mail the executives received reveals an interesting picture—only 13% was of specific and immediate use. So now we have another piece in the puzzle: not much of the mail provides live, current information—the action of a competitor, the mood of a government legislator, or the rating of last night's television show. Yet this is the information that drove the managers, interrupting their meetings and rescheduling their workdays.

Consider another interesting finding. Managers seem to cherish "soft" information, especially gossip, hearsay, and speculation. Why? The reason is its timeliness; today's gossip may be tomorrow's fact. The manager who misses the telephone call revealing that the company's biggest customer was seen golfing with a main competitor may read about a dramatic drop in sales in the next quarterly report. But then it's too late.

To assess the value of historical, aggregated, "hard" MIS information, consider two of the manager's prime uses for information—to identify problems and opportunities[8] and to build mental models (e.g., how the organization's budget system works, how customers buy products, how changes in the economy affect the organization). The evidence suggests that the manager identifies decision situations and builds models not with the aggregated abstractions an MIS provides but with specific tidbits of data.

Consider the words of Richard Neustadt, who studied the information-collecting habits of Presidents Roosevelt, Truman, and Eisenhower: "It is not information of a general sort that helps a President see personal stakes; not summaries, not surveys, not the *bland amalgams*. Rather . . . it is the odds and ends of *tangible detail* that pieced together in his mind illuminate the underside of issues put before him. To help himself he must reach out as widely as he can for every scrap of fact, opinion, gossip, bearing on his interests and relationships as President. He must become his own director of his own central intelligence."[9]

The manager's emphasis on this verbal media raises two important points. First, verbal information is stored in the brains of people. Only when people write this information down can it be stored in the files of the organization—whether in metal cabinets or on magnetic tape—and managers apparently do not write down much of what they hear. Thus the strategic data bank of the organization is not in the memory of its computers but in the minds of its managers.

Second, managers' extensive use of verbal media helps to explain why they are reluctant to delegate tasks. It is not as if they can hand a dossier over to subordinates; they must take the time to "dump memory"—to tell subordinates all about the subject. But this could take so long that managers may find it easier to do the task themselves. Thus they are damned by their own information system to a "dilemma of delegation"—to do too much or to delegate to subordinates with inadequate briefing.

Folklore: Management is, or at least is quickly becoming, a science and a profession. By almost any definition of *science* and *profession*, this statement is false. Brief observation of any manager will quickly lay to rest the notion that managers practice a science. A science involves the enaction of systematic, analytically determined procedures or programs. If we do not even know what procedures managers use, how can we prescribe them by scientific analysis? And how can we call management a profession if we cannot specify what managers are to learn? For after all, a profession involves "knowledge of some department of learning or science" *(Random House Dictionary).*[10]

Fact: The managers' programs—to schedule time, process information, make decisions, and so on—remain locked deep inside their brains. Thus, to describe these programs, we rely on words like *judgment* and *intuition*, seldom stopping to realize that they are merely labels for our ignorance.

I was struck during my study by the fact that the executives I was observing—all very competent—are fundamentally indistinguishable from their counterparts of a hundred years ago (or a thousand years ago). The information they need differs, but they seek it in the same way—by word of mouth. Their decisions concern modern technology, but the procedures they use to make those decisions are the same as the procedures used by nineteenth century managers. Even the computer, so important for the specialized work of the organization, has apparently had no influence on the work procedures of general managers. In fact, the manager is in a kind of loop, with increasingly heavy work pressures but no aid forthcoming from management science.

Considering the facts about managerial work, we can see that the manager's job is enormously complicated and difficult. Managers are overburdened with obligations yet cannot easily delegate their tasks. As a result, they are driven to overwork and forced to do many tasks superficially. Brevity, fragmentation, and verbal communication characterize their work. Yet these are the very characteristics of managerial work that have impeded scientific attempts to improve it. As a result, management scientists have concentrated on the specialized functions of the organization, where it is easier to analyze the procedures and quantify the relevant information.[11]

But the pressures of a manager's job are becoming worse. Where before managers needed to respond only to owners and directors, now they find that subordinates with democratic norms continually reduce their freedom to issue unexplained orders, and a growing number of outside influences (consumer groups, government agencies, and so on) demand attention. Managers have had nowhere to turn for help. The first step in providing such help is to find out what the manager's job really is.

BACK TO A BASIC DESCRIPTION OF MANAGERIAL WORK

Earlier, I defined the manager as that person in charge of an organization or subunit. Besides CEOs, this definition would include vice presidents, bishops, foremen, hockey coaches, and prime ministers. All these "managers" are vested with formal authority over an organiza-

The Manager's Roles

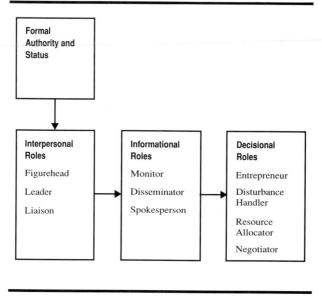

tional unit. From formal authority comes status, which leads to various interpersonal relations, and from these comes access to information. Information, in turn, enables the manager to make decisions and strategies for the unit.

The manager's job can be described in terms of various "roles," or organized sets of behaviors identified with a position. My description, shown in "The Manager's Roles," comprises ten roles. As we shall see, formal authority gives rise to the three interpersonal roles, which in turn give rise to the three informational roles; these two sets of roles enable the manager to play the four decisional roles.

INTERPERSONAL ROLES

Three of the manager's roles arise directly from formal authority and involve basic interpersonal relationships. First is the *figurehead* role. As the head of an organizational unit, every manager must perform some ceremonial duties. The president greets the touring dignitaries. The foreman attends the wedding of a lathe operator. The sales manager takes an important customer to lunch.

The chief executives of my study spent 12% of their contact time on ceremonial duties; 17% of their incoming mail dealt with acknowledgments and requests related to their status. For example, a letter to a company president requested free merchandise for a crippled schoolchild; diplomas that needed to be signed were put on the desk of the school superintendent.

Duties that involve interpersonal roles may sometimes be routine, involving little serious communication and no important decision making. Nevertheless, they are important to the smooth functioning of an organization and cannot be ignored.

Managers are responsible for the work of the people of their unit. Their actions in this regard constitute the *leader* role. Some of these actions involve leadership directly—for example, in most organizations the managers are normally responsible for hiring and training their own staff.

In addition, there is the indirect exercise of the leader role. For example, every manager must motivate and encourage employees, somehow reconciling their individual needs with the goals of the organization. In virtually every contact with the manager, subordinates seeking leadership clues ask: "Does she approve?" "How would she like the report to turn out?" "Is she more interested in market share than high profits?"

The influence of managers is most clearly seen in the leader role. Formal authority vests them with great potential power; leadership determines in large part how much of it they will realize.

The literature of management has always recognized the leader role, particularly those aspects of it related to motivation. In comparison, until recently it has hardly mentioned the *liaison* role, in which the manager makes contacts outside the vertical chain of command. This is remarkable in light of the finding of virtually every study of managerial work that managers spend as much time with peers and other people outside their units as they do with their own subordinates—and, surprisingly, very little time with their own superiors.

In Rosemary Stewart's diary study, the 160 British middle and top managers spent 47% of their time with peers, 41% of their time with people inside their unit, and only 12% of their time with their superiors. For Robert H. Guest's study of U.S. foremen, the figures were 44%,

46%, and 10%. The chief executives of my study averaged 44% of their contact time with people outside their organizations, 48% with subordinates, and 7% with directors and trustees.

The contacts the five CEOs made were with an incredibly wide range of people: subordinates; clients, business associates, and suppliers; and peers—managers of similar organizations, government and trade organization officials, fellow directors on outside boards, and independents with no relevant organizational affiliations. Guest's study of foremen shows, likewise, that their contacts were numerous and wide-ranging, seldom involving fewer than 25 individuals, and often more than 50.

INFORMATIONAL ROLES

By virtue of interpersonal contacts, both with subordinates and with a network of contacts, the manager emerges as the nerve center of the organizational unit. The manager may not know everything but typically knows more than subordinates do.

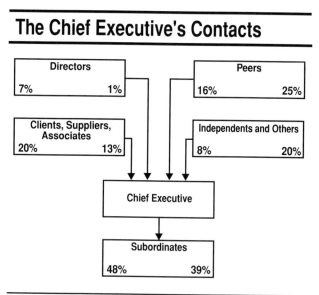

The Chief Executive's Contacts

Directors		Peers	
7%	1%	16%	25%

Clients, Suppliers, Associates		Independents and Others	
20%	13%	8%	20%

Chief Executive

Subordinates	
48%	39%

Note: The first figure indicates the proportion of total contact time spent with each group and the second figure, the proportion of mail from each group.

Studies have shown this relationship to hold for all managers, from street gang leaders to U.S. presidents. In *The Human Group*, George C. Homans explains how, because they were at the center of the information flow in their own gangs and were also in close touch with other gang leaders, street gang leaders were better informed than any of their followers.[12] As for presidents, Richard Neustadt observes: "The essence of [Franklin] Roosevelt's technique for information-gathering was competition. 'He would call you in,' one of his aides once told me, 'and he'd ask you to get the story on some complicated business, and you'd come back after a couple of days of hard labor and present the juicy morsel you'd uncovered under a stone somewhere, and *then* you'd find out he knew all about it, along with something else you *didn't* know. Where he got this information from he wouldn't mention, usually, but after he had done this to you once or twice you got damn careful about your information.' "[13]

We can see where Roosevelt "got this information" when we consider the relationship between the interpersonal and informational roles. As leader, the manager has formal and easy access to every staff member. In addition, liaison contacts expose the manager to external information to which subordinates often lack access. Many of these contacts are with other managers of equal status, who are themselves nerve centers in their own organization. In this way, the manager develops a powerful database of information.

Processing information is a key part of the manager's job. In my study, the CEOs spent 40% of their contact time on activities devoted exclusively to the transmission of information; 70% of their incoming mail was purely informational (as opposed to requests for action). Managers don't leave meetings or hang up the telephone to get back to work. In large part, communication *is* their work. Three roles describe these informational aspects of managerial work.

As *monitor*, the manager is perpetually scanning the environment for information, interrogating liaison contacts and subordinates, and receiving unsolicited information, much of it as a result of the network of personal contacts. Remember that a good part of the information the manager collects in the monitor role arrives in verbal form, often as gossip, hearsay, and speculation.

In the *disseminator* role, the manager passes some privileged information directly to subordinates, who would otherwise have no access to it. When subordinates lack easy contact with one another, the manager may pass information from one to another.

In the *spokesperson* role, the manager sends some information to people outside the unit—a president makes a speech to lobby for an organization cause, or a foreman suggests a product modification to a supplier. In addition, as a spokesperson, every manager must inform and satisfy the influential people who control the organizational unit. For the foreman, this may simply involve keeping the plant manager informed about the flow of work through the shop.

The president of a large corporation, however, may spend a great amount of time dealing with a host of influences. Directors and shareholders must be advised about finances; consumer groups must be assured that the organization is fulfilling its social responsibilities; and government officials must be satisfied that the organization is abiding by the law.

DECISIONAL ROLES

Information is not, of course, an end in itself; it is the basic input to decision making. One thing is clear in the study of managerial work: the manager plays the major role in the unit's decision-making system. As its formal authority, only the manager can commit the unit to important new courses of action; and as its nerve center, only the manager has full and current information to make the set of decisions that determines the unit's strategy. Four roles describe the manager as decision maker.

As *entrepreneur*, the manager seeks to improve the unit, to adapt it to changing conditions in the environment. In the monitor role, a president is constantly on the lookout for new ideas. When a good one appears, he initiates a development project that he may supervise himself or delegate to an employee (perhaps with the stipulation that he must approve the final proposal).

There are two interesting features about these development projects at the CEO level. First, these projects do not involve single decisions or even unified clusters of decisions. Rather, they emerge as a series of small decisions and actions sequenced over time. Apparently, chief executives prolong each project both to fit it into a busy, disjointed schedule, and so that they can comprehend complex issues gradually.

Second, the chief executives I studied supervised as many as 50 of these projects at the same time. Some projects entailed new products or processes; others involved public relations campaigns, improvement of the cash position, reorganization of a weak department, resolution of a morale problem in a foreign division, integration of computer operations, various acquisitions at different stages of development, and so on.

Chief executives appear to maintain a kind of inventory of the development projects in various stages of development. Like jugglers, they keep a number of projects in the air; periodically, one comes down, is given a new burst of energy, and sent back into orbit. At various intervals, they put new projects on-stream and discard old ones.

While the entrepreneur role describes the manager as the voluntary initiator of change, the *disturbance handler* role depicts the manager involuntarily responding to pressures. Here change is beyond the manager's control. The pressures of a situation are too severe to be ignored—a strike looms, a major customer has gone bankrupt, or a supplier reneges on a contract—so the manager must act.

Leonard R. Sayles, who has carried out appropriate research on the manager's job, likens the manager to a symphony orchestra conductor who must "maintain a melodious performance,"[14] while handling musicians' problems and other external disturbances. Indeed, every manager must spend a considerable amount of time responding to high-pressure disturbances. No organization can be so well run, so standardized, that it has considered every contingency in the uncertain environment in advance. Disturbances arise not only because poor managers ignore situations until they reach crisis proportions but also because good managers cannot possibly anticipate all the consequences of the actions they take.

The third decisional role is that of *resource allocator*. The manager is responsible for deciding who will get what. Perhaps the most important resource the manager allocates is his or her own time. Access to the manager constitutes exposure to the unit's nerve center and decision maker. The manager is also charged with designing the unit's structure, that pattern of formal relationships that determines how work is to be divided and coordinated.

Also, as resource allocator, the manager authorizes the important decisions of the unit before they are implemented. By retaining this power, the manager can ensure that decisions are interrelated. To fragment this power encourages discontinuous decision making and a disjointed strategy.

There are a number of interesting features about the manager's authorization of others' decisions. First, despite the widespread use of capital budgeting procedures—a means of authorizing various capital expenditures at one time—executives in my study made a great many authorization decisions on an ad hoc basis. Apparently, many projects cannot wait or simply do not have the quantifiable costs and benefits that capital budgeting requires.

Second, I found that the chief executives faced incredibly complex choices. They had to consider the impact of each decision on other decisions and on the organization's strategy. They had to ensure that the decision would be acceptable to those who influence the organization, as well as ensure that resources would not be overextended. They had to understand the various costs and benefits as well as the feasibility of the proposal. They also had to consider questions of timing. All this was necessary for the simple approval of someone else's proposal. At the same time, however, the delay could lose time, while quick approval could be ill-considered and quick rejection might discourage the subordinate who had spent months developing a pet project.

One common solution to approving projects is to pick the person instead of the proposal. That is, the manager authorizes those projects presented by people whose judgment he or she trusts. But the manager cannot always use this simple dodge.

The final decisional role is that of *negotiator*. Managers spend considerable time in negotiations: the president of the football team works out a contract with the holdout superstar; the corporation president leads the company's contingent to negotiate a new strike issue; the foreman argues a grievance problem to its conclusion with the shop steward.

These negotiations are an integral part of the manager's job, for only he or she has the authority to commit organizational resources in "real time" and the nerve-center information that important negotiations require.

THE INTEGRATED JOB

It should be clear by now that these ten roles are not easily separable. In the terminology of the psychologist, they form a gestalt, an integrated whole. No role can be pulled out of the framework and the job be left intact. For example, a manager without liaison contacts lacks external information. As a result, that manager can neither disseminate the information that employees need nor make decisions that adequately reflect external conditions. (This is a problem for the new person in a managerial position, since he or she has to build up a network of contacts before making effective decisions.)

Here lies a clue to the problems of team management.[15] Two or three people cannot share a single managerial position unless they can act as one entity. This means that they cannot divide up the ten roles unless they can very carefully reintegrate them. The real difficulty lies with the informational roles. Unless there can be full sharing of managerial information—and, as I pointed out earlier, it is primarily verbal—team management breaks down. A single managerial job cannot be arbitrarily split, for example, into internal and external roles, for information from both sources must be brought to bear on the same decisions.

To say that the ten roles form a gestalt is not to say that all managers give equal attention to each role. In fact, I found in my review of the various research studies that sales managers seem to spend relatively more of their time in the interpersonal roles, presumably a reflection of the extrovert nature of the marketing activity. Production managers, on the other hand, give relatively more attention to the decisional roles, presumably a reflection of their concern with efficient work flow. And staff managers spend the most time in the informational roles, since they are experts who manage departments that advise other parts of the organization. Nevertheless, in all cases, the interpersonal, informational, and decisional roles remain inseparable.

TOWARD MORE EFFECTIVE MANAGEMENT

This description of managerial work should prove more important to managers than any prescription they might derive from it. That is to say, *the managers' effectiveness is significantly influenced by their insight into their own work.* Performance depends on how well a manager understands and responds to the pressures and dilemmas of the job. Thus managers who can be introspective about their work are likely to be effective at their jobs.

Let us take a look at three specific areas of concern. For the most part, the managerial logjams—the dilemma of delegation, the database centralized in one brain, the problems of working with the management scientist—revolve around the verbal nature of the manager's information.

There are great dangers in centralizing the organization's data bank in the minds of its managers. When they leave, they take their memory with them. And when subordinates are out of convenient verbal reach of the manager, they are at an informational disadvantage.

The manager is challenged to find systematic ways to share privileged information. A regular debriefing session with key subordinates, a weekly memory dump on the dictating machine, maintaining a diary for limited circulation, or other similar methods may ease the logjam of work considerably. The time spent disseminating this information will be more than regained when decisions must be made. Of course, some will undoubtedly raise the question of confidentiality. But managers would be well advised to weigh the risks of exposing privileged information against having subordinates who can make effective decisions.

If there is a single theme that runs through this article, it is that the pressures of the job drive the manager to take on too much work, encourage interruption, respond quickly to every stimulus, seek the tangible and avoid the abstract, make decisions in small increments, and do everything abruptly.

Here again, the manager is challenged to deal consciously with the presures of superficiality by giving serious attention to the issues that require it, by stepping back in order to see a broad picture, and by making use of analytical inputs. Although effective managers have to be adept at responding quickly to numerous and varying problems, the danger in managerial work is that they will respond to every issue equally (and that means abruptly) and that they will never work the tangible bits and pieces of information into a comprehensive picture of their world.

To create this comprehensive picture, managers can supplement their own models with those of specialists. Economists describe the functioning of markets, operations researchers simulate financial flow processes, and behavioral scientists explain the needs and goals of people. The best of these models can be searched out and learned.

In dealing with complex issues, the senior manager has much to gain from a close relationship with the organization's own management scientists. They have something important that the manager lacks—time to probe complex issues. An effective working relationship hinges on the resolution of what a colleague and I have called "the planning dilemma."[16] Managers have the information and the authority; analysts have the time and the technology. A successful working relationship between the two will be effected when the manager learns to share information and the analyst learns to adapt to the manager's needs. For the analyst, adaptation means worrying less about the elegance of the method and more about its speed and flexibility.

Analysts can help the top manager schedule time, feed in analytical information, monitor projects, develop models to aid in making choices, design contingency plans for disturbances that can be anticipated, and conduct "quick and dirty" analyses for those that cannot. But there can be no cooperation if the analysts are out of the mainstream of the manager's information flow.

The manager is challenged to gain control of his or her own time by turning obligations into advantages and by turning those things he or she wishes to do into obligations. The chief executives of my study initiated only 32% of their own contacts (and another 5% by mutual agreement). And yet to a considerable extent they seemed to control their time. There were two key factors that enabled them to do so.

First, managers have to spend so much time discharging obligations that if they were to view them as just that, they would leave no mark on the organization. Unsuccessful managers blame failure on the obligations. Effective managers turn obligations to advantages. A speech is a chance to lobby for a cause; a meeting is a chance to reorganize a weak department; a visit to an important customer is a chance to extract trade information.

Second, the manager frees some time to do the things that he or she—perhaps no one else—thinks important by turning them into obligations. Free time is made, not found. Hoping to leave some time open for contemplation or general planning is tantamount to hoping that the pressures of the job will go away. Managers who want to innovate initiate projects and obligate others to report back to them. Managers who need certain environmental information establish channels that will automatically keep them informed. Managers who have to tour facilities commit themselves publicly.

THE EDUCATOR'S JOB

Finally, a word about the training of managers. Our management schools have done an admirable job of training the organization's specialists—management scientists, marketing researchers, accountants, and organizational development specialists. But for the most part, they have not trained managers.[17]

Management schools will begin the serious training of managers when skill training takes a serious place next to cognitive learning. Cognitive learning is detached and informational, like reading a book or listening to a lecture. No doubt much important cognitive material must be assimilated by the manager-to-be. But cognitive learning no more makes a manager than it does a swimmer. The latter will drown the first time she jumps into the water if her coach never takes her out of the lecture hall, gets her wet, and gives her feedback on her performance.

In other words, we are taught a skill through practice plus feedback, whether in a real or a simulated situation. Our management schools need to identify the skills managers use, select students who show potential in these skills, put the students into situations where these skills can be practiced and developed, and then give them systematic feedback on their performance.

My description of managerial work suggests a number of important managerial skills—developing peer relationships, carrying out negotiations, motivating subordinates, resolving conflicts, establishing information networks and subsequently disseminating information, making decisions in conditions of extreme ambiguity, and allocating resources. Above all, the manager needs to be introspective in order to continue to learn on the job.

No job is more vital to our society than that of the manager. The manager determines whether our social institutions will serve us well or whether they will squander our talents and resources. It is time to strip away the folklore about managerial work and study it realistically so that we can begin the difficult task of making significant improvements in its performance.

REFERENCES

1. All the data from my study can be found in Henry Mintzberg, *The Nature of Managerial Work* (New York: Harper & Row, 1973).

2. Robert H. Guest, "Of Time and the Foreman," *Personnel*, May 1956, p. 478.

3. Rosemary Stewart, *Managers and Their Jobs* (London: Macmillan, 1967); see also Sune Carlson, *Executive Behaviour* (Stockholm: Strombergs, 1951).

4. Francis J. Aguilar, *Scanning the Business Environment* (New York Macmillan, 1967), p. 102.

5. Unpublished study by Irving Choran, reported in Mintzberg, *The Nature of Managerial Work*.

6. Robert T. Davis, *Performance and Development of Field Sales Managers* (Boston: Division of Research, Harvard Business School, 1957); George H. Copeman, *The Role of the Managing Director* (London: Business Publications, 1963).

7. Stewart, *Managers and Their Jobs*; Tom Burns, "The Directions of Activity and Communication in a Departmental Executive Group," *Human Relations* 7, no. 1 (1954): 73.

8. H. Edward Wrapp, "Good Managers Don't Make Policy Decisions," *HBR* September-October 1967, p. 91. Wrapp refers to this as spotting opportunities and relationships in the stream of operating problems and decisions; in his article, Wrapp raises a number of excellent points related to this analysis.

9. Richard E. Neustadt, *Presidential Power* (New York: John Wiley, 1960), pp. 153–154; italics added.

10. For a more thorough, though rather different, discussion of this issue, see Kenneth R. Andrews, "Toward Professionalism in Business Management," *HBR* March-April 1969, p. 49.

11. C. Jackson Grayson, Jr., in "Management Science and Business Practice," *HBR* July-August 1973, p. 41, explains in similar terms why, as chairman of the Price Commission, he did not use those very techniques that he himself promoted in his earlier career as a management scientist.

12. George C. Homans, *The Human Group* (New York: Harcourt, Brace & World, 1950), based on the study by William F. Whyte entitled *Street Corner Society*, rev. ed. (Chicago, University of Chicago Press, 1995).

13. Neustadt, *Presidential Power*, p. 157.

14. Leonard R. Sayles, *Managerial Behavior* (New York: McGraw-Hill, 1964), p. 162.

15. See Richard C. Hodgson, Daniel J. Levinson, and Abraham Zaleznik, *The Executive Role Constellation* (Boston, Division of Research, Harvard Business School, 1965), for a discussion of the sharing of roles.

16. James S. Hekimian and Henry Mintzberg, "The Planning Dilemma," *The Management Review*, May 1968, p. 4.

17. See J. Sterling Livingston, "Myth of the Well-Educated Manager," *HBR* January-February 1971, p. 79.

The Ambiguity of Leadership

Jeffrey Pfeffer

Leadership has for some time been a major topic in social and organizational psychology. Underlying much of this research has been the assumption that leadership is causally related to organizational performance. Through an analysis of leadership styles, behaviors, or characteristics (depending on the theoretical perspective chosen), the argument has been made that more effective leaders can be selected or trained or, alternatively, the situation can be configured to provide for enhanced leader and organizational effectiveness.

Three problems with emphasis on leadership as a concept can be posed: (a) ambiguity in definition and measurement of the concept itself; (b) the question of whether leadership has discernible effects on organizational outcomes; and (c) the selection process in succession to leadership positions, which frequently uses organizationally irrelevant criteria and which has implications for normative theories of leadership. The argument here is that leadership is of interest primarily as a phenomenological construct. Leaders serve as symbols for representing personal causation of social events. How and why are such attributions of personal effects made? Instead of focusing on leadership and its effects, how do people make inferences about and react to phenomena labelled as leadership (5)?

THE AMBIGUITY OF THE CONCEPT

While there have been many studies of leadership, the dimensions and definition of the concept remain unclear. To treat leadership as a separate concept, it must be distinguished from other social influence phenomena. Hollander and Julian (24) and Bavelas (2) did not draw distinctions between leadership and other processes of social influence. A major point of the Hollander and Julian review was that leadership research might develop more rapidly if more general theories of social influence were incorporated. Calder (5) also argued that there is no

54

unique content to the construct of leadership that is not subsumed under other, more general models of behavior.

Kochan, Schmidt, and DeCotiis (33) attempted to distinguish leadership from related concepts of authority and social power. In leadership, influence rights are voluntarily conferred. Power does not require goal compatibility—merely dependence—but leadership implies some congruence between the objectives of the leader and the led. These distinctions depend on the ability to distinguish voluntary from involuntary compliance and to assess goal compatibility. Goal statements may be retrospective inferences from action (46, 53) and problems of distinguishing voluntary from involuntary compliance also exist (32). Apparently there are few meaningful distinctions between leadership and other concepts of social influence. Thus, an understanding of the phenomena subsumed under the rubric of leadership may not require the construct of leadership (5).

While there is some agreement that leadership is related to social influence, more disagreement concerns the basic dimensions of leader behavior. Some have argued that there are two tasks to be accomplished in groups—maintenance of the group and performance of some task or activity—and thus leader behavior might be described along these two dimensions (1, 6, 8, 25). The dimensions emerging from the Ohio State leadership studies—consideration and initiating structure—may be seen as similar to the two components of group maintenance and task accomplishment (18).

Other dimensions of leadership behavior have also been proposed (4). Day and Hamblin (10) analyzed leadership in terms of the closeness and punitiveness of the supervision. Several authors have conceptualized leadership behavior in terms of the *authority and discretion subordinates are permitted* (23, 36, 51). Fiedler (14) analyzed leadership in terms of the least-preferred-co-worker scale (LPC), but the meaning and behavioral attributes of this dimension of leadership behavior remain controversial.

The proliferation of dimensions is partly a function of research strategies frequently employed. Factor analysis on a large number of items describing behavior has frequently been used. This procedure tends to produce as many factors as the analyst decides to find, and permits the development of a large number of possible factor structures. The resultant factors must be named and further imprecision is introduced.

Deciding on a summative concept to represent a factor is inevitably a partly subjective process.

Literature assessing the effects of leadership tends to be equivocal. Sales (45) summarized leadership literature employing the authoritarian-democratic typology and concluded that effects on performance were small and inconsistent. Reviewing the literature on consideration and initiating structure dimensions, Korman (34) reported relatively small and inconsistent results, and Kerr and Schriesheim (30) reported more consistent effects of the two dimensions. Better results apparently emerge when moderating factors are taken into account, including subordinate personalities (50), and situational characteristics (23, 51). Kerr, et al. (31) list many moderating effects grouped under the headings of subordinate considerations, supervisor considerations, and task considerations. Even if each set of considerations consisted of only one factor (which it does not), an attempt to account for the effects of leader behavior would necessitate considering four-way interactions. While social reality is complex and contingent, it seems desirable to attempt to find more parsimonious explanations for the phenomena under study.

THE EFFECTS OF LEADERS

Hall asked a basic question about leadership: is there any evidence on the magnitude of the effects of leadership (17, p. 248)? Surprisingly, he could find little evidence. Given the resources that have been spent studying, selecting, and training leaders, one might expect that the question of whether or not leaders matter would have been addressed earlier (12).

There are at least three reasons why it might be argued that the observed effects of leaders on organizational outcomes would be small. First, those obtaining leadership positions are selected, and perhaps only certain, limited styles of behavior may be chosen. Second, once in the leadership position, the discretion and behavior of the leader are constrained. And third, leaders can typically affect only a few of the variables that may impact organizational performance.

Homogeneity of Leaders

Persons are selected to leadership positions. As a consequence of this selection process, the range of behaviors or characteristics exhibited by leaders is reduced, making it more problematic to empirically discover an effect of leadership. There are many types of constraints on the selection process. The attraction literature suggests that there is a tendency for persons to like those they perceive as similar (3). In critical decisions such as the selections of persons for leadership positions, compatible styles of behavior probably will be chosen.

Selection of persons is also constrained by the internal system of influence in the organization. As Zald (56) noted, succession is a critical decision, affected by political influence and by environmental contingencies faced by the organization. As Thompson (49) noted, leaders may be selected for their capacity to deal with various organizational contingencies. In a study of characteristics of hospital administrators, Pfeffer and Salancik (42) found a relationship between the hospital's context and the characteristics and tenure of the administrators. To the extent that the contingencies and power distribution within the organization remain stable, the abilities and behaviors of those selected into leadership positions will also remain stable.

Finally, the selection of persons to leadership positions is affected by a self-selection process. Organizations and roles have images, providing information about their character. Persons are likely to select themselves into organizations and roles based upon their preferences for the dimensions of the organizational and role characteristics as perceived through these images. The self-selection of persons would tend to work along with organizational selection to limit the range of abilities and behaviors in a given organizational role.

Such selection processes would tend to increase homogeneity more within a single organization than across organizations. Yet many studies of leadership effect at the work group level have compared groups within a single organization. If there comes to be a widely shared, socially constructed definition of leadership behaviors or characteristics which guides the selection process, then leadership activity may come to be defined similarly in various organizations, leading to the selection of only those who match the constructed image of a leader.

Constraints on Leader Behavior

Analyses of leadership have frequently presumed that leadership style or leader behavior was an independent variable that could be selected or trained at will to conform to what research would find to be optimal. Even theorists who took a more contingent view of appropriate leadership behavior generally assumed that with proper training, appropriate behavior could be produced (51). Fiedler (13), noting how hard it was to change behavior, suggested changing the situational characteristics rather than the person, but this was an unusual suggestion in the context of prevailing literature which suggested that leadership style was something to be strategically selected according to the variables of the particular leadership theory.

But the leader is embedded in a social system, which constrains behavior. The leader has a role set (27), in which members have expectations for appropriate behavior and persons make efforts to modify the leader's behavior. Pressures to conform to the expectations of peers, subordinates, and superiors are all relevant in determining actual behavior.

Leaders, even in high-level positions, have unilateral control over fewer resources and fewer policies than might be expected. Investment decisions may require approval of others, while hiring and promotion decisions may be accomplished by committees. Leader behavior is constrained by both the demands of others in the role set and by organizationally prescribed limitations on the sphere of activity and influence.

External Factors

Many factors that may affect organizational performance are outside a leader's control, even if he or she were to have complete discretion over major areas of organizational decisions. For example, consider the executive in a construction firm. Costs are largely determined by operation of commodities and labor markets; and demand is largely affected by interest rates, availability of mortgage money, and economic conditions which are affected by governmental policies over which the executive has little control. School superintendents have little control over birth rates and community economic development, both of which profoundly affect school system budgets. While the leader may react to contingencies as they arise, or may be a better or worse forecaster, in accounting for variation in organizational outcomes, he or she may account for relatively little compared to external factors.

Second, the leader's success or failure may be partly due to circumstances unique to the organization but still outside his or her control.

Leader positions in organizations vary in terms of the strength and position of the organization. The choice of a new executive does not fundamentally alter a market and financial position that has developed over years and affects the leader's ability to make strategic changes and the likelihood that the organization will do well or poorly. Organizations have relatively enduring strengths and weaknesses. The choice of a particular leader for a particular position has limited impact on these capabilities.

Empirical Evidence

Two studies have assessed the effects of leadership changes in major positions in organizations. Lieberson and O'Connor (35) examined 167 business firms in 13 industries over a 20 year period, allocating variance in sales, profits, and profit margins to one of four sources: year (general economic conditions), industry, company effects, and effects of changes in the top executive position. They concluded that compared to other factors, administration had a limited effect on organizational outcomes.

Using a similar analytical procedure, Salancik and Pfeffer (44) examined the effects of mayors on city budgets for 30 U.S. cities. Data on expenditures by budget category were collected for 1951–1968. Variance in amount and proportion of expenditures was apportioned to the year, the city, or the mayor. The mayoral effect was relatively small, with the city accounting for most of the variance, although the mayor effect was larger for expenditure categories that were not as directly connected to important interest groups. Salancik and Pfeffer argued that the effects of the mayor were limited both by absence of power to control many of the expenditures and tax sources, and by construction of policies in response to demands from interests in the environment.

If leadership is defined as a strictly interpersonal phenomenon, the relevance of these two studies for the issue of leadership effects becomes problematic. But such a conceptualization seems unduly restrictive, and is certainly inconsistent with Selznick's (47) conceptualization of leadership as strategic management and decision making. If one cannot observe differences when leaders change, then what does it matter who occupies the positions or how they behave?

Pfeffer and Salancik (41) investigated the extent to which behaviors selected by first-line supervisors were constrained by expectations of others in their role set. Variance in task and social behaviors could be accounted for by role-set expectations, with adherence to various demands made by role-set participants a function of similarity and relative power. Lowin and Craig (37) experimentally demonstrated that leader behavior was determined by the subordinate's own behavior. Both studies illustrate that leader behaviors are responses to the demands of the social context.

The effect of leadership may vary depending upon level in the organizational hierarchy, while the appropriate activities and behaviors may also vary with organizational level (26, 40). For the most part, empirical studies of leadership have dealt with first line supervisors or leaders with relatively low organizational status (17). If leadership has any impact, it should be more evident at higher organizational levels or where there is more discretion in decisions and activities.

THE PROCESS OF SELECTING LEADERS

Along with the suggestion that leadership may not account for much variance in organizational outcomes, it can be argued that merit or ability may not account for much variation in hiring and advancement of organizational personnel. These two ideas are related. If competence is hard to judge, or if leadership competence does not greatly affect organizational outcomes, then other, person-dependent criteria may be sufficient. Effective leadership styles may not predict career success when other variables such as social background are controlled.

Belief in the importance of leadership is frequently accompanied by belief that persons occupying leadership positions are selected and trained according to how well they can enhance the organization's performance. Belief in a leadership effect leads to development of a set of activities oriented toward enhancing leadership effectiveness. Simultaneously, persons managing their own careers are likely to place emphasis on activities and developing behaviors that will enhance their own leadership skills, assuming that such a strategy will facilitate advancement.

Research on the bases for hiring and promotion has been concentrated in examination of academic positions (e.g., 7, 19, 20). This is possibly the result of availability of relatively precise and unambiguous measures of performance, such as number of publications or citations.

Evidence on criteria used in selecting and advancing personnel in industry is more indirect.

Studies have attempted to predict either the compensation or the attainment of general management positions of MBA students, using personality and other background information (21, 22, 54). There is some evidence that managerial success can be predicted by indicators of ability and motivation such as test scores and grades, but the amount of variance explained is typically quite small.

A second line of research has investigated characteristics and backgrounds of persons attaining leadership positions in major organizations in society. Domhoff (11), Mills (38), and Warner and Abbeglin (52) found a strong preponderance of persons with upper-class backgrounds occupying leadership positions. The implication of these findings is that studies of graduate success, including the success of MBA's, would explain more variance if the family background of the person were included.

A third line of inquiry uses a tracking model. The dynamic model developed is one in which access to elite universities is affected by social status (28) and, in turn, social status and attendance at elite universities affect later career outcomes (9, 43, 48, 55).

Unless one is willing to make the argument that attendance at elite universities or coming from an upper class background is perfectly correlated with merit, the evidence suggests that succession to leadership positions is not strictly based on meritocratic criteria. Such a conclusion is consistent with the inability of studies attempting to predict the success of MBA graduates to account for much variance, even when a variety of personality and ability factors are used.

Beliefs about the bases for social mobility are important for social stability. As long as persons believe that positions are allocated on meritocratic grounds, they are more likely to be satisfied with the social order and with their position in it. This satisfaction derives from the belief that occupational position results from application of fair and reasonable criteria, and that the opportunity exists for mobility if the person improves skills and performance.

If succession to leadership positions is determined by person-based criteria such as social origins or social connections (16), then efforts to enhance managerial effectiveness with the expectation that this will lead to career success divert attention from the processes of stratification actually operating within organizations. Leadership literature has been implicitly aimed at two audiences. Organizations were told how to become more effective, and persons were told what behaviors to acquire in order to become effective, and hence, advance in their careers. The possibility that neither organizational outcomes nor career success are related to leadership behaviors leaves leadership research facing issues of relevance and importance.

THE ATTRIBUTION OF LEADERSHIP

Kelley conceptualized the layman as:

> an applied scientist, that is, as a person concerned about applying his knowledge of causal relationships in order to *exercise control* of his world (29, p. 2).

Reviewing a series of studies dealing with the attributional process, he concluded that persons were not only interested in understanding their world correctly, but also in controlling it.

> The view here proposed is that attribution processes are to be understood not only as a means of providing the individual with a veridical view of his world, but as a means of encouraging and maintaining his effective exercise of control in that world (29, p. 22).

Controllable factors will have high salience as candidates for causal explanation, while a bias toward the more important causes may shift the attributional emphasis toward causes that are not controllable (29, p. 23). The study of attribution is a study of naive psychology—an examination of how persons make sense out of the events taking place around them.

If Kelley is correct that individuals will tend to develop attributions that give them a feeling of control, then emphasis on leadership may derive partially from a desire to believe in the effectiveness and importance of individual action, since individual action is more controllable than contextual variables. Lieberson and O'Connor (35) made essentially the same point in introducing their paper on the effects of top management changes on organizational performance. Given the desire for control and a feeling of personal effectiveness, organizational outcomes are more likely to be attributed to individual actions, regardless of their actual causes.

Leadership is attributed by observers. Social action has meaning only through a phenomenological process (46). The identification of certain organizational roles as leadership positions guides the construction of meaning in the direction of attributing effects to the actions of those positions. While Bavelas (2) argued that the functions of leadership, such as task accomplishment and group maintenance, are shared throughout the group, this fact provides no simple and potentially controllable focus for attributing causality. Rather, the identification of leadership positions provides a simpler and more readily changeable model of reality. When causality is lodged in one or a few persons rather than being a function of a complex set of interactions among all group members, changes can be made by replacing or influencing the occupant of the leadership position. Causes of organizational actions are readily identified in this simple causal structure.

Even if, empirically, leadership has little effect, and even if succession to leadership positions is not predicated on ability or performance, the belief in leadership effects and meritocratic succession provides a simple causal framework and a justification for the structure of the social collectivity. More importantly, the beliefs interpret social actions in terms that indicate potential for effective individual intervention or control. The personification of social causality serves too many uses to be easily overcome. Whether or not leader behavior actually influences performance or effectiveness, it is important because people believe it does.

One consequence of the attribution of causality to leaders and leadership is that leaders come to be symbols. Mintzberg (39), in his discussion of the roles of managers, wrote of the symbolic role, but more in terms of attendance at formal events and formally representing the organization. The symbolic role of leadership is more important than implied in such a description. The leader as a symbol provides a target for action when difficulties occur, serving as a scapegoat when things go wrong. Gamson and Scotch (15) noted that in baseball, the firing of the manager served a scapegoating purpose. One cannot fire the whole team, yet when performance is poor, something must be done. The firing of the manager conveys to the world and to the actors involved that success is the result of personal actions, and that steps can and will be taken to enhance organizational performance.

The attribution of causality to leadership may be reinforced by organizational actions, such as the inauguration process, the choice process, and providing the leader with symbols and ceremony. If leaders are chosen by using a random number table, persons are less likely to believe in their effects than if there is an elaborate search or selection process followed by an elaborate ceremony signifying the changing of control, and if the leader then has a variety of perquisites and symbols that distinguish him or her from the rest of the organization. Construction of the importance of leadership in a given social context is the outcome of various social processes, which can be empirically examined.

Since belief in the leadership effect provides a feeling of personal control, one might argue that efforts to increase the attribution of causality to leaders would occur more when it is more necessary and more problematic to attribute causality to controllable factors. Such an argument would lead to the hypothesis that the more the *context* actually effects organizational outcomes, the more efforts will be made to ensure attribution to *leadership*. When leaders really do have effects, it is less necessary to engage in rituals indicating their effects. Such rituals are more likely when there is uncertainty and unpredictability associated with the organization's operations. This results both from the desire to feel control in uncertain situations and from the fact that in ambiguous contexts, it is easier to attribute consequences to leadership without facing possible disconfirmation.

The leader is, in part, an actor. Through statements and actions, the leader attempts to reinforce the operation of an attribution process which tends to vest causality in that position in the social structure. Successful leaders, as perceived by members of the social system, are those who can separate themselves from organizational failures and associate themselves with organizational successes. Since the meaning of action is socially constructed, this involves manipulation of symbols to reinforce the desired process of attribution. For instance, if a manager knows that business in his or her division is about to improve because of the economic cycle, the leader may, nevertheless, write recommendations and undertake actions and changes that are highly visible and that will tend to identify his or her behavior closely with the division. A manager who perceives impending failure will attempt to associate the division and its policies and decisions with others, particularly persons in higher organizational positions, and to disassociate himself or herself from the division's performance, occasionally even transferring or moving to another organization.

CONCLUSION

The theme of this article has been that analysis of leadership and leadership processes must be contingent on the intent of the researcher. If the interest is in understanding the causality of social phenomena as reliably and accurately as possible, then the concept of leadership may be a poor place to begin. The issue of the effects of leadership is open to question. But examination of situational variables that accompany more or less leadership effect is a worthwhile task.

The more phenomenological analysis of leadership directs attention to the process by which social causality is attributed, and focuses on the distinction between causality as perceived by group members and causality as assessed by an outside observer. Leadership is associated with a set of myths reinforcing a social construction of meaning which legitimates leadership role occupants, provides belief in potential mobility for those not in leadership roles, and attributes social causality to leadership roles, thereby providing a belief in the effectiveness of individual control. In analyzing leadership, this mythology and the process by which such mythology is created and supported should be separated from analysis of leadership as a social influence process, operating within constraints.

REFERENCES

1. Bales, R.F. *Interaction Process Analysis: A Method for the Study of Small Groups* (Reading, Mass.: Addison-Wesley, 1950).

2. Bavelas, Alex. "Leadership: Man and Function," *Administrative Science Quarterly*, Vol. 4 (1960), 491–498.

3. Berscheid, Ellen, and Elaine Walster. *Interpersonal Attraction* (Reading, Mass.: Addison-Wesley, 1969).

4. Bowers, David G., and Stanley E. Seashore. "Predicting Organizational Effectiveness with a Four-Factor Theory of Leadership," *Administrative Science Quarterly*, Vol. 11 (1966), 238–263.

5. Calder, Bobby J. "An Attribution Theory of Leadership," in B. Staw and G. Salancik (Eds.), *New Directions in Organizational Behavior* (Chicago: St. Clair Press, 1976), in press.

6. Cartwright, Dorwin C., and Alvin Zander. *Group Dynamics: Research and Theory*, 3rd ed. (Evanston, Ill.: Row, Peterson, 1960).

7. Cole, Jonathan R., and Stephen Cole. *Social Stratification in Science* (Chicago: University of Chicago Press, 1973).

8. Collins, Barry E., and Harold Guetzkow. *A Social Psychology of Group Processes for Decision-Making* (New York: Wiley, 1964).

9. Collins, Randall. "Functional and Conflict Theories of Stratification," *American Sociological Review*, Vol. 36 (1971), 1002–1019.

10. Day, R. C., and R. L. Hamblin. "Some Effects of Close and Punitive Styles of Supervision," *American Journal of Sociology*, Vol. 69 (1964), 499–510.

11. Domhoff, G. William. *Who Rules America?* (Englewood Cliffs, N.J.: Prentice-Hall, 1967).

12. Dubin, Robert. "Supervision and Productivity: Empirical Findings and Theoretical Considerations," in R. Dubin, G. C. Homans, F. C. Mann, and D. C. Miller (Eds.), *Leadership and Productivity* (San Francisco: Chandler Publishing Co., 1965), pp. 1–50.

13. Fiedler, Fred E. "Engineering the Job to Fit the Manager," *Harvard Business Review*, Vol. 43 (1965), 115–122.

14. Fiedler, Fred E. *A Theory of Leadership Effectiveness* (New York: McGraw-Hill, 1967).

15. Gamson, William A., and Norman A. Scotch. "Scapegoating in Baseball," *American Journal of Sociology*, Vol. 70 (1964), 69–72.

16. Granovetter, Mark. *Getting a Job* (Cambridge, Mass.: Harvard University Press, 1974).

17. Hall, Richard H. *Organizations: Structure and Process* (Englewood Cliffs, N.J.: Prentice-Hall, 1972).

18. Halpin, A. W., and J. Winer. "A Factorial Study of the Leader Behavior Description Questionnaire," in R. M. Stogdill and A. E. Coons (Eds.), *Leader Behavior: Its Description and Measurement* (Columbus, Ohio: Bureau of Business Research, Ohio State University, 1957), pp. 39–51.

19. Hargens, L. L. "Patterns of Mobility of New Ph.D.'s Among American Academic Institutions," *Sociology of Education*, Vol. 42 (1969), 18–37.

20. Hargens, L. L., and W. O. Hagstrom. "Sponsored and Contest Mobility of American Academic Scientists," *Sociology of Education*, Vol. 40 (1967), 24–38.

21. Harrell, Thomas W. "High Earning MBA's," *Personnel Psychology*, Vol. 25 (1972), 523–530.

22. Harrell, Thomas W., and Margaret S. Harrell. "Predictors of Management Success." *Stanford University Graduate School of Business, Technical Report No. 3 to the Office of Naval Research.*

23. Heller, Frank, and Gary Yukl. "Participation, Managerial Decision-Making, and Situational Variables," *Organizational Behavior and Human Performance*, Vol. 4 (1969), 227–241.

24. Hollander, Edwin P., and James W. Julian. "Contemporary Trends in the Analysis of Leadership Processes," *Psychological Bulletin*, Vol. 71 (1969), 387–397.

25. House, Robert J. "A Path Goal Theory of Leader Effectiveness," *Administrative Science Quarterly*, Vol. 16 (1971), 321–338.

26. Hunt, J. G. "Leadership-Style Effects at Two Managerial Levels in a Simulated Organization," *Administrative Science Quarterly*, Vol. 16 (1971), 476–485.

27. Kahn, R. L., D. M. Wolfe, R. P. Quinn, and J. D. Snoek. *Organizational Stress: Studies in Role Conflict and Ambiguity* (New York: Wiley, 1964).

28. Karabel, J., and A. W. Astin. "Social Class, Academic Ability, and College 'Quality'," *Social Forces*, Vol. 53 (1975), 381–398.

29. Kelley, Harold H. *Attribution in Social Interaction* (Morristown, N.J.: General Learning Press, 1971).

30. Kerr, Steven, and Chester Schriesheim. "Consideration, Initiating Structure and Organizational Criteria—An Update of Korman's 1966 Review," *Personnel Psychology*, Vol. 27 (1974), 555–568.

31. Kerr, S., C. Schriesheim, C. J. Murphy, and R. M. Stogdill, "Toward A Contingency Theory of Leadership Based Upon the Consideration and Initiating Structure Literature," *Organizational Behavior and Human Performance*, Vol. 12 (1974), 62–82.

32. Kiesler, C., and S. Kiesler. *Conformity* (Reading, Mass.: Addison-Wesley, 1969).

33. Kochan, T. A., S. M. Schmidt, and T. A. DeCotiis. "Superior-Subordinate Relations: Leadership and Headship," *Human Relations*, Vol. 28 (1975), 279–294.

34. Korman, A. K. "Consideration, Initiating Structure, and Organizational Criteria—A Review," *Personnel Psychology*, Vol. 19 (1966), 349–362.

35. Lieberson, Stanley, and James F. O'Connor. "Leadership and Organizational Performance: A Study of Large Corporations," *American Sociological Review*, Vol. 37 (1972), 117–130.

36. Lippitt, Ronald. "An Experimental Study of the Effect of Democratic and Authoritarian Group Atmospheres," *University of Iowa Studies in Child Welfare*, Vol. 16 (1940), 43–195.

37. Lowin, A., and J. R. Craig. "The Influence of Level of Performance on Managerial Style: An Experimental Object-Lesson in the Ambiguity of Correlational Data," *Organizational Behavior and Human Performance*, Vol. 3 (1968), 440–458.

38. Mills, C. Wright. "The American Business Elite: A Collective Portrait," in C. W. Mills, *Power, Politics, and People* (New York: Oxford University Press, 1963), pp. 110–139.

39. Mintzberg, Henry. *The Nature of Managerial Work* (New York: Harper and Row, 1973).

40. Nealey, Stanley M., and Milton R. Blood. "Leadership Performance of Nursing Supervisors at Two Organizational Levels," *Journal of Applied Psychology*, Vol. 52 (1968), 414–442.

41. Pfeffer, Jeffrey, and Gerald R. Salancik. "Determinants of Supervisory Behavior: A Role Set Analysis," *Human Relations*, Vol. 28 (1975), 139–154.

42. Pfeffer, Jeffrey, and Gerald R. Salancik. "Organizational Context and the Characteristics and Tenure of Hospital Administrators," *Academy of Management Journal*, Vol. 20 (1977), in press.

43. Reed, R. H., and H. P. Miller. "Some Determinants of the Variation in Earnings for College Men," *Journal of Human Resources*, Vol. 5 (1970), 117–190.

44. Salancik, Gerald R., and Jeffrey Pfeffer. "Constraints on Administrator Discretion: The Limited Influence of Mayors on City Budgets," *Urban Affairs Quarterly*, in press.

45. Sales, Stephen M. "Supervisory Style and Productivity: Review and Theory," *Personnel Psychology*, Vol. 19 (1966), 275–286.

46. Schutz Alfred. *The Phenomenology of the Social World* (Evanston, Ill.: Northwestern University Press, 1967)

47. Selznick, P. *Leadership in Administration* (Evanston, Ill.: Row, Peterson, 1957).

48. Spaeth, J. L., and A. M. Greeley. *Recent Alumni and Higher Education* (New York: McGraw-Hill, 1970).

49. Thompson, James D. *Organizations in Action* (New York: McGraw-Hill, 1967).

50. Vroom, Victor H. "Some Personality Determinants of the Effects of Participation," *Journal of Abnormal and Social Psychology*, Vol. 59 (1959), 322–327.

51. Vroom, Victor H., and Phillip W. Yetton. *Leadership and Decision-Making* (Pittsburgh: University of Pittsburgh Press, 1973).

52. Warner, W. L., and J. C. Abbeglin. *Big Business Leaders in America* (New York: Harper and Brothers, 1955).

53. Weick, Karl E. *The Social Psychology of Organizing* (Reading, Mass.: Addison-Wesley, 1969).

54. Weinstein, Alan G., and V. Srinivasan. "Predicting Managerial Success of Master of Business Administration (MBA) Graduates," *Journal of Applied Psychology*, Vol. 59 (1974), 207–212.

55. Wolfle, Dael. *The Uses of Talent* (Princeton: Princeton University Press, 1971).

56. Zald, Mayer N. "Who Shall Rule? A Political Analysis of Succession in a Large Welfare Organization," *Pacific Sociological Review*, Vol. 8 (1965), 52–60.

PART II

Power and Influence

Power does not corrupt men; fools, however, if they get into a position of power, corrupt power.

George Bernard Shaw

Nearly all men can stand adversity, but if you want to test a man's character, give him power.

Abraham Lincoln

One measure of leadership is the caliber of people who choose to follow you.

Dennis A. Peer

Charlatanism is to some degree indispensable to effective leadership.

Eric Hoffer

Power is the ultimate aphrodisiac.

Henry Kissinger

You can get more with a kind word and a gun, than with a kind word alone.

An American gangster

The first reading in this section, entitled "Power, Politics, and Influence," provides an overview of fundamental social dynamics. The reading initially defines power, authority and influence, and then moves on to a description of bases of power and techniques people use to gain power and influence. The article concludes with a consideration of the ethics of exercising power and how people respond to influence exercised by legitimate authority.

The next article takes up the topic of how subordinates relate to authority figures, and suggests that subordinates have opportunities to project upward influence on their bosses. Authors John J. Gabarro and

John P. Kotter underscore the mutual dependence that exists in work groups. The following article, on effective followership, considers the neglected topic of dimensions or styles of followership and argues for greater attention to appreciating how followers can dictate the responses of leaders.

David Kipnis and Stuart Schmidt then explore ways in which people try to influence others at work. Their results are most interesting in that their inductive approach identifies the tendency of people to choose among such tactics as assertiveness, ingratiation, rationality, sanctions, exchange, upward appeals, blocking, and coalitions when seeking to influence others.

The final article in this section, by Mario Sussmann and Robert Vecchio, integrates several major views of employee behavior in response to supervisory influence efforts. Their framework suggests that employee motivation can be understood in terms of employee acceptance or rejection of social influence efforts.

Power, Politics, and Influence

Robert P. Vecchio

DISTINGUISHING POWER AND INFLUENCE

Power is an essential feature of a manager's role. Without some degree of power, a manager would find it very difficult to direct the efforts of subordinates. Thus, power underlies a manager's effectiveness. Subordinates also possess forms and degrees of power. For example, subordinates can control the work flow or withhold support from their manager. Therefore, to some extent, each member of an organization possesses power.

Because power is intangible, it is very difficult to define clearly and precisely. Also, our language has several similar terms that we tend to confuse with power, such as authority and influence. In the interest of clarity, we shall define *power* as the ability to change the behavior of others. It is the ability to cause others to perform actions that they might not otherwise perform.[1]

Power is not always legitimate. Therefore, we speak of *authority* as the *right* to try to change or direct others. Authority includes the notion of legitimacy. It is the right to influence others in the pursuit of common goals that are agreed upon by various parties. Power, in contrast, does not always pursue common goals and may, at times, be clearly directed to pursuing only a single individual's goals.

Another term, *influence*, is also frequently used when discussing the notion of power. Influence tends to be subtler, broader, and more general than power. Although both influence and power can be defined as the ability to change the behavior of others, power embodies the ability to do so with regularity and ease. Influence is weaker and less reliable than power. Also, power rests on a number of specific sources or foundations, which will be examined in a subsequent section of this chapter. Influence relies on particular tactics and often employs face-to-face interactions. Thus, the exercise of influence tends to be more subtle than the exercise of power.

71

Interpersonal Influence Processes

In a classic article, Kelman distinguished among three primary reasons for an individual to yield to another person's attempt to be directive.[2] If an employee accepts a manager's influence attempt because she believes she will be rewarded or avoid being punished, her response is one of *compliance*. For example, an employee may skip lunch in order to finish typing a report for her supervisor. She may actually hope to receive an expression of appreciation from the supervisor or she may merely wish to avoid the hard feelings that will result if the report is not finished on time. The employee's behavior is strictly motivated by concern with rewards and punishments. Supervisors who strive for consistent compliance must (1) be certain that they can in fact deliver rewards or punishments and (2) be in a position to frequently monitor their subordinates' behavior.

A second influence process, *identification*, occurs when one person follows another's direction because of a desire to establish or maintain a personally satisfying relationship. When a subordinate admires his manager, seeks his approval, and perhaps tries to imitate him, we infer that the subordinate has a strong desire to identify with the manager. One example of this process occurs when a junior executive who greatly admires the CEO of his organization espouses the CEO's philosophy and beliefs when addressing the employees in his own work unit.

In both compliance and identification, the performance of an action in itself is not necessarily personally satisfying. Rather, the action may be due to a desire for specific outcomes (compliance) or an attraction to the source of influence (identification).

Sometimes employees' actions stem from a third reason: the belief that the behavior is congruent with their value systems. *Internalization* occurs when an employee accepts an influence attempt because he or she believes that the resulting behavior is correct and appropriate. For instance, assume that a high-level executive announces that the organization is participating in a United Way fund-raising campaign. Some of her managers may actively encourage subordinates to contribute to the fund because they strongly believe in the goals of United Way. These managers are not motivated by threats or rewards or admiration for their superior but rather by a personal commitment to a set of values.

The Five Bases of Power

Who gets what, when, and how are important concerns for every member of an organization. People at all levels are interested in and affected by the acquisition and distribution of rewards and resources. Of course, power plays a central role in such allocation processes. To explain how power operates, we will first examine the five distinct sources of power proposed by John French and Bertram Raven: reward power, coercive power, legitimate power, referent power, and expert power.[3]

Reward Power

Reward power is the ability to determine who will receive particular rewards. As long as the rewards are valued, a person who is able to distribute or withhold them can enjoy strong power over other's behavior. Granting promotions, giving raises, and conferring preferred job assignments are some typical rewards most managers can control. Unfortunately, this is not always the case. For example, when a work force is unionized, salary increases and job assignments are based more on seniority and the specifics of a labor contract than on the judgment of a manager or supervisor. The relationship between performance and rewards should always be clear. When a manager lacks the ability to administer both extrinsic and intrinsic rewards, it becomes extremely difficult to direct subordinates' behavior. Reward power gives a manager a distinct advantage in obtaining desired ends from his or her work group.

Coercive Power

If reward power can be termed "the carrot," then coercive power is "the stick." *Coercive power* stems from the capacity to produce fear in others. The threat of punishment can be a strong means of invoking compliance. The most obvious examples of punishments are demotions, salary cuts, suspension, removal of such perquisites as a company car or an expense account, and dismissal. However, coercive power can also be more subtle. For example, criticism and the denial of emotional support and friendship may also be effective forms of coercion.

The application of coercive power requires good social judgment. In some instances, a manager is actually expected to be coercive—as when a subordinate is extremely unproductive or interferes with the productivity of others. In such a situation, other employees and managers will rightly expect the supervisor to take firm action.

On the other hand, a manager must be careful when applying coercive power. If he or she is too heavy-handed and indiscriminately inflicts punishment on all employees, morale and productivity are likely to suffer. Such a manager may find that the unit's turnover rate is very high as people seek employment elsewhere. In addition, injured employees may retaliate by sabotaging the unit's operations or withholding useful suggestions for improving the unit's performance.

Despite its potentially negative effects, coercive power underlies much of the routine compliance that occurs in organizations. Decisions to arrive at work on time, meet deadlines, and so forth are often largely due to fear of being fired, ridiculed, or reprimanded. Rightly or wrongly, coercive power is frequently used in most organizations.

Legitimate Power

Legitimate power stems from the willingness of others to accept an individual's direction. They feel an obligation to follow the individual's lead and submit to his authority. There are two sources of legitimate power. The first is social conditioning: From early childhood, people are conditioned to accept the direction of authority figures. They learn that teachers and crossing guards, as well as foremen and managers, have the right to lead or direct others. The second source of legitimate power is designation: A person can gain power by being designated an authority figure by someone who already possesses legitimate authority. For example, the president of a company may assign a vice president the authority to make important decisions on the company's behalf. The president thus gives the vice president legitimate power to act as his representative and exercise authority accordingly.

Legitimate power can be effective only if it is accepted by the people it is intended to control. If the people withdraw their support from the system that is the basis of power, the power ceases to exist. Such withdrawals of support occur in revolutions, when ruling classes and their social systems are overthrown, and in riots, when a spontaneous but limited rebellion is made against authority.

Referent Power

People with attractive personalities or other special qualities possess a form of power. Their appearance, poise, interpersonal style, or values can inspire admiration and cause others to identify with them. The resulting ability to influence behavior is called *referent power*. It is often easy to identify an individual who possesses such power. For example, most people would agree that successful politicians, athletes, and entertainers—such as Bill Clinton, Michael Jordan, and Oprah Winfrey—have this attribute. However, it is extremely difficult to define exactly what gives these people their charisma. Usually, vigor and the appearance of success play important roles. But other characteristics that contribute to referent power can be very difficult to pinpoint (consider, for example, that Adolf Hitler was judged to be charismatic in the eyes of his countrymen).

Referent power derives from people's desire to identify with the qualities of an attractive individual. Advertising that uses a celebrity to endorse a product is based on referent power, since the sponsor hopes that the audience will buy the product in an attempt to imitate the celebrity's behavior and attitudes.

Expert Power

Individuals with *expert power* are able to direct others because they are perceived as knowledgeable or talented in a given area. Most of us readily seek and follow the advice of experts, such as our family physician or athletic coach. So too are we likely to follow the directions of a coworker who is seen as having expertise in our field of work. This form of power is usually limited to a fairly narrow and specific realm, however, and does not spread to other areas of social interaction.

Most subordinates presume that their superiors possess expert power in the form of understanding all jobs in the work unit. Generally, greater levels of experience and job-relevant knowledge do give a manager an edge in expertise. However, in highly technical job settings, it may happen that some subordinates have more expert knowledge about certain aspects of their jobs than do their managers. In fact, some managers may be highly dependent on the technical expertise of their subordinates in order to successfully manage their work units. In such a situation, expert power can lead to an atypical reversal of the usual manager-subordinate relationship.

Interplay among the Power Bases

A manager can possess each of the five sources of power to varying degrees, and his or her use of one power base can affect the strength of another. For example, a person can gain greater legitimacy by being promoted to a higher-level position. Of course, a position of greater legitimate power usually entails more opportunities to use rewards and coercion. The exercise of coercion, however, could reduce the manager's referent power because coercion tends to produce immediate compliance but may have negative side effects.

Above all, the manager should bear in mind that the tendency to use power can lead to greater effectiveness, while the failure to use power can have the opposite effect. Managers who exercise power with some frequency can be counted on to continue such behavior in future settings and are, therefore, given greater deference by subordinates. More passive managers may have difficulty if they suddenly decide to use their power because their subordinates will have become accustomed to their lack of assertiveness.

Distinctions can be drawn among the five power bases. Expert and referent power bases are more informal in nature, while legitimate, reward, and coercive power bases are more formal. The informal power bases have a greater capacity to affect overall employee satisfaction and performance. The formal power bases, in contrast, have potentially greater impact on immediate behavior. Although formal power can elicit a quick response from an employee, it will not necessarily produce agreement and commitment. For example, a worker may comply with a manager's order but still resent having been coerced.

Many centuries ago, the Italian philosopher Machiavelli contended that people who have formal power tend to remain in their positions of authority longer than people who rely on informal power. This observation makes some sense in that the informal bases of power can be more easily eroded, since they depend on people's perceptions. For example, a manager may lose his expertise due to changes in technology or his appeal may diminish following a series of unpopular actions or personnel changes. While expert power can be regained through technical training, there are no surefire ways of increasing referent power.

In general, informal power resides in the personal characteristics of the manager, whereas formal power resides in the position itself. It can be forcefully argued, however, that all sources of power can really be reduced to a single category: control over reinforcers. The most effective way to control others' behavior is to control when and how they receive reinforcement.

AN ORGANIZATIONAL ANALYSIS OF POWER

In his analysis of how complex organizations attempt to direct the behavior of their members, Etzioni identified three kinds of organizational power.[4] One type of organizational power can be characterized as coercive. Such organizations try to extract compliance from members through threats and punishment. Examples of coercive organizations include prisons, some mental institutions, and divisions within the military (such as boot camp).

Most business organizations, of course, do not rely on coercion, but instead offer contingent incentives: If employees follow directives, they can expect to be rewarded. Such organizations are said to use *utilitarian power* because of their emphasis on the utility of conforming to directives.

A third set of organizations relies on *normative power*. In this type of organization, members accept directives because of their sense of affiliation with the organization and its espoused values. Professional associations (such as the American Dental Association) and religious organizations typically use normative power to influence their members.

All three types of power can be useful in obtaining people's cooperation in organizations. However, the relative effectiveness of each approach depends on the organizational members' orientation or involvement. Etzioni contends that members' involvement can be broadly categorized as alienative, calculative, or moral. Members with *alienative involvement* have hostile, rejecting, and extremely negative attitudes. Members with *calculative involvement* are rational and oriented toward maximizing personal gain. And members with *moral involvement* are committed to the socially beneficial features of their organizations.

According to Etzioni, the three types of organizational power can be matched with the three types of involvement. According to this logic, only one type of power is most appropriate for each type of member involvement. Attempts to use types of power that are inappropriate for the type of involvement can reduce effectiveness. Figure 1 illustrates Etzioni's model of power and involvement.

TYING IT ALL TOGETHER

Sussmann and Vecchio formally compared the three models of power and influence put forth by French and Raven, Kelman, and Etzioni.[5] A good deal of similarity was identified among all three views. For example, French and Raven's concepts of reward and coercive power have a strong similarity to Kelman's notions of compliance. Referent power, in turn, is allied to Kelman's notion of identification, and legitimate and expert power overlap to a great extent with the process of internalization. Both Etzioni and Kelman identify three forms of power (or influence), but while Etzioni focuses on the organizational level of analysis, Kelman focuses on the interpersonal level. Table 1 summarizes the comparison of the three views.

In a sense, the multiple forms of power identified correspond to the need-level views of Maslow and others. The correspondence lies in the

Figure 1
Etzioni's Model of Power and Involvement

Types of Power

Types of Involvement	Coercive	Utilitarian	Normative
Alienative	X		
Calculative		X	
Moral			X

Table 1
A Comparison of Three Views of Power and Influence

Interpersonal Influence Process (Kelman)	Power Bases (French and Raven)	Organizational Power (Etzioni)
Internalization	Legitimate Power Expert Power	Normative
Identification	Referent Power	Normative
Compliance (reward-based)	Reward Power	Utilitarian
Compliance (punishment-based)	Coercive Power	Coercive

recognition that there are several levels of motivation or forms of influence. One level is fairly rudimentary: reward and punishment. A higher level is more social in nature: referent or identification. And the highest level is fairly psychological in nature: internalization or legitimacy.

A SOCIAL INFLUENCE VIEW OF SUPERVISOR BEHAVIOR

Sussmann and Vecchio also proposed that a supervisor's attempts to exert influence follow a cycle in which he or she tries one of three approaches to influence a subordinate in accordance with the three levels of needs and the three forms of power.[6] This view suggests that a supervisor (or evaluator) will attempt to use compliance, identification, or internalization to influence an individual. Respectively, he or she may try threats, appeals to a subordinate's sense of organizational membership or affiliation, or appeals to the subordinate's value system.

Such attempts will succeed or fail to the extent that the individual is disposed to accept incentives or threats, identity-related appeals, or value-related appeals. For certain types of subordinates, a particular type of disposition may be more prevalent, as is suggested by Etzioni's notion of involvement. Acceptance of the supervisor's influence attempt leads to behavioral intentions on the part of the subordinate to act in the desired direction. The actual behavior of the subordinate is then compared to the standards that are held in the mind of the supervisor. If the influence attempt is judged to have failed, the supervisor will likely try another attempt, but perhaps with a different type of influence (for example, appealing on a different level). This model suggests that supervisors need to be sensitive to differences in subordinates' preferences for inducement schemes. It is possible that supervisors who are aware of and make use of subordinate preferences for inducements are relatively more effective than other supervisors.

POLITICS: THE FACTS OF ORGANIZATIONAL LIFE

The terms *politics* and *power* are sometimes used interchangeably. Though they are related, they are nonetheless distinct notions. Pfeffer defines *organizational politics* as "those activities taken within organizations to acquire, develop, and use power and other resources to obtain one's preferred outcomes in a situation in which there is uncertainty or [disagreement] about choices."[7] In a sense, the study of organizational politics constitutes the study of power in action. It may also be said that politics involves the playing out of power and influence.

The word *politics* has a somewhat negative connotation. It suggests that someone is attempting to use means or to gain ends that are not sanctioned by the organization. Actually, political behavior, as we've defined it, is quite neutral. Similarly, power is not inherently negative. Whether a person views power and politics as unsavory topics depends on a number of considerations, most important perhaps being where the individual stands on a specific issue in a given situation. Nonetheless, most managers are reluctant to admit to the political character of their own work settings.

A further point is that all members of an organization may exhibit political behavior. In our previous discussion of power, we took a fairly formal and traditional approach to the topic of influence. Thus, we looked at power from the perspective of a supervisor or manager who directs others. Yet, in the area of politics, everyone is a player. Subordinates, as well as their managers, can engage in the give-and-take of organizational politics.[†]

[†] Nonetheless, it is widely believed that political behavior is far less common and less intense among employees in lower-level positions than among employees in higher-level positions.

Political Tactics

Several authors have identified a variety of political tactics used by employees at virtually all levels.[8] In this section, we will examine a number of these activities.

Ingratiation

This tactic involves giving compliments to or doing favors for superiors or coworkers. Most people have a difficult time rejecting the positive advances of others. Ingratiation usually works as a tactic insofar as the target often feels positive toward the source even if the ingratiation attempt is fairly blatant and transparent.

In the behavioral sciences, the notion of "social reciprocity" has been offered to help explain the process of ingratiation. In social reciprocity, there is a feeling of a social obligation to repay the positive actions of others with similar actions. For example, if someone pays you a compliment, there is a strong expectation that you should respond with a compliment of your own. If you fail to do so, you may be judged as being rude. Similarly, ingratiation involves giving positive strokes to a person with the expectation that he or she will feel obligated to return them in some form.

Forming Coalitions and Networks

Another political tactic consists of befriending important people. These people may not be in positions of any obvious political value. However, their jobs may provide them with information that could be useful to have. Some people find that forming friendships with people in upper-level management can help them gain access to important information. They may also find that by being on good terms with their boss's secretary, they can sometimes gain inside information and easier access to the boss.

Impression Management

A simple tactic that virtually everyone uses from time to time is the management of their outward appearance and style. Generally, most organizations prefer a particular image that consists of being loyal, attentive, honest, neatly groomed, sociable, and so forth. By deliberately trying to exhibit this preferred image, an individual can make a positive impression on influential members of the organization.

Information Management

A further tactic consists of managing the information that is shared with others. The nature, as well as the timing, of information given out can have strong effects on others' conduct. Releasing good or bad news when it is likely to have its fullest impact can greatly promote one person's self-interest or defeat the hopes of others. Similarly, an individual can ask for information (such as sales data or a production report) when it is most likely to make things appear particularly good or bad. People who play the information management game are not likely to lie or spread misinformation, however, because their future credibility would be jeopardized. Instead, they rely on the carefully planned release of valid information to obtain their ends.

Promote the Opposition

It may sound strange, but one way to eliminate opposition is to aid political rivals. For example, it is possible to eliminate a political rival by helping that person become so successful that he or she is transferred to a desirable position someplace else in the organization. Recommending a rival for a new assignment or even a promotion within another division of the organization can make one's own work life easier.

Pursue Line Responsibility

Within virtually every organization, some positions are more closely tied to the primary mission of the organization; these jobs are called line positions. They are at the very heart of the organization. People who occupy support positions are said to be in staff positions. Examples of line positions include engineering, manufacturing, and sales in a customer-oriented firm. People in departments such as public relations, market research, and personnel are usually in staff positions. While staff people may come to wield great power within their own territories, it is the line people who usually "call the shots" on major issues. Line people not only make the more important decisions within the organization, they are also more likely to be promoted to top-level executive positions. In many organizations, there is a preferred department of origin and career path for top-level managers. These are usually line positions. Therefore, one way to gain influence within an organization is to be assigned initially to, or be transferred to a line position. It will often provide more visibility, influence, and upward mobility.

Devious Political Tactics

Some political tactics are quite honest in nature. For example, accumulating seniority, providing copies of your accomplishments to your boss, and hitching your wagon to yourself are all respectable means for gaining influence.[‡] Some other tactics, however, are difficult to defend on moral grounds. In the interest of self-defense, it is worth examining several of these devious political tactics.[9]

Take No Prisoners

Sometimes it is necessary to do something unpopular or distasteful, such as demote or transfer someone or announce pay cuts. During corporate takeovers, many unpopular actions may be necessary. As a result, political enemies are likely to be made. One tactic for dealing with this potential problem is to ruthlessly eliminate *all* individuals who may resent your past actions by having them fired or transferred.

Divide and Conquer

This tactic involves creating a feud among two or more people so that they will be continually off balance and thus unable to mount an attack against you. This is a very old idea that is still practiced in some work settings. An unscrupulous individual who employs this tactic usually encourages bickering between possible rivals by spreading rumors or promoting competition between subordinates or factions. This is a risky tactic, however, as the opponents may eventually compare notes

---

[‡] Pure and simple performance remains an essential ingredient of a successful career in virtually all fields of endeavor.

and conclude that someone else is really responsible for creating and maintaining their bad feelings.

Exclude the Opposition

Another devious tactic involves keeping rivals away from important meetings and social occasions. This can be done simply by scheduling important affairs when the opposition is out of town (on vacation or a business trip) or attending another meeting. With the opposition absent, it is possible to influence decision making or to take credit for a rival's efforts.

Political Blunders

Although certain tactics can promote desired ends, others can be costly political mistakes. Among the most common are violating the chain of command, losing your cool, saying no to top management, upstaging your supervisor, and challenging cherished beliefs. These activities constitute serious political blunders or mistakes.

Violating Chain of Command

Occasionally, a person will feel that it is his duty to see his boss's boss, either to complain about his treatment at the hands of his own boss or to serve as an informant. A person may even feel that such an "end run" is justified because he is fervently convinced of the rightness of his position. However, going over the boss's head is often a very strong organizational taboo. Generally, it is expected that an employee will ask the boss's permission before seeing his superior on any matter.

Losing Your Cool

Throwing temper tantrums and acting aggressively toward others are often seen as acceptable and sometimes effective tactics in settings such as sports events. But in office settings, these tactics do not work well at all. Fist pounding and snide remarks usually earn a person a reputation for being hard to deal with, a label that can be extremely difficult to overcome. One devious twist on this tactic is to goad a person who tends to be acerbic and aggressive into displaying these tendencies at the wrong times. In this way, such a person's peers help him or her to commit political suicide.

Saying No to Top Management

One of the surest ways to stop your own career progress is to reject a request from top-level management. Instead of feeling fortunate to be selected for an assignment, some individuals believe that they are over-burdened and that they are being "dumped on," or that they can afford to defy top management because they are indispensable. This represents poor judgment on two counts: First, people in the lower ranks of an organization are rarely indispensable. Second, if workers are overbur-dened, they should explain the situation to the manager and try to arrange for additional help.

Upstaging Your Supervisor

Generally speaking, one should avoid publicly criticizing others. For example, it is not considered appropriate for a supervisor to criticize a subordinate in public view. However, the reverse is also true. A subordinate should refrain from implicitly criticizing the boss by upstaging him or her. Upstaging often takes the form of bragging about one's own accomplishments or claiming credit for a unit's success.

Challenging Cherished Beliefs

In many firms, there are a number of cherished beliefs about the nature of the organization, and it is generally considered "poor form" to criticize or challenge such folklore within earshot of company loyalists. Examples of such fond beliefs include "This organization is the best in its field," "Our founder was (or is) an outstanding individual," and "People who leave our organization are people that we are better off without." To be sure, all people are entitled to their own opinions, but it can be politically foolish to engage in an open debate about the truth of certain widely held beliefs.

Coping with Organizational Politics

Political gamesmanship, when carried to the extreme, has many dysfunctional effects: Morale is weakened, victors and victims are created, and energy and time are spent on planning attacks and counterattacks instead of on productivity. Thus, combating politics must be part of a manager's job.

Set an Example

When a manager plays political games, such as distorting the facts or manipulating people, he or she conveys to subordinates a message that such conduct is acceptable. A manager can create a climate either tolerant or intolerant of dirty tricks. Clearly, a department is better served by a manager who provides a positive role model by encouraging truthfulness and the even-handed treatment of others.

Give Clear Job Assignments

Politics seem to be more prevalent when overall purposes are unclear and it is difficult to assess the performance of individual employees.[§] One way to counter political activities is to give well-defined, discrete work assignments. When expectations are clear and subordinates understand how they will be assessed, game playing becomes less necessary as a device for gaining personal recognition.

Eliminate Coalitions and Cliques

Coalitions and cliques that are detrimental to unit performance can often be reduced in influence or eliminated. Although dismissal and transfer are two possible solutions, individuals may also be rotated through different job assignments. Job rotation encourages an employee's perception of the larger enterprise and helps to counter an us-them view of other departments.

[§] The attributes of an open-ended purpose and difficulty in measuring individual performance are especially relevant to academic departments.

Confront Game Players

Even in a climate of trust and openness, individuals may make suggestive comments or offer information that has an ulterior motive. A good response in such a situation is simply to ask, "Why are you telling me this about Sam?" or "Why don't you and I go see Sam's boss about this right now? I think you should tell her what you've just told me." Another useful response is to offer to discuss questionable information in a public forum. A manager may say, for example, "I think I understand your concerns on this issue. Let's bring it up for discussion at our next department meeting." Using a public forum to discuss and choose a course of action is an excellent defense to most dubious suggestions. As a rule, a manager should not get involved in any scheme that he or she is unwilling to have discussed in public. Knowing that all suggestions are subject to open discussion invariably discourages people who hope to engage a manager in political games.

Machiavellianism

Niccolò Machiavelli, an Italian philosopher and statesman (1469–1527), was one of the earliest writers on the topic of political behavior. In his works, Machiavelli examined political effectiveness without regard for ethics or morality. Machiavelli simply ignored moral considerations in exploring not how people *should* behave, but how they actually *do* behave. Because of his uncompromising view of political reality, Machiavelli has sometimes been called the ultimate pragmatist. In recent years, his name has come to be synonymous with the use of political treachery and maneuvering. Thus, to say that someone is Machiavellian is a serious insult.**

Christie and Geis have tried to assess the extent to which an individual's personal style is Machiavellian in nature.[10] To do so, they converted certain basic tenets of Machiavelli's writings into an attitude scale that can be used to measure the extent to which an individual

---

** Other world cultures have also had their own version of Niccolò Machiavelli. About 300 B.C., both Lord Shang of China and Koutilya, a prime minister in the south of India, wrote much the same philosophy as Machiavelli. All three writers shared several common themes: Humankind is basically weak, fallible, and gullible; therefore, a rational person takes advantage of situations and protects himself or herself from the implicit untrustworthiness of others.

agrees with Machiavelli's views. The statements of the Machiavellian scale (or *Mach Scale* for short) focus on several factors. Chief among them are (1) the use of manipulative interpersonal tactics ("It is wise to flatter important people" and "Never tell anyone the real reason you did something unless it is useful to do so") and (2) an unfavorable view of human nature ("Generally speaking, people won't work hard unless they are forced to do so" and "Anyone who completely trusts anyone else is asking for trouble").

A good deal is known about people who score high in agreement with Machiavelli's views.[11] Generally, they are able to control social interactions and effectively manipulate others. They are also especially effective in using their skills in face-to-face settings. A series of studies among college students found that highly Machiavellian students were more likely to be involved in medicine as a career and were more critical of their fellow students.[12] They also admitted to having strong feelings of hostility. In one contrived study, when students were induced to cheat and then accused of doing so, highly Machiavellian individuals looked their accuser in the eye and denied cheating longer than did less Machiavellian individuals.

Still other research indicates that Machiavellianism is positively correlated with occupational attainment (that is, job prestige and income) for individuals with above-average education, while for individuals with below-average education Machiavellianism is inversely related to occupational attainment. These results make sense in that highly Machiavellian individuals require situations that offer considerable latitude for improvisation and interpersonal manipulation (as is characteristic of white-collar jobs). Individuals in blue-collar jobs, where standards of performance are more objective and disciplinary measures are relatively coercive, may be penalized in proportion to their degree of Machiavellianism.[13]

In general, Machiavellian individuals are thought to be socially domineering and manipulative, and they are assumed to engage in political behavior more often than other organizational participants. They are lacking in (1) emotional display in interpersonal relations (that is, they remain cool and distant, and treat others as objects to be manipulated), (2) concern for traditional morality (that is, they find deceit useful rather than reprehensible), and (3) ideological commitments (that is, they prefer to maintain personal power in situations, rather than adhere to relatively inflexible ideals).

Consequences of Using Influence Tactics

Research on attempts to influence others has begun to focus on the specific techniques people use at work. After conversations with employees, David Kipnis and Stuart Schmidt developed a questionnaire for measuring six tactics for influencing others.[14] These tactics include:

1. Reason: relies on using data, logic, and discussion
2. Friendliness: interest, goodwill, and esteem are demonstrated to create a favorable impression
3. Coalition formation: other people in the organization are mobilized to support requests
4. Bargaining: relies on negotiation and exchanging favors
5. Assertiveness: relies on directness and forcefulness in communication
6. Appeal to higher authority: the influence of those higher in the organization is invoked to back up a request.

From responses to their questionnaire, Kipnis and Schmidt grouped employees into four influence styles:

1. Shotguns: people who refuse to take "no" for an answer and who use all of the preceding tactics to achieve their ends
2. Tacticians: people who try to influence others through reason and logic
3. Ingratiators: people who rely on ingratiation and flattery
4. Bystanders: people who watch the action rather than attempt to influence it[15]

Comparisons of performance evaluations for the four types of employees revealed that people who assertively attempted to influence their supervisors (Shotguns) were viewed less favorably. Both male and female Shotguns received equally low evaluations from their supervisors. Male supervisors tended to give the highest ratings to male Tacticians, who relied on reason and logic. Women who received the highest ratings were likely to be Ingratiators and Bystanders. In responding to these findings, male supervisors explained that both male Tacticians and female Ingratiators were seen as deferential and thoughtful.

Salary was also found to be associated with influence style. In a comparison of the income of 108 male CEOs, Tacticians earned the most

($73,240), followed by Bystanders (60,270), Shotguns ($56,480), and Ingratiators ($52,700). Based on both evaluations and income, it seems that Tacticians are valued more than their peers who use other styles. Also, Shotgun-style individuals reported more job tension and personal stress than their counterparts.

Kipnis and Schmidt argue, from these and other findings, that books and training programs that are designed to "put people in charge" (in essence, teach a Shotgun style) are questionable. They contend that people should not be taught to be overly assertive as the best tactic for achieving their desires. Instead, training programs should emphasize less vigorous influence styles that rely on reason and logic.[16] Also, it is interesting to contrast managers' preferred styles when trying to influence superiors versus subordinates. Kipnis and Schmidt report that reason is preferred for trying to influence both superiors and subordinates. However, assertiveness is far more likely to be used with subordinates than with superiors, while coalition formation is more likely to be used to influence superiors than to influence subordinates.

Other Influence Techniques

Beyond the influence tactics discussed thus far are several other, more subtle, mechanisms by which people can be influenced. One effective technique is to create the appearance of higher *status*. Research has shown that people who merely appear to have higher status by virtue of their manner of dress or the use of titles exert greater influence. For example, in one study, a man violated the traffic light when crossing the street. In half the instances, the man was dressed in a well-tailored business suit, while in the remaining instances, he wore a work shirt and trousers. Of interest was the number of pedestrians who would cross the street with the man. As would be predicted from a status influence view, the well-dressed jaywalker influenced 3½ times as many people to cross the street with him.[17]

A second subtle form of influence is to create the appearance that a behavior is *normative*. For example, bartenders often place a few dollars into a tip glass to create the appearance that tipping is a proper action, and that greenbacks, not change, are commonly given. Also, "ringers" are sometimes planted in the audiences of preachers, with instructions to come forward on cue with donations or "cures."‡ The apparent popularity of an action generally tends to induce compliance. For example, in one study, several individuals stared upward at the sky over New York City for a prolonged period of time. Within a short while, most passersby were also gazing at the empty sky.[18]

Lastly, people can sometimes be influenced to comply with a request for a sizable favor that they would otherwise not agree to, if they are first asked to do a small favor. This foot-in-the-door principle was once demonstrated in a study in which researchers asked people to install a large "Drive Carefully" sign in their front yards. Only 17 percent agreed to post a large sign. However, individuals who were initially asked to display a small 3-inch sign in their windows (which nearly all agreed to do) yielded 76 percent of the time when asked two weeks later to post the large sign.[19]

The Ethics of Organizational Politics

Figure 2 presents a model for incorporating ethical considerations into deciding whether to act in a political manner. This model, proposed by Gerald Cavanagh, Dennis Moberg, and Manuel Velasquez, provides guidance on whether a political behavior (PB), or course of action, should be followed in a particular situation.[20] From their perspective, a political behavior is ethical and appropriate only if (1) the behavior respects the rights of all affected parties and (2) the behavior respects the canons of justice—a self-evidently correct judgment of what is equitable and fair. In essence, the model encourages the adoption of nonpolitical behaviors (where such alternatives exist), and the rejection of behaviors that interfere with the canons of justice.

To illustrate their model, Cavanagh and his associates suggest a case in which two research scientists, Sam and Bill, are in competition in a new-product development lab. Each has prepared a proposal to win a significant cash award for the best new-product idea. Blind reviews of the proposals by other scientists indicate that both are equally meritorious.

---

‡ The use of ringers to induce behavior in others in a calculated fashion dates from Parisian opera houses in the 1820s, where members of the audience were paid to applaud or cheer on cue during the performance. The modern descendent of this practice is the television laugh track.

Figure 2
A Decision Tree for Incorporating Ethics into Political Behavior Decisions

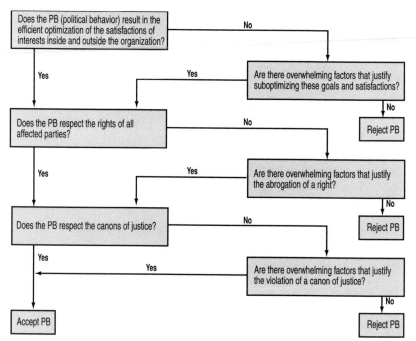

Sam inquires periodically about the outcome of the bidding process, while Bill wages an open campaign in support of his proposal. Specifically, Bill seizes every opportunity to point out the relative advantages of his proposal to individuals who may have some impact on the final decision. He does this after freely admitting his intention to Sam and others. His campaign of informal pressure is effective and his proposal is funded, while Sam's is not.

Using the decision tree, we first ask whether the outcome, in terms of the broad interests of society and the company, will be optimal. Since both proposals were judged to be equivalent in the blind reviews, we must answer yes to the first question. The second question focuses on whether Bill's behavior respected the rights of Sam. Because Bill told Sam he intended to campaign actively for his proposal, Bill cannot be accused of deceit. Also, Sam's inaction may be viewed as implied consent. The third question highlights the suspect nature of Bill's actions in pointing out irrelevant differences between the proposals. Given the equivalent merit of the proposals, other considerations (for example, which scientist was most qualified to implement the proposal, or other evidence of past performance) should have been incorporated in the funding decision.

RESPONDING TO AUTHORITY: OBEDIENCE

For managers to meet their goals, they must rely on their subordinates to obey their directions. Obedience to authority is a strongly ingrained predisposition for most people. Without this predisposition, society would not be able to function. Usually, the depth of our predisposition to obey orders can only be guessed at. Occasionally, we hear of instances of blind obedience to authority, as in the war-crime trials of Adolf Eichmann and Lieutenant William Calley, but we tend to discount such cases as extreme and unusual.

In the early 1960s, Stanley Milgram of Yale University conducted a series of studies to examine the extent to which people would obey, even if the demands of authority violated their moral responsibilities.[21] As part of this research, 40 adult males from a wide variety of occupations were paid to serve as subjects in a learning experiment. Each subject was told that he was participating in a study of the effects of punishment on learning. The subject was then asked to help another adult (actually the researcher's confederate) learn a lengthy list of word pairs by using electric shock as a penalty for each incorrect answer.

The subject (teacher) met with the alleged learner and then watched as the learner was strapped into an apparatus that looked like an electric chair. The experimenter then took the subject into the next room and showed him how to communicate with the learner through an intercom system. The experimenter also explained how to administer the punishment for any errors the learner might make in responding to stimulus words in the list of word pairs. The shock generator contained 30 switches, one for each of 30 different voltage levels ranging from 15 to 450 volts. The switches were also labeled in terms of the increasing strength of the voltage: slight shock, moderate shock, strong shock, very strong shock, intense shock, extreme intensity shock, danger: severe shock, and XXX.

After reading the list of word pairs to the learner, the teacher was to begin quizzing the learner. For each incorrect response, the teacher was to administer an electric shock, and for each additional incorrect response, the teacher was to apply the next higher voltage level on the generator.

The trials passed uneventfully until the learner began to make numerous mistakes. Then, in short order, the teacher found himself administering fairly high levels of voltage to the learner. At that point, the learner would begin to protest, saying that he wanted to drop out of the experiment because his heart was bothering him and the pain of the shocks was too much for him. If the teacher hesitated, the experimenter would encourage him to proceed, saying, for example, "Please go on" or "It is essential that you continue." If the teacher refused to proceed after four verbal encouragements, the experiment was discontinued.

As the voltage levels increased, the confederate (in accord with the experiment's protocol) would voice even stronger objections: He would pound on the wall and, at one point, scream loudly. Beyond a certain voltage level, the learner would no longer answer any of the teacher's questions, giving the impression that he was injured or dead. When this silence occurred, the experimenter would tell the teacher to treat the learner's failure to respond as an incorrect response, to administer the punishment, and to continue on with the next word pair.

Given these conditions, you would probably assume that very few subjects would obey the experimenter. But the actual results revealed that a majority of the subjects administered the maximum voltage on the shock generator and continued their participation in the experiment despite the learner's objections.

We should note, however, that although most subjects gave the maximum level of shock to the learner, they did not enjoy doing so. Typically, the subjects displayed strong signs of nervous tension, such as nail biting, trembling, and groaning. Many of them also laughed nervously whenever the learner protested or pleaded. However, the constraints of the situation compelled the subjects to continue their participation.[‡‡]

The high level of obedience displayed by Milgram's subjects suggests that the predisposition to follow authority is very strong. In this case, the

---

[‡‡] When each subject completed the experiment, he met with the learner and discovered that in fact no shocks had been given. The true purpose of the study was then explained to each subject.

experimenter relied on his expertise and legitimacy to give the subject orders. Despite the fact that all subjects received their pay in advance and participated voluntarily, most felt a strong desire to avoid disobeying authority, even in light of the suffering they inflicted on another person.

These results suggest that society may be too successful at socializing its members to obey authority. When people take on roles that prescribe obedience (such as those of research subject, student, soldier, or employee), the sense of responsibility for the outcomes of their own conduct is likely to be diminished. The evidence from Milgram's work implies that human conscience cannot be relied on to step in and halt activities that are injurious to others. It can be inferred that organizational members generally will carry out orders given by those in authority, regardless of the content or consequences of the actions. This suggests that forms of socialization that emphasize personal responsibility to others may be lacking in our society.

Milgram's findings have raised a number of questions. One of the more intriguing is whether there are cultural differences in the predisposition to obey authority. For example, considering the Holocaust—the persecution and extermination of European Jews by Nazi Germany— one might hypothesize that the level of obedience would be higher in Germany than in other countries. To test this notion, the conditions of Milgram's original study were recreated in several different countries: Canada, England, Jordan, and the former West Germany. The results yielded essentially similar findings, suggesting that the level of obedience to authority in the Milgram condition is fairly constant across different societies.[22] By inference, the atrocities that occurred in Nazi Germany could happen elsewhere in the world.[§§]

In addition, the level of obedience in the Milgram study may have been near the "baseline" for injurious behavior. The victim (learner) in

[§§] Such mass atrocities have in fact happened again—witness Cambodia, Uganda, Mao's China, and Stalin's Russia. In an interview with Morley Safer for the news program "Sixty Minutes," Milgram stated that "if a system of death camps were set up in the United States of the sort we had seen in Nazi Germany, one would be able to find sufficient personnel for those camps in any medium-sized American town".[23] However, other evidence from cross-national studies is somewhat suggestive of cultural differences. In a less well publicized self-decision condition (wherein the "teacher" was allowed to choose the shock level in each trial), various studies found extremely low levels of total shock administered by all national samples. However, the levels administered for German and Jordanian samples were somewhat higher than those observed for Australian and U.S. samples.[24]

Milgram's original study was an innocent 47-year-old man. If the victim had been someone whom the subject disliked for any number of possible reasons (race, religion, or politics) or had the subject possessed a strong commitment to the purpose of the study in which he was involved, or expected to be continually involved with persons in the study, the level of obedience might well have been much higher.

The study of the personalities of participants in the Milgram experiments has yielded some interesting findings. Subjects who were relatively more obedient were significantly more authoritarian. This result confirms the notion that a major component of the authoritarian personality is one of uncritical submission to an idealized authority.[25] Individuals who defied the experimenter were at a higher stage of moral development than those who were obedient, as measured in Kohlberg's system of moral development. Yet another correlate of defiance of authority was social intelligence. In one study, it was found that subjects who did not comply fully with the experimenter's commands were individuals who scored higher on a measure of social intelligence.[26] People who are more socially intelligent (that is, who are more astute observers of others and who have the ability to effectively influence the outcomes of situations) are probably better able to understand and manage situations using available social cues.

Since the time of Milgram's studies, greater concern has arisen over research ethics and specifically the need to protect subjects from traumatic experiences. Because of these concerns about the rights of subjects, it has become exceedingly difficult to obtain peer approval to conduct and publish similar research. Therefore, something of a moratorium exists on conducting studies such as Milgram's that may involve unpleasant experiences for the subject. As a result, it cannot be determined whether the present level of obedience is lower than in the past. Some national experiences, such as the Watergate scandal and the Vietnam War protests, have certainly made it more socially acceptable to oppose authority. It is probably safe to say that it is now somewhat more difficult to extract conformity in a variety of settings (including work, school, and government) than it has been in the past.

In summary, Milgram's research suggests that people placed in a conflict situation pitting moral values against authority will tend to follow the dictates of authority. Perhaps the most sobering aspect of this discovery lies in how little real power an authority figure needs in order to succeed in directing others. Of course, opportunities for the abuse of authority also occur in business organizations. Because of this reality, it is essential that managers recognize the magnitude of their power over others and act in accordance with the responsibility that such power entails.

NOTES

1. D. C. McClelland, *Power: The Inner Experience* (New York: Irvington, 1975); D. C. McClelland, "Power Is the Great Motivation," *Harvard Business Review* 54 (1976): 100–110.

2. H. C. Kelman, "Processes of Opinion Change," *Public Opinion Quarterly* 25 (1961): 57–78.

3. J. R. P. French, Jr., and B.H. Raven, "The Bases of Social Power," in *Studies in Social Power*, ed. D. Cartwright (Ann Arbor: University of Michigan, Institute for Social Research, 1959); T. Hinkin and C. Schriesheim, "Development and Application of New Scales to Measure the French and Raven Bases of Social Power," *Journal of Applied Psychology* 74 (1989): 561–567.

4. A. Etzioni, *A Comparative Analysis of Complex Organizations*, rev. ed. (New York: Free Press, 1975); R. Mayer, "Understanding Employee Motivation through Organizational Commitment" (Ph. D. diss., Purdue University, 1989).

5. M. Sussmann and R.P. Vecchio, "A Social Influence Interpretation of Worker Motivation," *Academy of Management Review* 7 (1982): 177–186; R. P. Vecchio and M. Sussmann, "Preference for Forms of Supervisory Social Influence," *Journal of Organizational Behavior* 10 (1989): 135–143.

6. Ibid.

7. G. R. Ferris and K.M. Kacmar, "Perceptions of Organizational Politics," *Journal of Management* 10 (1992): 93–116; J. Pfeffer, *Power in Organizations* (Boston: Pitman Publishing Co., 1981).

8. R. W. Allen, D. L. Madison, L. W. Porter et al., "Organizational Politics: Tactics and Characteristics of Its Actors," *California Management Review* 12 (Fall 1979): 77–83; A. J. DuBrin, *Winning at Office Politics* (New York: Ballantine, 1978); R. H. Miles, *Macro Organizational Behavior* (Santa Monica, Calif.: Goodyear, 1980), 174–175; Pfeffer, *Power in Organizations*.

9. DuBrin, *Winning at Office Politics*.

10. R. Christie and F. L. Geis, eds., *Studies in Machiavellianism* (New York: Academic Press, 1970).

11. G. R. Gemmil and W.J. Heisler, "Machiavellianism as a Factor in Managerial Job Strain, Job Satisfaction, and Upward Mobility," *Academy of Management Journal* 15 (1972): 53–67.

12. R. V. Exline, J. Thibaut, C. O. Hickey et al., "Visual Interaction in Relation to Machiavellianism and an Unethical Act," in *Studies in Machiavellianism*, eds. R. Christie and F. L. Geis (New York: Academic Press, 1970), 53–75; D. Kipnis and

S.M. Schmidt, *Profiles of Organizational Influence Strategies* (San Diego: University Associates, 1982); S. M. Schmidt and D. Kipnis, "The Perils of Persistence," *Psychology Today*, November 1987, 32–34; D. Kipnis, *The Powerholders* (Chicago: University of Chicago Press, 1976); P. Block, *The Empowered Manager* (San Francisco: Jossey-Bass, 1988).

13. C. F. Turner and D. C. Martinez, "Socioeconomic Achievement and the Machiavellian Personality," *Sociometry* 40 (1977): 325–336.

14. Kipnis and Schmidt, *Profiles of Organizational Influence Strategies*; C. Schriescheim and T. Hinkin, "Influence Tactics Used by Subordinates: A Theoretical and Empirical Analysis and Refinement of the Kipnis, Schmidt, and Wilkinson Subscales," *Journal of Applied Psychology* 75 (1990): 246–252; G. Yukl and J. B. Tracey, "Consequences of Influence Tactics Used with Subordinates, Peers, and the Boss," *Journal of Applied Psychology* 76 (1992): 525–535; C. Falbe and G. Yukl, "Consequences for Managers of Using Single Influence Tactics and Combinations of Tactics," *Academy of Management Journal* 35 (1992): 638–652; D. Brass and M. Burkhardt, "Potential Power and Power Use: An Investigation of Structure and Behaviors," *Academy of Management Journal* 36 (1993): 441–470.

15. Schmidt and Kipnis, "The Perils of Persistence."

16. Kipnis, *The Powerholders*; Block, *The Empowered Manager*; D. Kipnis, S. M. Schmidt, C. Swaffin-Smith, and I. Wilkenson, "Patterns of Managerial Influence: Shotgun Managers, Tacticians, and Bystanders," *Organizational Dynamics* (1984): 58–67; S. M. Farmer, D. B. Fedor, J .S. Goodman, and J. M. Maslyn, "Factors Affecting the Use of Upward Influence Strategies," *Proceedings of the Academy of Management* (1993): 64–68.

17. M. Lefkowitz, R. A. Blake, and J. S. Mouton, "Status Factors in Pedestrian Violation of Traffic Signals," *Journal of Abnormal and Social Psychology* 51 (1955): 704–706.

18. S. Milgram, L. Bickman, and L. Berkowitz, "Note on the Drawing Power of Crowds of Different Size," *Journal of Personality and Social Psychology* 13 (1969): 79–82.

19. J. C. Freedman and S. C. Fraser, "Compliance Without Pressure: The Foot-in-the-Door Technique," *Journal of Personality and Social Psychology* 4 (1966): 195–202.

20. G. F. Cavanagh, D. J. Moberg, and M. Velasquez, "The Ethics of Organizational Politics," *Academy of Management Review* 6 (1981): 363–374.

21. S. Milgram, "Behavioral Study of Obedience," *Journal of Abnormal and Social Psychology* 67 (1963): 371–378.

22. S. Milgram, *Obedience to Authority* (New York: Harper, 1974); M. E. Shanah and K. A. Yahya, "A Behavioral Study of Obedience in Children," *Journal of Personality and Social Psychology* 35 (1977): 530–536.

23. CBS News, Transcript of "Sixty Minutes" segment, "I Was Only Following Orders," (March 31, 1979): 2–8; D. M. Mantell, "The Potential for Violence in Germany," *Journal of Social Issues* 27 (1971): 101–112; M. E. Shanah and K. A. Yahya, "A Cross-Cultural Study of Obedience," *Bulletin of the Psychonomic Society* 11 (1978): 267–269; W. Kilham and L. Mann, "Level of Destructive

Obedience as a Function of Transmitter and Executant Roles in the Milgram Obedience Paradigm," *Journal of Personality and Social Psychology* 29 (1974): 696–702; S.R. Shalala, "A Study of Various Communication Settings Which Produce Obedience by Subordinates to Unlawful Superior Orders" (Ph.D. diss, University of Kansas, 1974).

24. T. Blass, "Obedience to Authority: Some Issues and Significance," in *Perspectives on Stanley Milgram's Contributions to Social Psychology* (Symposium conducted at the Annual Meeting of the American Psychological Association, Boston, Mass., August 24, 1990).

25. A. C. Elms and S. Milgram, "Personality. Characteristics Associated with Obedience and Defiance toward Authoritative Command," *Journal of Experimental Research in Personality* 1 (1966): 282–289; A. C. Elms, *Social Psychology and Social Relevance* (Boston: Little, Brown, 1972); S. Milgram, *Obedience to Authority: An Experimental View* (New York: Harper and Row, 1974).

26. P. M. Burley and J. McGuiness, "Effects of Social Intelligence on the Milgram Paradigm," *Psychological Reports* 40 (1977): 767–770.

Managing Your Boss

John J. Gabarro and John P. Kotter

To many people, the phrase *managing your boss* may sound unusual or suspicious. Because of the traditional top-down emphasis in most organizations, it is not obvious why you need to manage relationships upward—unless, of course, you would do so for personal or political reasons. But we are not referring to political maneuvering or to apple polishing. We are using the term to mean the process of consciously working with your superior to obtain the best possible results for you, your boss, and the company.

Recent studies suggest that effective managers take time and effort to manage not only relationships with their subordinates but also those with their bosses. These studies also show that this essential aspect of management is sometimes ignored by otherwise talented and aggressive managers. Indeed, some managers who actively and effectively supervise subordinates, products, markets, and technologies assume an almost passively reactive stance vis-à-vis their bosses. Such a stance almost always hurts them and their companies.

If you doubt the importance of managing your relationship with your boss or how difficult it is to do so effectively, consider for a moment the following sad but telling story:

Frank Gibbons was an acknowledged manufacturing genius in his industry and, by any profitability standard, a very effective executive. One year, his strengths propelled him into the position of vice president of manufacturing for the second largest and most profitable company in its industry. Gibbons was not, however, a good manager of people. He knew this, as did others in his company and his industry. Recognizing this weakness, the president made sure that those who reported to Gibbons were good at working with people and could compensate for his limitations. The arrangement worked well.

Later, Philip Bonnevie was promoted into a position reporting to Gibbons. In keeping with the previous pattern, the president selected Bonnevie because he had an excellent track record and a reputation for being good with people. In making that selection, however, the president neglected to notice that, in his rapid rise through the organization, Bonnevie had always had good-to-excellent bosses. He had never been forced to manage a relationship with a difficult boss. In retrospect, Bonnevie admits he had never thought that managing his boss was a part of his job.

Fourteen months after he started working for Gibbons, Bonnevie was fired. During that same quarter, the company reported a net loss for the first time in seven years. Many of those who were close to these events say that they don't really understand what happened. This much is known, however: while the company was bringing out a major new product—a process that required sales, engineering, and manufacturing groups to coordinate decisions very carefully—a whole series of misunderstandings and bad feelings developed between Gibbons and Bonnevie.

For example, Bonnevie claims Gibbons was aware of and had accepted Bonnevie's decision to use a new type of machinery to make the new product; Gibbons swears he did not. Furthermore, Gibbons claims he made it clear to Bonnevie that introduction of the product was too important to the company in the short run to take any major risks.

As a result of such misunderstandings, planning went awry: a new manufacturing plant was built that could not produce the new product designed by engineering, in the volume desired by sales, at a cost agreed on by the executive committee. Gibbons blamed Bonnevie for the mistake. Bonnevie blamed Gibbons.

Of course, one could argue that the problem here was caused by Gibbons's inability to manage his subordinates. But one can make just as strong a case that the problem was related to Bonnevie's inability to manage his boss. Remember, Gibbons was not having difficulty with any other subordinates. Moreover, given the personal price paid by Bonnevie (being fired and having his reputation within the industry severely tarnished), there was little consolation in saying the problem was that Gibbons was poor at managing subordinates. Everyone already knew that.

We believe that the situation could have turned out differently had Bonnevie been more adept at understanding Gibbons and at managing his relationship with him. In this case, an inability to manage upward was unusually costly. The company lost $2 million to $5 million, and Bonnevie's career was, at least temporarily, disrupted. Many less costly cases similar to this probably occur regularly in all major corporations, and the cumulative effect can be very destructive.

MISREADING THE BOSS-SUBORDINATE RELATIONSHIP

People often dismiss stories like the one we just related as being merely cases of personality conflict. Because two people can on occasion be psychologically or temperamentally incapable of working together, this can be an apt description. But more often, we have found, a personality conflict is only a part of the problem—sometimes a very small part.

Bonnevie did not just have a different personality from Gibbons, he also made or had unrealistic assumptions and expectations about the very nature of boss-subordinate relationships. Specifically, he did not recognize that his relationship to Gibbons involved *mutual dependence* between two *fallible* human beings. Failing to recognize this, a manager typically either avoids trying to manage his or her relationship with a boss or manages it ineffectively.

Some people behave as if their bosses were not very dependent on them. They fail to see how much the boss needs their help and cooperation to do his or her job effectively. These people refuse to acknowledge that the boss can be severely hurt by their actions and needs cooperation, dependability, and honesty from them.

Some people see themselves as not very dependent on their bosses. They gloss over how much help and information they need from the boss in order to perform their own jobs well. This superficial view is particularly damaging when a manager's job and decisions affect other parts of the organization, as was the case in Bonnevie's situation. A manager's immediate boss can play a critical role in linking the manager to the rest of the organization, making sure the manager's priorities are consistent with organizational needs, and in securing the resources the manager needs to perform well. Yet some managers need to see themselves as practically self-sufficient, as not needing the critical information and resources a boss can supply.

Many managers, like Bonnevie, assume that the boss will magically know what information or help their subordinates need and provide it to them. Certainly, some bosses do an excellent job of caring for their subordinates in this way, but for a manager to expect that from all bosses is dangerously unrealistic. A more reasonable expectation for managers to have is that modest help will be forthcoming. After all, bosses are only human. Most really effective managers accept this fact and assume primary responsibility for their own careers and development. They make a point of seeking the information and help they need to do a job instead of waiting for their bosses to provide it.

In light of the foregoing, it seems to us that managing a situation of mutual dependence among fallible human beings requires the following:

1. That you have a good understanding of the other person and yourself, especially regarding strengths, weaknesses, work styles, and needs.
2. That you use this information to develop and manage a healthy working relationship—one that is compatible with both people's work styles and assets, is characterized by mutual expectations, and meets the most critical needs of the other person. This combination is essentially what we have found highly effective managers doing.

UNDERSTANDING THE BOSS

Managing your boss requires that you gain an understanding of the boss and his or her context, as well as your own situation. All managers do this to some degree, but many are not thorough enough.

At a minimum, you need to appreciate your boss's goals and pressures, his or her strengths and weaknesses. What are your boss's organizational and personal objectives, and what are his or her pressures, especially those from his or her own boss and others at the same level? What are your boss's long suits and blind spots? What is the preferred style of working? Does your boss like to get information through memos, formal meetings, or phone calls? Does he or she thrive on conflict or try to minimize it?

Without this information, a manager is flying blind when dealing with the boss, and unnecessary conflicts, misunderstandings, and problems are inevitable.

In one situation we studied, a top-notch marketing manager with a superior performance record was hired into a company as a vice president "to straighten out the marketing and sales problems." The company, which was having financial difficulties, had recently been acquired by a larger corporation. The president was eager to turn it around and gave the new marketing vice president free rein—at least initially. Based on his previous experience, the new vice president correctly diagnosed that greater market share was needed for the company and that strong product management was required to bring that about. Following that logic, he made a number of pricing decisions that were aimed at increasing high-volume business.

When margins declined and the financial situation did not improve, however, the president increased pressure on the new vice president. Believing that the situation would eventually correct itself as the company gained back market share, the vice president resisted the pressure.

When by the second quarter, margins and profits had still failed to improve, the president took direct control over all pricing decisions and put all items on a set level of margin, regardless of volume. The new vice president began to find himself shut out by the president, and their relationship deteriorated. In fact, the vice president found the president's behavior bizarre. Unfortunately, the president's new pricing scheme also failed to increase margins, and by the fourth quarter, both the president and the vice president were fired.

What the new vice president had not known until it was too late was that improving marketing and sales had been only *one* of the president's goals. His most immediate goal had been to make the company more profitable—quickly.

Nor had the new vice president known that his boss was invested in this short-term priority for personal as well as business reasons. The president had been a strong advocate of the acquisition within the parent company, and his personal credibility was at stake.

The vice president made three basic errors. He took information supplied to him at face value, he made assumptions in areas where he had no information, and—what was most damaging—he never actively tried to clarify what his boss's objectives were. As a result, he ended up taking actions that were actually at odds with the president's priorities and objectives.

Managers who work effectively with their bosses do not behave this way. They seek out information about the boss's goals and problems and pressures. They are alert for opportunities to question the boss and others around him or her to test their assumptions. They pay attention to clues in the boss's behavior. Although it is imperative that they do this especially when they begin working with a new boss, effective managers also do this on an ongoing basis because they recognize that priorities and concerns change.

Being sensitive to a boss's work style can be crucial, especially when the boss is new. For example, a new president who was organized and formal in his approach replaced a subordinate who was informal and intuitive. The new president worked best when he had written reports. He also preferred formal meetings with set agendas.

One of his division managers realized this need and worked with the new president to identify the kinds and frequency of information and reports that the president wanted. This manager also made a point of sending background information and brief agendas ahead of time for their discussions. He found that with this type of preparation their meetings were very useful. Another interesting result was, he found that with adequate preparation his new boss was even more effective at brainstorming problems than his more informal and intuitive predecessor had been.

In contrast, another division manager never fully understood how the new boss's work style differed from that of his predecessor. To the degree that he did sense it, he experienced it as too much control. As a result, he seldom sent the new president the background information he needed, and the president never felt fully prepared for meetings with the manager. In fact, the president spent much of this time when they met trying to get information that he felt he should have had earlier. The boss experienced these meetings as frustrating and inefficient, and the subordinate often found himself thrown off guard by the questions that the president asked. Ultimately, this division manager resigned.

The difference between the two division managers just described was not so much one of ability or even adaptability. Rather, one of them was more sensitive to the boss's work style than the other and to the implications of the boss's needs.

UNDERSTANDING YOURSELF

The boss is only one-half of the relationship. You are the other half, as well as the part over which you have more direct control. Developing an effective working relationship requires, then, that you know your own needs, strengths and weaknesses, and personal style.

You are not going to change either your basic personality structure or that of your boss. But you can become aware of what it is about you that impedes or facilitates working with your boss and, with that awareness, take actions that make the relationship more effective.

For example, in one case we observed, a manager and the superior ran into problems whenever they disagreed. The boss's typical response was to harden his position and overstate it. The manager's reaction was then to raise the ante and intensify the forcefulness of his argument. In doing this, he channeled his anger into sharpening his attacks on the logical fallacies he saw in his boss's assumptions. His boss in turn would become even more adamant about holding his original position. Predictably, this escalating cycle resulted in the subordinate avoiding whenever possible any topic of potential conflict with his boss.

In discussing this problem with his peers, the manager discovered that his reaction to the boss was typical of how he generally reacted to counterarguments—but with a difference. His response would overwhelm his peers but not his boss. Because his attempts to discuss this problem with his boss were unsuccessful, he concluded that the only way to change the situation was to deal with his own instinctive reactions. Whenever the two reached an impasse, he would check his own impatience and suggest that they break up and think about it before getting together again. Usually when they renewed their discussion, they had digested their differences and were more able to work them through.

Gaining this level of self-awareness and acting on it are difficult but not impossible. For example, by reflecting over his past experiences, a young manager learned that he was not very good at dealing with difficult and emotional issues where people were involved. Because he disliked those issues and realized that his instinctive responses to them were seldom very good, he developed a habit of touching base with his boss whenever such a problem arose. Their discussions always surfaced ideas and approaches the manager had not considered. In many cases, they also identified specific actions the boss could take to help.

Although a superior-subordinate relationship is one of mutual dependence, it is also one in which the subordinate is typically more dependent on the boss than the other way around. This dependence inevitably results in the subordinate feeling a certain degree of frustration, sometimes anger, when his actions or options are constrained by his boss's decisions. This is a normal part of life and occurs in the best of relationships. The way in which a manager handles these frustrations largely depends on his or her predisposition toward dependence on authority figures.

Some people's instinctive reaction under these circumstances is to resent the boss's authority and to rebel against the boss's decisions. Sometimes a person will escalate a conflict beyond what is appropriate. Seeing the boss almost as an institutional enemy, this type of manager will often, without being conscious of it, fight with the boss just for the sake of fighting. The subordinate's reactions to being constrained are usually strong and sometimes impulsive. He or she sees the boss as someone who, by virtue of the role, is a hindrance to progress, an obstacle to be circumvented or at best tolerated.

Psychologists call this pattern of reactions counterdependent behavior. Although a counterdependent person is difficult for most superiors to manage and usually has a history of strained relationships with superiors, this sort of manager is apt to have even more trouble with a boss who tends to be directive or authoritarian. When the manager acts on his or her negative feelings, often in subtle and nonverbal ways, the boss sometimes does become the enemy. Sensing the subordinate's latent hostility, the boss will lose trust in the subordinate or his or her judgment and then behave even less openly.

Paradoxically, a manager with this type of predisposition is often a good manager of his or her own people. He or she will many times go out of the way to get support for them and will not hesitate to go to bat for them.

At the other extreme are managers who swallow their anger and behave in a very compliant fashion when the boss makes what they know to be a poor decision. These managers will agree with the boss even when a disagreement might be welcome or when the boss would easily alter a decision if given more information. Because they bear no relationship to the specific situation at hand, their responses are as much an overreaction as those of counterdependent managers. Instead of seeing the boss as an enemy, these people deny their anger—the other extreme—and tend to see the boss as if he or she were an all-wise parent who should know best, should take responsibility for their careers, train them in all they need to know, and protect them from overly ambitious peers.

Both counterdependence and overdependence lead managers to hold unrealistic views of what a boss is. Both views ignore that most bosses, like everyone else, are imperfect and fallible. They don't have unlimited time, encyclopedic knowledge, or extrasensory perception; nor are they evil enemies. They have their own pressures and concerns that are sometimes at odds with the wishes of the subordinate—and often for good reason.

Altering predispositions toward authority, especially at the extremes, is almost impossible without intensive psychotherapy (psychoanalytic theory and research suggest that such predispositions are deeply rooted in a person's personality and upbringing). However, an awareness of these extremes and the range between them can be very useful in understanding where your own predispositions fall and what the implications are for how you tend to behave in relation to your boss.

If you believe, on the one hand, that you have some tendencies toward counterdependence, you can understand and even predict what your reactions and overreactions are likely to be. If, on the other hand, you believe you have some tendencies toward overdependence, you might question the extent to which your overcompliance or inability to confront real differences may be making both you and your boss less effective.

DEVELOPING AND MANAGING THE RELATIONSHIP

With a clear understanding of both your boss and yourself, you can *usually* establish a way of working together that fits both of you, that is characterized by unambiguous mutual expectations, and that helps you both be more productive and effective. The "Checklist for Managing Your Boss" summarizes some things such a relationship consists of. Following are a few more.

Compatible Work Styles

Above all else, a good working relationship with a boss accommodates differences in work style. For example, in one situation we studied, a manager (who had a relatively good relationship with his superior) realized that during meetings his boss would often become inattentive and sometimes brusque. The subordinate's own style tended to be discursive and exploratory. He would often digress from the topic at hand to deal with background factors, alternative approaches, and so forth. His boss preferred to discuss problems with a minimum of background detail and became impatient and distracted whenever his subordinate digressed from the immediate issue.

Recognizing this difference in style, the manager became terser and more direct during meetings with his boss. To help himself do this, before meetings, he would develop brief agendas that he used as a guide.

Checklist for Managing Your Boss

Make sure you understand your boss and his or her context, including:

- ☐ Goals and objectives
- ☐ Pressures
- ☐ Strengths, weaknesses, blind spots
- ☐ Preferred work style

Assess yourself and your needs, including:

- ☐ Strengths and weaknesses
- ☐ Personal style
- ☐ Predisposition toward dependence on authority figures

Develop and maintain a relationship that:

- ☐ Fits both your needs and styles
- ☐ Is characterized by mutual expectations
- ☐ Keeps your boss informed
- ☐ Is based on dependability and honesty
- ☐ Selectively uses your boss's time and resources

Whenever he felt that a digression was needed, he explained why. This small shift in his own style made these meetings more effective and far less frustrating for both of them.

Subordinates can adjust their styles in response to their bosses' preferred method for receiving information. Peter Drucker divides bosses into "listeners" and "readers." Some bosses like to get information in report form so they can read and study it. Others work better with information and reports presented in person so they can ask questions. As Drucker points out, the implications are obvious. If your boss is a listener, you brief him or her in person, *then* follow it up with a memo. If your boss is a reader, you cover important items or proposals in a memo or report, *then* discuss them.

Other adjustments can be made according to a boss's decision-making style. Some bosses prefer to be involved in decisions and problems as they arise. These are high-involvement managers who like to keep their hands on the pulse of the operation. Usually their needs (and your own) are best satisfied if you touch base with them on an ad hoc basis. A boss who has a need to be involved will become involved one way or another, so there are advantages to including him or her at your initiative. Other bosses prefer to delegate—they don't want to be involved. They expect you to come to them with major problems and inform them about any important changes.

Creating a compatible relationship also involved drawing on each other's strengths and making up for each other's weaknesses. Because he knew that the boss—the vice president of engineering—was not very good at monitoring his employees' problems, one manager we studied made a point of doing it himself. The stakes were high: the engineers and technicians were all union members, the company worked on a customer-contract basis, and the company had recently experienced a serious strike.

The manager worked closely with his boss, along with people in the scheduling department and the personnel office, to make sure that potential problems were avoided. He also developed an informal arrangement through which his boss would review with him any proposed changes in personnel or assignment policies before taking action. The boss valued his advice and credited his subordinate for improving both the performance of the division and the labor-management climate.

Mutual Expectations

The subordinate who passively assumes that he or she knows what the boss expects is in for trouble. Of course, some superiors will spell out their expectations very explicitly and in great detail. But most do not. And although many corporations have systems that provide a basis for communicating expectations (such as formal planning processes, career planning reviews, and performance appraisal reviews), these systems never work perfectly. Also, between these formal reviews, expectations invariably change.

Ultimately, the burden falls on the subordinate to find out what the boss's expectations are. They can be both broad (such as what kinds of problems the boss wishes to be informed about and when) as well as very specific (such things as when a particular project should be completed and what kinds of information the boss needs in the interim).

Getting a boss who tends to be vague or not explicit to express expectations can be difficult. But effective managers find ways to get that information. Some will draft a detailed memo covering key aspects of their work and then send it to their boss for approval. They then follow this up with a face-to-face discussion in which they go over each item in the memo. A discussion like this will often surface virtually all of the boss's expectations.

Other effective managers will deal with an inexplicit boss by initiating an ongoing series of informal discussions about "good management" and "our objectives." Still others find useful information more indirectly through those who used to work for the boss and through the formal planning systems in which the boss makes commitments to his or her own superior. Which approach you choose, of course, should depend on your understanding of your boss's style.

Developing a workable set of mutual expectations also requires that you communicate your own expectations to the boss, find out if they are realistic, and influence the boss to accept the ones that are important to you. Being able to influence the boss to value your expectations can be particularly important if the boss is an overachiever. Such a boss will often set unrealistically high standards that need to be brought into line with reality.

A Flow of Information

How much information a boss needs about what a subordinate is doing will vary significantly depending on the boss's style, the situation he or she is in, and the confidence the boss has in the subordinate. But it is not uncommon for a boss to need more information than the subordinate would naturally supply or for the subordinate to think the boss knows more than he or she really does. Effective managers recognize that they probably underestimate what their bosses need to know and make sure they find ways to keep them informed through processes that fit their styles.

Managing the flow of information upward is particularly difficult if the boss does not like to hear about problems. Although many people would deny it, bosses often give off signals they want to hear only good news. They show great displeasure—usually nonverbally—when someone tells them about a problem. Ignoring individual achievement, they may even evaluate more favorably subordinates who do not bring problems to them.

Nevertheless, for the good of the organization, the boss, and the subordinate, a superior needs to hear about failures as well as successes. Some subordinates deal with a good-news-only boss by finding indirect ways to get the necessary information to him or her, such as a management information system. Others see to it that potential problems, whether in the form of good surprises or bad news, are communicated immediately.

Dependability and Honesty

Few things are more disabling to a boss than a subordinate on whom he cannot depend, whose work he cannot trust. Almost no one is intentionally undependable, but many managers are inadvertently so because of oversight or uncertainty about the boss's priorities. A commitment to an optimistic delivery date may please a superior in the short term but become a source of displeasure if not honored. It's difficult for a boss to rely on a subordinate who repeatedly slips deadlines. As one president (describing a subordinate) put it: "I'd rather he be more consistent even if he delivered fewer peak successes—at least I could rely on him."

Nor are many managers intentionally dishonest with their bosses. But it is easy to shade the truth and play down issues. Current concerns often become future surprise problems. It's almost impossible for bosses to work effectively if they cannot rely on a fairly accurate reading from their subordinates. Because it undermines credibility, dishonesty is perhaps the most troubling trait a subordinate can have. Without a basic level of trust, a boss feels compelled to check all of a subordinate's decisions, which makes it difficult to delegate.

Good Use of Time and Resources

Your boss is probably as limited in his or her store of time, energy, and influence as you are. Every request you make of your boss uses up some of these resources, so it's wise to draw on these resources selectively. This may sound obvious, but many managers use up their boss's time (and some of their own credibility) over relatively trivial issues.

One vice president went to great lengths to get his boss to fire a meddlesome secretary in another department. His boss had to use considerable influence to do it. Understandably, the head of the other department was not pleased. Later, when the vice president wanted to tackle more important problems, he ran into trouble. By using up his chips on a relatively trivial issue, he had made it difficult for him and his boss to meet more important goals.

No doubt, some subordinates will resent that on top of all their other duties, they also need to take time and energy to manage their relationships with their bosses. Such managers fail to realize the importance of this activity and how it can simplify their jobs by eliminating potentially severe problems. Effective managers recognize that this part of their work is legitimate. Seeing themselves as ultimately responsible for what they achieve in an organization, they know they need to establish and manage relationships with everyone on whom they depend—and that includes the boss.

Effective Followership:
Leadership Turned Upside Down

Robert P. Vecchio

The twelve members of a professional association recently met to select a new president. Each member had a hand in pressuring the former president to resign. As a result of a number of minor actions and omissions of actions the members had made the president's task so difficult that he had found it nearly impossible to function as the head of the association. Now, each member was prepared to fight for a preferred candidate for the presidential position. When the group's discussion came to the selection of a new president, one member observed, "Who can we find that will be able to lead us?" Unexpectedly, one clever member replied, "More importantly, who can we find that we will be able to follow?"

This wry reply provides an insight to a much neglected feature of the process of leadership: followership. Traditionally, studies of leadership have focused on leader behaviors and leader attributes. Omitted in these writings is a serious consideration of the impact of followership as a determinant of effective leadership. Yet, the activities of leadership and followership are inextricably related. The concepts are intertwined in Ying-Yang fashion: one concept implies (and, in fact, requires) the other. For example, consider the following propositions developed by Trudy Heller and Jon VanTil:[3]

- The leader must lead, and do it well to retain leadership; the follower must follow, and do it well to retain followership.
- Where all seek to lead, or all seek to follow, there can be no leadership or followership.
- Good leadership enhances followers, just as good followership enhances leaders.
- Leadership, and followership, may be an art in which people can become more highly skilled.

A good argument can be made that when we commonly speak of effective leadership, we are really speaking of effective followership.

As evidence of this, consider that we typically measure a manager's effectiveness by examining the performance of his or her unit. The performance of a unit, however, is often more a function of the talents and desires of the followers than the leader. A given level of subordinate talent and motivation can have far more to do with the unit's performance than the leader's efforts.

As an essential element in the development and management of an effective business strategy, the human resources configuration of those units comprising an organization is critical. In this article, the importance and dynamics of effective followership will be explored. In addition, techniques for fostering and maintaining effective followership will be considered.

THE LIMITS OF LEADERSHIP

In many situations, it can be extremely difficult for a leader to influence, easily or directly, the performance of a unit. Social scientists have recently come to recognize that many factors can serve as "substitutes" for and "neutralizers" of a leader's efforts.[5] Substitutes for leadership include explicit rules and procedures, rigid reward structures which a leader cannot affect, and physical distance between a leader and his subordinates. For example, subordinates who are given explicit goals and rules for performing their jobs, will not need to be given direction by a leader. Characteristics of individuals can serve to neutralize a leader's influence. For example, subordinates who are highly experienced, possess sufficient training and knowledge, and have a high need for independence or a sense of professionalism will not need, or may even resent, a leader who tries to be directive. Task characteristics, such as routineness, frequent feedback, and a high degree of structure can also undercut a leader's potential influence.

What we typically think of as being failures in leadership, may also be rightly characterized as failures in followership. A degree of responsibility for unit performance rests squarely on subordinates. Superiors, where their influence can make a difference, cannot be effective if subordinates do not subscribe to unit goals, or exert sufficient effort. Subordinates have a responsibility to be conscientious, and to expend energies for unit goals. In an enlightened view, both leaders and followers share in the responsibility of being productive and effective.

LEADERSHIP AND FOLLOWERSHIP: SOME POPULAR FICTIONS

The traditional view of leadership assumes that leaders are responsible for motivating subordinates and eliciting their commitment—that subordinates are initially lacking in responsibility and a willingness to commit. Of course, a leader's success at eliciting commitment depends on many factors. It is partly a function of individual differences in subordinates' willingness of predisposition to be committed, loyal, etc. An individual's upbringing can play an important role in determining the degree of his or her willingness to follow[8]. Whether or not, and to what degree, specific values are emphasized in a child's home can influence that individual's attitude toward superiors, as an adult. The emerging findings from the social sciences also suggest that managers are seldom fully in command (as frequently portrayed), and subordinates are rarely as submissive or faceless as is generally assumed.

Much has been made of the need to avoid being deceived by yes-men. A variation of this notion is popularly referred to as group-think, wherein a leader is surrounded by yea-sayers and devotees who contribute to the group's self-deception about its invulnerability.[4] In a unit that is victimized by the group-think phenomenon, the leader may make a disastrous decision because his or her followers have total conviction of the ultimate success of the group's efforts. Such a group will not seriously entertain the possibility of failure. The Bay of Pigs fiasco of the Kennedy Administration and the early escalation of U.S. military involvement in Vietnam by the Johnson Administration have often been attributed to group-think. In both the Bay of Pigs and Vietnam escalation decisions, the respective leaders and their supportive followers unconsciously conspired to create a mindset that inhibited their ability to foresee obstacles to the success of their plans.

The group-think phenomenon is most likely to occur in a highly cohesive work unit where the members are already strongly committed to their leader and the group's objectives. The message portrayed by the group-think examples is largely overstated since, in reality, the preconditions for group-think (i.e., extreme cohesion and total followership) are rare. More typically, managers must wrestle with a situation wherein their subordinates are far less loyal, and far less attracted to other members of the work unit than group-think requires. There is a good deal of *potential* followership held in reserve by subordinates.

Various anecdotal accounts of the group-think phenomenon have made it possible, and popular, to criticize the notion of followership. Similarly, well-publicized accounts of the predisposition of some individuals to blindly submit to authority in experimental settings have contributed to a criticism of followership. One famous study by Stanley Milgram[9] found that a majority of normal adults would administer seemingly painful electric shocks to another participant in a research study, even if the recipient of the shock protested and demanded to be set free. A related study by Phil Zimbardo[12] reported that college students who participated in role playing the job of prison guard would all too readily engage in the more cruel and sadistic activities stereotypically thought to characterize the treatment of prisoners by prison guards. In addition, the predisposition of some individuals to follow authority has been denigrated by the reports of social scientists in early research on the "obedient personality." Specifically, researchers during World War II sought to better understand the so-called "Nazi personality" and thus attempted to study fascist tendencies via a personality scale.[10] This research on the obedient (or fascist) personality, of course, represents an attempt to understand an aberrant style of behavior. Omitted in these classic studies were attempts to understand followership within normal settings (that is, hospitals, profit-oriented organizations, etc.).

While these studies provide fascinating insights into the more bizarre aspects of human behavior, their results do not have firm implications for life in organizations. Although laboratory experiments can offer insights to employee behavior, these popular studies often involved the creation of brief, transitory episodes, wherein people were placed in highly ambiguous and tension-charged settings of very short duration. Normal, adult behavior in the ongoing role of employee/subordinate does not readily lend itself to cruelty and blind obedience. The social norms and codes of personal conduct that exist in the real world (and are largely suspended in the temporary setting created in a research laboratory), inhibit tendencies toward excessive cruelty and blind obedience. In addition, most managers do not deliberately seek to be surrounded by blindly obedient and subservient individuals. The traits of good followership (that is, a sense of responsibility, adult-orientation, commitment, openness, and loyalty) are what most managers desire.

STYLES OF FOLLOWERSHIP

All managers are familiar with the notion of "styles of leadership." When this expression is used, we typically think of such terms as auto-cratic, participative, laissez-faire, etc. We can also extend this per-spective to include styles of followership. Although a neglected topic, it is useful to consider the major dimensions along which subordinates differ, and to consider how follower styles may be developed and maintained.*

Figure 1 displays a framework for conceptualizing styles of fol-lowership. The framework incorporates two dimensions: compliance-defiance, and loyalty-hostility. The dimension of compliance-defiance is a behavioral dimension, and reflects the extent to which a follower conforms to the directives of a superior, versus undermines or counters the supervisor's desires. Loyalty-hostility is an attitudinal dimension

Figure 1
Dimensions of Followership

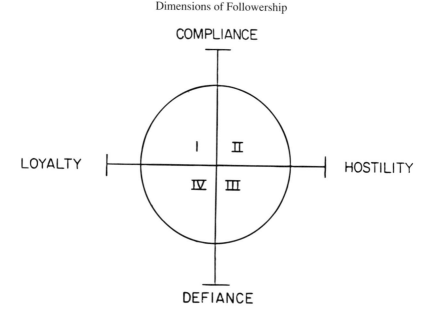

* One useful framework, which was developed by Zaleznik,[11] served as the starting point for developing the present scheme

which represents the degree to which a subordinate is supportive of, versus antagonistic toward, a supervisor and his or her goals. By crossing the two dimensions, we create a set of quadrants, each of which has a unique meaning.

In quadrant I (loyal, compliant), we are dealing with a supportive and conforming individual. Quadrant II refers to a compliant, but hostile individual. This would be the case of a subordinate who is maliciously obedient. Quadrant III is a person who is both hostile and defiant, while quadrant IV is a person who is defiant, but loyal (such as a conscientious objector would be). In the extremes of each quadrant (i.e., outside the circle), we are dealing with a form of mental illness. In their most exaggerated forms, the blindly obedient follower and the extremely hostile subordinate (quadrants I and III) represent forms of illness. An extremely hostile but obedient individual is being logically inconsistent, and is perhaps only compliant because of external constraints (for example, fear of being terminated or having difficulty finding another position). An individual in quadrant III is also, in the extreme, experiencing distress. Such a person (who is simultaneously defiant, but committed to a supervisor's goals) may eventually be called to explain his or her actions, perhaps before a disciplinary board or a court. Eventual separation from the unit is the most likely outcome for an individual who is caught in the dilemma of supporting a supervisor, but defying his directives. At the extreme, this may be thought of as a situation which induces a form of mental illness. Finally, it should be noted that although the two dimensions are, in the "real world," likely to be highly correlated (such that loyal employees are likely to be compliant, and so on), there are certainly many occasions wherein attitudes and behaviors are not highly correlated.

DEVELOPING AND MAINTAINING EFFECTIVE FOLLOWERSHIP

Managers, of course, have a responsibility for developing and maintaining the followership of their subordinates (Note: being a follower and being a subordinate are not equivalent notions, as being a leader and being a supervisor also are not equivalent terms). The framework displayed in Figure 1 provides a guide for understanding how to approach the task of developing followership. The compliant-defiant (that is, behavioral) aspect of followership can be best attended to by rewarding subordinates for engaging in appropriate action and withholding rewards for inappropriate action. Volumes have been written on the importance and utility of tying rewards more closely to performance[6]. Generally, making rewards contingent on performance tends to enhance productivity. Simple compliance can also be more reliably predicted from contingent rewards. Enhancing the attitudinal aspect of followership (i.e., the dimension of loyalty-hostility) is far more complicated, in terms of the social processes that are involved. Nonetheless, several recommendations can be deduced from the available literature in the social sciences.

The Cost of Admission

Making the expense of attaining group membership more costly to the individual is a powerful means of inducing employee commitment. That is to say, individuals will have a more positive attitude toward group membership if they are compelled to expend more time, money, or effort to attain and maintain membership. A dramatic illustration of this phenomenon comes from a classic social science study by Eliott Aronson and Judson Mills.[1] As part of their research, these investigators had research subjects engage in an unpleasant activity as a prerequisite for admission to a group. Specifically, individual female college students, who were interested in joining a group that discussed topics related to human sexuality, were asked to read a written passage into a tape recorder (ostensibly to test their voice for maturity of reaction). Several groups of subjects were run in the study. One group was given a fairly innocuous passage to read (i.e., a mild initiation experience), while other groups read relatively more explicit and relatively sexually detailed passages in order to gain admission to the group (i.e., more severe initiation experience). All students were then asked to listen to a tape-recording of the group discussion (the group had allegedly already met several times). The discussion was deliberately staged so as to be extremely boring and unattractive (e.g., the members dryly and haltingly discussed the sexual habits of grasshoppers and other insects).

The investigators were primarily interested in how each applicant for group membership would evaluate the group. Intriguingly, the females who were put through the more difficult initiation experience rated the group more highly (i.e., gave higher ratings of the members' attractiveness, and intelligence, based on the tape). In a replication of this study by Gerard and Mathewson, subjects were required to demonstrate their ability to control their emotions by being given varying degrees of electric shock. The results were identical: the more electric shock a subject received, the more favorably she rated the group.[2] Thus, it appears that the more costly it is to individuals to gain admittance to a group, the more they will value their membership. This form of rationalization can be found in other varieties of group membership. For example, fraternities and sororities require "pledges" for membership to undergo a hazing period, where distasteful initiation experiences are forced on the would-be members. The resulting loyalty of the members of these organizations is well known.

Participation in Decision Making

A second method for inducing loyalty is to involve subordinates in the decision-making process. Participation in decision making increases an individual's sense of involvement and, thereby, dedication to the ultimate course of action. If the participation is genuine, participation can lead to a sense of "ownership" for a goal. A manager must be careful not to merely create an illusion of participation by asking for advice and input from subordinates which he or she does not intend to incorporate into the final decision. Many popular motivational schemes (e.g., MBO and quality circles) incorporate the notion of involving subordinates in planning, goal setting, and suggesting improvements in work methods.

Creating a Sense of Identification

A third device for soliciting loyalty is to create a sense of identity with a group or its leader. Many organizations try to elicit a sense of identity by having group members wear uniforms, or by emblazoning a company logo on paychecks, stationery, and I.D. cards. Beyond these simple techniques, a sense of identity can be fostered by first understanding the value system of employees. If employees value certain notions (such as the importance of being a part of a "family," or the importance of self-reliance), a manager can appeal to these notions by frequently relating to and highlighting these values as part of the theme of his or her administration. For example, as part of his election campaigns, President Reagan skillfully managed to identify his administration with the values of a strong defense and self-reliance (themes which were attractive to the American populace, especially at the end of President Carter's term in office). In short, a sense of identity can be achieved by frequent use of symbols (both tangible and verbal).

Accenting the Importance of Followership

Finally, a manager can enhance loyalty by demonstrating to his unit that loyalty and commitment are highly valued. For example, he or she can highlight the history of the organization and what makes for success and failure in the organization; a manager can stress the importance of loyalty and commitment in attaining both personal and corporate success. By their own conduct, managers communicate the extent to which loyalty is likely to be valued in their own units. If a manager is cynical and critical of superiors, he is more likely to create within his own unit a belief that sarcasm and second-guessing of superiors is an acceptable norm. That is not to say, of course, that a manager should be blindly devoted and praiseworthy of superiors. Rather, a manager should be respectful toward and considerate of the reputation of superiors (and all others) and predisposed to offer support and aid to help the organization achieve its goals.

To be sure, organizations would come to a grinding halt without a minimal degree of followership. Yet, the level of followership in the United States over the past two decades appears to be at an historically low level.[†] Our capacity for greater levels of effective followership is not completely utilized. Perhaps our readiness to follow is at a low ebb because the level of leadership (as distinct from headship) has not also been maximal. Our country has come through a difficult era for top-level leaders, a period characterized by assassinations and assassination attempts, near-impeachments, and questioning of traditional values. Also, employees are better educated, more outspoken, and more conscious of rights and entitlements than in the past. However, it is still popular to call for more effective leadership. Yet, organizational

---

[†] Followership in the United States is also noticeably suboptimal when one considers the apparent level of followership in other industrialized nations, such as Japan and Germany.

performance will not be maximal without the necessary condition of responsible followership.

The principle of followership is perhaps best understood at the U.S. Military Academy at West Point, where leadership is a central focus of the curriculum—the interrelated nature of leadership and followership is acknowledged. As they say at West Point, "(i)f you wish to develop people into leaders, you must begin by teaching them to be followers."[7]

REFERENCES

1. Aronson, E. and Mills, J. "The Effect of Severity of Initiation on Liking for a Group." *Journal of Abnormal and Social Psychology*, vol. 59, pp. 177–181 (1959).

2. Gerard, H. B. and Mathewson, G. C. "The Effects of Severity of Initiation on Liking for a Group: A Replication." *Journal of Experimental Social Psychology*, vol. 2, pp. 278–287 (1966).

3. Heller, T. and VanTil, J. V. "Leadership and Followership: Some Summary Propositions." *Journal of Applied Behavioral Science*, vol. 18, pp. 405–414 (1982).

4. Janis, I. L. *Groupthink*, second edition. Boston, MA: Houghton Mifflin (1982).

5. Kerr, S. and Jermier, J. "Substitutes for Leadership: Their Meaning and Measurement." *Organizational Behavior and Human Performance*, pp. 375–403 (1978).

6. Lawler, E. E., III. "Whatever Happened to Incentive Pay?" *New Management*, vol. 1, pp. 37–41 (1984).

7. Litzinger, W. and Schaeffer, T. "Leadership Through Followership." *Business Horizons*, (1982).

8. McClelland, D. *The Achieving Society*. Princeton, NJ: VanNostrand (1961).

9. Milgram, S. *Obedience to Authority*. London: Tavistock Publications (1974).

10. Sanford, F. H. *Authoritarianism and Leadership*. Philadelphia, PA: Stephenson (1950).

11. Zaleznik, A. "The Dynamics of Subordinancy." *Harvard Business Review*, May–June 1965, pp. 119–131.

12. Zimbardo, P. G. "The Power and Pathology of Imprisonment." *Congressional Research, Serial No. 15*, Washington, DC: U.S. Government Printing Office (1971).

Intraorganizational Influence Tactics: Explorations in Getting One's Way

David Kipnis, Stuart M. Schmidt,
and Ian Wilkinson

Organizational psychologists have not been particularly interested in studying the ways in which people at work influence their colleagues and superiors to obtain personal benefits or to satisfy organizational goals. For the most part, interest has centered on the ways subordinates can be influenced to improve subordinate productivity and morale. This latter use of influence is customarily called the study of leadership, whereas the former can be called the study of organizational politics.

A consequence of this focus on leadership is that there is little systematic information available about how people use power to influence their colleagues or superiors. With but few exceptions (e.g., Izraeli, 1975; Schein, 1977), our thinking about this topic is guided by anecdotal evidence or armchair speculations that have been organized into rational classifications of power tactics (e.g., Etzioni, 1968, pp. 94–109; French & Raven, 1959). One problem with these classifications of power tactics, as Raven (1974) has pointed out, is that they overlap with each other, though each varies in the number of influence dimensions that are described. A further problem with existing classifications of power tactics is that when influence acts are actually studied, it is found that people do not exercise influence in ways predicted by rational classification schemes. This point was first explicitly made in a study by Goodchild, Quadrado, and Raven (Note 1) in which college students wrote brief essays on the topic "How I got my way." It was found that many of the influence tactics described by these students could not be classified into preexisting categories. Several tactics thought to be basic when classifying influence, such as the use of expert power, were not even mentioned by the students.

There is a need, therefore, for empirical studies of the use of influence within organizations. The purpose of this article is to report two studies that sought to examine the tactics of influence used by people at work when attempting to change the behavior of their superiors, co-workers, and subordinates. In the first study, the range of tactics that people use at work was identified by applying content analysis to written descriptions by managers of their attempts to influence their bosses, co-workers, or subordinates. The second study sought to identify through factor analysis the dimensions of influence underlying the specific tactics that were uncovered in the first study.

STUDY 1: DETERMINING INTRAORGANIZATIONAL INFLUENCE TACTICS

Method

The data for this study were collected from 165 respondents, 25% women and 75% men. All respondents were taking graduate business courses part-time, in the evening. They were told to refer to their current employment experience when supplying the requested information.

The respondents were employed mainly in managerial roles as engineers, technicians, and professionals. Since most respondents came from different organizations, there were almost as many organizations as respondents represented.

Respondents were asked to describe an incident in which they actually succeeded in getting either their boss, a co-worker, or a subordinate to do something they wanted; 62 described how they got their way with their boss, 49 with a co-worker, and 54 with a subordinate. The reason for the unequal distribution of respondents over status levels was that fewer respondents had subordinates or co-workers than had bosses.

In their description of an incident, each respondent wrote in essay form what they wanted from a target person, what they did, whether there was resistance from the target, and what further influence tactics were used in response to resistance from the target. Each respondent also completed a structured questionnaire containing demographic and specific organizational job-situation questions.

The incidents were sorted first in terms of the goal sought from the target person. This sorting yielded five general categories of goals: *assistance with own job*—obtaining the assistance of the target in helping the respondent do his or her job, when it was not part of the target's legitimate job duties; *get others to do their job*—getting the target to do his or her own work; *obtain benefits*—goals that personally benefited the respondent, such as salary increase, promotion, and improved work schedule; *initiate change*—initiating new organizational programs and systems or improving the coordination of organizational activities (e.g., changing a scheduling procedure); and *improve performance*—improving the target's on-the-job performance.

These goals varied as a function of the target's job status, as shown in Table 1. Respondents sought mostly self-interest goals from their superiors. The primary goal sought from co-workers was to get assistance with the respondent's own job. The most prevalent reason for influencing subordinates was to get them to do their jobs. Finally, the goal of initiating change was sought both from bosses and from subordinates in almost equal proportion. However, the changes sought from superiors focused on job-related organizational changes, such as launching a new accounting procedure or starting a special project. But with subordinates, the changes sought dealt with job performance, such as changes in the way a job should be done or the manner of working in the organization.

Next, the influence tactics reported by the respondents in attempting to achieve these goals were identified. A total of 370 influence tactics were reported by the 165 respondents. The authors sorted these tactics into 14 categories (see Table 2). Consensus among the coders was used as the criterion for assigning a given tactic to a category. The 14 categories ranged from the use of administrative sanctions and personal threats through the use of logic and rational discussions to clandestine, dependency appeal, and ingratiating tactics. The individual tactics

Table 1
Reasons for Exercising Influence, by Target Status (Study 1) in Percentages

| Reasons | Target status | | | |
	Boss (62)	Co-worker (49)	Subordinate (54)	Total (165)
Obtain assistance on own job	3	48	9	18
Get others to do their jobs	13	23	46	27
Obtain personal benefits	58	10	0	25
Initiate change in work	26	15	28	23
Improve target's job performance	0	4	17	7

Note. Numbers in parentheses are *N*s.

Table 2
Classification of Influence Tactics by Category (Study 1)

Category/tactic	%[a]	Category/tactic	%[a]
Clandestine	8	Exchange	8
Challenged the ability of the target		Contributed in exchange for compliance	
Lied to the target		Compromised	
Acted in a pseudo-democratic manner		Offered to make sacrifice	
Puffed up the importance of the job		Offered help to get the job done	
Manipulated information		Invoked past favors	
Made the target feel important		Persistence	7
Cajoled the target		Repeated reminders	
Showed understanding (pretended) of the target's problem		Argued	
		Repeated previous actions	
		Surveillance	
Personal negative actions	8	Training	6
Fait accompli/went ahead on own		Explained how it was to be done	
Chastised the target		Showed how to do it	
Became a nuisance		Reward	2
Slowed down on the job		Verbal reinforcement	
Held personal confrontation with target		Salary raise	
Threatened withdrawal of help		Gave benefits	
Expressed anger		Self-presentation	5
Threatened to leave job		Demonstrated competence	
Blocked target's actions		Performed well, then asked	
Ignored target		Waited until target was in the right mood	
		Was humble	
		Was friendly	
Administrative negative actions	3	Direct request	10
Filed a report with supervisor		Weak ask	6
Sent target to superior for conference		Showed dependency	
Gave unsatisfactory performance evaluations		Weak request	
Gave no salary increase		Demand	7
Threatened with unsatisfactory performance ratings		Invoked rules	
Threatened job security		Ordered	
Threatened loss of promotion		Convened formal conference	
		Set time deadline	
		Told target that it must be done as I said or better proposed	

(continued)

Table 2   *Continued*

Category/tactic	%[a]	Category/tactic	%[a]
Explained rationale for request	17	Obtained support from subordinates	
Gathered supporting data	6	Threatened to notify an outside agency	
Coalitions	7	Made formal appeals to higher levels	
Obtained support from co-workers			
Obtained support informally from superiors			

[a] Percentage of the 370 tabulated influence tactics reported by respondents.

illustrating these 14 categories are also shown in Table 2. To determine the reliability of the assignment of items to these 14 categories, three coders who were not associated with the research independently sorted the 370 influence tactics into the 14 categories. Raters 1 and 2 agreed on the placement of items 61% of the time; Raters 1 and 3 agreed 64% of the time; and Raters 2 and 3 agreed 65% of the time. Since there were 14 categories into which any item could be placed, the degree of agreement between the three raters suggests modestly high reliability for the classification scheme. The areas of disagreement between the raters involved primarily the three categories "weak ask," "explain," and "request."

In addition to identifying influence tactics, the analyses of Study 1 focused on the correlates of the 14 categories of influence. To this end, a unit weight of 1 was assigned if the respondent reported using any of the items comprising a given influence tactic category; a score of 0 was assigned if none of the items comprising a category were mentioned. Thus, each respondent had 14 scores of 1 or 0. Next, multivariate analyses of variance, which if significant were followed by univariate analyses, were carried out to examine the relationship among the 14 categories of influence, the status of the target person, and the goals sought by respondents in exercising influence.

The influence tactics used by the respondents varied with the goal sought from the target person. When the goal was self-interest, the most frequently reported tactics were self-presentation and personal negative actions; when the goal was to initiate change, the most frequently reported tactics were the use of logic and rational discussions; when the goal was to improve a target's performance, respondents reported using administrative sanctions, training, and simply demanding compliance. Finally, when the goal was to get others to do the respondent's own work, the most frequently reported tactic was the use of requests. All of the above findings were statistically reliable beyond the .05 level.

The kinds of influence tactics used by the respondents varied with the power of the target person. Respondents significantly more often used the tactics of self-presentation, supporting data, and coalitions when attempting to influence their bosses. Different tactics, however, were used to influence subordinates; then respondents significantly more often used clandestine tactics, administrative sanctions, training, demanding, and explaining. Finally, the data showed that only one tactic was significantly associated with influencing co-workers— the tactic of requesting help. At the .10 level, however, the tactics of exchange, requests, and rewards were also associated with influencing co-workers.

The use of influence tactics also varied with the amount of resistance shown by target persons. When the respondents stated that the target at first refused to comply, the subsequent actions of respondents included an increase in persistence and the use of personal negative actions. Additionally, when confronting resisting bosses and co-workers, the respondents reported an increase in the use of coalitions with fellow employees. If the person resisting was a subordinate, however, the respondents reported using more administrative sanctions such as giving unsatisfactory performance evaluations.

Results

The findings of the study suggest that in organizational settings the choice of influence tactics is associated with what the respondents are trying to get from the target person, the amount of resistance shown, and the power of the target person. Combining these findings suggests that administrative sanctions and personal negative actions are more likely to be used when the target is a subordinate who is actively resisting the request of the manager and when the reasons for exercising influence are based on the respondent's role in the organization (e.g., improve target's performance).

It is also important to note that many of the tactics reported by the respondents have received little mention in the organizational literature (e.g., the use of deceit, self-presentation, and clandestine tactics). In fact, the tactics shown in Table 2 represent a bewildering combination of several classification schemes from the exchange theories of Michener and Schwertfeger (1972) to the schemes described by French and Raven (1959) and by Cartwright (1965, pp. 1–47). It is clear that the many influence tactics described here do not fit easily into any single classification scheme currently found in the literature on power usage. Based on these findings, we believe that new ways of classifying such tactics are needed that use the actual influence behaviors of organizational members as the starting point. An effort in this direction is reported in the next study.

STUDY 2

Method

Many of the 14 categories of influence tactics in the first study overlapped either conceptually or empirically or both (e.g., "weak ask" vs. "request"). The purpose of Study 2 was to determine the factor structure of the tactics found in the previous study. To this end, 58 items were developed from Study 1's tactics. These items were included in a questionnaire administered to 754 employed respondents. Respondents were asked to describe on a 5-point scale how frequently during the past 6 months they had used each item to influence a target person at work. The 5-point scale had verbal anchors as follows: usually use this tactic to influence him/her (5), frequently use this tactic to influence him/her (4), occasionally use this tactic to influence him/her (3), seldom use this tactic to influence him/her (2), and never use this tactic to influence him/her (1).

There were three forms of the questionnaire: One asked respondents to describe how they influenced their bosses, another asked how they influenced their co-workers, and the third asked how they influenced their subordinates. The instructions read:

This questionnaire is a way of obtaining information about how you go about changing your boss's (or co-worker's or subordinate's) mind so that he or she agrees with you. Below are described various ways of doing this. Please do not answer in terms of what you would like to do.

Respondents were also told that if the tactics did not apply in their work to leave the space blank; blank responses were coded as "never used this tactic."

Sample. The respondents were drawn from the same managerial population as in Study 1 and were taking graduate business courses part-time: 690 were enrolled in evening courses at Temple University and 64 were enrolled at the Bernard Baruch Graduate Center in New York City. Of the 754 respondents, 225 described how they influenced their bosses, 285 described how they influenced co-workers, and 244 described how they influenced subordinates.

Reasons for exercising influence. In addition to describing how frequently each influence tactic was used, a separate scale presented respondents with five possible reasons for influencing the target person. These reasons were based on those found in Study 1 and read as follows: (a) have my boss (co-worker or subordinate) assist me on my job or do some of my work; (b) assign work to my boss (co-worker or subordinate) or tell him or her what to do; (c) have my boss (co-worker or subordinate) give me benefits, such as raises, better hours of work, time off, better job assignments, and so on; (d) have my boss (co-worker or subordinate) do his or her own work better or do what they are supposed to do; (e) have my boss (co-worker or subordinate) accept my ideas for changes, for example, to accept a new way of doing the work more efficiently or a new program or project.

For each of the five reasons, the respondents were asked to rate on a 5-point scale ranging from "very often" (5) to "never" (1) how frequently each reason had been the cause of their trying to influence the target person to do something.

Paralleling the findings of Study 1, the reasons for exercising influence varied with whether the target person was a superior, co-worker, or subordinate. Table 3 shows that the major reasons for influencing subordinates were that respondents more frequently attempted to assign them work, to improve their task performance, and to have them assist the respondents in their own work ($p < .01$ compared to co-workers or superiors). Superiors were influenced most frequently to receive personal benefits ($p < .01$). Finally, respondents reported that they attempted to influence both their subordinates and their superiors with almost equal frequency to convince them to initiate change. This last result was also found in Study 1.

Table 3
Mean Frequency of Reasons for Respondents Exercising Influence (Study 2)

Reason for exercising influence	Target status			F
	Subordinate (244)	Co-worker (285)	Superior (225)	
Assistance on own job	3.15_a	2.75_b	2.09_c	64.36**
Assign work	4.08_a	2.47_b	1.86_c	329.69**
Obtain benefits	1.33_a	1.65_b	2.42_c	90.41**
Improve performance	3.93_a	2.88_b	2.39_c	135.19**
Initiate change	3.54_a	3.27_b	3.47_a	6.66*

Note. Numbers in parentheses are Ns. Groups with different subscripts differ beyond the .05 level. High scores indicate that the goal was rated as a frequent reason for the respondent to influence the target person.

* $p < .05$ ** $p < .01$.

Additional background data. The questionnaire also obtained information about the sex of the respondent, the sex of the respondent's boss, whether the organization was unionized, the number of persons employed in the respondent's work unit, and the job level of the respondent. Job level information was based on the respondent's description of his or her own work. This information was coded into four groups: clerical/sales, professional (e.g., engineer, computer technician), first-line and middle managers (e.g., supervisor, manager of clerical unit, etc.), and top-level managers (e.g., vice president of marketing).

Results

The 58 influence tactic items were factor analyzed using a principal component factor solution, with iterations for communality and varimax rotation. Forced two-factor through eight-factor solutions were carried out to aid in interpreting the findings.

Factor analyses were carried out for the entire sample and separately for each of the three target status levels (superior, co-worker, subordinate). This was done to examine the possibility that dimensions of influence would emerge at each target status level that did not emerge in the overall analysis. A second reason for carrying out separate factor analyses at each target status level was to ensure that any factors that emerged in the combined analysis also appeared in at least one of the separate factor analyses. It was assumed that a factor that did not appear in any of the separate analyses, yet appeared in the overall analysis, only reflected differences between target status levels in the exercise of influence.

The factor analysis of the entire sample yielded six interpretable factors. These six factors accounted for 38% of the total item variance. Table 4 lists the tactics presented in the questionnaire. The data in Table 4 are based on the overall factor analysis utilizing all 754 respondents.

Factor 1 is identified by highest loadings on the influence tactics, including demanding, ordering, and setting deadlines. This factor is labeled *Assertiveness*. The factor emerged as a dimension of influence at all target status levels (superior, co-worker, and subordinate).

Factor 2 is described by the highest loadings on weak and nonobtrusive influence tactics. Included here were such tactics as "acting humble" and "making the other person feel important." This factor is labeled *Ingratiation*. The factor emerged as a dimension of influence at all levels of target status.

Factor 3 is characterized by loadings on the use of rationality influence tactics and is labeled *Rationality*. It includes such tactics as "writing a detailed plan" and "explaining the reasons for my request." This factor emerged at each target status level. In the analysis of tactics directed toward subordinates, however, additional items that involved group pressure also loaded highly on this factor. These latter items will be discussed subsequently.

Factor 4 involved the use of administrative sanctions to induce compliance. Tactics with high loadings included "prevented salary increases" and "threatened job security." This factor is labeled *Sanctions*. It emerged as a dimension of influence at all levels of target status.

Factor 5 loaded on tactics involving the exchange of positive benefits. Included here were such tactics as "offering an exchange" and "offering to make personal sacrifices." This factor is labeled *Exchange of Benefits*. This factor only emerged in the factor analysis of influence tactics directed toward superiors.

Factor 6 is described by loadings on tactics that bring additional pressure for conformity on the target by invoking the influence of higher levels in the organization. Included here were such tactics as "making a formal appeal to higher levels" and "obtaining the informal support of

Table 4
Rotated Factors and Items

Dimension of influence/tactic

Assertiveness
51. Kept checking up on him or her.
45. Simply ordered him or her to do what was asked.
18. Demanded that he or she do what I requested.
39. Bawled him or her out.
11. Set a time deadline for him or her to do what I asked.
19. Told him or her that the work must be done as ordered or he or she should propose a better way.
53. Became a nuisance (kept bugging him/her until he/she did what I wanted).
43. Repeatedly reminded him or her about what I wanted.
54. Expressed my anger verbally.
41. Had a showdown in which I confronted him or her face to face.
30. Pointed out that the rules required that he or she comply.

Ingratiation
46. Made him or her feel important ("only you have the brains, talent to do this").
 9. Acted very humbly to him or her while making my request.
17. Acted in a friendly manner prior to asking for what I wanted.
28. Made him or her feel good about me before making my request.
37. Inflated the importance of what I wanted him or her to do.
36. Praised him or her.
 3. Sympathized with him/her about the added problems that my request has caused.
44. Waited until he or she appeared in a receptive mood before asking.
10. Showed my need for their help.
29. Asked in a polite way.
22. Pretended I was letting him or her decide to do what I wanted (act in a pseudo-democratic fashion).

Rationality
40. Wrote a detailed plan that justified my ideas.
38. Presented him or her with information in support of my point of view.
31. Explained the reasons for my request.
13. Used logic to convince him or her.
24. Wrote a memo that described what I wanted.
42. Offered to compromise over the issue (I gave in a little).
16. Demonstrated my competence to him or her before making my request.

Sanctions
49. Gave no salary increase or prevented person from getting a pay raise.
26. Threatened his or her job security (e.g., hint of firing or getting him or her fired).

(continued)

Table 4   *Continued*

Dimension of influence/tactic

15. Promised (or gave) a salary increase.
 6. Threatened to give him or her an unsatisfactory performance evaluation.
34. Threatened him or her with loss of promotion.

Exchange
35. Offered an exchange (e.g., if you do this for me, I will do something for you).
27. Reminded him or her of past favors that I did for them.
50. Offered to make a personal sacrifice if he or she would do what I wanted (e.g., work late, work harder, do his/her share of the work, etc).
55. Did personal favors for him or her.
 7. Offered to help if he/she would do what I wanted.

Upward appeal
58. Made a formal appeal to higher levels to back up my request.
20. Obtained the informal support of higher-ups.
25. Filed a report about the other person with higher-ups (e.g., my superior).
33. Sent him or her to my superior.

Blocking
47. Threatened to notify an outside agency if he or she did not give in to my request.
48. Threatened to stop working with him or her until he or she gave in.
 4. Engaged in a work slowdown until he or she did what I wanted.
 5. Ignored him or her and/or stopped being friendly.
14. Distorted or lied about reasons he or she should do what I wanted.

Coalitions
12. Obtained the support of co-workers to back up my request.
56. Had him or her come to a formal conference at which I made my request.
32. Obtained the support of my subordinates to back up my request.

Unclassified items
52. Kept kidding him or her until they did what I wanted.
23. Ignored him or her and went ahead and did what I wanted.
 8. Provided him or her with various benefits that they wanted.
 1. Challenged his or her ability ("I bet you can't do that").
21. Pretended not to understand what needed to be done so that he or she would volunteer to do it for me.
 2. Concealed some of my reasons for trying to influence him/her.

Note. $N = 754$. Item numbers denote the items' original position in the questionnaire.

higher-ups." This factor only emerged in the factor analysis of influence tactics directed toward superiors; it is labeled *Upward Appeal*.

Two additional factors (Factors 7 and 8) did not emerge in the overall factor analysis but were found in the subanalyses. It was decided to retain these factors for heuristic purposes.

Factor 7 emerged in the factor analysis of influence directed toward superiors. Items that loaded on this factor included "engaging in a work slowdown" and "threatening to stop working with the target person." Essentially, these tactics are attempts to stop the target person from carrying out some action by various kinds of blocking tactics. This factor is labeled *Blocking*.

Factor 8 emerged from the factor analysis of tactics directed toward subordinates. Items in this factor were part of the previously described factor Rationality. However, this subset of items described the use of steady pressure for compliance by "obtaining the support of co-workers" and by "obtaining the support of subordinates." This is labeled *Coalitions*.

Scale construction

To aid further analysis, scales were constructed whose items were selected to represent each of the eight dimensions of influence. Selection was made on the basis of two criteria. First, items were selected that loaded over .40 on a given dimension and did not load above .25 on any of the remaining dimensions. Second, from the pool of items that were selected to represent each dimension, items were selected based on an examination of each item's correlation with other items representing the factor and their correlations with items in the remaining factors. High item intercorrelation within a factor and low item intercorrelation with the remaining items were used as the final criteria for selecting items.

Correlates of Influence Tactics

Target status

Table 5 shows the means and standard deviations of each influence dimension as a function of the status of the target. Seven of the eight

Table 5
Target Status and Average Frequency of Tactic Use

Dimension of influence	Target status			F
	Subordinate	Co-worker	Superior	
Ingratiation				
M	15.92$_b$	16.08$_b$	14.52$_a$	16.69**
SD	3.97	4.73	4.48	
Rationality				
M	14.04$_b$	13.74$_b$	14.72$_a$	7.17**
SD	2.47	3.20	3.01	
Assertiveness				
M	12.04$_a$	8.06$_b$	6.94$_c$	243.91**
SD	3.00	2.67	2.25	
Sanctions				
M	6.39$_a$	5.27$_b$	5.16$_b$	68.18**
SD	1.95	0.91	0.62	
Exchange				
M	9.83$_b$	10.08$_b$	8.56$_a$	13.52**
SD	3.10	3.65	3.53	
Upward appeal				
M	7.05$_b$	6.83$_b$	5.43$_a$	37.16**
SD	2.31	2.29	1.99	
Blocking				
M	3.31$_a$	3.50$_b$	3.29$_a$	4.05*
SD	0.82	1.04	0.91	
Coalitions				
M	4.37	4.30	4.53	.079
SD	2.04	2.05	2.14	

Note. Groups with different subscripts differ beyond the .05 level.

* $p < .05$. ** $p < .01$.

dimensions were significantly associated with the relative status of the target. Basically, the findings suggest that as the status of the target person increased, respondents placed more reliance on rationality tactics. An analysis using Duncan's multiple-range test found that Assertive tactics and Sanctions were used more often to influence subordinates than co-workers or superiors ($ps < .01$). The tactics of Ingratiation, Exchange of Benefits, and Upward Appeal were used with equal frequency among subordinates and co-workers but significantly less often when attempting to influence superiors ($p < .01$). Finally, respondents reported that they used Rationality tactics more frequently to convince superiors than co-workers or subordinates ($p < .01$). As will be shown later, these differences in choice of tactics in part reflect the fact that respondents have different reasons for influencing target persons at different status levels.

Goals

It will be recalled that respondents in the present study rated the importance of five possible reasons for exercising influence. To determine whether different combinations of tactics were used as the reasons for influencing varied, a set of stepwise regression analyses was performed. These stepwise regression analyses examined the relation between the eight tactic scores and the rated importance of each reason for exercising influence. A restriction put on the analysis was that only tactics that correlated significantly ($p < .05$) with a given reason were entered into the regression analysis. Since we have already found that the type of tactic used and the reasons for exercising influence both varied with the status of the target person, separate regression analyses were carried out at each target status level. Table 6 shows these findings in terms of the particular combination of influence tactics that best predicted each reason for exercising influence. In addition, Table 6 presents the multiple correlations of these influence tactics with each reason for exercising influence.

Table 6 shows that at all target status levels, the respondent's choice of influence tactics varied with the respondents' reasons for exercising influence. That is, respondents who frequently sought personal assistance from target persons used Ingratiation tactics; respondents who frequently assigned work to target persons used Assertiveness; and respondents who frequently tried to improve a target person's performance used Assertiveness and Rationality tactics. Finally, respondents who frequently tried to convince target persons to accept new ideas used Rationality tactics.

Another finding of interest in Table 6 is that respondents showed the least variation in choice of tactics when attempting to influence their subordinates. No matter what the reason for influencing subordinates, the use of Assertiveness was associated with each of the five reasons

Table 6
Multiple Correlations Between Tactics and Rated Importance
of Reasons for Exercising Influence

Reason for exercising influence/target	Tactic category used	R
Receive assistance on own job		
boss	Ingratiation	.20
co-worker	Ingratiation	.16
subordinate	Assertiveness	
	Ingratiation	.29
Assign work to target		
boss	Assertiveness	.51
co-worker	Assertiveness	.28
subordinate	Assertiveness	.31
Obtain benefits from target		
boss	Exchange	
	Ingratiation	.38
co-worker	Exchange	
	Blocking	
	Ingratiation	.32
subordinate	Assertiveness	
	Coalitions	.21
Improve target's performance		
boss	Assertiveness	
	Blocking	
	Rationality	.43
co-worker	Assertiveness	
	Exchange	
	Coalitions	
	Rationality	.46
subordinate	Assertiveness	
	Rationality	.34
Initiate change		
boss	Rationality	
	Coalition	
	Ingratiation	
	Exchange	.57
co-worker	Rationality	
	Coalitions	
	Exchange	.45
subordinate	Assertiveness	
	Rationality	.42

Note. Tactics are listed in order of their entry into the stepwise multiple regression equations. All correlations are significant beyond the .05 level.

and accounted for the most variance for each reason. In contrast, when influencing co-workers and superiors, the use of Assertiveness was associated only with two of the five reasons.

Other Situational Factors

So far it has been shown that use of the eight dimensions of influence was associated with the relative power of the target person and the reasons why the respondents wanted to influence the target person. In this section we examine the relationship between the use of tactics and five personal or situational characteristics of the respondent: sex, level in the organization, whether the respondent's unit was unionized, number of people in respondent's work unit, and sex of respondent's boss.

The findings showed that the respondent's own level in the organization was closely associated with use of influence tactics. Compared to those with low job status, respondents with higher job status reported greater use of Rationality and Assertiveness tactics when influencing both their subordinates and their superiors ($ps < .01$). In addition, respondents with higher job status used Sanctions more frequently and sought aid from their superiors less frequently when influencing their subordinates ($ps < .01$). Thus, as the respondents' own job status rose, they were more likely to use more direct tactics of influence and be less dependent upon superiors.

Size of work unit also related to the use of tactics on subordinates. In large work units, respondents more frequently used Assertiveness ($p < .01$), Sanctions ($p < .01$), and Upward Appeal ($p < .05$) when influencing subordinates. These findings are consistent with the general idea that as the number of persons in a work unit increases, a greater reliance is placed on strong and impersonal means of control.

Finally, the presence of unions was associated with the use of certain tactics. If the organization was unionized, respondents were more likely to use Ingratiating tactics to influence subordinates ($p < .01$), to avoid the use of Assertiveness when influencing co-workers ($p < .05$), and to use Rationality tactics less frequently ($p < .01$) and Blocking tactics more frequently ($p < .01$) when influencing bosses.

There were no significant relations associated with the sex of the respondent and the sex of the respondent's boss in terms of the frequency of use of the eight dimensions of influence. Thus, in the present study men and women chose similar tactics when attempting to get their way.

DISCUSSION

In Study 1, influence tactics were sorted into 14 categories, but we suspected that a more parsimonious classification system was likely to exist. The results of Study 2 yielded eight dimensions of influence.

Four of these dimensions emerged at all status levels. These dimensions were Assertiveness, Sanctions, Ingratiation, and Rationality. The remaining dimensions were uniquely associated with influencing either superiors or subordinates. The tactics of Exchange of Benefits, Blocking, and Upward Appeal emerged when respondents described how they influenced their bosses. These dimensions did not appear in the analysis of influence tactics used among subordinates. Finally, the use of Coalitions tactics appeared only when respondents described how they influenced their subordinates.

Unfortunately, there are few studies available with which to compare the present findings. Within organizational settings, the major empirical studies of influence tactics have been based on the Ohio State–Navy leadership studies (Fleishman, 1973). These studies could identify only two dimensions of influence—consideration and initiating structure. However, this early program of research was only concerned with how leaders exercised influence over subordinates and was not concerned with the use of influence tactics among peers and bosses. Hence, the range of influence tactics used in that early research covered fewer areas than those included here.

Other factorial studies of influence tactics have focused on dimensions of influence in interpersonal settings (Falbo, 1977; Kipnis, Cohen, & Catalano, Note 2). These studies have uncovered only two or three dimensions of influence. For example, Kipnis et al. reported that dating couples used three dimensions of influence—strong, weak, and rational—as ways of changing their dating partner's behavior. The items loading on these three dimensions closely resemble the dimensions we have labeled *Assertiveness, Rationality*, and *Ingratiation* tactics. Thus, instead of acting "more loving" in order to influence, organizational members act "humble" and offer to "make sacrifices." The parallel is clearly there. The additional factors found in the present study suggest that organizational resources extend the range of tactics that organizational members can use. Thus, organizational members can invoke formal sanctions or the added authority of higher management as compliance-gaining strategies.

It is recognized, of course, that findings presented here are based on self-report measures and require replication using different methodologies. Nevertheless, the picture portrayed by these data is of organizational members actively seeking to influence peers, superiors, and subordinates for a variety of reasons, some personal and some based on their management roles. This picture supports the view of those who argue that organizational leadership is more complicated than is represented in organizational behavior textbooks (Kochan, Schmidt, & DeCotiis, 1976). Such texts mainly focus on the ways in which higher levels in the organization influence lower levels. This is called the leadership process. In fact, we would suggest that everyone is influencing everyone else in organizations, regardless of job title. People seek benefits, information, satisfactory job performance, the chance to do better than others, to be left alone, cooperation, and many other outcomes too numerous to mention.

In fact, there may be very little difference in the frequency with which people try to influence their bosses, co-workers, and subordinates, given all these various reasons for trying to influence others. What shows remarkable variation, however, are the kinds of tactics that are chosen when trying to obtain these various outcomes. The present article has shown that these tactics vary with the particular wants of the influencing agent and his or her degree of control over the target of influence. The implications of these findings for the understanding of organizational politics remain to be explored.

As a final point, the scales that have been developed to measure the various dimensions of influence can be useful in further research. Even though the use of influence within organizations is a topic of considerable interest, there have been few systematic attempts to develop a means of measuring such behavior. The present dimensions provide the potential for profiling the use of influence in a variety of organizational settings and at different levels as well as between various groups.

REFERENCE NOTES

1. Goodchild, J. D., Quadrado, C., & Raven, B. H. *Getting one's way*. Paper presented at the meeting of the Western Psychological Association, Sacramento, California, April 1975.

2. Kipnis, D., Cohen, E., & Catalano, R. *Power and affection*. Paper presented at the meeting of the Eastern Psychological Association, Philadelphia, April 1979.

REFERENCES

Cartwright, D. Influence, leadership and control. In J. G. March (Ed.), *Handbook of organizations*. Chicago: Rand McNally, 1965.

Etzioni, A. Organizational dimensions and their interrelationship. In B. Indik & F. K. Berrien (Eds.), *People, groups and organizations*. New York: Teachers College Press, 1968.

Falbo, T. The multidimensional scaling of power strategies. *Journal of Personality and Social Psychology*, 1977, *35*, 537–547.

Fleishman, E. A. Twenty years of consideration and structure. In E. A. Fleishman & J. G. Hunt (Eds.), *Current developments in the study of leadership*. Carbondale: Southern Illinois University Press, 1973.

French, J. R. P., & Raven, B. H. The bases of social power. In D. Cartwright (Ed.), *Studies in social power*. Ann Arbor: University of Michigan Press, 1959.

Izraeli, D. N. The middle manager and the tactics of power expansion. *Sloan Management Review*, 1975, *16*, 57–70.

Kochan, T. A., Schmidt, S. M., & DeCotiis, T. A. Superior-subordinate relations: Leadership and headship. *Human Relations*, 1976, *28*, 279–294.

Michener, A., & Schwertfeger, M. Liking as a determinant of power tactic preference. *Sociometry*, 1972, *35*, 190–202.

Raven, B. H. The comparative analysis of power and influence. In J. T. Tedeschi (Ed.), *Perspective on social power*. Chicago: Aldine, 1974.

Schein, V. E. Individual power and political behavior. *Academy of Management Review*, 1977, *2*, 64–72.

A Social Influence Interpretation of Worker Motivation

Mario Sussmann and Robert P. Vecchio

When considering the topic of worker motivation, one is initially overwhelmed by the abundance of different theories and approaches that are present in the organizational literature (Adams, 1965; Campbell & Pritchard, 1976; Campbell, Dunnette, Lawler, & Weick, 1970; Lawler, 1973; Porter & Lawler, 1968; Vroom, 1964). However, the major theories of worker motivation (both mechanistic and cognitive) have largely ignored a fundamental issue concerning the origins of worker behavior. Specifically, this omission stems from an assumption that factors which appear to precede changes in behavior operate in a unilateral fashion, and workers (it is assumed) do not exercise an appreciable degree of personal volition, that is, they *do not decide to accept influence attempts.* This theoretical omission sidesteps the question of the process whereby influence attempts are accepted/rejected as well as the varieties of influence that exist. Rather than define "influence processes," one can instead attempt to define the "basis of acceptance." However, the latter view does not present the worker as an active participant in the determination of his or her behavior. Presented in this paper is a process view of social influence that specifies the manner and nature of socially induced changes in worker behavior.

An influence attempt is defined here as a social occasion wherein one individual exhibits behaviors, emits verbal utterances, and so on, with the intent of altering the behavior of another or others to a desired end. The scope of this discourse is restricted to work related behaviors (especially, but not exclusively, behaviors related to worker productivity). Of concern here are occasions of socially dependent influence. That is to say, influence that originates from outside the target person can be distinguished from influence that originates primarily from within the target person (e.g., the socially independent process of a competency motive or exploratory motive). Furthermore, it is recognized that influence is unlikely to be unilateral. Rather, it is most commonly a reciprocal process in that the target person's response to an influence attempt likely will alter the variety, frequency, intensity, and/or direction of future influence attempts.

For the moment, the focus is on the behavior (i.e., response to an influence attempt) of the person who occupies a "subordinate" position (i.e., in the formal, organizational sense of subordinate) because subordinate behavior traditionally has been the primary interest of theories of worker motivation. However, as will be illustrated, influence can be more broadly conceptualized so as to include the impact of subordinate behavior on supervisor behavior (specifically, supervisor's influence attempts).

SOCIAL INFLUENCE PROCESSES

Kelman's (1961) work on identifying qualitatively distinct processes of opinion change has particular relevance to the goals of this paper. These processes are termed compliance, identification, and internalization. If Kelman's terms are extended to work settings, it may be said that *compliance* is concerned with whether a worker accepts an influence attempt because of a desire to obtain a favorable outcome or to avoid an unfavorable outcome. *Identification* refers to whether a worker exhibits behaviors derived from another or others because these behaviors contribute to a person's self-image. The third type of influence process, *internalization*, refers to whether a worker accepts an influence attempt because the encouraged actions are congruent with a personal value system and/or are intrinsically rewarding to the individual.

French and Raven's (1959) view of social power suggests five major sources of influence: reward, coercive, legitimate, referent, and expert. Each of these five may be viewed as being relatively more closely aligned with one of the three processes proposed by Kelman. Specifically, French and Raven's reward and coercive power possesses a strong conceptual similarity with Kelman's notion of compliance. Also, the social power bases of referent power are most in allegiance with Kelman's process of identification. And, finally, legitimate power may be viewed as being potentially the power source for an internalization influence process. Therefore, French and Raven's analysis of social power may be viewed as overlapping with Kelman's typology such that French and Raven's power bases provide a more elaborate conceptual foundation for influence attempts. These influence attempts, in turn, are directed at (or, perhaps more properly, are translated into) specific psychological processes (Kelman, 1961) and succeed or fail in altering behavior as a function of individual and situational contingencies.

Etzioni (1975) has offered an approach that examines social power and worker response within the framework of a structurally oriented organizational analysis. Etzioni considered the influence-motivation problem as one of *compliance*, a term that indicates the relation between the influence agent's power and the influencee's involvement (by involvement is meant a cathectic-evaluative orientation of an actor to an object).

In Etzioni's typology of power, coercive power refers to the administration of pain or the threat to do so. Remunerative or utilitarian power refers to allocation of rewards such as pay, benefits, services, and commodities. Among two types of normative power, pure normative power refers to the allocation of symbolic rewards based on prestige, esteem, and ritualistic symbols, and social power refers to the apportionment of interpersonal rewards and acceptance. There also are four types of involvement: alienative (a negative and hostile orientation); calculative (based on the material gain in an economic relationship); and two types of moral involvement (devotion to ideas, groups, movements, organizations, leaders), with a distinction between "pure moral" commitment and "social" commitment, paralleling the distinction between pure normative and social power. In a proposal that anticipated contingency theories, congruent types of compliance are defined as occasions in which a type of power is paired with a corresponding type of involvement (coercive with alienative, remunerative-utilitarian with calculative, normative with moral); all other combinations are incongruent.

A comparison of Kelman's and Etzioni's typologies shows that Etzioni offers two types of relationship (coercive power and remunerative-utilitarian power) but Kelman writes only of compliance. On the other hand, Kelman's distinction between identification (social power, social commitment) and internalization (pure normative power—pure moral commitment) appears to be particularly useful because Kelman also postulates a cost difference between identification and internalization: the internalization process clearly is the one that does not require surveillance (in contrast with compliance) or the presence/salience (in contrast with identification) of the power agent and might be seen as the most effective and parsimonious means of control. Yet, an important difference remains: Kelman's three processes are located at the individual level of analysis, whereas Etzioni's compliance is defined as a relation between an individual process (involvement) and an organizational process (power).

INDIVIDUAL AND SITUATIONAL MODERATORS

Individual differences variables, one may reasonably assume, moderate the impact of influence attempts such that a given type of influence attempt will be more successful with a given group of individuals. Imagine, for example, the outcome of the use of coercive/reward power in order to bring about simple compliance. In such an instance, one would find that the influence attempt was or was not successful as a partial function of such predispositions as willingness to comply with incentives, intimidation, bribery, or threats. It would be suspected that animals, children, and those adults who possess little desire for autonomy would be most responsive to influence attempts that are designed to bring about simple compliance and that are based on coercive/reward power.

Some individual differences moderators that have been the focus of considerable organizational research include growth need strength (Hackman & Oldham, 1976), Protestant work ethic (Blood, 1969; Mirels & Garrett, 1971), and internal versus external locus-of-control (Rotter, 1966). It is suspected that these value system indices are likely to be most relevant for social influence attempts directed at an internalization process. That is to say, influence attempts that essentially are appeals to the target's value system will be differentially effective as a function of the target's value system.

A value system having implications across all three influence modes has been advanced by Kohlberg (1963, 1969). Kohlberg proposes that an individual passes through three identifiable stages of value maturity. At the first level, the preconventional, an individual is most concerned with the consequences of his or her behavior. At the second (conventional) level, an individual is most concerned with meeting the expectations of family, immediate group, or nation because it is valuable as an end in itself. The final, or postconventional, level is characterized by an individual's effort to define and apply these values or principles apart from external norms and potential sanctions.

It can be argued that Kohlberg's typology maps, aptly, into the social influence processes. Specifically, the more an influence attempt is based on simple reward/coercive power and seeks to evoke compliance, the more successful the influence attempt will be if it is directed towards individuals whose value system is best characterized as hedonistic/utilitarian. Influence attempts based on referent power should be most effective with individuals who have a strong desire for social conformity. And, finally, influence heavily directed toward appealing to an individual's values will be most effective with persons who are strongly concerned with value issues. It is worthy of note that a motivational study that employed the Kohlberg typology (Vecchio, 1981) reported support for the hypothesis that individual values moderate worker response to incentive schemes.

In addition to individual differences moderators, one might expect situational factors to play an important role in moderating the differential effectiveness of the various influence approaches. Situational attributes of possible importance include job autonomy and job challenge. Organizational level (a potentially significant situational factor) may be of particular importance to the influence process view of motivation. For example, one might find that different influence processes are used more frequently at different organizational levels, such that internalization influence attempts are used more frequently in higher organizational levels and compliance-based influence attempts are employed more commonly at lower organizational levels. Although such a finding would be of a purely descriptive nature, it should be possible to document the differential effectiveness of these influence processes at different levels.

At a still broader level of conceptualization, the organizational power types proposed by Etzioni offer a further framework for matching the type of influence attempt with situational attributes. That is to say, specific types of influence attempts may appear most appropriate (congruent) and be most effective within specific organizational power structures.

Up to this point, the importance has been shown of several situational and individual attributes as moderators of the relationship between influence attempts and individual motivation. However, the translation of individual motivation (often conceptualized as effort and/or strength of a behavioral intention) into performance requires the specification of individual and situational attributes that serve as moderators of the relationship between individual motivation and performance (Lawler, 1971; Porter & Lawler, 1968; Vroom, 1964). These specific attributes can be best summarized by the terms "ability" and "availability of the behavior."

The intersection of situational attributes, individual differences attributes, and influence attempts yields a complex and theoretically rich framework for hypothesizing specific interactions. However, before discussing such effects it is necessary to link the influence processes with clusters of relevant dependent variables. That is to say, not only is the presently proposed model deliberately explicit with respect to the impact of situational and individual differences moderators (and their interactions), but it also explicitly specifies theoretically relevant intermediate variables and it ties relevant dependent variables to associated processes. Therefore, it is suggested that each influence process is most directly relevant for only certain outcome/process variables.

RELEVANT VARIABLES

Before linking intermediary variables to their associated processes, one must consider the constructs and variables commonly investigated in the area of worker motivation. These constructs and variables have various conceptual commonalities that permit a simple clustering in the interest of parsimony.

The intermediary process variables may be defined as those dimensions that describe individuals' behaviors, intentions, and cognitive and emotional states within an organizationally relevant setting. These process variables appear to describe the specific details of Etzioni's "involvement." Two trends have emerged within the literature for identifying these variables. For the first approach, clusters of these variables are identified and relationships with their antecedents, concomitants, and consequents are explored (Porter & Steers, 1973). Alternatively, many authors have dropped the strict dichotomy between overt behaviors and attitudinal, conative, and cognitive antecedents/concomitants. These authors tend (implicitly) to conceive of acts as including both overt and covert aspects, and they describe work behavior as a process involving a sequence of stages (Mobley, 1977; Mobley, Horner, & Hollingsworth, 1978; Mobley, Griffith, Hand, & Meglino, 1979; Porter

& Lawler, 1968; Steers & Rhodes, 1978). The second approach has the potential advantage of emphasizing the importance of individual processes that mediate overt actions and observable outcomes. Thus, the second route of viewing behavior as a unit of overt and covert processes (by covert is meant those latent processes that can reasonably be deduced from overt behaviors) has been adopted for this paper.

Based on a review of the recent literature, three sets of intermediary process variables and a suspected sequence were derived. The first set of variables centers on the issue of the extent to which work events and attributes are related to the individual's value system. Therefore, these variables are termed *value-related*. This set is similar to Katz's (1964) motivational patterns of intrinsic satisfaction, goal internalization, and acceptance of organizational rules. Four variables were identified for this set: (a) importance of success versus failure at work for a person's self-esteem—a variable identified by Rabinowitz and Hall (1977) as one conceptualization of job involvement; (b) the extent to which one's job and/or work is a "central life interest" (Dubin, 1956)—a variable also interpreted by Rabinowitz and Hall (1977) as a manifestation of the "importance of self-esteem" conceptualization of job involvement; (c) the worker's expectation of pleasant/unpleasant feelings as a result of success versus failure (Lawler, 1969)—a variable best summarized as intrinsic motivation; and (d) the extent of belief in and acceptance of values pertinent to the work role—these values can consist of organizational goals, but they may be specific to a particular profession or occupation (Gouldner, 1957). As "acceptance of organizational goals and values," this variable is identical to the first component of "organizational commitment" (Porter, Steers, Mowday, & Boulian, 1974).

The second set, which includes two variables, represents the extent to which work role, occupation, and organizational membership mark the individual's self-image and the degree to which the individual derives satisfaction from interpersonal relations and primary-group relationships (Katz, 1964) in organizations. This set therefore may be labeled *identity-related*. More specifically, the variables in this set may be termed: (a) importance of the job or the work role for a person's self-concept; and (b) social attachment to the organization. Importance of the job for self-concept is the second conceptualization of job involvement as elaborated by Rabinowitz and Hall (1977). According to these authors, this variable also can be understood as the degree of psychological identification with work. Social attachment refers to the desire to remain within one's organization and to remain a member of the organization. It corresponds therefore to the third component of "organizational commitment" (Porter et al., 1974).

The third set of variables is comprised of utility-related aspects of the job—for example Katz's (1964) instrumental system and individual rewards. These aspects will be referred to with the inclusive variable label of "job outcome utility." This variable consists of extrinsic factors and is reflected in terms such as role attraction (Mobley, Hand, Baker, & Meglino, 1979) and valence of the work role (Vroom, 1964). Also, it is parallel to satisfaction with specific extrinsic facets of the job (Lawler, 1973). Subjective evaluations of job outcomes are thought to be a function not only of the absolute attractiveness of outcomes, but also of social comparisons (Adams, 1965; Katzell, 1964; Locke, 1969).

These three sets of variables—value-related, identity-related, and utilitarian—may be understood as antecedents of those *behavioral intentions* that are, in turn, related to overt behavior. Thus, the variable now considered corresponds to Fishbein's (1967) "behavioral intentions" (BI). This variable is used in Mobley's turnover model (Miller, Katerberg, & Hulin, 1979; Mobley, 1977; Mobley et al., 1978). In the Porter et al. (1974) "organizational commitment" scheme, this variable appears as "willingness to exert effort on behalf of the organization." It must be noted that Porter et al.'s "willingness to exert effort" is far less specific than are such variables as intentions to quit, attend, and produce efficiently, which usually are criteria for prediction. Thus, willingness to exert effort might appear as an antecedent to specific intentions.

Lastly, the proposed process generates overt activity. Examples of this variable are production behavior, quitting, attending, and job performance (the latter is defined as production behavior projected on an evaluative dimension of effectiveness).

A SOCIAL INFLUENCE FRAMEWORK

The entire sequence, consisting of the influence attempts, the three sets of antecedent variables, BI, and overt behavior, is portrayed in Figure 1. Cardinal emphasis is placed on the concept that BI is determined by the three categories of antecedents identified herein. A major corollary of this contention is that in order to change motivation, one has to alter one,

Figure 1
Influence Processes and Sequence

[a] Includes desire for competence, mastery.

two, or all three of these categories. That is to say, motivation change is mediated by changes in the three sets of antecedent variables.

Logically, the question then must be asked as to how these antecedent variables can be modified. Kelman's (1961) aforementioned processes of influence appear to correspond closely to the character of the three BI-antecedent categories.

1. Compliance is defined by Kelman as acceptance of influence in order to gain specific rewards and to avoid punishments. It is a process wherein behavior is controlled by its contingencies; or, in the terminology of expectancy theory, by expectancies of differently valued outcomes. These notions are similar to the variable "utility of work outcomes." It is proposed here, therefore, that motivation is influenced through the mediary of *utility* by the process of *compliance*.

2. Identification refers to the process of accepting influence in order to engage in a satisfying role-relationship with another person or a group. It is behavior controlled by role acceptance, the involvement in the work role in terms of its importance for the self-concept, the commitment to a group, or the attractiveness of membership in an organization. Therefore, this variety of motivation is influenced through the mediary of *identity-related* variables (i.e., importance of the work role for the self-concept, and social attachment to the organization) by the process of *identification*.

3. Internalization refers to the acceptance of influence because it is congruent with a worker's value system and/or because it is intrinsically rewarding. With regard to the work behavior variables listed above, internalization can be understood to exert control through the importance of success and failure for self-esteem, the place of work as a central life interest, the importance of intrinsic rewards, and acceptance of organizational goals and values. Thus, in such cases, motivation is influenced through the mediary of *value-related* variables by the process of *internalization*.

The relationship between the Kelman influence processes and the dependent and process variables is shown at the left-hand side of Figure 1. The incorporation of the dependent and process variables within the Kelman scheme represents an important elaboration of Kelman's work. The proposed framework and inherent process may be summarized as follows: Among the three variables that influence overt behavior directly, BI is the motivational construct. Motivation, in turn, is a function of value-related, identity-related, and/or utility-related categories of person variables. These three categories are controlled by the interpersonal influence process of internalization, identification, and compliance, respectively.

A relationship exists between Kelman's interpersonal influence processes and Etzioni's types of organizational power. Pure normative organizational power (Etzioni) parallels an internalization interpersonal influence process (Kelman), social power corresponds to identification, and utilitarian and coercive power correspond to Kelman's compliance. In the present framework, this paper proposes to distinguish between *positive* (reward based) and *negative* (punitive oriented) compliance, in order to provide the connections with utilitarian and coercive power. Figure 2 portrays this integration of structural (macro-level) with interpersonal and individual (micro-level) processes. On the left-hand side of Figure 2 are Etzioni's types of power, which at the level of interpersonal influence attempts appear as Kelman-type influence processes (second column). The dependent and process variables are clustered, as in Figure 1, with the difference that now the corresponding involvement labels are: pure moral commitment for the value-related variables, social commitment for the identity-related variables, and calculative involvement for the utility-related variables. A cluster is added to describe alienative involvement (consisting of responses such as fear,

Figure 2
An Expanded Motivation Framework[a]

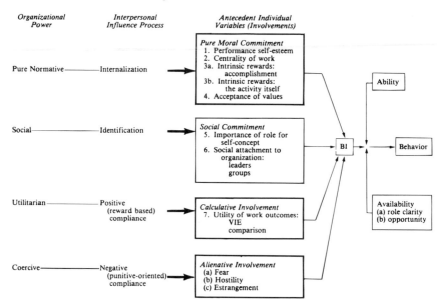

[a]Solid arrows indicate congruent (appropriate) links.

hostility, and estrangement). These clusters are then seen as antecedents of BI. The right-hand side of Figure 2 is identical to the right-hand side of Figure 1.

The *validity* of the proposed view of social influence is suggested by a consideration of popular methods of motivating workers. For example, O. B. Mod and incentive-type schemes appear to be representative of influence attempts that are based on a simple compliance process. Such approaches seek to use extrinsic factors to bring about behavior change (with little or no attention given to appealing to higher order processes).

Identification-based motivational techniques are best represented by modeling techniques. For example, Goldstein and Sorcher (1974) proposed the use of behavioral modeling, which recently was tested by Latham and Saari (1979) and found to be an effective training technique. Also, studies reported by Burnaska (1976) and Kraut (1976) exemplify the social-learning theory approach to modifying work behavior (Davis & Luthans, 1980a).

Job enrichment, by contrast, appears to be directed toward altering the behavior of workers who are more seriously concerned with value-related issues (by offering opportunities for psychological rewards via job redesign). Job enrichment investigators have reported difficulty with respect to motivating individuals who are low on higher-order growth need strength (e.g., the case of the hard-core unemployed). This gives testimony to the validity of the proposition that an internalization influence attempt is most effective with only certain individuals (Hulin, 1971).

In summary, the major approaches to motivating workers (i.e., organizational intervention approaches) can be viewed as being aligned with each of the proposed influence processes. Although the effectiveness of the various intervention approaches is potentially *moderated* by individual and situational contingencies, the possibility exists that the simultaneous use of multiple approaches may result in relatively greater effectiveness (relative to employing a single motivational approach). This second, *additive* strategy is based on evidence—reviewed by Porras (1979) and Porras and Berg (1978)—that suggests that the number of OD techniques employed in intervention projects (or intervention mix) is positively related with effectiveness.

A SOCIALLY-INDEPENDENT MOTIVATIONAL PROCESS

There is a motivational process that has received little consideration in the organizational literature. This process has been ignored, perhaps, because it may be accurately described as a process that is somewhat socially independent. "Socially independent" here means that the relevant behavior originates within the worker with little (at least apparent) external inducement. Nonetheless, the behavior can be characterized as purposeful and seemingly goal-oriented, although the goal is totally internal to the worker. This socially independent motivational process has been termed a competence or mastery motive (White, 1959). This motivational process also encompasses exploratory behavior. Despite its generally socially independent nature, it nonetheless is possible to imagine an influence attempt directed at an individual's competence motive. Such an influence attempt would be one that offered novel and challenging job assignments.

In the vein of socially-independent motivational processes, the recently proposed concept of behavioral self-managment should be mentioned (Davis & Luthans, 1980b; Luthans & Davis, 1979; Manz & Sims, 1980). Based on concepts derived from cognitive behavior modification (Meichenbaum, 1977), behavioral self-management has been offered as a device for self-directing one's own behavior in desired directions.

IMPLICATIONS

By extending and elaborating the proposed framework, it is possible to deduce several implications for supervisory behaviors that would be directed toward motivating workers. For this extension, it is necessary to introduce a feedback loop from worker behavior to a supervisor or, more generally, an evaluator. In this process (see Figure 3), the supervisor compares the observed behavior of the worker with a standard or prior expectations. The supervisor then determines whether a further influence attempt is warranted. If so, the supervisor decides the nature of the influence attempt (compliance, internalization, and/or identification). From a purely descriptive standpoint, the framework represents a cyclical view of social influence, with the supervisor changing influence strategies as a function of worker behavior. It might be argued that this view places a substantial emphasis on worker behavior as a determinant of supervisor behavior. At first glance, this seems like supervision turned upside-down in that the supervisor's influence attempts are "shaped" by the behavior of the worker. However, once the cycle begins, a reciprocal causation process is set in motion so that

Figure 3
A Social Influence View of Supervisor Behavior

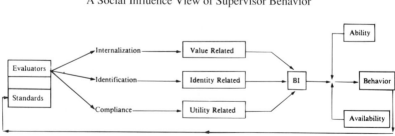

the question of primary control of one person over the other becomes pointless.

Taking the descriptive stance a bit further, it might be demonstrated empirically that different types of supervisors prefer different influence modes. For example, highly authoritarian supervisors might prefer to use compliance influence modes; human-relations oriented supervisors might prefer to use identification influence modes. Also, supervisors might be observed to use different modes of influence when operating in different levels of an organization.

From a prescriptive standpoint, the proposed influence framework suggests that supervisors should be attentive to individual worker differences for preferred inducements. For example, to increase worker motivation, a supervisor should be sensitive to differences in subordinates' preferences for compliance-identification-internalization inducement schemes. It might be possible to demonstrate that more effective supervisors are aware of and make use of subordinate's inducement preferences when attempting to influence the latter's behavior. Such a finding would have important implications for a prescriptive application of the proposed framework.

The above-mentioned extension to supervisor behavior is consistent with the currently popular contingency view of leadership. Clearly, the framework's implications for supervision point to an optimal "matching" of (a) supervisor's preferred style of influence, (b) individual predisposition to respond to specific influence modes, and (c) situational variables that dictate what is socially-appropriate (i.e., normative) for the employment of specific influence modes. The view of the supervisor within the proposed framework, in essence, is best summarized as a view of the supervisor "as motivator."

SUMMARY

This paper has outlined a viewpoint that argues that worker motivation cannot be adequately understood without relating the concept of motivation to attempts on the part of organizational agents to "motivate" people. Such attempts usually take place by means of manipulating outcomes that are made contingent on the actions of individuals. The variables were identified that operate at the individual level (motivation), the interpersonal level (influence), and the organizational level (power).

A framework was presented for tying these variables together, and concepts from both micro-level and macro-level approaches were integrated in a relatively meso-level approach. Also, specific testable predictions were generated from a proposed theoretical integration.

REFERENCES

Adams, J. S. Inequity in social exchange. In L. Berkowitz (Ed.), *Advances in experimental social psychology* (Vol. 2). New York: Academic Press, 1965, 267–299.

Blood, M. R. Work values and job satisfaction. *Journal of Applied Psychology*, 1969, 53, 456–459.

Burnaska, R. F. The effects of behavior upon managers' behaviors and employees' perceptions. *Personnel Psychology*, 1976, 29, 329–335.

Campbell, J. P., & Pritchard, R. D. Motivation theory in industrial and organizational psychology. In M. Dunnette (Ed.), *Handbook of industrial and organizational psychology*. Chicago: Rand-McNally, 1976, 63–130.

Campbell, J. P., Dunnette, M. D., Lawler, E. E., & Weick, K. E. *Managerial behavior, performance, and effectiveness.* New York: McGraw-Hill, 1970.

Davis, T. R. V., & Luthans, F. A social learning approach to organizational behavior. *Academy of Management Review*, 1980a, 5, 281–290.

Davis, T. R. V., & Luthans, F. A social learning approach to training and development: Guidelines for application. *Proceedings of the 12th Annual Meeting of the American Institute for Decision Sciences*, 1980b, 1, 399–401.

Dubin, R. Industrial workers' worlds: A study of the "central life interests" of industrial workers. *Social Problems*, 1956, 3, 131–142.

Etzioni, A. *A comparative analysis of complex organizations* (Rev. ed.). New York: Free Press, 1975.

Fishbein, M. (Ed.). *Readings in attitude theory and measurement.* New York: Wiley, 1967.

French, J. R. P., & Raven, B. The bases of social power. In D. Cartwright (Ed.), *Studies in social power*. Ann Arbor, Mich.: Institute for Social Research, 1959, 150–167.

Goldstein, A. P., & Sorcher, M. *Changing supervisory behavior.* New York: Pergamon Press, 1974.

Gouldner, A. W. Cosmopolitans and locals: Toward an analysis of latent social roles. *Administrative Science Quarterly*, 1957, 2, 281–292.

Hackman, J. R., & Oldham, G. R. Motivation through the design of work: Test of a theory. *Organizational Behavior and Human Performance*, 1976, 16, 250–279.

Hulin, C. L. Individual differences and job enrichment: The case against general treatments. In J. R. Maher (Ed.), *New perspectives in job enrichment.* New York: Van Nostrand, 1971, 159–191.

Katz, D. The motivational basis of organizational behavior. *Behavioral Science*, 1964, 9, 131–146.

Katzell, R. A. Personal values, job satisfaction, and job behavior. In H. Borow (Ed.), *Man in a world of work.* Boston: Houghton Mifflin, 1964, 314–363.

Kelman, H. C. Processes of opinion change. *Public Opinion Quarterly*, 1961, 25, 57–78.

Kohlberg, L. Moral development and identification. In H. Stevenson (Ed.), *Child psychology*, 62nd Yearbook of the National Society for the study of Education. Chicago: University of Chicago Press, 1963, 383–431.

Kohlberg, L. The cognitive-developmental approach to socialization. In D. A. Goslin (Ed.), *Handbook of socialization theory and research.* Chicago: Rand-McNally, 1969, 347–480.

Kraut, A. I. Developing managerial skills via modeling techniques: Some positive research findings—a symposium. *Personnel Psychology*, 1976, 29, 325–369.

Latham, G. P., & Saari, L. M. Application of social-learning theory to training supervisors through behavioral modeling. *Journal of Applied Psychology*, 1979, 64, 239–246.

Lawler, E. E., III. Job design and employee motivation. *Personnel Psychology*, 1969, 22, 426–435.

Lawler, E. E., III. *Pay and organizational effectiveness.* New York: McGraw-Hill, 1971.

Lawler, E. E., III. *Motivation in work organizations.* Monterey, Cal.: Brooks/Cole, 1973.

Locke, E. A. What is job satisfaction? *Organizational Behavior and Human Performance*, 1969, 4, 309–336.

Luthans, F., & Davis, T. R. V. Behavioral self-management—the missing link in managerial effectiveness. *Organizational Dynamics*, 1979, 8, 42–60.

Manz, C. C., & Sims, H. P. Self-management as a substitute for leadership: A social learning theory perspective. *Academy of Management Review*, 1980, 5, 361–367.

Meichenbaum, D. *Cognitive behavior modification: An integrative approach.* New York: Plenum, 1977.

Miller, E. E., Katerberg, R., & Hulin, C. L. Evaluation of the Mobley, Horner, and Hollingsworth model of employee turnover. *Journal of Applied Psychology*, 1979, 64, 509–517.

Mirels, H. L., & Garrett, J. B. The Protestant ethic as a personality variable. *Journal of Consulting and Clinical Psychology*, 1971, 36, 40–44.

Mobley, W. H. Intermediate linkages in the relationship between job satisfaction and employee turnover. *Journal of Applied Psychology*, 1977, 62, 237–240.

Mobley, W. H., Horner, S. O., & Hollingsworth, A. T. An evaluation of precursors of hospital employee turnover. *Journal of Applied Psychology*, 1978, 63, 408–414.

Mobley, W. H., Griffeth, R. W., Hand, H. H., & Meglino, B. M. Review and conceptual analysis of the employee turnover process. *Psychological Bulletin*, 1979, 86, 493–522.

Mobley, W. H., Hand, H. H., Baker, R. L., & Meglino, B. M. Conceptual and empirical analysis of military recruit training attrition. *Journal of Applied Psychology*, 1979, 64, 10–18.

Porras, J. I. The comparative impact of different OD techniques and intervention intensities. *Journal of Applied Behavioral Sciences*, 1979, 15, 156–178.

Porras, J. I., & Berg, P. O. The impact of organization development. *Academy of Management Review*, 1978, 3, 249–266.

Porter, L. W., & Lawler, E. E., III. *Managerial attitudes and performance.* Homewood, Ill.: Irwin, 1968.

Porter, L. W., & Steers, R. M. Organizational, work and personal factors in employee turnover and absenteeism. *Psychological Bulletin*, 1973, 80, 151–176.

Porter, L. W., Steers, R. M., Mowday, R. T., & Boulian, P. V. Organizational commitment, job satisfactions and turnover among psychiatric technicians. *Journal of Applied Psychology*, 1974, 59, 603–609.

Rabinowitz, S., & Hall, D. T. Organizational research and job involvement. *Psychological Bulletin*, 1977, 84, 265–288.

Rotter, J. B. Generalized expectancies for internal versus external control of reinforcement. *Psychological Monographs*, 1966, 80, (1, Whole No. 609).

Steers, R. M., & Rhodes, R. S. Major influences on employee attendance: A process model. *Journal of Applied Psychology*, 1978, 63, 391–407.

Vecchio, R. P. An individual differences interpretation of conflicting predictions generated by equity theory and expectancy theory. *Journal of Applied Psychology*, 1981, 66, 470–481.

Vroom, V. H. *Work and motivation.* New York: Wiley, 1964.

White, R. Motivation reconsidered: The concept of competence. *Psychological Review*, 1959, 66, 297–334.

PART III

Dysfunctional Aspects of Leadership

I don't want any yes-men around me. I want everyone to tell me the truth even if it costs them their jobs.

Samuel Goldwyn

The President doesn't want any yes-men and yes-women around him. When he says no, we all say no.

Elizabeth Dole

The secret of success is sincerity. Once you can fake that, you've got it made.

Jean Giraudoux

Remember, you can do everything right, and do absolutely nothing wrong, and still fail.

Captain Jean-Luc Picard

Although we tend to think of leadership in positive and heroic terms, many times leadership processes operate in a dysfunctional manner. In this set of readings, we explore social problems that arise and work to undermine a group's best interest. The initial reading considers how the drive for consensus in a group can result in the suppression of dissent and honest discussion of alternatives. In "Groupthink" Irving Janis provides concrete examples of how the tendency to internalize group norms and to seek approval has resulted in defective decision making. Dov Eden, of Tel Aviv University, then provides an overview of research on self-fulfilling prophecies as they occur in work groups. The so-called Pygmalion effect, if not properly managed, constitutes a potential pitfall for managers who may be the unwitting victims (and victimizers) of their own delusions. The selection by Manfred Kets de Vries and Danny Miller on narcissism and leadership, explores self-destructive tendencies

that reside in self-absorbed leaders. Jay Conger considers potential liabilities in a leader's skills that can simultaneously give rise to achievement while providing opportunities for self-destruction. The causes and
cures of leader self-destruction are then examined in another article by
Manfred Kets de Vries, who considers how leaders may unconsciously
cause themselves to fail. Finally, Steven Kerr, now with General
Electric, provides some interesting illustrations from society in general
and organizations in particular, on how reward systems that are thought
to guide employee behavior toward one goal may, in fact, lead to unexpected and undesired consequences.

Groupthink

Irving L. Janis

"How could we have been so stupid?" President John F. Kennedy asked after he and a close group of advisers had blundered into the Bay of Pigs invasion. For the last two years I have been studying that question, as it applies not only to the Bay of Pigs decision-makers but also to those who led the United States into such other major fiascos as the failure to be prepared for the attack on Pearl Harbor, the Korean War stalemate and the escalation of the Vietnam War.

Stupidity certainly is not the explanation. The people who participated in making the Bay of Pigs decision, for instance, comprised one of the greatest arrays of intellectual talent in the history of American Government—Dean Rusk, Robert McNamara, Douglas Dillon, Robert Kennedy, McGeorge Bundy, Arthur Schlesinger Jr., Allen Dulles and others.

It also seemed to me that explanations were incomplete if they concentrated only on disturbances in the behavior of each individual within a decision-making body: temporary emotional states of elation, fear, or anger that reduce a person's mental efficiency, for example, or chronic blind spots arising from a person's social prejudices or idiosyncratic biases.

I preferred to broaden the picture by looking at the fiascos from the standpoint of group dynamics as it has been explored over the past three decades, first by the great social psychologist Kurt Lewin and later in many experimental situations by myself and other behavioral scientists. My conclusion after poring over hundreds of relevant documents—historical reports about formal group meetings and informal conversations among the members—is that the groups that committed the fiascos were victims of what I call "groupthink."

"Groupy"

In each case study, I was surprised to discover the extent to which each group displayed the typical phenomena of social conformity that are regularly encountered in studies of group dynamics among ordinary citizens. For example, some of the phenomena appear to be completely in line with findings from social-psychological experiments showing that powerful social pressures are brought to bear by the members of a cohesive group whenever a dissident begins to voice his objections to a group consensus. Other phenomena are reminiscent of the shared illusions observed in encounter groups and friendship cliques when the members simultaneously reach a peak of "groupy" feelings.

Above all, there are numerous indications pointing to the development of group norms that bolster morale at the expense of critical thinking. One of the most common norms appears to be that of remaining loyal to the group by sticking with the policies to which the group has already committed itself, even when those policies are obviously working out badly and have unintended consequences that disturb the conscience of each member. This is one of the key characteristics of groupthink.

1984

I use the term groupthink as a quick and easy way to refer to the mode of thinking that persons engage in when *concurrence-seeking* becomes so dominant in a cohesive ingroup that it tends to override realistic appraisal of alternative courses of action. Groupthink is a term of the same order as the words in the newspeak vocabulary George Orwell used in his dismaying world of *1984*. In that context, groupthink takes on an invidious connotation. Exactly such a connotation is intended, since the term refers to a deterioration in mental efficiency, reality testing and moral judgments as a result of group pressures.

The symptoms of groupthink arise when the members of decision-making groups become motivated to avoid being too harsh in their judgments of their leaders' or their colleagues' ideas. They adopt a soft line of criticism, even in their own thinking. At their meetings, all the members are amiable and seek complete concurrence on every important issue, with no bickering or conflict to spoil the cozy, "we-feeling" atmosphere.

Kill

Paradoxically, soft-headed groups are often hard-hearted when it comes to dealing with outgroups or enemies. They find it relatively easy to resort to dehumanizing solutions—they will readily authorize bombing attacks that kill large numbers of civilians in the name of the noble cause of persuading an unfriendly government to negotiate at the peace table. They are unlikely to pursue the more difficult and controversial issues that arise when alternatives to a harsh military solution come up for discussion. Nor are they inclined to raise ethical issues that carry the implication that *this fine group of ours, with its humanitarianism and its high-minded principles, might be capable of adopting a course of action that is inhumane and immoral.*

Norms

There is evidence from a number of social-psychological studies that as the members of a group feel more accepted by the others, which is a central feature of increased group cohesiveness, they display less overt conformity to group norms. Thus we would expect that the more cohesive a group becomes, the less the members will feel constrained to censor what they say out of fear of being socially punished for antagonizing the leader or any of their fellow members.

In contrast, the groupthink type of conformity tends to increase as group cohesiveness increases. Group-think involves nondeliberate suppression of critical thoughts as a result of internalization of the group's norms, which is quite different from deliberate suppression on the basis of external threats of social punishment. The more cohesive the group, the greater the inner compulsion on the part of each member to avoid creating disunity, which inclines him or her to believe in the soundness of whatever proposals are promoted by the leader or by a majority of the group's members.

In a cohesive group, the danger is not so much that each individual will fail to reveal objections to what the others propose but that the individual will think the proposal is a good one, without attempting to carry out a careful, critical scrutiny of the pros and cons of the alternatives. When groupthink becomes dominant, there also is considerable suppression of deviant thoughts, but it takes the form of each person's deciding that his or her misgivings are not relevant and should be set aside, that the benefit of the doubt regarding any lingering uncertainties should be given to the group consensus.

Stress

I do not mean to imply that all cohesive groups necessarily suffer from groupthink. All ingroups may have a mild tendency toward group-think, displaying one or another of the symptoms from time to time, but it need not be so dominant as to influence the quality of the group's final decision. Neither do I mean to imply that there is anything necessarily inefficient or harmful about group decisions in general. On the contrary, a group whose members have properly defined roles, with traditions concerning the procedures to follow in pursuing a critical inquiry, prob-ably is capable of making better decisions than any individual group member working alone.

The problem is that the advantages of having decisions made by groups are often lost because of powerful psychological pressures that arise when the members work closely together, share the same set of values and, above all, face a crisis situation that puts everyone under intense stress.

The main principle of groupthink, which I offer in the spirit of Parkinson's Law, is this: *The more amiability and esprit de corps there is among the members of a policy-making ingroup, the greater the dan-ger that independent critical thinking will be replaced by groupthink, which is likely to result in irrational and dehumanizing actions directed against outgroups.*

Symptoms

In my studies of high-level governmental decision-makers, both civilian and military, I have found eight main symptoms of groupthink.

1 Invulnerability.   Most or all of the members of the ingroup share an *illusion* of invulnerability that provides for them some degree of reas-surance about obvious dangers and leads them to become over opti-mistic and willing to take extraordinary risks. It also causes them to fail to respond to clear warnings of danger.

The Kennedy ingroup, which uncritically accepted the Central Intelligence Agency's disastrous Bay of Pigs plan, operated on the false assumption that they could keep secret the fact that the United States was responsible for the invasion of Cuba. Even after news of the plan began to leak out, their belief remained unshaken. They failed even to consider the danger that awaited them: a worldwide revulsion against the U.S.

A similar attitude appeared among the members of President Lyndon B. Johnson's ingroup, the "Tuesday Cabinet," which kept escalating the Vietnam War despite repeated setbacks and failures. "There was a belief," Bill Moyers commented after he resigned, "that if we indicated a willingness to use our power, they [the North Vietnamese] would get the message and back away from an all-out confrontation. . . . There was a confidence—it was never bragged about, it was just there—that when the chips were really down, the other people would fold."

A most poignant example of an illusion of invulnerability involves the ingroup around Admiral H. E. Kimmel, which failed to prepare for the possibility of a Japanese attack on Pearl Harbor despite repeated warnings. Informed by his intelligence chief that radio contact with Japanese aircraft carriers had been lost, Kimmel joked about it: "What, you don't know where the carriers are? Do you mean to say that they could be rounding Diamond Head (at Honolulu) and you wouldn't know it?" The carriers were in fact moving full-steam toward Kimmel's command post at the time. Laughing together about a danger signal, which labels it as a purely laughing matter, is a characteristic manifestation of groupthink.

2 Rationale. As we see, victims of groupthink ignore warnings; they also collectively construct rationalizations in order to discount warnings and other forms of negative feedback that, taken seriously, might lead the group members to reconsider their assumptions each time they recommit themselves to past decisions. Why did the Johnson ingroup avoid reconsidering its escalation policy when time and again the expectations on which they based their decisions turned out to be wrong? James C. Thompson Jr., a Harvard historian who spent five years as an observing participant in both the State Department and the White House, tells us that the policymakers avoided critical discussion of their prior decisions and continually invented new rationalizations so that they could sincerely recommit themselves to defeating the North Vietnamese.

In the fall of 1964, before the bombing of North Vietnam began, some of the policymakers predicted that six weeks of air strikes would induce the North Vietnamese to seek peace talks. When someone asked, "What if they don't?" the answer was that another four weeks certainly would do the trick.

Later, after each setback, the ingroup agreed that by investing just a bit more effort (by stepping up the bomb tonnage a bit, for instance), their course of action would prove to be right. *The Pentagon Papers* bear out these observations.

In *The Limits of Intervention*, Townsend Hoopes, who was acting Secretary of the Air Force under Johnson, says that Walt W. Rostow in particular showed a remarkable capacity for what has been called "instant rationalization." According to Hoopes, Rostow buttressed the group's optimism about being on the road to victory by culling selected scraps of evidence from news reports or, if necessary, by inventing "plausible" forecasts that had no basis in evidence at all.

Admiral Kimmel's group rationalized away their warnings, too. Right up to December 7, 1941, they convinced themselves that the Japanese would never dare attempt a full-scale surprise assault against Hawaii because Japan's leaders would realize that it would precipitate an all-out war which the United States would surely win. They made no attempt to look at the situation through the eyes of the Japanese leaders—another manifestation of groupthink.

3 Morality. Victims of groupthink believe unquestioningly in the inherent morality of their ingroup; this belief inclines the members to ignore the ethical or moral consequences of their decisions.

Evidence that this symptom is at work usually is of a negative kind—the things that are left unsaid in group meetings. At least two influential persons had doubts about the mortality of the Bay of Pigs adventure. One of them, Arthur Schlesinger Jr., presented his strong objections in a memorandum to President Kennedy and Secretary of State Rusk but suppressed them when he attended meetings of the Kennedy team. The other, Senator J. William Fulbright, was not a member of the group, but the President invited him to express his misgivings in a speech to the policymakers. However, when Fulbright finished speaking, the President moved on to other agenda items without asking for reactions of the group.

David Kraslow and Stuart H. Loory, in *The Secret Search for Peace in Vietnam*, report that during 1966 President Johnson's ingroup was concerned primarily with selecting bomb targets in North Vietnam. They based their selections on four factors—the military advantage, the risk to American aircraft and pilots, the danger of forcing other countries into the fighting, and the danger of heavy civilian casualties. At their regular Tuesday luncheons, they weighed these factors the way school teachers grade examination papers, averaging them out. Though evidence on this point is scant, I suspect that the group's ritualistic adherence to a standardized procedure induced the members to feel morally justified in their destructive way of dealing with the Vietnamese people—after all, the danger of heavy civilian casualties from U.S. air strikes was taken into account on their checklists.

4 Stereotypes.   Victims of groupthink hold stereotyped views of the leaders of enemy groups: they are so evil that genuine attempts at negotiating differences with them are unwarranted, or they are too weak or too stupid to deal effectively with whatever attempts the ingroup makes to defeat their purposes, no matter how risky the attempts are.

Kennedy's groupthinkers believed that Premier Fidel Castro's air force was so ineffectual that obsolete B-26s could knock it out completely in a surprise attack before the invasion began. They also believed that Castro's army was so weak that a small Cuban-exile brigade could establish a well-protected beach-head at the Bay of Pigs. In addition, they believed that Castro was not smart enough to put down any possible internal uprisings in support of the exiles. They were wrong on all three assumptions. Though much of the blame was attributable to faulty intelligence, the point is that none of Kennedy's advisers even questioned the CIA planners about these assumptions.

The Johnson advisers' sloganistic thinking about "the Communist apparatus" that was "working all around the world" (as Dean Rusk put it) led them to overlook the powerful nationalistic strivings of the North Vietnamese government and its efforts to ward off Chinese domination. The crudest of all stereotypes used by Johnson's inner circle to justify their policies was the domino theory ("If we don't stop the Reds in South Vietnam, tomorrow they will be in Hawaii and next week they will be in San Francisco," Johnson once said). The group so firmly accepted this stereotype that it became almost impossible for any adviser to introduce a more sophisticated viewpoint.

In the documents on Pearl Harbor, it is clear to see that the Navy commanders stationed in Hawaii had a naive image of Japan as a midget that would not dare to strike a blow against a powerful giant.

5 Pressure.   Victims of groupthink apply direct pressure to any individual who momentarily expresses doubts about any of the group's shared illusions or who questions the validity of the arguments supporting a policy alternative favored by the majority. This gambit reinforces the concurrence-seeking norm that loyal members are expected to maintain.

President Kennedy probably was more active than anyone else in raising skeptical questions during the Bay of Pigs meetings, and yet he seems to have encouraged the group's docile, uncritical acceptance of defective arguments in favor of the CIA's plan. At every meeting, he allowed the CIA representatives to dominate the discussion. He permitted them to give their immediate refutations in response to each tentative doubt that one of the others expressed, instead of asking whether anyone shared the doubt or wanted to pursue the implications of the new worrisome issue that had just been raised. And at the most crucial meeting, when he was calling on each member to give his vote for or against the plan, he did not call on Arthur Schlesinger, the one man there who was known by the President to have serious misgivings.

Historian Thomson informs us that whenever a member of Johnson's ingroup began to express doubts, the group used subtle social pressures to "domesticate" him. To start with, the dissenter was made to feel at home, provided that he lived up to two restrictions: 1) that he did not voice his doubts to outsiders, which would play into the hands of the opposition; and 2) that he kept his criticisms within the bounds of acceptable deviation, which meant not challenging any of the fundamental assumptions that went into the group's prior commitments. One such "domesticated dissenter" was Bill Moyers. When Moyers arrived at a meeting, Thomson tells us, the President greeted him with, "Well, here comes Mr. Stop-the-Bombing."

6 Self-censorship.   Victims of groupthink avoid deviating from what appears to be group consensus; they keep silent about their misgivings and even minimize to themselves the importance of their doubts.

As we have seen, Schlesinger was not at all hesitant about presenting his strong objections to the Bay of Pigs plan in a memorandum to the President and the Secretary of State. But he became keenly aware of his tendency to suppress objections at the White House meetings. "In the months after the Bay of Pigs, I bitterly reproached myself for having kept so silent during those crucial discussions in the cabinet room,"

Schlesinger writes in *A Thousand Days*. "I can only explain my failure to do more than raise a few timid questions by reporting that one's impulse to blow the whistle on this nonsense was simply undone by the circumstances of the discussion."

7 Unanimity.   Victims of groupthink share an *illusion* of unanimity within the group concerning almost all judgments expressed by members who speak in favor of the majority view. This symptom results partly from the preceding one, whose effects are augmented by the false assumption that any individual who remains silent during any part of the discussion is in full accord with what the others are saying.

When a group of persons who respect each other's opinions arrives at a unanimous view, each member is likely to feel that the belief must be true. This reliance on consensual validation within the group tends to replace individual critical thinking and reality testing, unless there are clear-cut disagreements among the members. In contemplating a course of action such as the invasion of Cuba, it is painful for the members to confront disagreements within their group, particularly if it becomes apparent that there are widely divergent views about whether the preferred course of action is too risky to undertake at all. Such disagreements are likely to arouse anxieties about making a serious error. Once the sense of unanimity is shattered, the members no longer can feel complacently confident about the decision they are inclined to make. Each person must then face the annoying realization that there are troublesome uncertainties and he must diligently seek out the best information he can get in order to decide for himself exactly how serious the risks might be. This is one of the unpleasant consequences of being in a group of hardheaded, critical thinkers.

To avoid such an unpleasant state, the members often become inclined, without quite realizing it, to prevent latent disagreements from surfacing when they are about to initiate a risky course of action. The group leader and the members support each other in playing up the areas of convergence in their thinking, at the expense of fully exploring divergencies that might reveal unsettled issues.

"Our meetings took place in a curious atmosphere of assumed consensus," Schlesinger writes. His additional comments clearly show that, curiously, the consensus was an illusion—an illusion that could be maintained only because the major participants did not reveal their own reasoning or discuss their idiosyncratic assumptions and vague reservations. Evidence from several sources makes it clear that even the three principals—President Kennedy, Rusk and McNamara—had widely differing assumptions about the invasion plan.

8 Mindguards. Victims of groupthink sometimes appoint themselves as mindguards to protect the leader and fellow members from adverse information that might break the complacency they shared about the effectiveness and morality of past decisions. At a large birthday party for his wife, Attorney General Robert F. Kennedy, who had been constantly informed about the Cuban invasion plan, took Schlesinger aside and asked him why he was opposed. Kennedy listened coldly and said, "You may be right or you may be wrong, but the President has made his mind up. Don't push it any further. Now is the time for everyone to help him all they can."

Rusk also functioned as a highly effective mindguard by failing to transmit to the group the strong objections of three "outsiders" who had learned of the invasion plan—Undersecretary of State Chester Bowles, USIA Director Edward R. Murrow, and Rusk's intelligence chief, Roger Hilsman. Had Rusk done so, their warnings might have reinforced Schlesinger's memorandum and jolted some of Kennedy's ingroup, if not the President himself, into reconsidering the decision.

Products

When a group of executives frequently displays most or all of these interrelated symptoms, a detailed study of their deliberations is likely to reveal a number of immediate consequences. These consequences are, in effect, products of poor decision-making practices because they lead to inadequate solutions to the problems under discussion.

First, the group limits its discussions to a few alternative courses of action (often only two) without an initial survey of all the alternatives that might be worthy of consideration.

Second, the group fails to reexamine the course of action initially preferred by the majority after they learn of risks and drawbacks they had not considered originally.

Third, the members spend little or no time discussing whether there are nonobvious gains they may have overlooked or ways of reducing the

seemingly prohibitive costs that made rejected alternatives appear undesirable to them.

Fourth, members make little or no attempt to obtain information from
experts within their own organizations who might be able to supply
more precise estimates of potential losses and gains.

Fifth, members show positive interest in facts and opinions that support their preferred policy; they tend to ignore facts and opinions that do
not.

Sixth, members spend little time deliberating about how the chosen
policy might be hindered by bureaucratic inertia, sabotaged by political
opponents, or temporarily derailed by common accidents. Consequently,
they fail to work out contingency plans to cope with foreseeable setbacks
that could endanger the overall success of their chosen course.

Support

The search for an explanation of why groupthink occurs has led me
through a quagmire of complicated theoretical issues in the murky area of
human motivation. My belief, based on recent social psychological
research, is that we can best understand the various symptoms of groupthink as a mutual effort among the group members to maintain self-esteem
and emotional equanimity by providing social support to each other, especially at times when they share responsibility for making vital decisions.

Even when no important decision is pending, the typical administrator will begin to doubt the wisdom and morality of past decisions each
time information is received about setbacks, particularly if the information is accompanied by negative feedback from prominent people who
originally had been his supporters. It should not be surprising, therefore,
to find that individual members strive to develop unanimity and esprit
de corps that will help bolster each other's morale, to create an optimistic outlook about the success of pending decisions, and to reaffirm
the positive value of past policies to which all of them are committed.

Pride

Shared illusions of invulnerability, for example, can reduce anxiety
about taking risks. Rationalizations help members believe that the risks
are really not so bad after all. The assumption of inherent morality helps

the members to avoid feelings of shame or guilt. Negative stereotypes function as stress-reducing devices to enhance a sense of moral right-eousness as well as pride in a lofty mission.

The mutual enhancement of self-esteem and morale may have func-tional value in enabling the members to maintain their capacity to take action, but it has maladaptive consequences insofar as concurrence-seeking tendencies interfere with critical, rational capacities and lead to serious errors of judgment.

While I have limited my study to decision-making bodies in govern-ment, groupthink symptoms appear in business, industry and any other field where small, cohesive groups make the decisions. It is vital, then, for all sorts of people—and especially group leaders—to know what steps they can take to prevent groupthink.

Remedies

To counterpoint my case studies of the major fiascos, I have also inves-tigated two highly successful group enterprises, the formulation of the Marshall Plan in the Truman Administration and the handling of the Cuban missile crisis by President Kennedy and his advisers. I have found it instructive to examine the steps Kennedy took to change his group's deci-sion-making processes. These changes ensured that the mistakes made by his Bay of Pigs ingroup were not repeated by the missile-crisis ingroup, even though the membership of both groups was essentially the same.

The following recommendations for preventing groupthink incorpo-rate many of the good practices I discovered to be characteristic of the Marshall Plan and missile-crisis groups:

1   The leader of a policy-forming group should assign the role of critical evaluator to each member, encouraging the group to give high priority to open airing of objections and doubts. This practice needs to be reinforced by the leader's acceptance of criticism of his own judgments in order to discourage members from soft-pedaling their disagreements and from allowing their striving for concurrence to inhibit critical thinking.

2   When the key members of a hierarchy assign a policy-planning mis-sion to any group within their organization, they should adopt an impar-tial stance instead of stating preferences and expectations at the beginning. This will encourage open inquiry and impartial probing of a wide range of policy alternatives.

3 The organization routinely should set up several outside policy-planning and evaluation groups to work on the same policy question, each deliberating under a different leader. This can prevent the insulation of an ingroup.

4 At intervals before the group reaches a final consensus, the leader should require each member to discuss the group's deliberations with associates in the same unit of the organization—assuming that those associates can be trusted to adhere to the same security regulations that govern the policymakers—and then to report back their reactions to the group.

5 The group should invite one or more outside experts to each meeting on a staggered basis and encourage the experts to challenge the views of the core members.

6 At every general meeting of the group, whenever the agenda calls for an evaluation of policy alternatives, at least one member should play devil's advocate, functioning as a good lawyer in challenging the testimony of those who advocate the majority position.

7 Whenever the policy issue involves relations with a rival nation or organization, the group should devote a sizable block of time, perhaps an entire session, to a survey of all warning signals from the rivals and should write alternative scenarios on the rivals' intentions.

8 When the group is surveying policy alternatives for feasibility and effectiveness, it should from time to time divide into two or more sub-groups to meet separately, under different discussion leaders and then come back together to hammer out differences.

9 After reaching a preliminary consensus about what seems to be the best policy, the group should hold a "second-chance" meeting at which every member expresses as vividly as possible all residual doubts, and rethinks the entire issue before making a definitive choice.

How

These recommendations have their disadvantages. To encourage the open airing of objections, for instance, might lead to prolonged and costly debates when a rapidly growing crisis requires an immediate solution. It also could cause rejection, depression and anger. A leader's failure to set a norm might create cleavage between leader and members that could develop into a disruptive power struggle if the leader looks on the emerging consensus as anathema. Setting up outside evaluation groups might increase the risk of security leakage. Still, inventive executives who know their way around the organizational maze probably can figure out how to apply one or another of the prescriptions successfully, without harmful side effects.

They also could benefit from the advice of outside experts in the administrative and behavioral sciences. Though these experts have much to offer, they have had few chances to work on policy-making machinery within large organizations. As matters now stand, executives innovate only when they need new procedures to avoid repeating serious errors that have deflated their self-images.

Leadership and Expectations: Pygmalion Effects and Other Self-Fulfilling Prophecies in Organizations

Dov Eden

Expectations play an important role in determining leadership effectiveness. Scholars and practitioners have assumed for a long time that leaders who expect more get more (e.g., Likert, 1961, 1967; McGregor, 1960). Despite this general awareness, until recently there was little empirical research illuminating how and why leader expectation effects operate, and how they can be profitably utilized in practice. In parallel, work motivation theorists have long postulated the central role of self-expectations in motivating the exertion of effort in job performance and in determining the level of productivity achieved (Atkinson, 1957; Atkinson & Feather, 1966; Atkinson & Raynor, 1974; McClelland, Atkinson, Clark, & Lowell, 1953; Rotter, 1943, 1945; Vroom, 1964; Zuroff & Rotter, 1985). There is a consensus among scholars that expectations and motivation are positively associated. However, none of these theoreticians has proposed that we apply knowledge of this relationship by purposely raising worker expectations in order to boost work motivation. Moreover, theory and research have largely ignored the interface between the manager's expectations of the subordinate and the subordinate's self-expectations. The manager-as-Pygmalion model is unique in focusing on the interlinking expectations of managers and subordinates as a key to understanding—and enhancing—the motivational power of effective leadership. The purposes of the present article are to review the experimental findings demonstrating the power of expectation effects in leadership, to present a model of leader expectation effects, and to propose ways in which expectations can be utilized to improve leadership practice.

The leader expectation effect is a special case of self-fulfilling prophecy (SFP). Merton (1948) gave us the SFP concept. SFP is the process through which the expectation that an event will occur increases its likelihood of occurrence. Expecting something to happen, we act in ways that make it more likely to occur. (Note the misnomer; the prophecy does not fulfill itself. Rather, it is the prophet who, due to his expectations, acts unwittingly to bring about the expected event. This makes it appear to be self-fulfilling) SFP is ubiquitous in human inter-course (Jones, 1977).

SFP in management shares much common ground with concepts of charismatic and transformational leadership (Bass, 1985; Conger & Kanungo, 1987; House, 1977). A unique feature of SFP in manage-ment, which distinguishes it from other leadership phenomena, is that SFP operates by and large beyond the awareness of the players, both leaders and followers, whose behavior is so profoundly affected by it. The elusiveness of SFP is at once fascinating and frustrating, and it undoubtedly explains why such an important leadership phenomenon has been neglected by scholars for so long. The SFP approach to man-agement is also unique in proposing raising leader expectations as a way of increasing transformational leadership. In presenting a summary model of SFP in management, integrating all the relevant variables, I hope to stoke up the interest of leadership theorists and researchers. I also hope practitioner readers will devise innovative SFP applications to boost productivity.

SFP AND EXPECTATION EFFECTS

Early Research on SFP and Expectation Effects

The first SFP to be investigated extensively in psychology was the experimenter effect. Serendipitously discovered by Rosenthal (1976), the experimenter effect refers to hypothesis confirmation that results from the experimenter's influencing subjects to respond to the treatment in a way that conforms to the experimenter's expectations. Rosenthal (1963) summarized a dozen experimenter-effect studies and wondered in print whether similar interpersonal expectation effects occur among physicians, psychotherapists, employers, and teachers. This led to Rosenthal and Jacobson's (1968) landmark experiment published under the title "Pygmalion in the Classroom." They showed that by raising teachers' expectations regarding the academic potential of some ran-domly designated pupils, those pupils actually learned more than con-trol pupils in the same classes. They dubbed this boost in achievement the "Pygmalion effect." Igniting the imagination of a generation of classroom researchers, the Pygmalion effect was studied intensively (see Dusek, Hall, & Meyer, 1985; Rosenthal & Rubin, 1978 for reviews), and is now an undisputed feature of teacher-pupil relations. However, the application of the Pygmalion concept to leader-follower relations in general, and to manager-worker relations in particular, was much slower in emerging.

THE FIRST PYGMALION EXPERIMENTS IN INDUSTRY

King (1971) replicated the Pygmalion effect in a training program for disadvantaged persons using the experimental approach pioneered by Rosenthal and Jacobson. He designated four pressers, five welders, and five mechanics as high aptitude personnel (HAPs), leading the instructors to expect superior performance from these individuals. In reality, the HAPs had been chosen at random. The designations produced the hypothesized SFP. The HAPs obtained higher test scores, higher supervisor and peer ratings, and shorter learning times, and had lower dropout rates, evidencing the Pygmalion effect.

Organizationwide Expectation-raising

King (1974) next shifted his focus from the individual to SFP at the organizational level. He hypothesized that managers' expectations regarding the outcomes of organizational innovations produce effects on those outcomes that are distinguishable from the effects of the innovations themselves. He tested this hypothesis experimentally in four similar industrial plants in one company. The firm's director of manufacturing presented the same changes differently in each plant. Job enlargement was the innovation installed in two plants and withheld from the two enlargement-control plants, which got job rotation as a sham innovation. The second independent factor was management's productivity expectations, which were raised in one enlargement plant and in one rotation plant, and unchanged in the two remaining plants. Thus, four comparable plants got different treatment combinations: a high-expectation enlargement plant, a high-expectation rotation plant, a control-expectation enlargement plant, and a control-expectation rotation plant.

The results were that neither enlargement nor rotation had any effect but expectations did. Over the follow-up period, both high-expectation plants increased output by similar amounts irrespective of whether they had gotten enlargement or rotation, whereas output in both control-expectation plants remained unchanged. King concluded that manager expectations for performance due to the innovations had produced an SFP. He neither measured or speculated about the leadership behaviors through which the managers increased output.

King's findings have important practical implications for management and consulting. Those who expect more from a program—any program—are likely to benefit more from it. This implies that one way to create productive SFP willfully is for leaders to get followers to expect positive outcomes from programs and organizational changes of all sorts. However, organization-wide SFP is not a Pygmalion effect. There are two different varieties of SFP that are distinguishable in terms of how the high expectations are anchored. To produce a Pygmalion effect, one gets a leader to expect more of a follower on the basis of some characteristic of the follower. In creating organization-wide SFP, King took advantage of his expert role to anchor leader expectations in properties of the new program. This can be an effective, alternative way to create productive SFP when leaders know, or think they know, their followers' limitations well. Firmly crystallized expectations are hard to change, rendering those who hold to them resistant to Pygmalion effects.

King's rotation plants got what in medical science would be called a placebo, and the high-expectation rotation plant showed a placebo effect: even the "sugar capsules" (i.e., rotation) proved to be an efficacious remedy if the "patients" believed they could improve productivity. A menace to valid inference, placebo effects must be controlled in research evaluating the effectiveness of new treatments (Critelli & Neumann, 1984). However, practice is not research. We should harshly judge the clinician who abstains from using the placebo effect as an aid to treatment. If smiling, nodding reassuringly, and saying to a patient, "I'm sure the treatment I've prescribed will make you feel a lot better" can augment the drug in promoting the healing process, then physicians should add these placebo interventions to their treatment repertoire. Refraining from creating physician expectation effects on methodological grounds is wrong both practically and ethically. The same reasoning applies to willful creation of leader expectation effects.

PYGMALION AND CHARISMA

To conclude the discussion of Pygmalion, expectations, and leadership, let us return to a related concept: charisma. A new conceptualization of leadership emerged in the 1980's, as management scholars began renewing their interest in Weber's (1947) concept. Some theorists articulated charisma in concrete terms in order to demystify it and make it more amenable to research and application (e.g., Conger & Kanungo, 1987; House, 1977; House, Howell, Shamir, Smith, & Spangler, 1990). Some have explicitly pointed out the common ground shared by the Pygmalion and charismatic formulations.

As part of this "new look" at charisma, the concept of transformational leadership emerged. Transformation addresses a leadership phenomenon broader than the rewards-for-performance exchange of transactional leadership, and extends well beyond the confines of previous conceptualization of managerial style. Charismatic and inspirational leadership are dubbed "transformational" because they radically alter followers' beliefs in their capacity to achieve outstanding levels of performance, levels that far exceed their previous achievements and expectations. Such leadership transforms followers by changing their values, ideals, motives, and concepts of what levels of achievement are possible. Hence Bass (1985) titled his book on transformational leadership *Leadership and Performance beyond Expectations*. Borrowing from political science and psychohistory, and acknowledging a heavy debt to Burns (1978), Bass described transformational leadership as encompassing both charisma and Pygmalion: "Charismatics take advantage of the Pygmalion effect . . and reciprocate in their confidence in their followers and in their optimistic expectations about their followers' performance. Follower self-esteem and enthusiasm are raised as a consequence, and the effort is increased among followers to fulfill the leaders' expressed expectations" (p 47). Expanding charisma to include inspirational leadership, Bass included "making use of the Pygmalion effect" as an inspirational behavior: "In its most general form, the Pygmalion effort (sic) is a performance-stimulating effect. People who are led to expect that they will do well, will be better than those who expect to do poorly or who do not have any expectations about how well or poorly they will do. . . . The leader who arouses in subordinates confidence in their own capabilities and confidence in those with whom they work, all things being equal, by raising expectations about the success of their efforts, will increase such efforts to succeed" (p. 71).

The concept of visionary leadership (Sashkin, 1988a, 1988b, 1990; Sashkin & Burke, 1990) dovetails with charismatic and transformational theories, as well as with the Pygmalion approach. In Sashkin's (1988b) words:

> Only if there exists the belief that the organization can control its destiny is it likely to even try. Moreover, such trials may well change the 'reality,' so that the organization *becomes* more capable of controlling its environment and its ultimate destiny. Thus, while it is foolish and perhaps even destructive to hold to values that are in obvious conflict with reality, there is much to be said for taking 'optimistic' positions, even when one realizes that there may be some question about whether the value is, in fact, consistent with objective reality. (p 242)

Sashkin thus described the effective leader's impact in terms of getting people in the organization to share in an optimistic vision (i.e., high expectations) of the organization's future. Adopting a rosy vision sparks an organizationwide SFP that contributes to the ultimate realization of the vision. Through the concerted action of the individuals affected, the vision ultimately transforms reality.

In a similar vein, Bennis and Nanus (1985) described the "transformative" leaders whom they interviewed as visionary: "The visions these various leaders conveyed seemed to bring about a confidence on the part of the employees, a confidence that instilled in them a belief that they were capable of performing the necessary acts" (p. 30). Believing one is capable of performing the necessary acts is precisely Bandura's (1986) definition of self-efficacy. "Positive self-regard seems to exert its force by creating in others a sense of confidence and high expectations, not very different from the fabled Pygmalion effect" (Bennis & Nanus, 1985, p. 65).

Thus, both Bass, and Bennis and Nanus have incorporated the Pygmalion effect into their descriptions of how inspirational and visionary leaders transform their subordinates and bring out the best in them. Transformational leadership creates productive SFP on a grand scale, as each individual worker touched by the transformational leader's confidence becomes a party to a positive expectation effect. The more visible the inspirational manager and the greater the number of individuals affected by his positive vision, the larger the number of individual

Pygmalion effects that combine in producing the dramatic boost in organizational effectiveness. Through the collective action of the individuals affected, the vision ultimately transforms reality.

Creating productive SFP is thus centered at the confluence of much current thinking in the fields of leadership, organization development, and organizational culture. Conceptualizing these processes in terms of SFP links them all together and gives the manager a tool that can be used at many levels under highly varied circumstances. That tool is expectancy raising.

Molding the organization's culture is a prime means for exercising transformational leadership. Thus, transformational leadership and organizational culture are intimately related. By changing culture, the transformational leader influences many members with whom he never even comes into direct personal contact. This is the crossroads at which SFP, transformational leadership, and the management of culture, all meet. By creating a high-expectancy culture, the transformational leader produces productive SFP at many levels in the organization. Changing organizational culture is an act of transformational leadership, and transformational leadership is implemented most effectively by means of culture change.

Thus, since Livingston's early application of the Pygmalion notion to managerial leadership, through the growing research base, Pygmalion has become an integral part of the latest and most far-reaching approaches to leadership. Pygmalion and the other transformational models share recognition of the role of leader expectations in inspiring followers to give their best efforts. However, the Pygmalion model is unique in its emphasis on *raising* leader expectations as a means of initiating a more effective leadership process. Being focused on expectation raising, it is relatively easy to propose myriad practical ways of effectuating transformational leadership.

CREATING PRODUCTIVE SFP: PYGMALION LEADERSHIP STYLE

The Pygmalion Leadership Style (PLS) is comprised of the behaviors that facilitate productive SFP effects in organizations. Based on evidence for the interplay between leadership, culture, and SFP, some components of PLS are described below. They are intended to provide practitioners with suggestions for expectation raising in their field work and to stimulate further thinking about expectation effects on the part of leadership scholars.

Create the Pygmalion Effect

The prime practical implication of the leader expectation research is that leaders should create the Pygmalion effect by expecting high performance from their followers. At the same time, they should do all in their power to get followers to feel more efficacious and to expect more of themselves. In the course of day-to-day interaction with subordinates, the manager who wants to be a more positive Pygmalion should point out to the subordinates that they have untapped potential, and in general get them to believe that they can achieve more. Many of the proposals below are variations on this theme.

Expectation and Self-efficacy Training

This is the practical application that comes closest to qualifying as a stand-alone SFP intervention, as it most literally grabs the expectation bull by its horns. Rather than seeking some surreptitious channel to convey high expectations to unwitting managers, expectation training educates them about SFP, expectation effects, and Pygmalion, and teaches them how judicious utilization of this knowledge might improve motivation and boost productivity.

Expectation training is best illustrated by the United States Navy's Pygmalion-at-Sea project. Crawford, Thomas, and Fink (1980) at the Navy Personnel Research and Development Center undertook a novel SFP intervention aimed at improving the productivity of low performing sailors on a combatant ship. They targeted chronically low performers for remedial treatment designed to improve their motivation and performance. While the ship was docked, supervisory personnel were given a leadership workshop intended to change their negative expectations toward the problem sailors. The high expectations aroused among the supervisors were buttressed by behavioral skill building. Crawford et al. taught the supervisors the principles of behavior modification and then had them brainstorm actions that the low performers would perceive as positive reinforcers. This training gave the supervisors tools to support their newly acquired high expectations. This procedure is not only sensible; it is essential. It is unfeasible to convince managers to expect more of their subordinates by merely lecturing to them, showing them a film, and exhorting them to expect more. An expectation-raising program needs solid moorings. Second, 15 additional senior enlisted supervisors, who had been carefully selected to serve as mentors for the low performers, were given a workshop in counseling and guidance skills. Finally, 12 low performers participated in a workshop devoted to personal growth and self-improvement.

The communication and cultivation of high performance expectations—among both the supervisors and the subordinates themselves—were the hallmark of this intervention. One of Crawford et al.'s underlying assumptions was that if the low performers could be made aware of the role of negative expectations in depressing their performance, they would be able to overcome these debilitating SFP effects and improve their performance.

The low performers on the experimental ship were compared to some of their shipmates and to similarly low performers on other ships. There were significant improvements in the experimental sailors in overall performance as rated by their supervisors. The authors concluded that the program succeeded in engendering SFP in the sailors and their supervisors. Crawford et al. pioneered in practical application of leader expectation effects. Their example is worthy of emulation. In several field experiments now in progress, my students and I are testing the effectiveness of SFP workshop training among leaders. Our field experiment (Eden & Aviram, in press) among unemployed persons demonstrated that self-efficacy training can increase the performance of requisite behaviors and speed reemployment. Together with other recent field-experimental research on self-efficacy training, it is clear that self-efficacy training is emerging as a practical tool to aid individuals in mustering the wherewithal to tackle challenges in the workplace. The leader who facilitates this is fulfilling a Pygmalion role.

Immunize Potential Victims against the Golem Effect

Individuals who perform far below their ability due to the negative influence of their superiors' low expectations on their own expectations (the "Golem effect") may be unaware of the process, and therefore defenseless. Training could make them conscious of the process, immunize them against it, and thereby help prevent its recurrence.

Fight Negative Stereotypes

Stereotypes produce SFP because they involve expectations toward individuals on the basis of their belonging to some social group or class (Snyder, Tanke, & Berscheid, 1977). Two of Merton's (1948) classic examples of SFP involve blacks and Jews who, as targets, come to behave in ways that fulfill the expectations of those who hold the stereotypes. When individuals are expected to perform poorly because of their race, age, sex, or any other ascribed characteristic not related to actual competence, a Golem effect is likely. The locations in organizations where counterproductive stereotypes are most likely to be operating are those staffed by racial and ethnic minorities, women, very old and very young employees, and others about whom stereotypes abound.

Not all stereotypes are negative. Positive stereotypes should not be discouraged. Belonging to a minority group that is stereotyped as industrious or intelligent can be a boon to individual members of that group and help make them more productive. There is no reason to deprive either individuals or organizations of this SFP-based blessing.

Set Challenging Goals and Objectives

The goal-setting and the Management-by-Objectives (MBO) approaches converge in dealing more or less explicitly with performance expectations and in prescribing that performance goals and output objectives be high and difficult to achieve. "Objectives are statements of *expected output*" (Odiorne, 1969, p. 20, italics in original.) Successful MBO may be SFP. Challenging objectives are explicit expressions of high expectations. Similarly, goal-setting experimentation has shown that difficult goals, when clearly stated, result in greater output than do intermediate or easy goals (Locke & Latham, 1990). Furthermore, Garland (1984) revealed how expectations mediate the influence of goals on output. Setting hard goals raises expectations, which in turn spur improved performance. In other words, one effective way to produce a Pygmalion effect is to set difficult goals, or, in MBO terminology, to set high objectives.

Conversely, setting easy goals or low objectives produces a Golem effect in which subordinates realize that little is expected of them and adjust their efforts downward accordingly. Thus, MBO and goal setting trigger SFP and owe much of their success to expectation effects. However, MBO and goal setting share a limitation; output must be specifiable, and preferably quantifiable, in order to set goals or objectives. This limitation is not shared by other approaches to expectation-raising.

Clear the Record

Individuals who get off to a bad start in school, in a job, or in life, are often locked in to their past by an unforgetting—and unforgiving—record. Worse perhaps even than the living memory of teachers, supervisors, and peers who have witnessed past failure, the written record remains as an indelible reminder that refreshes memories and contaminates—lowers—the expectations of persons who had no involvement in the original disgrace. Perusing a record rife with failure creates expectations for "more of the same." Many people never realize their potential because they are victimized by their past record. Managers' ready access to the record thus contributes materially to low-performer recidivism through the operation of self-sustaining prophecy. Although the present leader had no part in producing the record, his or her expectations for future achievements are influenced by it. A record of failure leads one to expect more poor performance and to treat the individual accordingly as a poor performer, thereby sustaining the underachievement. This self-sustaining Golem scenario is most widespread "in nature."

We need to find ways of freeing individuals from the shackles of their records. This could be done by clearing the record of entries likely to arouse negative expectations in a new supervisor. Information retained in dossiers is often notoriously mistaken, ambiguous, irrelevant, outdated, and meaningless (Laudon, 1986). Stigmatizing labels, if they must be used at all, should be expunged at the end of a reasonable period of time. Like foodstuffs on the supermarket shelf and moving-violation points on the driving record, a diagnostic, disciplinary, or evaluative entry in an employee's record should include an expiration date. Furthermore, a company could withhold the record of a new hire or a new transfer from the supervisor for an initial period of, say, a month or two, during which time expectations would be formed on the basis of first-hand experience rather than on the basis of the past preserved in the record. An obvious limitation to this kind of solution exists in companies in which it is easy for a manager to phone a new transfer's previous supervisor and obtain a quick evaluation. It is more applicable to new hires.

Organizations could install "worker protection programs," akin to the witness protection programs used by the FBI and INTERPOL to save the lives of criminals who turn State's evidence and then have to be obscured from the long arm of mob revenge. Employees with a bad performance record could be relocated in the same company or elsewhere, be given a new occupational identity, and get "another chance" at a job free from the persecution of their own work history and the inevitable Golem effect that it triggers each time anew. The recurrence of a destructive SFP would be blocked and their chances of utilizing their potential would be greater. Both the supervisor and the organization would enjoy the benefits of having a more productive employee.

Piggyback on Changes in Personnel and Organization

The interminable changes in organizational structure, personnel assignments, product lines, work methods, and operating procedures provide virtually limitless opportunities for raising expectations. The unfreezing of expectations wrought by organizational changes, whether "natural" or planned, can be utilized opportunistically for expectation-raising. Any nontrivial change unfreezes expectations, as members anticipate repercussions that might impact positively or negatively on their work and career. These vague moments of unclear expectations, when members are unsure what is in store for them, invite the alert leader to intervene with timely words of assurance, encouragement, and optimism, to implant positive expectations. When members are apprehensive due to their anticipation of an imminent turn for the worse in their situation, the reassuring words of a sanguine leader can reduce the suspense and potentially avert a Golem effect as negative expectations are replaced by positive ones.

There are countless examples of changes whose success was augmented by positive expectations and changes that failed at least in part due to negative expectations. Elsewhere I have mustered documentation in support of the argument that even the classical Hawthorne experiments may have succeeded in boosting productivity by unwittingly raising expectations (Eden, 1986). It is also possible that participative management, when it succeeds, owes part of its success to raised expectations. When participation is implemented properly, participants have higher post-decision performance expectations than those who have not participated. Such expectation effects may contribute as much to the success of participation as the mediating variables commonly cited, such as psychological "ownership" and acceptance of the decisions and improved information flow (Sashkin, 1976). The practical implication is that leaders using participation, as other management techniques, should piggyback and use these opportunities deliberately to raise participants' expectations.

Ruinous debilitating effects can be wrought on any change program by individuals who harbor negative expectations toward it. A strategically placed skeptic can doom a program by saying to peers and subordinates, "Those Whiz Kids up there have cooked up another one of their ingenious inventions for us; personally, I don't think it has a chance." The added thrust of the piggyback proposal is that even changes undertaken for extraneous reasons and unanticipated changes initiated by force majeure should be seized upon as opportunities for creating productive SFPs. Announcing that the new computer system, the friendlier software, the redesigned office layout, the revised procedure, the improved routing, the replacement engineer, the new warehouse forms, the change in materials suppliers, the week-end retreat, the divisional reorganization, the new chief of accounting, or any other change should be expected to improve productivity may make such changes more productive. The cost of piggybacking is nil, and the potential payoff is appreciable.

Foster High-expectation Culture

Culture is intimately involved in organizational SFP because it is a rich source of performance expectations. Schein (1985) has described how organizational culture influences organizational effectiveness. In his words, "productivity is a cultural phenomenon par excellence, both at the small-work-group level and at the level of the total organization" (pp. 43–44).

Myth making is a promising way of molding organizational culture to create productive SFP. Boje, Fedor, and Rowland (1982) have proposed ways of intervening in the myth-making process in the interests of organizational effectiveness. Their recommendations can be applied to building up the stock of myths that convey high performance expectations and to rooting out negative myths that imply organizational impotence or helplessness. Consider the positive SFP inspired by the widespread belief that "we are in a can-do organization" or that we are "lean and mean" compared to the collective Golem effect that flows from myths such as "Nothing ever gets done right around here" or "We operate on Murphy's Law and the Peter Principle."

Mastery of myth making requires macro-level leverage over a pervasive, systemwide source of expectations. The impact of myths on expectations can be particularly insidious and persistent because, as part of the organization's culture, myths summarize complex, underlying beliefs and assumptions about the organization's capabilities and frailties, assumptions that have slipped out of awareness and become highly resistant to change. In short, it is tough to change culture. Top executives wield unique leverage over organizational culture, and the performance expectations that it implies. Therefore, it is the job of the CEO and other top leaders with high visibility and credibility to change organizational culture and replace pernicious myths with positive ones. Managing myths is a worthy task for those at the organization's pinnacle, for ". . . *the unique and essential function of leadership is the manipulation of culture*" (Schein, p. 317, italics in original).

Symbolic expressions of a high-achievement culture should be devised and enhanced where they already exist. Properly arranged props can be used to fortify performance-oriented leadership. Clinical psychologists are aware of the effects of physical artifacts such as office location, decor, dress, and grooming on client expectations, and use them deliberately. Coe (1980) has discussed how to arrange props for maximal positive impact under the heading "Techniques for Enhancing Expectation Effects." Similarly, some managers are masters at arranging furniture, visual aids, schedules, and other nonverbal, environmental cues in ways that create and sustain high expectations. We need research on the effectiveness of various such arrangements.

Undaunted by the elusiveness of culture, some investigators have devised tools for quantitative cultural analysis. Cooke and Rousseau's (1988) *Organizational Culture Survey* assesses culture in terms of the dominant norms and expectations in organizations. One of their dimensions is "achievement culture," a feature of high expectation culture. Using such tools, we may achieve a better grasp of the nature of organizational culture than its qualitative explorers have given us so far. This will make it possible to diagnose an organization's culture in terms of its potential for SFP and to spell out in more operational terms the SFP applications that target culture.

REFERENCES

Atkinson, J. W. (1957). Motivational determinants of risk-taking behavior. *Psychological Review, 10*, 209–232.

Atkinson, J. W., & Feather, N. T. (1966). *A theory of achievement motivation.* New York: Wiley.

Atkinson, J. W., & Raynor, J. O. (1974). *Motivation and achievement.* Washington, DC: Winston.

Bandura, A. (1986). *Social foundations of thought and action. A social-cognitive view.* Englewood Cliffs, NJ: Prentice-Hall.

Bass, B. M. (1985). *Leadership and performance beyond expectations.* New York: Free Press.

Bennis, W. G., & Nanus, B. (1985). *Leaders: The strategies for taking charge.* New York: Harper & Row.

Boje, D. M., Fedor, D. B., & Rowland, K. M. (1982). Myth making: A qualitative step in OD interventions. *Journal of Applied Behavioral Science, 18*, 17–28.

Burns, J. M. (1978). *Leadership.* New York: Harper & Row.

Coe, W. C. (1980). Expectations, hypnosis, and suggestion in behavior change. In F. H. Kanfer & A. P. Goldstein (Eds.), *Helping people change: A textbook of methods* (2nd ed., pp. 423–469). New York: Pergamon.

Conger, J. A., & Kanungo, R. N. (1987). Toward a behavioral theory of charismatic leadership in organizational settings. *Academy of Management Review, 12*, 637–647.

Cooke, R. A., & Rousseau, D. M. (1988). Behavioral norms and expectations: A quantitative approach to the assessment of organizational culture. *Group & Organization Studies, 13*, 245–273.

Crawford, K. S., Thomas, E. D., & Fink, J. J. (1980). Pygmalion at sea: Improving the work effectiveness of low performers. *Journal of Applied Behavioral Science, 16*, 482–505.

Critelli, J. W., & Neumann, K. F. (1984). The placebo: Conceptual analysis of a construct in transition. *American Psychologist, 39*, 32–39.

Dusek, J. B., Hall, V. C., & Meyer, W. J. (Eds.). (1985). *Teacher expectations.* Hillsdale, NJ: Lawrence Erlbaum.

Eden, D. (1986). OD and self-fulfilling prophecy: Boosting productivity by raising expectations. *Journal of Applied Behavioral Science, 22,* 1–13.

Eden, D., & Aviram, A. (in press). Self-efficacy training to speed reemployment. *Journal of Applied Psychology.*

Garland, H. (1984). Relation of effort-performance expectancy to performance in goal-setting experiments. *Journal of Applied Psychology, 69,* 79–84.

House, R. J. (1977). A 1976 theory of charismatic leadership. In J. G. Hunt & L. L. Larson (Eds.), *Leadership: The cutting edge* (pp. 189–207). Carbondale, IL: Southern Illinois University Press.

House, R. J., Howell, J., Shamir, B., Smith, B., & Spangler, D. (1990). Charismatic leadership: A 1990 theory and four empirical tests. Working Paper, Department of Management, The Wharton School of Management, University of Pennsylvania.

Jones, R. A. (1977). *Self-fulfilling prophecies: Social, psychological, and physiological effects of expectancies.* Hillsdale, NJ: Lawrence Erlbaum.

King, A. S. (1971). Self-fulfilling prophecies in training the hard-core: Supervisors' expectations and the underprivileged workers' performance. *Social Science Quarterly, 52,* 369–378.

King, A. S. (1974). Expectation effects in organization change. *Administrative Science Quarterly, 19,* 221–230.

Laudon, K. C. (1986). *Dossier society: Value choices in the design of national information systems.* New York: Columbia University Press.

Likert, R. (1961). *New patterns of management.* New York: McGraw-Hill.

Likert, R. (1967). *The human organization: Its management and value.* New York: McGraw-Hill.

Locke, E. A., & Latham, G. P. (1990). *A theory of goal setting and task performance.* Englewood Cliffs, NJ: Prentice-Hall.

McClelland, D. C., Atkinson, J. W., Clark, R. A., & Lowell, E. L. (1953). *The achievement motive.* New York: Appleton-Century-Crofts.

McGregor, D. (1960). *The human side of enterprise.* New York: McGraw-Hill.

Merton, R. K. (1948). The self-fulfilling prophecy. *Antioch Review, 8,* 193–210.

Odiorne, G. S. (1969). *Management decision by objectives.* Englewood Cliffs, NJ: Prentice-Hall.

Rosenthal, R. (1963). On the social psychology of the psychological experiment: The experimenter's hypothesis as unintended determinant of experimental results. *American Scientist, 51,* 268–283.

Rosenthal, R. (1976). *Experimenter effects in behavioral research: Enlarged edition.* New York: Irvington Publishers, Halstead Division of Wiley.

Rosenthal, R., & Jacobson, L. (1968). *Pygmalion in the classroom: Teacher expectation and pupils' intellectual development.* New York: Holt, Rinehart & Winston.

Rosenthal, R., & Rubin, D.B. (1978). Interpersonal expectancy effects: The first 345 studies. *Behavioral and Brain Sciences, 3,* 377–386.

Rotter, J. B. (1943). Level of aspiration as a method of studying personality. III. Group validity studies. *Character and Personality, 11*, 254–274.

Rotter, J. B. (1945). Level of aspiration as a method of studying personality. IV. The analysis of patterns of response. *Journal of Social Psychology, 21*, 159–177.

Sashkin, M. (1976). Changing toward participative management approaches: A model and methods. *Academy of Management Review, 1*, 75–86.

Sashkin, M. (1988a). The visionary leader. In J.A. Conger & R.N. Kanungo (Eds.), *Charismatic leadership: The elusive factor in organizational effectiveness* (pp. 120–160). San Francisco: Jossey-Bass.

Sashkin, M. (1988b). The visionary principal: School leadership for the next century. *Education and Urban Society, 20*, 239–249.

Sashkin, M. (1990). *The Leader Behavior Questionnaire* (3rd. ed.). King of Prussia, PA: Organization Design and Development.

Sashkin, M., & Burke, W.W. (1990). Understanding and assessing organizational leadership. In K.E. Clark & M.B. Clark (Eds.), *Measures of leadership* (pp. 297–325). West Orange, NJ: Leadership Library of America.

Schein, E. H. (1985). *Organizational culture and leadership*. San Francisco: Jossey-Bass.

Snyder, M., Tanke, E. D., & Berscheid, E. (1977). Social perception and interpersonal behavior: On the self-fulfilling nature of social stereotypes. *Journal of Personality and Social Psychology, 35*, 656–666.

Vroom, V. H. (1964). *Work and motivation*. New York: Wiley.

Weber, M. (1947). *The theory of social and economic organizations* (T. Parsons, Trans.). New York: Free Press. (Original work published 1924)

Zuroff, D. C., & Rotter, J. B. (1985). A history of the expectancy construct in psychology. In J. B. Dusek, V. C. Hall, & W. J. Meyer (Eds.), *Teacher expectations* (pp. 9–36). Hillsdale, NJ: Lawrence Erlbaum.

Narcissism and Leadership:
An Object Relations Perspective

Manfred F. R. Kets de Vries
and Danny Miller

When we think of leaders and leadership, a wide array of images come to mind, often conveying emotional reactions. Some leaders elicit thoughts of strength, power, and care, others recall the forces of terror, malevolence, and destructiveness. Our ubiquitous judgments of a leader's degree of "goodness" or evil are reflected in epithets such as Akbar the Great or Ivan the Terrible. We shall attempt in this paper to show that leadership effectiveness and dysfunction can often be explained by the narcissistic dispositions of the leader. We shall discuss and contrast three types of leaders and probe the etiology and consequences of their narcissistic orientations. The task will be to show the relationships between the intrapsychic development of the leader (using an object relations perspective), his or her subsequent narcissistic orientation, and the concrete manifestations of this orientation in leadership behavior. In no sense will our method be positivistic. We draw upon our experiences as practicing psychoanalysts, professors of management, and management consultants to demonstrate the linkages between early developmental experiences, types of narcissism, and leader behavior (Kets de Vries, 1980). The framework we shall employ is based on our clinical experiences with individuals who play a leadership role. It therefore goes without saying that our conclusions are to be viewed more as hypotheses than findings.

LEADERS AND FOLLOWERS

The dynamics of leadership have remained very much a puzzle. We still know little about what makes a good leader. But this is not for any lack of research on the subject. The late scholar of leadership, Ralph Stogdill, made the discouraging statement that "there are almost as many definitions of leadership as there are persons who have attempted to define the concept" (Bass, 1981, p. 7). Stogdill in his *Handbook of Leadership* reviewed 72 definitions proposed by scholars between 1902–1967. But this lack of consensus has not discouraged researchers. The proliferation of literature on leadership is amply reflected by the increase in the number of articles listed in the *Handbook*. While the old (1974) *Handbook* referred to only 3000 studies, 7 years later, the number exceeded 5000. Unfortunately, as Mintzberg (1981) has suggested, the popularity of leadership research was not equaled by its relevance. He states: "Even the titles of the theories—new no less than old—reveal the nature of their content—plodding and detached. Since the beginning, there seems to have been a steady convergence on the peripheral at best, and all too often on the trivial and the irrelevant" (p. 250). Mintzberg was not alone in criticizing excessive abstraction in the study of leadership. Bass (1981, p. 26), in his new edition of the *Handbook of Leadership*, noted that "if a theory of leadership is to be used for diagnosis, training, and development, it must be grounded theory— grounded in the concepts and assumptions acceptable to and used by managers, officials, and emergent leaders."

Competing theories abound. We find great men theories, trait theories, environmental theories, person-situation theories, interaction-expectation theories, humanistic theories, exchange theories, behavioral theories, and perceptual and cognitive theories. This confused state of affairs caused some scholars to abandon the subject altogether and focus on more specific problems such as power or motivation. Other researchers, however, are less pessimistic, anticipating that the wealth of results constitutes some basis for a cogent theory of leadership. They attempt to escape the labyrinth of contradictory findings and theories of leadership by proposing a contingency paradigm (House & Baetz, 1979). They try to explain the discrepancies in the research, noting that "leadership has an effect under some conditions and not under others and also that the causal relationships between leader behavior and commonly accepted criteria of organizational performance are two-way" (House & Baetz, 1979, p. 348). But in spite of its real merits, one wonders if this contingency paradigm will by itself be sufficient to breathe new life into this often discredited field.

Far richer characterizations of leadership are needed, those taking into consideration both its cognitive and affective dimensions. These are suggested by the psychoanalytic and psychiatric literature. Here, the "inner world" of leaders is analyzed and their personalities and characters are related to their behavior and situation. This, of course, is a time-honored practice among many historians and biographers. Research that aims to decipher intrapsychic thought processes and resulting actions thus involves the study of "psycho-political drama" (Zaleznik & Kets de Vries, 1975) that relates managerial personality both to role behavior and to the administrative setting.

What most leaders seem to have in common is the ability to reawaken primitive emotions in their followers. Leaders, particularly those who are charismatic, are masters at manipulating certain symbols. Followers, when under the "spell" of certain types of leaders, often feel powerfully grandiose and proud, or helpless and acutely dependent. Max Weber (1947) used the term *charisma* to elucidate this strange influence of some leaders over followers which, for him, consisted of

> a certain quality of an individual personality by virtue of which he is set apart from ordinary men and treated as endowed with supernatural, superhuman, or at least specifically exceptional powers or qualities. These are such as are not accessible to the ordinary person, but are regarded as of divine origin or as exemplary, and on the basis of them, the individual concerned is treated as a leader. (pp. 358–359)

We don't have to go so far as Weber, but whatever strange "quality" leaders possess, some have the power to induce regressive behavior among their followers. They have the uncanny ability to exploit, not necessarily in full awareness, the unconscious feelings of their subordinates. In this process, some followers may try to embrace an idealized, "omnipotent" leader, one who will fulfill their dependency needs. This may lead to the destructive suspension of their own rational faculties. The mesmerizing influence of some leaders may also cause the common good to be sacrificed for personal folly. Rituals of adulation can supplant task-related activity. Form tends to dominate substance, as the followers become pawns to be manipulated, like the gullible spectators in Andersen's "The Emperor's New Clothes." Thus, functional requirements pertaining to common purposes or ideals may be neglected in favor of fleeting narcissistic gratifications.

In spite of the regressive potential of some leaders, there are others who transcend petty concerns, who are able to create a climate of constructiveness, involvement, and care, who engender initiative, and spur creative endeavors. This is the kind of person Zaleznik (1977) had in mind when he said:

> One often hears leaders referred to in adjectives rich in emotional content. Leaders attract strong feelings of identity and difference, or of love and hate. Human relations in leader-dominated structures often appear turbulent, intense, and at times even disorganized. Such an atmosphere intensifies individual motivation and often produces unanticipated outcomes. (p. 74)

James MacGregor Burns (1978) probably had similar thoughts when he compared transactional with transforming leadership. While the first type of leader motivates followers by exchanging rewards for services rendered, whether economic, political, or psychological, the latter type of leader recognizes and exploits an existing need or demand of a potential follower. But, beyond that, the successful transforming leader looks for potential motives in followers, seeks to satisfy their higher needs, and engages their full potential. The result of the most adept transforming leadership is a relationship of mutual stimulation and elevation that converts followers into leaders and leaders into moral agents (Burns, 1978, p. 4).

To conclude, leadership can be pathologically destructive or most inspiring. But what is it about the leaders themselves that makes it so? What differentiates styles of leadership? Our theme will be that the degree of narcissism, and its genesis, stand central.

THE NARCISSISTIC DISPOSITION

In studying leaders, we soon recognized that one critical component of their orientation is the quality and intensity of their narcissistic development. If there is one personality constellation to which leaders tend to gravitate it is the narcissistic one. Freud (1921, pp. 123–124), in his study of the relationship between leaders and followers already confirmed this, stating that "the leader himself need love no one else, he may be of a masterful nature, absolutely narcissistic, self-confident and independent." Later, he introduced a narcissistic libidinal personality, an individual whose main interest is self-preservation, who is independent and impossible to intimidate. Significant aggressiveness is possible, which sometimes manifests itself in a constant readiness for activity. People belonging to this type impress others as being strong personalities. They are especially suited to act as moral ideological bastions for others, in short, as true leaders (Freud, 1931, p. 21).

In a similar context, Wilhelm Reich referred to a phallic-narcissistic character which he portrayed as being "self-confident, often arrogant, elastic, vigorous and often impressive. . . . The outspoken types tend to achieve leading positions in life and resent subordination. . . . If their vanity is hurt, they react either with cold reserve, deep depression or lively aggression" (Reich, 1949, p. 201).

Narcissism became a particularly important topic for study when new developments in psychoanalytic theory occurred. The introduction of object relations theory and self-psychology was especially fruitful. The most important revisions concerning narcissism were formulated by clinicians such as Otto Kernberg (1975) and Heinz Kohut (1971).

For the purpose of this paper, we will not dwell on the theoretical controversies about whether narcissism is a result mainly of developmental arrest or regression, or whether it possesses its own developmental lines. Our aim is to explore the relationships between narcissism and leadership, a connection recognized by both Kernberg and Kohut. For example, Kernberg states that "because narcissistic personalities are often driven by intense needs for power and prestige to assume positions of authority and leadership, individuals with such characteristics are found rather frequently in top leadership positions" (Kernberg, 1979, p. 33). Kohut, in focusing on leaders as objects of identification, mentions that "certain types of narcissistically fixated personalities with their apparently absolute self-confidence and certainty lend themselves specifically to this role" (Kohut, 1971, p. 316).

Narcissism is often the driving force behind the desire to obtain a leadership position. Perhaps individuals with strong narcissistic personality features are more willing to undertake the arduous process of attaining a position of power. A central theme of our discussion will be that the kind of behavior we encounter in a leader will be likely to reflect the nature and degree of his narcissistic tendencies.

Although the narcissistic type of personality has long been recognized, only recently has it come under critical scrutiny. For example, the latest version of the *Diagnostic and Statistical Manual of Mental Disorders* (DSM III, American Psychiatric Association, 1980) lists a large number of criteria to describe narcissistic personality disorders. There are overtones of mental illness and impairment of functioning:

symptoms include extremes of grandiosity, exploitativeness, exhibition-ism, and so on. Many of these characteristics are also applicable, albeit in smaller measure, to narcissistic individuals who adopt a more "nor-mal" mode of functioning.

Narcissists feel they must rely on themselves rather than on others for the gratification of life's needs. They live with the assumption that they cannot reliably depend on anyone's love or loyalty. They pretend to be self-sufficient, but in the depth of their beings they experience a sense of deprivation and emptiness. To cope with these feelings and, perhaps, as a cover for their insecurity, narcissists become preoccupied with estab-lishing their adequacy, power, beauty, status, prestige, and superiority. At the same time, narcissists expect others to accept the high esteem in which they hold themselves, and to cater to their needs. What is striking in the behavior of these people is their interpersonal exploitativeness. Narcissists live under the illusion that they are entitled to be served, that their own wishes take precedence over those of others. They think that they deserve special consideration in life.

It must be emphasized, however, that these characteristics occur with different degrees of intensity. A certain dose of narcissism is necessary to function effectively. We all show signs of narcissistic behavior. Among individuals who possess only limited narcissistic tendencies, we find those who are very talented and capable of making great contributions to soci-ety. Those who gravitate toward the extremes, however, give narcissism its pejorative reputation. Here we find excesses of rigidity, narrowness, resistance, and discomfort in dealing with the external environment. The managerial implications of narcissism can be both dramatic and crucial.

THREE TYPES OF NARCISSISM: ETIOLOGY, DEFENSES, AND MANIFESTATIONS

We shall proceed to discuss three types of narcissistic orientations beginning with the most pernicious or pathological and proceeding toward the more adaptive or functional: these we shall call *reactive, self-deceptive*, and *constructive*. We will first discuss the general etiology and common defenses of these types, using an object relations perspec-tive. We shall then present a discussion of the behavioral manifestations of the types in a leadership situation. Each type is based on examples from our clinical experiences which confirm how executives with different formative backgrounds manifest narcissistic behavior in various leadership situations. Table 1 summarizes our major findings for each of the three types.

Object Relations and the Etiology of Narcissism

Leaders may be said to occupy different positions on a spectrum ranging from healthy narcissism to pathology. We are by no means dealing with distinct categories. The factors that distinguish between health and dysfunction are the intrapsychic and interpersonal dynamics of the leader.

Over time, most people develop relatively stable ways of representing the experiences of themselves and others. These psychic representations in one's private inner world are known as *internal objects*; they are accumulated perceptions. They are composed of fantasies, ideals, thoughts, and images which create a kind of cognitive map of the world (Klein, 1948; Fairbairn, 1952; Jacobson, 1964; Guntrip, 1969; Mahler, Pine, & Bergman, 1975; Kernberg, 1976). The term "object relations" thus refers to theories, or aspects of theories, concerned with exploring the relationships between real, external people, the mental images retained of these people, and the significance of these mental residues for psychic functioning (Greenberg & Mitchell, 1983). Our interactions with actual people depend not only on how we view them, but also on our views of internal others. These psychic representations profoundly influence our affective states as well as our behavior. Good internal objects have a generative and restorative function, and serve as a source of sustenance in dealing with life's adversities. They constitute the underpinnings of healthy functioning. But in the absence of good internal objects, various dysfunctions accrue. Therein lies the genesis of pathological narcissism. Naturally, the earliest "objects" are the parents whose nurturing gives rise to different kinds of "internal worlds." Since parents are not always consistent in dealing with their children, this world can be highly complex and turbulent. We shall proceed to discuss the etiology or early object relations of three types of narcissistic leaders.

Reactive Narcissism

In describing messianic and charismatic leaders, Kohut (1971) argues that such leaders suffer from a pathology of narcissistic develop-

Table 1
"Ideal" Varieties of Narcissism

Reactive	Self-deceptive	Constructive
Early object relations (etiology)		
Rejecting, unresponsive parenting	Overburdening parenting	"Good enough" care
Absence of secure attachment	Absence of secure attachment	Sense of acceptance
Defensive reactions (splitting projective identification idealization/devaluation)		
Pervasive	Manifestation,	Rare
Severe	frequency, and	Mild
Frequent	intensity varies	Infrequent
Exploitativeness	Manipulation	
Symptomatology		
Exhibitionism	Lack of empathy	Sense of humor
Grandiosity	Machiavellianism	Creativity
Ruthlessness	Fear of failure	Self-confidence
Coldness	"Ideal-hungry"	Ambition
Entitlement	Preoccupation	Energy
(want to dominate)	with own needs	Stubbornness
	(want to be loved)	Pride (want to achieve)
Manifestation in organizational functioning		
1. Leadership		
Transforming orientation	Transactional orientation	Transforming/transactional orientation
Expelling mode	Binding mode	Reciprocal mode
Tolerate only sycophants	Prefer non-critical subordinates	Meritocratic
Cruel taskmaster	Diplomatic	Inspirational
Ignore subordinates' needs	Instrumental consideration of subordinates	Mentor role
Enraged by criticism	Hurt by criticism	Learns from criticism
2. Decision-making		
Major, risk-laden, spectacular projects	Conservative, risk averse, overcautious	Consultative in information-gathering, independent in decision-making
Consults no one	Consults too many	Inner-directed
Crushes opponents	Lacks resolve	
Uses scapegoats		
Never admits defeat		

ment. He attributes it to their failure during early childhood to integrate two important spheres of the self, namely, *the grandiose self* and *the idealized parental image* (Kohut, 1978, p. 826). The first construct refers to early feelings of grandiose omnipotence, when a child wishes to display his evolving capabilities and wants to be admired for it. The second construct applies to the equally illusory wishes about the idealized powers attributed to the parents, the desire to experience a sense of merger with an idealized person. Typically, the child's "I am perfect and you admire me," gradually changes into "you are perfect and I am part of you."

Clinical studies indicate that these early experiences, which are a part of everyone's maturation, become mitigated and neutralized through phase-appropriate development (Winnicott, 1975). By this process, the child is gradually able to reduce frustration from the inevitable failures of parents to live up to his or her archaic expectations, and through experience, comes gradually to understand the difference between the ideal of perfection and just being good enough. He or she learns that the parent is neither completely good nor completely bad. A more balanced and integrated image of the parent is internalized to make for a more realistic appreciation. This fusion of originally split "good and bad" objects is said to be essential for the development of trust in the permanence, "constancy," or reliability of the parental figures (Klein, 1948). In turn, this early success in creating secure interpersonal attachments makes for confident self-esteem and for stable relationships. Kohut (1971) calls this a process of "transmuting internalization." He believes it to be the basis of the development of a permanent and durable psychic structure.

Unfortunately, phase-appropriate development does not always occur. Parental behavior may be experienced as cold and unempathic, even at the earliest stage of development. Parents might not be sufficiently sensitive to the needs of the growing child. In these cases, children acquire a defective sense of self and are unable to maintain a stable level of self-esteem. Consequently, childhood needs are not modified or neutralized, but continue to prevail. This, in turn, results in a persistent longing and a search for narcissistic recognition throughout adulthood. The stage is thus set for "reactive" narcissism. In a classic article, Kohut and Wolf (1978) refer to the understimulated and fragmented self that results from too few stimulating and integrating parental responses during childhood.

The legacy for the child of such deficient interactions may be a lingering sense of inadequacy. To cope with such feelings some individuals create for themselves a self-image of "specialness." This can be viewed as a compensatory, reactive refuge against an ever-present feeling of never having been loved by the parent. The illusion of uniqueness will vitally affect how the individual deals with his external environment. Any discrepancies between capacities and wants are likely to contribute to anxiety and to impaired reality testing, the inability to distinguish wish from perception or, in other words, "inside" from "outside." Individuals with this "reactive" kind of orientation will frequently distort outside events to manage anxiety and to prevent a sense of loss and disappointment. If they are in a position of leadership this can have grave consequences. Reactive narcissism caused by emotionally unresponsive, rejecting parents is the severest type. This will become obvious from our discussion of defenses and symptoms.

In making these inferences, we should bear in mind that early experiences in themselves rarely have a direct impact on adult functioning. There are many mediating experiences during one's life. Early experiences do, however, play a substantial role in shaping the core personality which influences the kind of environment sought out by the individual. This has an effect on experience and, in turn, will influence personality. We are thus talking about an interactive cycle of personality, behavior, and situation (Erikson, 1963; McKinley Runyan, 1982).

Self-Deceptive Narcissism

We often find a second type of narcissistic leader with a very different type of early childhood development. These individuals were once led by one or both parents to believe that they were completely lovable and perfect, regardless of their actions and in spite of any basis in reality. Such self-deceptive leaders probably suffer from what Kohut and Wolf (1978) describe as an overstimulated or overburdened self. Because the responses of the figures of early childhood were inappropriate given the children's age, the latter never learn to moderate their grandiose self-images or their idealized parental images. Ideals of perfection have been too demanding to allow them to internalize soothing, stabilizing internal objects. These children become the proxies of their parents, entrusted with the mission to fulfill many unrealized parental hopes. What may appear as indulgence on the part of the parents is, in fact, exactly the opposite. The parents use their children to take care of their own needs, overburdening them with their implicit desires. When parents impose their unrealistic hopes onto their children, they engender delusions. They confuse the children about their true abilities.

Such unrealistic beliefs may sometimes be the original impetus which differentiates these individuals from others and makes them successful. Perhaps Freud (1917, p. 156) had this in mind when he noted that "if a man has been his mother's undisputed darling, he retains throughout life the triumphant feeling, the confidence in success, which not seldom brings actual success along with it." In those rare instances when such encouragements work out, the child may be sufficiently talented to live up to the parents' exaggerated expectations. A person who in more normal circumstances might have led an ordinary life has used the expectations imposed on him as a child as a basis for excellence.

In general, however, the self-delusory quality of the unrealistic beliefs created by the parents will lead to problems. An exalted self-image is usually difficult to sustain in the light of external circumstances such as disappointment and failure. Thus, even though the early internalized objects are benign, disturbing interpersonal encounters when the child ventures forth from the protective family environment will give them an element of instability, of frailty. The overvalued image of the self that was garnered from an idealizing parent becomes more realistic after interactions with more honest and critical peers. Still, the traumas of early disappointments may have left a somewhat fragile and distorted concept of self. Self-deceiving narcissists are likely to suffer from interpersonal difficulties due to their desire to live up to the now internalized parental illusions of self-worth. They tend to demonstrate emotional superficiality and poverty of affect. Their behavior has an "ideal-hungry" quality resulting from difficulties in identity formation.

Conceptually, we have to be able to differentiate between the etiology of the reactive and self-deceptive modes of narcissism. In practice, however, a distinction is more difficult to make. Parents might each have responded differently toward the developing child. One parent might have taken a cold, hostile, rejecting attitude, while the other might have been supportive. Thus could have been created different gradations of benign and vicious internal objects, which accounts for mixtures of narcissistic styles. In addition, instead of being frustrated when ambitious parental expectations are incongruent with external reality, the child can sometimes strive successfully to bring his abilities up to his perceived capacity, as Freud notes so poignantly. Moreover, as we have pointed out, learning experiences later in life may also have buffering or mitigating effects.

Constructive Narcissism

Miller (1981), in describing the childhood object relations of healthy or constructive narcissists, stated:

> Aggressive impulses [were] neutralized because they did not upset the confidence and self-esteem of the parents.
>
> Strivings toward autonomy were not experienced [by parents] as an attack.
>
> The child was allowed to experience and express "ordinary" impulses (such as jealousy, rage, defiance) because his parents did not require him to be "special," for instance, to represent their own ethical attitudes.
>
> There was no need to please anybody (under optimal conditions), and the child could develop and exhibit whatever was active in him during each developmental phase. . . .
>
> Because the child was able to display ambivalent feelings, he could learn to regard both himself and the subject [the other] as "both good and bad," and did not need to split off the "good" from the "bad" object. (pp. 33–34)

The constructive narcissists do not behave in a reactive or self-deceptive manner. They do not feel the same need to distort reality to deal with life's frustrations. Nor are they so prone to anxiety. They make less frequent use of primitive defenses, and are less estranged from their feelings, wishes, or thoughts. In fact, they often generate a sense of positive vitality that derives from confidence about their personal worth. Such people have internalized relatively stable and benign objects, which sustain them in the face of life's adversities. They are willing to express their wants and to stand behind their actions, irrespective of the reactions of others. When disappointed, they do not act spitefully, but are able to engage in reparative action. That is, they have the patience to wait, to search out the moment when their talents will be needed (Erikson, 1978). Boldness in action, introspection, and thoughtfulness are common.

Defensive Systems

How do these three types of narcissistic leaders use their defensive systems? What struck us most in observing their behavior was how primitive the defenses of the first two types tend to be (Kernberg, 1975). At the core of the defensive systems is a mental process called *splitting*. All other defenses can be seen as derivatives of this very primitive mechanism.

What we mean by splitting is the tendency to see everything as either ideal (all good) or persecutory (all bad). When the individual has not sufficiently integrated or synthesized the opposite qualities of internal objects, these representations are kept separate to avoid contamination of "good" with "bad." Individuals with a tendency toward splitting possess affective and cognitive representations of themselves and others that are dramatically oversimplified. They fail to appreciate the real complexity and ambiguity of human relationships. Relationships are polarized between unbridled hatred, fear, or aggression on the one hand, and those of omnipotence and over-idealization on the other. Splitting thus avoids conflicts and preserves an illusory sense of being good. All evil is ascribed unto others. The price of maintaining this illusory sense of goodness is, of course, an impaired conception of reality.

Closely related to this defense are primitive *idealization* and *devaluation*. First, there is a need to create unrealistic, all-good, all-powerful representations of others. This process can be viewed as a protection against persecutory objects. A sense of intense helplessness and insignificance creates the need for all-powerful protectors. In the long run, however, no one can sustain these exaggerated expectations. A vengeful devaluation of the idealized figure then occurs when needs are not met.

Other derivatives of splitting are *projection* and *projective identification* (Ogden, 1982). These defense mechanisms serve to defend against persecution by bad internal objects. The person tries to get rid of unwanted aspects of the self. Consequently, internal representations of self and others are externalized and attributed (projected) to others. Blame is always placed on someone or something else. Never is there any sense of personal responsibility. Again, all this is associated with distortions of reality.

As we can see from Table 1, the frequency, severity, and intensity of these defensive mechanisms vary among the types of narcissism. The reactive type shows the highest frequency and intensity, the constructive type, the lowest.

Symptoms of Narcissism

The most extreme symptoms of this developmental legacy and these defenses are summarized in the *DSM III* (American Psychiatric Association, 1980, p. 317) which lists the following diagnostic criteria for narcissistic personality disorders:

A. Grandiose sense of self-importance or uniqueness, for example, exaggeration of achievements and talents, focus on the special nature of one's problems.
B. Preoccupation with fantasies of unlimited success, power, brilliance, beauty, or ideal love.
C. Exhibitionism: the person requires constant attention and administration.
D. Cool indifference or marked feelings of rage, inferiority, shame, humiliation, or emptiness in response to criticism, indifference of others, or defeat.
E. At least two of the following characteristics of disturbances in interpersonal relationships:
   1. Entitlement: expectation of special favors without assuming reciprocal responsibilities, for example, surprise and anger that people will not do what one wants.
   2. Interpersonal exploitativeness: taking advantage of others to indulge one's own desires or for self-aggrandizement, disregard for the personal integrity and rights of others.
   3. Relationships that characteristically alternate between the extremes of over-idealization and devaluation.
   4. Lack of empathy: inability to recognize how others feel, for example, one may be unable to appreciate the distress of someone who is seriously ill.

It is important once again to realize that particularly the first two types of narcissistic leaders will show many of these clinical indications, but each to a different extent. In our experience, reactive narcissists will be cold, ruthless, grandiose, and exhibitionistic. They will show a desire to dominate and control and will be extremely exploitative. Self-deceptive narcissists will be milder, they want to be liked and are much less tyrannical. Still, they lack empathy, are obsessed mainly with their own needs, and are given to being discreetly Machiavellian.

Their behavior has an "as if" quality, because they lack a strong sense of inner conviction and identity (Deutsch, 1965). Finally, constructive narcissistic leaders are also quite ambitious and can be manipulative and hypersensitive to criticism. But they have enough self-confidence, adaptability, and humor to stress real achievements. They get on well with others because of their insights into relationships.

ORGANIZATIONAL FUNCTIONING

The Reactive Leader

We shall describe two managerial situations in which we have seen the reactive narcissistic (RN) personality in operation. The first is in *leadership* or interpersonal relations. The second relates to their efforts at *environmental scanning, analysis*, and *decision-making*. The reactive narcissist can be an extremely demanding taskmaster. His grandiosity and exhibitionism cause him to gravitate toward subordinates who are sycophants. The arguments of others are ignored if they run counter to the ideas of the boss. Solicitous subordinates seem to be the only ones who are tolerated by a reactive narcissist, all others are "expelled." A strong Machiavellian streak runs through these situations: the leader cares little about hurting and exploiting others in the pursuit of his own advancement. The followers play politics simply to survive. The RN leader surpasses all other types in his total lack of empathy. He completely ignores the needs of subordinates and peers alike, reserving his attention to matters that concern him and him alone. The fluctuations in attitude toward his people will be extreme. Consequently, the level of employee turnover tends to be very high. Projects that require teamwork or subordinate initiative are seriously jeopardized.

The RN leader exhibits characteristic dysfunctions in making important decisions for his organization. He tends to do very little scanning or analysis of the internal and external environment before making decisions. The RN leader feels that he can manipulate and act upon his environment so that he need not study it very closely. The environment is somehow "beneath him," it is assumed to pose no challenges that cannot easily be met. The RN's grandiosity, exhibitionism, and preoccupation with fantasies of unlimited success cause him to undertake extremely bold and venturesome projects. The quality of his leadership style is transforming rather than transactional. He wishes to attract the attention of an invisible audience, to demonstrate his mastery and brilliance. Projects are undertaken on a grand scale, but they are often doomed to fail. First, their overblown scale reflects the desires of the leader more than the realities of the situation, too many resources are placed at risk for too little reason. Second, the leader doesn't listen to his advisors, peers, or subordinates. He feels that only he is sufficiently informed to make judgments. A potentially crucial forum is thereby lost. Third, even when it is clear that things are not going well with the project, the RN leader is reluctant to admit the evidence. He will not own up to having made any errors and he becomes especially rigid and sensitive to criticism. Thus, he initiates a momentum that is difficult to reverse (Miller & Friesen, 1980, 1984). When the leader finally realizes how fast the situation is deteriorating, his penchant for splitting causes him to blame others. He never sees himself as being responsible for anything that is at all negative.

The Self-Deceptive Leader

These individuals have many of the traits of the reactive executives, but these are less evident in a managerial situation. We can again explore the categories of leadership, environmental scanning, and decision-making. As leaders, self-deceptive (SD) executives are much more approachable than their RN counterparts. They care more about their subordinates, are more given to listening to the opinions of others, and are not nearly as exploitative as the RNs. However, they also show a hypersensitivity to criticism, extreme insecurity, and a strong need to be loved. SD leaders will be more tolerant of dissenting opinions in that they may seem to react sympathetically when the opinions are expressed. But they will tend to carry a grudge, to be less available to habitual critics and to promote weaker-willed subordinates over their vocal peers.

While the SD leader will often express interest in his subordinate's preoccupations, it will be out of a desire to appear sympathetic rather than out of a genuine sense of concern. He will want to do the right thing, but does not feel very enthusiastic about it. An exception to this pattern occurs in cases where the leader becomes attached to a subordinate that he has come to idealize. He will do all in his power to "bind" this person, to develop and bring him along in his own image. It is not surprising of course that this treasured subordinate generally idolizes the boss and is not usually a very strong or opinionated individual. If the subordinate were to show personal initiative, it would be interpreted as treason. The leader's idealization would then quickly change into devaluation, with predictable results for the subordinate's future in the organization.

The SD leader, in contrast to his RN counterpart, may be very eager to discover opportunities, and particularly threats, in his environment. He is insecure and therefore does a great deal of scanning of the internal and external environment to make sure that he will be able to neutralize threats and avoid costly mistakes. Competitors are watched, customers are interviewed, and information systems are established. A good deal of analysis and assessment takes place, so much so that it might sometimes paralyze action.

In making strategic decisions, the SD leader has a degree of performance anxiety. He wants to do the best job he possibly can so that he will be respected and admired, but he worries about his ability to do so. He is afraid of failure. This tends to make him much more conservative than the reactive executive. The SD executive studies the situation very thoroughly and solicits the opinions of others. Decision-making is done in response to exchanges of various types, quite in contrast to the pernicious transforming style of the reactive leader. The SD leader's orientation is thus predominantly of a transactional nature. Of course, conservative (like-minded) managers are much more likely to get a receptive hearing than the more venturesome ones. They have a general tendency to procrastinate, to put things off just a bit too long, and their perfectionism and hesitancy can give rise to organizational stagnation. Note that the RN narcissist was working to impress the broader political or business community, to be revered, to fulfill bold, impossible, visionary dreams. The SD narcissist just wants to be loved and admired by the people he interacts with. Also his symptoms will wax and wane according to his degree of anxiety to a greater extent than those of the RN leader.

The Constructive Leader

These leaders are no strangers to manipulation and are not beyond occasional acts of opportunism. But they generally are able to get on fairly well with their subordinates. Constructive narcissists possess a high degree of confidence in their abilities and are highly task and goal oriented. Thus they may sometimes come across as lacking in warmth or consideration.

Although constructive leaders enjoy being admired, they have a realistic appreciation of their abilities and limitations. Their attitude is one of give and take, and they recognize the competence of others. Constructive leaders are good listeners and appreciate the opinions of their subordinates, even though they are content to assume the ultimate responsibility for collective actions. They are willing to take a stand and stick to their decisions. This attitude may cause subordinates to complain that CLs are unsociable or uncooperative. In fact, constructive leaders sometimes do lack true empathy and may be prone to using others as mere instruments to accomplish their own objectives.

These leaders possess a sense of inner direction and self-determination that makes them confident. They have the ability to inspire others and to create a common cause, thereby transcending petty self-interests. Their inner directedness, however, can also be reflected by coldness, arrogance, or a stubborn insensitivity to the needs of others. Abstract concerns, such as "the good of the company" or "helping the worker," may replace reciprocity in interpersonal relations and the building of a team. In general, however, constructive narcissists have a sense of humor that makes it possible for them to put things in perspective. Their independence can make for the creativity and vision necessary to energize subordinates to engage in ambitious endeavors. Since it lacks the rigidity of the other two types, the dominant leadership style has both a transforming and transactional quality.

The constructive leaders vary a good deal in their decision-making styles which are more reflections of the situation facing the firm than the personal foibles of the executive. Their flexibility allows them to do a good deal of analysis, environmental scanning, and consultation before making strategic decisions of far-reaching consequences. But it also enables them to handle more routine situations with dispatch, entrusting matters to subordinates. They also tend to avoid extremes of boldness and conservatism, operating more in "the middle range."

ORGANIZATIONAL THERAPY

Constructive narcissistic leaders pose few organizational problems. But what can a firm's healthy managers do about the two more dysfunctional types of leaders? Where the organization is centralized and the narcissistic leader is dominant, poor performance and subsequent dismissal by a strong board of directors may be the only effective catalysts for change. And even these mutative influences are ruled out when a leader has strong financial control. But the outlook is much brighter where organizational power is more broadly distributed or where the narcissist occupies a less elevated position (Kets de Vries & Miller, 1984).

In fact, there are a number of organizational measures that can be taken to minimize the damage done by *lower level* narcissistic leaders. The first might be to try to become aware of their existence. In this pursuit, it may be useful to bear in mind that single indicators of each of the neurotic types are not sufficient to warrant a diagnosis of narcissism. But when these combine to form a syndrome this may indicate trouble.

It is very difficult to change a narcissist's personality. The primary emphasis must be to transfer the individual out of harm's way or to reduce his influence. A number of structural devices may be used to accomplish the latter. For example, power can be more broadly distributed in the organization so that many people get involved in strategic decisions, and lower level managers are induced to take responsibility for more routine concerns. Cross-functional committees, task forces, and executive committees can provide a useful forum in which a multitude of managers can express their viewpoint, providing opportunities for the narcissistic leaders (and especially their subordinates) to learn from and have their influence mitigated by others. Monolithic and unrealistic perspectives are thereby discouraged.

Regular leader appraisals in which subordinates have a chance to express their opinions to a third party about their boss may also be useful. Where a consensus of dissatisfaction emerges, particularly if it coincides with poor unit performance, it might be time to transfer or release the leader. Such an appraisal policy might inhibit overtly narcissistic exploitation.

When the top decision makers in an organization become aware of the narcissistic proclivities of some of the organization's managers, they can use this information in carrying out personnel policy. This is especially true when assigning subordinates to a narcissistic leader. One of the greatest dangers is to engage insecure, inexperienced managers to work for the narcissist. These employees will have too little strength or resolve to be able to cope, and still less potential to act as useful counterbalancing forces. In contrast, it might be useful to assign strong, confident, and secure personalities to work with the narcissistically inclined executive, those who are not afraid to express their opinions and can help to introduce more "reality" into the decision-making process.

It is particularly important, also, to look for signs of excessive narcissism in recruiting and making promotions. Psychological tests by trained clinicians and interviews with a candidate's previous superiors and subordinates might flag a narcissistic leader. There is no doubt that the easiest way to deal with these managers is to avoid hiring them, or failing that, to refrain from giving them much power.

REFERENCES

American Psychiatric Association. *DSM III: Diagnostic and statistical manual of mental disorders* (3rd ed.). Washington, 1980.

Bass, B. B. *Stogdill's handbook of leadership.* New York: The Free Press, 1981.

Burns, J. M. *Leadership.* New York: Harper and Row, 1978.

Deutsch, H. *Neuroses and character types.* New York: International Universities Press, 1965.

Erikson, E. H. *Childhood and society.* New York: W. W. Norton and Co., 1963.

Erikson, E. H. *Life history and the historical moment.* New York: W. W. Norton and Co., 1978.

Fairbairn, W. R. D. *An object-relations theory of personality.* New York: Basic Books, 1952.

Freud, S. *A childhood recollection from Dichtung und Wahrheit, The standard edition of the complete psychological works of Sigmund Freud* (Vol. XVII). London: The Hogarth Press and the Institute of Psychoanalysis, 1917.

Freud, S. *Group psychology and the analysis of the ego, The standard edition of the complete psychological works of Sigmund Freud* (Vol. XVIII). London: The Hogarth Press and the Institute of Psychoanalysis, 1921.

Freud, S. *Libidinal types, The standard edition of the complete psychological works of Sigmund Freud* (Vol. XXI). London: The Hogarth Press and the Institute of Psychoanalysis, 1931.

Greenberg, J. R., & Mitchell, S. A. *Object relations in psychoanalytic theory.* Cambridge, Massachusetts: Harvard University Press, 1983.

Guntrip, H. *Schizoid phenomena, object relations and the self.* New York: International Universities Press, 1969.

House, R. J., & Baetz, M. L. Leadership: Some empirical generalizations and new research directions. *Research in Organizational Behavior*, 1979, *1*, 341–423.

Jacobson, E. *The self and the object world.* New York: International Universities Press, 1964.

Kernberg, O. *Borderline conditions and pathological narcissism.* New York: Jason Aronson, 1975.

Kernberg, O. *Object relations theory and clinical psychoanalysis.* New York: Jason Aronson, 1976.

Kernberg, O. Regression in organizational leadership. *Psychiatry,* 1979, *42,* 29–39.

Kets de Vries, M. F. R. Leadership in a narcissistic age. Faculty of Management, *McGill University Working Paper,* 1980.

Kets de Vries, M. F. R., & Miller, D. *The neurotic organization: Diagnosing and changing counterproductive styles of management.* San Francisco: Jossey Bass, 1984.

Klein, M. *Contributions to psychoanalysis, 1921–1945.* London: The Hogarth Press, 1948.

Kohut, H. *The analysis of the self.* New York: International Universities Press, 1971.

Kohut, H. Creativeness, charisma, group psychology. In Paul H. Ornstein (Ed.), *The search for the self* (Vol. 2). New York: International Universities Press, 1978.

Kohut, H. & Wolf, E. S. The disorders of the self and their treatment: An outline. *The International Journal of Psychoanalysis,* 1978, *59,* 413–426.

Mahler, M. S., Pine, F. & Bergman, A. *The psychological birth of the human infant.* New York: Basic Books, 1975.

McKinley Runyan, W. *Life histories and psychobiography.* New York: Oxford University Press, 1982.

Miller, A. *Prisoners of childhood.* New York: Basic Books, 1981.

Miller, D. & Friesen, P. H. Momentum and revolution in organizational adaptation. *Academy of Management Journal,* 1980, *24,* 591–614.

Miller, D. & Friesen, P. H. *Organizations: A quantum view.* Englewood Cliffs, N.J.: Prentice-Hall, 1984.

Mintzberg, H. If you're not serving Bill and Barbara, then you're not serving leadership. In J. G. Hunt, U. Sekaran, & C. A. Schriesheim (Eds.), *Leadership: Beyond establishment views.* Carbondale Illinois: Southern Illinois University Press, 1981.

Ogden, T. H. *Projective identification and psychotherapeutic technique.* New York: Jason Aronson, 1982.

Reich, W. *Characteranalysis.* New York: Farrar, Strauss and Giroux, 1949.

Weber, M. *The theory of social and economic organizations.* New York: Oxford University Press, 1947.

Winnicott, D. W. *Through paediatrics to psycho-analysis.* New York: Basic Books, 1975.

Zaleznik, A. Managers and leaders: Are they different? *Harvard Business Review,* 1977, *55,* 67–78.

Zaleznik, A. & Kets de Vries, M. F. R. *Power and the corporate mind.* Boston: Houghton Mifflin, 1975.

The Dark Side of Leadership

Jay A. Conger

In recent years, business leaders have gained great popularity: Lee Iaccoca and Steven Jobs, for example, have stepped into the limelight as agents of change and entrepreneurship. But though we tend to think of the positive outcomes associated with leaders, certain risks or liabilities are also entailed. The very behaviors that distinguish leaders from managers also have the potential to produce problematic or even disastrous outcomes for their organizations. For example, when a leader's behaviors become exaggerated, lose touch with reality, or become vehicles for purely personal gain, they may harm the leader and the organization.

How do leaders produce such negative outcomes—and why? Three particular skill areas can contribute to such problems. These include leaders' strategic vision, their communications and impression-management skills, and their general management practices. We will examine each to discover its darker side.

PROBLEMS WITH THE VISIONARY LEADER

As we know, there have been tremendous changes in the world's competitive business environment. Previously successful organizations that had grown huge and bureaucratic were suddenly faced with pressures to innovate and alter their ways. Out of these turbulent times came a new breed of business leader: the strategic visionary. These men and women, like Ross Perot of Electronic Data Systems and Mary Kay Ash of Mary Kay Cosmetics, possessed a twofold ability: to foresee market opportunities and to craft organizational strategies that captured these opportunities in ways that were personally meaningful to employees. When their success stories spread, "vision" became the new byword. Yet though many of these leaders led their organizations on to great successes, others led their organizations on to great failures. The very qualities that distinguished the visionary leader contained the potential for disaster.

Generally speaking, unsuccessful strategic visions can often be traced to the inclusion of the leaders' personal aims that did not match their constituents' needs. For example, leaders might substitute personal goals for what should be shared organizational goals. They might construct an organizational vision that is essentially a monument to themselves and therefore something quite different from the actual wishes of their organizations or customers.

Moreover, the blind drive to create this very personal vision could result in an inability to see problems and opportunities in the environment. Thomas Edison, for example, so passionately believed in the future of direct electrical current (DC) for urban power grids that he failed to see the more rapid acceptance of alternating power (AC) systems by America's then-emerging utility companies. Thus the company started by Edison to produce DC power stations was soon doomed to failure. He became so enamoured of his own ideas that he failed to see competing and, ultimately, more successful ideas.

In addition, such personal visions encourage the leader to expend enormous amounts of energy, passion, and resources on getting them off the ground. The higher their commitment, the less willing they are to see the viability of competing approaches. Because of the leader's commitment, the organization's investment is also likely to be far greater in such cases. Failure therefore will have more serious consequences.

Fundamental errors in the leader's perceptions can also lead to a failed vision. Common problems include (1) an inability to detect important changes in markets (e.g., competitive, technological, or consumer needs); (2) a failure to accurately assess and obtain the necessary resources for the vision's accomplishment; and (3) a misreading or exaggerated sense of the needs of markets or constituents. For example, with a few exceptions like the Chrysler minivan, Lee Iacocca inaccurately believed that automobile style rather than engineering was the primary concern of automotive buyers. At Chrysler, he relied on new body styles and his charisma to market cars built on an aging chassis (the K car). The end result was that, after several initial years of successful sales, Chrysler's sales plunged 22.8%. Today, the future of Chrysler looks equally cloudy.

Ultimately, then, the success of a leader's strategic vision depends on a realistic assessment of both the opportunities and the constraints in the organization's environment and a sensitivity to constituents' needs. If the leader loses sight of reality or loses touch with constituents, the vision becomes a liability. Visions may fail for a wide variety of reasons; Exhibit 1 outlines some of the more significant ones. We will examine several of these categories and illustrate them with the experiences of some prominent business leaders.

Making the Leader's Personal Needs Paramount

As mentioned, one of the most serious liabilities of a visionary leader occurs when he or she projects purely personal needs and beliefs onto those of constituents. A common example is the inventor with a pet idea who acquires sufficient resources to initiate a venture that fails to meet the market's needs. When a leader's needs and wishes diverge from those of constituents, the consequences can be quite costly. Consider, for example, Edwin Land, inventor of the Polaroid camera. Dr. Land's experiences with a camera he developed called the SX-70 illustrate how a leader can get side-tracked by his own personal goals.

As we know, Land's company, Polaroid, held a monopoly on the instant photography market for some three decades and became the household word for such cameras. Throughout the 1960s and 1970s, Polaroid's sales climbed with astonishing speed. By 1973, four million of the company's Colorpack cameras were being sold annually at $30 a piece. But Dr. Land was not content. His dream was to create what he called "absolute one-step photography"; the SX-70 camera was to embody his dream. "Photography will never be the same . . . With the gargantuan effort of bringing SX-70 into being, the company has come fully of age," Land remarked on the day of the camera's inauguration.

In setting the parameters for his new vision, Land outlined several demanding criteria: The camera was to be totally automatic and would have to fold to fit into a purse or pocket, possess a single-lens reflex-

Exhibit 1
The Sources of Failed Vision

The vision reflects the internal needs of leaders rather than those of the market or constituents.

The resources needed to achieve vision have been seriously miscalculated.

An unrealistic assessment or distorted perception of market and constituent needs holds sway.

A failure to recognize environmental changes prevents redirection of the vision.

viewing system, and focus from less than a foot to infinity. It was to be a radically new design, making earlier versions of instant photography obsolete.

The SX-70 also represented a major strategic shift for the company. Before its advent, the manufacturing of Polaroid products, especially films, was subcontracted to outsiders. Plant and equipment were usually leased or rented. But Land's dream of the SX-70 required total integration of the company. A color-negative and camera-assembly plant were designed and built, and the company's existing chemical production and films-packaging facilities were expanded.

Although the total cost of the SX-70 strategy was never formally disclosed, Land responded in an interview that it was a half-billion-dollar investment. Other estimates have put it higher. In any case, the SX-70 was a design masterpiece. It was estimated that the reflex-viewing system cost millions of dollars and required more than two-and-a-half years of engineering effort. Engineering for the eye-piece alone cost $2 million.

Land's expectations of the camera's success were as lavish as his investment in the camera. At $180 per camera, company projections were that first-year sales would reach several million. By some accounts, sales of 5,000,000 units were predicted. Yet despite such optimism, the camera met with only limited public support. By the end of its first year in 1973, only 470,000 SX-70 cameras had been sold. It would take several years, many design changes, and significant price cuts before the camera would gain widespread market acceptance—all at the cost of sacrificing many of the camera's original features. Land's personal vision of the instant camera had missed what the market wanted.

Most important, in his quest for the perfect instant camera he had failed to take into account lessons that his company had already learned about consumers' needs. Before the SX-70, Polaroid's experience with both its black-and-white and its color cameras was that demand was intimately tied to price. Consumers wanted an inexpensive, easy-to-use, instant camera. Their foremost desire was not a perfect picture but a relatively good instant picture at a low price.

In the 1960s, the marketplace had powerfully demonstrated its needs to Polaroid after the company first introduced its color system in 1963. When the Colorpack cameras priced at $100 met with only limited market interest, Polaroid introduced a version at $75 and, by 1969, a $30

Colorpack. At the $30 price level, volume dramatically expanded, and 4,000,000 units were sold by 1973. Consumers wanted instant photography but only at an inexpensive price. So how could 5,000,000 SX-70s at $180 a piece be sold when only 4,000,000 Colorpack cameras had been sold at $30 each? Clearly they could not. Dr. Land's vision was a personal ideal, one that was not shared by consumers at a price of $180 per camera.

What happened to Land that he failed to learn from the past? There are several possible explanations. For one, his initial vision of instant photography had been correct; people really did want instant photographs. This initial success, however, may have convinced him of the invincibility of his ideas. Second, Land was an engineer at heart; he loved the technology more than the marketing of the product. His very background made him product- and technology-driven, not so much marketplace-driven. Finally and most important, I believe that Land, like other leaders, came to identify with his vision to an unhealthy extreme: The vision personified him.

A similar example is seen in Henry Ford, who was willing to build a Model T of any color as long as it was black. The vision in essence becomes so much a part of the leader's personality that he or she is unwilling or unable to consider information to the contrary from staff members or from the marketplace. Convinced by past successes of their invincibility, such leaders plow ahead without considering other viewpoints—a sure course toward failure.

Becoming a "Pyrrhic Victor"

In the quest to achieve a vision, a leader may be so driven as to ignore the costly implications of his strategic aims. Ambition and the miscalculation of necessary resources can lead to a "Pyrrhic victory" for the leader. The term "Pyrrhic victory" comes from an incident in Ancient Greece: Pyrrhus, the King of Epirus, sustained such heavy losses in defeating the Romans that despite his numerous victories over them, his entire empire was ultimately undermined. Thus the costs of a "Pyrrhic" victory deplete the resources that are needed for future success.

In this scenario, the leader is usually driven by a desire to expand or accelerate the realization of his vision. The initial vision appears correct, and early successes essentially delude or weaken the leader's ability to realistically assess his resources and marketplace realities. The costs that must be paid for acquisitions or market share ultimately become unsustainable and threaten the long-term viability of the leader's organization.

Robert Campeau is the quintessential Pyrrhic victor. After amassing a fortune as a real estate developer, he proceeded to expand his empire into retailing with a series of purchases in the mid-1980s totalling $13.4 billion. He did this despite the fact that he knew little about the business of retailing itself. His celebrated purchase of the Allied and Federated Department Stores alone cost him some $400 million in bankers' and lawyers' fees and added $11.7 billion of debt to the Campeau Corporation. They also transformed him overnight into the most powerful retailer in the world. The price of course was an enormous amount of debt—much of it in the form of high-interest junk bonds that would soon demand most of the company's operating cash to service.

When asked how he planned to successfully integrate and enhance the profitability of these new and unrelated acquisitions, Campeau explained that it was only a matter of consolidating various operations, selling off assets to pay off company debt, and motivating management by giving them stock options. With an air of great confidence, he commented: "I own the best department stores in the world, and they will be damned profitable." He also envisioned enormous potential for synergy between his retailing and real estate operations. His plans included the building of some 50 U.S. shopping malls anchored by his newly acquired retail stores. These projects, which included 17 new Bloomingdale's stores, were estimated at a cost of $1.5 billion. In comments to the press, he stated: "Most retail managements don't know much about real estate and finance . . . [but] real estate is the gravy on top of these great retailing deals." For Campeau, his newly acquired stores sat on prime land—ripe for future deals. It was an intriguing and untried dream.

Ironically, these bold strategic moves were all made during a sales slowdown in the department store industry and in a country glutted with shopping malls. As well, the two chains he had acquired were prestigious but also notoriously inefficient. None of these factors seemed to impede Campeau, who was intent on building an empire.

Despite his rosy projections for the future, Campeau's kingdom quickly unraveled within a few years. After struggling to meet a crushing debt load, Campeau's retail operations ran out of operating cash in August 1989. By January 1990 his company stood on the edge of bankruptcy, and so did Campeau himself. The projections of great profitability for the retail operations had never materialized. New and last-minute junk-bond financing to keep the company alive came at a dear price, with interest rates as high as 17.75%. But this would not save the company as soaring debt-servicing costs forced Campeau to sell off company stock to others and to default on company loans. Even the company's crown jewel—Bloomingdale's—was soon put up for sale. Campeau's own personal fortune of $500 million was said to have all but evaporated by February 1990.

Campeau's tragic error in this case was tied as much to blind ambition as it was to poor strategic and financing decisions. His history of successes in the real estate field, in combination with an ambitious personality, led this visionary leader to dream of ever-greater expansion, but in new and unfamiliar territories. The idea of an "empire" became more important than the satisfaction of enjoying his present successes. Failing to see that he lacked the long-term resources or skills needed to sustain his grand plan, he continued to acquire companies and debt at an alarming rate.

Then, too, in wishing to maintain an image of self-confidence, he may have denied or minimized the existence of any problems. Already an autocratic leader, Campeau became even more autocratic. For example, he himself assumed the position of chairman of the board at both Federated and Allied, a job he had originally and sensibly promised to an executive of a highly successful retail chain. He wanted to run his new and glamorous acquisitions personally. Sadly, this scenario is all too typical of the Pyrrhic victor whose ambitions stymie his ability to assess goals and resources realistically. Investment bankers and subordinates may further encourage visions of grandeur. As serious problems emerge, their importance is minimized. Once a crisis stage is reached, the leader exerts greater personal control and becomes less able to hear the counsel of advisors or staff members who might be helpful. In the worst case, such as Campeau's, the organization's resources are exhausted and the company fails.

Chasing a Vision Before Its Time

Sometimes a leader's perceptions of the market are so exaggerated or so significantly ahead of their time that the marketplace fails to sustain the leader's venture. The organization's resources are mobilized and spent on a mission that ultimately fails to produce the expected results. In this case, the leader is perhaps too visionary or too idealistic. He or she is unable to see that the time is not ripe, so the vision goes on to failure or, at best, a long dormancy.

Robert Lipp, former president of Chemical Bank, is an example of a visionary charismatic who in one project was essentially too far ahead of his time. He had championed a vision of home banking in the early 1980s. Sensing that the personal computer was revolutionizing many aspects of everyday life, Lipp and others at Chemical Bank expected personal banking to be the next beneficiary of the personal computer revolution. Through a modem, phone line, software supplied by the bank, and a personal computer at home, individuals could instruct their banks to carry out certain transactions. A service fee of $8 to $15 a month was charged for personal users and $20 to $50 a month for small businesses. From the user's viewpoint, home banking provided convenience in bill paying and ease of access to accounts. While on travel, the user could instruct the system to pay bills on exact due dates.

For banks, electronic home banking was very appealing. The printing, processing, and return of some 41 billion checks annually in the United States amounted to $41 billion. This figure represented 20% of the annual revenues of banks belonging to the Federal Reserve System. Home banking offered the possibility of a tremendous reduction in operating costs.

In 1983, Chemical Bank under Lipp's guidance introduced a home banking system called the Pronto Two with a goal of four million customers within several years. By 1988, however, the total nationwide users of home banking systems had reached only 100,000 people. An article in *Business Week* (February 29, 1988) remarked: "When Chemical Bank unveiled the idea of home banking in 1983, it projected that 10% of its customers would eventually pay bills and make banking transactions from their home computer. Talk about misplaced optimism. Today, if you're among those who deal with any bank by personal computer, you're in a minority of a mere 100,000 people—and that includes a number of small business operators." Only 30 banks were offering the service by 1988, out of a total of 14,000 banks nationwide.

What Chemical and others later discovered was that several inherent problems with home banking led to consumer resistance. First, customers were reluctant to give up the "float" between when they wrote a check and when it was cashed. With home banking, once the computer authorizes a payment, it is immediately debited from the customer's account.

Second, some investment—for a computer and a modem—was required on the customer's part. It is estimated that only 10% of personal computer owners had modems—and the number of personal computers in homes was limited. Finally, it was a matter of opinion whether writing a paper check was not just as simple and convenient as paying bills by personal computer. Given the costs of such computer systems, it was believed that only by providing a wider range of services, such as home shopping services, would home banking's appeal increase—and that a period of 10 to 15 years was required for market acceptance.

In Lipp's case, his vision was essentially premature for its market. Part of the problem could be attributed to the difficulty of trying to predict a future event for which there is no history. It is extremely difficult to accurately estimate the demand for a particular product or service; the leader is essentially relying on his or her forecast of resources and market trends. The margin for error in these situations is high, and the costs and time horizons for introducing a new product or service are often underestimated. Such miscalculations can forestall a vision.

Two other factors may play important roles. In their own excitement over an idea, leaders may fail to adequately test-market a new product or service, or fail to hear naysayers or overlook contrary signs from the environment. Again, because of successes in other projects (Lipp had had several outstanding ones), they may delude themselves into believing they know their markets more accurately than they actually do. Or their spellbinding ability to lead may not be backed up by an adequate understanding of marketplace trends.

HOW LEADERS COME TO DENY FLAWS IN THEIR VISIONS

All three of these cases share certain characteristics that cause leaders to deny the flaws in their visions. Often, for example, leaders will perceive that their course of action is producing negative results, yet they persist. Why this happens can be explained by a process called "cognitive dissonance," which prevents the leader from changing his course. Simply put, individuals act to keep the commitments they have made because failing to do so would damage their favorable perceptions of themselves. For example, studies have found that executives will sometimes persist in an ineffective course of action simply because they feel they have committed themselves to the decision. This same process, I suspect, occurs with leaders.

Others in the organization, who tend to become dependent on a visionary leader, may perpetuate the problem through their own actions. They may idealize their leader excessively and thus ignore negative aspects and exaggerate the good qualities. As a result, they may carry out their leader's orders unquestioningly—and leaders may in certain cases encourage such behavior because of their needs to dominate and be admired. The resulting sense of omnipotence encourages denial of market and organizational realities. The danger is that leaders will surround themselves with "yes people" and thus fail to receive information that might be important but challenging to the mission. Their excessive confidence and the desire for heroic recognition encourages them to undertake large, risky ventures—but because of their overreliance on themselves and their cadre of "yes people," strategic errors go unnoticed. Bold but poorly thought-out strategies will be designed and implemented. The leader's vision, in essence, becomes a vehicle for his or her own needs for attention and visibility.

Finally, problems with "group-think" can occur where the leader's advisors delude themselves into agreement with the leader or dominant others. In such a case, decision-making becomes distorted, and a more thorough and objective review of possible alternatives to a problem are all but precluded. This is especially true of groups that are very cohesive, highly committed to their success, under pressure, and possessing favorable opinions of themselves—common characteristics in the organizations of powerful and charismatic leaders. When group-think occurs, the opinions of the leader and advisors with closely allied views come to dominate decision making. Doubts that others might have are kept hidden for fear of disapproval. It is more important "to go along to get along" rather than to consider contrary viewpoints.

John DeLorean is an example of a leader who may have purposely created group-think situations. One executive of the DeLorean Motor Company, after being dismissed by DeLorean from the company board, commented: "He told me he knew how some of the things the board was doing bothered my conscience. He said he wanted me to keep a clear conscience and not to worry as much as I did, so he had dropped me from the board. . . . When I told him he couldn't bear having anyone disagree with him so he had to stack the board his way, John . . . just nodded and said, 'That's right. It's my company and I'm going to do what I want to do—when you get your own company, you can do the same' " (Hill Levin, *Grand Delusions*, Viking, 1983, pg. 248).

MANIPULATION THROUGH IMPRESSION MANAGEMENT AND COMMUNICATION SKILLS

Because some leaders are gifted at communicating, it may be quite easy for them to misuse this ability. For instance, they may present information that makes their visions appear more realistic or more appealing than the visions actually are. They may also use their language skills to screen out problems in the larger environment or to foster an illusion of control when, in reality, things are out of control. Exhibit 2 highlights a number of these possible problem areas.

While at General Motors John DeLorean was particularly adept at employing skills of articulation and impression management to promote himself. For example, he would often claim responsibility for projects without acknowledging the contributions of others. His aim was simply to manipulate information so that he appeared as the originating genius. In the case of the highly successful Pontiac GTO, DeLorean claimed to be the engineer at Pontiac who conceived the idea of combining a lighter version of the Tempest body with a powerful engine to create the GTO. In reality, the idea was suggested by a GM colleague.

Exhibit 2
Potential Liabilities in the Leader's Communications
and Impression Management Skills

Exaggerated self-descriptions.

Exaggerated claims for the vision.

A technique of fulfilling stereotypes and images of uniqueness to manipulate audiences.

A habit of gaining commitment by restricting negative information and maximizing positive information.

Use of anecdotes to distract attention away from negative statistical information.

Creation of an illusion of control through affirming information and attributing negative outcomes to external causes.

In *Current Biography*, DeLorean is described as owning "more than 200 patents, including those for the recessed windshield wipers and the overhead-cam engine." However, Hill Levin in his biography of DeLorean reported that the U.S. Patent Office listed a total of 52 patents, none for the wipers or for the overhead cam. Exaggeration of personal deeds was perhaps DeLorean's way of building the legend. What we see with some leaders is that their need for personal recognition and visibility is so high that they feel compelled to distort reality to enhance their own image.

When leaders rely greatly on their impression management skills in communicating, they do themselves a disservice. For instance, research in impression management indicates not only that one's self-descriptions are effective in deceiving an audience, but also that they may deceive the presenter as well. This is especially true when an audience reinforces and approves of the individual's image. Such positive responses encourage leaders to internalize their own self-enhancing descriptions. Especially when exaggeration is only moderate, leaders tend to internalize and believe such claims. So DeLorean may ultimately have come to believe in his own responsibility for the Pontiac GTO.

Considerable research has also been performed on people who are ingratiators—people who play to their audiences by telling them what they want to hear. Two particular tactics that I suspect charismatic leaders use to ingratiate themselves with their audiences are to (1) fulfill stereotypes and (2) create an image of uniqueness.

Research shows that if individuals behave in ways that fulfill the positive stereotypes of an audience, they are more likely to interact successfully with them. This can be achieved by espousing the beliefs, values, and behaviors associated with the stereotype and appearing as the stereotype is expected to look. For example, DeLorean supposedly went to great efforts to present the image of a young, highly successful executive with an entrepreneurial spirit. He underwent cosmetic surgery, dieted from 200 pounds to 160, lifted weights, dyed his grey hair black. He flew only first class. When he ate out, he always obtained the best table. To many, his image fulfilled the stereotype of the successful businessman.

DeLorean used the second tactic—to demonstrate uniqueness—through his unconventional actions while working at General Motors and his tales of innovations at the automobile giant. These stories created the image of a highly successful, unique individual excelling in the corporate world.

In terms of how or what a leader communicates, according to Charles Schwenk, there are several tactics that individuals can use to gain commitment from others even when the circumstances are unethical. Because our ability to process information is limited, we rely on simple biases to reduce the amount of information needed to make a decision. By playing on these biases, a leader can create or heighten commitment to a course of action. They may manipulate information so as to encourage biases in others that will increase confidence in and commitment to the leader's strategic choices. For example, leaders can withhold information that is not favorable to a cause and present instead more positive information. Or they may relate anecdotes designed to draw attention away from statistical information that reflects negatively on their plans.

DeLorean's management of investors in his automobile venture offers one example of this process. If investors had looked at history, they would have found that the odds of his succeeding were slim. Not since the founding of the four major auto companies had a new automobile company succeeded, and there had been many attempts in the interim. Moreover, there was negative statistical information in the company prospectus that might have dissuaded investors. But instead of focusing on such important statistical information, the investors allowed themselves to be swayed by DeLorean's personal character and his impressive press coverage while at General Motors. Could it be that DeLorean aimed to create a flashy image in the minds of investors in order to draw their attention away from other sources of information?

Anecdotal information may be used by the leader not only to influence decision makers' choices, but also to increase their confidence in a choice. The sheer amount of information the leader provides may act to build overconfidence. Various studies of decision making indicate that more information apparently permits people to generate more reasons for justifying their decisions and, in turn, increases the confidence of others in the decisions. Leaders might also create an illusion of control by selectively providing information that affirms they are in control and attributes failures or problems to external causes. All of these tactics may be used by leaders to mislead their direct reports and their investors.

MANAGEMENT PRACTICES THAT BECOME LIABILITIES

The managerial practices of leaders also have certain inherent liabilities. Some leaders are known for their excessively impulsive, autocratic management style. Others become so disruptive through their unconventional behavior that their organizations mobilize against them. Moreover, leaders can at times be poor at managing their superiors and peers. In general, some of the very management practices that make leaders unique may also lead to their downfall.

Leaders' liabilities fall into several categories: (1) the way they manage relations with important others, (2) their management style with direct reports, and (3) their thoroughness and attention to certain administrative detail. Typical problems associated with each of these categories are shown in Exhibit 3. We will start with the first category: managing relations with important others.

Managing Upwards and Sideways

Some leaders—particularly charismatic leaders in large organizations—seem to be very poor at managing upwards and sideways. Because they are usually unconventional advocates of radical reform, they may often alienate others in the organization, including their own bosses. The charismatic leader's unconventional actions may trigger the ire of forces within the organization which then act to immobilize him

Exhibit 3
Potential Liabilities of a Leader's Management Practices

Poor management of people networks, especially superiors and peers.
Unconventional behavior that alienates.
Creation of disruptive "in group/out group" rivalries.
An autocratic, controlling management style.
An informal/impulsive style that is disruptive and dysfunctional.
Alternation between idealizing and devaluing others, particularly direct reports .
Creation of excessive dependence in others.
Failure to manage details and effectively act as an administrator.
Attention to the superficial.
Absence from operations.
Failure to develop successors of equal ability.

or her. Leaders' aggressive style may also alienate many potential supporters and ultimately leave them without sufficient political support for their ambitious plans. This problem is common when charismatic leaders are brought in from the outside; their radically different values and approaches may alienate the rest of the organization.

This kind of situation occurred at General Motors when Ross Perot was made a board member. Once on the board, Perot became one of the company's most outspoken critics. As an entrepreneur, he was quite naturally accustomed to running his own show, and after his company, Electronic Data Systems (EDS), merged with GM he insisted that any changes made in EDS procedures be cleared through him. His style and outspokenness were so much at odds with the General Motors culture that the company offered Perot $700 million in stock to step down from the board—an offer he finally accepted.

A second problem related to managing relations within large organizations is the tendency of certain leaders to cultivate a feeling of being "special" among members of their operating units. This practice is often accompanied by a corresponding depreciation of other parts of the corporation. In short, the leader creates an "us versus them" attitude. Although this heightens the motivation of the leader's group, it further alienates other groups that may be important for resources or political support. Steven Jobs did this with the MacIntosh division at Apple Computer. Even though the company's Apple II Computer provided the profits, Jobs consistently downplayed that division's importance. He essentially divided the company into two rivals. He was fond of telling people in the MacIntosh division, "This is the cream of Apple. This is the future of Apple." He even went so far as telling marketing managers for Apple II that they worked for an outdated, clumsy organization. Jobs's later departure from Apple stemmed in part from morale problems he created within the company by using this tactic.

In another case, the charismatic president of a division in a large corporation used as his group's emblem a mascot symbol of the TV cartoon character Roadrunner. (In the cartoons, Roadrunner was particularly adept at outwitting a wily coyote.) To him, his division managers were the "roadrunners" who were smarter and faster than the corporate "coyotes" who laid roadblocks in their path. He also had a habit of ignoring corporate staff requests for reports or information, and he returned their reports with "STUPID IDEA" stamped on the front cover. Although such behaviors and tactics fostered a sense of camaraderie and aggressiveness within the charismatic leader's division, they were ultimately detrimental both to the leader and to the organization. In this case, the executive eventually stepped down from the organization.

Relationships with Subordinates

Highly directive and visionary leaders are often described as autocratic. Jobs, for example, has been described as dictatorial. I suspect that in many cases the vision is such a personification of the leader that he or she becomes obsessed about its perfection or implementation. Leaders' natural impatience with the pace of the vision's achievement exacerbates the problem and encourages them to be more hands-on, more controlling.

There also appears to be, at times, an impulsive dynamic at work in the way leaders manage—and at such times they will override subordinates' suggestions or insights. Again, this occurs especially in relation to accomplishing the vision. DeLorean is described as increasing his production of the DeLorean car by 50% in the belief that his product would become an overnight sensation. Production went to an annual rate of 30,000 cars. This was done in spite of market research that showed total annual sales of between 4,000 and 10,000 cars. A company executive lamented, "Our figures showed that this was a viable company with half the production. If the extravagence had been cut out of New York, we could have broken even making just 6,000 cars a year. But that wasn't fast enough for John. First he had to build his paper empire in the stock market. A creditable success was not enough for him" (ibid., pg. 282).

Steven Jobs is known to have darted in and out of operations causing havoc: "He would leap-frog back and forth among various projects, dictating designs, with little or no knowledge of whether or not the technology even existed to make his ideas work" (L. Butcher, *Accidental Millionaire*, Paragon House, 1988, pp. 140–141).

Another potential problem can arise from a style of informality when managing the hierarchy of an organization—this is especially true of charismatic leaders. Advantages of this style are that leaders are highly visible, approachable, and able to react quickly to issues and problems. The drawback is that they often violate the chain of command by going around direct reports and thus undercut their direct reports' authority. If a particular project or idea interests them, they do not hesitate to become involved, sometimes to the detriment of the project managers' responsibilities. DeLorean would drop in on his engineers to suggest what seemed trivial ideas. One company engineer said: "He came in one day to say we should hook into the cooling system and make a little icebox for a six-pack of beer behind the driver's seat. Or, another time, he told us to work on a sixty-watt radio speaker that could be detached and hung outside the car for picnics" (H. Levin, ibid., pg. 267).

Administrative Skills

Some visionary leaders are so absorbed by the "big picture" that they fail to understand essential details—except for "pet" projects in which they become excessively involved. Iaccoca, for instance, turned over most of the day-to-day operations to others as he became increasingly famous. As a result, he lost touch with new model planning. He himself admitted: "If I made one mistake, it was delegating all the product development and not going to a single meeting" (ibid., pg. 267). A DeLorean executive complained: "He [John DeLorean] just didn't have time for the details of the project. But attention to detail is everything" (ibid., p. 267). Then, too, leaders may get so caught up in corporate stardom that they become absentee leaders. Again, Iaccoca is an example. His success at Chrysler led to his becoming a best-selling author, a U.S. presidential prospect, and the head of the $277 million fund-raising campaign for the Statue of Liberty—all of which distracted him from the important task of leading Chrysler.

Because these individuals are often excited by ideas, they may at times be poor implementors. Once an idea begins to appear as a tangible reality, I suspect they feel the need to move on to the next challenge, thereby leaving subordinates scrambling to pick up the pieces. Furthermore, because some leaders have high needs for visibility, they gravitate toward activities that afford them high people contact and recognition. Such activities are generally not performed at a desk while paying careful attention to the details.

Succession Problems

A true leader is usually a strong figure and, as noted, often one upon whom subordinates develop dependencies. Thus it is difficult for others with leadership potential to develop fully in the shadow of such leaders. For while they may actively coach their subordinates, I suspect that it is extremely difficult for them to develop others to be leaders *of equal power*. Leaders simply enjoy the limelight too much to share it, so when they ultimately depart, a leadership vacuum is created. Moreover, under charismatic leadership authority may be highly centralized around the leader—and this is an arrangement that, unfortunately, weakens the authority structures that are normally dispersed throughout an organization.

It's clear that many of the qualities of a strong leader have both a positive and a negative face. That's why the presence of leaders entails risks for their direct reports, their organizations, and at times their societies. They must be managed with care. The negatives, however, must always be weighed in light of the positives. For companies and society, the need for organizational change and strategic vision may be so great that the risks of confrontation, unconventionality, and so on may seem a small price to pay. It is also possible that organizations and educational institutions can train, socialize, and manage future leaders in ways that will minimize their negative qualities.

Leaders Who Self-Destruct: The Causes and Cures

Manfred F. R. Kets de Vries

Why do some people derail when they reach the top? What psychological forces affect executives when they attain a position of power? Why does an executive who seems bright, likeable, and well adjusted, suddenly resort to strange behavior when he or she becomes chief executive officer?

There are no simple answers to these questions. In order to address them, we must deepen our understanding of the psychodynamics of leadership and the vicissitudes of power. A number of clinical insights from dynamic psychiatry and psychoanalysis may help in our analysis.

First, however, consider an example that illustrates the kind of irrational behavior described above. Before Robert Clark[1] assumed the presidency of the Solan Corporation, he had always been well liked. His supervisors had been impressed by his capacity for work, his helpful attitude, his dedication, and his imaginative method of solving problems. He eventually crowned his seemingly brilliant career by being selected to succeed Solan's former CEO.

In the period immediately after Clark took over, he received many accolades for his role in taking a number of long overdue steps. Gradually, however, after the initial enthusiasm had cleared up, many of his old colleagues concluded that he had apparently undergone a personality change. He had become less accessible; his once widely acclaimed open-door policy and advocacy of participative management had disappeared. He had become increasingly authoritarian, impatient, and careless of the feelings of others.

The organizational effects of Clark's transformation were quickly forthcoming. In their desire to please him, key executives would jostle

---

[1] "Robert Clark" is a pseudonym, and the name "the Solan Corporation" is fictitious. The following individuals and organizations mentioned in this article are also identified by pseudonyms or fictitious names: Peter Harris and the Noro Corporation; Ted Howell and the Larix Corporation; and Ted Nolan and the Dalton Corporation.

for his attention and waste time and energy on power games and intra-company squabbles rather than on strategic decisions. Company morale sank to an all-time low, and the financial results were predictably dismal.

What happened to Clark—and *why* did it happen? Certain psychological forces—his own and those of his followers—came into play, creating a multitude of problems. Here are three reasons why this occurred:

- Succession to the top leadership position in an organization is necessarily isolating in that it separates leaders from others (who now directly report to them) and leaves them without peers. As a result, their own normal dependency needs for contact, support, and reassurance rise up and overwhelm them.
- Whether consciously or unconsciously, employees expect their organization's leaders to be infallible and even gifted to some degree with "magical" powers.
- Troubled by guilt feelings about their success and fearful that it may not last, leaders may unconsciously cause themselves to fail.

To some degree, every human being suffers from these reactions and feelings. History has provided us with many examples of leaders whose behavior became pathological in the extreme once they attained power: political leaders such as King Saul, Caligula, Adolf Hitler, and Colonel Quaddafi, or business leaders such as Howard Hughes.

I am not suggesting that each business leader will resort to pathological behavior upon reaching the top of his or her organization. What differentiates those who "crash" from those who don't is the latter's ability to stay in touch with reality and take these psychological forces in stride. Many leaders are very good at handling the pressures that leadership brings; indeed, some individuals who may previously have been rather colorless turn into great leaders when they attain positions of power. However, some leaders just can't manage; the regressive pulls simply become too strong. Since we are all susceptible to these psychological forces, I will discuss their dynamics.

ISOLATION FROM REALITY

On June 18, 1982, the body of Roberto Calvi, Chairman of Ambrosiano, Italy's largest private bank, was found hanging under Black-friars

Bridge in London. The exact circumstances of his death may never be known; however, this was certainly an ignominious ending for one of Italy's most prominent bankers. It was also one of the saddest developments in modern Italy's largest financial scandal.

Although the extent of Calvi's involvement may never be known, he certainly carried a heavy responsibility. His secretive, control-oriented management style didn't help, and his remoteness was an added complication. In newspaper accounts of that time, Calvi was described as the most private of financiers, an individual who was very reserved and formal, a man for whom communication was a difficult task. From the various descriptions we have of him, he was apparently a person who would internalize his problems rather than confide in anyone. Here was an individual who had a very detached way of dealing with others.

Why did Calvi get himself into this situation? We cannot really answer this question; however, we do know that, in spite of the sea of executives reporting to Calvi, he apparently ended up very much alone in dealing with his problems. There was apparently no one he could turn to, which seems paradoxical in light of his contacts and his very active life. Unfortunately, this kind of isolation seems all too common among people who head organizations, and it can affect their sense of reality.

The term "loneliness of command" has been used frequently in the context of leadership. The inability to test one's perceptions, the tendency to lose touch with reality because one occupies a top position, is a danger anyone can fall victim to when in a leadership position.

For example, when Peter Harris became president of the Noro Corporation, he thought that his personal and professional lives would continue more or less as they had before. The appointment had been very routine; as one of the senior vice-presidents of his company, he had been the logical choice for the job.

In reality, however, Harris had to deal with more changes in his lifestyle than he had expected. Soon after he assumed the presidency, he realized that, in spite of his efforts to maintain his previous amicable working style, he was creating more distance between himself and his employees. Although he tried for a while to be one of the boys, he discovered that this was no longer possible. In short, Harris now had difficulty socializing with and having to make tough career decisions about the same person; life seemed much simpler if he retained some distance. He had also discovered that friendliness to an employee was quickly interpreted by others as favoritism; attempts at closeness by an employee were similarly viewed as a lobbying effort.

Although Harris simplified matters by keeping his distance, this had a price. He increasingly felt a sense of isolation, a loss of intimacy. He could talk to his wife, but that didn't seem to be enough. He wanted to confide in someone more familiar with what happened in the business, someone on whom he could test his ideas.

Sometimes he would think nostalgically of the time before he became president. Occasionally, he found himself longing for a way to resurrect the broken network of relationships, searching for a way of sharing, but this had become impossible. A side-effect was that he was becoming increasingly irritated about having gotten himself into this position; it was not what he had expected. He began to wonder if his increasing aloofness was affecting his ability to make decisions.

The examples of Roberto Calvi and Peter Harris show us one of the pitfalls of assuming the position of CEO; for some it becomes a mixed blessing. The organization's leaders are supposed to take care of their organization's existing strategic and structural needs; they are expected to articulate a vision of the future and show others how to achieve it. But there are a number of other aspects to leadership; one of these is that leaders should take care of the dependency needs of their employees. Given the universal nature of these needs, however, one must ask who takes care of the *leaders'* dependency needs? When no such person is available, some leaders may suffer from anxiety associated with loneliness and disconnectedness; some may even lose touch with reality.

When leaders reach the top of their organizations, they may be dismayed to learn that their network of complex mutual dependencies has been changed forever. Some leaders can overcome this and find other forms of gratification; others may even enjoy experiencing a certain degree of detachment. However, many leaders become upset at finding themselves in this situation and may react accordingly. They may feel frustrated and angry and may even experience a seemingly irrational desire to "get even" with those who have not fulfilled their dependency needs. The resulting scapegoating behavior can create a very politicized organization torn by interdepartmental rivalry.

However, aggression can also be turned inward, which can lead to depression and to alcohol and drug abuse. If these extreme responses continue, they can have dire consequences for the organization.

THE DANGERS OF TRANSFERENCE

Apart from acting as catalysts in the achievement of their organizations' objectives, leaders can also become the embodiment of their employees' ideals, wishes, feelings, and fantasies. By transforming their subjective fantasies into objective reality, employees may imbue their leaders with mystical qualities—a phenomenon that may occur despite their leaders' attempts to resist it. Employees may consciously or unconsciously perceive and respond to their leaders not according to objective reality, but as though the leader were a significant authority figure from their past, such as a parent or teacher. When this occurs, the boundaries between the past and present may disappear.

As with any authority figure, leaders are a prime outlet for such emotional reactions. Given their position, they can easily retrigger in their employees previously unresolved conflicts with significant figures from their past. When this happens, regressive behavior may occur: Employees may endow their leaders with the same omniscience that they attributed in childhood to parents or other significant figures.

This psychological process—the distortion of the whole context of one's relationship—is called *transference* and is present in all meaningful human interactions. Although leaders may find it hard to accept, all interpersonal exchanges involve both realistic *and* transference reactions—and leaders are particularly susceptible to this kind of confusion.

Transference reactions can be acted out in several ways and can affect both leaders and their employees. One common manifestation is for employees to "idealize" their leaders in an attempt to recreate the sense of security and importance they felt in childhood, when they were cared for by apparently omnipotent and perfect parents. As authority figures, leaders fall easily into an employee's subconscious definition of a "parent" role. Employees may therefore want to endow their leaders with unrealistic powers and attributes, which in turn can inflate their leaders' self-esteem.

During periods of organizational upheaval such as cutbacks or expansions, employees are particularly anxious to cling to their beliefs in their leaders' powers as a way of maintaining their own sense of security and identity. For this reason, employees will do anything to please or charm their leaders—including giving in to their extravagant whims. Thus, in times of organizational crisis, leaders may conceivably be surrounded by "yes-men." This lack of critical opinion can obviously have dire consequences for their organizations. If leaders get too much uncritical admiration from their employees, they may begin to believe that they really are as perfect, intelligent, or powerful as others think. Losing one's grasp on reality in this way is a common human failing, but it can be particularly dangerous for leaders since they often have the power to act on their delusions of grandeur. When a CEO stops listening to criticism and embarks on an overambitious expansion or orders the unnecessary construction of a new company headquarters, this process may indeed be at work.

As a result of their grandiose delusions, some leaders will favor highly dependent employees who are in search of an all-knowledgeable, all-powerful leader. However, such leaders can be very callous about these employees' needs; they may exploit them and then drop them when they no longer serve their purposes.

Such employees may legitimately react angrily to this type of behavior. However, another less obvious process may also be at work: Employees may subconsciously blame their leaders for failing to live up to their own exaggerated expectations. Angry about this, and perhaps aggravated by callous, exploitative behavior, these employees may find their attitudes quickly turning from admiration to hostility and rebellion. Like children, such people tend to divide all experiences, perceptions, and feelings into unambiguously "good" and "bad" categories. Thus, although new CEOs may initially have been welcomed as messiahs, they may be surprised to find out how suddenly their employees' mood can shift. After one setback, employees may view their leader as being responsible for all the company's problems, even if these problems developed long before his or her arrival.

Faced with this transition in employee attitudes from admiration to rebellion and anger, leaders may become irritated and even develop slight feelings of persecution. But leaders have to realize that this is to a certain extent inevitable and that they must exert a certain amount of self-control.

Some leaders, however, may be tempted to retaliate—possibly by firing their critics. There are some leaders who tend to mentally divide their employees into those who are "with" them and those who are "against" them; such an outlook is liable to breed an organizational culture of fear and suspicion. Employees who are "with" their leaders share their outlooks and support them even if they engage in unrealistic, grandiose schemes or imagine the existence of malicious plots, sabotage, and enemies. Effective leaders, however, know how to contain their excessive emotional reactions and avoid being caught up in groundless fears.

The Case of Ted Howell

To illustrate how these psychological forces can affect a leader, consider the following incident. As a result of the unexpected death of his predecessor, Ted Howell was appointed president of the Larix Corporation, a company in the electronics equipment field. Howell had been found with the help of a headhunter who had highly recommended him. He had previously held a senior staff position in a company in the same line of business; Howell's knowledge of the industry had been a key factor in convincing Larix's board to take him on.

Soon after his arrival, Larix's board members saw signs that Howell was having difficulties dealing with the pressures of the job. A number of rash decisions made in his first week at the office were the first indications of trouble. But in spite of these mistakes, everything initially turned out better than expected. First, one of the company's main competitors went out of business, which freed up an important segment of the market. In addition, one of Howell's employees came up with an excellent marketing idea that he quickly adopted and that proved very successful. Some executives were disturbed because their colleague never received credit for it; nevertheless, these two factors helped to get Larix back into the black.

Unfortunately, this success apparently went to Howell's head. After the turnaround, he embarked on a dramatic expansion program, ignoring cautionary remarks made by his employees, consultants, and bankers. Other steps were taken, including the relocation of the company's headquarters to what Howell thought were more suitable surroundings and the acquisition of an expensive company plane. These two actions put a heavy strain on the company's finances. Those executives who expressed disagreement or concern about the new moves were fired; consultants who suggested that Howell change course suffered the same fate. In the end, only sycophants who were willing to share his grandiose ideas and accept his aggressive outbursts were left.

As expected, the unrealistic plans and high expenditures put the company into the red. However, Howell was unwilling to admit his role in the debacle. When questioned at directors' meetings, he would become defensive and deny any responsibility for the losses; instead, he would blame them on faulty moves made by his predecessor or on vindictive action by executives no longer in his employ. In his opinion, a turnaround was just around the corner. To an increasing number of board members, however, Howell's behavior was becoming unacceptable. Eventually, having become impatient with the continuing losses and with Howell's imperious, paranoid behavior, they managed to remove him.

As in the case of Robert Clark, here was an individual who was apparently well adjusted and who had performed well in his previous job. After his promotion, however, when he was subjected to the pressures of being a leader, this same individual began to behave irrationally.

One contributing factor was apparently the excessively high expectations that Howell's employees had for him. Overwhelmed by all the attention that he was suddenly receiving, he apparently allowed his sense of reality to become distorted. Perhaps because he couldn't withstand these psychological pressures, he may have assumed that some of the qualities ascribed to him were true and behaved accordingly. When his grandiose actions backfired and he couldn't deliver, his employees reacted with anger. Howell began to show signs of paranoid behavior and retaliated by putting the blame on others.

This distortive reaction pattern is another factor that contributes to this strange, irrational behavior we sometimes find in leaders. These reaction patterns are semidormant tendencies with which we all have to deal and which arise easily in leadership situations. As I have indicated, some leaders find it very difficult to withstand these pressures.

THE FEAR OF SUCCESS

In a success-oriented society, failure is looked upon as a catastrophe, and to some extent we all fear it. But while the fear of failure is quite understandable as a reactivating mechanism for feelings of incompetence, fear of success is more of a mystery. In fact, Sigmund Freud tried to demystify some of the dynamics behind this fear in an article entitled

"Those Wrecked by Success" (1916). He noted that some people become sick when a deeply rooted and longed-for desire comes to fulfillment. He gave as an example a professor who cherished a wish to succeed his teacher. When this wish eventually came true, the professor became plagued by feelings of depression and self-deprecation and found that he was unable to work.

The Case of Ted Nolan

Sometimes we can see how top executives fall victim to this form of anxiety. Reflecting on his career, Ted Nolan recalled being surprised when he was asked to succeed Larry Fulton as president of the Dalton Corporation. Like many of his colleagues, he had thought that the vice-president of marketing was the person most likely to be chosen by the board; however, he certainly didn't protest when asked.

When his appointment came through, however, Nolan noticed that he felt slightly ill at ease, a feeling that didn't go away when he took over. He became increasingly preoccupied with the question of whether he could hack it. He began to have difficulties sleeping at night, tormenting himself by wondering whether his previous day's actions had been correct. He often felt like an impostor, having just been "lucky" to get the job. To make matters worse, he also developed a full-fledged drinking problem. At work he found it increasingly difficult to concentrate and make decisions. He wondered how many of his problems in handling the top job were noticed by his board members. When were they going to realize that they had made a mistake, and that he was really an incompetent fake?

However, as Nolan said himself, he had been fortunate. His wife had been a great support to him. Because of the changes in his behavior, she had encouraged him to see a psychotherapist. As he explored the underlying causes of his anxiety with the therapist, he began to realize that he had always been anxious whenever he was put in a position of responsibility; previously, however, he had handled it better because there had always been others in a similar situation with whom he could talk. This time, however, he was really on his own.

With the psychotherapist's help, Nolan discovered the relationship between his past and his present feelings. In reviewing his life, he realized how successful he had been, having overcome tremendous handicaps to work himself up to a position far above those held by his parents and siblings. He also recognized that this success had come with feelings of guilt and betrayal of his origins. Having risen so far above his roots apparently contributed to his current anxiety. He had explored these feelings with his psychotherapist and had succeeded in becoming more objective by integrating these feelings with his current situation. Being able to see those connections and working through these insights had brought him greater peace of mind. What's more, he felt he was now doing a fairly good job in his new position.

What Nolan's experience exemplifies is that some people believe, whether consciously or unconsciously, that success can only be attained by displacing someone else. For them, success is perceived as a symbolic victory over the parents or siblings of childhood. This is particularly true for those individuals who have never resolved rivalrous feeling towards the latter. If this is the case, to be successful and to have tangible accomplishments in adulthood can turn into a Pyrrhic victory.

In a case like this, success becomes symbolically equated with betrayal. Success makes these individuals stand out and be noticed; it becomes a provocative, hostile act that not only leads to feelings of guilt but also invites retribution. As in childhood, being in such a position may arouse the envy and resentment of others. Retaliation will be feared from those individuals with whom the person is competing. Thus unresolved competitive feelings from the past become confused with present-day reality. Since success is feared to have negative consequences, these successful individuals may downgrade their accomplishments or even view themselves as impostors. They may have difficulty believing that they have achieved success through their own abilities.

In management situations, these irrational thoughts and behavior patterns may not become evident as long as the executive in question is one out of many. As long as such patterns are not particularly noticeable, the problem may be subdued. But as soon as these people reach a leadership position, they may become anxious, deprecate their accomplishments, and even engage in self-defeating behavior.

STAYING ON COURSE

I have described some of the more problematic aspects of leadership, as well as depicted a number of psychological forces that can negatively affect individuals in leadership positions. Many of these forces will often be brought to bear simultaneously; leaders who cannot withstand them will be the ones who cannot manage. Stress reactions may follow, and such individuals may lose touch with reality.

Leaders should be aware of the psychological forces and should be able to identify potential signs of trouble. To prevent stress reactions and irrational behavior from coming to the fore, leaders should engage in a regular process of critical self-evaluation. Those who are interested in the vicissitudes of leadership may want to reflect on the following questions:

- How accessible is the leader?
- How does the leader react to bad news or criticism from an employee?
- Is the leader able to discuss any problems or ideas with colleagues?
- Does the leader think of employees in terms of those who are "with" and those who are "against" him or her?
- How realistic is the leader's vision of the company's future? Is there a large discrepancy between his or her own and others' points of view?
- Is the leader willing to accept responsibility if things go wrong, or does he or she blame "the others?"
- Is the leader quick to take offense and feel unfairly treated? Does he or she have a great need to "blow his or her own horn?"
- Does the leader feel anxious and guilty when he or she is successful and have difficulties believing that his or her professional success is caused by his or her own accomplishments and not by sheer luck?

In considering these questions, we should not forget that the ability to change fantasy into reality, given the power leaders have, can be like the mythological siren's call and may cause an individual to change as soon as he or she attains a leadership position. The potential for losing touch with reality and behaving irrationally is dormant in all of us.

Paradoxically enough, it is sometimes this very irrational quality that is needed to make some leaders effective. Paranoid reactions and visionary experiences may feed very well into certain types of situations, and many political and religious leaders have acted in just this way (consider Joseph Stalin or the Ayatollah Khomeini).

However, in spite of what may have been an initially enthusiastic reception, there is a dark side to this behavior. To evoke regressive tendencies in others and to provoke aggression is to set in motion that which may be impossible to stop.

What Organizations—and Their Leaders—Can Do

This cautionary note—on a somewhat lesser scale—is also true in business situations. Here, however, it may be somewhat easier to set up safeguards against the excess of leadership. Leaders in contemporary society have to deal with the government, unions, banks, or other stakeholders that may take on the role of a countervailing power, helping to keep the leaders in touch with reality. In many large organizations, leaders will inherit an organizational structure with different checks and balances in the form of distribution of key policy decisions over a number of individuals and various agencies that will circumscribe their behavior. Moreover, in large organizations, organizational processes find their own momentum and are resistant to dramatic change. Social systems have their own way of providing a "safety belt" for individuals through their inherent structure.

Apart from the various external checks on leaders' actions that may prevent these irrational manifestations from coming to the fore, leaders themselves can take preventive action. Encouraging frank feedback from outsiders such as external directors, bankers, and consultants is one way of preventing these regressive forces from gaining the upper hand. Individuals from outside the organization usually possess a very different frame of reference, and their vision will be considerably less distorted by the existing organizational dynamics. They can provide more of an overall view and warn about potential sources of trouble. Board members in particular can play a critical role; selecting a strong, independent board that is really willing to enforce its auditing role rather than just acting as a rubber stamp is one of the best ways to keep an organization on course and prevent it from losing touch with reality.

Another useful countervailing force can be participation in top executive training programs. These programs can provide a nonthreatening environment in which leaders can discuss their working experience with colleagues and professionals exposed to similar problems; such situations will enhance reality testing. Mutual comparison of potential problem areas may provide leaders with a revelation, and insight is the first step toward constructive change.

A SHARED RESPONSIBILITY

Leaders and their employees are like partners in a dance: The experience can be very exhilarating, but the dancers can also fall over each others' feet. Both parties carry a heavy responsibility for the interchange to work. To make this possible, they must be willing to listen and have respect for each other's point of view. This requires a certain amount of self-knowledge and a preparedness to reflect on their actions. Empathetic listening becomes a *sine qua non* to a real understanding of the leader-employee dialogue. Thus in spite of all the countervailing forces mentioned, in the end it is the relationship of equity, consistency, and trust that will make for frank interchange between leaders and employees and will constitute the strongest force in preventing regressive behavior in leadership. And given the nature of power in organizations, making this relationship work is the real challenge for all concerned.

On the Folly of Rewarding A, While Hoping for B

Steven Kerr

Whether dealing with monkeys, rats, or human beings, it is hardly controversial to state that most organisms seek information concerning what activities are rewarded, and then seek to do (or at least pretend to do) those things, often to the virtual exclusion of activities not rewarded. The extent to which this occurs of course will depend on the perceived attractiveness of the rewards offered, but neither operant nor expectancy theorists would quarrel with the essence of this notion.

Nevertheless, numerous examples exist of reward systems that are fouled up in that behaviors which are rewarded are those which the rewarder is trying to *discourage*, while the behavior he desires is not being rewarded at all.

In an effort to understand and explain this phenomenon, this paper presents examples from society, from organizations in general, and from profit making firms in particular.

SOCIETAL EXAMPLES

Politics

Official goals are "purposely vague and general and do not indicate . . . the host of decisions that must be made among alternative ways of achieving official goals and the priority of multiple goals . . ." (6, p. 66). They usually may be relied on to offend absolutely no one, and in this sense can be considered high acceptance, low quality goals. An example might be "build better schools." Operative goals are higher in quality but lower in acceptance, since they specify where the money will come from, what alternative goals will be ignored, etc.

The American citizenry supposedly wants its candidates for public office to set forth operative goals, making their proposed programs "perfectly clear," specifying sources and uses of funds, etc. However, since operative goals are lower in acceptance, and since aspirants to public office need acceptance (from at least 50.1 percent of the people), most politicians prefer to speak only of official goals, at least until after the election. They of course would agree to speak at the operative level if "punished" for not doing so. The electorate could do this by refusing to support candidates who do not speak at the operative level.

Instead, however, the American voter typically punishes (withholds support from) candidates who frankly discuss where the money will come from, rewards politicians who speak only of official goals, but hopes that candidates (despite the reward system) will discuss the issues operatively. It is academic whether it was moral for Nixon, for example, to refuse to discuss his "secret plan" to end the Vietnam war, his operative goals concerning the lifting of price controls, the reshuffling of his cabinet, etc. The point is that the reward system made such refusal rational.

It seems worth mentioning that no manuscript can adequately define what is "moral" and what is not. However, examination of costs and benefits, combined with knowledge of what motivates a particular individual, often will suffice to determine what for him is "rational."[1] If the reward system is so designed that it is irrational to be moral, this does not necessarily mean that immorality will result. But is this not asking for trouble?

War

If some oversimplification may be permitted, let it be assumed that the primary goal of the organization (Pentagon, Luftwaffe, or whatever) is to win. Let it be assumed further that the primary goal of most individuals on the front lines is to get home alive. Then there appears to be an important conflict in goals—personally rational behavior by those at the bottom will endanger goal attainment by those at the top.

But not necessarily! It depends on how the reward system is set up. The Vietnam war was indeed a study of disobedience and rebellion, with terms such as "fragging" (killing one's own commanding officer)

---

[1] In Simon's (8, pp. 76–77) terms, a decision is "subjectively rational" if it maximizes an individual's valued outcomes so far as his knowledge permits. A decision is "personally rational" if it is oriented toward the individual's goals.

and "search and evade" becoming part of the military vocabulary. The difference in subordinates' acceptance of authority between World War II and Vietnam is reported to be considerable, and veterans of the Second World War often have been quoted as being outraged at the mutinous actions of many American soldiers in Vietnam.

Consider, however, some critical differences in the reward system in use during the two conflicts. What did the GI in World War II want? To go home. And when did he get to go home? When the war was won! If he disobeyed the orders to clean out the trenches and take the hills, the war would not be won and he would not go home. Furthermore, what were his chances of attaining his goal (getting home alive) if he obeyed the orders compared to his chances if he did not? What is being suggested is that the rational soldier in World War II, *whether patriotic or not*, probably found it expedient to obey.

Consider the reward system in use in Vietnam. What did the man at the bottom want? To go home. And when did he get to go home? When his tour of duty was over! This was the case *whether or not* the war was won. Furthermore, concerning the relative chance of getting home alive by obeying orders compared to the chance if they were disobeyed, it is worth noting that a mutineer in Vietnam was far more likely to be assigned rest and rehabilitation (on the assumption that fatigue was the cause) than he was to suffer any negative consequence.

In his description of the "zone of indifference," Barnard stated that "a person can and will accept a communication as authoritative only when . . . at the time of his decision, he believes it to be compatible with his personal interests as a whole" (1, p. 165). In light of the reward system used in Vietnam, would it not have been personally irrational for some orders to have been obeyed? Was not the military implementing a system which *rewarded* disobedience, while *hoping* that soldiers (despite the reward system) would obey orders?

Medicine

Theoretically, a physician can make either of two types of error, and intuitively one seems as bad as the other. A doctor can pronounce a patient sick when he is actually well, thus causing him needless anxiety and expense, curtailment of enjoyable foods and activities, and even physical danger by subjecting him to needless medication and surgery. Alternately, a doctor can label a sick person well, and thus avoid treating what may be a serious, even fatal ailment. It might be natural to conclude that physicians seek to minimize both types of error.

Such a conclusion would be wrong.[2] It is estimated that numerous Americans are presently afflicted with iatrogenic (physican *caused*) illnesses (7). This occurs when the doctor is approached by someone complaining of a few stray symptoms. The doctor classifies and organizes these symptoms, gives them a name, and obligingly tells the patient what further symptoms may be expected. This information often acts as a self-fulfilling prophecy, with the result that from that day on the patient for all practical purposes is sick.

Why does this happen? Why are physicians so reluctant to sustain a type 2 error (pronouncing a sick person well) that they will tolerate many type 1 errors? Again, a look at the reward system is needed. The punishments for a type 2 error are real: guilt, embarrassment, and the threat of lawsuit and scandal. On the other hand, a type 1 error (labeling a well person sick) "is sometimes seen as sound clinical practice, indicating a healthy conservative approach to medicine" (7, p. 69). Type 1 errors also are likely to generate increased income and a stream of steady customers who, being well in a limited physiological sense, will not embarrass the doctor by dying abruptly.

Fellow physicians and the general public therefore are really *rewarding* type 1 errors and at the same time *hoping* fervently that doctors will try not to make them.

GENERAL ORGANIZATIONAL EXAMPLES

Rehabilitation Centers and Orphanages

In terms of the prime beneficiary classification (2, p. 42) organizations such as these are supposed to exist for the "public-in-contact," that is, clients. The orphanage therefore theoretically is interested in placing

---

[2] In one study (4) of 14,867 films for signs of tuberculosis, 1,216 positive readings turned out to be clinically negative; only 24 negative readings proved clinically active, a ratio of 50 to 1.

as many children as possible in good homes. However, often orphan-ages surround themselves with so many rules concerning adoption that it is nearly impossible to pry a child out of the place. Orphanages may deny adoption unless the applicants are a married couple, both of the same religion as the child, without history of emotional or vocational instability, with a specified minimum income and a private room for the child, etc.

If the primary goal is to place children in good homes, then the rules ought to constitute means toward that goal. Goal displacement results when these "means become ends-in-themselves that displace the origi-nal goals" (2, p. 229).

To some extent these rules are required by law. But the influence of the reward system on the orphanage's management should not be ignored. Consider, for example, that the:

1. Number of children enrolled often is the most important determinant of the size of the allocated budget.
2. Number of children under the director's care also will affect the size of his staff.
3. Total organizational size will determine largely the director's pres-tige at the annual conventions, in the community, etc.

Therefore, to the extent that staff size, total budget, and personal prestige are valued by the orphanage's executive personnel, it becomes rational for them to make it difficult for children to be adopted. After all, who wants to be the director of the smallest orphanage in the state?

If the reward system errs in the opposite direction, paying off only for placements, extensive goal displacement again is likely to result. A common example of vocational rehabilitation in many states, for exam-ple, consists of placing someone in a job for which he has little interest and few qualifications, for two months or so, and then "rehabilitating" him again in another position. Such behavior is quite consistent with the prevailing reward system, which pays off for the number of individuals placed in any position for 60 days or more. Rehabilitation counselors also confess to competing with one another to place relatively skilled clients, sometimes ignoring persons with few skills who would be harder to place. Extensively disabled clients find that counselors often prefer to work with those whose disabilities are less severe.

Universities

Society *hopes* that teachers will not neglect their teaching responsibilities but *rewards* them almost entirely for research and publications. This is most true at the large and prestigious universities. Cliches such as "good research and good teaching go together" notwithstanding, professors often find that they must choose between teaching and research oriented activities when allocating their time. Rewards for good teaching usually are limited to outstanding teacher awards, which are given to only a small percentage of good teachers and which usually bestow little money and fleeting prestige. Punishments for poor teaching also are rare.

Rewards for research and publications, on the other hand, and punishments for failure to accomplish these, are commonly administered by universities at which teachers are employed. Furthermore, publication oriented resumés usually will be well received at other universities, whereas teaching credentials, harder to document and quantify, are much less transferable. Consequently it is rational for university teachers to concentrate on research, even if to the detriment of teaching and at the expense of their students.

By the same token, it is rational for students to act based upon the goal displacement which has occurred within universities concerning what they are rewarded for. If it is assumed that a primary goal of a university is to transfer knowledge from teacher to student, then grades become identifiable as a means toward that goal, serving as motivational, control, and feedback devices to expedite the knowledge transfer. Instead, however, the grades themselves have become much more important for entrance to graduate school, successful employment, tuition refunds, parental respect, etc., than the knowledge or lack of knowledge they are supposed to signify.

It therefore should come as no surprise that information has surfaced in recent years concerning fraternity files for examinations, term paper writing services, organized cheating at the service academies, and the like. Such activities constitute a personally rational response to a reward system which pays off for grades rather than knowledge.

BUSINESS RELATED EXAMPLES

Ecology

Assume that the president of XYZ Corporation is confronted with the following alternatives:

1. Spend $11 million for antipollution equipment to keep from poisoning fish in the river adjacent to the plant; or
2. Do nothing, in violation of the law, and assume a one-in-ten chance of being caught, with a resultant $1 million fine plus the necessity of buying the equipment.

Under this not unrealistic set of choices it requires no linear program to determine that XYZ Corporation can maximize its probabilities by flouting the law. Add the fact that XYZ's president is probably being rewarded (by creditors, stockholders, and other salient parts of his task environment) according to criteria totally unrelated to the number of fish poisoned, and his probable course of action becomes clear.

Evaluation of Training

It is axiomatic that those who care about a firm's well-being should insist that the organization get fair value for its expenditures. Yet it is commonly known that firms seldom bother to evaluate a new GRID, MBO, job enrichment program, or whatever, to see if the company is getting its money's worth. Why? Certainly it is not because people have not pointed out that this situation exists; numerous practitioner-oriented articles are written each year to just this point.

The individuals (whether in personnel, manpower planning, or wherever) who normally would be responsible for conducting such evaluations are the same ones often charged with introducing the change effort in the first place. Having convinced top management to spend the money, they usually are quite animated afterwards in collecting arigorous vignettes and anecdotes about how successful the program was. The last thing many desire is a formal, systematic, and revealing evaluation. Although members of top management may actually *hope* for such systematic evaluation, their reward systems continue to *reward* ignorance in this area. And if the personnel department abdicates its responsibility, who is to step into the breach? The change agent himself? Hardly! He is likely to be too busy collecting anecdotal "evidence" of his own, for use with his next client.

Miscellaneous

Many additional examples could be cited of systems which in fact are rewarding behaviors other than those supposedly desired by the rewarder. A few of these are described briefly below.

Most coaches disdain to discuss individual accomplishments, preferring to speak of teamwork, proper attitude, and a one-for-all spirit. Usually, however, rewards are distributed according to individual performance. The college basketball player who feeds his teammates instead of shooting will not compile impressive scoring statistics and is less likely to be drafted by the pros. The ballplayer who hits to right field to advance the runners will win neither the batting nor home run titles, and will be offered smaller raises. It therefore is rational for players to think of themselves first, and the team second.

In business organizations where rewards are dispensed for unit performance or for individual goals achieved, without regard for overall effectiveness, similar attitudes often are observed. Under most Management by Objectives (MBO) systems, goals in areas where quantification is difficult often go unspecified. The organization therefore often is in a position where it *hopes* for employee effort in the areas of team building, interpersonal relations, creativity, etc., but it formally *rewards* none of these. In cases where promotions and raises are formally tied to MBO, the system itself contains a paradox in that it "asks employees to set challenging, risky goals, only to face smaller paychecks and possibly damaged careers if these goals are not accomplished" (5, p. 40).

It is *hoped* that administrators will pay attention to long-run costs and opportunities and will institute programs which will bear fruit later on. However, many organizational reward systems pay off for short-run sales and earnings only. Under such circumstances it is personally rational for officials to sacrifice long-term growth and profit (by selling off equipment and property, or by stifling research and development) for short-term advantages. This probably is most pertinent in the public sector, with the result that many public officials are unwilling to implement programs which will not show benefits by election time.

As a final, clear-cut example of a fouled-up reward system, consider the cost-plus contract or its next of kin, the allocation of next year's budget as a direct function of this year's expenditures. It probably is conceivable that those who award such budgets and contracts really hope for economy and prudence in spending. It is obvious, however, that adopting the proverb "to him who spends shall more be given," rewards not economy, but spending itself.

CONCLUSIONS

Modern organization theory requires a recognition that the members of organizations and society possess divergent goals and motives. It therefore is unlikely that managers and their subordinates will seek the same outcomes. Three possible remedies for this potential problem are suggested.

Selection

It is theoretically possible for organizations to employ only those individuals whose goals and motives are wholly consonant with those of management. In such cases the same behaviors judged by subordinates to be rational would be perceived by management as desirable. State-of-the-art reviews of selection techniques, however, provide scant grounds for hope that such an approach would be successful (for example, see Ref. 10).

Training

Another theoretical alternative is for the organization to admit those employees whose goals are not consonant with those of management and then, through training, socialization, or whatever, alter employee goals to make them consonant. However, research on the effectiveness of such training programs, though limited, provides further grounds for pessimism (for example, see Ref. 3).

Altering the Reward System

What would have been the result if:

1. Nixon had been assured by his advisors that he could not win reelection except by discussing the issues in detail?

2. Physicians' conduct was subjected to regular examination by review boards for type 1 errors (calling healthy people ill) and to penalties (fines, censure, etc.) for errors of either type?
3. The President of XYZ Corporation had to choose between (a) spending 11 million dollars for antipollution equipment, and (b) incurring a fifty-fifty chance of going to jail for five years?

Managers who complain that their workers are not motivated might do well to consider the possibility that they have installed reward systems which are paying off for behaviors other than those they are seeking. This, in part, is what happened in Vietnam, and this is what regularly frustrates societal efforts to bring about honest politicians, civic-minded managers, etc.

A first step for such managers might be to find out what behaviors currently are being rewarded. In fact, such undesirable behavior by organizational members as they have observed may be explained largely by the reward systems in use.

This is not to say that all organizational behavior is determined by formal rewards and punishments. Certainly it is true that in the absence of formal reinforcement some soldiers will be patriotic, some presidents will be ecology minded, and some orphanage directors will care about children. The point, however, is that in such cases the rewarder is not *causing* the behaviors desired but is only a fortunate bystander. For an organization to *act* upon its members, the formal reward system should positively reinforce desired behaviors, not constitute an obstacle to be overcome.

It might be wise to underscore the obvious fact that there is nothing really new in what has been said. In both theory and practice these matters have been mentioned before. Thus, in many states Good Samaritan laws have been installed to protect doctors who stop to assist a stricken motorist. In states without such laws it is commonplace for doctors to refuse to stop, for fear of involvement in a subsequent lawsuit. In college basketball additional penalties have been instituted against players who foul their opponents deliberately. It has long been argued by Milton Friedman and others that penalties should be altered so as to make it irrational to disobey the ecology laws, and so on.

By altering the reward system the organization escapes the necessity of selecting only desirable people or of trying to alter undesirable ones.

In Skinnerian terms (as described in 9, p. 704), "As for responsibility and goodness—as commonly defined—no one . . . would want or need them. They refer to a man's behaving well despite the absence of positive reinforcement that is obviously sufficient to explain it. Where such reinforcement exists, 'no one needs goodness.' "

REFERENCES

1. Barnard, Chester I. *The Functions of the Executive* (Cambridge, Mass.: Harvard University Press, 1964).

2. Blau, Peter M., and W. Richard Scott. *Formal Organizations* (San Francisco: Chandler, 1962).

3. Fiedler, Fred E. "Predicting the Effects of Leadership Training and Experience from the Contingency Model," *Journal of Applied Psychology*, Vol. 56 (1972), 114–119.

4. Garland, L. H. "Studies of the Accuracy of Diagnostic Procedures," *American Journal Roentgenological, Radium Therapy Nuclear Medicine*, Vol. 82 (1959), 25–38.

5. Kerr, Steven. "Some Modifications in MBO as an OD Strategy," *Academy of Management Proceedings*, 1973, pp. 39–42.

6. Perrow, Charles. "The Analysis of Goals in Complex Organizations," in A. Etzioni (Ed.), *Readings on Modern Organizations* (Englewood Cliffs, N. J.: Prentice-Hall, 1969).

7. Scheff, Thomas J. "Decision Rules, Types of Error, and Their Consequences in Medical Diagnosis," in F. Massarik and P. Ratoosh (Eds.), *Mathematical Explorations in Behavioral Science* (Homewood, Ill.: Irwin, 1965).

8. Simon, Herbert A. *Administrative Behavior* (New York: Free Press, 1957).

9. Swanson, G. E. "Review Symposium: Beyond Freedom and Dignity," *American Journal of Sociology*, Vol. 78 (1972), 702–705.

10. Webster, E. *Decision Making in the Employment Interview* (Montreal: Industrial Relations Center, McGill University, 1964).

PART IV

Models of Leadership

Being in politics is like being a football coach, you have to be smart enough to understand the game, and dumb enough to think it's important.

                                                                    Eugene McCarthy

We have, I fear, confused power with greatness.

                                                                    Stewart Udall

To be clever enough to gain real power over others, one must be dumb enough to want it.

                                                                    G. K. Chesterton

Rank times IQ equals a mathematical constant.

                                                                    Anonymous

This section overviews some of the major models of leadership that have been developed during the past several decades. Path-goal theory, by Robert House and Terence Mitchell suggests a manager's behavior is motivating to the extent that the behavior increases a subordinate's goal attainment and helps to clarify the paths to these goals. The next article, "Are you *In* or *Out* with Your Boss?" reviews an approach created by George Graen of the University of Cincinnati. This approach contends that each subordinate develops a unique working relationship with the leader, and the varying quality of these relationships influences individual responses to work, such as individual motivation and individual emotional reactions. This approach is quite distinct from early views of leadership as it argues for examining leadership as a dyadic process (i.e., between two people), rather than as a group-wide process. The following article, by Victor Vroom, demonstrates that the ideal type of

257

leader style depends on aspects of the situation and offers a model for understanding the requirements of a situation, including ways to modify one's style to satisfy these requirements. Robert Sternberg of Yale University presents a three-part theory of managerial intelligence that is intuitively appealing and supported by data. His theory is gaining attention from academics and practitioners, in part because of its suggestion that the early trait approach to studying leadership may have some merit if suitably modified to take account of job demands and a more refined understanding of mental abilities.

The article by Bernard Bass asks us to consider the topic of charismatic leadership, by offering terms and a framework for analyzing the potential influence of charisma on leader effectiveness.

The role of situational influences is examined in the final two readings of this section. The first, by Robert Vecchio, investigates the validity of one of the more popular models used in today's leadership training programs and suggests that the model may require some modification. Next, Roya Ayman, Martin Chemers, and Fred Fiedler review the research literature that relates to the Contingency Model of Leadership. The model has had a stormy history and has been the subject of substantial debate. Nonetheless, the model is worth some consideration because of the related effort to better understand how the situation in which a person operates as head may dictate the appropriate style of leadership.

Path-Goal Theory of Leadership

Robert J. House and Terence R. Mitchell

The path-goal approach has its roots in a more general motivational theory called expectancy theory.[1] Briefly, expectancy theory states that an individual's attitudes (e.g., satisfaction with supervision or job satisfaction) or behavior (e.g., leader behavior or job effort) can be predicted from: (1) the degree to which the job, or behavior, is seen as leading to various outcomes (expectancy) and (2) the evaluation of these outcomes (valences). Thus, people are satisfied with their job if they think it leads to things that are highly valued, and they work hard if they believe that effort leads to things that are highly valued. This type of theoretical rationale can be used to predict a variety of phenomena related to leadership, such as why leaders behave the way they do, or how leader behavior influences subordinate motivation.[2]

This latter approach is the primary concern of this article. The implication for leadership is that subordinates are motivated by leader behavior to the extent that this behavior influences expectancies (e.g., goal paths) and valences (e.g., goal attractiveness).

Several writers have advanced specific hypotheses concerning how the leader affects the paths and the goals of subordinates.[3] These writers focused on two issues: (1) how the leader affects subordinates' expectations that effort will lead to effective performance and valued rewards, and (2) how this expectation affects motivation to work hard and perform well.

While the state of theorizing about leadership in terms of subordinates' paths and goals is in its infancy, we believe it is promising for two reasons. First, it suggests effects of leader behavior that have not yet been investigated but which appear to be fruitful areas of inquiry. And, second, it suggests with some precision the situational factors on which the effects of leader behavior are contingent.

The initial theoretical work by Evans asserts that leaders will be effective by making rewards available to subordinates and by making these rewards contingent on the subordinate's accomplishment of specific goals.[4] Evans argued that one of the strategic functions of the

leader is to clarify for subordinates the kind of behavior that leads to
goal accomplishment and valued rewards. This function might be
referred to as path clarification. Evans also argued that the leader
increases the rewards available to subordinates by being supportive
toward subordinates, i.e., by being concerned about their status, welfare,
and comfort. Leader supportiveness is in itself a reward that the leader
has at his or her disposal, and the judicious use of this reward increases
the motivation of subordinates.

Evans studied the relationship between the behavior of leaders and
the subordinates' expectations that effort leads to rewards and also studied the resulting impact on ratings of the subordinates' performance. He
found that when subordinates viewed leaders as being supportive (considerate of their needs) and when these superiors provided directions
and guidance to the subordinates, there was a positive relationship
between leader behavior and subordinates' performance ratings.

However, leader behavior was only related to subordinates' performance when the leader's behavior also was related to the subordinates'
expectations that their effort would result in desired rewards. Thus,
Evans' findings suggest that the major impact of a leader on the performance of subordinates is clarifying the path to desired rewards and
making such rewards contingent on effective performance.

Stimulated by this line of reasoning, House, and House and Dessler
advanced a more complex theory of the effects of leader behavior on the
motivation of subordinates.[5] The theory intends to explain the effects of
four specific kinds of leader behavior on the following three subordinate attitudes or expectations: (1) the satisfaction of subordinates, (2)
the subordinates' acceptance of the leader and (3) the expectations of
subordinates that effort will result in effective performance and that
effective performance is the path to rewards. The four kinds of leader
behavior included in the theory are: (1) directive leadership, (2) supportive leadership, (3) participative leadership and (4) achievement-oriented leadership. Directive leadership is characterized by a leader who
lets subordinates know what is expected of them, gives specific guidance as to what should be done and how it should be done, makes his or
her part in the group understood, schedules work to be done, maintains
definite standards of performance, and asks that group members follow
standard rules and regulations. Supportive leadership is characterized
by a friendly and approachable leader who shows concern for the status,

well-being, and needs of subordinates. Such a leader does little things to make the work more pleasant, treats members as equals, and is friendly and approachable. Participative leadership is characterized by a leader who consults with subordinates, solicits their suggestions, and takes these suggestions seriously into consideration before making a decision. An achievement-oriented leader sets challenging goals, expects subordinates to perform at their highest level, continuously seeks improvement in performance *and* shows a high degree of confidence that the subordinates will assume responsibility, put forth effort, and accomplish challenging goals. This kind of leader constantly emphasizes excellence in performance and simultaneously displays confidence that subordinates will meet high standards of excellence.

A number of studies suggest that these different leadership styles can be shown by the same leader in various situations.[6] For example, a leader may show directiveness toward subordinates in some instances and be participative or supportive in other instances.[7] Thus, the traditional method of characterizing a leader as either highly participative and supportive *or* highly directive is invalid; rather, it can be concluded that leaders vary in the particular fashion employed for supervising their subordinates. Also, the theory, in its present stage, is a tentative explanation of the effects of leader behavior—it is incomplete because it does not explain other kinds of leader behavior and does not explain the effects of the leader on factors other than subordinate acceptance, satisfaction, and expectations. However, the theory is stated so that additional variables may be included in it as new knowledge is made available.

PATH-GOAL THEORY

General Propositions

The first proposition of path-goal theory is that leader behavior is acceptable and satisfying to subordinates to the extent that the subordinates see such behavior as either an immediate source of satisfaction or as instrumental to future satisfaction.

The second proposition of this theory is that the leader's behavior will be motivational, i.e., increase effort, to the extent that (1) such behavior makes satisfaction of subordinates' needs contingent on effective performance and (2) such behavior complements the environment of subordinates by providing the coaching, guidance, support, and rewards necessary for effective performance.

These two propositions suggest that the leader's strategic functions are to enhance subordinates' motivation to perform, satisfaction with the job, and acceptance of the leader. From previous research on expectancy theory of motivation, it can be inferred that the strategic functions of the leader consist of: (1) recognizing and/or arousing subordinates' needs for outcomes over which the leader has some control, (2) increasing personal payoffs to subordinates for work-goal attainment, (3) making the path to those payoffs easier to travel by coaching and direction, (4) helping subordinates clarify expectancies, (5) reducing frustrating barriers and (6) increasing the opportunities for personal satisfaction contingent on effective performance.

Stated less formally, the motivational functions of the leader consist of increasing the number and kinds of personal payoffs to subordinates for work-goal attainment and making paths to these payoffs easier to travel by clarifying the paths, reducing road blocks and pitfalls, and increasing the opportunities for personal satisfaction en route.

Contingency Factors

Two classes of situational variables are asserted to be contingency factors. A contingency factor is a variable which moderates the relationship between two other variables such as leader behavior and subordinate satisfaction. For example, we might suggest that the degree of structure in the task moderates the relationship between leaders' directive behavior and subordinates' job satisfaction. Figure 1 shows how such a relationship might look. Thus, subordinates are satisfied with directive behavior in an unstructured task and are satisfied with nondirective behavior in a structured task. Therefore, we say that the relationship between leader directiveness and subordinate satisfaction is contingent upon the structure of the task.

The two contingency variables are (a) personal characteristics of the subordinates and (b) the environmental pressures and demands with which subordinates must cope in order to accomplish the work goals and to satisfy their needs. While other situational factors also may operate to determine the effects of leader behavior, they are not presently known.

Figure 1
Hypothetical Relationship Between Directive Leadership
and Subordinate Satisfaction with Task Structure as a Contingency Factor

With respect to the first class of contingency factors, the characteristics of subordinates, path-goal theory asserts that leader behavior will be acceptable to subordinates to the extent that the subordinates see such behavior as either an immediate source of satisfaction or as instrumental to future satisfaction. Subordinates' characteristics are hypothesized to determine this perception partially. For example, Runyon[8] and Mitchell[9] show that the subordinate's score on a measure called Locus of Control moderates the relationship between participative leadership style and subordinate satisfaction. The Locus of Control measure reflects the degree to which an individual sees the environment as systematically responding to his or her behavior. People who believe that what happens to them occurs because of their behavior are called internals; people who believe that what happens to them occurs because of luck or chance are called externals. Mitchell's findings suggest that internals are more satisfied with a participative leadership style and externals are more satisfied with a directive style.

A second characteristic of subordinates on which the effects of leader behavior are contingent is subordinates' perception of their own ability with respect to their assigned tasks. The higher the degree of perceived ability relative to task demands, the less the subordinate will view leader directiveness and coaching behavior as acceptable. Where the subordinate's perceived ability is high, such behavior is likely to have little positive effect on the motivation of the subordinate and to be perceived as excessively close control. Thus, the acceptability of the leader's behavior is determined in part by the characteristics of the subordinates.

The second aspect of the situation, the environment of the subordinate, consists of those factors that are not within the control of the subordinate but which are important to need satisfaction or to ability to perform effectively. The theory asserts that effects of the leader's behavior on the psychological states of subordinates are contingent on other parts of the subordinates' environment that are relevant to subordinate motivation. Three broad classifications of contingency factors in the environment are:

The subordinates' tasks.
The formal authority system of the organization.
The primary work group.

Assessment of the environmental conditions makes it possible to predict the kind and amount of influence that specific leader behaviors will have on the motivation of subordinates. Any of the three environmental factors could act upon the subordinate in any of three ways: first, to serve as stimuli that motivate and direct the subordinate to perform necessary task operations; second, to constrain variability in behavior. Constraints may help the subordinate by clarifying expectancies that effort leads to rewards or by preventing the subordinate from experiencing conflict and confusion. Constraints also may be counterproductive to the extent that they restrict initiative or prevent increases in effort from being associated positively with rewards. Third, environmental factors may serve as rewards for achieving desired performance, e.g., it is possible for the subordinate to receive the necessary cues to do the job and the needed rewards for satisfaction from sources other than the leader, e.g., coworkers in the primary work group. Thus, the effect of the leader on subordinates' motivation will be a function of how deficient the environment is with respect to motivational stimuli, constraints, or rewards.

With respect to the environment, path-goal theory asserts that when goals and paths to desired goals are apparent because of the routine nature of the task, clear group norms or objective controls of the formal authority systems, attempts by the leader to clarify paths and goals will be both redundant and seen by subordinates as imposing unnecessary, close control. Although such control may increase performance by preventing soldiering or malingering, it also will result in decreased satisfaction (see Figure 1). Also with respect to the work environment, the theory asserts that the more dissatisfying the task, the more the subordinates will resent leader behavior directed at increasing productivity or enforcing compliance to organizational rules and procedures.

Finally, with respect to environmental variables the theory states that leader behavior will be motivational to the extent that it helps subordinates cope with environmental uncertainties, threats from others or sources of frustration. Such leader behavior is predicted to increase subordinates' satisfaction with the job context and to be motivational to the extent that it increases the subordinates' expectations that their effort will lead to valued rewards.

These propositions and specification of situational contingencies provide a heuristic framework on which to base future research. Hopefully, this will lead to a more fully developed, explicitly formal theory of leadership.

Figure 2 presents a summary of the theory. It is hoped that these propositions, while admittedly tentative, will provide managers with

Figure 2
Summary of Path-Goal Relationships

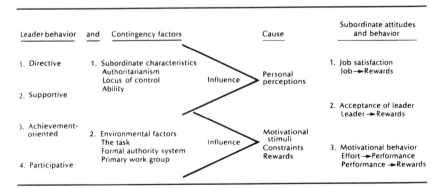

some insights concerning the effects of their own leader behavior and that of others.

EMPIRICAL SUPPORT

The theory has been tested in a limited number of studies which have generated considerable empirical support for our ideas and also suggest areas in which the theory requires revision. A brief review of these studies follows.

Leader Directiveness

Leader directiveness has a positive correlation with satisfaction and expectancies of subordinates who are engaged in ambiguous tasks and has a negative correlation with satisfaction and expectancies of subordinates engaged in clear tasks. These findings were predicted by the theory and have been replicated in seven organizations. They suggest that when task demands are ambiguous or when the organization procedures, rules, and policies are not clear, a leader behaving in a directive manner complements the tasks and the organization by providing the necessary guidance and psychological structure for subordinates.[10] However, when task demands are clear to subordinates, leader directiveness is seen more as a hindrance.

However, other studies have failed to confirm these findings.[11] A study by Dessler[12] suggests a resolution to these conflicting findings—he found that for subordinates at the lower organizational levels of a manufacturing firm who were doing routine, repetitive, unambiguous tasks, directive leadership was preferred by closed-minded, dogmatic, authoritarian subordinates and nondirective leadership was preferred by nonauthoritarian, open-minded subordinates. However, for subordinates at higher organizational levels doing nonroutine, ambiguous tasks, directive leadership was preferred for both authoritarian and nonauthoritarian subordinates. Thus, Dessler found that two contingency factors appear to operate simultaneously: subordinate task ambiguity and degree of subordinate authoritarianism. When measured in combination, the findings are as predicted by the theory; however, when the subordinate's personality is not taken into account, task ambiguity does not always operate as a contingency variable as predicted by the theory. House, Burill, and Dessler recently found a similar interaction between subordinate authoritarianism and task ambiguity in a second manufacturing firm, thus adding confidence in Dessler's original findings.[13]

Supportive Leadership

The theory hypothesizes that supportive leadership will have its most positive effect on subordinate satisfaction for subordinates who work on stressful, frustrating, or dissatisfying tasks. This hypothesis has been tested in 10 samples of employees,[14] and in only one of these studies was the hypothesis disconfirmed.[15] Despite some inconsistency in research on supportive leadership, the evidence is sufficiently positive to suggest that managers should be alert to the critical need for supportive leadership under conditions where tasks are dissatisfying, frustrating, or stressful to subordinates.

Achievement-Oriented Leadership

The theory hypothesizes that achievement-oriented leadership will cause subordinates to strive for higher standards of performance and to have more confidence in the ability to meet challenging goals. A recent study by House, Valency, and Van der Krabben provides a partial test of this hypothesis among white-collar employees in service organizations.[16] For subordinates performing ambiguous, nonrepetitive tasks, they found a positive relationship between the amount of achievement orientation of the leader and subordinates' expectancy that their effort would result in effective performance. Stated less technically, for subordinates performing ambiguous, nonrepetitive tasks, the higher the achievement orientation of the leader, the more the subordinates were confident that their efforts would pay off in effective performance. For subordinates performing moderately unambiguous, repetitive tasks, there was no significant relationship between achievement-oriented leadership and subordinate expectancies that their effort would lead to effective performance. This finding held in four separate organizations.

Two plausible interpretations may be used to explain these data. First, people who select ambiguous, nonrepetitive tasks may be different in personality from those who select a repetitive job and may, therefore, be more responsive to an achievement-oriented leader. A second explanation is that achievement orientation only affects expectancies in ambiguous situations because there is more flexibility and autonomy in such tasks. Therefore, subordinates in such tasks are more likely to be able to change in response to such leadership style. Neither of the above interpretations have been tested to date; however, additional research is currently under way to investigate these relationships.

Participative Leadership

In theorizing about the effects of participative leadership, it is necessary to ask about the specific characteristics of both the subordinates and their situation that would cause participative leadership to be viewed as satisfying and instrumental to effective performance.

Mitchell recently described at least four ways in which a participative leadership style would impact on subordinate attitudes and behavior as predicted by expectancy theory.[17] First, a participative climate should increase the clarity of organizational contingencies. Through participation in decision making, subordinates should learn what leads to what. From a path-goal viewpoint participation would lead to greater clarity of the paths to various goals. A second impact of participation would be that subordinates, hopefully, should select goals they highly value. If one participates in decisions about various goals, it makes sense that this individual would select goals he or she wants. Thus, participation would increase the correspondence between organization and subordinate goals. Third, we can see how participation would increase the control the individual has over what happens on the job. If our motivation is higher (based on the preceding two points), then having greater autonomy and ability to carry out our intentions should lead to increased effort and performance. Finally, under a participative system, pressure towards high performance should come from sources other than the leader or the organization. More specifically, when people participate in the decision process, they become more ego-involved; the decisions made are in some part their own. Also, their peers know what is expected and the social pressure has a greater impact. Thus, motivation to perform well stems from internal and social factors as well as formal external ones.

A number of investigations prior to the above formulation supported the idea that participation appears to be helpful,[18] and Mitchell presents a number of recent studies that support the above four points.[19] However, it is also true that we would expect the relationship between a participative style and subordinate behavior to be moderated by both the personality characteristics of the subordinate and the situational demands. Studies by Tannenbaum and Allport and Vroom have shown that subordinates who prefer autonomy and self-control respond more positively to participative leadership in terms of both satisfaction and performance than subordinates who do not have such preferences.[20] Also, the studies mentioned by Runyon[21] and Mitchell[22] showed that subordinates who were external in orientation were less satisfied with a participative style of leadership than were internal subordinates.

House also has reviewed these studies in an attempt to explain the ways in which the situation or environment moderates the relationship between participation and subordinate attitudes and behavior.[23] His analysis suggests that where participative leadership is positively related to satisfaction, regardless of the predispositions of subordinates, the tasks of the subjects appear to be ambiguous and ego-involving. In the studies in which the subjects' personalities or predispositions moderate the effect of participative leadership, the tasks of the subjects are inferred to be highly routine and/or nonego-involving.

House reasoned from this analysis that the task may have an overriding effect on the relationship between leader participation and subordinate responses, and that individual predispositions or personality characteristics of subordinates may have an effect only under some tasks. It was assumed that when task demands are ambiguous, subordinates will have a need to reduce the ambiguity. Further, it was assumed that when task demands are ambiguous, participative problem solving between the leader and the subordinate will result in more effective decisions than when the task demands are unambiguous. Finally, it was assumed that when the subordinates are ego-involved in their tasks they are more likely to want to have a say in the decisions that affect them. Given these assumptions, the following hypotheses were formulated to account for the conflicting findings reviewed above:

When subjects are highly ego-involved in a decision or a task and the decision or task demands are ambiguous, participative leadership will have a positive effect on the satisfaction and motivation of the subordinate, *regardless* of the subordinate's predisposition toward self-control, authoritarianism, or need for independence.

When subordinates are not ego-involved in their tasks and when task demands are clear, subordinates who are not authoritarian and who have high needs for independence and self-control will respond favorably to leader participation and their opposite personality types will respond less favorably.

These hypotheses were derived on the basis of path-goal theorizing, i.e., the rationale guiding the analysis of prior studies was that both task characteristics and characteristics of subordinates interact to determine the effect of a specific kind of leader behavior on the satisfaction, expectancies, and performance of subordinates. To date, one major investigation has supported some of these predictions[24] in which personality variables, amount of participative leadership, task ambiguity, and job satisfaction were assessed for 324 employees of an industrial manufacturing organization. As expected, in nonrepetitive, ego-involving tasks, employees (regardless of their personality) were more satisfied under a participative style than a nonparticipative style. However, in repetitive tasks which were less ego-involving, the amount of authoritarianism of subordinates moderated the relationship between leadership style and satisfaction. Specifically, low authoritarian subordinates were *more satisfied* under a participative style. These findings are exactly as the theory would predict; thus, it has promise in reconciling a set of confusing and contradictory findings with respect to participative leadership.

SUMMARY AND CONCLUSIONS

We have attempted to describe what we believe is a useful theoretical framework for understanding the effect of leadership behavior on subordinate satisfaction and motivation. Most theorists today have moved away from the simplistic notions that all effective leaders have a certain set of personality traits or that the situation completely determines performance. Some researchers have presented rather complex attempts at matching certain types of leaders with certain types of situations . . . But, we believe that a path-goal approach goes one step further. It not only suggests what type of style may be most effective in a given situation—it also attempts to explain *why* it is most effective.

We are optimistic about the future outlook of leadership research. With the guidance of path-goal theorizing, future research is expected to unravel many confusing puzzles about the reasons for and effects of leader behavior that have, heretofore, not been solved. However, we add a word of caution: the theory, and the research on it, are relatively new to the literature of organizational behavior. Consequently, path-goal theory is offered more as a tool for directing research and stimulating insight than as a proven guide for managerial action.

REFERENCES

1. T. R. Mitchell, "Expectancy Model of Job Satisfaction, Occupational Preference and Effort: A Theoretical, Methodological and Empirical Appraisal," *Psychological Bulletin* (1974).

2. D. M. Nebeker and T. R. Mitchell, "Leader Behavior: An Expectancy Theory Approach," *Organization Behavior and Human Performance*, 11(1974): 355–67.

3. M. G. Evans, "The Effects of Supervisory Behavior on the Path-Goal Relationship," *Organization Behavior and Human Performance*, 55(1970): 277–98; T. H. Hammer and H. T. Dachler, "The Process of Supervision in the Context of Motivation Theory," Research Report no. 3 (University of Maryland, 1973); F. Dansereau, Jr., J. Cashman, and G. Graen, "Instrumentality Theory and Equity Theory as Complementary Approaches in Predicting the Relationship of Leadership and Turnover among Managers," *Organization Behavior and Human Performance*, 10(1973): 184–200; R. J. House, "A Path-Goal Theory of Leader Effectiveness," *Administrative Science Quarterly*, 16, 3(September 1971): 321–38; T. R. Mitchell, "Motivation and Participation: An Integration," *Academy of Management Journal*, 16 4(1973): 160–79; G. Graen, F. Dansereau, Jr., and T. Minami, "Dysfunctional Leadership Styles," *Organization Behavior and Human Performance*, 7(1972): 216–36; G. Graen, F. Dansereau, Jr. and T. Minami, "An Empirical Test of the Man-in-the-Middle Hypothesis among Executives in a Hierarchical Organization Employing a Unit Analysis," *Organization Behavior and Human Performance*, 8(1972): 262–85; R. J. House and G. Dessler, "The Path-Goal Theory of Leadership: Some Post Hoc and A Priori Tests," to appear in J. G. Hunt, ed, *Contingency Approaches to Leadership* (Carbondale, III.: Southern Illinois University Press, 1974).

4. M. G. Evans, "Effects of Supervisory Behavior"; M. G. Evans, "Extensions of a Path-Goal Theory of Motivation," *Journal of Applied Psychology*, 59 (1974): 172–78.

5. R. J. House, "A Path-Goal Theory"; R. J. House and G. Dessler, "Path-Goal Theory of Leadership."

6. R. J. House and G. Dessler, "Path-Goal Theory of Leadership"; R. M. Stogdill, *Managers, Employees, Organization* (Ohio State University, Bureau of Business Research, 1965); R. J. House, A. Valency, and R. Van der Krabben, "Some Tests and Extensions of the Path-Goal Theory of Leadership" (in preparation).

7. W. A. Hill and D. Hughes, "Variations in Leader Behavior as a Function of Task Type," *Organization Behavior and Human Performance*, 11, 1(1974): 83–96.

8. K. E. Runyon, "Some Interactions between Personality Variables and Management Styles," *Journal of Applied Psychology*, 57, 3(1973): 288–94; T. R. Mitchell, C. R. Smyser, and S. E. Weed, "Locus of Control: Supervision and Work Satisfaction," *Academy of Management Journal*, 18, 3(1975): 623–31.

9. T. R. Mitchell, "Locus of Control."

10. R. J. House, "A Path-Goal Theory"; R. J. House and G. Dessler, "Path-Goal Theory of Leadership"; A. D. Szalagyi and H. P. Sims, "An Exploration of the Path-Goal Theory of Leadership in a Health Care Environment," *Academy of Management Journal* (in press); J. D. Dermer, "Supervisory Behavior and Budget Motivation" (Cambridge, Mass.: unpublished, MIT, Sloan School of Management, 1974); R. W. Smetana, "The Relationship between Managerial Behavior and Subordinate Attitudes and Motivation: A Contribution to a Behavioral Theory of Leadership" (Ph.D. dissertation, Wayne State University, 1974).

11. S. E. Weed, T. R. Mitchell, and C. R. Smyser, "A Test of House's Path-Goal Theory of Leadership in an Organizational Setting" (paper presented at Western Psychological Assn., 1974); J. D. Dermer and J. P. Siegel, "A Test of Path-Goal Theory: Disconfirming Evidence and a Critique" (unpublished, University of Toronto, Faculty of Management Studies, 1973); R. S. Schuler, "A Path-Goal Theory of Leadership: An Empirical Investigation" (Ph.D. dissertation, Michigan State University, 1973); H. K. Downey, J. E. Sheridan, and J. W. Slocum, Jr., "Analysis of Relationships among Leader Behavior, Subordinate Job Performance and Satisfaction: A Path-Goal Approach" (unpublished mimeograph, 1974); J. E. Stinson and T. W. Johnson, "The Path-Goal Theory of Leadership: A Partial Test and Suggested Refinement," *Proceedings* (Kent, Ohio: 7th Annual Conference of the Midwest Academy of Management, April 1974): 18–36.

12. G. Dessler, "An Investigation of the Path-Goal Theory of Leadership" (Ph. D. dissertation, City University of New York, Bernard M. Baruch College. 1973).

13. R. J. House, D. Burrill, and G. Dessler, "Tests and Extensions of Path-Goal Theory of Leadership, I" (unpublished, in process).

14. R. J. House, "A Path-Goal Theory"; R. J. House and G. Dessler, "Path-Goal Theory of Leadership"; A. D. Szalagyi and H. P. Sims, "Exploration of Path-Goal"; J. E. Stinson and T. W. Johnson, *Proceedings*; R. S. Schuler, "Path-Goal: Investigation"; H. K. Downey, J. E. Sheridan, and J. W. Slocum, Jr., "Analysis of Relationships"; S. E. Weed, T. R. Mitchell, and C R. Smyser, "Test of House's Path-Goal."

15. A. D. Szalagyi and H. P. Sims, "Exploration of Path-Goal."

16. R. J. House, A. Valency, and R. Van der Krabben, "Tests and Extensions of Path-Goal Theory of Leadership, II" (unpublished, in process).

17. T. R. Mitchell, "Motivation and Participation."

18. H. Tosi, "A Reexamination of Personality as a Determinant of the Effects of Participation," *Personnel Psychology*, 23(1970): 91–99; J. Sadler "Leadership Style, Confidence in Management and Job Satisfaction," *Journal of Applied*

Behavioral Sciences, 6(1970): 3–19; K. N. Wexley, J. P. Singh, and G. A. Yukl, "Subordinate Personality as a Moderator of the Effects of Participation in Three Types of Appraisal Interviews," *Journal of Applied Psychology*, 83 1(1973): 54–59.

19. T. R. Mitchell, "Motivation and Participation."

20. A. S. Tannebaum and F. H. Allport, "Personality Structure and Group Structure: An Interpretive Study of Their Relationship through an Event-Structure Hypothesis," *Journal of Abnormal and Social Psychology*, 53(1956): 272–80; V. H. Vroom, "Some Personality Determinants of the Effects of Participation," *Journal of Abnormal and Social Psychology*, 59(1959): 322–27

21. K. E. Runyon, "Some Interactions between Personality Variables and Management Styles," *Journal of Applied Psychology*, 57, 3(1973): 288–94.

22. T. R. Mitchell, C. R. Smyser, and S. E. Weed, "Locus of Control."

23. R. J. House, "Notes on the Path-Goal Theory of Leadership" (University of Toronto, Faculty of Management Studies, May 1974).

24. R. S. Schuler, "Leader Participation, Task Structure, and Subordinate Authoritarianism" (unpublished mimeograph, Cleveland State University, 1974).

Are You *In* or *Out* with Your Boss?

Robert P. Vecchio

At one time or another, each of us has had the feeling of being relatively *in* or *out* with an immediate supervisor. Perhaps more than anything else, the sense of being accepted or rejected by your boss makes or breaks your confidence. The tendency of supervisors to divide their subordinates into in-group members and out-group members is only beginning to be understood. Researchers are reporting insights that are important to both supervisor and subordinate.[1]

Until recently, the literature on how to be an effective manager has argued that there is one appropriate style of management for most situations, or that there is a best style for any given specific situation. Regardless of the theory of supervision you consider, it is generally assumed that a manager can and does display a uniform style of supervision toward all subordinates.

However, this assumption is in error. Different subordinates often report far different views of the same immediate supervisor. And supervisors do not describe their individual subordinates or relate to them in the same way. Often, they differentiate among subordinates by the kinds of assignments they entrust and the degree of freedom from supervision that they allow. Although such popular views of supervision as Theory X and Y, Managerial Grid, and Fiedler's Contingency Model assume that a leader exhibits a particular dominant style, recent research suggests that a given supervisor will show a far different "face" to certain subordinates.

THE INS AND OUTS

The existence of in-groups and out-groups within a given department or work unit is easy to document. Studies show that subordinates can

[1] See, for example, Fred Dansereau, Jr., George Graen, and William J. Haga, "A Vertical Dyad Linkage Approach to Leadership within Formal Organizations: A Longitudinal Investigation of the Role Making Process," *Organizational Behavior and Human Performance* 13 (February 1975): 46–78; John B. Miner, *Theories of Organizational Behavior* (Hinsdale, Ill.: Dryden, 1980); Robert P. Vecchio and Bruce C. Gobdel, "The Vertical Dyad Linkage Model of Leadership: Problems and Prospects," *Organizational Behavior and Human Performance* 34 (August 1984): 5–20.

readily agree on who is relatively in or out with the boss. And the boss can quickly list which employees are currently in or out of favor.

By and large, in-groups can be labeled as the boss's *trusted assistants*. Out-group members can best be termed *hired hands*. *Trusted assistants* are given considerable freedom in their jobs. They are asked to give their opinions about various matters and have ready access to their supervisors. *Hired hands*, in contrast, are treated with courtesy and perhaps respect, but they are not considered loyal or capable of handling critical assignments. In a sense, the *hired hands*, in accordance with a written or unwritten labor contract, are merely supervised. In-groupers are given considerable responsibility, support, and encouragement. Out-groupers are denied valuable opportunities and displays of confidence.

WHY DO IN-GROUPS AND OUT-GROUPS DEVELOP?

The origins of in-groups and out-groups are not completely understood. It is likely, however, that something occurs fairly early in the relationship between each new employee and a supervisor.

The boss tries out each new employee by offering small but challenging assignments. The subordinate's reaction to these additional responsibilities is then closely watched. If the employee reacts negatively (by saying, "It's not *my* job") or positively (by replying, "I'm happy to help"), then a cycle of trust or distrust is begun. In short, supervisors learn quickly who is reliable and who is not. Frequently, this discovery process is not even conscious or intentional; supervisors may be unaware that this process is occurring.

In addition to these displays of loyalty and cooperation, a certain degree of personal bias may play a role in determining who is in or out. Supervisors may be more willing to offer desirable job assignments and be more available to subordinates whom they find attractive, or regard as similar to themselves in terms of attitudes, sex, and/or race. Still, though personal bias may play a role, it is perhaps more likely that employee competence and early manifestations of cooperation are the major determinants in most superior-subordinate relations.

Performance appraisal systems can create or cement a person's membership in an in-group or an out-group. The annual or semiannual task of sorting out employees for purposes of making decisions on raises or sending employees to training programs influences a supervisor's beliefs about the merit of a given employee. If a supervisor is unduly influenced by the realization that a given employee did not fare well in a performance assessment, and if the supervisor does not try to help in that employee's development, then the supervisor's later behavior may be influenced by the negative appraisal.

Lastly, it appears that some employees *want* to be out. Apparently not everyone wants to have a good working relationship with the boss. Some people are antagonistic to authority figures. For such people, this negative predisposition is present regardless of who their supervisor happens to be. Such individuals will take a relatively defiant and unco-operative stance as long as their jobs are secure (thanks to a union con-tract, the threat of a lawsuit, longevity, or being relatively indispensable because of their expert knowledge).

No one has yet offered a solution on how to reach or turn around such extremely negative individuals. Perhaps the only practical advice for coping with them is to try to arrange for their transfer to another unit or to redefine their job responsibilities so that their negative influence is minimized.

THE CONSEQUENCES OF BEING IN OR OUT

Studies of the in-out phenomenon show that in-groupers are more satisfied with their bosses and their jobs than are out-groupers. In-groupers may be less likely to quit than out-group members (although this finding of reduced turnover is less reliable than the findings for employee satisfaction).

Furthermore, in-group members have higher performance levels than out-group members. Regardless of how performance is measured (that is, by hard, objective measures of performance or by subjective ratings), in-groupers are generally better performers. These findings suggest that real gains may result from creating a sense of in-ness among subordinates. Marginal employees may be motivated to become superior performers.

IN OR OUT: WHAT TO DO ABOUT IT

In truth, the best time to manage the in or out phenomenon is very early in a person's employment. If you are a new employee or if you are developing a relationship with a newly assigned boss, it is a good idea to offer your loyalty and provide expressions of cooperativeness.

If your status as an out-member is already well established, it may be difficult or impossible to break the status quo. Short of confronting the supervisor and asking for a new start, an out-group employee's only options are to:

- Accept the current situation;
- Try to become an in-group member by being cooperative and loyal (this is an unattractive option for many out-groupers because they may have to swallow their pride); or
- Quit.

Out-group members typically—but resentfully—come to accept the status quo.

Supervisors should be mindful that in-groups and out-groups exist within their work units, and they should control potential conflict between the two divisions. Supervisors should consciously try to expand their in-groups. This means not giving up on people who may gradually be coming to see themselves as marginal members of the work unit. Supervisors who create a greater sense of in-ness among their subordinates can expect to have more effective work units.

Can Leaders Learn to Lead?

Victor H. Vroom

Like my fellow authors, I start with certain preconceptions. These preconceptions—some may call them biases—influence the way in which I view issues of leadership, particularly leadership training. I have tried to depict these preconceptions in Figure 1.

The central variable in this figure is the behavior of the leader, which I believe is determined by two classes of variables, attributes of the leader and attributes of the situation. Furthermore, I assume that many of the differences in the behavior of leaders can be explained only by examining their joint effects, including interactions between these two classes of variables.

The left-hand portion of the diagram is the descriptive side of the leader behavior equation. Much of my research has focused on these relationships in an attempt to understand the ways in which managers actually respond to situations that vary in a number of dimensions. If you examine the right-hand side of Figure 1, however, you encounter issues that are potentially normative or prescriptive in character. They deal with the consequences of leader behavior for the organization and here I share with Fiedler (and probably disagree with Argyris) a conviction that a contingency model is required. I do not see any form of leader behavior as optimal for all situations. The contribution of a leader's actions to the effectiveness of the organization cannot be determined without considering the nature of the situation in which that behavior is displayed.

WORKING WITH THE CONTINGENCY MODEL

I am going to assume that most of you are familiar with the model that Phil Yetton and I developed and have described in detail in our recent book. As a normative model, it deals with the right-hand side of Figure 1, but it is a limited model because it deals with only one facet of leadership behavior—the extent to which the leader shares decision-making power with subordinates.

Figure 1
Schematic Representation of Variables Used in Leadership Research

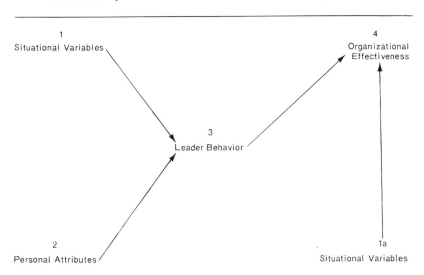

Figure 2 shows the latest version of our model. For purposes of simplicity, the presentation here is restricted to the model for group problems, that is, problems or decisions that affect all or a substantial portion of the manager's subordinates. At the top of the figure are problem attributes—that is, situational variables that ought to influence the decision process used by the leader—specifically, the amount of opportunity that the leader gives his or her subordinates to participate in the making of a decision. To use the model, one first selects an organization problem to be solved or decision to be made. Starting at the left-hand side of the diagram, one asks oneself the question pertaining to each attribute that is encountered, follows the path developed, and finally determines the problem type (numbered 1 through 12). This problem type specifies one or more decision processes that are deemed appropriate to that problem. These decision processes are called the "feasible set" and represent the methods that remain after a set of seven rules has been applied. The first three of these rules eliminate methods that threaten the quality of the decisions, while the last four rules eliminate methods that are likely to jeopardize acceptance of the decision by subordinates.

Figure 2
Decision Process Flowchart (Feasible Set)

A. Does the problem possess a quality requirement?
B. Do I have sufficient information to make a high-quality decision?
C. Is the problem structured?
D. Is acceptance of the decision by subordinates important for effective implementation?
E. If I were to make the decision by myself, am I reasonably certain that it would be accepted by my subordinates?
F. Do subordinates share the organizational goals to be attained in solving this problem?
G. Is conflict among subordinates likely in preferred solutions?

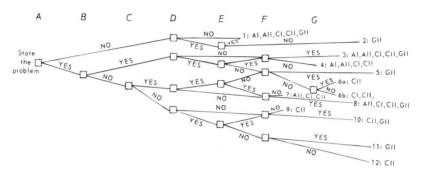

For those who are unfamiliar with the Vroom-Yetton model, let me point out that the decision processes are described here in a kind of code. AI and AII are variants of an autocratic process. In AI the manager solves the problem alone using whatever information is available at that time; in AII the manager obtains any necessary information of a specific nature from subordinates before making the decision alone. CI and CII are variants of a consultative process. In CI the manager shares the problem with relevant subordinates individually, getting their ideas and suggestions before making the decision; CII is similar, but the consultation takes place within the context of a group meeting. Finally, GII corresponds with Norman Maier's concept of group decision in which the manager's role is that of chairperson of a group meeting aimed at reaching consensus on the action to be taken.

The part of the model described so far specifies how decisions should *not* be made, not how they should be made. For most problem types, there exists more than one decision process consistent with the rules and therefore contained in the feasible set. We have also been concerned with the consequences of various ways of choosing from these alternatives. There is considerable evidence that the time required to make the decision (defined either as the elapsed time or the number of work hours needed to make the decision) increases with the intensity of involvement or participation of subordinates. Thus a time-efficient model (which we term Model A) would select the most autocratic alternative within the feasible set, a choice that would be clearly indicated in crisis or emergency situations, and in situations in which one seeks to minimize the number of work-hours that enter into making the decision.

Of course, time is not the only dimension to include in deciding the degree to which the leader should encourage the participation of subordinates in decision making. In addition to the possibilities that participation may increase decision quality or its acceptance (considerations that are incorporated into the rules referred to previously), there are also grounds for believing that participation contributes to individual and team development and is likely to result in more informed and responsible behavior by subordinates in the future. Hence Model B, which could be thought of as a time-investment or developmental model, dictates the choice of the most participative process within the feasible set. It is important to note that Models A and B are consistent with the same rules (to protect decision quality and acceptance) but represent extremely different ways of operating within these rules. Model A maximizes a short-run value—time; Model B maximizes a long-run value—development.

What is the image of the effective leader portrayed by this normative model? It is one that is neither universally autocratic nor universally participative but utilizes either approach in response to the demands of a situation *as he or she perceives them.* Above all, the leader has thought through his or her values and has a repertoire of skills necessary to execute effectively each of the decision processes.

VALIDATING THE MODEL

When Philip Yetton and I wrote our book, we had no evidence validating the model other than the consistency of our rules with existing empirical evidence concerning the consequences of alternative approaches. During the past six months, Art Jago and I have been working to remedy this deficiency. We have asked managers, all of whom were unfamiliar with the model, to select two decisions that they had made—one that proved to be successful and one that proved to be unsuccessful. Each manager wrote up each decision situation as a case and specified the decision process he used in solving the problem. Later these managers were trained in the problem attributes and went back over each of these two cases, coding each in a manner that would permit the researcher to determine the problem type and the feasible set of methods for that problem type.

The data for this study are still coming in. To date, we have written accounts of 46 successful decisions and 42 unsuccessful ones. (It seems that some managers have difficulty in recalling the decisions they made that did not turn out too well!) Figure 3 shows the results available so far. These results clearly support the validity of the model. If the manager's method of dealing with the case corresponded with the model, the probability of the decision's being deemed successful was 65 percent; if the method disagreed with the model, the probability of its being deemed successful was only 29 percent.

It is important to note, however, that behavior that corresponds with the model is no guarantee that the decision will ultimately turn out to be successful—nor is behavior outside the feasible set inevitably associated with an unsuccessful decision.

To create a model of decision processes that completely predicts decision outcomes (that is, which generates 100 percent observations in upper left and lower right cells) is an impossibility. Any fantasies that we may have entertained about having created a model of process that would completely determine decision outcomes have been permanently dashed against the rocks of reality! Insofar as organizations are open systems and decisions within them are made under conditions of risk

Figure 3
Relationship Between Model Agreement
and Decision Outcome

	Percent Successful	Percent Unsuccessful	Total
Method used agrees with feasible set	65	35	100%
Method used disagrees with feasible set	29	71	100%

and uncertainty, it will be impossible to generate complete predictability for a model such as ours. To be sure, we may be able to use the data from the study I have described to improve the "batting average" of the model, but the limit of success must be less than perfection.

IMPLICATIONS FOR TRAINING

I would now like to turn to a central issue, the use of the model in leadership training. Over the past few years, several thousand managers have received training in the concepts underlying the model. The workshops have ranged from two to over five days in length, and the participants have included admirals, corporation presidents, school superintendents, and senior government officials. I have been personally involved in enough of this training to have learned some important things about what to do and what not to do. And because I believe that there are substantial but understandable misconceptions about how training based on the Vroom and Yetton model works, I would like to describe the things I have learned.

It would have been possible to build a training program around the model that was completely cognitive and mechanistic. Participants would be sold on the model and then trained in its use through intensive practice—first on standardized cases and later on real problems drawn from their own experiences. Such an approach would represent a new domain for Taylorism and could even be accomplished through Skinnerian programmed learning. I believe that, at best, this behavioral approach would influence what Argyris calls espoused theories and would not have any long-lasting behavioral effects.

Our methods have been much more influenced by Carl Rogers than by B. F. Skinner. We have assumed that behavioral changes require a process of self-discovery and insight by each individual manager.

One method of stimulating this process is to provide the participants with a picture of their leadership style. This picture includes a comparison of one's style with that of others, the situational factors that influence one's willingness to share power with others, and similarities and differences between one's own "model" and the normative models.

In advance of the training program, each participant sits down with a set of cases, each of which depicts a leader confronted with an actual organizational problem. We call these cases "problem sets," and the number of cases in different problem sets ranges from 30 to 54. The common feature in each of the eight or nine problem sets that have been developed is that the cases vary along each of the situational dimensions used in the construction of the normative model. The set is designed so that the variation is systematic and that the effects of each situational attribute on a given manager's choice of decision process can be readily determined. This feature permits the assessment of each of the problem attributes in the decision processes used by a given manager.

The manager's task is to select the decision process that comes closest to depicting what he or she would do in each situation. Responses are recorded on a standardized form and processed by computer along with other participants' responses in the same program.

Instead of writing about information contained on a printout, I thought that it might be more efficient to let you see what it looks like. The next figure reproduces several pages of feedback that a manager recently received. Examine the first page of the printout shown in Figure 4. Consider A first in that figure. The first row opposite "your frequency"

Figure 4
Page 1 of Printout

NAME OR I.D. -- JOHN DOE

A -- PROPORTION OF CASES IN WHICH EACH DECISION PROCESS IS USED

	AI	AII	CI	CII	GII
YOUR FREQUENCY	43%	3%	23%	30%	0%
PEER FREQUENCY	25%	14%	19%	27%	15%
MODEL A (MINIMIZE PARTICIPATION)	40%	13%	3%	23%	20%
MODEL B (MAXIMIZE PARTICIPATION)	0%	0%	0%	40%	60%

B --SCALED PARTICIPATION SCORES

	MEAN	SD
YOUR RESPONSES	3.60*	3.48
PEER AVERAGE	4.73	3.66
MODEL A	4.17	4.31
MODEL B	9.20	0.98

* - YOUR SCORE IN FIGURE 1

C --FREQUENCY DISTRIBUTION OF SCALE SCORES (MEAN LEVELS OF PARTICIPATION)

Figure 4 *Continued*

D ---- BEHAVIOR BY PROBLEM TYPE

PROBLEM TYPE	PROBLEM NUMBERS	MODEL "A"	MODEL "B"	FEASIBLE SET	YOUR BEHAVIOR
1	14,15,17,28	AI	GII	AI,AII,CI,CII,GII	AI AI AI
2	3,5,	GII	GII	GII	CII AI
3	2,22,27,30	AI	GII	AI,AII,CI,CII,GII	AI AI CII
4	12,25,26,29	AI	CII	AI,AII,CI,CII	CI CI AI
5	7,8,20	GII	GII	GII	CII CI
6A	1,10	CI	CII	CI	CII CI
6B	11	CI	CII	CI,CII	CII CI
7	21,24	AII	GII	AII,CI,CII	CII AI
8	19,23	AII	GII	AII,CI,CII,GII	AI AII
9	4,16	CII	GII	CII	CII CI
10	6,9	CII	GII	CII	AI CI
11	13	GII	GII	CII,GII	CII
12	18	CII	CII	CII	CII

E ---- FREQUENCY OF AGREEMENT WITH THE NORMATIVE MODEL

	YOUR MEAN	PEER AVERAGE		PROBLEM NUMBERS
AGREEMENT WITH FEASIBLE SET	17 (57%)	20.8 (69%)		
AGREEMENT MODEL A (MINIMUM PARTICIPATION)	12 (40%)	12.1 (40%)	6 19 24	
AGREEMENT MODEL B (MAXIMUM PARTICIPATION)	4 (13%)	6.3 (21%)	9 16	

F ---- FREQUENCY OF RULE VIOLATIONS

	RULE	RESPONSES IN VIOLATION	YOUR FREQUENCY	PEER AVERAGE	PROBLEM NUMBERS
1	LEADER INFORMATION RULE	AI	3.0 (25%)*	0.7 (6%)	6 19 24
2	GOAL CONGRUENCE RULE	GII	0.0 (0%)	1.3 (10%)	0
3	UNSTRUCTURED PROBLEM RULE	AI,AII,CI	3.0 (50%)	2.8 (47%)	6 9 16
4	ACCEPTANCE RULE	AI,AII	1.0 (10%)	1.3 (13%)	5
5	CONFLICT RULE	AI,AII,CI	3.0 (60%)	1.9 (39%)	1 5 10
6	FAIRNESS RULE	AI,AII,CI,CII	2.0 (100%)	1.3 (63%)	3 5
7	ACCEPTANCE PRIORITY RULE	AI,AII,CI,CII	4.0 (100%)	2.9 (72%)	7 8 13 20

*----PROBABILITY OF RULE VIOLATION (THAT IS, FREQUENCY OF VIOLATION EXPRESSED AS A PERCENTAGE OF RULE APPLICABILITY)

285

Figure 4 *Continued*

		YOUR MEAN = X	MODEL A MEAN = A
		PEER MEAN = P	MODEL B MEAN = B

G----MAIN EFFECTS OF PROBLEM ATTRIBUTES

PARTICIPATIVENESS ON PROBLEMS WITH ATTRIBUTE

< LOW PARTICIPATION   HIGH PARTICIPATION >

PROBLEM ATTRIBUTES		(means)	chart	PROBLEMS WITH ATTRIBUTE
IMPORTANCE OF THE QUALITY OF THE FINAL SOLUTION (ATTRIBUTE A)	HIGH	X=4.17 P=4.97 A=4.38	----XA---P-------A---P------- B-------	(1,2,4,6,7,8,9,10,11,12,13, 16,18,19,20,21,22,23,24,25, 26,27,29,30)
	LOW	X=1.33 P=3.75 A=3.33	--------X-------A---P------- B	(3,5,14,15,17,28)
ADEQUACY OF MANAGER'S INFORMATION AND EXPERTISE (ATTRIBUTE B)	HIGH	X=3.67 P=4.24 A=2.75	A----X---P------- B-------	(1,2,8,11,12,20,22,25,26, 27,29,30)
	LOW	X=4.67 P=5.71 A=6.00	X----P-A------- B-------	(4,6,7,9,10,13,16,18,19, 21,23,24)
DEGREE OF STRUCTURE IN PROBLEM (ATTRIBUTE C)	HIGH	X=3.67 P=4.97 A=3.67	X----P------- B-------	(7,10,19,21,23,24)
	LOW	X=5.67 P=6.46 A=8.33	X----P---- A----B-------	(4,6,9,13,16,18)
IMPORTANCE OF SUBORDINATE ACCEPTANCE (ATTRIBUTE D)	HIGH	X=3.80 P=5.30 A=5.35	X----P------- B-------	(1,3,5,6,7,8,10,11,12,13,14, 15,16,18,19,20,22,24,29,30)
	LOW	X=3.20 P=3.59 A=1.80	X---A---P------- B-------	(2,4,9,17,21,23,25,26,27,28)
PROBABILITY OF LEADER'S SELLING HIS OWN SOLUTION (ATTRIBUTE E)	HIGH	X=1.30 P=3.68 A=1.80	X---A----P------- B-------	(6,12,14,15,16,19,22,24,29,30)
	LOW	X=6.30 P=6.91 A=8.90	X----A---B-------	(1,3,5,7,8,10,11,13,18,20)
DEGREE TO WHICH SUBORDINATES SHARE GOALS (ATTRIBUTE F)	HIGH	X=3.58 P=5.45 A=4.83	X----A---P------- B-------	(2,6,7,8,9,13,19,20,22, 23,27,30)
	LOW	X=4.75 P=4.49 A=3.92	A---P-X------- B-------	(1,4,10,11,12,16,18,21,24, 25,26,29)
PROBABILITY OF CONFLICT AMONG SUBORDINATES (ATTRIBUTE G)	HIGH	X=3.27 P=3.99 A=4.27	X-P-A------- B-------	(1,2,5,8,9,10,13,15,16,19, 21,22,26,28,29)
	LOW	X=3.93 P=5.47 A=4.07	X----P------- B-------	(3,4,6,7,11,12,14,17,18, 20,23,24,25,27,30)

•••••••   NOTE: THE THREE ATTRIBUTES WITH THE GREATEST EFFECT ON YOUR RESPONSES ARE A, C, AND E. •••••••

286

shows the proportion of cases in which the manager indicated he would use each of the five decision processes. The next row (opposite "peer frequency") shows the average use of these processes by the 41 managers constituting his training group. A comparison of these two rows indicates the methods the manager used more and less frequently than average.

The third row shows the distribution of decision processes that would be used by a manager using Model A, the time-efficient model in the 30 cases. The final row shows a distribution for Model B, the developmental or time-investment model.

To obtain an overall picture of how participative this manager's responses are in relation to other members of the training group and to Models A and B, it is necessary to assign scale values to each of the five decision processes. The actual numbers used for this purpose are based on research on the relative amounts of participation perceived to result from each process. AI is given a value of 0; AII a value of 1; CI a value of 5; CII a value of 8; and GII a value of 10.

With the aid of these scale values, a mean score can be computed for the manager, peers, and both models. These are obtained by multiplying the percentage of times each process is used by its scale value and dividing by 100. These mean scores are shown in B along with the standard deviation (SD), a measure of dispersion around the mean—that is, an indicator of how much behavior is varied over situations.

These mean scores are shown graphically in the figure at the bottom. Each asterisk is the mean score of one of the group members. The symbol X is printed underneath this manager's mean score, the symbol P under the group average, and the symbols A and B show the location on the scale of Models A and B respectively.

D through F in Figure 4 are on the second page of the printout. As we previously mentioned, the normative model identifies 12 problem types corresponding to the terminal nodes of the decision tree shown in Figure 2. There is at least one case within the set of 30 problems that has been designated by the authors and most managers as representative of each type. The problem types and corresponding problem numbers are shown in the two left-hand columns of D. In the third and fourth columns, the prescriptions of Models A and B are given, and the fifth column shows the feasible set for that problem type. The last column, marked "your behavior," indicates the manager's responses to each of the cases of the indicated problem type. If there is more than one case of that type, the methods used are shown in the same order as the problem numbers at the left-hand side.

E reports the frequency with which the manager's behavior agreed with the feasible set, with Model A, and with Model B. For comparison purposes, the average rates of agreement for members of the manager's training group are also presented.

Each time our manager chose a decision process that was outside the feasible set, he violated at least one of the seven rules underlying the model. F in Figure 4 reports the frequencies with which each rule was violated both by this manager and by his or her peer group. The right-hand column shows the specific cases in which the rule violations occurred. It should be noted that each manager understands the seven rules by the time he or she receives the feedback, and it is possible to re-examine the problems with the appropriate rule in mind.

We have previously noted that the cases included in a problem set are selected in accordance with a multifactorial experimental design. Each of the problem attributes is varied in a manner that will permit the manager to examine its role in his or her leadership style. Figure 4 (page 3 of printout) depicts these results. Consider problem attribute A—the importance of the quality of the final solution. The problem set contains cases that have a high quality requirement and those without a quality requirement (the identifying numbers of these cases are shown at the right-hand side of this table).

The mean scores for the manager's behavior on these two sets of cases are specified at the left-hand side of each row and are designated by the symbol X. They are also designated by the symbol X on each of the scales, and the slope of the line made by connecting the two letters (X) provides a visual representation of that difference.

If the score opposite "high" is greater (that is, more toward the right-hand side of the scale), it means that the manager encourages more participation from his subordinates on important decisions than on so-called "trivial" ones. However, if the score opposite "high" is lower, it means that the manager is willing to use more participative methods on problems for which the course of action adopted makes little difference and is more autocratic on "important" decisions.

The letter P shown on both scales designates the average effects of this attribute on the manager's peer group, and the letters A and B designate the effects on Models A and B respectively.

A similar logic can be used in interpreting the effects of each of the other attributes in the model. At the bottom of the page, the computer prints out the three attributes that have the greatest effect on the manager's behavior—magnitude of effect referring to the amount of difference the attribute makes in willingness to share decision-making power with subordinates.

The results shown in Figure 4 pertain to only one manager and to his or her peer group. Similar data have been obtained from several thousand managers, a sufficient number to provide the basis for some tentative generalizations about leadership patterns. One of our conclusions is that differences among managers in what might be termed a general trait of participativeness or authoritarianism are small in comparison with differences within managers. On the standardized cases in the problem sets, no manager has indicated that he or she would use the same decision process on all problems or decisions—and most use all methods under some circumstances.

It is clear that no one score computed for a manager and displayed on the printout adequately represents one's leadership style. To begin to understand one's style, the entire printout must be considered. For example, two managers may appear to be equally participative or autocratic on the surface, but a close look at the third page of the printout (Figure 4) may reveal crucial differences. One manager may limit participation by subordinates to decisions where the quality element is unimportant, such as the time and place of the company picnic, while the other manager may limit participation by subordinates to those decisions with a demonstrable impact on important organizational goals.

In about two-thirds of the cases we have examined—both those used in the problem sets and those reported to us by managers from their experiences—the manager's behavior was consistent with the feasible set of methods given by the model. Rules that helped ensure the acceptance of or commitment to a decision tend to be violated much more frequently than rules that protect the quality of the decision. Our findings suggest strongly that decisions made by typical managers are more likely to prove ineffective because subordinates don't fully accept decisions than because decision quality is deficient.

Let me now turn to another thing that we have learned in the design of this training—the usefulness of the small, informal group as a vehicle in the change process. The first four or five hours in the training process are spent in creating six- to eight-person teams operating under conditions of openness and trust. Each participant spends more than 50 percent of the training time with his or her small group before receiving feedback. Group activities include discussing cases in the problem set and trying to reach agreement on their mode of resolution, practicing participative leadership styles within their own groups, analyzing videotapes of group problem-solving activities; then group members give one another feedback on the basis of predictions of one another's leadership styles.

After feedback, group members compare results with one another and with their prior predictions and share with one another what they have learned as well as their plans to change. The use of small, autonomous groups greatly decreases the dependence of participants on the instructor for their learning and increases the number of people who can undergo the training at the same time. I have personally worked with as many as 140 managers at the same time (22 groups), and 40 to 50 is commonplace.

One criticism that has been correctly leveled at the Vroom and Yetton work stems from the fact that the data on which the feedback is based are, at best, reports of intended actions rather than observations of actual behavior. While we have evidence that most managers honestly try to portray what they think they would do in a particular situation rather than what they think they should do, I am persuaded by Argyris's evidence that many people are unaware of discrepancies between their espoused theories and their actions. Small groups can be helpful in pointing out these discrepancies. I have seen managers who were universally predicted by other group members to have a highly autocratic style, who were provided with very specific evidence of the ground for this assumption by other group members, but who later received a printout reflecting a much more participative style. I am less concerned about the relative validity of these discrepant pieces of data than I am about the fact that they are frequently confronted and discussed in the course of the training experience.

In fact, we have begun using a different source of potential inconsistencies, and it is logical to assume that this source will have more information about a manager's behavior than do the other members of his or her small group. I am referring to the manager's subordinates.

In a recent variant of the training program, subordinates were asked to predict their manager's behavior on each of the cases in the problem set. These predictions were made individually and processed by computer, which generated for each manager a detailed comparison of perceptions of leadership style with the mean perception of his or her subordinates. Not surprisingly, these two sources of information are not always in perfect agreement. Most managers, as seen by their subordinates, are substantially more autocratic (about one point on the 10-point scale) and in substantially less agreement with the model. Once again, I am less concerned with which is the correct description of the leader's behavior than I am with the fact that discrepancies generate a dialogue between the manager and subordinates that can be the source of mutual learning.

We are still experimenting with methods of using the Vroom-Yetton model in leadership training and, I believe, still learning from the results of this experimentation. How effective is the training in its present form? Does it produce long-lasting behavioral changes? I must confess that I do not know. Art Jago and I are in the first stages of designing an extensive follow-up study of almost 200 managers in 20 different countries who have been through a four-or five-day version of the training within the past two and one-half years. If we can solve the incredible logistical and methodological problems in a study of this kind, we should have results within a year.

On the basis of the evidence, I am optimistic on two counts: first, as to the leader's potential to vary style to meet the requirements of a situation; second, as to the leader's ability, through training and development, to enlarge the repertoire of his or her styles. In short, like Argyris and unlike Fiedler, I believe that managers can learn to become more effective leaders. But like Fiedler (and unlike Argyris), I believe that such effectiveness requires matching of one's leadership style to the demands of the situation. I also am confident that 50 years from now both contingency models will be found wanting in detail if not in substance. If we are remembered at that time, it will be for the kinds of questions we posed rather than the specific answers we provided.

Managerial Intelligence:
Why IQ Isn't Enough

Robert J. Sternberg

"Pssst! You want to recruit the brightest college students to be managers in your organization? Here's a hot tip: Then hire math majors."

This apocryphal "hot tip" has a certain logic, despite the fact that the so-called tip is unlikely to be whispered in the inner-sanctum of a managerial-recruiting office. Every organization wants the best possible managers it can find. To the extent its managerial recruiters believe that academic aptitude, or so-called "general intelligence" (g), is the single best predictor of managerial performance, then it would be quite reasonable for the recruiters to go first after mathematics majors. In an analysis of *Graduate Record Examination* subject-matter tests, for which scores are equated to *GRE* aptitude examinations, mathematics majors come out on top, with physics and then chemistry majors close behind, especially those who receive good grades in college (Briel, O'Neill, & Scheuneman, 1993). Yet there seems to be no rush among managerial recruiters to besiege the math, physics, and chemistry departments of colleges and universities with recruiting efforts. Why not? After all, these departments house those students who do best on conventional tests of abilities. Perhaps it is because even those who verbally espouse a conventional model of human intelligence do not quite, or at least fully, believe in it.

This article will show that, although conventional IQ is one part of managerial intelligence, it is not all there is to managerial intelligence. The conventional model of psychometrically measured intelligence needs to be superseded by a broader, more encompassing model of the kind proposed here.

TWO MODELS OF THE INTELLECTUAL ANTECEDENTS OF JOB SUCCESS

Model I

Conventional tests of intelligence contain a variety of abstract and usually rather academic kinds of problems—difficult vocabulary words, number series, figural matrices, and so on. According to the traditional psychometric model of the intellectual antecedents of job success—referred to here as Model I—scores on conventional intelligence tests are the best and perhaps the only consistent cognitive predictors of performance across a wide variety of jobs (Ree & Earles, 1993; Schmidt & Hunter, 1981).

The claim is sometimes even stronger. A number of psychologists have argued that scores based on solving problems from these tests—which are often summarized by a single number estimating g—provide the best single predictor of practically everything, but most importantly for present purposes, job performance (e.g., Barrett & Depinet, 1991; Gottfredson, 1986; Herrnstein & Murray, 1994; Hunter & Hunter, 1984; Jensen, 1993; Ree & Earles, 1993; Schmidt & Hunter, 1981, 1993). None of these psychologists have argued that g is the only meaningful predictor. But they are generally of accord that, if there are other intellectual abilities (as opposed to, say, personality traits such as conscientiousness) that predict job performance, their role is minimal to nonexistent. Indeed, so many psychologists have made this claim that one could not help wondering how they all could be wrong. Perhaps, however, they are all wrong.

Model II

The goal of this article is to show that better prediction of job performance, in general, and of managerial performance, in particular, is to be attained by broadening our conception of intelligence. One way to broaden this conception is to include practical and creative abilities in addition to the memory-analytical abilities that many psychologists already consider when they speak of g (Sternberg, 1985, 1988). I will refer to this model as Model II. Elsewhere, I have referred to this model as one of "successful intelligence" (Sternberg, 1996).

By maintaining a narrow conception of intelligence, and empirically testing only this narrow conception, psychologists espousing the conventional view do not allow themselves an opportunity to disconfirm or at least expand upon what I believe is a limited conception both of human abilities and of how these abilities affect job performance.

Where Models I and II Converge and Diverge

At one level, there is no disagreement between the two models: clearly scores on conventional intelligence tests do predict performance on many, and probably most jobs. Indeed, as Herrnstein and Murray (1994) have pointed out, performance on these tests predicts many kinds of outcomes in society, including income, entrance into the job market, job placement in the job market, and likelihood of going on welfare, among other things. What is at issue are two things: what the prediction means in the first place—whether the value of Model I might be inflated by considering predictive validity outside the context of construct validity; and whether the prediction couldn't be even better with Model II than with Model I. I will consider each of these issues in turn.

WHY CONSTRUCT VALIDITY IS MORE IMPORTANT THAN JUST PREDICTIVE VALIDITY

A test is predictively valid to the extent that it predicts some criterion. A test is construct valid to the extent that it veridically measures a construct. Predictive validity is an aspect of construct validity. For example, one way of determining whether a test truly measures intelligence is to assess whether the test predicts some form of behavior that is deemed to require intelligence. The argument here is that the Model-II conception of intelligence ultimately will result in higher construct validity overall with respect to intelligence, including higher predictive validity for job placement and performance.

It is important to consider a concept of intelligence, whether of managers or anyone else, from the standpoint of construct validity, in general, and not just of predictive validity. The reason is that a test can be predictively valid, but for reasons that are not relevant to its construct validity. Consider how, both with respect to quality of job placement and with respect to quality of job performance, predictive validity can lead to a false conclusion that a test has construct validity for measuring intelligence that it does not, in fact, have.

Job Placement

Herrnstein and Murray (1994), among others, have shown that if one classifies jobs according to various socioeconomic criteria, tests based on Model I predict job placement, or even whether one is employed in the first place. These statistics may be correct, but their interpretation of the statistics is not correct.

The interpretation that some Model-I theorists, including Herrnstein and Murray, have proposed is one of the invisible guiding hand of nature (their term). The idea, to put it somewhat crudely, is that the cream rises to the top and the dregs sink to the bottom. Those higher in scores on traditional measures of intelligence are at an advantage and so are able to perform at the level required by higher level, more demanding jobs; those lower in scores on traditional intelligence tests are at a disadvantage in being able to meet the requirements of intellectually demanding jobs, and so end up in less demanding jobs, or at the extreme, with no jobs at all. Higher measured intelligence is thereby viewed as the causal antecedent of better job placement and performance.

Certainly, a person with an IQ of 150 will be at an advantage over a person with an IQ of 50 for virtually any intellectually demanding job. But when we get away from extremes, the argument becomes fuzzier. Consider why.

In order to be admitted to a reasonably selective college—the kind that provides a fast track to managerial and other higher prestige jobs—one typically has to take a college-admissions test, such as the *Scholastic Assessment Test* (*SAT*) or the *American College Test* (*ACT*). These Model-I tests, whatever they may be called, are very similar in form and content to conventional intelligence tests. Some colleges use formulas employing the test scores to determine admissions; others use the test scores in a more advisory capacity. However the scores are used, higher scores will be associated with higher probabilities of college admission. The predictive function may or may not be linear. In many cases, the function will more resemble a cutoff function than a linear function: Below a certain score point, the college just will not consider a candidate.

The result is that students who test poorly on Model-I tests are at a disadvantage in applying to selective colleges. Moreover, they are at a disadvantage in applying not to just one of these colleges, but to virtually all of them, because the tests are almost universally required. Even the few selective colleges that do not mandate the tests—such as Bates and Bowdoin—welcome scores from those who wish to submit them.

So low scorers will see their educational options reduced, and the chances of making it to the fast track to job and especially managerial opportunities will be reduced as well.

Some individuals will score high enough to be admitted to a selective, or at least, reasonably selective college, but then will not make it into a selective graduate program—in business, in law, in economics, or whatever—because requirements for selective graduate programs are even higher than they are for selective colleges. The funnel has narrowed, with the result that it is even harder to get into the very best graduate programs than it is to get into the very best undergraduate programs. Now individuals who do not score high on the tests are again disadvantaged. Some who may have made it into a selective college will not have the same luck the next time around.

The point, quite simply, is that the access routes to the occupations and placements within these occupations of highest prestige, and ultimately, income, are blocked to those who do not score highly on Model-I tests. Even among high scorers, there is a filtering process such that those with the highest scores will be, on average, at an advantage over those with high but not truly superior scores. The implication is that, by virtue of a societal decision to weigh these tests heavily in the selection processes of colleges and universities, those who do not score well on Model-I tests find that it is very difficult to gain entrance into the jobs of higher socioeconomic status and rewards. This fact, curiously, has nothing to do with the validity of the tests, as can be shown by the changing criteria for selection decisions over time and place.

In the past, parental socioeconomic status served much of the function in the U.S. that test scores presently serve, so that students from the "right" families found themselves at a great advantage for admission to selective universities. Those of the wrong socioeconomic status—or religion, race, or ethnic group, for that matter—were likely to find the doors closed, regardless of their Model-I intelligence.

Consider a hypothetical example. Suppose we decided as a society to use height rather than Model-I test scores as a basis for admission to selective universities (Sternberg, 1995a). Height has the advantage of being more reliably measured than does Model-I intelligence, so it has at least that one advantage. Moreover, we apparently do use height as a measure of ability, in that CEOs and other people in high-status jobs do, in fact, tend to be taller than those in low-status jobs.

Now, to get into Harvard as an undergraduate, perhaps one would have to be 6 feet, 4 inches tall. To be admitted to the Harvard graduate program in business or law, however, one might have to be as tall as 6′ 6″. Now, what will happen after, say, 25 years? Clearly, people in higher status jobs for which university training provides access will tend to be relatively tall, and those in lower status jobs will tend to be relatively short. This effect will occur, regardless of the validity of height for the use to which it is placed. Indeed, it may not predict either school or job performance at all.

The use of this example is not to argue that Model-I abilities should be irrelevant to job placement, but rather, that their present relevance to job placement may or may not reflect the validity of these abilities to predict job performance. Because tests are heavily used for a given purpose does not necessarily mean that they are valid for that purpose.

Job Performance

The case for using Model-I tests to predict job performance might seem tighter than that for using them to predict job placement. If these tests predict job performance, does not this relation indicate that higher Model-I abilities cause better job performance? Not necessarily. Indeed, perhaps not at all.

There are many factors that could mediate the correlation between test performance and job performance. One possible factor is the existence of a self-fulfilling prophecy, if the evaluators are aware of the test scores (Rosenthal & Jacobson, 1968). A second possible factor is any variable that may mediate both test scores and job performance, such as number of years of education (Ceci, 1996). A third possible factor includes sources of variation that result in higher test scores and in higher job evaluations, but not necessarily in better job performance. For example, higher verbal ability may lead to higher test scores as well as to higher evaluations of performance. But sometimes individuals use verbal ability not to express, but to hide their true level of performance, especially when there are no objective measures of job performance available. Higher verbal ability thus may lead to higher test scores, and later, to higher evaluations of job performance than an individual merits.

I wish to emphasize that I am not stating that any of these factors plays a major role in mediating the correlation of Model-I tests with job performance, or necessarily even any role. The point, rather, is that the fact that a correlation exists tells us little or nothing about why it exists. At times, people may draw causal inferences that are simply wrong with regard to the reason for a correlation.

Consider a concrete and, I believe, plausible example. Model-I tests do not assess creativity. People who are creative are at no particular advantage on conventional ability tests, and may actually be at a disadvantage, seeing response options that may not be allowed or rewarded by those who constructed or will score the tests. Now suppose that two individuals take a battery of conventional (Model-I) tests. The first individual scores higher than the second one, despite the second one's being more creative. When the job performances of the two individuals are considered, the same factor that led the second individual nowhere on the Model-I test may also lead him or her nowhere in terms of a job evaluation. Indeed, the evaluator may be unfavorably impressed with the performance of the creative individual, seeing it as incompatible with company norms. Even good ideas may be punished because they are seen as thus incompatible (see Sternberg & Lubart, 1995). In contrast, the first, more conventional thinker may be seen as better approaching the company ideal.

The result is that the pattern of performance of the first individual leads both to better test scores and to better evaluations on the job. This second individual, however, with another boss, might be someone who would be viewed as capable of contributing quite a bit more to the company than could the first individual. In essence, the test (which provides the predictor measurement) and the evaluator (who provides the criterion measurement) share the same bias in favor of more conventional types of thinkers and against less conventional types.

In sum, we need to go beyond correlations to a theory of what constitutes intelligence, in general, or managerial intelligence, in particular. In the next section, I propose such a theory.

A TRIARCHIC THEORY OF MANAGERIAL INTELLIGENCE

The triarchic theory of human intelligence (Sternberg, 1985, 1988, 1996) holds that intelligence comprises three aspects: analytical, practical, and creative. All three of these aspects are keys to managerial intelligence, but Model-I tests measure only the first aspect, despite the fact that all three aspects are measurable and, I will argue, contribute to managerial performance.

Analytical Intelligence

Although Model-I tests measure analytical intelligence, and probably do so reasonably well, they nevertheless do so in a more limited sense than would be ideal for the prediction of managerial performance. What, exactly, are analytical skills, and how are they important to managerial performance?

Components of Intelligence

The triarchic theory distinguishes among three kinds of information-processing components that, together, constitute the building blocks of the analytical aspect of intelligence. These three kinds of components are referred to as metacomponents, performance components, and knowledge-acquisition components.

Metacomponents are used to plan, monitor, and evaluate one's problem solving. Performance components are used to execute the plans for problem solving devised by the metacomponents. Knowledge-acquisition components are used to learn how to solve the problems in the first place. Consider some examples of each of the components, without any attempt to be exhaustive (see Sternberg, 1985, for more details).

Real-world Examples of Components in Action

An important aspect of coping with problem situations arises before problem solving even begins. This aspect is problem definition—realizing what the problem is in the first place. Problem definition is important in the corporate world. Managers at Intel, for example, recognized that they had a problem when Intel's Pentium chip turned out to make rare calculation errors. But they initially failed to define the problem appropriately, resulting in a massive public-relations fiasco. Indeed, the problem was at least as much one of public relations as one of computation. But because the managers initially did not see the problem this way, they tried to shrug off the problem. When it didn't go away when ignored and when initial attempts to solve it—corrections for selected users—faltered, the company eventually offered to correct the problem for all users.

Misdefinition of a problem has cost companies more than it cost Intel. For example, the A. H. Robins Company went into bankruptcy over its failure to define properly the problem with its Dalkon Shield Intrauterine Device. Later, it could not afford the lawsuits for damages caused by the defective product. In contrast, the Coca-Cola Company recognized that it had a serious problem with its new Coke, and the company redefined the problem: It reintroduced the old Coke as "Classic Coke," and thereby pulled a victory from what had seemed to be the jaws of defeat. The company now had two products instead of just one.

Similarly, Johnson and Johnson realized the full extent of the problem they had with the Tylenol brand name when someone started spiking Extra-Strength Tylenol with cyanide. The company officers eventually decided to remove all Tylenol products from the store shelves. What to many seemed like a public-relations disaster in fact proved to be a temporary glitch: Johnson and Johnson's excellent management of the problem resulted in their regaining their first-place market share.

In each of these cases, correct definition of a problem resulted in a gain for management, whereas incorrect definition of a problem resulted in a loss. Proper analysis of a problem, therefore, is essential to management success.

A second metacomponent is formulating a strategy for problem solving. Strategic planning is recognized as important by management in almost all businesses, of course. The question is whether they do it, and whether they do it well.

IBM and Apple both devised strategies for maximizing the sales of their microcomputer hardware. But the strategies were, to a large extent, diametrically opposed. IBM allowed an open system, which clones could then copy. Apple did not, and aggressively pursued companies that tried to make use of their operating system (an irony, because their product was quite similar to an earlier product, Xerox's Star System).

Obviously, both products had advantages and disadvantages. But today IBM has largely come out of an extremely difficult turnaround period, whereas Apple has not. Clones produced competition in the marketing of hardware but also yielded a software explosion for IBM-compatible machines. As people bought more and more of these machines, more and more software was produced to work on them. When IBM started competing on price, the company was able to capture a decent share of an increasing market, whereas Apple found itself isolated with an operating system that could not be found on other machines. Worse, when WINDOWS appeared, people became able to do on IBM-compatible machines some of the graphics that formerly had been easier on the Apple products. Today, Apple has started opening up its design systems, and the question is whether it is too late.

Consider a knowledge-acquisition component—selective comparison. This component is used when one draws on past experience in order to help solve problems in the present. It is part of what makes managers who are successful in one company attractive to another company. The assumption in hiring such managers is that they will draw on a large knowledge base of experience, which will help them to solve the problems in the new company in the way they solved them in the old company.

Sometimes managers who succeeded in the previous company succeed in the new company, but other times they are spectacular failures. There are a number of reasons they may fail in a new setting, of course, but selective comparison is probably one of them. As futile as is the lack of selective comparison is its overuse or misuse. Each company is different—with its own set of working conditions, its own organizational culture, its own competitive context, and so on. The result is that someone who succeeds in one environment may not succeed particularly well in another.

This problem applies not only across companies, but across jobs. For example, a very successful businessman, such as Ross Perot, may find that skills that led to success in business do not necessarily lead to success in politics. In Mexico, some members of the leading party, the Partido Revolucionario Institucional (PRI), have just attempted (unsuccessfully) to pass a rule that would require candidates for top offices to have run for other offices. The rationale, similar to that presented here, is that many of the technocrats who were being selected for top positions were not successfully able to make the transition from the demands of being technocrats to the demands of being in political positions. Individuals in the United States, such as McGeorge Bundy and Robert McNamara, showed during the Vietnam War that this country is not immune from the same transition failures.

To summarize, if we wish to understand intelligence as it applies in the real world of management, it is useful to think beyond a narrow and unitary index such as IQ, and to think in terms of broader abilities that are directly relevant in a management context.

Measurement of Components

Various attempts have been made to measure the individual components of intellectual functioning that are specified by the triarchic theory of intelligence (see Sternberg, 1985). For example, in an analogical-reasoning task, separate scores might be computed for individuals with respect to performance components of encoding of stimuli and inference of relations (Sternberg, 1977). At one level, these attempts have been successful, but at another level, they have been less so. The way in which they have been successful has been in terms of internal validity. It has been possible to construct models of performance on information-processing tasks that account for much of the variation in response-time and response-accuracy data. The way in which they have been less than successful has been in terms of external validity. Prediction of test or other kinds of performance using component scores has been no better than prediction using conventional factor scores, and in some cases, it has been worse.

In retrospect, the failure to improve upon prediction obtained by conventional factor scores is probably due to the fact that the analyses of component scores used conventional measures, such as measures of analogical or syllogistic reasoning. Although the subscores were different, the tests were not. Hence, what was done, basically, was to redistribute the sources of variation in the scores. Without a fundamental expansion of the kinds of testing done, improvement in prediction was not likely. One way to expand testing is through the measurement of practical intelligence.

Practical Intelligence

Perhaps even more important to managerial intelligence than the analytical aspect of intelligence is the practical aspect of intelligence. A number of investigators have studied practical intelligence, or common sense, and suggested that it differs from the kind of intelligence measured by Model-I tests of intelligence. Practical intelligence involves not just adaptation to environments, but also shaping and selection of environments. It is not possible to review here all of the available work on practical intelligence. For reviews of some of this work, see Sternberg and Wagner (1986) and Sternberg, Wagner, Williams, and Horvath (1995).

Real-World Examples of Practical Intelligence in Action

The best place to see practical intelligence in action is in any workplace. Most of the important rules of the workplace are unspoken. Some people learn them; others do not. A few people excel way above the rest. For example, in the financial world, few people have met with the kind of success that Warren Buffet or Peter Lynch have achieved, despite the efforts of many individuals to figure out the rules under which the stock market operates. Similarly, individuals such as Jack Welch at General Electric, Michael Eisner at Disney, or Robert Allen at AT&T, for whatever mistakes they may have made, have moved their companies forward at a remarkable rate during a variety of business climates.

The Nature of Tacit Knowledge

Much of our own work (as reviewed in Sternberg, Wagner, & Okagaki, 1993; Sternberg et al., 1995) has concentrated on the notion of tacit knowledge for management. Tacit knowledge refers to action-oriented knowledge, acquired without direct help from others, that allows individuals to achieve goals they personally value. The acquisition and use of such knowledge appears to be uniquely important to competent performance in real-world endeavors, including management.

There are three main characteristic features of tacit knowledge. These features address, respectively, the structure of tacit knowledge, the conditions of its use, and the conditions under which it is acquired. First, tacit knowledge is procedural in nature. Second, tacit knowledge is relevant to the attainment of goals people value. Third, tacit knowledge is acquired with little help from others. Knowledge containing these three properties is called tacit because it often must be inferred from actions or statements.

We have expressed tacit knowledge in terms of production systems (Sternberg et al., 1995), or ordered series of if-then statements. Tacit knowledge is thus always wedded to particular uses in particular situations or in classes of situations. It is also knowledge that is practically useful, and further, is instrumental to the attainment of goals people value. The more highly valued a goal is, and the more directly the knowledge supports the attainment of the goal, the more useful is the knowledge. For example, knowledge about how to make subordinates feel valued is practically useful for managers who value that outcome, but is not practically useful for those who are unconcerned with making their subordinates feel valued. Thus, tacit knowledge is distinguished from knowledge, even "how to" knowledge, that is irrelevant to goals that people care about personally.

Tacit knowledge is acquired without direct help from others. It is usually acquired on one's own. The knowledge is unspoken, underemphasized, and typically poorly conveyed relative to its importance for practical success. Thus, it is acquired under conditions of minimal environmental support. In the typical organizational environment, tacit knowledge may be hidden—for example, how one really gets a promotion as opposed to how one is supposed to get the promotion.

Construct Validation

We have developed an instrument that measures tacit knowledge in managers (Wagner & Sternberg, 1991), as well as instruments that measure tacit knowledge for other occupations, including sales people and academic psychologists (see Sternberg, Wagner, & Okagaki, 1993). Table 1 shows a typical type of item for a business-management scale. The scale was constructed through a rather elaborate procedure described elsewhere (see Sternberg, 1995b). Items are scored by comparing individual responses to those of an expert group that is nominated by top executives in a given company setting. Several questions arise with regard to the tacit-knowledge construct.

First, are individual differences in tacit knowledge domain-general, or common across various aspects of the work environment? Two kinds of factor analysis were performed on the tacit-knowledge scores of a sample of 64 business managers (Wagner, 1987). These techniques enable one to determine the latent constructs that underlie a measured construct.

First, a principal-components analysis yielded a first principal component that accounted for 44% of the total variance, and for 76% of total

Table 1

An Example of an Item Measuring Tacit Knowledge for Management

---

It is your second year as a mid-level manager in a company in the communications industry. You head a department of about thirty people. The evaluation of your first year on the job has been generally favorable. Performance ratings for your department are at least as good as they were before you took over, and perhaps even a little better. You have two assistants. One is quite capable. The other just seems to go through the motions but to be of little help.

You believe that although you are well liked, there is little that would distinguish you in the eyes of your superiors from the nine other managers at a comparable level in the company.

Your goal is rapid promotion to the top of the company. The following is a list of things you are considering doing in the next two months. You obviously cannot do them all. Rate the importance of each by its priority as a means of reaching your goal.

_____ a. Find a way to get rid of the "dead wood" (e.g., the less helpful assistant and three or four others).

_____ b. Participate in a series of panel discussions to be shown on the local public television station.

_____ c. Find ways to make sure your superiors are aware of your important accomplishments.

_____ d. Make an effort to better match the work to be done with the strengths and weaknesses of individual employees.

---

variance after the correlations among scores were corrected for unreliability. The residual matrix was not significant after extracting the first principal component, meaning that the first factor appears to have accounted for all meaningful variation in the data.

Second, a confirmatory factor analysis was performed to test alternative models of the factor structure of the tacit knowledge inventory more formally. The results supported the generality of tacit knowledge. A model consisting of a single general factor provided the best fit to the data and yielded a small and nonsignificant difference between predicted and observed covariances.

The domain generality of tacit knowledge was given additional support when the identical tacit-knowledge framework was used to construct an inventory to measure tacit knowledge for the domain of academic psychology. In a group of 60 undergraduates, the correlation between scores on the business and psychology inventories was .58 for total score, and almost as high for three subscores: .52 for managing oneself, .47 for managing tasks, and .52 for managing others, all significant at the .001 level. These results further support the domain generality of tacit knowledge.

Second, given this domain-generality (i.e., high level of correlation across scores in different aspects of work), are tacit-knowledge inventories just Model-I intelligence tests in disguise, rather than measures yielding some incremental variance obtainable only through Model II? Results from several studies of tacit knowledge, in which participants were given a traditional measure of cognitive abilities in addition to a tacit-knowledge inventory, suggest that this is not the case.

For example, Wagner and Sternberg (1985) gave the Verbal Reasoning subtest of the *Differential Aptitudes Tests* to a sample of 22 undergraduates. The correlation between tacit knowledge and verbal reasoning was .16 ($p > .05$). In subsequent studies a deviation scoring system, in which lower scores indicated better performance than higher scores, was used to quantify tacit knowledge. Thus, a positive relation between tacit knowledge and cognitive ability would be represented by a negative correlation. For a sample of 60 undergraduates, the correlation between tacit knowledge and verbal reasoning was $-.12$ ($p > .05$).

An important limitation of these results is that the participants were Yale undergraduates and thus represented a restricted range of verbal abilities. We also administered the Tacit Knowledge Inventory to a sample of 45 managers who participated in a leadership development program at the Center for Creative Leadership in Greensboro, North Carolina (Wagner & Sternberg, 1990). Participants in this program routinely completed a battery of tests, including an intelligence test. For this sample, the correlation between tacit knowledge and IQ was $-.14$ ($p > .05$).

But even business managers represent a restricted range in IQ, and perhaps in tacit knowledge as well. What would be the relation between tacit knowledge and IQ in a more general sample? In a study at the Human Resources Laboratory at Brooks Air Force Base that was supervised by Malcolm Ree, Eddy (1988) examined relations between our *Tacit Knowledge Inventory for Managers* and the *Armed Services Vocational Aptitude Battery (ASVAB)* for a sample of 631 Air Force recruits, 29% of whom were women, and 19% of whom were members of a minority group.

The median correlation of subtest scores with the tacit-knowledge inventory was −.07, with a range from .06 to −.15. Of the 10 correlations, only 2 correlations were significantly different from 0, despite the large sample size of 631 recruits. A factor analysis of all the test data, followed by oblique rotations (which allow correlated axes), yielded the usual four *ASVAB* factors (vocational-technical information, clerical speed, verbal ability, and mathematics) and a distinct factor for tacit knowledge. The factor loading for the *Tacit Knowledge Inventory for Managers* score on the tacit-knowledge factor was .9, with a maximum loading for the score on the four *ASVAB* factors of only .06. Upon oblique rotation, the four *ASVAB* factors were moderately intercorrelated, but the correlations between the tacit-knowledge factor and the four *ASVAB* factors were near 0 and all less than .1 in absolute value. Thus, the abilities measured by a test of tacit knowledge appear to be distinct from the more traditional abilities measured by the *ASVAB*.

As an incidental result, although Eddy (1988) did not report scores separately by race and sex, correlations were reported between scores and coded variables that indicated race and sex. Significant correlations in the .2–.4 range between *ASVAB* subtest scores and both race and sex indicated that, on the *ASVAB*, minority group members had poorer scores than did majority group members, and that women scored lower than men. However, nonsignificant correlations between tacit knowledge and both race (.03) and sex (.02) indicated comparable levels of performance on the tacit-knowledge measures between minority and majority group members and between women and men.

Third, and most importantly, does performance on measures of tacit knowledge uniquely predict performance in management? In several early studies, we gave our tacit-knowledge measure to samples of business managers and examined correlations between tacit-knowledge scores and criterion referenced measures of performance in business (i.e., objective measures of performance, such as number of employees supervised or merit salary increases). For example, in samples of 54 (Wagner & Sternberg, 1985) and 64 (Wagner, 1987) business managers, we found correlations ranging from .2 to .4 between tacit-knowledge scores and criteria such as salary, years of management experience, and whether the manager worked for a company at the top of the Fortune 500 list. These uncorrected correlations were in the range of the average correlation between cognitive ability test scores and job performance (Wigdor & Garner, 1982).

In these studies, the managers were from a wide range of companies, and only global criterion measures—such as salary and years of management experience—were available for study. When more precise criterion measures have been available, higher correlations between tacit knowledge and managerial performance have been found. For example, in a study of bank branch managers (Wagner & Sternberg, 1985), the simple correlation between tacit knowledge and average percentage of merit-based salary increase was .48 ($p < .05$). The simple correlation between tacit knowledge and average performance rating for the category of "generating new business for the bank" was .56 ($p < .05$).

Further support for the predictive validity of tacit-knowledge measures was provided by the previously mentioned study of business managers who participated in the Leadership Development Program at the Center for Creative Leadership (Wagner & Sternberg, 1990). In this study, we were able to examine correlations among a variety of measures.

The dependent variable was performance on two managerial simulation tasks, called Earth II and Energy International. Trained observers rated the performance of the managers in eight categories: activity level, discussion leading, influencing others, problem analysis, task orientation, motivating others, verbal effectiveness, and interpersonal skills. Independent variables included our tacit-knowledge inventory, as well as tests of intelligence (*Shipley Institute for Living Scale*), personality (*California Psychological Inventory*), styles (*Myers-Briggs Type Indicator* and *Kirton Adaptation Innovation Inventory*), interpersonal orientation (*Fundamental Interpersonal Relations Orientation— Behavior*), a measure of field independence (*Hidden Figures Test*), and a measure of job satisfaction (the *Managerial Job Satisfaction Questionnaire*).

Beginning with zero-order correlations, we found that the best predictors of the criterion score of managerial performance were tacit knowledge ($r = -.61, p < .001$), followed by IQ ($r = .38, p < .001$). The correlation between tacit knowledge and IQ was not significantly different from 0 ($r = -.14, p > .05$). In a series of hierarchical regressions, tacit knowledge contributed significantly to prediction of the dependent measure, even after all other independent variables were placed in the equation first.

In sum, these and other studies suggest that a part of practical intelligence, utilization of tacit knowledge, plays an important part in management success. Two points should be made clear, however, about the relation of practical to more conventional forms of intelligence.

First, although we did not find statistically significant correlations with IQ, such correlations would very likely be found if the full range of IQs, with a mean of 100 and a standard deviation of 15, were used. At the same time, these population parameters apply to the general population, not to the population of people who actually become managers, which is probably better represented by the samples we studied than would be a sample with a mean of 100 and a standard deviation of 15.

Second, the results suggest to us that analytical intelligence (Model I) and practical intelligence (as added by Model II) both contribute to prediction of job performance. The situation is not an "either-or" one, but rather, a "both-and" one: Prediction is improved by using both kinds of tests, at the same time that one obtains measurement that is more construct valid, representing a more nearly complete range of intellectual abilities (at least according to Model II). But there is still a third aspect of intelligence that needs to be considered.

Creative Intelligence

With the rate at which the world is changing, and the explosion in both procedural and declarative knowledge, the ability to think creatively has become important, perhaps more so than ever before. Because the business environment is changing rapidly as well, creativity is particularly important in a management setting.

According to our investment theory of creativity (Sternberg & Lubart, 1991, 1992, 1995, 1996), creative people are individuals who are willing and able to "buy low and sell high" in the realm of ideas. Buying low means pursuing ideas that are unknown or out of favor but that have growth potential. Often, when these ideas are first presented, they encounter resistance. The creative individual persists in the face of this resistance and eventually sells high, moving on to the next new or unpopular idea. Sometimes creativity is thwarted because a person puts forth an idea prematurely or holds an idea so long that it becomes common or obsolete.

According to the investment theory, creativity requires a confluence of six distinct but interrelated resources: intellectual ability, knowledge, styles of thinking, personality, motivation, and environment. Because the focus of this article is on managerial intelligence, I will deal here only with the intellectual aspect of creativity.

The intellectual aspect requires especially the synthetic ability to see problems in new ways and to escape the bounds of conventional thinking. An example illustrates this point.

Real-World Examples of Creative Intelligence in Action

A high-level executive in one of the Big Three automobile firms in the United States was faced with a dilemma. On the one hand, he loved his job and the money he made doing it. On the other hand, he absolutely detested his boss. After carefully considering his options, he decided to visit a headhunter. The headhunter indicated that there would be no problem in finding him another position.

The executive told his wife (from whom I learned this story) how the appointment had gone and that he was confident he would find another job. She then told him that she had taught that day a unit in her college class on applied intelligence that dealt with redefining problems. The basic idea is that you take a problem you are facing and turn it on its head. In other words, you look at the problem in a totally new way—one that is different not only from how you have seen it in the past, but that is also different from how other people would be likely to see it in the present. As she described her lesson, the executive realized how he could apply what his wife had told him to his own problem at work.

The next day the executive returned to the headhunter and gave the headhunter his boss's name. He asked the headhunter to look for another job—not for himself this time, but for his boss. The headhunter agreed and, before long, found something for the boss. The boss received a phone call offering him another job, not realizing, of course, that the offer was the result of the teamwork of his subordinate and the headhunter. The boss accepted the position, and the boss's old position was later offered to the executive who had arranged for the headhunter to find the job.

This example illustrates the importance of creative intelligence, and particularly, of the ability to see old problems in new ways. Of course, there are many other examples. For example, a group working on automobile safety at Tennessee Technological University realized that the problem of protecting people from injury during a crash had always been taken as the need to keep people in their seats—to stop the passengers from moving around and hitting parts of the car. The Tennessee group was able to generate a creative approach to automobile safety by redefining the problem. They shifted the focus from the person to the car and worked on making the interior of the car less likely to hurt a person if a crash occurred (Stein, 1989).

Management often does not display creativity in operating a business. A case study of lack of creative intelligence, at least at the corporate level, can be found, perhaps ironically, in the ability-testing industry.

The first well-known computer, UNIVAC, was created at about the same time as the first edition of the *Wechsler Adult Intelligence Scale* (*WAIS*). At the time, both inventions were certainly highly creative. But UNIVAC, which had less power than even the most basic current desktop computers, filled a large room with its hardware. UNIVAC would not even be recognizable today to the younger generation of computer-users, and anyone who used it or a similar device would be met with incredulity.

In stark contrast, the latest revised edition of the Wechsler differs little from the first edition and contains largely the same type of material, in updated form. Some other intelligence tests, such as the Stanford-Binet, have undergone only slightly more of an evolutionary process. When one looks at computers that have increased millions of times in terms of speed and power, the lack of progress in intelligence testing is flabbergasting. Indeed, it is questionable whether any other major technology has evolved so slowly.

Why has high technology moved at light-speed in comparison with the glacial development of intelligence tests? There may be many reasons, but one is almost certainly the different competitive landscape in the computer industry versus the intelligence-testing industry. Manufacturers in each case define their problem in terms of economic viability—the bottom line. With thousands of viable companies competing in the hardware and software markets, the competition in the computing business is extremely intense. A company that does not move forward very quickly soon dies, as many computing companies, in fact, have.

The competition in the testing industry is much less intense, with the result that testing companies have been able to succeed in selling products that, except for minor facelifts, are basically 50 years old. If one compares the new Wechsler (or Stanford-Binet) to the old, one will see little meaningful difference. A further problem is that a less competitive industry is likely to attract individuals who would not, for whatever reasons, be likely to thrive in the rapidly-changing world of a highly competitive industry.

Construct Validation

Can creative intelligence of the sort described above be measured? We have sought to test the investment theory in several studies (Sternberg & Lubart, 1995).

In one study, 48 adults equally divided by gender and ranging in age from 18 to 65 years (with a mean age of 33 years) were asked to produce two creative products in each of four domains. They were also asked to complete cognitive tests measuring intellectual processes related to creativity and to fill out other measures as well.

The four domains in which creative production were assessed were writing, art, advertising, and science. In each domain, participants were given between 3 and 10 options, from which they had to select 2. In the writing domain, participants were asked to provide sketches of short stories for titles such as "Beyond the Edge" and "The Octopus's Sneakers." In the artistic domain, participants were asked to produce drawings, given topics such as "hope," "rage," and "the Earth from an insect's point of view." Topics for potential television commercials in the advertising domain were (intentionally boring) ones such as "bowties," "brussels sprouts," and the "Internal Revenue Service." And topics for scientific problems to be solved included "How could we detect extraterrestrial aliens among us?" and "How could we tell if someone had been on the moon in the past month?"

All products were rated by multiple raters for overall creativity as well as for novelty, aptness to the topic chosen, aesthetic value, integration of disparate elements, technical skill, and perceived effort. The various ratings all tended to be moderately to highly intercorrelated with each other. What did we find?

First, as in previous research (Amabile, 1982, 1983), we found that creativity can be reliably assessed. Interrater reliabilities for the four domains ranged from .81 to .89, with a median of .86. Averaging over domains, mean interrater reliability was .92.

The high interrater reliability is promising, but there is a caveat. In a related study (Lubart & Sternberg, 1995), we found that sometimes raters agree that a response is not very creative, but apparently, their agreement is based on the unpopularity of the point of view taken. Thus, ratings may be reliable across raters, but not necessarily always valid. Scoring can be no better than those doing the scoring.

Second, correlations between products within domains were generally moderate: .63 for writing, .37 for art, .65 for advertisements, .52 for science, and .67 for overall creative performance across products. Levels of creativity were thus moderately correlated within a given domain.

Third, creativity appears to be relatively domain-specific. Correlations across domains ranged from .23 to .62, with a median of .36. Although five of six cross-domain correlations were statistically significant, they could at best be categorized as weak to moderate.

Fourth, intellectual functioning (as well as the other resources we tested) correlated significantly with creative performance. Using nonentrenched tests of intelligence (i.e., tests requiring coping with novelty, such as the *Cattell Culture-Fair Test of g*), the multiple correlation of the tests of intelligence with rated creativity of products was .75. However, it is important to note that we used only tests of intelligence that measured nonentrenched kinds of thinking. In another study, high-school students completed other measures of creativity, including both multiple-choice and essay items. For example, the multiple-choice items might ask the individuals to solve mathematics problems using new numerical operations (created just for the test). The essay item asked students to design an ideal school. When the correlation was computed with conventional analytical Model-I tests, the correlation between analytical and creative abilities was only .49—statistically significant, but nowhere near as high (Sternberg, Ferrari, Clinkenbeard, & Grigorenko, 1996) as in the Sternberg-Lubart study.

Much of the time, as noted earlier, creative people are unrewarded for the demonstration of their abilities. This lack of reward results in wasted talent. In one study (Sternberg, Ferrari, Clinkenbeard, & Grigorenko, 1996), we taught a college-level course on introductory psychology to high-school students pretested with a test based on the triarchic theory of human abilities (Sternberg, 1993). We found that students who were identified as creative and who were then taught and assessed in their course performance in a way that permitted the students to be creative and rewarded them for their creativity performed better than did creative students who were not so recognized.

Thus, to the extent that creative people often do not succeed in school, in management, or anywhere else, it may be not because they lack the ability for success, but because their successes are not perceived as such. Teaching them the declarative knowledge as well as the useful skills they need may be facilitated by allowing them to express their creativity during the learning process.

CONCLUSION

Intelligence of the narrow kind—the kind measured by Model-I tests—is important for many kinds of life pursuits, including management. But this aspect of intelligence—the memory-analytical aspect of the triarchic theory—represents only a portion of the intellectual spectrum that can contribute to success in management. Managerial intelligence comprises practical and creative abilities too. The most successful managers will have and be able to utilize effectively a blend of all three aspects of intelligence.

Ultimately, virtually no one is good at everything. Although some people test higher than others, all have their strengths and weaknesses. According to the triarchic theory, the successfully intelligent person is someone who goes beyond just any one particular static profile of intellectual skills. Rather, successfully intelligent people are those who have the dynamic abilities to (a) figure out their strengths, (b) figure out their weaknesses, (c) capitalize on their strengths, and (d) compensate for or repair their weaknesses. In other words, they make the most of what they have, and find ways around what they don't.

The best managers do not follow any one-size-fits-all approach. If they did, somewhere there would be that one book that could turn anyone into a successful manager. Rather, successful managers adopt a variety of approaches to their work, and suit their behavior flexibly to fit the occasion. What they have in common, though, is an appreciation of their own strengths as well as an understanding of their own limitations. They do what they do well, and either find other people to do what they do not do well, find other ways around their weaknesses, or make themselves good enough to get by. Realizing that there is no one formula for success, they find a formula that works for them. Finding this individual path to success is the hallmark of true managerial intelligence.

The implication for managers is that they need both to find their own strengths and weaknesses and those of their employees, and to find ways of capitalizing on strengths and of compensating for weaknesses. Future research needs to be devoted to the illumination of ways to help managers evaluate strengths and weaknesses, and to help themselves and their employees make the most of their patterns of abilities. Such research would move us away from static notions of academic intelligence, and toward a more dynamic notion of managerial intelligence.

REFERENCES

Amabile, T. M. (1982). Social psychology of creativity: A consensual assessment technique. *Journal of Personality and Social Psychology, 43*, 997–1013.

Amabile, T. M. (1983). *The social psychology of creativity.* New York: Springer-Verlag.

Barrett, G. V., & Depinet, R. L. (1991). A reconsideration of testing for competence rather than for intelligence. *American Psychologist, 46*, 1012–1024.

Briel, J. B., O'Neill, K., & Scheuneman, J. D. (Eds.) (1993). *GRE Technical Manual.* Princeton, N.J.: Educational Testing Service.

Ceci, S. J. (1996). *On intelligence* (2nd ed.). Cambridge, Mass.: Harvard University Press.

Eddy, A. S. (1988). *The relationship between the Tacit Knowledge Inventory for Managers and the Armed Services Vocational Aptitude Battery.* Unpublished master's thesis, St. Mary's University, San Antonio, Tex.

Gottfredson, L. S. (1986). Societal consequences of the g factor. *Journal of Vocational Behavior, 29*, 379–410.

Herrnstein, R., & Murray, C. (1994). *The bell curve: Intelligence and class structure in American life.* New York: Free Press.

Hunter, J. E., & Hunter, R. F. (1984). Validity and utility of alternative predictors of job performance. *Psychological Bulletin, 96*, 72–98.

Jensen, A. R. (1993). Test validity: g versus "tacit knowledge." *Current Directions in Psychological Science, 1*, 9–10.

Lubart, T. I., & Sternberg, R. J. (1995). An investment approach to creativity: Theory and data. In S. M. Smith, T. B. Ward, & R. A. Finke (Eds.), *The creative cognition approach* (pp. 269–302). Cambridge, Mass.: MIT Press.

Ree, M. J., & Earles, J. A. (1993). g is to psychology what carbon is to chemistry: A reply to Sternberg and Wagner, McClelland, and Calfee. *Current Directions in Psychological Science, 1*, 11–12.

Rosenthal, R., & Jacobson, L. (1968). *Pygmalion in the classroom: Teacher expectation and pupils' intellectual development*. New York: Holt, Rinehart, & Winston.

Schmidt, F. L., & Hunter, J. E. (1981). Employment testing: Old theories and new research findings. *American Psychologist, 36*, 1128–1137.

Schmidt, F. L., & Hunter, J. E. (1993). Tacit knowledge, practical intelligence, general mental ability, and job knowledge. *Current Directions in Psychological Science, 1*, 8–9.

Stein, B. S. (1989). Memory and creativity. In J. A. Glover, R. R. Ronning, & C. R. Reynolds (Eds.), *Handbook of creativity* (pp. 163–176). New York: Plenum.

Sternberg, R. J. (1977). *Intelligence, information processing, and analogical reasoning: The componential analysis of human abilities*. Hillsdale, N.J.: Erlbaum.

Sternberg, R. J. (1985). *Beyond IQ: A triarchic theory of human intelligence*. New York: Cambridge University Press.

Sternberg, R. J. (1988). *The triarchic mind: A new theory of intelligence*. New York: Viking-Penguin.

Sternberg, R. J. (1993). *Sternberg triarchic abilities test*. Unpublished test.

Sternberg, R. J. (1995a). For whom the bell curve tolls: A review of *The bell curve*. *Psychological Science, 6*, 257–261.

Sternberg, R. J. (1995b). Theory and measurement of tacit knowledge as a part of practical intelligence. *Zeitschrift fur Psychologie, 203*, 319–334.

Sternberg, R. J. (1996). *Successful intelligence: How practical and creative intelligence determine success in life*. New York: Simon & Schuster.

Sternberg, R. J., Ferrari, M., Clinkenbeard, P., & Grigorenko, E. (1996). Identification, instruction, and assessment of gifted children: A construct validation of a triarchic model. *Gifted Child Quarterly, 40*, 129–137.

Sternberg, R. J., & Lubart, T. I. (1991). An investment theory of creativity. *Human Development, 34*, 1–32.

Sternberg, R. J., & Lubart, T. I. (1992). Buy low and sell high: An investment approach to creativity. *Current Directions in Psychological Science, 1*, 1–5.

Sternberg, R. J., & Lubart, T. I. (1995). *Defying the crowd: Cultivating creativity in a culture of conformity*. New York: Free Press.

Sternberg, R. J., & Lubart, T. I. (1996). Investing in creativity. *American Psychologist, 51*, 677–688.

Sternberg, R. J., & Wagner, R. K. (Eds.) (1986). *Practical intelligence: Nature and origins of competence in the everyday world*. New York: Cambridge University Press.

Sternberg, R. J., Wagner, R. K., & Okagaki, L. (1993). Practical intelligence: The nature and role of tacit knowledge in work and at school. In H. Reese & J. Puckett (Eds.), *Advances in lifespan development* (pp. 205–227). Hillsdale, N.J.: Erlbaum.

Sternberg, R. J., Wagner, R. K., Williams, W. M., & Horvath, J. A. (1995). Testing common sense. *American Psychologist, 50*, 912–927.

Wagner, R. K. (1987). Tacit knowledge in everyday intelligent behavior. *Journal of Personality and Social Psychology, 52*, 1236–1247.

Wagner, R. K., & Sternberg, R. J. (1985). Practical intelligence in real-world pursuits: The role of tacit knowledge. *Journal of Personality and Social Psychology, 49*, 436–458.

Wagner, R. K., & Sternberg, R. J. (1990). Street smarts. In K. E. Clark & M. B. Clark (Eds.), *Measures of leadership* (pp. 493–504). West Orange, N.J.: Leadership Library of America.

Wagner, R. K., & Sternberg, R. J. (1991). *Tacit knowledge inventory for managers.* San Antonio, Tex.: The Psychological Corporation.

Wigdor, A. K., & Garner, W. R. (Eds.) (1982). *Ability testing: Uses, consequences, and controversies.* Washington, D.C.: National Academy Press.

From Transactional
to Transformational Leadership:
Learning to Share the Vision

Bernard M. Bass

Sir Edmund Hillary of Mount Everest fame liked to tell a story about one of Captain Robert Falcon Scott's earlier attempts, from 1901 to 1904, to reach the South Pole. Scott led an expedition made up of men from the Royal Navy and the merchant marine, as well as a group of scientists. Scott had considerable trouble dealing with the merchant marine personnel, who were unaccustomed to the rigid discipline of Scott's Royal Navy. Scott wanted to send one seaman home because he would not take orders, but the seaman refused, arguing that he had signed a contract and knew his rights. Since the seaman was not subject to Royal Navy disciplinary action, Scott did not know what to do. Then Ernest Shackleton, a merchant navy officer in Scott's party, calmly informed the seaman that he, the seaman, was returning to Britain. Again the seaman refused—and Shackleton knocked him to the ship's deck. After another refusal, followed by a second flooring, the seaman decided he would return home. Scott later became one of the victims of his own inadequacies as a leader in his 1911 race to the South Pole. Shackleton went on to lead many memorable expeditions; once, seeking help for the rest of his party, who were stranded on the Antarctic Coast, he journeyed with a small crew in a small open boat from the edge of Antarctica to South Georgia Island.

LEADERSHIP TODAY

Most relationships between supervisors and their employees are quite different today. Few managers depend mainly on their legitimate power, as Scott did, or on their coercive power, as Shackleton did, to persuade people to do as they're told. Rather, managers engage in a transaction with their employees: They explain what is required of them and what compensation they will receive if they fulfill these requirements.

A shift in management style at Xerox's Reprographic Business Group (RBG) provides a good example. In the first step toward establishing management in which managers take the initiative and show consideration for others, 44 specific, effective management behaviors were identified. Two factors that characterize modern leadership were found in many of these behaviors. One factor—initiating and organizing work—concentrates on accomplishing the tasks at hand. The second factor—showing consideration for employees—focuses on satisfying the self-interest of those who do good work. The leader gets things done by making, and fulfilling, promises of recognition, pay increases, and advancement for employees who perform well. By contrast, employees who do not do good work are penalized. This transaction or exchange—this promise and reward for good performance, or threat and discipline for poor performance—characterizes effective leadership. These kinds of transactions took place in most of the effective 44 leadership behaviors identified at Xerox's RBG. This kind of leadership, which is based on transactions between manager and employees, is called "transactional leadership."

In many instances, however, such transactional leadership is a prescription for mediocrity. This is particularly true if the leader relies heavily on passive management-by-exception, intervening with his or her group only when procedures and standards for accomplishing tasks are not being met. My colleagues and I have arrived at this surprising but consistent finding in a number of research analyses. Such a manager espouses the popular adage, "If it ain't broken, don't fix it." He or she stands in back of the caboose of a moving freight train and says, "Now I know where we are going." This kind of manager may use disciplinary threats to bring a group's performance up to standards—a technique that is ineffective and, in the long run, likely to be counterproductive.

Moreover, whether the promise of rewards or the avoidance of penalties motivates the employees depends on whether the leader has control of the rewards or penalties, and on whether the employees want the rewards or fear the penalties. In many organizations, pay increases depend mainly on seniority, and promotions depend on qualifications and policies about which the leader has little to say. The breaking of regulations may be the main cause of penalties. Many an executive has found his or her hands tied by contract provisions, organizational politics, and inadequate resources.

TRANSFORMATIONAL LEADERSHIP

Superior leadership performance—transformational leadership—occurs when leaders broaden and elevate the interests of their employees, when they generate awareness and acceptance of the purposes and mission of the group, and when they stir their employees to look beyond their own self-interest for the good of the group. Transformational leaders achieve these results in one or more ways: They may be charismatic to their followers and thus inspire them; they may meet the emotional needs of each employee; and/or they may intellectually stimulate employees. Exhibit 1 lists the characteristics of transformational and transactional leadership; these listings are based on the findings of a series of surveys and on clinical and case evidence.

Attaining charisma in the eyes of one's employees is central to succeeding as a transformational leader. Charismatic leaders have great power and influence. Employees want to identify with them, and they have a high degree of trust and confidence in them. Charismatic leaders inspire and excite their employees with the idea that they may be able to accomplish great things with extra effort. Further, transformational

Exhibit 1
Characteristics of Transformational and Transactional Leaders

Transformational Leader

Charisma: Provides vision and sense of mission, instills pride, gains respect and trust.

Inspiration: Communicates high expectations, uses symbols to focus efforts, expresses important purposes in simple ways.

Intellectual Stimulation: Promotes intelligence, rationality, and careful problem solving.

Individualized Consideration: Gives personal attention, treats each employee individually, coaches, advises.

Transactional Leader

Contingent Reward: Contracts exchange of rewards for effort, promises rewards for good performance, recognizes accomplishments.

Management by Exception (active): Watches and searches for deviations from rules and standards, takes corrective action.

Management by Exception (passive): Intervenes only if standards are not met.

Laissez-Faire: Abdicates responsibilities, avoids making decisions.

leaders are individually considerate, that is, they pay close attention to differences among their employees; they act as mentors to those who need help to grow and develop. Intellectual stimulation of employees is a third factor in transformational leadership. Intellectually stimulating leaders are willing and able to show their employees new ways of looking at old problems, to teach them to see difficulties as problems to be solved, and to emphasize rational solutions. Such a leader was Lorenz Iversen, a former president of the Mesta Machine Company, who said to his employees, "We got this job because you're the best mechanics in the world!" He practiced management-by-walking-around and stimulated the development of many of Mesta's patented inventions. He is remembered for instilling pride and commitment in his employees.

THE BIG PAYOFF

Managers who behave like transformational leaders are more likely to be seen by their colleagues and employees as satisfying and effective leaders than are those who behave like transactional leaders, according to their colleagues', supervisors', and employees' responses on the Multifactor Leadership Questionnaire (MLQ). Similar results have been found in various organizational settings. Leaders studied have come from an extremely broad variety of organizations: chief executive officers and senior and middle level managers in business and industrial firms in the United States, Canada, Japan, and India; research and development project leaders; American, Canadian, and British Army field grade officers; United States Navy senior officers and junior surface fleet officers; Annapolis midshipmen; educational administrators; and religious leaders.

Moreover, various types of evaluations—including performance ratings by both supervisors and direct reports, as well as standard financial measures—have produced a similar correlation between transformational behavior and high ratings. Managers tagged as high performers by their supervisors were also rated, in a separate evaluation by their followers, as more transformational than transactional. Their organizations do better financially. The same pattern emerged between followers' descriptions of shipboard Naval officers and those officers' supervisors' performance appraisals and recommendations for early promotion. And among Methodist ministers, transformational—not transactional—

leadership behavior was positively related to high church attendance among congregants and growth in church membership.

Results were the same for evaluation of team performance in complex business simulations. Considerable credit for Boeing's turn-around since its 1969 crisis can be given to its chief executive, T. A. Wilson, who has emphasized technological progress, aggressive marketing, and a willingness to take calculated business risks. The confidence that Boeing employees have in Wilson, and their respect for him as a brilliant engineer and an outstanding leader, have instilled in them great pride in the company and its products.

EXTRA EFFORT FROM BELOW

Transformational leaders have better relationships with their supervisors and make more of a contribution to the organization than do those who are only transactional. Moreover, employees say that they themselves exert a lot of extra effort on behalf of managers who are transformational leaders. Organizations whose leaders are transactional are less effective than those whose leaders are transformational— particularly if much of the transactional leadership is passive management-by-exception (intervening only when standards are not being met). Employees say they exert little effort for such leaders. Nevertheless, leader-follower transactions dependent on contingent reward may also work reasonably well if the leaders can provide rewards that are valued by the followers.

Exhibit 2 illustrates the effect that transformational, as compared with transactional, leadership has on employee effort. The data were collected from 228 employees of 58 managers in a large engineering firm. The managers were ranked according to their leadership factor scores, which were based on descriptions of leaders by their employees and colleagues on the Multifactor Leadership Questionnaire. "Four-star" leaders were those who ranked in the top 25% on a leadership factor score; "one-star" leaders were among the bottom 25% of managers on the leadership factor score. From 75% to 82% of the "four-star" transformational managers had employees who indicated they frequently exerted extra effort on their jobs. Of the "one-star" transformational managers, only 22% to 24% had employees who said they frequently exerted extra effort.

Exhibit 2
Employees' Efforts Under Various Leaders

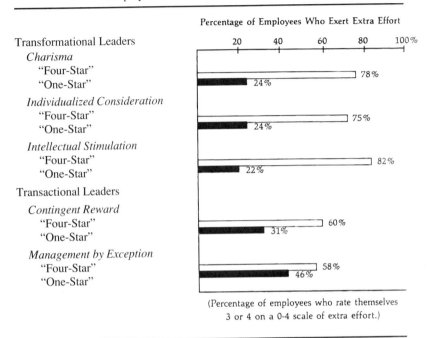

Percentage of Employees Who Exert Extra Effort

Transformational Leaders
  Charisma
    "Four-Star" — 78%
    "One-Star" — 24%
  Individualized Consideration
    "Four-Star" — 75%
    "One-Star" — 24%
  Intellectual Stimulation
    "Four-Star" — 82%
    "One-Star" — 22%
Transactional Leaders
  Contingent Reward
    "Four-Star" — 60%
    "One-Star" — 31%
  Management by Exception
    "Four-Star" — 58%
    "One-Star" — 46%

(Percentage of employees who rate themselves
3 or 4 on a 0-4 scale of extra effort.)

It is interesting to note that, as Exhibit 2 illustrates, being rated as "four-star" rather than "one-star" in *transactional* leadership did not have the same impact on employees' extra effort as a high rating had for the transformational leaders. Similar findings have emerged from studies of leaders and their immediate employees at a diverse range of organizations, including Digital Equipment Corporation and Federal Express.

DIFFERENT STYLES OF TRANSFORMATIONAL LEADERSHIP

As noted earlier, certain types of behavior characterize the transformational leader. Yet transformational leaders vary widely in their personal styles. H. Ross Perot is self-effacing: "I don't look impressive," he says. "To a lot of guys I don't look like I could afford a car." But Perot created the $2.5 billion EDS organization from his vision, initiative, emphasis on hard work, and a special organizational culture with strict codes of morality and dress and quasi-military management. His personal involvement in the rescue of two of his employees trapped as hostages in Iran in 1979 is an extreme example of individualized consideration, a transformational factor. Leslie Wexner of The Limited, Inc. enjoys a more flamboyant lifestyle. But like Perot, Wexner converted his vision of a nationwide chain of women's sportswear stores into a reality through his own hard work. He stimulates employee participation in discussions and decisions and encourages them to share his vision of the company's future.

Many on *Fortune*'s list of the ten toughest bosses would not live up to modern behavioral science's prescriptions for the good leader: one who initiates the structure for interaction among his colleagues, and who does so with consideration for their welfare. Nevertheless, these tough bosses are highly successful as a consequence of the transformational qualities they display; Boeing's Wilson is a case in point. Although they do initiate structure and may be considerate of their employees, these leaders succeed through such transformational factors as charisma and the ability and willingness to treat different subordinates differently, as well as by providing intellectual stimulation for the employees. They frequently raise standards, take calculated risks, and get others to join them in their vision of the future. Rather than work within the organizational culture, they challenge and change that culture, as Roger Smith of General Motors Corporation did. Self-determination and self-confidence are characteristic of them. They succeed because of these transformational elements—even if they, like Wilson, have authoritarian tendencies.

TRANSFORMATIONAL LEADERS MAKE THE DIFFERENCE BETWEEN SUCCESS AND FAILURE

Fighting with far fewer men and tanks than his enemy had, against superior equipment, Ernst Rommel, the Desert Fox, won a series of victories in 1941 and 1942 against the British in North Africa, until he was overwhelmed at El Alamein. Because he was up front at the scene of the action, he could make more rapid assessments and decisions than could his British counterparts, who stayed 20 miles back in headquarters. This, and his willingness to accept calculated risks, contributed to his legendary speed, surprise, and boldness, as well as to the continuing high morale of his troops.

Napoleon declared that an army of rabbits commanded by a lion could do better than an army of lions commanded by a rabbit. He was not far from the truth. With all due respect to social, economic, political, and market forces, and to human resources policies that affect an organization's health, having a lion—or, in Rommel's case, a fox—in command rather than a rabbit frequently means success for the organization. Lee Iacocca of Chrysler Corporation and John Welch of General Electric, who have become folk heroes (or folk devils, to some), are contemporary examples of the importance of transformational leaders to their organizations.

Leadership makes its presence felt throughout the organization and its activities. We have found that employees not only do a better job when they believe their supervisors are transformational leaders, but they also are much more satisfied with the company's performance appraisal system. Likewise, mass communications directed toward individual employees are much more likely to have an impact if the messages are reinforced face-to-face by their supervisors at all organizational levels.

Transformational leadership should be encouraged, for it can make a big difference in the firm's performance at all levels. Managers need to do more than focus on the exchange of material, social, and personal benefits for services satisfactorily rendered. The charismatic leader, like the flamboyant Ted Turner of Turner Broadcasting System, Inc. can instill a sense of mission; the individually considerate leader, like the shy and self-effacing Roberto Goizueta of the Coca Cola Corporation, can lead employees to take an interest in higher-level concerns; the intellectually stimulating leader, like the innovative Roger Smith at General Motors Corporation, can articulate a shared vision of jointly acceptable possibilities. This is not to say that transformational leaders are always prosocial in their efforts, for some fulfill grandiose dreams at the expense of their followers.

Despite the many successes with management development programs and the leadership development programs in our military academies, many executives still feel that leadership is like the weather—something to talk about, but about which not much can be done. Others say leadership ability is mystical—one needs to be born with it.

In fact, much can be done to improve leadership in an organization and to change the presiding style from transactional to transformational. The overall amount of transformational leadership in an organization can be increased substantially by suitable organizational and human resources policies. The new model of transformational leadership presents opportunities for enhancing a corporation's image and for improving its success in recruitment, selection, and promotion. This model also has implications for the organization's training and development activities and for the design of its jobs and organizational structure.

Implications for Corporate Image

It is no accident that many of the firms identified in Tom Peters and Robert Waterman's *In Search of Excellence* (Warner Books, 1982) as excellently managed have large numbers of transformational leaders. Conversely, the poorly managed "dinosaurs" among the firms they describe need to implement a lot more transformational leadership. A firm that is permeated with transformational leadership from top to bottom conveys to its own personnel as well as to customers, suppliers, financial backers, and the community at large that it has its eyes on the future; is confident; has personnel who are pulling together for the common good; and places a premium on its intellectual resources and flexibility and on the development of its people.

Implications for Recruiting

Increasing transformational leadership within the organization may help in recruitment. Candidates are likely to be attracted to an organization whose CEO is charismatic and enjoys a public image as a confident, successful, optimistic, dynamic leader. In addition, prospects are likely to be attracted by interview experiences with other members of management who exhibit individualized consideration. More intelligent prospects will be particularly impressed with intellectually stimulating contacts they make during the recruiting and hiring process.

Implications for Selection, Promotion, and Transfer

Since we can identify and measure the factors associated with transformational leadership, these factors should be incorporated into managerial assessment, selection, placement, and guidance programs—along with related assessments of relevant personal dimensions and individual differences. Somewhat more transformational leadership is generally expected and found as managers move to successively higher levels in the organization, but it is reasonable to expect that an individual's performance at one level will be similar to his or her performance at the next. Direct reports, peers, and/or supervisors can be asked to describe the manager's current leadership with the Multifactor Leadership Questionnaire; their responses should be considered when decisions are made regarding a manager's promotion or transfer into a position of greater supervisory responsibility. Feedback from these results can also be used for counseling, coaching, and mentoring.

Further, the organization can tap the personal characteristics and strengths that underlie the manager's transformational behavior. Charismatic leaders are characterized by energy, self-confidence, determination, intellect, verbal skills, and strong ego ideals. Each of these traits can be assessed in individual managers. Similarly, we can assess some of the traits underlying individualized consideration, such as coaching skills; preference for two-way, face-to-face communication; and willingness to delegate. Again, in the area of intellectual stimulation, candidates for promotion could be assessed with an eye toward the type of intellectual stimulation—general, creative, or mathematical—that would be most effective at the higher level of management. Appropriate intelligence tests may be used to select intellectually stimulating candidates.

Research findings indicate that when employees rate their managers on the MLQ, they describe new business leaders as significantly more transformational than established business leaders. Thus MLQ scores can be used profitably to identify executives to head new ventures.

Implications for Development

A management trainee's first supervisor can make a big difference in his or her subsequent career success. For example, six years after they joined Exxon, many managers who were highly rated by their supervisors reported that they had been given challenging assignments by their initial supervisor (i.e., they had received individualized consideration). Many had been assigned to supervisors with good reputations in the firm. It is important to note that managers tend to model their own leadership style after that of their immediate supervisors. Thus if more higher-ups are transformational, more lower-level employees will emulate transformational behavior—and will be likely to act as transformational leaders as they rise in the organization.

Organizational policy needs to support an understanding and appreciation of the maverick who is willing to take unpopular positions, who knows when to reject the conventional wisdom, and who takes reasonable risks. For example, when R. Gordon McGovern took over as president of Campbell Soup, he introduced the "right to fail" policy, which shook up the stodgy organization. On the other hand, the fine line between self-confidence and obstinacy needs to be drawn. The determined Winston Churchill who contributed so much to the survival of Britain in 1940 was the same Churchill whose obstinacy contributed to the mistakes in 1941 of failing to prepare Singapore adequately and of committing British troops to unnecessary disaster in Crete and Greece.

Intellectual stimulation also needs to be nurtured and cultivated as a way of life in the organization. The "best and the brightest" people should be hired, nourished, and encouraged. Innovation and creativity should be fostered at all levels in the firm.

Implications for Training

Despite conventional wisdom to the contrary, transformational leadership is a widespread phenomenon. True, more of it occurs at the top than at the bottom of an organization; but it has also been observed by many employees in their first-level supervisors. Transformational leadership can be learned, and it can—and should—be the subject of management training and development. Research has shown that leaders at all levels can be trained to be charismatic in both verbal and nonverbal performance. Successful programs have been conducted for first-level project leaders in hi-tech computer firms as well as for senior executives of insurance firms.

That transformational leadership can be increased through training was verified in an experiment when Multifactor Leadership Questionnaire scores were obtained on shop supervisors from their trainees, who were inmates in minimum, medium, and maximum security prisons. The supervisors worked directly with the inmates in industrial shops to produce various products for sale within and outside the prison system. The experiment compared four groups of supervisors on their pre- and post-training effectiveness in various industrial and vocational shops in the prison. One group was trained in transformational leadership, one group was trained in transactional leadership, one was untrained but measured "before and after," and one was untrained and measured only "after." The performances of both trained groups improved, but in comparison to the three other groups of supervisors, those who were trained in transformational leadership did as well or better at improving productivity, absenteeism, and "citizenship" behavior among the inmates; they also won more respect from the inmates.

TRAINING MANAGERS

Practical training that teaches people how to be transformational is similar to that used in the Xerox RPG strategy to modify management style. A counselor, mediator, or supervisor gives a manager a detailed, standardized description of his or her transformational and transactional leadership performance as rated by the manager's employees and/or colleagues. The Multifactor Leadership Questionnaire is used for this purpose. The manager also sees a chart showing the effects of his or her leadership on employee satisfaction, motivation, and perception of organizational effectiveness. Anonymity is maintained, although the manager sees the individual differences among the responses.

Participating managers complete a parallel questionnaire about their own leadership. The discrepancies between how they rate themselves and how their employees rate them may be examined scale-by-scale and item-by-item. The counselor may pose such questions as: "Why do you think you gave yourself a much higher score than your employees gave you in individualized consideration?" and "Why did your employees disagree with you on how rapidly you get to the heart of complex problems or the extent to which they trust you to overcome any obstacles?" It is important for managers to be aware of and accept their employees' view of their performance. A study of United States Naval officers found that those who agreed with their direct reports about their transformational leadership behavior were also likely to earn higher fitness ratings and recommendations for early promotion from their supervisors.

The manager and the counselor discuss in detail why certain results may have appeared and what can be done to improve ratings. For example, a manager may be asked: "What specific behavior on your part makes your employees say they are proud to work with you?" or "What have you done that results in your colleagues' saying you foster a sense of mission?" The collected responses to these questions can create a useful picture of what the manager can do to raise his or her performance on particular items.

In addition to working individually with a counselor, the manager also may participate in a workshop with other managers who are working toward becoming more transformational leaders. Workshop participants who received high ratings from their employees on a particular item are asked what they, the participants, specifically did to achieve these ratings. Questions might include: "Why did all of your employees say that you frequently enabled them to think about old problems in new ways?" or "Why did they all say that you increased their optimism for the future?"

Conversely, questions may focus on why a participant's employees varied widely in their ratings. If the data printout shows a wide divergence of opinion about whether a manager made the employees enthusiastic about assignments, he or she might be asked to suggest possible reasons for such differences of opinion among the employees.

Other Approaches to Training

Several other approaches to teaching transformational leadership make use of the specific data gathered in the workshop. For instance, participants are asked to think of an effective leader they have known and the behavior the leader displayed. Many examples of charisma, individualized consideration, and intellectual stimulation are usually noted. The effective leaders who are mentioned typically come from many levels inside and outside the organization; the workshop leader may point out that transformational leadership is neither particularly uncommon nor limited only to world class leaders. Moreover, these leaders' specific behaviors can be described, observed, and adopted. After viewing videotapes of charismatic, individually considerate, and intellectually stimulating managers in action, workshop participants may be asked to create their own scenarios and videotapes, in which they emulate the transformational leaders they have observed. The other participants may then offer critiques and suggest improvements.

The workshop also aims to increase other aspects of transformational leadership. The transformational leader develops and changes the organizational culture, and to show participants that they have such capabilities, the workshop leader asks them to imagine what the organization might be like in two to five years if it were fully aligned with their own ideas and interests. Then, in small teams based on their actual functions at work, they proceed to redesign the organization.

Similarly, training in mentoring can be used to promote the transformational factor of individualized consideration. For example, one participant can counsel another while a third acts as an observer and a source of feedback about the performance. And many creativity exercises show a manager how he or she can be more intellectually stimulating. Action plans emerge from workshop sessions. Examples include the following:

- I am going to sit down with all my employees and review these data with them.
- I am going to ask for another "reading" in a year; in the meantime I will try to reduce the discrepancies between where I am and where I should be.
- I'm going to talk with my mentor about these results and ask what I should do about them.

Implications for Leadership Education

Military academies have traditionally emphasized leadership education, and today we are seeing a surge of interest in leadership courses in liberal arts colleges as well. At least 600 such courses were being offered, according to a recently completed survey of colleges. The Center for Creative Leadership holds conferences on leadership courses in undergraduate education, most recently in the summer of 1986. The subject of transformational leadership also has been added to leadership courses at the U.S. Air Force Academy at Colorado Springs. In one such course, both faculty and students examined how Air Force officers who are transformational leaders serve as role models for cadets. Scales from the Multifactor Leadership Questionnaire were used to show that the transformational leaders among the instructors and staff provided role models for their students. The faculty and students discussed the questionnaire results and their implications.

Clearly, training cannot turn a purely transactional leader into a transformational leader. Moreover, some managers, while striving to be transformational leaders, misuse their training; their pseudotransformational efforts only further the manager's self-interest and values. Under the influence of such a manager, employees can be misdirected away from their own best interests and those of the organization as a whole. In one such case, Donald Burr of People's Express Airlines displayed many transformational qualities that rapidly built and then rapidly ruined the firm.

For too long, leadership development has been seen as mainly a matter of skill development. But leadership—particularly transformational leadership—should be regarded as an art and a science. It is encouraging to see that the Council for Liberal Learning of the Association of American Colleges now sponsors week-long conferences on leadership for scholars, prominent citizens, and national leaders.

Implications for Job Design and Job Assignment

As we have noted earlier, the results of a study of Exxon managers showed that highly rated managers had had challenging tasks delegated to them by their supervisors when they first joined the company. Jobs can—and should—be designed to provide greater challenges. Delegation with guidance and follow-up can become an individualizing and developmental way of life in a firm.

Transformational leaders show individualized consideration by paying attention to the particular development needs of each of their employees. Employees' jobs are designed with those needs in mind, as well as the needs of the organization. One employee needs experience leading a project team. Another needs an opportunity to reinforce what she has learned in an advanced computer programming class. Their transformational leader assigns them tasks accordingly.

Leaders can be intellectually stimulating to their employees if their own jobs allow them to explore new opportunities, to diagnose organizational problems, and to generate solutions. Leaders whose jobs force them to focus on solving small, immediate problems are likely to be less intellectually stimulating than those who have time to think ahead and in larger terms.

Implications for Organizational Structure

Transformational leadership is not a panacea. In many situations, it is inappropriate and transactional processes are indicated. In general, firms that are functioning in stable markets can afford to depend on their "one-minute" managers to provide the necessary, day-to-day leadership. If the technology, workforce, and environment are stable as well, then things are likely to move along quite well with managers who simply promise and deliver rewards to employees for carrying out assignments. And in stable organizations, even management-by-exception can be quite effective if the manager monitors employee performance and takes corrective action as needed. Rules and regulations for getting things done, when clearly understood and accepted by the employees, can eliminate the need for leadership under some circumstances.

But when the firm is faced with a turbulent marketplace; when its products are born, live, and die within the span of a few years; and/or when its current technology can become obsolete before it is fully depreciated; then transformational leadership needs to be fostered at all levels in the firm. In order to succeed, the firm needs to have the flexibility to forecast and meet new demands and changes as they occur—and only transformational leadership can enable the firm to do so.

Problems, rapid changes, and uncertainties call for a flexible organization with determined leaders who can inspire employees to participate enthusiastically in team efforts and share in organizational goals. In short, charisma, attention to individualized development, and the ability and willingness to provide intellectual stimulation are critical in leaders whose firms are faced with demands for renewal and change. At these organizations, fostering transformational leadership through policies of recruitment, selection, promotion, training, and development is likely to pay off in the health, well-being, and effective performance of the organization.

Situational Leadership Theory: An Examination of a Prescriptive Theory

Robert P. Vecchio

Hersey and Blanchard's (1982) Situational Leadership Theory (SLT) embodies one of the more widely known and, at the same time, least researched views of managerial effectiveness. Throughout this article, the term *managerial* will be used interchangeably with the term *leadership* as SLT focuses on the effectiveness of nominal heads rather than on emergent or incremental forms of power and influence (i.e., leadership per se). As noted by Graeff (1983), the theory is often cited in academically oriented management textbooks. However, we can offer little advice to our students, or to practicing managers, on the utility of the theory. Before we can endorse or critique the theory to our constituencies, a rigorous test of the theory's propositions is, of course, required. In this article, the origins and central elements of the theory, the available evidence of the theory's validity, and the requirements for a rigorous test of the theory's propositions are considered.

ORIGINS AND ELEMENTS OF SITUATIONAL LEADERSHIP THEORY

Situational Leadership Theory developed from the writings of Reddin (1967). Reddin's 3-Dimensional Management Style Theory posits the importance of a manager's relationship orientation and task orientation in conjunction with effectiveness. From the interplay of these dimensions, Reddin proposed a typology of management styles (e.g., the autocrat, the missionary, the deserter). Although Reddin suggested that his framework explained effectiveness as a function of matching style to situation, his approach did not identify specific situational attributes that could be explicitly incorporated into a predictive scheme.

Building on Reddin's (1967) suggestion that leader or manager effectiveness varies according to style, Hersey and Blanchard (1969) proposed a life-cycle theory of leadership. According to life-cycle theory, degrees of task orientation and relationship orientation must be examined in conjunction with the dimension of follower maturity to account for leader effectiveness. The central precept of life-cycle theory (Hersey and Blanchard, 1969, p. 29) is that as the level of follower maturity increases, effective leader behavior will involve less structuring (task orientation) and less socio-emotional support (relationship orientation). However, the decline in need for both of these leader behaviors is not straightforward. During the early stages of an employee's tenure, a low level of relationship orientation coupled with high task orientation is considered to be ideal. As an employee (or group of employees of roughly equal maturity) gains in maturity, the need for supervisory social-emotional support increases, while the need for structuring declines. Beyond a certain level of maturity, the need for both social-emotional support and structuring declines. At the highest levels of employee maturity, supervisory task and social behaviors become superfluous to effective employee performance.

In a popular text (evidenced by its being in multiple editions), Hersey and Blanchard (1982) attempted to provide still greater precision to these precepts. They suggested that follower maturity can be broken into benchmark categories of high, moderate, and low, and that appropriate leader style can be summarized in terms of a leader primarily telling, selling, participating, or delegating in relations with subordinates.

EVIDENCE OF THE MODEL'S VALIDITY

At a purely theoretical level, SLT has been suggested as having a good deal of overlap with other popular views of leader and group behavior. In a comparison of their views with those offered by other perspectives, Hersey and Blanchard (1982, chap. 13) achieved a synthesis of their concepts with those contained in McGregor's (1960) Theory X and Y, Argyris's (1957) maturity-immaturity continuum, Likert's (1967) management systems, Maslow's (1954) need hierarchy, Herzberg's (1966) two-factor theory, McClelland's (1961) achievement theory, Schein's (1970) assumptions of human nature, transactional analysis (Berne, 1964; Harris 1969), French and Raven's (1959) power bases, parent effectiveness training concepts (Gordon, 1970), Greiner's (1972) phases of organizational growth, Lewin's (1947) views of achieving behavioral change, behavior modification (Skinner, 1953), and force field analysis (Lewin, 1947). Although one can cynically argue that this high degree of overlap suggests that SLT is not saying much that is new or original, it can also be contended that many of the above theories can also be shown to contain a high degree of overlap. More positively, one can argue that SLT is focusing on critical features of behavior that have been previously identified.

The fact that SLT can be shown to overlap to varying degrees with other theories is not in itself sufficient evidence of SLT's validity. This point is of clear importance when one considers that many of the previously cited theories have not achieved a high degree of empirical support (e.g., Herzberg's two-factor theory), despite a fair amount of attention in the academic literature. In terms of internal theoretical coherence, Graeff (1983) has provided the most comprehensive critique of the theory. In his review of SLT, Graeff argued that the theory may actually have been derived from a passage in an article by Korman (1966), in which the suggestion of curvilinear relationships between dimensions of leader behavior and other variables was taken to mean that a curvilinear relationship may exist between dimensions of leader behavior. In addition, Graeff (1983) suggested that the manner in which components of dimensions in SLT are combined and the manner of graphic presentation of a four-dimensional model (task orientation, relationship orientation, follower maturity, and effectiveness) in only two dimensions are critical problems for the theory. Also, he has suggested that the popularly advocated measurement device for studying leader behaviors (the LEAD instrument) possesses unknown psychometric qualities. In the theory's favor, Graeff argued, however, that SLT correctly focuses on issues of leader flexibility and the importance of subordinate attributes as the key situational determinant of appropriate leader behavior.

At an empirical level, the theory has received little attention. One of the earliest published studies devoted to SLT concepts focused on the development of a measure of follower maturity, yet it did not use the measure in a test of the model (Moore, 1976). In a study that approximated a test of the theory, Hambleton and Gumpert (1982) asked managers to select at random 4 of their subordinates to complete a survey instrument. For 65 participating managers (of 159 who were contacted), manager ratings of subordinate maturity were coded in conjunction with manager self-assessments of leadership style (high vs. low task and relationship orientation). From this coding, matches and mismatches were identified. Matches occurred in only 29% of the cases. A comparison of mean performance ratings—given for each employee by the managers—for the matches and mismatches revealed that the matches received somewhat higher mean evaluations ($t = 6.47$, $p < .01$).

Although the findings of Hambleton and Gumpert (1982) are the only available supportive evidence for the model, they raise several concerns. First, the sample suffered severe attrition (i.e., less than half of the managers provided data). Second, the managers provided self-assessments of their own style. Such self-assessments of leader behavior are not regarded as being highly accurate (Schriesheim & Kerr, 1974). In addition, these assessments were taken on a version of the LEAD instrument, rather than on a more widely studied and accepted measure of leader behavior. Last, the respondents were highly cognizant of SLT precepts (as evidenced by their having been asked to rate their knowledge of SLT and to assess the extent to which they used SLT in their work). This awareness of SLT principles on the part of the participants may have induced some respondents to attempt to complete their surveys in conformity with the theory (i.e., in order to appear to be applying their knowledge of the theory). Also, all of the respondents reported at least fair knowledge of and some use of SLT.

The most recently reported study of SLT (Blank, Weitzel, & Green, 1986) involved 27 hall directors and 353 resident advisors (subordinates) at two large universities. Respondents completed the Leader Behavior Description Questionnaire (LBDQ-XII; Stogdill & Coons, 1957) and a measure of maturity. Directors provided performance ratings of resident advisors, and each resident advisor completed subscales of the Job Description Index (JDI) satisfaction measure (Smith, Kendall, & Hulin, 1969). In their analysis of these data, Blank, Weitzel, and Green did not report the results of matching subordinate maturity and leader behaviors to predict subordinate performance and satisfaction, but instead examined interactions between maturity and each of the two leader behavior dimensions (consideration and structuring) in an attempt to predict subordinate performance and satisfaction. In general, their search for two-way interactions did not reveal support for the theory. However, it should be noted that the theory predicts a three-way interaction, and not separate two-way interactions, among the key variables (i.e., the interaction of maturity with structuring should not be examined independently of consideration, but jointly).

In summary, investigations of the theoretical and empirical robustness of SLT have been rare. Although the theory contains strong intuitive appeal, the veracity of the theory has not been assessed via a rigorous empirical test.

ISSUES SURROUNDING A TEST OF THE SITUATIONAL LEADERSHIP THEORY

In order to test SLT, several issues must be addressed that relate to the clarity of the theory's prediction. One major issue surrounds the unit of analysis for SLT: the individual versus the group. Although the theory is often stated in terms of group maturity, there are also many references to individual maturity as well. For example, in their definition of maturity, Hersey and Blanchard (1982, p. 151) stated that an "individual or a group" is their focus. They also recognized that when one relates to an entire group (e.g., a teacher speaking to a class of students), it is the maturity level of the group that is important. However, when one deals with an employee in a one-to-one setting (e.g., a teacher speaking with a single student), the maturity level of the individual is most important. This recognition of the need for leaders to behave differently with individual group members than when they relate to an entire group is an important statement. Much of the recent research in the area of leadership has, in fact, focused on the issue of universal versus differential leadership style (cf. research on the Vertical Dyad Linkage Model; Liden & Graen, 1980). That the dynamics of SLT are presumed to operate at both levels is an important feature of the SLT framework. In the context of a test of SLT, it is necessary to specify and be consistent in studying leadership phenomena at a given level (and not across levels) of analysis. It seems likely—in light of the preponderance of research at the individual level and the suspicion that group processes may mask individual process—that SLT will be most robust at the individual level of social dynamics (i.e., leadership behavior that is in accord with the prescriptions of SLT will be more effective when it is targeted to a given individual's level of maturity).

An extended issue that is beyond the present investigation is whether individual maturity interacts with group maturity in determining leader effectiveness. It is easy to envision a situation in which a subordinate is significantly more mature than his or her peers in a given position, yet the leader's behaviors (if they are often displayed for the benefit of the group) may be grossly inappropriate. In such settings, the incongruent subordinate will likely be dissatisfied with the leader's directions and may be resentful of the limits that his peers indirectly set via the leader's actions.

Perhaps the least clear feature of SLT surrounds the definition of effectiveness. In their book, Hersey and Blanchard (1982, pp. 96–99) define effectiveness and ineffectiveness as occurring when a leader's style is appropriate and inappropriate, respectively. Although they recognize that effectiveness can be viewed as a continuum, they do not acknowledge the multifaceted nature of the concept. Also, the definition of effectiveness in terms of appropriateness of leader style is somewhat circular in its use of logic. In order to test SLT, it is useful to define effectiveness in broader, more traditional terms. For example, effectiveness can be defined in terms of output, cost reduction, enhancement of employee motivation, morale, and so forth. This restatement of effectiveness implies that SLT should be restated so that effectiveness is a possible outcome of appropriateness of leader behavior. The use of the word *possible* is important in the foregoing sentence because an appropriate combination of leader style (in terms of SLT's prescription) may still not enhance subordinate behavior and attitudes. As noted by Kerr and Jermier (1978), situational attributes can offset and substitute for leader behaviors. In a sense, subordinate maturity in SLT is a substitute for leadership, in that subordinates of higher maturity need less attention or direction from leaders. Increases in subordinate self-sufficiency (maturity), which likely result from relevant work experience and training, can make leader behaviors increasingly irrelevant to subordinate performance and morale. Therefore, SLT's prediction that highly mature employees require a low-structure-low-consideration style of supervision may be partially misstated. It may be more correct to say that supervisory style is comparatively more irrelevant, in terms of its impact on highly mature subordinates. In short, the conduct of highly mature subordinates may simply be less predictable than that of other employees, from supervisory attributes.

A further issue centers on how to test in a statistical sense, the predictive accuracy of SLT. At its heart, the theory forecasts a three-way interaction of leader consideration, leader structuring, and subordinate maturity. If one imagines the form of this hypothesized interaction by trying to graph the hyperplane that is predicted, it becomes apparent that the predicted interaction does not satisfy the statistical assumption of homoscedascity. That is to say, the regression-based assumption of equal variance around the regression plane does not hold, by definition, for SLT as the predictions of superior performance only hold for specific points in the multidimensional space. In all other locations in the space, the data are free to vary. Therefore, the theory only makes predictions for specific combinations of variables. For all other combinations, the theory is silent. In essence, a test of the theory that uses the statistical technique of multiple regression may lead, erroneously, to the conclusion that the theory is incorrect for a given data set (i.e., a Type II error). To more fairly test the theory, it would be worthwhile to examine the predictions in the manner proposed by the theory's developers (i.e., to compare the effectiveness of leaders whose styles are "appropriate" for given settings to leaders whose styles are predicted to be "inappropriate" for the same settings). Although one may test whether a given data set violates the requirement of homoscedascity, the results of such a test would not, of course, shed light on the validity of Situational Leadership Theory, per se.

The purpose of the present investigation was (a) to test SLT in a study that was designed to capture the critical variables proposed by the theory and (b) to explore SLT with analytic techniques that reflect traditional practice in organizational research (i.e., regression) as well as accommodate the need to study leadership as a situation-specific phenomena (i.e., subgrouping analysis).

METHOD

Subjects and Procedure

Subjects were 303 full-time high school teachers, who represented 14 high schools in a large midwestern city and provided data in response to a confidential survey. Because of the support of the head of the school district, cooperation was readily obtained from the principals of all 14 schools in the district. During monthly meetings with faculty, the principals distributed surveys to their teachers. At the meetings, time was devoted to the completion of the surveys. Both teachers and principals completed similar surveys, which focused on the behavior of the school principal (leader) and the individual teacher (subordinate). To ensure anonymity for the teachers, the surveys were coded with ID numbers. In addition, the completed surveys of both teachers and principals were collected at the meeting, placed in an envelope, and mailed directly to the author. With the exception of 34 teachers who did not attend their school's monthly meeting in January 1986, all of the principals and teachers responded to the survey.

Measures

Each teacher provided responses to the following scales: (a) JDI, satisfaction with supervision (Smith et al., 1969); (b) Leader-Member Exchange, quality of leader-member relationship (Liden & Graen, 1980); (c) LBDQ-XII, leader consideration (Stogdill & Coons, 1957); and (d) LBDQ-XII, leader initiating structure (Stogdill & Coons, 1957). Modified versions of the LBDQ-XII measures of leader behavior were used in place of the LEAD instrument because of the relative psychometric advantages of the LBDQ-XII (i.e., its reliability and construct validity have received more attention than the LEAD instrument, and it is a more widely accepted index of leader behavior than the LEAD instrument). In addition, the stems of the items in the LBDQ-XII used in this study were modified to incorporate an individualized format (cf. Vecchio & Gobdel, 1984): sample item, "My principal acts without consulting me." Furthermore, each teacher was asked to complete a follower maturity index that contained items related to both task-relevant (e.g., understanding of job requirements) and psychological (e.g., commitment) forms of maturity (Hambleton, Blanchard, & Hersey, 1977).

Principals provided ratings for each teacher on dimensions of follower maturity and performance. Maturity was assessed on items related to task-relevant and psychological maturity, whereas performance was assessed by summing ratings across dimensions of dependability, planning, know-how, present performance, and expected performance (Liden & Graen, 1980).

Analytic Techniques

The accuracy of the principles of SLT was examined with several statistical techniques. As will be shown, each technique represents a somewhat different phrasing of the central research question. The first technique used was hierarchical regression analysis, in which a three-way multiplicative interaction term was created (Maturity × Consideration × Structuring). This interaction term was entered into a regression equation following the inclusion of main effects and two-way interaction terms to determine whether the inclusion of the three-way interaction term appreciably increased the variance accounted for in the performance criterion. As was noted earlier, the use of multiple regression for testing SLT can be critiqued on the grounds that certain assumptions of regression cannot be met when the principles of SLT are, in fact, correct. Nonetheless, the robustness of regression techniques and our present uncertainty as to just what would result with the use of the technique warrant the exploratory use of multiple regression to test the theory.

A second approach to testing SLT involves the creation of subgroups of employees for whom the theory is expected to hold or not to hold. This requires the creation of subgroups based on the combination of consideration, structuring, and maturity. For employees whose situations are designated "matches," their mean performance should be superior to that of subordinates for whom the situations are "mismatches." This comparison of matches and mismatches represents an omnibus test of SLT in that it ignores differences within specific categories of maturity in favor of an overall test.

It can be argued, however, that an omnibus test is not the best possible device for assessing SLT. If the distribution of cases is not uniform across categories, then the results of the omnibus test may be biased. For example, no (or very few) cases may exist for some combinations of maturity and leader behavior. The peculiarities of these distributions and the possible associated mean differences for the categories could, thereby, produce spurious results. A third, more direct, assessment of SLT involves the creation of several categories on the dimension of follower maturity. After creating these categories, comparisons could then be made within categories to determine whether subordinates who match on the leader dimensions are superior performers, relative to those who do not match on these dimensions. The need to first create categories of maturity is perhaps critical in that different levels of follower maturity are likely to be related to different levels of overall performance (although SLT does not directly address this critical issue). Therefore, the likely correlation of maturity with performance needs to be controlled by conducting comparisons within levels of maturity.

To be sure, only the third, partitioned, technique is the most defensible approach to assessing SLT. However, we presently know so little about SLT-related phenomena that all three techniques are reported here in the interest of completeness and in order to gain further understanding.

RESULTS

The internal consistency coefficients for the measures of interest were all of reasonable magnitude (ranging from .82 to .94). Evidence that the maturity measure at least partially taps work-relevant experience was obtained by correlating individual maturity with self-reported years of teaching experience. The obtained correlation suggested that years of experience was related to the index ($r = .15, p < .01$). It should also be noted that the range of professional teaching experience for the sample was substantial (range = 1–31 years; $M = 20.5$ years).

The results of the hierarchical regression analyses are presented in Table 1 for the criteria of supervisor rating, leader-member exchange, and satisfaction with supervision. For each analysis, the three predictors of consideration, structuring, and maturity were entered simultaneously at the first step. Next, the two-way interaction terms were entered into the equation. Last, the three-way interaction term was included. The increment in R^2 at each step (i.e., in variance accounted for) was calculated and tested for significance (Cohen & Cohen, 1975). As the results in Table 1 indicate, none of the three criteria tested yielded support for a three-way interaction.

Omnibus tests of mean differences on the criteria were also conducted. For these analyses, the distribution of follower maturity was trichotomized into high, moderate, and low maturity by cutting at the values of 44 and 40. Three categories, rather than four, of maturity were created to ensure a sufficient number of cases for each subgroup. The predictions for the middle-range groups on maturity are identical (i.e., high consideration coupled with moderate structuring is prescribed). Next, the dimensions of consideration and structuring were trichotomized and dichotomized, respectively. Cuts on the structuring dimension were made at the values of 19 and 15. On the consideration dimension, the split was made at the value of 19. This resulted in a 3×2 cross tabulation, in accord with the SLT model. Employees whose values on maturity coincided with the prescribed levels of consideration

Table 1
Summary of Regression Analyses

Source	Performance R^2	Performance ΔR^2	Leader-member quality R^2	Leader-member quality ΔR^2	Satisfaction R^2	Satisfaction ΔR^2
Consideration (C), structuring (S), maturity (M)	.743**		.686**		.639**	
C × S, C × M, S × M	.744**	.001	.697**	.011*	.641**	.012*
C × S × M	.744**	.000	.697**	.000	.641**	.000

* $p < .05$. ** $p < .01$.

and structuring were designated matches; all remaining employees were designated mismatches. It is, of course, predicted that mean values for the outcome variables will be higher for the matched group, relative to the mismatched group.

As Table 2 reveals, a large percentage of the employees were in the mismatched group (i.e., their situations were those for which the theory predicts lower effectiveness). This finding, in itself, is of some importance in that it suggests that the positive SLT prescriptions may have little relevance to a majority of employees (i.e., the natural occurrence of

Table 2
Results of Omnibus Tests

Group	M	SD	n	F	p	Estimated effect size
Performance						
Match	30.4	3.91	50	1.61	.21	.002
Mismatch	29.5	5.03	252			
Leader-member quality						
Match	22.8	22.80	50	5.25	.02	.014
Mismatch	21.2	21.18	245			
Satisfaction with supervision						
Match	51.0	6.25	46	7.35	.01	.022
Mismatch	46.3	11.52	238			

the preferred combinations may be fairly low). Alternatively, it can be argued that there is a great untapped potential or significant need for creating circumstances that the theory prescribes. To test this later point, mean differences were tested for significance for the matched versus mismatched groups. If the theory is correct, we can expect the matched group (albeit a smaller group) to have higher values on the outcome measures.

As the results reported in Table 2 indicate, the means were in the predicted direction for all three comparisons. In two of these comparisons, the means were significantly different (although the estimates of the effects' sizes were not substantial). The results suggest that employees who describe their superiors' behavior on the dimensions of consideration and structuring in accord with SLT prescriptions, given their specific level of maturity, tend to have somewhat higher performance ratings, and to report higher quality relationships with their supervisor, as well as greater satisfaction with their supervisor.

Although the omnibus tests provided evidence of the accuracy of SLT, they do not tell us precisely where these differences are occurring in the framework. Also, the supportive results of the omnibus tests may have capitalized on unique, sample-specific differences that are correlated with uneven distributions of attributes. Therefore, sets of partitioned tests of the theory were conducted. These tests involved making mean difference comparisons within maturity groups. That is to say, matches and mismatches were designated within each of the three levels of maturity. The results of these comparisons (see Table 3) indicate that the mean differences were in the correct direction in six of nine comparisons. Of these six, four were significantly different. The effect sizes for these differences ranged from .032 to .160. In one instance, the mean difference was significant in the reverse direction of that which was hypothesized. Also, the results were more generally supportive in the low-maturity category, somewhat mixed in the moderate-maturity category, and generally nonsignificant in the high-maturity category. This suggests a very different picture of the results, in which the theory is only correct for low-maturity employees and less correct for more mature employees. The implication is that low consideration coupled with high structuring is a superior combination for low-maturity employees. For moderate- and especially high-maturity employees, it is not clear that the combinations prescribed by SLT are associated with superior outcomes. Furthermore, it is worth noting that the mismatched

Table 3
Summary of Partitioned Tests

Group	M	SD	n	F	p	Estimated effect size
Low maturity						
Performance						
Match	27.3	3.50	21	4.68	.03	.032
Mismatch	25.0	4.54	92			
Leader-member quality						
Match	24.2	3.06	21	22.18	.00	.160
Mismatch	19.1	4.79	92			
Satisfaction with supervision						
Match	53.4	3.86	19	16.80	.00	.129
Mismatch	41.3	12.68	88			
Moderate maturity						
Performance						
Match	32.1	2.37	15	5.65	.02	.048
Mismatch	30.1	3.11	78			
Leader-member quality						
Match	19.6	3.20	15	4.18	.04	.034
Mismatch	22.1	4.54	75			
Satisfaction with supervision						
Match	47.0	7.51	13	<1		
Mismatch	48.6	9.84	72			
High maturity						
Performance						
Match	33.4	2.10	14	1.20	.28	.002
Mismatch	33.9	1.70	82			
Leader-member quality						
Match	24.1	2.81	14	1.65	.20	.007
Mismatch	22.7	3.89	80			
Satisfaction with supervision						
Match	51.4	6.15	14	<1		
Mismatch	49.6	9.66	78			

groups (Tables 2 and 3) were somewhat more variable than the matched groups. This is evidenced by the often larger standard deviations for the mismatched groups. This difference in variability confirms the earlier suggestion that the more stringent assumptions of parametric statistical tests (e.g., regression analysis) may not be satisfied by the data generated by—as well as the logic attendant to—tests of Situational Leadership Theory.

DISCUSSION

The present study represents one of the first comprehensive tests of Situational Leadership Theory. As such, it is not possible to contrast the current findings with those obtained in other investigations. Therefore, the present evidence must be taken, for the moment, as providing the best available test of the theory's principles. In general, the present study provides partial support for the theory in that the omnibus tests and several of the partitioned tests point to the theory being partially accurate in its prescriptions. The results of the regression analyses are perhaps suspect in that various assumptions of regression analysis are contrary to the essential features of SLT. Furthermore, the predictor variables that were used in the regression analysis were intercorrelated. This may be more than a common source effect problem because the predictor constructs may not be logically or empirically independent of one another.

The finding that SLT was most strongly supported in the low-maturity condition appears reasonable in that employees who are relatively lacking in task-relevant knowledge or commitment should require more structuring on the part of their supervisor. Displays of considerateness by superiors for low-maturity subordinates would be tantamount to sending improper signals to such subordinates. For subordinates of moderate maturity, it is not clear what style of supervision works best. The present data suggest that performance is greater for these same employees if moderate structuring is combined with high consideration. However, the same sample provides evidence that the quality of leader-member relationships may be significantly lower when this particular combination of styles is reported.

For high-maturity employees, the theory appears to be unable to predict. Perhaps the theory needs to be rephrased to accommodate such high-maturity types. As it stands, the theory seems to suggest that highly mature employees can be relatively free from direction and do not need to receive "strokes" from their supervisors. Such a scenario is highly doubtful, as most employees probably appreciate supervisor considerateness and occasional signs of supervisor interest (as manifested by supervisor direction or structuring). In addition, the measurement of maturity poses a unique problem for testing Situational Leadership Theory. Self-reports of maturity are highly suspect. Similarly, peer ratings may largely reflect popularity rather than task orientation. Yet, the construct is so broad that a rating seems the most appropriate technique for addressing it. It is interesting that in the present sample, years of teaching was somewhat associated with supervisor ratings of maturity. However, experience can still be regarded as independent of supervisor ratings. This makes sense as long-tenured employees may be, on the average, more competent than are more recently hired individuals. Yet, the job-relevant maturity of long-tenured employees can still be quite variable (i.e., years of experience and job-relevant maturity are not likely to be highly correlated across situations). Of further interest, the correlation of teachers' self-ratings of maturity were significantly correlated with their superiors' ratings on the same instrument ($r = .28$, $p < .01$).

It is possible that SLT is not well suited to making predictions in any given job category, in that a full range of maturity and leader behaviors may not be manifested in one job classification. Perhaps SLT is better viewed as being prescriptive *across* job categories. In this view, high to low maturity represents various classes of jobs (e.g., professional to unskilled). For professional (high-maturity) jobs, supervisors should display relatively less consideration and less structuring. Professionals, as the reasoning goes, should be capable and desirous of greater self-direction. For unskilled (low-maturity) jobs, supervisors should provide significantly greater structuring and less consideration. Unskilled workers perhaps expect, and may prefer, greater direction and less social-emotional attention on the part of supervisors (cf. Vroom & Mann, 1960). This restatement of SLT suggests that the underlying principles of SLT may be valid but that the theory may be improperly conceptualized, such that the current focus is on maturity differences within jobs rather than across jobs.

An across-jobs perspective offers possibly greater ranges of maturity and, therefore, a greater likelihood of identifying systematic relationships. However, this across-jobs perspective requires a modification of the term *maturity*. As it is used in a within-job perspective, its meaning is fairly clear (i.e., employee level of task-relevant knowledge and commitment). In an across-job perspective, maturity may have to be replaced with a more level-appropriate concept such as normative expectations. This across-jobs view suggests that job prestige (or job quality) dictates specific norms for preferred styles of supervision. To be effective, a supervisor should be conscious of and responsive to these norms. The above viewpoint also can be seen as incorporating notions from Kerr and Jermier's (1979) suggestion of substitutes for leadership. In professional and highly skilled positions, experience and knowledge can make a supervisor's influence less important. In less skilled positions in which employees lack experience and acquired knowledge, supervisory influences can be of far greater importance. However, a testing of an across-jobs perspective should perhaps not be undertaken without further testing of the within-job view of Situational Leadership Theory. In addition, future tests of the theory should, to the degree possible, use independent measures of predictors.

In summary, the present study provided partial support for principles contained in Situational Leadership Theory. As is not uncommon in organizational research, an initial, seemingly simple research question yielded a complex set of results that only substantiated a portion of a set of propositions. Furthermore, the results underscored the somewhat disheartening observation that the approach taken in analyzing a theory determines, to an extent, the form and degree of support that is obtained for the propositions. The present results most strongly suggest that more recently hired employees may require greater structuring from their superior. Nonetheless, the present results are sufficiently intriguing so as to suggest that SLT be studied further, with an across-jobs perspective and with a recognition that high-maturity conditions may obviate the need for supervision, rather than specify a particular style of supervision.

REFERENCES

Argyris, C. (1957). *Personality and organization.* New York: Harper & Row.

Berne, E. (1964). *Games people play.* New York: Grove Press.

Blank, W., Wietzel, J., & Green, S. G. (1986). Situational leadership theory: A test of underlying assumptions. *Proceedings of the Academy of Management, 384.*

Cohen, J., & Cohen, P. (1975). *Applied multiple regression/correlation analysis for the behavioral sciences.* Hillsdale, NJ: Erlbaum.

French, J. R. P., & Raven, B. (1959). The bases of social power. In D. Cartwright (Ed.), *Studies in social power* (pp. 150–167). Ann Arbor, MI: Institute for Social Research.

Gordon, T. (1970). *Parent effectiveness training.* New York: P. H. Wyden.

Graeff, C. L. (1983). The situational leadership theory: A critical view. *Academy of Management Review, 8,* 285–291.

Greiner, L. E. (1972, July–August). Evolution and revolution as organizations grow. *Harvard Business Review*, 37–46.

Hambleton, R. K., Blanchard, K. H., & Hersey, P. (1977). *Maturity Scale—Self-rating form*. San Diego, CA: Learning Resources Corporation.

Hambleton, R. K., & Gumpert, R. (1982). The validity of Hersey and Blanchard's theory of leader effectiveness. *Group and Organization Studies, 7*, 225–242.

Harris, T. (1969). *I'm OK—You're OK: A practical guide to transactional analysis*. New York: Harper & Row.

Herzberg, F. (1966). *Work and the nature of man*. New York: World Publishing.

Hersey, P., & Blanchard, K. (1969). Life-cycle theory of leadership. *Training and Development Journal, 23*, 26–34.

Hersey, P., & Blanchard, K. (1982). *Management of organizational behavior* (4th ed.). Englewood Cliffs, NJ: Prentice-Hall.

Kerr, S., & Jermier, J. M. (1978). Substitutes for leadership: Their meaning and measurement. *Organizational Behavior and Human Performance, 22*, 375–403.

Korman, A. K. (1966). Consideration, initiating structure, and organization criteria— A review. *Personnel Psychology, 19*, 349–361.

Lewin, K. (1947). Frontiers in group dynamics: Concept, method, and reality in social science; social equilibria and social change. *Human Relations, 1*, 5–41.

Liden, R. C., & Graen, G. (1980). Generalizability of the vertical dyad linkage model of leadership. *Academy of Management Journal, 23*, 451–465.

Likert, R. (1967). *The human organization*. New York: McGraw-Hill.

Maslow, A. (1954). *Motivation and personality*. New York: Harper & Row.

McClelland, D. C. (1961). *The achieving society*. Princeton, NJ: Van Nostrand.

McGregor, D. (1960). *The human side of enterprise*. New York: McGraw-Hill.

Moore, L. I. (1976). The FMI: Dimensions of follower maturity. *Group and Organization Studies, 1*, 203–222.

Reddin, W. J. (1967). The 3-D Management Style Theory. *Training and Development Journal, 21*, 8–17.

Schein, E. H. (1970). *Organizational psychology* (2nd ed.). Englewood Cliffs, NJ: Prentice Hall.

Schriesheim, C. A., & Kerr, S. (1974). Psychometric properties of the Ohio State leadership scales. *Psychological Bulletin, 81*, 756–765.

Skinner, B. F. (1953). *Science and human behavior*. New York: MacMillan.

Smith, P., Kendall, L., & Hulin, C. L. (1969). *The measurement of satisfaction in work and retirement*. Chicago: Rand-McNally.

Stogdill, R., & Coons, A. (1957). *Leader behavior: Its description and measurement* (Research Monograph No. 88). Columbus: Ohio State University, Bureau of Business Research.

Vecchio, R. P., & Gobdel, B. C. (1984). The vertical dyad linkage model of leadership: Problems and prospects. *Organizational Behavior and Human Performance, 34*, 5–20.

Vroom, V. H., & Mann, F. C. (1960). Leader authoritarianism and employee attitudes. *Personnel Psychology, 13*, 125–140.

The Contingency Model
of Leadership Effectiveness:
Its Levels of Analysis

Roya Ayman, Martin M. Chemers,
and Fred Fiedler

The contingency model of leadership effectiveness was presented in its most complete form in Fiedler (1967) and Fiedler and Chemers (1974). The evolution of the model and the development of its constructs covers three decades of research. This article examines the model from a theoretical and methodological perspective. It focuses on the levels of analysis used to determine the various components of the model, to measure effective leadership, and to define the sources of information for its central variables.

The model predicts that a leader's effectiveness is based on two main factors: a leader's attributes, referred to as task or relationship motivational orientation (formerly referred to as style), and a leader's situational control (formerly referred to as situational favorability). The model predicts that leaders who have a task motivational orientation compared to those who have a relationship orientation or motivation will be more successful in high- and low-control situations. Relationship oriented leaders compared to task-oriented leaders will be more effective in moderate control situations (Fiedler, 1978). A leader is designated as "in match" in situations where the model predicts high group performance and "out of match" in situations of low group performance (Fiedler & Chemers, 1984).

The model is, by design, multi-level and multi-source. That is, measures of the leader's motivational orientation are based on the leader's responses (individual level); characteristics of the situation have been measured by the leader's report and/or that of subordinates and experimenters (multi-level and multi-source), and outcomes have been assessed at the group level, primarily group performance (Fiedler, 1978) as determined by objective measures, supervisor ratings, and averaged follower satisfaction (Rice, 1981). A few studies used outcomes related

351

to the leader as an individual (e.g., stress, performance). A few studies have examined the model at the dyadic, leader-subordinate level (e.g., Fiedler, Potter, Zais, & Knowlton, 1979). Most generally, the model has defined the leadership effectiveness at the group level of analysis. In fact, it may be appropriate to say that this is the first model in leadership effectiveness research that was designed in a multi-level-of-analysis framework (Dansereau, personal communication).

The model has been the target of numerous criticisms through its evolution (e.g., Ashour, 1973; Graen, Alvares, Orris, & Martella, 1971; Graen, Orris, & Alvares, 1971; Schriesheim & Kerr 1977; Vecchio, 1977) and has been an impetus for over 200 empirical studies. After three decades of research, two meta-analyses (i.e., Peters, Hartke, & Pohlmann, 1985; Strube & Garcia, 1981) have tested its criteria-related validity. The results, overall, have supported the model. Both meta-analyses agreed that the laboratory studies yielded stronger support than the field studies, and both provided recommendations for improvement. Most of the recommendations suggested a need to expand and refine the definitions of situational control and of the factors that contribute to situational control.

This article defines the constructs which determine the model and reviews the operational definitions. Although there have been several reviews of the model, it has been about 16 years since the last complete review (Fiedler, 1978). Confusion still exists regarding the model's components and their relationship with each other. In this article, new and old evidence is discussed to clarify these misunderstandings. The model's constructs are: (1) leader's characteristics, (2) situational control, and (3) leadership effectiveness. Table 1 gives a summary of the way each of these variables in the model has been defined and measured.

This article seeks to demonstrate that the strength of the contingency model lies in its use of a multi-level and multiple-sources approach in defining leadership effectiveness. Specifically, as presented in Table 1, measures of the leader's orientation are drawn from the leader; outcome measures are typically taken from sources independent of the leader, such as supervisor ratings or objective performance measures. Situational variables have been specified in a number of ways, many of which are conceptually and operationally independent both from leader variables and sources of the outcome criteria (e.g., experimental manipulations, observer ratings of organizational characteristics).

Table 1
Summary of Contingency Model's Variables with Their Conceptual
Level of Analysis, Measure, and Source of Information

Variables	Level	Measure	Source
Leader's Motivational Orientation	Individual	Least Preferred Coworker (LPC) Scale	Leader
Situational Control			
Group Climate	Group	Group Atmosphere (GA) Leader-Member Relation Sociometric Method	Leader or Averaged Group Score
Task Structure	Individual	Task Structure Scale or Type of Job	Leader or Experimenter
Authority	Individual	Position Power Scale	Leader Experiment Superior
Effectiveness			
Satisfaction	Group or Dyadic	Job Descriptor Index (JDI)	Subordinate
Performance	Group	Supervisory Rating Archival Data	Superior Experimenter Org. Records
Stress	Individual	Fiedler's Job Stress Scale	Leader

The independence of the theoretical variables reduces the model's vulnerability to validity threats attendant to single-source ratings and overlapping common-method variance. Furthermore, even when leader's characteristics and situational and outcome variables are provided by leader ratings, as in studies of leader stress (Chemers, Hays, Rhodewalt, & Wysocki, 1985), the predicted interactions among the variables are of a nature (i.e., both complex and counterintuitive) such that the interactions are unlikely to be the result of consistency factors or demand characteristics (Orne, 1962).

In the sections that follow, we address the levels of analysis and sources of information with respect to: (1) the leader's motivational orientation, (2) the variables that contribute to the leader's situational control, (3) various individual, group, and organizational outcomes, (4) the new directions, and (5) the applications of the contingency model.

LEADERSHIP MOTIVATIONAL ORIENTATION

Although past reviews (e.g., Rice 1978a, 1978b) have been quite thorough, there are a few issues regarding the conceptualization of the scale and its use that were not clarified. In order to address these points, this section presents key evidence that elucidates these issues. The leader's orientation is measured by a scale referred to as "least preferred coworker" (LPC) scale. The scale's instructions ask the respondent to identify within the context of all the persons with whom the respondent has ever worked:

> the one person in your life with whom you could work least well. This individual may or may not be the person you also dislike most. It must be the one person with whom you had the most difficulty getting a job done, the one single individual with whom you would least want to work—a boss, a subordinate, or a peer (Fiedler & Chemers, 1984, p. 17).

Various closely related forms of the LPC scale have consisted of from 16 to 22, eight-point, bipolar adjective scales on which the respondent's least preferred coworker is described. Regardless of the version, the respondent's score is calculated by summing across all items. When the LPC score has been treated categorically, the cutoff points to categorize the score have not always been consistent across studies. In some cases, extreme scores have been used (cutoffs usually have been based on a standard deviation on each side of the mean or the top and bottom 10% or thirds of the distribution). In other cases, a median or mean split has been used to categorize high and low LPC scores. In recent years, a few studies have used the LPC score as a continuous score, examining the magnitude of its relation to outcome variables.

Psychometric Questions Concerning the LPC Scale

This section discusses the validity and reliability of the LPC scale, with the special intent of clarifying past misconceptions with respect to the measurement and meaning of the construct. We address both the psychometric properties of the scale and its validity and utility as a research tool. Rather than measuring a leader's attitudes, expectations, and self-reported behaviors, the LPC scale seeks to infer a respondent's (leader's) investment in task accomplishment through his/her reactions to a coworker who thwarts accomplishment. The degree to which the respondent gives a negative rating of the "least preferred coworker" presumably reflects the respondent's frustration or anger.

Two terms in the instructions are especially important—that is, "least" and "coworker." The term "least" demands that the person rated is not just any undesirable coworker in the rater's experience but the single worst ever encountered. The intent is to create a strong stimulus that will draw the greatest level of reaction from the respondent. Asking a respondent to describe two different coworkers as a means of assessing the reliability of the measure is not appropriate. For each rater, there should be only one appropriate stimulus: the least preferred coworker.

The term "coworker" rather than "subordinate" or "follower" is intentionally vague, allowing the respondent to rate a peer, superior, or subordinate. Finally, the frame of reference for identifying this poor coworker is the respondent's entire working history, avoiding an emphasis on the current situation. Here, the attempt is to obtain a stable, affective reaction. The items on which the least preferred coworker are rated are not descriptors of particular behaviors or task-related abilities. They are global, evaluative adjectives. The ratings of the stimulus thus reflect a general evaluative response (i.e., an attitude) toward a person who has interfered with the attainment of a more or less highly valued goal (e.g., task accomplishment). In sum, the LPC reflects a broad emotional reaction to a poor coworker, revealing how important the rater considers task success to be.

The LPC score clearly has been the most controversial component of the contingency model. It has been interpreted as a measure of psychological distance, leader orientation, and motivational hierarchy. All of these interpretations apply to some extent. This lack of consensus has been very disturbing to those with a low tolerance for ambiguity. Whether we now call LPC a measure of leader orientation, the term favored by Ayman and Chemers (1991), or a motivational index, the term favored by Fiedler (1978), is not of critical importance. As we shall see, the difference in operational terms turns out to be one of emphasis rather than of substance.

Questions of the construct validity of the LPC scale have engendered debates and controversies. Three approaches have been taken to respond to these debates. One has examined the scale's item content. A second has addressed issues of convergent and divergent validity, and a third has studied the relationship between the LPC score and leader behavior. Each of these approaches is now considered.

Item Content

The discussion surrounding the nature of the adjectives included in the scale has been concerned with the different number of adjectives that were descriptors of work-related traits (e.g., lazy or industrious) versus the number of relationship-relevant descriptors (e.g., friendly or close). Rice (1978b) referred to a series of studies (published and unpublished) demonstrating that the scale has two factors (task and people orientation). He also demonstrated that the structure has varied for high and low LPC respondents, and the intercorrelation between the factors across studies has also varied. Edwards, Rode, and Ayman (1989) compared the responses of ROTC cadets to the leader behavior questionnaire (LBDQ), leader opinion questionnaire (LOQ or LEAD), and LPC scale, using confirmatory factor analyses. They found that the three scales of LBDQ, LOQ, and LEAD had similar two-factor structures (consideration and initiation of structure) and that the LPC scale did not match this factor structure.

Rice (1978b) argued that "the potential importance of these factor analytic data is indicated by examining the relationship between LPC factor scores and external criteria" (p. 110). Rice and Seaman (1981) explored the relationship of task versus relationship adjective sets with outcome variables. Using a 22-item scale, they found that an overall score and a score based only on task items seemed to have quite similar relationships to outcome criteria. Apparently, the variations in item content of the scale do not threaten the criterion-related validity of the total LPC scale.

Convergent-Divergent Validity

During the past 30 years of research on LPC, several studies have examined the LPC scale's construct validity through convergent and divergent validity studies in which LPC scores are associated with other trait measures. The earlier studies reported correlations below .30 between the various traits and the LPC scale, establishing the LPC scale as an independent construct (Fiedler, 1967). Recent studies have shown that respondents' self-monitoring score (Ayman & Chemers, 1991; Ayman & Abenate, 1994), gender (Powell, Butterfield, Mainiero, 1981; Schneier, 1978), values and intelligence (Kennedy, Houston, Korsgaard, & Gallo, 1987) are non-linearly related to the LPC scale.

Rice (1978a) reported a low negative linear relationship between the LPC score (that is, a low LPC person scoring higher) and measures of self-evaluation, including intelligence (Bons, Bass, & Komorita, 1970), achievement (Burke, 1965), and being agreeable (Shima, 1968). He also reported a positive relationship (that is, high LPC person scoring higher) with social cognitive complexity. A pattern of results relating the LPC score to measures of confidence, attention, and cognitive complexity, revealed that low LPC persons were more interested in, and knowledgeable about, variables in the task domain, whereas high LPC persons evidenced a similar involvement with aspects of the interpersonal or relationship domain. Rice concluded that the LPC scale reflects a basic value orientation (toward task achievement in low LPCs and toward interpersonal relations in high LPCs) and these values influence attitudes toward various factors in the leadership environment.

Two studies of job satisfaction provide direct support of the value-attitude interpretation of the LPC construct. In both a laboratory experiment (Rice, Marwick, Chemers, & Bentley, 1982) and an organizational survey (Chemers & Ayman, 1985), low LPC leaders showed a significantly stronger relationship between performance measures and job satisfaction than did high LPC leaders. The high LPCs showed a stronger relationship than the lows between job satisfaction and measures of group atmosphere and interpersonal harmony. Consistent with other studies that have demonstrated a moderating effect of work values (e.g., growth need strength, need for achievement) on satisfaction-performance relationships (e.g., Abdel-Halim, 1980), these findings reinforce the view of LPC as a measure of values or motivational orientations of the respondents.

Leader Behavior

The third construct validity technique involves relating the LPC scale to leader behavior measures. Fiedler and Chemers (1974) referred to the

LPC score as a measure of the leader's style. Whereas it may have seemed rational then to relate the LPC score to leader behavior, several issues of concern need to be addressed. First, as already established, the LPC scale measures a respondent's attitudes, values, and motivational orientation, not his or her behavior. Although attitudes and values may be the basis for an individual's behavior, attitude/values and behavior do not bear an isomorphic relationship, and therefore, the relationship between a leader's LPC score and a particular leader behavior is an empirical question. Second, recognition of the strong effect of cognitive and information processing biases in the perception of leader behavior (Lord & Maher, 1991) has called into question the role of behavioral measures as valid indicators of "actual" leader behavior.

Given these caveats related to the measurement of leader behavior, the relationship between the LPC and leaders' behaviors is important not only from a leadership-process perspective but also because it can assist in clarifying two dominant hypotheses about the LPC: the Value-Attitude (Rice 1978a) and the Motivational Hierarchy (Fiedler, 1978) hypotheses. For the value-attitude hypothesis to be supported, the research should show significant and consistent main effects for the LPC scale and measures of leader behavior. For the motivational hierarchy hypothesis to be validated, the results should have demonstrated an interaction effect of a leader's LPC score with his or her situational control predicting the leader's behavior. Rice (1978a), by including main effects that were present in studies with significant interaction effects, concluded that across studies there were an equal number of findings supporting both hypotheses. This conclusion may have been premature because some of these main effects were part of results that supported interaction effects.

We argued earlier that the LPC scale is an attitude measure with a strong emphasis on the affective component. However, evidence also supported the fact that although the LPC reflects the respondent's reaction to a person in a situation, it also reflects the respondent's values and goals (i.e., emphasis on task accomplishment or relationship with people), which are the motivational forces behind his/her actions. The results of the interaction effects of leader's LPC score and situational control on measures of leader behavior demonstrate that the relationship of the leader's LPC score to the leader's behavior is moderated by the situation (e.g., Bons & Fiedler, 1976; Borden, 1980; Chemers, 1969;

Frost, 1981; Fiedler, 1967, 1972; Fiedler & Garcia, 1987; Larson & Rowland, 1973; Sample & Wilson, 1965). For example, high LPC leaders behaved more considerately toward group members in moderately stressful conditions than low LPC leaders; low LPC leaders behaved more considerately than highs in situations where they felt in control. On the other hand, high LPC leaders behaved with more emphasis on the task than low LPC leaders in situations where they felt in control, and the low LPC leaders behaved with more focus on the task than high LPC leaders when they were in moderately stressful conditions. These shifts in behavioral manifestations of LPC score may be indicative of a hierarchy of the leaders' goals motivating them to act. That is, in situations where individuals feel that their primary values, goals, or motivational orientations are not met, they act in a way to satisfy them, and if they are satisfied, their secondary goals or values will direct their behavior. It is important to note that in several of the above-mentioned studies, leader's behavior was measured by objective techniques—for example, in-basket exercise responses (Larson & Rowland, 1973).

In summary, the value-attitude and motivational hierarchy are not incompatible hypotheses. Rather, one focuses on the measure of LPC and the other on the construct it represents. They both agree that LPC measures values or goals. However, the former assumed that individual's values will always be manifested in specific behaviors (Rice, 1978a) and the latter (Fiedler, 1978) assumed that values or goals may or may not be manifested in a particular behavior. In the latter case, the vehicle that moderates the behavioral manifestation is the situation. The motivational hierarchy is more in line with other social-psychological views on the relationship between attitude and behavior (Ajzen, 1987; Fazio, 1990).

In addition, the relationship of the LPC score and leader behavior can only be studied when the issues of measurement of leader behavior are considered with great care. Therefore, although we concur with Rice's position that research on this relationship may provide a better understanding of the LPC score, the path is not as smooth and clear as it may seem.

Although the evidence on the construct validity of the LPC scale is not conclusive, some conclusions do seem reasonable. A low LPC score is a reflection of a negative affect emanating from frustration with the inability to complete the task at hand. A low score may represent those individuals who have a self-concept that is strongly associated with accomplishment. The evidence suggests that LPC is a measure of a respondent's inner state, not a measure of his/her behavior patterns.

Reliability

As a final note to the review of the LPC scale's psychometric properties, its reliability is now discussed. The reliability of the LPC scale has been measured both by examining its internal consistency and test-retest reliability. The internal consistency of the scale has always been fairly high. The average internal consistency coefficient reported is .88 (Rice, 1978b), and more recently, Ayman and Chemers (1991) reported Cronbach's alpha of .90. The test-retest reliability of the scale parallels other personality measures with a median stability coefficient of .67 (Rice, 1978b; Fiedler, 1978). Rice's (1978b) review included 23 studies on test-retest reliability of the scale. The time lapse in these studies ranged from two days to two-and-a-half years. The scale seems to meet the established criteria for reliability.

Summary of the Review on the LPC Scale

Overall, the findings about the psychometric properties of the LPC scale have demonstrated that the nature of the adjectives included in the scale may affect its structure, but it is not critical to the scale's functionality. Based on the existing evidence, it is safe to say that the LPC scale is a measure of the internal state of the leader. Whether it measures values, motivation attitude, or goals is not totally resolved. However, based on Markus and Wurf (1987), all of these concepts are variables that operate in determining the working self, though they vary in their level of specificity.

The LPC scale is a measure whose history and approach creates unique advantages and disadvantages. As an indirect measure of values and/or motivational orientation, it is less susceptible to demand characteristics or social desirability effects. On the other hand, the lack of a clear theoretic-deductive explanation makes the LPC construct appear mysterious and unscientific. The predictive utility of the construct as evidenced in the comprehensive meta-analyses (Strube & Garcia, 1981; Peters, Hartke, & Pohlmann, 1985) does encourage us to continue attempts to understand the concept better.

SITUATIONAL CONTROL

The other central construct in contingency model research, situational control, has been operationalized in various ways. It is conceptually defined as the leader's sense of influence and control afforded by the situation (Fiedler, 1978). In most of the research, three components of the situation have been identified as contributors to a sense of predictability and control: Leader-Member Relationship (formerly referred to as Group Atmosphere), Task Structure, and Position Power.

In the following sections, each of the three components of situational control is discussed. Each component is defined both theoretically and methodologically. From a methodological perspective, both the measurements and the source of information for the component across studies are examined. Finally, the relationship among the three components is presented, as well as their relationship with the leader's motivational orientation.

Leader-Member Relations

This construct refers to the amount of cohesiveness in the work team and the support of the team for the leader. Leader-member relations is the most important aspect of the situation, because if the leader lacks group support, energy is diverted to controlling the group rather than toward planning, problem-solving, and productivity. Under these conditions, the leader's influence is weakened, and he or she can not rely on the team to achieve and implement the goal.

In early laboratory research of the model, the group-atmosphere scale (Fiedler, 1967) was used to assess either experimentally manipulated or naturally occurring work team cohesion. The measure was completed by all participants. The scale consisted of 10 eight-point bipolar items. In studies where sociometric choice was used to manipulate group cohesion, the statistical relationship between the score on the group atmosphere scale and sociometric manipulation was positive and substantial (e.g., Chemers & Skrzypek, 1972).

More recently, the Leader-Member Relation (LMR) scale has been used to assess this construct. This measure was first introduced as a training tool (Fiedler, Chemers, & Mahar, 1976). It consists of eight five-point scale items describing the relationship of the team members with each other and their loyalty and responsiveness to the leader. The LMR scale has good internal reliability—Cronbach's alpha of .80 (e.g., Ayman & Chemers, 1991).

Leader-member relations is theoretically conceptualized at the group level. In much of the experimental and field studies a group average on Group Atmosphere scale was used to determine group cohesion (e.g., Chemers & Skrzypek, 1972, Geyer & Julian, 1973, Csoka & Fiedler, 1972). In some of the more recent field studies, the leader has been the source of information about this construct. However, the leaders' scores represented their experiences with their group as a whole, not with individual subordinates in dyadic relationships (e.g., Ayman & Chemers, 1991).

The leader-member relations scale has shown strong construct validity. The Group Atmosphere scale and the Leader-Member Relation scale are highly correlated—$r = .88$ (Fiedler, 1978). Neither of the scales has shown a correlation with the leader's LPC scale (e.g., Chemers, Hays, Rhodewalt, & Wysoki, 1985; Fiedler, 1978; McNamara, 1968). However, Group Atmosphere has been correlated with some outcome variables like leader's experience of stress with the subordinates (Chemers et al., 1985). The construct validity of the Leader-Member Relations scale demonstrates that it is a valid measure depicting the group's cohesion and loyalty to the leader. The test of validity has been ascertained by high correlations between two different measures and from multiple sources (i.e., the group and/or the leader). It is independent of the leader's orientation even when the leader has been the source of information for both the LPC score and the leader-member relation score. This is a significant strength in the model because in field studies, the leader is typically the source of this information.

Task Structure

This second component of Situational Control represents the clarity and certainty in task goals and procedures that allow the leader confidently to guide the group's activities. In laboratory studies, the variable was usually manipulated by the choice of assigned tasks that varied on Shaw's (1963) criteria for task structure (Fiedler, 1978). In field studies, task structure ratings can be provided by a knowledgeable observer, such as a superior. A scale for rating task structure by a supervisor or investigator was developed by Hunt (1967).

More recent field research has employed the Task Structure Rating Scale developed as part of the "Leader Match" training program (Fiedler, Chemers, & Mahar, 1976; Fiedler & Chemers, 1984). The self-report scale consists of 10 items incorporating Shaw's (1963) dimensions of goal clarity, goal-path multiplicity, solution specificity, and outcome quantifiability. Based on research that indicated that task-relevant experience and training enhanced task structure (Fiedler, 1970; Chemers, Rice, Sundstrom, & Butler, 1975), an additional two-item subscale assessing the leader's experience and training was added to the scale. Information on the total scale's reliability is not available. However, Ayman and Chemers (1991) reported a Cronbach's alpha of .81 for the first section of the scale.

In studies where the measure of task structure has been based on the leader's perception, the intercorrelation of LPC score and task structure score has not been reported. Part of the reason may be due to the fact that task structure is a single component of the situational control dimension and only the correlations between situational control and other variables are usually reported. In addition, until recently, task structure was objectively rated by the experimenter or the leader's supervisor in most studies.

The sense of predictability and certainty provided by a task with clear goals and procedures contributes to the overall level of situational control experienced by the leader. Conceptually, task structure is a group-level variable. The task being measured includes all the activities that the leader must accomplish to move the group toward its collective goal. In contrast to some models, the task being measured is the leader's task, not the task of individual subordinates being supervised by the leader. For example, a task requiring high levels of interdependence among subordinates might increase complexity and reduce task structure for the leader.

Operationally, task structure has been defined by leader self-reports, by ratings of observers or superiors, or by manipulation of assigned tasks. Although the measurement of the variable sometimes occurs at the individual level, in combination with other situational control variables, it represents an aspect of the group environment in which the leader functions. As shown in Table 1, however, it is an individual-level variable about the Leader's Task.

Position Power

This component of situational control is defined as the administrative authority bestowed on the leader by the organization or other source of authority—for example, the experimenter. Fiedler (1978) advised that position power assessments should be supplied by the leader's supervisor, due to the possibility of distortion of information by self-report. However, in most field studies, the leader's self-report has been used (Fiedler & Chemers, 1984). This is a five-item scale that measures the leader's discretionary power to reward and punish, job-relevant expertise, and official status. Internal reliability data are available for only one study (Ayman & Chemers, 1991), where it had a low Cronbach's Alpha of .31. While a single reliability coefficient is not conclusive, it may be that the low internal consistency is the result of the multidimensional nature of the scale, which measures several bases of power. In most field research, leaders are chosen from a single organizational level with similar position power. No relationship has been found between leader's LPC score and the leader's reported Position Power score.

Similar to the Task Structure, Position Power has been defined at the individual level, for the leader. It has been manipulated by experimental design, described by the leader's supervisor, or measured through the leader's perception (see Table 1). Like Task Structure, it contributes to the overall level of control in the leader's situation, and may be conceptualized as either a group- or individual-level variable depending on the analysis.

Summary of Situational Control and Social Power

The three components of situational control parallel French and Raven's (1959) five bases of power. Power has been defined as the ability to influence others. Situational Control has also been defined as providing the leader with the ability to influence and gain control (Bass, 1991). French and Raven identified the expert and referent sources of power as sources based on knowledge and expertise regarding the task and the strength or solidity of the social relationships. Research has indicated that these two sources of power have the most efficacious and lasting effects in social influence (Podsakoff & Schriesheim, 1985; Yukl &

Taber, 1983). Referent power based on the quality of the social relationship is most similar to the contingency model variable of "Leader-Member Relations." Expert power with its emphasis on task knowledge bears much in common with "Task Structure." The three other sources of power—coercive, reward, and legitimate—reflect on an individual's authority. These three sources have shown to be inter-correlated to the point that some have referred to it as position power (Bass, 1991). Their effects have been debated. Thus, they do not seem to have as robust and lasting an effect as the referent and expert sources (Podsakoff & Schrieshiem, 1985). In the contingency model, these power sources are given the least weight in the assessment of situational control.

The weighing of the three components of situational control was originally ordinal. Fiedler (1967) specified Group Atmosphere (leader-member relations) to be most important. Task Structure came second, and Position Power was third. The analytic strategy typically involved dividing groups at the median on each variable and combining the resultant designations into one of eight cells, or "octants." This approach had the ad hoc effect of weighing Leader-Member Relations twice as strongly as Task Structure, which was weighted twice as strongly as Position Power (i.e., 4:2:1 weighing ratio). Later empirical research related measures of each variable to a rating of overall control and predictability and found that the inductively derived weights were very close to the 4:2:1 ratios (Nebeker, 1975).

The self-rating Leader Match scales (Fiedler & Chemers, 1984) are adjusted for the prescribed weights by the maximum number of points possible on each scale (i.e., LMR scale, 40 points; TS scale, 20; PP scale, 10). The summed scale values provide a measure of overall Situational Control, which can be compared to the cutting points for high, moderate, and low levels of control. Recent field studies have used the normative cutoff points (e.g., Giffort & Ayman, 1989) or median (e.g., Ayman & Chemers, 1991) or tripartite splits (e.g., Chemers et al., 1985) of sample distributions to assign leaders to conditions.

THE RELATIONSHIP AMONG THE INDEPENDENT VARIABLES WITHIN THE CONTINGENCY MODEL

The variables that define the leader's personal characteristic (the LPC) and the leader's situational control (leader-member relations, task structure, and position power) are both conceptually and psycho-metrically independent. This is one of the most valuable and unique properties of the contingency model. In studies where the leader is the only source of information for both personal and situational variables, or where the situation is defined by an independent observer, the LPC and situational control scores are not statistically related. Problems of multi-colinearity and single-source biases, which bedevil much current leadership-research methodology (Podsakoff & Organ, 1986; Spector, 1987), are not a serious problem for contingency model research. Although LPC and situational control are uncorrelated, some dependency does appear among the three situational variables.

In laboratory experiments, the situational control variables were manipulated and their relationship was, by design, independent. In field studies, task structure and position power have been found to be correlated between $r = .75$ (Chemers & Fiedler, 1986) and $r = .33$ (Chemers et al., 1985). The actual level of interdependence of the three factors may have varied from study to study because of the level of the manager, the type of company, or the source of information on each factor. Overlap among the situational control variables provides a strong rationale for employing the composite situational control score.

Relationship of the Model to Outcome (Dependent) Variables

The contingency model of leadership effectiveness has defined its criterion of effectiveness primarily as work group performance. However, some studies have examined effects on other criteria, such as subordinate satisfaction or leader's reported symptoms of stress.

The operational definition of performance has been based partially on the nature of task and the level of the leader's position. Wherever possible, productivity was defined by objective measures, such as win-lose records for basketball teams, tons per person-hour for steel production crews, and accuracy for bombing crews. In cases where the nature of the tasks required a subjective evaluation, at least two raters evaluated the quality of performance. Such tasks typically consisted of composing a story, developing a report, or recommending a program. In most of the organizational field studies, the manager's performance was rated by a superior.

The important point to note is that the contingency model has used a variety of performance measures that have been relevant to the work group objective. However, regardless of whether the performance was measured subjectively or objectively and whether it was a measure of quality or quantity, it was always assessed by an agent outside of the work team.

We pointed out earlier that the contingency model was designed primarily to predict work team performance. The empirical development of the model made clear that only the interaction of personal and situational parameters could predict group performance. One of the most important premises of the contingency principle is that neither leader characteristics nor situational factors alone can predict performance. The reviews and meta-analyses have established the essential validity of that premise. Person-situation match, but neither person nor situation alone, has been consistently predictive of performance outcomes.

In the early stages of the development of the model, Fiedler (1967) argued that group productivity was the most important and appropriate outcome variable in leadership research. He pointed out that chief executive officers, football coaches, and symphony conductors are not retained and rewarded for making their subordinates happy and satisfied but for making them productive and profitable. This point is still apt today, but organizational theorists and practitioners have come to recognize that variables such as commitment, loyalty, and satisfaction can have important implications for organizational performance and profitability.

In 1977, Schriesheim and Kerr criticized the contingency model for its lack of attention to subordinate satisfaction. If we turn our attention to the prediction and explanation of subordinate satisfaction and other attitudinal and affective states, what might be the most useful ways to proceed? A logical approach might be to look for the same confluence of person and situational variables that are effective in the prediction of performance—that is, leader-situation match.

In 1981, Rice responded to Schriesheim and Kerr's (1977) criticism with a review of existing studies examining the relationship of the contingency model variables to job satisfaction. Although some inconsistencies exist across studies, Rice concluded that the bulk of the evidence supports the view that subordinate satisfaction is highest when leaders are in match. Subsequent studies of managers in the United

States (Giffort & Ayman, 1989) and in Mexico (Ayman & Chemers, 1991) have supported Rice's conclusions. Subordinates of low LPC managers in high-control situations and of high LPC managers in moderate-control situations were more satisfied than their "out-of-match" counterparts.

Job satisfaction is a multi-faceted construct. The contingency model effects reported here occur primarily on measures of satisfaction with the superior or satisfaction with coworkers (i.e., measures of work team cohesion) rather than on measures of satisfaction with pay or promotion which are variables frequently outside the leader's control. It is interesting to note that match (i.e., the interaction of LPC and Situational Control) is a better predictor of subordinate satisfaction than is the leader's score on the leader-member relations scale, indicating the importance of multiple, independent measures of group effects.

Although the validity of the contingency model in the prediction of group performance seems well established and its utility for predicting subordinate satisfaction is promising, many gaps in understanding remain which reduce the model's explanatory value. The model continues, however, to instigate research that may enrich our understanding of the processes that underlie match effects. The next section will briefly describe some new directions in contingency model research involving efforts at the individual level to understand the phenomenological and emotional effects of match; at the dyadic level to predict performance and satisfaction; and multi-trait approaches in which person-level variables besides the LPC are integrated into the model.

NEW DIRECTIONS

Individual-Level Analyses

A series of studies have examined the phenomenological experience of style-situation match on leaders. Garcia (1983) compared high and low LPC persons working on individual tasks that varied in the degree of certainty. Certainty was manipulated by providing half of the subjects with task-relevant training that increased task structure and subjective reports of certainty. Garcia reported that low LPC persons in the high-certainty condition (training) and high LPC persons in the low-certainty (no training) condition made stronger attributions to their own ability as the cause of performance than did low LPC persons in the low certainty condition or high LPCs in the high certainty condition. In a laboratory experiment on group leadership, Nahavandi (1983) found that "in-match" leaders, as defined by contingency model variables, reported higher levels of involvement and interest in the experience than did "out-of-match" leaders.

Chemers, Hays, Rhodewalt, and Wysocki (1985) measured the relationship of contingency model match to job stress and stress-related illness among university administrators. Department chairs who were out of match reported significantly higher levels of stress and stress-related illness than did their in-match counterparts. These findings were replicated in a follow-up study (Chemers, Hill, & Sorod, 1986) of high school administrators. As in the earlier studies, in-match leaders reported less stress and illness, as well as higher levels of job satisfaction, than did out-of-match leaders. Shirakashi (1991) closely replicated the results of these match-stress studies using a sample of managers in Japan.

A laboratory experiment by Chemers, Sorod, and Akimoto (reported in Chemers, 1993) found that in-match leaders as compared to out-of-match leaders reported: (1) more positive mood states, (2) greater confidence in their ability to lead, and (3) more internal attributions to their own ability and effort to explain group performance. A number of theorists and researchers have recently focused on the role of positive affective states, such as confidence and mood, on leadership performance (e.g., Murphy, 1992; May, 1993; Staw & Barsade, 1993; Bennis & Nanus, 1985; House & Shamir, 1993). Leadership match may be a powerful moderator of contemporaneous situational factors affecting such affective states.

Dyadic-Level Analyses

The study of dyads in the contingency model has not received much attention. Two studies that have examined dyads have shown trends that indicate that the nature of the task may interact with different compositions of leader's and follower's LPC score to predict subordinate satisfaction and performance.

Chemers, Goza, and Plumer (1978) conducted an experiment in which three- person groups solved a problem for which the leader and one follower had been given contradictory information in a pre-session briefing. The dyads that were most effective in solving the problem were those with a high LPC leader and low LPC follower, while the most ineffective dyads were those that were homogeneous with respect to leader and follower LPC. Tobey (1992) also found the high-LPC-leader/low-LPC-subordinate dyads to be most effective in performance on a similarly unstructured task. However, Tobey (1992) also found that dyads led by low LPCs outperformed dyads led by high LPCs when the task was more structured. It seems reasonable to expect that the effects of dyadic composition on both performance and satisfaction would be most productively addressed in a contingency framework.

Multi-Trait Approach

Weiss and Adler (1984) have suggested a multi-trait approach to organizational behavior theories. They advise the inclusion of traits that have a theoretical relationship to outcome criteria or have the potential for expanding the explanatory base of the theory. The most developed of the new expansions of the contingency model is the cognitive resource theory (Fiedler, 1993; Fiedler & Garcia, 1987). Fiedler and his associates have demonstrated that the leader's ability to make effective use of his or her cognitive resources (i.e., intellectual ability and job-relevant experience) depends on a number of contingencies. Job stress from any of several sources (including one's boss or subordinates, or the nature of one's task) interferes with a leader's ability to think creatively and use intellectual resources but enhances the value of the well-learned lessons of experience. The intellectual demands of the task, the cooperativeness of subordinates, and the leader's willingness to act directively also moderate the impact of cognitive resources on group productivity.

Unless the leader acts in a directive manner employing knowledge and insight to influence group activities, those cognitive resources will have little effect. Furthermore, compliant and supportive subordinates who respond positively to the leader's influence attempts increase the impact of the leader's directions on group outputs. Finally, intellectually demanding tasks that place a premium on thoughtful and creative ideas will increase the relative effects of cognitive processes.

Similar to the cognitive model, cognitive resource theory places an individual-level phenomenon (the effects of stress on cognition) in a context in which superiors, subordinates, and task influence relationships with group-level outcomes. Leadership as a group process, analyzable at the group level, seems to be the overriding emphasis of these two contingency theories.

Like the contingency model that preceded it, cognitive resource theory assesses the effects of individual-level variables (i.e., leader intelligence and experience) at a group level of analysis. Situational parameters, such as task demands, subordinate support, and environmental stress, moderate the relationships between the individual-level variables and group-level outcomes, for example, productivity. Cognitive resource theory adds the process variable of the leader's level of directiveness to tie together the leader and outcome variables. The centrality of job stress in the cognitive resource theory and in the recent work by Chemers and his associates on leadership match and job stress suggests the potential for integrating the two models. Future research in that direction seems warranted.

Another multi-trait approach to contingency-model research has investigated the moderating role of self-monitoring (Snyder, 1979). Kenny and Zaccaro (1983) have argued that a leader's flexibility in adapting to situational characteristics may be a leadership trait with broad applicability. The self-monitoring construct reflects an individual's sensitivity and responsiveness to the social expectations across varying situations. Since leadership match is based on the degree of fit between the leader's motivational orientation and situational characteristics, a leader's ability to adapt to situations might moderate the effects of match. Specifically, high self-monitors who are able to change their behavior to adjust to the expectations of others may be less susceptible to leader-situation mismatches than would be low self-monitors whose behavioral style is more rigidly determined by internal values and attitudes.

A recent study by Ayman and Chemers (1991) included the self-monitoring scale with the contingency model measures administered to 85 middle managers in Mexican companies. The predicted effects of match on several outcome measures, including subordinate satisfaction with work and the leader's effectiveness in conflict management, were moderated by self-monitoring as expected. Other measures in the same study, such as subordinate satisfaction with the leader, showed straight match effects, unaffected by self-monitoring.

These results indicate that multi-trait approaches to leadership effects have great potential. However, the choice of traits for inclusion must be theoretically driven (Weiss & Adler, 1984).

SUMMARY AND CONCLUSIONS

The contingency model of leadership has stimulated and guided research for more than 30 years. The greatest strengths of the model reside in: (1) the conceptual and statistical independence of its central constructs, LPC and Situational Control; (2) its emphasis on independent and, where possible, objective measures of important organizational outcomes such as group productivity; (3) its relatively lesser vulnerability to the invalidation of its constructs and findings as a result of information-processing biases and methodological weaknesses; and, of course, (4) its proven predictive validity.

The model's greatest weaknesses arise from its inductive development. The LPC construct has little face or concurrent validity, and even evidence for its construct validity requires some faith. The lack of process-based explanations for performance effects makes both the understanding and application of the model more difficult.

One of the major strengths of the contingency model in practical application is that about 15 minutes worth of questionnaire administration provides a multi-level analysis of person-situation match that can be used in selection, placement, training, and organizational development. Based on the contingency model, the Leader Match training program (Fiedler & Chemers, 1984) provides a framework for organizational intervention at the individual, dyadic, and group levels.

During the last three decades, the contingency model has been the subject of extensive research and vigorous controversy, and yet it is alive and still developing. The individual and dyadic levels of analysis are being added to the traditional focus on group-level effectiveness phenomena. Multi-trait approaches may help to illuminate the factors that underlie its impact. The power of the cognitive resource theory reveals productive avenues for bridging the gap between the contingency model and other psychological theories. Finally, the model's utility in creating practical approaches to leadership training and organizational development reinforces Kurt Lewin's dictum that "There is nothing so practical as a good theory."

Through training such as Leader Match, which is based on the contingency model of leadership effectiveness, the leader uses both personal and group data to assess his or her match in the situation. The validity of this training program has been presented in numerous documents (Fiedler & Mahar, 1979; Burke & Day, 1986). Using the model's existing research, the leader can then anticipate his or her effectiveness both at a personal and dyadic level (i.e., experienced stress or subordinate satisfaction) and at a group level (i.e., performance, subordinates' satisfaction and morale). With access to such wisdom, the leader can do "job engineering." This does not require major changes in the way the work is done but, through modifying the three situational control constructs, the leader can affect all levels of work team dynamics and alter group functioning.

REFERENCES

Abdel-Halim, A. A. (1980). Effects of higher order need strength on the job performance-job satisfaction relationship. *Personnel Psychology, 33*, 335–347.

Ajzen, I. (1987). Attitudes, traits, and actions: Dispositional prediction of behavior in personality and social psychology. In L. Berkowitz (Ed.), *Advances in Experimental Social Psychology* (Vol. 20, pp. 1–63). New York: Academic.

Ashour, A. S. (1973). The contingency model of leadership effectiveness: An evaluation. *Organizational Behavior and Human Performance, 9*, 339–355.

Ayman, R., & Abenate, D. C. (1994). An expansion of the contingency model: The moderating influence of self-monitoring. Unpublished manuscript, Illinois Institute of Technology, Chicago, IL.

Ayman, R., & Chemers, M. M. (1991). The effect of leadership match on subordinate satisfaction in Mexican organizations: Some moderating influences of self-monitoring. *Applied Psychology: An International Review, 40*, 299–314.

Bass, B. M. (1991). *Bass & Stogdill's handbook of leadership: Theory, research, & managerial applications.* 3rd edition. New York: Free Press.

Bennis, W., & Nanus, B. (1985). *Leaders: Strategies for taking charge.* New York: Harper & Row.

Bons, P. M., Bass, A. R., & Komorita, S. (1970). Changes in leadership style as a function of military experience and type of command. *Personnel Psychology, 23*, 551–568.

Bons, P.M., & Fiedler, F.E. (1976). Changes in organizational leadership and the behavior of relationship and task motivated leaders. *Administrative Science Quarterly, 21*, 453–473.

Borden, D. F. (1980). Leader-boss stress, personality job satisfaction and performance: Another look at the inter-relationship of some old constructs in the modern large bureaucracy. Unpublished Ph.D. dissertation, University of Washington, Seattle.

Burke, W. W. (1965). Leadership behavior as a function of the leader, the follower, and situation. *Journal of Personality, 33*, 60–81.

Burke, M. J., & Day, R. R. (1986). Acumulative study of the effectiveness of managerial training. *Journal of Applied Psychology, 71*, 232–246.

Chemers, M. M. (1969). Cross-cultural training as a means for improving situational favorableness. *Human Relations, 22*, 531–546.

Chemers, M. M. (1993). An integrative theory of leadership. In M. M. Chemers & R. Ayman (Eds.), *Leadership theory and research: Perspectives and directions* (pp. 293–319). San Diego, CA: Academic Press.

Chemers, M. M., and Ayman, R. (1985). Leadership orientation as a moderator of the relationship between job performance and job satisfaction of Mexican managers. *Personality and Social Psychology Bulletin, 11*, 359–367.

Chemers, M. M., and Fielder, F. E. (1986). The trouble with assumptions: A reply to Jago and Ragan. *Journal of Applied Psychology, 71*, 560–563.

Chemers, M. M., Goza, B., & Plumer, S. I. (1978). Leadership style and communication process. Paper presented at the annual meeting of the American Psychological Association, Toronto, Ontario, Canada.

Chemers, M. M., Hays, R. B., Rhodewalt, F., & Wysocki, J. (1985). A person-environment analysis of job stress: A contingency model explanation. *Journal of Personality and Social Psychology, 49*, 628–635.

Chemers, M. M., Hill, C., & Sorod, B. (1986). Personality-environment match and health: Support for the contingency model. Paper presented at the annual meetings of the American Psychological Association, Chicago, IL.

Chemers, M. M., Rice, R. W., Sundstrom, E., & Butler, W. (1975). Leader esteem for the least preferred co-worker score, training, and effectiveness: An experimental examination. *Journal of Personality and Social Psychology, 31*, 401–409.

Chemers, M. M., & Skrzypek, G.J. (1972). Experimental test of the contingency model of leadership effectiveness. *Journal of Personality and Social Psychology, 24*, 172–177.

Csoka, L. S., & Fiedler, F. E. (1972). The effect of military training: A test of the contingency model. *Organizational Behavior and Human Performance, 8*, 395–407.

Edwards, J. E., Rode, L. G., & Ayman, R. (1989). The construct validity of scales from four leadership questionnaires. *The Journal of General Psychology, 116*, 171–181.

Fazio, R. H. (1990). Multiple processes by which attitudes guide behavior: The MODE model as an integrative framework. In M. Zanna (Ed.), *Advances in Experimental Social Psychology* (Vol. 23, pp. 75–109). New York: Academic Press.

Fiedler, F. E. (1967). *A theory of leadership effectiveness.* New York: McGraw-Hill.

Fiedler, F. E. (1970). Leadership experience and leadership training—Some new answers to an old problem. *Administrative Science Quarterly, 17*, 453–470.

Fiedler, F. E. (1972). Personality, motivational systems, and the behavior of high and low LPC persons. *Human Relations, 25*, 391–412.

Fiedler, F. E. (1978). The contingency model and the dynamics of the leadership process. In L. Berkowitz (Ed.), *Advances in Experimental Social Psychology* (Vol. 11, pp. 59–96). New York: Academic Press.

Fiedler, F. E. (1993). The leadership situation and the black box in contingency theories. In M.M. Chemers & R. Ayman (Eds.), *Leadership theory and research: Perspectives and directions* (pp.2–28). New York: Academic Press.

Fiedler, F. E., & Chemers, M.M. (1974). *Leadership and effective management.* Glenview, IL: Scott, Foresman.

Fiedler, F. E., & Chemers, M.M. (1984). *Improving leadership effectiveness: The leader match concept.* 2nd edition, New York: Wiley.

Fiedler, F. E., Chemers, M. M., & Mahar, L. (1976). *Improving leadership effectiveness: The leader match concept.* New York: Wiley.

Fiedler, F. E., & Garcia, J. E. (1987). *New approach to effective leadership: Cognitive resources and organizational performance.* New York: John Wiley & Sons.

Fiedler, F. E., & Mahar, L. (1979). A field experiment validating contingency model leadership training. *Journal of Applied Psychology, 64,* 247–254.

Fiedler, F. E., Potter, E. H., Zais, M. M., & Knowlton, W. A. (1979). Organizational stress and the use and misuse of managerial intelligence and experience. *Journal of Applied Psychology, 64,* 635–647.

French, J. R., & Raven, B. (1959). The basis of social power. In D. Cartwright (Ed.), *Studies in social power.* Ann Arbor, MI: Institute for Social Research, University of Michigan.

Frost, D. E. (1981). The effects of interpersonal stress on leadership effectiveness. Unpublished Ph.D. dissertation, University of Washington, Seattle.

Garcia, J. E. (1983). An investigation of a person-situation match interpretation of the esteem for the least preferred coworker scale (LPC). Unpublished Ph.D. dissertation, Salt Lake City, University of Utah.

Geyer, L. J., & Julian, J.W. (1973). Manipulation of situational favorability in tests of the contingency model. *Journal of Psychology, 84,* 13–21.

Giffort, D. W., & Ayman, R. (1989). Contingency model and subordinate satisfaction: Mental health organizations. Paper presented at Academy of Management Annual Conference, Anaheim, CA.

Graen, G., Alvares, K. M., Orris, J. B., & Martella, J. A. (1971). Contingency model of leadership effectiveness: Antecedent and evidential results. *Psychological Bulletin, 74,* 285–296.

Graen, G., Orris, J. B., & Alvares, K. M. (1971). Contingency model of leadership effectiveness: Some experimental results. *Journal of Applied Psychology, 55,* 196–201.

House, R. J., & Shamir, B. (1993). Toward the integration of transformational, charismatic, and visionary theories. In M. M. Chemers & R. Ayman (Eds.), *Leadership theory and research: Perspectives and directions* (pp. 81–104). New York: Academic.

Hunt, J. G. (1967). Fiedler's leadership contingency model: An empirical test in three organizations. *Organizational Behavior and Human Performance, 2,* 290–308.

Kennedy, J. K., Houston, J. M., Korsgaard, M. A., & Gallo, D. D. (1987). Construct space of the least preferred coworker (LPC) scale. *Educational and Psychological Measurement, 47,* 807–814.

Kenny, D. A., & Zaccaro, S. J. (1983). An estimate of variance due to traits in leadership. *Journal of Applied Psychology, 68*, 678–685.

Larson, L. L., & Rowland, K. M. (1973). Leadership style, stress, and behavior in performance. *Organizational Behavior and Human Performance, 9*, 407–420.

Lord, R. G., & Maher, K. J. (1991). *Leadership and information processing.* Boston: Unwin Hyman.

Markus, H., and Wurf, E. (1987). The dynamic self-concept: A social psychological perspective. *Annual Review of Psychology, 38*, 299–337.

May, S. T. (1993). Heavy mettle: The effects of confidence and optimism on leader performance. Unpublished B.A. thesis, Claremont McKenna College, Claremont, CA.

McNamara, V. D. (1968). Leadership, staff and school effectiveness. Unpublished Ph.D. dissertation, University of Alberta.

Murphy, S. E. (1992). The contribution of leadership experience and self-efficacy to group performance under evaluation apprehension. Unpublished Ph.D. dissertation, University of Washington, Seattle, WA.

Nahavandi, A. (1983). The effect of personal and situational factors on satisfaction with leadership. Unpublished Ph.D. dissertation, University of Utah, Salt Lake City, UT.

Nebeker, D. M. (1975). Situational favoribility and environmental uncertainty: An integrative study. *Administrative Science Quarterly, 20*, 281–294.

Orne, M. T. (1962). On the social psychology of the psychological experiment: With particular reference to demand characteristics and their implications. *American Psychologist, 17*, 776–783.

Peters, L. H., Hartke, D. D., & Pohlmann, J. F. (1985). Fiedler's contingency theory of leadership: An application of the meta-analysis procedures of Schmitt and Hunter. *Psychological Bulletin, 97*, 274–285.

Podsakoff, P. M., and Schriesheim, C. A. (1985). Field studies of French and Raven's bases of power: Critique, reanalysis, and suggestions for future research. *Psychological Bulletin, 97*, 387–411.

Podsakoff, P. M., and Organ, D. W. (1986). Self-reports in organizational research: Problems and prospects. *Journal of Management, 12*, 31–41.

Powell, G. N., Butterfield, D. A., & Mainiero, L. A. (1981). Sex-role identity and sex as predictors of leadership style. *Psychological Reports, 49*, 829–830.

Rice, W. R. (1978a). Construct validity of the least preferred co-worker score. *Psychological Bulletin, 85*, 1199–1237.

Rice, W. R. (1978b). Psychometric properties of the esteem for the least preferred coworker (LPC Scale). *Academy of Management Review, 3*, 106–118.

Rice, W. R. (1981). Leader LPC and follower satisfaction: A review. *Organizational Behavior and Human Performance, 28*, 1–25.

Rice, R. W., Marwick, N. J., Chemers, M. M., & Bentley, J. C. (1982). Task performance and satisfaction: Least Preferred Coworker (LPC) as a moderator. *Personality and Social Psychology Bulletin, 8*, 534–541.

Rice, R. W., & Seaman, F. J. (1981). Internal analyses of the Least Preferred Coworker (LPC) scale. *Educational and Psychological Measurement, 41*, 109–120.

Sample, J. A., & Wilson, T. R. (1965). Leader behavior, group productivity, and rating of least preferred co-worker. *Journal of Personality and Social Psychology, 1*, 266–270.

Schneier, C. E. (1978). The contingency model of leadership: An extension to emergent leadership and leader's sex. *Organizational Behavior and Human Performance, 21*, 220–239.

Schriesheim, C. A., & Kerr, S. (1977). Theories and measures of leadership: A critical appraisal of current and future directions. In J. G. Hunt and L. L. Larson (Eds.), *Leadership: The cutting edge* (pp. 9–44). Carbondale, IL: Southern Illinois University Press.

Shaw, M. E. (1963). Scaling group tasks: A method of dimensional analysis: *JSAS Catalogue of Selected Documents in Psychology, 3*(8).

Shima, H. (1968). The leadership between the leader's modes of interpersonal cognition and the performance of the group. *Japanese Psychological Research, 10*, 13–30.

Shirakashi, S. (1991). Job stress of managers: A contingency model analysis. *Organizational Science, 25*, 42–51.

Snyder, M. (1979). Self-monitoring processes. In L. Berkowitz (Ed.), *Advances in experimental social psychology* (Vol. 12, pp. 81–104). New York: Academic Press.

Spector, P. E. (1987). Method variance as an artifact in self-report affect and perceptions at work: Myth or significant problem? *Journal of Applied Psychology, 72*, 438–443.

Staw, B. M., & Barsade, S. G. (1993). Affect and managerial performance: A test of the sadder-but-wiser vs. happier and smarter hypotheses. *Administrative Science Quarterly, 38*, 304–331.

Strube, M. J., & Garcia, J. E. (1981). A meta-analytic investigation of Fiedler's contingency model of leadership effectiveness. *Psychological Bulletin, 90*, 307–321.

Tobey, A. M. (1992). Subordinate satisfaction with supervision: A dyadic or group phenomenon. Unpublished M. A. thesis, Illinois Institute of Technology, Chicago, IL.

Vecchio, R. P. (1977). An empirical examination of the validity of Fiedler's model of leadership effectiveness. *Organizational Behavior and Human Performance, 19*, 180–206.

Vecchio, R. P. (1980). Alternatives to the least preferred co-worker construct. *The Journal of Social Psychology, 112*, 21–29.

Weiss, H. M., & Adler, S. (1984). Personality and organizational behavior. In B. M. Staw & L. L. Cummings (Eds.), *Research in organizational behavior* (Vol. 6, pp. 1–50). Greenwich, CT: JAI Press.

Yukl, G. A., & Taber, T. (1983). The effective use of managerial power. *Personnel, 60*, 37–44.

PART V

Alternative Views of Leadership

If you don't say anything, you won't be called on to repeat it.
                                    Calvin "Silent Cal" Coolidge

The people are the most important element, the land and grain are the next,
and the ruler is least important.
                                    Meng-Tse

There is no monument dedicated to the memory of a committee.
                                    Lester J. Pourciau

See everything, overlook much, correct little.

                                    Pope John XXIII

In this section, we turn our attention to views of leadership that are very recent, as well as very nontraditional. The first selection, "Substitutes for Leadership," suggests how attributes of a work setting (e.g., characteristics of subordinates, the task, the reward system, and the larger organization) may undermine the potential impact of a supervisor. These substitutes and neutralizers of leadership can virtually negate a supervisor's ability to influence a subordinate's performance. In the following article, Greg Stewart and Charles Manz extend the notions of self-management to self-managing work teams and offer an analysis of leadership within a team context. Then, Charles Manz and Henry Sims, Jr., offer a new view of management based on the notion of "SuperLeadership," wherein the leader of today teaches others to lead themselves. Clearly, these notions have much relevance to the contemporary interest in work teams and team leadership.

In the last three readings of this section, we carry the notion of the "un-leader" to the next level, that of the leader as enabler or the leader

as a person who sacrifices for others. This perspective is best embodied in the writings of Robert Greenleaf, in his treatment of "Servant
Leadership." A real-life example of a CEO who personified the notion
of a servant-leader, John F. Donnelly, Sr., is detailed in a lecture given
by one of his colleagues, Robert J. Doyle, of Delta Management
Group. Mr. Donnelly demonstrates that one can simultaneously devote
one's life to humanistic ideals and still operate an organization in a
profitable manner. Finally, we consider the life of an entrepreneur
who, while initially seeking a profit, came to appreciate the humanity
of his workers: Oskar Schindler. In "A Man of Transactions," Terrence
Rafferty provides a review of *Schindler's List* that is insightful as to
why leadership must be measured in terms that are beyond the simple
financial bottom line.

Substitutes for Leadership: Effective Alternatives to Ineffective Leadership

Jon P. Howell, David E. Bowen, Peter W. Dorfman, Steven Kerr, and Philip M. Podsakoff

Leadership has been recognized through the ages as a primary means of influencing the behavior of others. Research into the keys to effective and ineffective leadership has also been going on for quite some time. The earliest assumption was that effective leaders possessed particular traits that distinguished them from ineffective leaders. Effective leaders were thought to be dynamic, intelligent, dependable, high-achieving individuals—so, since traits are hard to change, problems caused by poor leadership were considered best solved by *replacing the leader* with someone who possessed more of the key traits. Regrettably, researchers were unable to identify leader traits that systematically improved organizational effectiveness. Yet leader replacement continues to be a very popular tool in the executive toolkit.

Partly in response to the limitations of trait theory, research in the late 1940s began to focus on relationships between leader behaviors and employee performance, in search of behaviors exhibited by effective leaders that were not displayed by those less effective. With this approach, effective leaders need not possess magical traits but, instead, provide strong direction and support while encouraging subordinates to participate in important decisions. This emphasis on leader behaviors still permitted replacement of a weak leader but allowed an additional remedy as well: namely, *changing the leader's behavior* through some form of training. Probably the most disappointing aspect of research on leader behaviors is that no strong, consistent relationships between particular leader behaviors and organizational effectiveness have ever been found. This has not prevented many off-the-shelf training programs from becoming popular, however, nor the marketers of such programs from becoming prosperous.

SITUATIONAL THEORIES

By the late 1950s it became evident that an approach was needed that didn't depend on ideal traits and universal behaviors. One answer was "situational theory," which starts with the assumption that there are no traits, and no behaviors, that automatically constitute effective leadership. The key is the fit between a leader's style and the situation the leader faces; thus the leader who is highly effective in one situation may be totally ineffective in another. For instance, although General George Patton led the 3rd Army to outstanding performance in World War II, one could hardly imagine the effective use of his leadership style in Mahatma Gandhi's situation against the British in India.

According to situational theories, effective leaders must correctly identify the behaviors each situation requires and then be flexible enough to exhibit these behaviors. Leaders who are behaviorally inflexible, or who lack the necessary diagnostic skills, must be either trained or replaced—the same remedies identified by researchers of leader traits and behaviors. An alternative is to let the leader alone but *change the situation so that the fit is improved.*

Various situational leadership theories have spawned a large number of intervention strategies, many of them competent and some of them useful. However, an assumption underlies all these theories that is wholly unsupported by the research literature. This assumption is that, though different situations require different leadership styles, in *every* situation there is *some* leadership style that will be effective. It has been shown in numerous studies, however, that circumstances often counteract the potential power of leadership, making it virtually impossible in some situations for leaders to have much impact regardless of their style or how good the fit is between leader and situation.

SUBSTITUTES FOR LEADERSHIP

Fortunately, additional remedies for problems stemming from weak leadership—remedies not articulated in any of the earlier trait, behavioral, or situational approaches—have been identified. Such remedies derive from acceptance of the conclusion, based on the research studies referenced earlier, that many organizations contain "substitutes for leadership"—attributes of subordinates, tasks, and organizations that provide task guidance and incentives to perform to such a degree that they virtually negate the leader's ability to either improve or impair subordinate performance. To the extent that powerful leadership substitutes exist, formal leadership, however displayed, tends to be unproductive and can even be counterproductive. In comparison with situational leadership approaches, research on leadership substitutes focuses on whether subordinates are receiving needed task guidance and incentives to perform without taking it for granted that the formal leader is the primary supplier.

Closely Knit Teams of Highly Trained Individuals

Consider the positive impact of substitutes in the following example. Todd LaPorte, Gene Rochlin, and Karlene Roberts are three researchers studying such highly stressful organizational situations as those involving pilots who land jet fighters on a nuclear carrier and air-traffic controllers who direct traffic into San Francisco. They have found that directive leadership is relatively unimportant compared with the work experience and training of individuals in closely knit work groups. This is particularly evident ". . . in the white heat of danger, when the whole system threatens to collapse. . . . The stress creates a need for competence among colleagues who by necessity develop close working relationships with each other." All such individuals are trained extensively and daily, regardless of their position in the hierarchy, to redirect operations or bring them to an abrupt halt. This can involve ignoring orders from managers who are removed from the front line of action. Here the experience and continuous training of individuals, along with the close relationships among members of a work group, substitute for the manager's directive leadership.

By creating alternate sources of task guidance and incentives to perform, substitutes for leadership may have a temporary negative effect on morale among leaders who perceive a loss of power. However, leadership substitutes can also serve as important remedies where there are organizational problems, particularly in situations where the leader is not the source of the problems or where, if the leader is the source, replacement, training, and improving the leader-situation fit are overly expensive, politically infeasible, or too time-consuming to be considered.

A principal advantage of the substitutes construct is that it identifies a remedy for problems stemming from weak leadership in addition to replacement, training, or situational engineering. The remedy is to intentionally, systematically *create substitutes for hierarchical leadership*. In fact, whereas weak, power-hungry leaders invariably regard substitutes as frustrating and necessarily dysfunctional (when they are aware of them at all), strong leaders understand and are comfortable with the idea that effective results can be achieved when task guidance and incentives to perform emanate from sources other than themselves. When other sources are deficient, the hierarchical superior is in a position to play a dominant role; when strong incentives and guidance derive from other sources, the hierarchical superior has less opportunity, but also less need, to exert his or her influence.

Intrinsic Satisfaction

The degree of intrinsic satisfaction that employees derive from their work task is a strong leadership substitute in a large manufacturer of camping equipment in the western United States. The company produces sleeping bags that range from top-of-the-line light-weight back-packers to low-cost models filled with floor sweepings from a mattress factory. Manufacturing personnel are required to rotate among all the lines, so no one group gains a territorial claim to a particular product. Management reports that for workers on the top-quality down-filled bags, supervisory direction has become relatively unnecessary, yet output and quality typically exceed management expectations. Workers report pride in working on this line and usually solve production problems themselves or with co-workers.

The production of bottom-line bags is very different. Quality problems are commonplace, workers cooperate less to overcome the problems, and workers seem to care little about meeting output or quality standards. The constant supervision required to address these problems raises indirect costs. Consultants observing the various production lines during a typical day report that supervisors slowly gravitate away from high-quality lines toward the lowest-quality lines. Thus the workers' intrinsic satisfaction from producing a high-quality product alleviates the need for most supervisory leadership.

Computer Technology

Edward E. Lawler III has noticed that companies with computer-integrated manufacturing and networked computer systems rely on computers to take over many of the supervisor's leadership functions. Feedback is provided by computerized productivity and quality data; directions for certain tasks are entered into the information system; even error detection and goal setting are incorporated in some interactive systems. When individual workers have access to operating data and to a network that allows them to ask employees at other locations to help solve problems, they become more independent of their managers and arrive at solutions among themselves. Spans of control greater than 100 are not unheard of in these organizations. Computerized information technology is therefore providing a substitute for certain types of managerial leadership.

Effective leadership, then, depends upon a leader's ability to supply subordinates with task guidance and incentives to perform to the extent that these are not provided by other sources. The inverse of this assertion is equally valid. Leadership substitutes can contribute to organizational effectiveness by supplying subordinates with task guidance and incentives to perform that are not being provided by the hierarchical superior. From this perspective it makes sense for a leader or someone above the leader to create substitutes when, for example, the leader must be frequently absent, has a large span of control, or is saddled with time-consuming nonmanagerial duties. Substitutes are also useful when a leader departs before a successor has been identified or there is a need to manage employees who are geographically dispersed or who, as in the following example, are culturally resistant to hierarchical supervision.

Extensive Professional Education

Professional employees may come to their firms with so much formal education that they can perform most work assignments without relying upon technical guidance from their hierarchical superior. Their education also often includes a strong socialization component, instilling in them a desire for autonomous, self-controlling behavior. The result may be that they neither need nor will readily accept a leader's direction. In such instances, professional education and socialization can serve as substitutes for formal leadership: A 1981 study by Jeffrey Ford found that extensive subordinate education acted as a substitute for directive and supportive leadership in a book publishing firm, a branch bank, and a midwestern university.

USING LEADERSHIP SUBSTITUTES TO SOLVE ORGANIZATIONAL PROBLEMS

The notion that professional education and socialization can substitute for traditional formal leadership identifies an important potential problem, but it can be turned to advantage if a leader is sensitive to the situation and builds collegial systems of task-related guidance and interpersonal support. This approach can be found in most well-run hospitals and universities, where deliberately designed substitutes for leadership abound.

Thus charges of medical malfeasance are often investigated by peer review teams, and university promotion and tenure decisions depend greatly on assessments by faculty colleagues who lack formal authority. Indeed, many a dean has learned that the same criticism that would be bitterly denied if it came from him or her is grudgingly accepted if the source is a peer-review committee. The trick is to develop norms and structures that consistently produce feedback when feedback is needed, rather than merely an occasional spontaneous outburst when circumstances become intolerable.

Team Approaches

Tracy Kidder's *The Soul of a New Machine* provides an excellent account of how a key manager at Data General utilized subordinates' professional norms and standards as a substitute for leadership to produce a faster computer than the competition's. The company at that time was competitive, highly political, and resource-poor, but the computer-design engineers were young, creative, well trained, and highly motivated. Recognizing the futility of relying on directive leadership and meager financial rewards, the leader obtained work space that encouraged considerable interaction among team members and discouraged interaction outside the team. He articulated key parameters and project deadlines, stayed out of members' personal disputes, obtained resources for the team, and buffered them from organization politics.

Reflecting the attitude of team members, Kidder observes, "They were building the machine all by themselves, without any significant help from their leader."

Task guidance and incentives to perform may derive from a number of sources other than the leader, including organized staff groups, internal and external consultants, and competent peers at all organizational levels. In the Columbus, Ohio Police Department, the creation of two-person patrol units and field-training officer positions effectively substituted for the guidance and support traditionally provided by hierarchical leaders, thus making time available for them to attend to other tasks. Where one-person patrols without field-training officers were utilized, leader guidance and support continued to be essential. (An ancillary benefit of substituting peer for hierarchical sources of task guidance is that it is often easier for subordinates to admit inadequacies to and request assistance from their co-workers than from their boss.)

High-Ability Independent Workers

Even when subordinates haven't much formal education, ability combined with experience can serve as a substitute for hierarchical leadership. Cummins Engine Company, General Motors Corporation, and Procter and Gamble all have reduced supervisory personnel and managerial overhead by selecting and developing high-ability, independent workers who require little or no supervision. Paul Reeves, a key production foreman for Harmon Auto Parts, taught workers to take over his job by helping them increase their ability and experience so that their responsibilities could also be increased. Each worker voluntarily spent half-days with him—asking questions, discussing his responses and, eventually, helping him perform his duties. When Reeves was promoted, the group continued to operate effectively without a foreman.

In Place of Hierarchical Feedback

Among the most important elements of task guidance is performance feedback. In the absence of feedback, ability to perform cannot be improved and motivation to perform cannot be sustained. Most organizations assign responsibility for feedback to the hierarchical superior, even in cases where the superior works at a physical distance from employees or doesn't know enough about their technical specialties to give them credible feedback.

However, many organizations have come to the realization that feedback from clients and peers, and feedback provided by the task itself, can serve as powerful substitutes for hierarchical feedback. Charles Manz and Hank Sims, two organizational researchers, described the operation of one such feedback system in a nonunion small-parts manufacturing plant. A subsidiary of a large U.S. corporation, the plant was organized around the concept of self-managed work teams from its inception in the early 1970s.

Each team of eight to twelve members is assigned a set of closely related production tasks, and the teams are buffered from each other by physical space and stores of in-process inventory. Each team prepares its own budgets, makes within-team job assignments, keeps track of quality control statistics and hours worked, and handles member absenteeism and discipline problems. Team members are trained in conducting meetings and in group problem solving. A hierarchical leader is responsible for each team, but this person is not supposed to supply either task guidance or interpersonal support, aside from encouraging self-observation, self-evaluation, and self-reinforcement. Manz and Sims found, in fact, that the most effective teams were those whose leaders did refrain from providing guidance and support. Leaders of effective teams spent much of their time representing the team to higher management, obtaining resources for the team, training new members, and coaching team members with respect to peer feedback and peer evaluation.

Substitutes by Procedure

The detailed work rules, guidelines, policies, and procedures existing in many organizations also serve to some extent as substitutes for hierarchical leadership by providing important non-leader sources of task guidance. Researchers Jon Howell and Peter Dorfman found this to be the case in a medium-size hospital, as did Robert Miles and M. M. Petty in county-level social service agencies. This type of leadership substitute can be particularly useful in situations where consistent behavior is imperative. For example, units of a firm increase the firm's legal exposure by acting inconsistently with respect to hiring, firing, leaves of absence, promotions, or other human resources actions. In other instances, such as pricing or purchasing activities, variation may be legal but cost-ineffective. It is quite common in these cases for organizations to install procedures, rules, and guidelines to replace or forestall managerial discretion.

LEADERSHIP NEUTRALIZERS

Thus far we have discussed only leadership substitutes, whose effect is to make it both less possible and less necessary for leaders to influence subordinates' satisfaction and performance, replacing the leader's impact with impact of their own. Leadership "neutralizers" are attributes of subordinates, tasks, and organizations that also interfere with a leader's attempts to influence subordinates. Unlike leadership substitutes, however, neutralizers do not replace the leader's impact over subordinates, but rather create an "influence vacuum" that can have serious negative consequences.

Physical Distances

For example, when subordinates work at a physical distance from their leader, many recommended leadership practices have limited usefulness or are nearly impossible to perform. A case in point is found at Kinko's, which provides professional copying services at widely dispersed locations nationwide. Regional managers at Kinko's are continually frustrated by not being able to provide enough direction, guidance, and personal support for the new store managers because physical distances are too great for much personal interaction. In other organizations, subordinates and leaders may not share a common time zone; indeed, they may scarcely share the same work day.

Spatial distance will be increasingly important as a potential leadership neutralizer in the future because, as the number of firms with international operations continues to rise, managers will increasingly be required to supervise subordinates across great distances. Furthermore, the growing importance of the U.S. service sector means that more and more employees will be working at home or at their client's work site.

Reward Systems

Organizational reward systems can also be important neutralizers of the hierarchical leadership's effects. Rewards may be awarded strictly according to seniority, for example, or attractive rewards may be unavailable to subordinates. Leaders tend to have little influence on corporate "rebels" because, in part, the rebels are not attracted to the typical rewards available in corporate bureaucracies. Union contracts also may mandate that all employees within a given job classification be paid the same wage rate, and civil service policies may require that promotions be based on objective examinations. In other cases, rewards may be controlled by higher management in ways that prevent the immediate supervisor from exerting influence. This occurs, for example, in firms requiring numerous one-over-one approvals before a salary recommendation takes effect. Other firms permit leaders to influence the amount of rewards, but their timing is wholly constrained by fiscal periods or employee anniversary dates.

Bypassing Management Structure

A very different type of neutralization occurs when someone at a higher level repeatedly bypasses a level of management to deal directly with that manager's subordinates. Another neutralizer is the continual countermanding by higher management of a leader's orders and instructions. These neutralizers often occur in instances where an organization's founder has finally, reluctantly, hired a subordinate manager to oversee operations and where a union's potential for mischief is so feared that supervisory efforts aimed at maintaining discipline are routinely reversed at higher levels.

Although normally dysfunctional, leadership neutralizers can occasionally be used to advantage. One such occasion occurred in a petro-chemical processing firm where, because of his technical expertise and involvement in several critical projects, an interpersonally incompetent director of design engineering could not be replaced. As an interim solution until he could be phased out, his day-to-day contact with employees was sharply curtailed, he was given numerous technical (nonleader) assignments, and his influence over salary and personnel decisions was considerably reduced. In this instance the "influence vacuum" caused by creating leadership neutralizers was deemed preferable to the state of leadership that previously existed.

LEADERSHIP ENHANCERS

Leader "enhancers" are attributes of employees, tasks, and organizations that amplify a leader's impact on the employees. For example, cohesive work groups with strong norms in support of cooperation with management can crystallize ambiguous goals and role definitions, augment overly subtle leader-provided feedback, and otherwise increase the power of weak, inconsistent leaders—for better or for worse. A study of four large hospitals found that development of a culture with strong performance norms greatly enhanced the impact of the head nurse's directive leadership style.

The creation of leadership enhancers makes particular sense when a leader has both the skill to manage effectively and personal goals consonant with organizational objectives but is prevented by one or more neutralizers from being effective. One way to amplify such a leader's power is to alter the organization's reward system. For example, make additional resources available, grant more discretion concerning the distribution of existing resources, or increase subordinates' dependency on the leader for desired physical and financial resources. Another type of enhancement is to give the leader access to key information and prestigious people at high levels—for example, as a member of a visible, prestigious task force. Enhancement in this case derives from connecting the leader to sources of power and important information, as well as from signaling to others that the leader probably has considerable influence with those at the top.

STRATEGIES FOR IMPROVING LEADERSHIP EFFECTIVENESS

Exhibit 1 outlines some typical leadership problems and effective coping strategies using leadership substitutes, neutralizers, and enhancers. Exhibit 2 provides specific information about how to implement these alternative leadership strategies.

Exhibit 1
Eleven Managerial Leadership Problems and Effective Coping Strategies*

Leadership Problems	Enhancer/Neutralizer	Substitutes
Leader doesn't keep on top of details in the department; coordination among subordinates is difficult.	Not useful.	Develop self-managed work teams; encourage team members to interact within and across departments.
Competent leadership is resisted through noncompliance or passive resistance.	*Enhancers:* Increase employees' dependence on leader through greater leader control of rewards/resources; increase their perception of leader's influence outside of work group.	Develop collegial systems of guidance for decision making.
Leader doesn't provide support or recognition for jobs well done.	Not useful.	Develop a reward system that operates independently of the leader. Enrich jobs to make them inherently satisfying.
Leader doesn't set targets or goals, or clarify roles for employees.	Not useful.	Emphasize experience and ability in selecting subordinates. Establish group goal-setting. Develop an organizational culture that stresses high performance expectations.
A leader behaves inconsistently over time.	*Enhancers:* These are dysfunctional. *Neutralizer:* Remove rewards from leader's control.	Develop group goal-setting and group rewards.
An upper-level manager regularly bypasses a leader in dealing with employees, or countermands the leader's directions.	*Enhancers:* Increase leader's control over rewards and resources; build leader's image via in-house champion or visible "important" responsibilities.	Increase the professionalization of employees.

Exhibit 1   *Continued*

Leadership Problems	Enhancer/Neutralizer	Substitutes
	Neutralizer: Physically distance subordinates from upper-level manager.	
A unit is in disarray or out of control.	Not useful.	Develop highly formalized plans, goals, routines, and areas of responsibility.
Leadership is brutal, autocratic.	*Enhancers:* These are dysfunctional. *Neutralizers:* Physically distance subordinates; remove rewards from leader's control.	Establish group goal-setting and peer performance appraisal.
There is inconsistency across different organizational units.	Not useful.	Increase formalization. Set up a behaviorally focused reward system.
Leadership is unstable over time; leaders are rotated and/or leave office frequently.	Not useful.	Establish competent advisory staff units. Increase profession-alism of employees.
Incumbent management is poor; there's no heir apparent.	*Enhancers:* These are dysfunctional. *Neutralizer:* Assign nonleader duties to problem managers.	Emphasize experience and ability in selec-ting employees. Give employees more training.

* The suggested solutions are examples of many possibilities for each problem.

Exhibit 2
Creative Strategies for Improving Leadership Effectiveness

Creating Substitutes for Leader Directiveness and Supportiveness	Creating Enhancers for Leader Directiveness and Supportiveness
Develop colleagial systems of guidance: • Peer appraisals to increase acceptability of feedback by subordinates. • Quality circles to increase workers' control over production quality. • Peer support networks; mentor systems.	Increase subordinates' perceptions of leader's influence/expertise: • Provide a visible champion of leader. • Give leader important organizational responsibilities. • Build leader's image through in-house publications and other means.
Improve performance-oriented organizational formalization: • Automatic organization reward system (such as commissions or gainsharing). • Group management-by-objectives (MBO) program. • Company mission statements and codes of conduct (as at Johnson & Johnson).	Build organizational climate: • Reward small wins to increase subordinates' confidence. • Emphasize ceremony and myth to encourage team spirit. • Develop superordinate goals to encourage cohesiveness and high performance norms.
Increase administrative staff availability: • Specialized training personnel. • Troubleshooters for human relations problems. • Technical advisors to assist production operators.	Increase subordinates' dependence on leader: • Create crises requiring immediate action. • Increase leader centrality in providing information. • Eliminate one-over-one approvals.
Increase professionalism of subordinates: • Staffing based on employee professionalism. • Development plans to increase employees' abilities and experience. • Encourage active participation in professional associations.	Increase leader's position power: • Change title to increase status. • Increase reward power. • Increase resource base.
Redesign jobs to increase: • Performance feedback from the task. • Ideological importance of jobs.	Create cohesive work groups with high performance norms: • Provide physical setting conducive to teamwork.

Exhibit 2 *Continued*

Creating Substitutes for Leader Directiveness and Supportiveness	Creating Enhancers for Leader Directiveness and Supportiveness
	• Encourage subordinates' participation in group problem solving. • Increase group's status. • Create intergroup competition.
Start team-building activities to develop group self-management skills such as: • Solving work-related problems on their own. • Resolving interpersonal conflicts among members. • Providing interpersonal support to members.	

Leadership for Self-Managing Work Teams: A Typology and Integrative Model

Greg L. Stewart and Charles C. Manz

A significant number of business organizations are currently taking action to increase employee involvement (Grootings, Gustavsen, & Héthy, 1989; Lawler, 1986, 1992; Verespej, 1990a; Versteeg, 1990; Walton, 1985). Included in many of these employee participation efforts is the implementation of some form of self-managing work teams. While teams are quite well established in European countries—particularly in Scandinavia (Gardell & Gustavsen, 1980; Grootings et al., 1989; Hofstede & Kassem, 1976), they are relatively new in the United States. Recent surveys, however, reveal that as many as 40% of U.S. employees will be working in self-managing teams by the year 2000 (Manz & Sims, 1993; Verespej, 1990a).

Yet, significant problems frequently accompany attempts to organize American workers into self-managing teams. Indeed, many team ventures fail when they are attempted within U.S. organizations (Lawler, 1986, 1988; Saporito, 1986; Verespej, 1990a; Walton, 1985). This suggests the necessity of increased research directed toward determining key factors that create obstacles for team development in the U.S.

One important difference seems to be leader behavior. More specifically, work team management or supervision is often identified as a primary reason why self-managing teams fail to properly develop and yield improvements in productivity, quality, and quality of life for American workers (Cummings, 1978; Klein, 1984; Letize & Donovan, 1990; Manz & Sims, 1987; Walton & Schlesinger, 1979).

While alternate methods of inquiry could be used to examine the difficulties associated with leadership of U.S. teams, we rely most heavily on a positivistic paradigm and attempt to find regularities that explain relationships among leadership, team development and performance, and characteristics of the leader and the organizational setting. The outcome of our analysis would be quite different if we had adopted an interpretive (Burrell & Morgan, 1979) or naturalistic (Lincoln, 1985) perspective, which might focus on ideographic perceptions and the unique circumstances of each team setting. Some differences between our positivistic view and the interpretive view will be noted throughout this paper, but the main focus of our discussion is description of nomothetic relationships. More specifically, we develop a typology explaining different approaches to team leadership.

LEADERSHIP IN A TEAM SETTING

Rationale Behind Team-Based Structure

An understanding of team-based organizational structure is required before the role of leadership within such a setting can be adequately explored. The logic for establishing self-managing teams stems primarily from socio-technical systems (STS) theory (Cummings, 1978; Emery & Trist, 1969; Susman, 1976). STS prescribes an effort to jointly optimize both the social and technical aspects of a work system. This joint optimization frequently results in a shift from individual to group-focused work methods. Employees are organized into small groups—or teams—based on natural divisions in the work flow process.

These teams are given increased autonomy in and control over their job tasks (Hackman, 1986; Manz, 1992a). Many responsibilities that have traditionally been reserved for managers and supervisors are delegated to the team. For instance, self-managing teams typically decide work methods and schedules, assign within-team job tasks, solve quality and interpersonal problems, and conduct team meetings (Lawler, 1986, 1988; Manz & Sims, 1990, 1993). Of course the extent to which teams are allowed to actually determine and regulate their behavior varies (Manz, 1992a). However, for purposes of theory development, self-managing teams are conceptualized here as work groups that are formally organized into teams and then, as a whole, given responsibility and authority beyond that traditionally experienced by line workers.

This increase in responsibility and authority allows individuals and teams to become empowered and thereby to have a wider repertoire of activity, which should help the organization better adapt to environmental turbulence (Emery & Trist, 1969; Weick, 1979). Empowerment has also been linked to intrinsic motivation (Deci, Connell, & Ryan, 1990), which causes employees to more willingly engage in job-related tasks (Manz, 1992b; Organ, 1988). Higher job satisfaction has additionally been found to accompany applications of STS (Herbst, 1962; Lawler, 1986; Trist, Susman, & Brown, 1977; Walton, 1977).

Although strong empirical evidence supporting the bottom-line benefits of team structure is still evolving, several case studies both within the U.S. and Europe have found self-managing teams to improve organizational performance. More specifically, self-managing teams have been credited with significant improvements in productivity, quality, cost savings, and employee morale; as well as reductions in absenteeism and turnover (Gustavsen & Héthy, 1989; Herbst, 1962; Lawler, 1986; Manz & Sims, 1987; Saporito, 1986; Trist et al., 1977; Verespej, 1990a; Versteeg, 1990; Walton, 1985). These benefits have been observed in both manufacturing and service settings. Specific studies have been conducted in the following: coal mines (Herbst, 1962; Trist et al., 1977), a pet food plant (Walton, 1977), a paint manufacturing plant (Poza & Markus, 1980), a hotel (Gustavsen & Hunnius, 1981), an airline (Cohen & Denison, 1990), a small parts manufacturer (Manz & Angle, 1986), a fertilizer plant (Rehnström & Gustavsen, 1989), a beer distributor (Saavedra, 1990), a warehouse (Manz, Keating, & Donnellon, 1990), a mental health hospital (Shaw, 1990), a financial investment firm (Sims, Manz, & Bateman, 1993), and paper mills (Manz & Newstrom, 1990).

Many of these teams struggle, however, through development stages. Initial problems with productivity and coordination are frequent (Lawler, 1986; Manz & Sims, 1993). These problems often result in the abandonment of teams long before their effectiveness can be properly determined (Hackman, 1990; Lawler, 1986).

Another important question concerns the extent to which these teams truly become self-managing. For instance, Barber (1993) found that a team-based structure did not actually increase behavioral control for line workers. This inability of workers to truly manage themselves seems especially prevalent in the U.S. (Kassem, 1976; Manz, 1992a; Walton, 1985). Several case studies conducted in U.S. organizations have further identified supervisor unwillingness to relinquish power and control to the team as a potential cause of these self-management failures (Hackman, 1986; Klein, 1984; Letize & Donovan, 1990; Manz,

Keating, & Donnellon, 1990; Manz & Sims, 1987; Walton & Schlesinger, 1979). The role of leadership for self-managing teams thus becomes a critical issue.

The Importance of Team Leadership

A plethora of research has been conducted on the topic of leadership; however, little has been done to develop theory specifically related to leadership of self-managing teams. We concentrate specifically on the influence of an individual who is formally designated as the team leader. This is quite different than the group-as-a-whole perspective (Wells, 1985), which would look at group-level interactions to describe how a leader emerges, behaves, and is perceived.

The existence of a formal leader (typically given a title such as facilitator, coordinator, or coach) may not be required, but is certainly common in attempts at team-based structure (Hackman, 1986; Lawler, 1986; Manz & Sims, 1987). In fact, Herbst (1962) found dominant individuals to naturally emerge as leaders, and Barber (1993) found teams in one organization unwilling to function without some type of formally designated leader.

Leadership is thus defined here as guidance and direction provided to a team by someone functioning in a role constituting formal authority to influence the team. This definition is objective in nature, and differs greatly from more interpretive definitions that see leadership as a socially constructed phenomenon (e.g., Gemmill & Oakley, 1992; Kets de Vries, 1989). Relying on the positive paradigm, we nevertheless focus on the role of a designated team leader.

This role is particularly difficult as team leaders are faced with the frequently ambiguous and difficult task of balancing leader guidance and direction with employee participation and discretion (Walton, 1977). The question, "How does one lead others who are supposed to lead themselves?" captures the essence of this leadership dilemma encountered by team supervisors. Moreover, attempts to cope with this difficult leadership role often result in negative supervisor reactions including resistance to change (Manz et al., 1990), role conflict (Letize & Donovan, 1990; Manz et al., 1990; Manz & Sims, 1987), unwillingness to relinquish power (Verespej, 1990a), fear of appearing incompetent (Manz et al., 1990) and fear of job termination (Mack, 1990;

Verespej, 1990a; Wagel, 1987). These responses frequently cause supervisors to engage in actions that inhibit team effectiveness. The following section, therefore, seeks to clearly define the leadership role within a team-based structure.

Integration of Leadership Research

Bass (1990) concludes that leadership practices fall on a continuum ranging from entirely autocratic to purely democratic. This clustering of widely recognized leader behaviors into either an autocratic or democratic style is empirically supported by factor analyses (e.g., Edwards & Rode, 1986; Sweeney, Fiechtner, & Samores, 1975). Summarizing the results of these analyses, Bass (1990) groups the following leadership styles into the autocratic cluster: authoritarian (Lewin & Lippitt, 1938), directive (Bass & Barrett, 1981), "Theory X" (McGregor, 1960), coercive (Bass, 1960), production oriented (Blake & Mouton, 1966), leader-derived decision making (Vroom & Yetton, 1973), initiating structure (Fleishman, 1953), production centered (Likert, 1961), goal emphasis (Bowers & Seashore, 1966), task oriented (Fiedler, 1967), and performance concern (Misumi, 1985). In contrast, Bass' (1990) participative cluster includes the following: consideration (Fleishman, 1953), democratic (Lewin & Lippitt, 1938), consultative (Bass, 1976), consensual (Zaleznik, 1974), employee centered (Likert, 1961), people oriented (Blake & Mouton, 1966), relations focused (Misumi, 1985), interaction facilitating (Bowers & Seashore, 1966), relations emphasis, (Fiedler, 1967), group-derived decision making (Vroom & Yetton, 1973), and "Theory Y" (McGregor, 1960). Autocratic leadership is thus displayed by leaders who seek sole possession of authority, power, and control; while democratic leadership is displayed by leaders who share authority, power, and control with their followers.

Bass (1990) also suggests that leader activity can range from highly involved to laissez-faire. This builds on the work of Lewin and Lippitt (1938) and Karmel (1978) who argue that some leaders adopt an active style, and others a passive style. For purposes of this paper, we define an active leader as one who is highly involved in team activities, and who is highly visible to team members. In contrast, a passive leader is one who is usually not involved in the day-to-day activities of the team, and whose influence is seldom directly felt by the team.

Extending the work of Bass (1990), Fig. 1 combines the active-passive dimension with the autocratic-democratic dimension. The resulting four cell taxonomy can be used for developing a theory of team leadership. Cell labels are used to provide insight into a leader's effect on the team; they do not describe specific leader activities.

Team Leader Behaviors

Overpowering Leadership

The cell representing active and autocratic leadership (labeled overpowering because it often overwhelms team autonomy) specifies leadership that is logically detrimental to team effectiveness. Active, autocratic leadership simply overpowers team effort to engage in self-regulation (Lawler, 1986; Manz, 1992a). A team being supervised by an active and autocratic leader is never given an opportunity (Blumberg & Pringle, 1982) to manage itself. The leader retains power through

Figure 1
A Typology of Leader Power Orientation and Leader
Involvement within a Team Setting

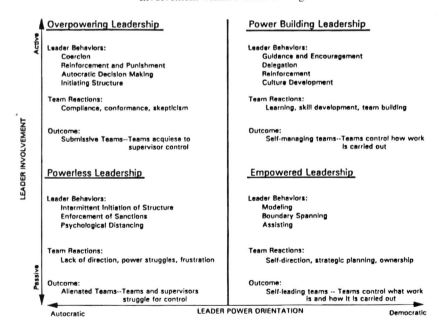

coercion (Bass, 1960), autocratic decision making (Vroom & Yetton, 1973), punishment (Bass, 1960), and initiation of structure (Fiedler, 1967; Fleishman, 1973).

Self-managing teams with an active, autocratic leader thus result in nothing more than an illusion of worker empowerment (Mulder, 1971, 1976). In reality, team members acquiesce to the leader's demands. Initiative and individual feelings of ownership are destroyed, and organizational performance likely remains unchanged (Lawler, 1986). Employees may also become skeptical and see team implementation as an attempt to deceive them into doing additional work (Trist et al., 1977). Each of these points suggests that a supervisor who actively engages in autocratic leadership will overwhelm team autonomy and thereby inhibit team effectiveness. The following proposition summarizes the predicted impact of active, autocratic leadership on teams.

Proposition 1

Self-managing work teams with active, autocratic leaders will not become autonomous and will thus fail to improve quality, productivity, and employee morale.

Powerless Leadership

Passive attempts at autocratic leadership leave a team powerless and can be just as harmful as active attempts. The existence of a passive (as opposed to active), autocratic leader is perhaps not intuitive. This approach, however, is exhibited when a supervisor practices "hands off" management, but continues to exert influence in an autocratic manner. The leader may initially provide the team with great latitude in decision making and behavioral choice, only to provide sanctions (Bales, 1958) and punishment (Bass, 1960) when results are not congruent with the leader's expectations. Passive leaders may also distance themselves psychologically from team members (Blau & Scott, 1962), while retaining subtle control over team activity (Manz, 1992a; Mulder, 1971, 1976).

General lack of leader activity can be detrimental to group development and productivity (Lewin, Lippitt, & White, 1939). Specifically, laissez-faire leadership has been shown to result in decreased productivity (Pelz, 1956), decreased quality (Kidd & Christy, 1961; Murningham &

Leung, 1976), reduced worker satisfaction (Aspergren, 1963), and dysfunctional group processes (Baumgartel, 1957). These outcomes are the opposite of benefits assumed to result from self-managing teams (Lawler, 1986).

Reasons for inability to accrue advantages from team structure likely revolve around the ambiguity created by a passive and autocratic leader. A team that intermittently receives commands is likely to become frustrated and lack clear direction (Manz & Sims, 1987). Confusion results from the team initially being given increased control over its activities but periodically losing that control to the leader. In the end, the team experiences a sense of powerlessness to manage itself. Moreover, a "hands off" approach fails to cultivate skills required for team self-management (Emery, 1959). These skills include self-reinforcement, self-criticism, self-goal-setting, self-observation, self-evaluation, self-expectation, and rehearsal (Manz & Sims, 1987). Without these critical skills teams lack the power to actually manage themselves. Proposition 2 summarizes these ideas.

Proposition 2

Self-managing work teams with passive, autocratic leaders may initially feel a sense of autonomy; but will come to feel powerless, subsequently having long-term reductions in quality, productivity, and employee morale.

Power-Building Leadership

An active, democratic style builds team power by providing guidance and teaching skills (Manz & Sims, 1987, 1990). These leaders provide the team with external encouragement and reinforcement for its attempts to achieve group-level control (Lawler, 1986; Manz, Mossholder, & Luthans, 1987). Organized delegation (Bass, 1985) helps the team learn how to coordinate its activities and work cooperatively. An active, democratic leader can also promote the creation of a culture (Wiener, 1988) that sustains team-level decision making and behavioral control (Manz & Sims, 1990).

An active, democratic leader teaches group interaction skills, as well as guides team-building efforts (Walton, 1977). This helps the team develop social skills (e.g., conflict reduction techniques) and builds a cooperative network that minimizes group process inefficiencies (Brickner, Harkins, & Ostrom, 1986). The resulting positive group interactions foster synergistic collaboration and allow the team to manage itself by solving its own problems and directing its own work (Lawler, 1992; Manz & Sims, 1987; Walton, 1977). The self-management established can lead to higher intrinsic motivation (Deci et al., 1990) and employee ownership (Lawler, 1986). An active leader, nevertheless, retains significant control over team behaviors and long-term strategic direction—even when the underlying style is democratic (Manz, 1992a; Mills, 1983). This control is maintained because the team continues to rely on the leader to set the overall direction for work activity. The predicted outcomes of power-building leadership are summarized in the following two propositions.

Proposition 3

Self-managing work teams with active, democratic leaders will develop self-management skills and thereby increase quality, productivity, and employee morale.

Proposition 4

A participative leader who is highly active will continue to retain significant control over team behavior, preventing the team from actually setting its own direction and governing itself.

Empowered Leadership

The passive form of democratic leadership is labeled empowered leadership, because it has the effect of truly empowering the team. These teams actually design their own work processes, and become self-governing (Hackman, 1986; Walton, 1985). Many supervisory functions are carried out by the team itself, and active involvement of the leader is no longer required (Lawler, 1986). In fact, active forms of leadership may inhibit the team from becoming truly autonomous and practicing advanced forms of team self-leadership (Manz, 1992a; Walton, 1985).

Some passive forms of democratic leadership can, nevertheless, facilitate team success. Modeling is one activity compatible with passive, democratic leadership. Leaders influence a team by presenting a living model of self-regulation (Manz & Sims, 1981, 1990). This passive influence may, in fact, be more powerful than active forms of leadership because it promotes continued learning and development (Bandura, 1986). Passive leaders can also facilitate team success by serving as boundary spanners (Gilmore, 1982; Tushman & Scanlan, 1981). A boundary spanner links the team with the rest of the organization (Likert, 1967). More specifically, Cummings (1978) suggests that a team leader can reduce uncertainty for the group by regulating environmental influences (cf. Thompson, 1967) and mediating relationships with other organizational units. In this sense, the team leader serves more as a resource and less as an authority figure attempting to influence behavior (Hackman, 1986; Walton, 1985).

Many of the criticisms of laissez-faire leadership will therefore not accompany properly applied passive forms of democratic team influence. Proper application implies that the team has the skills necessary for self-governance, and that the leader remains democratic—even if initial performance is not congruent with expectations (Manz & Sims, 1990). The leader also needs to assist the team when aid is sought (Cummings, 1978; Hackman, 1986). These arguments are summarized in the following proposition.

Proposition 5

Self-managing work teams with passive, democratic leaders will obtain the highest level of self-regulation; and will therefore realize the most significant long-term improvements in quality, productivity, and employee morale.

Transition From Active to Passive Leadership

Autocratic forms of leadership thus inhibit team success. The above discussion also implies a transition from active to passive forms of demographic leadership. This is because self-managing work teams have been shown to move through developmental stages that permit progressively increasing empowerment (Lawler, 1986, 1992; Manz &

Sims, 1993). As the team becomes more capable of self-regulation, leader involvement should decrease. In short, a team that has developed self-regulation skills is increasingly ready to direct itself (Lawler, 1986; Manz, 1992).

A successful transition from traditional to team structure, however, necessitates high leader involvement, especially in the early phases of change (Hackman, 1986). Empowerment is thus attained through the power building activities associated with active, democratic leadership. Yet, once self-regulation skills are developed, active leadership is no longer required. Leader activity is thus co-determined by team member ability, and passive forms of democratic leadership are seen as most effective when they follow active forms. Hersey and Blanchard's (1977) assertion that leader involvement should decrease as subordinate maturity increases is similar. These ideas lead to the sixth proposition.

Proposition 6

Passive forms of democratic leadership will fail to facilitate team effectiveness unless they are preceded by active forms of democratic leadership.

REFERENCES

Aspergren, R. E. A study of leadership behavior and its effects on morale and attitudes in selected elementary schools. *Dissertation Abstracts*, 1963, *23*, 3708.

Bales, R. F. Task roles and social roles in problem-solving groups. In E. E. Maccoby, T. M. Newcomb, and E. L. Hartley (Eds.), *Readings in social psychology*. New York: Holt, 1958.

Bandura, A. *Social foundations of thought and action: A social cognitive theory*. Englewood Cliffs, NJ: Prentice-Hall, 1986.

Barber, J. R. Tightening the iron cage: Concertive control in self-managing teams. *Administrative Science Quarterly*, 1993, *38*, 408–437.

Bass, B. M. *Leadership, psychology, and organizational behavior*. New York: Harper, 1960.

Bass, B. M. A systems survey research feedback for management and organizational development. *Journal of Applied Behavioral Science*, 1976, *12*, 215–229.

Bass, B. M. *Leadership and performance beyond expectations*. New York: Free Press, 1985.

Bass, B. M. *Bass & Stodgill's handbook of leadership: Theory, research, & managerial applications* (3rd ed.). New York: Free Press, 1990.

Bass, B. M., & Barrett, G. V. *People, work and organizations: An introduction to industrial and organizational psychology.* Boston: Allyn & Bacon, 1981.

Baumgartel, H. Leadership style as a variable in research administration. *Administrative Science Quarterly*, 1957, *2*, 344–360.

Blake, R. R., & Mouton, J. S. *The managerial grid.* Houston, TX: Gulf, 1966.

Blau, P. M., & Scott, W. R. *Formal organizations.* San Francisco: Chandler, 1962.

Blumberg, M., & Pringle, C. D. The missing opportunity in organizational research: Some implications for a theory of work performance. *Academy of Management Review*, 1982, *7*, 560–569.

Bowers, D. G., & Seashore, S. E. Predicting organizational effectiveness with a four-factor theory of leadership. *Administrative Science Quarterly*, 1966, *11*, 238–263.

Brickner, M. A., Harkins, S. G., & Ostrom, T. M. Effects of personal involvement: Thought-provoking implications for social loafing. *Journal of Personality and Social Psychology*, 1986, *51*, 763–770.

Burrell, G., & Morgan, G. *Sociological paradigms and organizational analysts.* London: Heinemann Educational Books, 1979.

Cohen, S. G., & Denison, D. R. Flight attendant teams. In J. R. Hackman (Ed.), *Groups that work (and those that don't).* San Francisco: Jossey-Bass, 1990.

Cummings, T. Self-regulated work groups: A socio-technical synthesis. *Academy of Management Review*, 1978, *3*, 625–634.

Deci, E. L., Connell, J. P., & Ryan, R. M. Self-determination in a work organization. *Journal of Applied Psychology*, 1990, *74*, 580–590.

Edwards, J. E., & Rode, L. G. *A Path Analytic Approach to the Construct Validation of Selected Leadership Scales.* Paper presented at the Annual Meetings of the Academy of Management, Chicago, IL, 1986.

Emery, F. E. *Characteristics of socio-technical systems.* London: Tavistock, 1959.

Emery, F. E., & Trist, E. L. Socio-technical systems. In F. E. Emery (Ed.), *Systems thinking.* London: Penguin, 1969.

Fiedler, F. E. *A Theory of Leadership Effectiveness.* New York: McGraw Hill, 1967.

Fleishman, E. A. The description of supervisory behavior. *Journal of Applied Psychology*, 1953, *37*, 1–6.

Gardell, B., & Gustavsen, B. Work environment research and social change: Current developments in Scandinavia. *Journal of Occupational Behavior*, 1980, *1*.

Gemmill, G., & Oakley, J. *Leadership: An alienating social myth? Human Relations*, 1992, *45*.

Gilmore, T. N. Leadership and boundary management. *Journal of Applied Behavioral Science*, 1982, *18*, 343–356.

Grootings, P., Gustavsen, B., & Héthy, L. *New forms of work organization in Europe.* Oxford, UK: Transaction Publishers, 1989.

Gustavsen, B., & Héthy, L. New forms of work organization: An overview. In P. Grootings, B. Gustavsen, and L. Héthy (Eds.), *New forms of work organization in Europe.* Oxford, UK: Transaction Publishers, 1989.

Gustavsen, B., & Hunnius, G. *New patterns of work reform. The case of Norway.* Oslo: Unieversitetsforlaget, 1981.

Hackman, J. R. The psychology of self-management in organizations. In M. S. Pollack and R. O. Perloff (Eds.), *Psychology and work: Productivity change and employment*. Washington, D. C.: American Psychological Association, 1986.

Hackman, J. R. *Groups that work (and those that don't)*. San Francisco: Jossey-Bass, 1990.

Herbst, P. G. *Autonomous group functioning and exploration in behavior theory and measurement*. London: Tavistock, 1962.

Hersey, P., & Blanchard, K. H. *Management and organizational behavior. Utilizing human resources*. Englewood Cliffs, NJ: Prentice-Hall, 1977.

Hofstede, G., & Kassem, M. S. *European contributions to organization theory*. Amsterdam, The Netherlands: Van Gorcum, 1976.

Karmel, B. Leadership: A challenge to traditional research methods and assumptions: *Academy of Management Review*, 1978, *3*, 475–482.

Kassem, M. S. Introduction: European versus American organization theories. In G. Hofstede and S. M. Kassem (Eds.), *European contributions to organization theory*. Amsterdam, The Netherlands: Van Gorcum, 1976.

Kets de Vries, M. F. R. *Prisoners of leadership*. New York: Wiley, 1989.

Kidd, J. A., & Christy, R. T. Supervisory procedures and work-team productivity. *Journal of Applied Psychology*, 1961, *45*, 388–392.

Klein, J. A. Why supervisors resist employee involvement. *Harvard Business Review*, 1984, *62*(5), 87–95.

Lawler, E. E. *High involvement management*. San Francisco: Jossey-Bass, 1986.

Lawler, E. E. Choosing an involvement strategy. *Academy of Management Executive*, 1988, *2*, 197–204.

Lawler, E. E. *The ultimate advantage: Creating the high involvement organization*. San Francisco: Jossey-Bass, 1992.

Letize, L., & Donovan, M. The supervisor's changing role in high involvement organizations. *Journal for Quality and Participation*, March, 1990, 62–65.

Lewin, K., & Lippitt, R. An experimental approach to the study of autocracy and democracy: A preliminary note. *Sociometry*, 1938, *1*, 292–300.

Lewin, K., Lippitt, R., & White, R. K. Patterns of aggressive behavior in experimentally created social climates. *Journal of Social Psychology*, 1939, *10*, 271–301.

Likert, R. *New patterns of management*. New York: McGraw-Hill, 1961.

Likert, R. *The human organization*. New York: McGraw-Hill, 1967.

Lincoln, Y. S. *Organizational theory and inquiry: The paradigm revolution*. London: Sage, 1985.

Mack, T. Oryx Energy Corp.: Energizing a bureaucracy. *Forbes*, February 17, 1990, 76–80.

Manz, C. C. Self-leading work teams: Moving beyond self-management myths. *Human Relations*, 1992, *45*, 1119–1139. (a)

Manz, C. C. *Mastering self-leadership: Empowering yourself for personal excellence*. Englewood Cliffs, NJ: Prentice-Hall, 1992. (b)

Manz, C. C., & Angle, H. Can group self-management mean a loss of personal control: Triangulating on a paradox. *Group and Organization Studies*, 1986, *11*, 309–334.

Manz, C. C., & Newstrom, J. W. Self-managing teams in a paper mill: Success factors, problems, and lessons learned. *International Human Relations Management Review*, 1990, *1*, 43–60.

Manz, C. C., & Sims, H. P., Jr. Vicarious learning: The influences of modeling on organizational behavior. *Academy of Management Review*, 1981, *6*, 105–113.

Manz, C. C., & Sims, H. P., Jr. Leading workers to lead themselves: The external leadership of self-managing work teams. *Administrative Science Quarterly*, 1987, *32*, 106–128.

Manz, C. C., & Sims, H. P., Jr. *Superleadership: Leading others to lead themselves*. New York: Berkley, 1990.

Manz, C. C., & Sims, H. P., Jr. *Business without bosses: How self-managing teams are building high performance companies*. New York: Wiley, 1993.

Manz, C. C., Mossholder, K. W., & Luthans, F. An integrated perspective of self-control in organizations. *Administration and Society*, 1987, *19*, 3–24.

Manz, C. C., Keating, D. E., & Donnellon, A. Preparing for organizational change to employee self-management: The managerial transition. *Organizational Dynamics*, 1990, *19*(2), 15–26.

McGregor, D. *The human side of enterprise*. New York: McGraw-Hill, 1960.

Mills, P. K. Self-management: Its control and relationship with other organizational properties. *Academy of Management Review*, 1983, *8*, 445–453.

Misumi, J. *The behavioral science of leadership: An interdisciplinary Japanese research program*. Ann Arbor, MI: University of Michigan Press, 1985.

Mulder, M. Power equalization through participation. *Administrative Science Quarterly*, 1971, *16*, 31–38.

Mulder, M. Reduction of power differences in practice. In G. Hofstede and M. S. Kassem, (Eds.), *European contributions to organization theory*. Amsterdam, The Netherlands: Van Gorcum, 1976.

Murningham, J. K., & Leung, T. K. The effects of leadership involvement and the importance of the task on subordinates' performance. *Organization Behavior and Human Performance*, 1976, *17*, 299–310.

Organ, D. W. *Organization citizenship behavior: The good soldier syndrome*. Lexington, MA: Lexington Books, 1988.

Pelz, D. C. Some social factors related to performance in a research organization. *Administrative Science Quarterly*, 1956, *1*, 310–325.

Poza, E. J., & Marcus, M. Success story: The team approach to work restructuring. *Organizational Dynamics*, Winter 1980, 3–25.

Rehnström, B., & Gustavsen, B. The development of new forms of work organization in Norway and Sweden. In P. Grootings, B. Gustavsen, and L. Hèthy (Eds.), *New forms of work organization in Europe*. Oxford, UK: Transaction Publishers, 1989.

Saavedra, R. Beer sales and delivery teams. In J. R. Hackman (Ed.), *Groups that work (and those that don't)*. San Francisco: Jossey-Bass, 1990.

Saporito, B. The revolt against "working smarter." *Fortune*, 1986, *114*(2), 58–65.

Shaw, R. B. Mental health treatment teams. In J. R. Hackman (Ed.), *Groups that work (and those that don't)*. San Francisco: Jossey-Bass, 1990.

Sims, H. P., Jr., Manz, C. C., & Bateman, B. The early implementation phase: Getting teams started in the office. In C. C. Manz and H. P. Sims, Jr. (Eds.), *Business without bosses: How self-managing teams are building high performance companies.* New York: Wiley, 1993.

Sweeney, A. B., Fiechtner, L. A., & Samores, R. J. An integrative factor analysis of leadership measures and theories. *Journal of Psychology*, 1975, *90*, 75–85.

Susman, G. I. *Autonomy at work: A sociotechnical analysis of participative management.* New York: Praeger, 1976.

Thompson, J. P. *Organizations in action.* New York: McGraw-Hill, 1967.

Trist, E. L. Susman, G. I., & Brown, G. R. An experiment in autonomous working in an American underground coal mine. *Human Relations*, 1977, *30*, 201–236.

Tushman, M. L., & Scanlan, T. J. Characteristics and external orientations of boundary spanning individuals. *Academy of Management Journal*, 1981, *24*, 83–98.

Verespej, M. A. When you put the team in charge. *Industry Week*, 1990, *239*(23), 30–32. (a)

Versteeg, A. Self-directed work teams yield long-term benefits. *Journal of Business Strategy*, 1990, *11*(6), 9–12.

Vroom, V. H., & Yetton, P. W. *Leadership and decision-making.* New York: Wiley, 1973.

Wagel, W. H. Working and managing without supervisors. *Personnel*, 1987, *64*(9), 8–11.

Walton, R. E. Work innovations at Topeka: After six years. *Journal of Applied Behavioral Science*, 1977, *13*, 422–433.

Walton, R. E. From control to commitment in the workplace. *Harvard Business Review*, 1985, *63*, 77–84.

Walton, R. E., & Schlesinger, L. A. Do supervisors thrive in participating work systems? *Organizational Dynamics*, 1979, *8*(3), 24–39.

Weick, K. E. *The social psychology of organizing* (2nd ed.). New York: Random House, 1979.

Wells, L., Jr. The group-as-a-whole perspective and its theoretical roots. In A. D. Colman and M. H. Geller (Eds.), *Group Relations Reader 2*, 1985. Washington, D. C.: A. K. Rice Institute.

Wiener, Y. Forms of value systems: A focus on organizational effectiveness and cultural change and maintenance. *Academy of Management Review*, 1988, *13*, 534–545.

Zaleznik, A. Charismatic and consensus leaders: A psychological comparison. *Bulletin of the Menninger Clinic*, 1974, *38*, 222–238.

SuperLeadership: Beyond the Myth of Heroic Leadership

Charles C. Manz and Henry P. Sims, Jr.

When most of us think of leadership, we think of one person doing something to another person. This is "influence," and a leader is someone who has the capacity to influence another. Words like "charismatic" and "heroic" are sometimes used to describe a leader. The word "leader" itself conjures up visions of a striking figure on a rearing white horse who is crying "Follow me!" The leader is the one who has either the power or the authority to command others.

Many historical figures fit this mold: Alexander, Caesar, Napoleon, Washington, Churchill. Even today, the turnaround of Chrysler Corporation by Lee Iacocca might be thought of as an act of contemporary heroic leadership. It's not difficult to think of Iacocca astride a white horse, and he is frequently thought of as "charismatic."

But is this heroic figure of the leader the most appropriate image of the organizational leader of today? Is there another model? We believe there is. In many modern situations, *the most appropriate leader is one who can lead others to lead themselves*. We call this powerful new kind of leadership "SuperLeadership."

Our viewpoint represents a departure from the dominant and, we think, incomplete view of leadership. Our position is that true leadership comes mainly from within a person, not from outside. At its best, external leadership provides a spark and supports the flame of the true inner leadership that dwells within each person. At its worst, it disrupts this internal process, causing damage to the person and the constituencies he or she serves.

Our focus is on a new form of leadership that is designed to facilitate the self-leadership energy within each person. This perspective suggests a new measure of a leader's strength—one's ability to maximize the contributions of others through recognition of their right to guide their own destiny, rather than the leader's ability to bend the will of others to his or her own. The challenge for organizations is to understand how to go about bringing out the wealth of talent that each employee possesses.

Many still operate under a quasi-military model that encourages conformity and adherence rather than one that emphasizes how leaders can lead others to lead themselves.

WHY IS SUPERLEADERSHIP AN IMPORTANT PERSPECTIVE?

This SuperLeadership perspective is especially important today because of several recent trends facing American businesses. First, the challenge to United States corporations from world competition has pressured companies to utilize more fully their human resources. Second, the workforce itself has changed a great deal in recent decades—for instance, "baby boomers" have carried into their organization roles elevated expectations and a need for greater meaning in their work lives.

As a consequence of these kinds of pressures, organizations have increasingly experimented with innovative work designs. Widespread introduction of modern management techniques, such as quality circles, self-managed work teams, Japanese business practices, and flatter organization structures, has led to the inherent dilemma of trying to provide strong leadership for workers who are being encouraged and allowed to become increasingly self-managed. The result is a major knowledge gap about appropriate new leadership approaches under conditions of increasing employee participation. The SuperLeadership approach is designed to meet these kinds of challenges.

Before presenting specific steps for becoming a SuperLeader, it is useful to contrast SuperLeadership with other views of leadership.

Viewpoints on what constitutes successful leadership in organizations have changed significantly over time. A simplified historical perspective on different approaches to leadership is presented in Figure 1. As it suggests, four different types of leader can be distinguished: the "strong man," the "transactor," the "visionary hero," and the "SuperLeader."

The *strong-man view* of leadership is perhaps the earliest dominant form in our culture. The emphasis with this autocratic view is on the strength of the leader. We use the masculine noun purposely because when this leadership approach was most prevalent it was almost a completely male-dominated process.

Figure 1
Four Types of Leaders

	Strong Man	Transactor	Visionary Hero	SuperLeader
Focus	Commands	Rewards	Visions	Self-leadership
Type of power	Position/authority	Rewards	Relational/inspirational	Shared
Source of leader's wisdom and direction	Leader	Leader	Leader	Most followers (self-leaders) and then leaders
Followers' response	Fear-based compliance	Calculative compliance	Emotional commitment based on leader's vision	Commitment based on ownership
Typical leader behaviors	Direction/command	Interactive goal setting	Communication of leader's vision	Becoming an effective self-leader
	Assigned goals	Contingent personal reward	Emphasis on leader's values	Modeling self-leadership
	Intimidation	Contingent material reward	Exhortation	Creating positive thought patterns
	Reprimand	Contingent reprimand	Inspirational persuasion	Developing self-leadership through reward & constructive reprimand
				Promoting self-leading teams
				Facilitating a self-leadership culture

413

The strong-man view of leadership still exists today in many organizations (and is still widely reserved for males), although it is not as highly regarded as it once was.

The strong-man view of leadership creates an image of a John Wayne type who is not afraid to "knock some heads" to get followers to do what he wants done. The expertise for knowing what should be done rests almost entirely in the leader. It is he who sizes up the situation and, based on some seemingly superior strength, skill, and courage, delivers firm commands to the workers. If the job is not performed as commanded, inevitably some significant form of punishment will be delivered by the leader to the guilty party. The focus is on the leader whose power stems primarily from his position in the organization. He is the primary source of wisdom and direction—strong direction. Subordinates simply comply.

One would think that the day of the strong-man leader has passed, but one apparently managed to work his way up the corporate hierarchy at Kellogg Co. This venerable Battle Creek cereal maker recently terminated its president in an unusual action. Accounts printed in the *Wall Street Journal* described this person as "abrasive and often unwilling to listen . . . , very abrupt . . . , more inclined to manage without being questioned." He was known for deriding unimpressive presentations as a "CE"—career ending—performance. As another example, we suspect that the majority of employees at Eastern Airlines would describe CEO Frank Lorenzo as a prototypical strong man.

The second view of leadership is that of a *transactor*.

As time passed in our culture, the dominance of the strong-man view of leadership lessened somewhat. Women began to find themselves more frequently in leadership positions. With the development of knowledge of the power of rewards (such as that coming from research on behavior modification), a different view of influence began to emerge. With this view, the emphasis was increasingly placed on a rational exchange approach (exchange of rewards for work performed) in order to get workers to do their work. Even Taylor's views on scientific management, which still influence significantly many organizations in many industries, emphasized the importance of providing incentives to get workers to do work.

With the transactor type of leader, the focus is on goals and rewards; the leader's power stems from the ability to provide rewards for followers doing what the leader thinks should be done. The source of wisdom and direction still rests with the leader. Subordinates will tend to take a calculative view of their work. "I will do what he (or she) asks as long as the rewards keep coming."

Perhaps one of the most prototypical (and successful) transactor organizations in the world today is PEPSICO. *Fortune* described the company with phrases like ". . . boot camp, . . . sixty-hour weeks . . . , back breaking standards that are methodically raised." Those who can't compete are washed out. Those who do compete successfully are rewarded very handsomely—first-class air travel, fully loaded company cars, stock options, bonuses that can hit 90% of salary. Those who are comfortable and effective in this culture receive the spoils. Those who are not comfortable tend to leave early in their career.

Perhaps the ultimate transactor leader is Chairman Larry Phillips of Phillips-Van Heusen, manufacturer of shirts, sweaters, and casual shoes. Phillips has set up a scheme whereby the 11 senior executives will each earn a $1 million bonus if the company's earnings per share grow at a 35% compound annual rate during the four years ending in January 1992. Not surprisingly, company executives are actively absorbed in striving to meet this goal.

The next type of leader, which probably represents the most popular view today, is that of the *visionary hero*. Here the focus is on the leader's ability to create highly motivating and absorbing visions. The leader represents a kind of heroic figure who is somehow able to create an almost larger-than-life vision for the workforce to follow. The promise is that if organizations can just find those leaders that are able to capture what's important in the world and wrap it up into some kind of purposeful vision, then the rest of the workforce will have the clarifying beacon that will light the way to the promised land.

With the visionary hero, the focus is on the leader's vision, and the leader's power is based on followers' desire to relate to the vision and to the leader himself or herself. Once again, the leader represents the source of wisdom and direction. Followers, at least in theory, are expected to commit to the vision and the leader.

The notion of the visionary hero seems to have received considerable attention lately, but the idea has not gone without criticism. Peter Drucker, for example, believes that charisma becomes the undoing of leaders. He believes they become inflexible, convinced of their own infallibility, and slow to really change. Instead, Drucker suggests that the most effective leaders are those not afraid of developing strength in their subordinates and associates. One wonders how Chrysler will fare when Iacocca is gone.

The final view of leadership included in our figure represents the focus of this article—the *SuperLeader*. We do not use the word "Super" to create an image of a larger-than-life figure who has all the answers and is able to bend others' wills to his or her own. On the contrary, with this type of leader, the focus is largely on the followers. Leaders become "super"—that is, can possess the strength and wisdom of many persons—by helping to unleash the abilities of the "followers" (self-leaders) that surround them.

The focus of this leadership view is on the followers who become self-leaders. Power is more evenly shared by leaders and followers. The leader's task becomes largely that of helping followers to develop the necessary skills for work, especially self-leadership, to be able to contribute more fully to the organization. Thus, leaders and subordinates (that are becoming strong self-leaders) together represent the source of wisdom and direction. Followers (self-leaders), in turn, experience commitment and ownership of their work.

SEVEN STEPS TO SUPERLEADERSHIP

For the SuperLeader, the essence of the challenge is to lead followers to discover the potentialities that lie within themselves. How can a SuperLeader lead others to become positive, effective self-leaders? How can a SuperLeader lead others to lead themselves?

We will present seven steps to accomplish these ends. As we will see, some of the elements included in the other leadership views summarized above are a part of SuperLeadership (for instance, the use of rewards), but as Figure 1 indicates, the focus of the leadership process and the basis of power and the relationship of the SuperLeader with followers are very different.

Step 1—Becoming a Self-Leader

Before learning how to lead others, it is important—make that essential—to first learn how to lead ourselves. Consequently, the first step to becoming a SuperLeader is to become an effective self-leader.

In a taped interview from the historical files of Hewlett-Packard, David Packard, co-founder of Hewlett-Packard, described how, as a young man, he used a daily schedule as a strategy to organize his own efforts. "I was resolved that I was going to have everything organized so, when I was a freshman, I had a schedule set for every day . . . what I was going to do every hour of the day . . . and times set up in the morning to study certain things. . . . You did have to allocate your time. . . ." At a very young age, David Packard was developing the self-leadership skills that became so critical to his later success as an executive.

Self-leadership is the influence we exert on ourselves to achieve the self-motivation and self-direction we need to perform. The process of self-leadership consists of an array of behavioral and cognitive strategies for enhancing our own personal effectiveness.

Self-leadership is also the essence of effective followership. As one Ford Motor Co. executive exclaimed to us, "We started participative management, but we didn't know what that meant for the subordinate!" What are the responsibilities of the follower? How does he or she behave in a participative management situation? Developing self-leadership skills is the answer to this question. From a SuperLeadership perspective, effective followers are leaders in their own right—they are skilled at leading themselves.

We will address two classes of self-leadership strategies. The first focuses mainly on effective behavior and action—"behavioral focused strategies"; the second focuses on effective thinking and feeling—"cognitive focused strategies." A summary of these strategies is provided in Figure 2.

Behavioral Focused Strategies

These self-leadership actions are designed to help individuals organize and direct their own work lives more effectively. Specifically, these strategies include self-observation, self-goal setting, cue management, self-reward, constructive self-punishment or self-criticism, and rehearsal.

The necessity for self-observation, for example, was dramatically brought forward at Harley Davidson, when the American motorcycle manufacturer instituted a Just-in-Time/employee involvement program. Management had to train workers to use statistical tools to monitor and

Figure 2
Self-Leadership Strategies

Behavior-Focused Strategies

Self-Observation—observing and gathering information about specific behaviors that you have targeted for change

Self-Set Goals—setting goals for your own work efforts

Management of Cues—arranging and altering cues in the work environment to facilitate your desired personal behaviors

Rehearsal—physical or mental practice of work activities before you actually perform them

Self-Reward—providing yourself with personally valued rewards for completing desirable behaviors

Self-Punishment/Criticism—administering punishments to yourself for behaving in undesirable ways

Cognitive-Focused Strategies

Building Natural Rewards into Tasks—self-redesign of where and how you do your work to increase the level of natural rewards in your job. Natural rewards that are part of, rather than separate from, the work (i.e., the work, like a hobby, becomes the reward) result from activities that cause you to feel:
   a sense of competence
   a sense of self-control
   a sense of purpose

Focusing Thinking on Natural Rewards—purposely focusing your thinking on the naturally rewarding features of your work

Establishment of Effective Thought Patterns—establishing constructive and effective habits or patterns in your thinking (e.g., a tendency to search for opportunities rather than obstacles embedded in challenges) by managing your:
   beliefs and assumptions
   mental imagery
   internal self-talk

---

control the quality of their own work—an effective prerequisite for helping employees to design and conduct their own self-observation system. The Harley story is a resounding success. This is one American company that has been extraordinarily successful in dealing with the Japanese incursion into their markets.

Each of these strategies, with the exception of self-criticism, when practiced consistently and effectively, has been found to be significantly related to higher performance. While self-criticism can at times serve a useful purpose, it tends to have a demoralizing and destructive impact when overused. Nevertheless, constructive self-criticism can sometimes send a signal to others that we are ready to accept responsibility for our own actions—and that we are sometimes human and make a mistake. Recently, basketball coach John Thompson of Georgetown University was ejected from a game when he protested too vigorously to game officials. Later he commented, "It was probably my fault more than the officials' fault. I have respect for all three of those men. I probably let my competitive juices overflow. . . . I made a mistake." Thompson's willingness to recognize some of his own flaws is one reason he is so widely respected.

Cognitive-Focused Strategies

In addition to behaviorally focused strategies, we can help ourselves to become more effective through the application of self-leadership strategies that promote effective thinking.

First, effective self-leaders can both physically and mentally redesign their own tasks to make them more naturally rewarding; that is, they can create ways to do tasks so that significant natural reward value is obtained from the enjoyment of doing the job itself. Natural rewards are derived from performing tasks in a way that allows us to experience (1) a sense of competence, (2) a sense of self-control, and (3) a sense of purpose. An example of this notion is embodied in the reply of a young girl featured in a recent news story who was asked why she had made a rock collection, and why she had tried to understand all about rocks. She replied, "Because it makes me feel good in my mind."

Other cognitive strategies help us by establishing constructive and effective habits or patterns of thinking—such as "opportunity thinking" as opposed to "obstacle thinking." For example, by studying and managing our beliefs and assumptions, we can begin to develop the ability to find opportunities in each new work challenge. Until managers began to believe that employees could be important participating partners in the success of American industry, much opportunity for progress was being wasted.

In summary, it's important to remember that if we want to lead others to be self-leaders, we must first practice self-leadership ourselves. If you want to lead somebody, the first critical step is to lead yourself.

Step 2—Modeling Self-Leadership

Once we have mastered self-leadership ourselves, the next step is to demonstrate these skills to subordinate employees; that is, our own self-leadership behaviors serve as a model from which others can learn. As Max DePree, chairman of Herman Miller, the office furniture maker, says, "It's not what you preach, but how you behave."

Modeling can be used to develop subordinate self-leadership on a day-to-day basis in two ways. The first use is to establish new behaviors—specifically self-leadership behaviors. The main point is that an employee can learn an entirely new behavior, especially self-leadership, without actually performing it. Executives that are self-starters and well-organized are likely to have subordinates who, in turn, are self-starters and well-organized. Executives, in particular, have a special responsibility to serve as the kind of self-leadership example that they wish subordinate employees to emulate.

The second use involves strengthening the probability of previously learned self-leadership behaviors. Self-leadership behaviors can be enhanced through observation of positive rewards received by others for desired behaviors. We observed, for example, an older woman react with delight when presented with a special achievement award for developing a new inspection procedure at Tandem Computer. She had developed this procedure using her own initiative—she had acted as a self-leader.

This incident served as a symbolic model for other employees at Tandem. Management made it clear that initiating the development of innovative cuing strategies (the inspection procedure) is desirable and that these types of actions are encouraged and rewarded. The hope and intention are that other employees will perceive innovative behavior to be desirable and potentially rewarding. Over time, the objective is to encourage and stimulate widespread incidents of innovative self-leadership.

The lesson from the Tandem incident is straightforward. Employees learn from and are motivated when they see rewards given to others for the performance of self-leadership behaviors. Public recognition to enhance a self-leadership model can be a powerful motivating force for others to initiate self-leadership actions.

Many learn the art of self-leadership from senior executives whom they admire and respect. The book *Eisenhower: Portrait of a Hero* by Peter Lyon (Little Brown, 1974) suggests that General Dwight Eisenhower formulated his own self-leadership style under the guidance of General George Marshall. "What General Marshall wanted most . . . were senior officers who would take the responsibility for action in their own areas of competence without coming to him for the final decision; officers who in their turn would have enough sense to delegate the details of their decisions to their subordinates." Learning to lead from those above him, Ike later carried this sense of delegation and control into his own military leadership style.

Sometimes a model of self-leadership can be inspiring. Who can forget the image of Jimmy Carter as he humbly went about building low-cost housing with his own hammer and nails. The sight of a former U.S. President actually engaging in a relatively minor self-leadership behavior had more influence than anything he could have said. Carter seems to be garnering more admiration as a former President than he acquired as a President.

Step 3—Encouraging Self-Set Goals

Goal setting, in general, has been one of the most actively investigated aspects of employee behavior and performance. Several general principles have been derived from this extensive research.

First, virtually any kind of goal setting seems to be better than none at all. The mere existence of a goal serves to focus employee attention and energy. This is one of the most pervasive findings of all organizational psychological research. Further, specific goals seem to be better than ambiguous or "fuzzy" ones. Also, in general, more difficult goals result in higher performance—provided the goals are accepted by the employee.

Last but not least, many believe that participation in setting goals will also enhance performance. The logic is that if an employee sees the goal as his or her own, the employee is more likely to give the effort required to attain the goal. Of course, the idea of participation is very closely connected with the essence of SuperLeadership.

Since the main aim of the SuperLeader is to improve the performance of subordinates through the development of their own self-leadership capabilities, employee self-goal setting is a key element. An important point to note is that goal setting is a *learned behavior*; that is, it is a skill or sequence of actions that an employee can develop over a period of time, not an innate behavior that every new employee brings to the job. Since self-goal setting is something to be learned, the role of the SuperLeader is to serve as a model, coach, and teacher. The Super-Leader helps employees learn to effectively set specific challenging goals for themselves.

Among the more interesting and extreme examples of institutional-ized self-set goals is the "Research Fellows" program at IBM. These high-status, high-performing scientists make their own decisions about how substantial resources will be allocated. Obviously, IBM believes its investment in the self-leadership capabilities of these eminent scientists will pay off in the long run. Other organizations would do well to learn from their example.

These ideas also have currency at the level of the shop floor. In a recent *Business Week* article (August 21, 1989), Alvin K. Allison, leader of a team of mechanics at Monsanto's Greenwood, South Carolina plant, says, "I knew 20 years ago that I could direct my own job, but nobody wanted to hear what I had to say." Today, Allison is a part of the upside-down revolution that seems to be driving dramatic improvements in quality and productivity at the Greenwood plant.

Step 4—Create Positive Thought Patterns

Constructive thought patterns are an important element in successful self-leadership. Part of the SuperLeader role is to transmit positive thought patterns to subordinates. Especially important is the process of facilitating positive self-expectation in subordinates.

Sometimes, but especially in the early stages of a new job, employ-ees do not have adequate natural habits of constructive thinking about themselves. They have doubts and fears—a general lack of confidence in themselves. At this stage, the actions of the SuperLeader are critical: His or her positive comments must serve as a temporary surrogate for the employee's own constructive thought patterns. As indicated in a recent *Fortune* article (March 26, 1990), Jack Welch, CEO of General Electric, thinks this issue is critical: "We need to drive self-confidence deep into the organization. . . . We have to undo a 100-year-old concept and convince our managers that their role is not to control people and stay 'on top' of things but rather to guide, energize, and excite."

The notion of constructing positive thought patterns may also be particularly critical when things are not going well. In the book *Joe Paterno: Football My Way* by Hyman & White (Collier, 1971), the very successful football coach emphasized that enhancing self-esteem is an important part of the equation: "When the staff is down . . . when the squad is down . . . when they are starting to doubt themselves . . . then it's gotta be a positive approach. The minute I have the feeling they have doubts concerning . . . [their] ability to do it . . . then I immediately want to jump in there and . . . talk about how good the kids are and what a great job they've done." He emphasizes confidence and pride: "A coach must be able to develop three things [in a team member] . . . pride, poise, and confidence in himself."

The SuperLeader creates productive thought patterns by carefully expressing confidence in the employee's ability to extend his or her present level of competence. Support and encouragement are necessary. In many ways, this expression of confidence is the essence of the "guided-participation" phase in which SuperLeaders teach each employee to lead himself or herself.

This SuperLeadership behavior is well founded in the results of research on the self-fulfilling prophecy: If a person believes something can be done, that belief makes it more likely that it *will* be done. Perhaps the SuperLeader plays "Professor Higgins" to an employee's "Eliza." Most of all, through expressions of confidence, the SuperLeader helps to create productive patterns of thinking—new constructive thought habits.

Step 5—Develop Self-Leadership Through Reward and Constructive Reprimand

One of the SuperLeader's most potent strategies in developing employee self-leadership is reward and reinforcement. For the most part, conventional viewpoints about using organizational rewards tend to focus on so-called extrinsic rewards as a means of reinforcing performance. One example is incentive pay systems.

We are basically in sympathy with this behavioral-management viewpoint and generally believe that material rewards should be used to reinforce desirable job-related behaviors. However, rewards take on a new perspective when seen through the eyes of the SuperLeader. If the purpose of the SuperLeader is to lead others to self-leadership, then an essential ingredient is to teach employees how to reward themselves and to build natural rewards into their own work. The SuperLeader attempts to construct a reward system that emphasizes self-administered and natural rewards and, in a comparative sense, de-empahsizes externally administered rewards. Thus the focus shifts from material types of rewards to a stronger emphasis on natural rewards that stem more from the task itself and on self-administration of rewards.

This usually means that people need to have the freedom to do their jobs in the ways they most value and can thrive in; that is, in the ways that they find most naturally rewarding. In the book *Our Story So Far* (3M Co., 1977), William McKnight, former CEO of 3M Company during perhaps 3M's most critical years in becoming an organizational success story, was quoted on the need for employees to do their jobs the way they want to do them. He stated, "Those men and women to whom we delegate authority and responsibility, if they are good people, are going to want to do their jobs in their own way. These are characteristics we want and should be encouraging."

In addition, a new type of reprimand is appropriate to develop employee self-leadership. We know that reprimand, in the short term, can keep somebody's nose to the grindstone, but the effectiveness of this mode of behavior is limited. Author Ken Blanchard was quoted in the *Minneapolis Star and Tribune* (May 27, 1987) as saying, "Most managers can get things done when they are around to nag and push. However, the real test of leadership is when management isn't present . . . which is about 70 percent of the time."

From a behavioral viewpoint, reprimand *should* be easy to understand. When an employee does something wrong, the manager provides a contingent aversive consequence, and the undesirable employee behavior *should* be reduced or eliminated. However, the long-term efficacy of reprimand is much more complex and leaves much to be desired. Most of all, a complex and sometimes confusing set of emotions typically accompanies reprimand, sometimes even leading to aggressive and disruptive behavior.

Reprimand is usually the opposite of what needs to be done to develop productive thought patterns in others. One objective of the SuperLeader is to encourage constructive self-confidence as an important part of the transition to self-leadership, but reprimand induces guilt and depression and diminishes self-confidence. On the other hand, if a SuperLeader treats a mistake as a learning opportunity, then employee self-esteem can be enhanced. After all, one sign of self-confidence is an individual objectively realizing that he has "made every mistake in the book" and has the experience and confidence to handle surprising situations.

We do recognize that reprimand is sometimes a necessary element in a SuperLeader's repertoire of behaviors, especially with careless or chronic underperformers. The most important lesson to remember is that the careless use of reprimand can be very discouraging to employees who are in their transition to self-leadership. The main focus should be to treat a mistake as a learning opportunity, to provide positive acceptance of the *person* despite the mistake, and to remember how the opportunity to make mistakes was a critical element in the Super-Leader's own development. Following these tips will result in a *constructive* feedback process that is more effective than the traditional use of reprimand and that positively influences employee self-leadership and long-term effectiveness.

Step 6—Promote Self-Leadership Through Teamwork

One of the more interesting examples of self-leadership systems is the team-oriented system of Volvo. Volvo has considerable experience with team assembly concepts, which were pioneered at its Kalmar plant. Further, the automobile assembly approach has been completely scrapped in the design of the new $315 million plant at Uddevalla. The key organizational philosophy at this plant is the work team, and the technical system has been designed to match the team concept. As Peter Gyllenhammar, Volvo's CEO, says, "I want the people in a team to be able to go home at night and really say, 'I built that car.' "

In the U.S., the self-managing team concept has had a slow but steady start. More recent media interest seems to indicate that the team idea is about to take off. The dramatic success of the team approach at the GM-Toyota joint venture in Fremont, California has been instructive to the U.S. automotive industry in general. In our own research, we have documented the leader characteristics that are necessary to make a team effort successful, the core of which are the basic principles of SuperLeadership.

Top-management teams are also important, as represented by this quote that appeared in *Fortune* (August, 1987) from Tom Watson, Jr., former CEO of IBM: "My most important contribution to IBM was my ability to pick strong and intelligent men and then hold the team together. . . ."

One of the more interesting indicators of a self-leadership culture is the presence of quite a few teams. The types of teams (not all work groups are called teams) include product teams, top-executive teams, ad hoc teams, and shop-floor self-managing teams. Of course, teams require a good deal of self-leadership at the group level to function correctly.

Teamwork is important at Hewlett-Packard when it comes to the precision timing and integration required for successful new product release. At H-P, a committee called "board of directors" serves to drive the process to completion. Representatives from every department involved in the project serve on these committees.

Step 7—Facilitate a Self-Leadership Culture

A major factor in developing SuperLeadership is the challenge of designing an integrated organizational culture that is conducive to high performance. Organizations will find it difficult to obtain initiative and innovation from employees without providing a pervasive environment that facilitates those elements of self-leadership.

For the most part, we focus on the one-on-one relationship between a SuperLeader and an employee: How can an executive lead that employee to lead himself or herself? For an organization, however, the best results derive from a total integrated system that is deliberately intended to encourage, support, and reinforce self-leadership *throughout* the system. Most of all, this is an issue that addresses the question of how top executives can create self-leadership cultures.

One company that has shown demonstrable results of an effort to develop a self-leadership culture is Xerox Corporation, recent winner of the Malcolm Baldrige National Quality Award. The award recognizes companies that attain preeminent leadership in quality control. At Xerox, the quality effort includes plant-level employee "family groups" that work with little direct supervision. But most of all, the award recognizes the effort of Xerox to build a total quality culture based on bottom-up employee involvement.

At another company, Dana Corporation, highly visible symbolic acts were instrumental in turning the organizational culture around. One of Rene McPherson's first concerns was to indicate the importance of giving discretion to make decisions down through the ranks. The most famous story is about one of his first actions: eliminating the procedures manual. According to one account, the procedures manual had risen to a height of 22.5 inches. McPherson was said to have dumped it in a wastebasket and replaced it with a one-page policy statement.

Rene McPherson used the following metaphor to describe his philosophy of a decentralized self-leadership culture at Dana as reported in an article in *Management Review* entitled "Hell Week—Or How Dana Makes its Managers Money Conscious" (1984). "You can control a business in one of two ways: You can institute a kind of martial law, with troops stationed in each hamlet or village standing guard; or you can sit back and let each village be self-governing. . . . What we are after is to help that person [the division manager] to be [his own] . . . manager." McPherson said of his division managers, "We didn't tell the guys what they were gonna do—they came in and told us!"

Through his radical change in culture, McPherson has left a meaningful legacy for Dana Corporation. He transformed a top-heavy, bureaucratic, sluggish organization into one of the most successful and competitive manufacturing businesses in the United States today. Self-leadership was a key ingredient: Rene McPherson demonstrated a special capacity to lead others to lead themselves.

SuperLeadership at the top requires the creation of positive organizational cultures within which self-leadership can flourish. Such environments consist of a host of factors, some observable and concrete, others more subtle and symbolic. Culture becomes particularly important when it comes to balancing the needs of individualism with the need for organized, coordinated effort. As Peter Drucker put it in the July 3, 1989 issue of *Fortune* ". . . it is important to build up the oboist as an oboist, but it is even more important to build up the oboist's pride in the performance of the orchestra . . . it puts a tremendous premium on having very clear goals and a very clear and demanding mission for the enterprise." Overreaching organizational values that support self-leadership are perhaps the most important factor.

Ford Motor Company, for example, has developed a set of guidelines that is widely circulated throughout the corporation and known as its

"Mission, Values and Guiding Principles." Among other things, they identify employee involvement and teamwork as Ford's "core human values."

In addition, training and development efforts that equip employees with both task-performance and self-leadership capabilities are important means of stimulating cultures based on leading others to lead themselves. Thus the SuperLeader's challenge is not limited to direct one-on-one leadership; the SuperLeader must also foster an integrated world in which self-leadership can survive and grow; in which self-leadership becomes an exciting, motivating, and accepted way of life. At lower levels, the challenge for aspiring SuperLeaders is to develop subcultures within their own control that stimulate the unique self-leadership strengths of subordinates.

The Servant as Leader

Robert K. Greenleaf

Servant and leader—can these two roles be fused in one real person, in all levels of status or calling? If so, can that person live and be productive in the real world of the present? My sense of the present leads me to say yes to both questions. This chapter is an attempt to explain why and to suggest how.

The idea of *The Servant as Leader* came out of reading Hermann Hesse's *Journey to the East*. In this story we see a band of men on a mythical journey, probably also Hesse's own journey. The central figure of the story is Leo who accompanies the party as the *servant* who does their menial chores, but who also sustains them with his spirit and his song. He is a person of extraordinary presence. All goes well until Leo disappears. Then the group falls into disarray and the journey is abandoned. They cannot make it without the servant Leo. The narrator, one of the party, after some years of wandering finds Leo and is taken into the Order that had sponsored the journey. There he discovers that Leo, whom he had known first as *servant*, was in fact the titular head of the Order, its guiding spirit, a great and noble *leader*.

One can muse on what Hesse was trying to say when he wrote this story. We know that most of his fiction was autobiographical, that he led a tortured life, and that *Journey to the East* suggests a turn toward the serenity he achieved in his old age. There has been much speculation by critics on Hesse's life and work, some of it centering on this story which they find the most puzzling. But to me, this story clearly says that *the great leader is seen as servant first*, and that simple fact is the key to his greatness. Leo was actually the leader all of the time, but he was servant first because that was what he was, *deep down inside*. Leadership was bestowed upon a man who was by nature a servant. It was something given, or assumed, that could be taken away. His servant nature was the real man, not bestowed, not assumed, and not to be taken away. He was servant first.

I mention Hesse and *Journey to the East* for two reasons. First, I want to acknowledge the source of the idea of *The Servant as Leader*. Then I want to use this reference as an introduction to a brief discussion of prophecy.

Fifteen years ago when I first read about Leo, if I had been listening to contemporary prophecy as intently as I do now, the first draft of this piece might have been written then. As it was, the idea lay dormant for eleven years until, four years ago, I concluded that we in this country were in a leadership crisis and that I should do what I could about it. I became painfully aware of how dull my sense of contemporary prophecy had been. And I have reflected much on why we do not hear and heed the prophetic voices in our midst (not a new question in our times, nor more critical than heretofore).

I now embrace the theory of prophecy which holds that prophetic voices of great clarity, and with a quality of insight equal to that of any age, are speaking cogently all of the time. Men and women of a stature equal to the greatest of the past are with us now addressing the problems of the day and pointing to a better way and to a personeity better able to live fully and serenely in these times.

The variable that marks some periods as barren and some as rich in prophetic vision is in the interest, the level of seeking, the responsiveness of the hearers. The variable is not in the presence or absence or the relative quality and force of the prophetic voices. Prophets grow in stature as people respond to their message. If their early attempts are ignored or spurned, their talent may wither away.

It is *seekers*, then, who make prophets, and the initiative of any one of us in searching for and responding to the voice of contemporary prophets may mark the turning point in their growth and service. But since we are the product of our own history, we see current prophecy within the context of past wisdom. We listen to as wide a range of contemporary thought as we can attend to. Then we *choose* those we elect to heed as prophets—*both old and new*—and meld their advice with our own leadings. This we test in real-life experiences to establish our own position.

Some who have difficulty with this theory assert that their faith rests on one or more of the prophets of old having given the "word" for all time and that the contemporary ones do not speak to their condition as the older ones do. But if one really believes that the "word" has been given for all time, how can one be a seeker? How can one hear the contemporary voice when one has decided not to live in the present and has turned that voice off?

Neither this hypothesis nor its opposite can be proved. But I submit that the one given here is the more hopeful choice, one that offers a significant role in prophecy to every individual. One cannot interact with and build strength in a dead prophet, but one can do it with a living one. "Faith," Dean Inge has said, "is the choice of the nobler hypothesis."

One does not, of course, ignore the great voices of the past. One does not awaken each morning with the compulsion to reinvent the wheel. But if one is *servant*, either leader or follower, one is always searching, listening, expecting that a better wheel for these times is in the making. It may emerge any day. Any one of us may find it out from personal experience. I am hopeful.

I am hopeful for these times, despite the tension and conflict, because more natural servants are trying to see clearly the world as it is and are listening carefully to prophetic voices that are speaking *now*. They are challenging the pervasive injustice with greater force and they are taking sharper issue with the wide disparity between the quality of society they know is reasonable and possible with available resources, and, on the other hand, the actual performance of the whole range of institutions that exist to serve society.

A fresh critical look is being taken at the issues of power and authority, and people are beginning to learn, however haltingly, to relate to one another in less coercive and more creatively supporting ways. A new moral principle is emerging which holds that the only authority deserving one's allegiance is that which is freely and knowingly granted by the led to the leader in response to, and in proportion to, the clearly evident servant stature of the leader. Those who choose to follow this principle will not casually accept the authority of existing institutions. *Rather, they will freely respond only to individuals who are chosen as leaders because they are proven and trusted as servants.* To the extent that this principle prevails in the future, the only truly viable institutions will be those that are predominantly servant-led.

I am mindful of the long road ahead before these trends, which I see so clearly, become a major society-shaping force. We are not there yet. But I see encouraging movement on the horizon.

What direction will the movement take? Much depends on whether those who stir the ferment will come to grips with the age-old problem of how to live in a human society. I say this because so many, having made their awesome decision for autonomy and independence from tradition, and having taken their firm stand against injustice and hypo-crisy, find it hard to convert themselves into *affirmative builders* of a better society. How many of them will seek their personal fulfillment by making the hard choices, and by undertaking the rigorous preparation that building a better society requires? It all depends on what kind of leaders emerge and how they—we—respond to them.

My thesis, that more servants should emerge as leaders, or should follow only servant-leaders, is not a popular one. It is much more com-fortable to go with a less demanding point of view about what is expected of one now. There are several undemanding, plausibly-argued alternatives to choose. One, since society seems corrupt, is to seek to avoid the center of it by retreating to an idyllic existence that minimizes involvement with the "system" (with the "system" that makes such withdrawal possible). Then there is the assumption that since the effort to reform existing institutions has not brought instant perfection, the remedy is to destroy them completely so that fresh new perfect ones can grow. Not much thought seems to be given to the problem of where the new seed will come from or who the gardener to tend them will be. The concept of the servant-leader stands in sharp contrast to this kind of thinking.

Yet it is understandable that the easier alternatives would be chosen, especially by young people. By extending education for so many so far into the adult years, the normal participation in society is effectively denied when young people are ready for it. With education that is pre-ponderantly abstract and analytical it is no wonder that there is a preoc-cupation with criticism and that not much thought is given to "What can *I* do about it?"

Criticism has its place, but as a total preoccupation it is sterile. In a time of crisis, like the leadership crisis we are now in, if too many poten-tial builders are taken in by a complete absorption with dissecting the wrong and by a zeal for instant perfection, then the movement so many of us want to see will be set back. The danger, perhaps, is to hear the analyst too much and the artist too little.

Albert Camus stands apart from other great artists of his time, in my view, and deserves the title of *prophet*, because of his unrelenting demand that each of us confront the exacting terms of our own exis-tence, and, like Sisyphus, *accept our rock and find our happiness in deal-ing with it*. Camus sums up the relevance of his position to our concern for the servant as leader in the last paragraph of his last published lecture, entitled *Create Dangerously*:

> One may long, as I do, for a gentler flame, a respite, a pause for musing. But perhaps there is no other peace for the artist than what he finds in the heat of combat. "Every wall is a door," Emerson correctly said. Let us not look for the door, and the way out, anywhere but in the wall against which we are living. Instead, let us seek the respite where it is—in the very thick of battle. For in my opinion, and this is where I shall close, it *is* there. Great ideas, it has been said, come into the world as gently as doves. Perhaps, then, if we listen attentively, we shall hear, amid the uproar of empires and nations, a faint flutter of wings, the gentle stirring of life and hope. Some will say that this hope lies in a nation, others, in a man. I believe rather that it is awakened, revived, nourished by millions of solitary individuals whose deeds and works every day negate frontiers and the crudest implications of history. As a result, there shines forth fleetingly the ever-threatened truth that each and every man, on the foundations of his own sufferings and joys, builds for them all.

One is asked, then, to accept the human condition, its sufferings and its joys, and to work with its imperfections as the foundation upon which the individual will build wholeness through adventurous creative achievement. For the person with creative potential there is no wholeness except in using it. And, as Camus explained, the going is rough and the respite is brief. It is significant that he would title his last university lecture *Create Dangerously*. And, as I ponder the fusing of servant and leader, it seems a dangerous creation: dangerous for the natural servant to become a leader, dangerous for the leader to be servant first, and dangerous for a follower to insist on being led by a servant. There are safer and easier alternatives available to all three. But why take them?

As I respond to the challenge of dealing with this question in the ensuing discourse I am faced with two problems.

First, I did not get the notion of the servant as leader from conscious logic. Rather it came to me as an intuitive insight as I contemplated Leo. And I do not see what is relevant from my own searching and experience in terms of a logical progression from premise to conclusion. Rather I see it as fragments of data to be fed into my internal computer from which intuitive insights come. Serving and leading are still mostly intuition-based concepts in my thinking.

The second problem, and related to the first, is that, just as there may be a real contradiction in the servant as leader, so my perceptual world is full of contradictions. Some examples: I believe in order, and I want creation out of chaos. My good society will have strong individualism amidst community. It will have elitism along with populism. I listen to the old and to the young and find myself baffled and heartened by both. Reason and intuition, each in its own way, both comfort and dismay me. There are many more. Yet, with all of this, I believe that I live with as much serenity as do my contemporaries who venture into controversy as freely as I do but whose natural bent is to tie up the essentials of life in neat bundles of logic and consistency. But I am deeply grateful to the people who are logical and consistent because some of them, out of their natures, render invaluable services for which I am not capable.

My resolution of these two problems is to offer the relevant gleanings of my experience in the form of a series of unconnected little essays, some developed more fully than others, with the suggestion that they be read and pondered on separately within the context of this opening section.

WHO IS THE SERVANT-LEADER?

The servant-leader *is* servant first—as Leo was portrayed. It begins with the natural feeling that one wants to serve, to serve *first*. Then conscious choice brings one to aspire to lead. That person is sharply different from one who is *leader* first, perhaps because of the need to assuage an unusual power drive or to acquire material possessions. For such it will be a later choice to serve—after leadership is established. The leader-first and the servant-first are two extreme types. Between them there are shadings and blends that are part of the infinite variety of human nature.

The difference manifests itself in the care taken by the servant-first to make sure that other people's highest priority needs are being served. The best test, and difficult to administer, is: Do those served grow as persons? Do they, *while being served*, become healthier, wiser, freer, more autonomous, more likely themselves to become servants? *And*, what is the effect on the least privileged in society; will they benefit, or, at least, not be further deprived?

As one sets out to serve, how can one know that this will be the result? This is part of the human dilemma; one cannot know for sure. One must, after some study and experience, hypothesize—but leave the hypothesis under a shadow of doubt. Then one acts on the hypothesis and examines the result. One continues to study and learn and periodically one re-examines the hypothesis itself.

Finally, one chooses again. Perhaps one chooses the same hypothesis again and again. But it is always a fresh open choice. And it is always an hypothesis under a shadow of doubt. "Faith is the choice of the nobler hypothesis." Not the *noblest*; one never knows what that is. But the *nobler*, the best one can see when the choice is made. Since the test of results of one's actions is usually long delayed, the faith that sustains the choice of the nobler hypothesis is psychological self-insight. This is the most dependable part of the true servant.

The natural servant, the person who is *servant first*, is more likely to persevere and refine a particular hypothesis on what serves another's highest priority needs than is the person who is *leader first* and who later serves out of promptings of conscience or in conformity with normative expectations.

My hope for the future rests in part on my belief that among the legions of deprived and unsophisticated people are many true servants who will lead, and that most of them can learn to discriminate among those who presume to serve them and identify the true servants whom they will follow.

EVERYTHING BEGINS WITH THE INITIATIVE OF AN INDIVIDUAL

The forces for good and evil in the world are propelled by the thoughts, attitudes, and actions of individual beings. What happens to our values, and therefore to the quality of our civilization in the future, will be shaped by the conceptions of individuals that are born of inspiration. Perhaps only a few will receive this inspiration (insight) and the rest will learn from them. The very essence of leadership, going out ahead to show the way, derives from more than usual openness to inspiration. Why would anybody accept the leadership of another except that the other sees more clearly where it is best to go? Perhaps this is the current problem: too many who presume to lead do not see more clearly and, in defense of their inadequacy, they all the more strongly argue that the "system" must be preserved—a fatal error in this day of candor.

But the leader needs more than inspiration. A leader ventures to say: "I will go; come with me!" A leader initiates, provides the ideas and the structure, and takes the risk of failure along with the chance of success. A leader says: "I will go; follow me!" while knowing that the path is uncertain, even dangerous. One then trusts those who go with one's leadership.

Paul Goodman, speaking through a character in *Making Do*, has said, "If there is no community for you, young man, young man, make it yourself."

WHAT ARE YOU TRYING TO DO?

"What are you trying to do?" is one of the easiest to ask and most difficult to answer of questions.

A mark of leaders, an attribute that puts them in a position to show the way for others, is that they are better than most at pointing the direction. As long as one is leading, one always has a goal. It may be a goal arrived at by group consensus, or the leader, acting on inspiration, may simply have said, "Let's go this way." But the leader always knows what it is and can articulate it for any who are unsure. By clearly stating and restating the goal the leader gives certainty and purpose to others who may have difficulty in achieving it for themselves.

The word *goal* is used here in the special sense of the overarching purpose, the big dream, the visionary concept, the ultimate consummation which one approaches but never really achieves. It is something presently out of reach; it is something to strive for, to move toward, or become. It is so stated that it excites the imagination and challenges people to work for something they do not yet know how to do, something they can be proud of as they move toward it.

Every achievement starts with a goal—but not just any goal and not just anybody stating it. The one who states the goal must elicit trust, especially if it is a high risk or visionary goal, because those who follow are asked to accept the risk along with the leader. Leaders do not elicit trust unless one has confidence in their values and competence (including judgment) and unless they have a sustaining spirit (entheos) that will support the tenacious pursuit of a goal.

Not much happens without a dream. And for something great to happen, there must be a great dream. Behind every great achievement is a dreamer of great dreams. Much more than a dreamer is required to bring it to reality; but the dream must be there first.

LISTENING AND UNDERSTANDING

One of our very able leaders recently was made the head of a large, important, and difficult-to-administer public institution. After a short time he realized that he was not happy with the way things were going. His approach to the problem was a bit unusual. For three months he stopped reading newspapers and listening to news broadcasts; and for this period he relied wholly upon those he met in the course of his work to tell him what was going on. In three months his administrative problems were resolved. No miracles were wrought; but out of a sustained intentness of listening that was produced by this unusual decision, this able man learned and received the insights needed to set the right course. And he strengthened his team by so doing.

Why is there so little listening? What makes this example so exceptional? Part of it, I believe, with those who lead, is that the usual leader in the face of a difficulty tends to react by trying to find someone else on whom to pin the problem, rather than by automatically responding: "I have a problem. What is it? What can *I* do about *my* problem?" The sensible person who takes the latter course will probably react by listening, and somebody in the situation is likely to say what the problem is and what should be done about it. Or enough will be heard that there will be an intuitive insight that resolves it.

I have a bias about this which suggests that only a true natural servant automatically responds to any problem by listening *first*. When one is a leader, this disposition causes one to be *seen* as servant first. This suggests that a non-servant who wants to be a servant might become a *natural* servant through a long arduous discipline of learning to listen, a discipline sufficiently sustained that the automatic response to any problem is to listen first. I have seen enough remarkable transformations in people who have been trained to listen to have some confidence in this approach. It is because true listening builds strength in other people.

Most of us at one time or another, some of us a good deal of the time, would really like to communicate, really get through to a significant level of meaning in the hearer's experience. It can be terribly important. The best test of whether we are communicating at this depth is to ask ourselves first: Are we really listening? Are we listening to the one we want to communicate to? Is our basic attitude, as we approach the confrontation, one of wanting to understand? Remember that great line from the prayer of St. Francis, "Lord, grant that I may not seek so much to be understood as to understand."

One must not be afraid of a little silence. Some find silence awkward or oppressive, but a relaxed approach to dialogue will include the welcoming of some silence. It is often a devastating question to ask oneself—but it is sometimes important to ask it—"In saying what I have in mind will I really improve on the silence?"

The Case of a Servant Leader: John F. Donnelly, Sr.

Robert J. Doyle

From a lecture presented at the University of Notre Dame, October 4, 1996

I would like to tell you a story; a story of a businessman, a story of a very successful CEO. There are, of course, lots of stories about successful CEO's. But this one was unique among his peers in two ways; unique in the way he defined success: service to others rather than profit; and unique in his personal driving force: love of neighbor rather than competition. John Fenlon Donnelly's story hasn't ended yet and, if you should find it interesting, you may help to write it. It is my hope that you will find it of sufficient value that you will be inspired to pick up the story line and add a new sentence, a new paragraph, a new chapter, or even a whole new volume.

To give you just a bit of background, Donnelly Corporation is the world's leading supplier of automotive glass parts such as rear view mirrors, windows and specialty glass parts. Because of their quality and reliability, they are one of the very few suppliers who are the single source of supply for the major auto companies. They have been listed in both editions of *The 100 Best Companies to Work For in America* and, in a recent edition, they are in the top 10 of the 100 best. Several years ago, they were voted one of the most admired companies in America by an association of human resource executives. They receive a steady stream of visitors, which over the years has included General Motors, Meade Corporation and Volvo, wanting to learn about their management and human resources systems. Using any criteria, this has been a very successful company.

I worked closely with John for 7 years as Personnel Director and we continued a correspondence on the subject for an additional 12 years. Of the more than 100 CEO's with whom I have worked, John's story is the most interesting, and the one most worthy of your careful examination and your emulation.

I want to tell you about John Donnelly, the man, because one can not fully appreciate his work unless one knows who he was and why he did the things he did. Then I will describe some of his work to establish participative management in his company and, finally, I will explain some of the things I have made of his legacy and encourage you to take his lessons to heart and in your own way continue to expand these efforts to make work and organizations serve the best interests of people.

John spent his entire adult life as the President and CEO of the Donnelly Corporation. He attended the University of Notre Dame in the late 1920's and early 1930's, where he studied engineering and, more importantly, was introduced to Thomistic philosophy by such great men as G.K. Chesterton and Jacques Maritain. He then entered the seminary in Baltimore, Maryland to study for the priesthood, but soon returned to Holland, Michigan to manage the family business when his father suddenly and unexpectedly died.

He applied himself diligently to the task of learning how to manage a business but he never gave up his drive to study philosophy, the arts, history and the natural and physical sciences. He was a voracious reader and the scope of his knowledge, as far as the rest of us could determine, was without limit.

A colleague, Jim Knister, and I used to lunch frequently with John at the Warm Friend Hotel and other restaurants in downtown Holland. We were amazed at the range of his understanding and knowledge. One day we decided to try to find a topic outside of his expertise. During lunch I began a conversation about offshore oil drilling in the Gulf of Mexico and Jim, according to our conspiracy, picked up the discussion. In no time, John had joined the discussion and neatly summarized the economic dimension, the environmental threat, and the technical difficulties of drilling under water. We were both stunned and, as you can well imagine, neither of us ever tried a stunt like that again. Typical of John, he did not enter the discussion to dominate it or to show how smart he was, he was just participating.

John was a leader and he wore the mantle of leadership with grace and charm in many roles. After his father's death he was needed to manage the company and he accepted that leadership responsibility willingly and continued it for more than fifty years. He was a community leader. He helped the Holland Chamber of Commerce become the first chartered Chamber in their size category in the U.S. He was a leader in his church at the parish and diocesan level and, in the early 1960's, he was elected President of the National Council of Catholic Men. He was a leader in his family, a responsibility more dear to him than anything else in his life. John gave great energy to his business and to a variety of social action causes but there was never a doubt that his primary responsibility and interest was the happiness and welfare of his wife, Kay, his children, and his brother and sisters and their families.

Michael Novak has written an excellent new book entitled *Business as a Calling*. By which he means business as a vocation. Novak didn't know John Donnelly but if he had, he could have written his book as a biography of John. In his book, Novak makes the point that human capital is the most important resource of a business. This is a point Rensis Likert made in 1960 which attracted John to Likert. Likert would ask CEO's: "What would happen to your business if I left you every asset that shows up on your balance sheet (land, buildings, machines, vehicles, computers, tools, inventory, cash and so on) but took away every one of your people? How long would it take, and what would be the cost to rebuild your company?" Likert, a social scientist, was thinking of human capital as the technical skills and organizational skills required by a business.

Novak, a theologian, takes this idea to a much higher level and points out that virtue and character are the important components of a business' human capital. Virtue and character, not technical and organizational skills, build the internal and external relationships of trust and service necessary to a successful business enterprise.

Novak applies the four cardinal virtues to the vocation of the modern businessman. These, he says, are the virtues upon which the good character of the business and business people must be built. By good character, he means the classic Greek philosophical ideal of good-Kalos, meaning a goal to aspire to, with a power of attraction and beauty drawing us onward by its radiance. We don't usually talk about business goals and strategic plans that draw us onward by their radiance, their goodness. But John was able to see things in that dimension, he had the good character hinged on the cardinal virtues. His goal was always Kalos—the good as he knew it and he worked hard to discover that which was truly good.

Novak names the cardinal virtues: tempered passions, the courage to quiet fears and inner terrors, practical wisdom, and the right touch in

giving to each person and each matter its due. If you have an old cate-
chism, the cardinal virtues were called temperance, fortitude, wisdom
and justice.

John Donnelly would receive a pretty good score on the cardinal
virtues. He was temperate in his passions; the first cardinal virtue. I've
seen him angry, but not out of control. His absence of visible vices and
his modesty were reasons he was so trusted and respected. I can remember production employees of the company saying about a new policy or
program or decision: "I don't really understand it but if John says it's
okay, that's good enough for me." That testimonial alone would set
John apart from most business leaders, indeed from leaders in almost all
professions.

The second virtue, his courage and ability to face adversity with
calmness was a product of his strong faith in a divine providence. One
Friday afternoon just before Christmas in the late 1950's, John received
a call from the Purchasing Department of General Motors. He was told
that beginning January 1st the company must lower the price of each
rear view mirror by 5 cents. That was about a 5% cut in revenues and
enough to wipe out any profit the company would make on GM's business. He was very upset with the harsh way the company was being
treated by its best customer: no warning, no discussion, no opportunity
to protect the company. He decided to keep this information to himself
rather than spoil everyone's Christmas holiday. He walked downstairs
to the factory and visited with the people on the floor. While talking
with the workers on the silvering line, he asked if anyone had ideas
about how they might take some cost out of production. One of the ideas
that came up was to purchase plate glass in a slightly larger size and get
five mirrors out of each blank rather than four. As soon as possible, he
had Purchasing check on the availability of the larger size. The answer
came back that the larger size was available and cheaper because the
larger size was a standard size. The company had been paying a premium for the smaller non-standard size. This amounted to a savings of
5 cents per mirror in material and labor costs. Incidents such as this
formed the rock-solid conviction John held about the power and benefits of employee participation.

In addition to his encyclopedic knowledge, he had the gift of practical wisdom, the third cardinal virtue. This enabled him to see the
practical value of the Scanlon Plan as a management tool to establish

the value of financial equity for the employees of the company. It was his practical wisdom that caused him to say yes when Rensis Likert asked the company to participate in a major research project on the use of employee diagnostic surveys as an organization development tool. It was his practical wisdom that prompted him to decline another Likert invitation to join a research project on Human Asset Accounting. John knew instinctively that the true value of the human organization could not be reduced to a mathematical fact. Likert's first project, Survey Guided Development, is alive and well. I use it often in my consulting. The Donnelly Corporation uses it to this day, 30 years later. Human Asset Accounting was tried for a few years in other companies and abandoned to the graveyard of intriguing, but unworkable, projects.

Another example of John's practical wisdom occurred in a discussion he was having with Art Thornbury, the Production and Manufacturing Engineering Manager for the then new Donnelly Mirrors, Ltd. factory in Ireland. John wanted to know Art's opinion of one of the more technical manufacturing processes. Art said the process had been explained to him in a way that contradicted what he considered to be good engineering practice, but he said he would withhold his concerns and see how the process worked out. John encouraged him not to acquiesce and not to withhold his knowledge and experience but to challenge everything until it made good practical sense to him. John not only possessed the virtue of practical wisdom but he encouraged it in others. This was a key element of John's idea of participation.

The fourth cardinal virtue, Novak describes as the right touch in giving each person and each matter its due; this is the virtue of justice. John was able to talk as easily with employees on the factory floor as with senior managers, major customers, government officials or even a council of bishops. He did not respect people of great status more than those with blue collars. He respected everyone very highly. He had a keen sense of justice and examined every aspect of his business to be sure that justice and equity were being served. Long before the environmental movement developed a head of steam, he moved at considerable expense to clean up a water discharge that was not toxic but was an esthetic problem. The water discolored a very minute portion of Lake Macatawa where the factory waste water emptied into the lake. No Department of Environmental Quality forced him to do it. The community loved its lake and it didn't look good, and that was enough for him to act.

Under John's leadership we never hesitated to act on a matter of social justice. We attempted a variety of affirmative action plans and participated in programs to employ the unemployable. John viewed the company as an institution of society and the community and, therefore, an institution with a responsibility to and for the community. His support of the Scanlon Plan was prompted by his sense of justice. His desire to see justice done was also the reason why he was so eager to promote the Scanlon Plan to other companies. In 1966, while I was Training Director of another Scanlon company, I convened a meeting of several western Michigan Scanlon companies and it was there that I first met John. John picked up on the idea and provided the leadership that changed that meeting into an association which, 30 years later, is still actively promoting the ideas of the Scanlon Plan.

John was not unique among CEO's in his extensive knowledge or in his practice of the cardinal virtues I have described, rare but not unique. Still he was considerably more successful than most in creating an organization whose hallmarks were participation, equity and trust. John had one more special ingredient that went beyond the cardinal virtues, a force that enabled him to be more consistent and more successful in his practice of management.

And, this is the major point I wish to make today: what made John Donnelly unique among business leaders, and the reason for his successes as a CEO, was his religion. For John, religion was not something saved for Sundays, it was the driving force in his life and in everything he did, including managing a manufacturing company. You cannot possibly understand John's actions and his successes without understanding his very strong religious motivations.

On the surface, we can characterize him as a typical devout American Irish Catholic. He attended church regularly and participated fully in the sacramental life of the Catholic Church. He was well read in philosophy and theology. In these, he was better educated than 99% of Catholic lay people and more than half of the clergy. He was very much a Thomist and strongly attracted to Aquinas' zealous pursuit of the truth. He was a serious student of two prominent 20th century Thomists: Jacques Maritain and Bernard Lonergan. He was first introduced to Thomistic philosophy by Maritain while he was a student here at Notre Dame.

Later he became a fan of Lonergan. In 1977, he wrote telling me of a new book by the Jesuit, Bernard Tyrell, entitled *Bernard Lonergan's Philosophy of God*. And I quote from John's letter:

"Lonergan, in my estimation, has done more for Thomism and truth seeking than any person since Aquinas. He is developing a following among philosophers and theologians both Catholic and Protestant. While he does not often address questions of the application of philosophy to life's problems, he is very much aware that the future of mankind depends on having a sound basis for our knowing."

He has what he calls the transcendental imperatives:

Be attentive
Be intelligent
Be reasonable
Be responsible
Be loving
Develop and, if necessary, change

These imperatives he says are the way to truth. They are also the way to love, to social justice and to the Omega point."

John's reference to the Omega point refers to the writing of Teilard de Chardin. John was very familiar with the work of Chardin and often made reference to Chardin's Omega point, that state of perfection toward which evolution is aimed.

The preceding list of John's intellectual interests in not exhaustive, but it does cover his major interests and I cite it to show that he was neither your average Catholic layman nor your average businessman. What I described above was the visible and intellectual side of his religious life, but it was the spiritual side of his religion that really set John apart.

As we explore this, let's listen to some of John's own words. In a company and family history John describes the religious character of his grandmother and of his father. About his grandmother he said: "Her outstanding trait, perhaps the source of her cheerfulness, was an abiding faith in God. Indeed, she appeared to live with Christ as a constant companion." And commenting on his father, he said: "Like his mother, he seemed to have God unobtrusively near."

Both of these statements could be made about John himself. He did not preach religion to his business associates, and many with whom he worked were never aware of the depth of his religious faith. Those who did not understand his deepest motivation simply saw a man who was kind, trustworthy, respectful, polite, and very smart. But today I cannot fully describe his legacy without explaining his religious motivation.

I discussed religion often with John and had the good fortune to be exposed to this powerful side of his character. John did live with Christ as a constant companion. John's religion was not a religion about Jesus, it was the religion of Jesus. Being a Christian to him meant very simply trying to live his life as Christ lived: serving others and in all matters, living the prayer "Thy will be done." Love one another is a basic tenet in all religions. John heard the whole of Jesus' message at the Last Supper: Love one another as I have loved you. It isn't enough to love on our terms. The ideal which John tried to practice was to love on Christ's terms.

Like all businessmen, John studied and practiced management, marketing, finance and technology, but as he did, he sought to use the knowledge and skills of the businessman in a Christlike manner. This was the dimension that gave John his edge.

For him, participation was not a search for a popular decision. It was always the search for truth, justice and excellence, popular or not. If you hadn't done your homework, you could be in trouble participating with John. Once an employee challenged John, asking him: "How much more improvement do you want? Aren't you ever satisfied?" John's answer was: "I won't ask for more improvement if you promise not to ask for more pay." On the other hand, if your position was sound, John would gladly support it. John's concept of participation was not a game to make people feel good. It was a way to discover truth and better ways of doing things. He expected participation to be a struggle. Achieving good things usually requires a struggle.

So now we have a CEO who was smart, who was virtuous, and whose secret ingredient was a very deep Christian faith.

So what's my point? Am I suggesting that you must be a Thomistic philosopher in order to succeed in business? No, I am not. Am I suggesting you must be a devout Catholic to be able to do the things John Donnelly did? No, I am not. But I don't want to get ahead of myself, so before I make my point, let's talk about John Donnelly's work and his achievements on the frontier of participative management.

In his first 20 years as President of Donnelly Mirrors, most of his attention was focused on the survival of the business. He took over at the depth of the Great Depression when things were anything but stable.

During WW II, he was able to get some war production which kept the company alive and provided a new product technology that put them into the automotive supply business following the war. This was the foundation upon which the current company is built.

In 1952, John installed the Scanlon Plan. The Scanlon Plan was then and still is a cutting-edge program that has three principal components: a highly participative management system, a formal employee involvement process, and an employee bonus to equitably share increases in productivity and profit with all of the company's employees. This was to be his first formal experience with participative management, but participative management was not his reason for adopting the Scanlon Plan. His main reason for adopting the Scanlon Plan was his sense of equity and fairness. Following WW II, Donnelly Mirrors, like many companies, had a myriad of out-of-control individual incentive plans. These, he said, were inequitable and divisive, and to replace the many individual incentive plans with one Scanlon bonus was more equitable and unifying. It was also practical in that it was more cost effective and administratively simpler. So he installed the Scanlon Plan to correct a compensation problem and then he began to discover and learn about participative management. Apparently he didn't learn fast enough because in 1960, he was shocked when the employees petitioned for a union election. He recognized immediately that the employees' interest in a union expressed their need to have a greater say in matters that affected them, their desire for greater participation. He opposed the union, but not in a typical competitive or adversarial way. He agreed that employees should have more say in matters of interest to them but he considered it management's responsibility to provide the means for appropriate participation. He was not willing to abdicate that responsibility to any outside third party. The employees voted not to have a union and John responded by becoming a much more serious student and practitioner of participative management.

He heard and understood de Tocqueville's observation that the more a people control their own government, the more it frees them to engage in cooperative efforts to improve their life situation. He created the Donnelly Committee, a representative group to review company policies and issues affecting the work community. And, as the Donnelly Committee gave people more influence in the company, they did participate and cooperate more in improving company performance.

He heard and learned from other authorities such as Drucker, McGregor, Likert, and Maslow. Before I started working for Donnelly Mirrors, I told John about Blake and Mouton's Managerial Grid; an intensive week-long training program in participative management. John saw value in this training and sent every Donnelly salaried employee, about 50 employees, to the week-long course. At that time this one decision resulted in an expenditure equal to about 20% of the company's annual profit. This was an example of his commitment and willingness to put his money where his heart was.

This also led to my joining the company. I had been unable to get anyone from my previous company to take an interest in Managerial Grid training. When I realized I was having more influence and success at Donnelly's, I asked John for a job.

With his guidance and support we made great strides in expanding employee participation. We pioneered the use of work teams in production and at all levels of the company. Work teams met regularly to solve problems and find ways to improve work. Prior to work teams, there was a traditional Scanlon production committee suggestion process. In its first year, work teams generated cost savings three times greater than under the old system. During this period employee bonuses averaged about 15% of their pay each month. The company consistently lowered product prices and profits grew to very healthy levels.

With a good participation process in place and good bonuses satisfying people's equity concerns, John turned his attention to the planning process as he felt this was a better source of motivation than the Scanlon bonuses. In a 1981 letter, he wrote:

> I believe a strong distinction should be drawn between incentives and motivation. Incentives encourage people to concentrate on the reward, not the work to be done. They encourage many non-productive behaviors. Motivation, on the other hand, is an internal drive that is released by worthwhile goals. Goals ought to start the process for humans. People will willingly work toward organizational goals if they believe them to be worthwhile. Providing a livelihood is a minimum goal. If the work involved is creative or helpful to others, the motivational forces become stronger. The more the CEO can provide a wholesome standard for the worth of company objectives, the more willingly the people will support these objectives.

He gave a great deal of attention to the whole planning process. Most business management planning processes are only concerned with the 'what' and 'how-to' of the company's work; the 'what' being sales and revenue goals, quality and customer satisfaction goals, and so on. The 'how-to' of planning includes budgets, staffing requirements, sales programs, etc. These, of course, are necessary for efficiency and productivity. The element John began to add was the 'why' of the company's work, the real meaning in human terms for all of the company's constituents. For John the 'why' was always defined as service to others, helping others. In religious terms it is: love one another. As John said in the preceding quote—when work is helpful to others, the motivation forces become stronger.

In the terms of the Maslow five-level motivation model, pay, benefits and job security address levels 1, 2 and 3. And, for most non-management workers, companies give very little attention to any needs beyond level 3. Interesting and challenging work, which is a component of most managerial and professional work, satisfies the self-esteem needs of Maslow's level 4. Maslow's level-5 needs get an honorable mention in management training programs but are not seriously addressed in the world of work. We have had several generations of managers who believe that people, at least the people they hire, are motivated solely by economic needs. Because John believed that people had a need for meaning in their lives well beyond economic needs, he tried to put more meaning into their work and the work of the company. He believed, with Victor Frankl, the author of *Man's Search for Meaning*, that the desire for meaning was more true to human nature than the desire for pleasure. He agreed with Maslow that the best managers help workers satisfy their needs for truth and beauty and goodness, as Maslow defined level 5. This was no easy task and I doubt that John was ever satisfied with his results in this area because his expectations were so high. However, his interest and efforts are there for us to see and they are part of the legacy he left for us to build upon. In a paper he wrote in 1977 to clarify the purpose and work of the company, he started with this John Ruskin quote: "The highest reward for man's work is not what he gets for it but what he becomes by it."

His interest in meaningfulness was not limited to employees of the company. Another thing that troubled John was the role of shareholders in the modern corporation. He felt that shareholders should be active and responsible participants in the business. He saw modern shareholders as investors with no more interest in the company, its affairs or its products than the financial return on their investment. Because he believed so strongly that people are much more than the wealth they might accumulate he felt that shareholders should be interested in more than how many dollars their investment might bring them. He tried to involve his own shareholders with more regular communications and special meetings. These efforts were somewhat successful and he never ceased to encourage responsible ownership or trusteeship.

It is a pity that John did not meet Robert Greenleaf while they were both alive. John was on the same "servant leadership" wave length as Greenleaf and I'm sure they could have been great collaborators on issues such as the stewardship responsibilities of boards, owners and managers. For those of you who are attracted to the Donnelly legacy, I recommend that you also look into the work of the Greenleaf Center for Servant Leadership located in Indianapolis. They are an advocacy and educational institute promoting the same kind of service to others and responsible business leadership that characterized the work of John Donnelly.

Using Greenleaf's concept of servant leadership I can now give you a simple model that puts John Donnelly's character and motivation into perspective.

Servant leader <—> Predatory leader

Starting with servant leadership or servant business management as an ideal of Christian service, as one pole of a continuum, we can identify its polar opposite as predator leadership or predatory business management. You can use this continuum from servant to predator to analyze company cultures, business practices and specific decisions. Everyday we see examples of predatory business practices. Some are truly mean, most are petty. We see downsizing, excessive executive pay, exploitation of third-world workers and petty office politics. We even have books entitled "How to Swim with Sharks." But John Donnelly was as far from the predator pole and as close to the servant pole as any CEO I have ever known. And this is my point in telling you about his very deep religious motivation. I believe his model of servant leadership to be the very essence of his legacy.

We have been trying to solve the problems of people at work with secular, humanistic behavioral science approaches for the past 50 years with very limited success. I don't believe we will make real progress until we recognize that man is truly a spiritual and religious being, and take the approach modeled by John Donnelly.

I am an unrepentant optimist and I see a shift away from predatory leadership and to servant leadership. I am encouraged by the Novak book, the Greenleaf Center, and by this lecture series. But I also want to make the point that John Donnelly was doing servant leadership when servant leadership wasn't cool. Predatory practices were the norm during most of John's career. He chose to break with the norm and move to higher ground. His courage and commitment are also part of his legacy.

The specifics of other activities to advance participative management at Donnelly's are not unique, they are typical of the many organizational changes and organizational development efforts of the past 30 years. As I have said repeatedly, the difference was the driving force, John's spirituality. Some of you may have seen and read the *Harvard Business Review* article that reports an interview with John, and contains additional details of the Donnelly experience.* As you follow the interview, note the number of changes mentioned in the article. He was learning as he went, so changes were frequent as new insights developed. What the article does not touch on is why he was so persistent in creating a human organization. I can tell you from my consulting experience that it is much more common for managers to fold when they encounter resistance or failure. Remember the transcendental imperatives from the Lonergan quote. The last one was: "Develop and, if necessary, change." John believed this imperative and he 'walked his talk.'

What we have covered are these major elements in John Donnelly's efforts to implement participative management.

- He first put the company on a sound product/financial foundation.
- He introduced the Scanlon Plan, developed it into one of the most successful and enduring of Scanlon Plans and contributed to the spread of this pioneering program of equity and participation to other companies.
- He encouraged the development of highly participative work teams which increased employee participation five-fold.
- He then turned his attention to better planning and creating meaningful work for the company, its workers and shareholders.

---

*Ewing, D. W., "Participative Management at Work: An interview with John F. Donnelly," *Harvard Business Review*, Jan–Feb. 1977, pp. 117–127.

These were his major thrusts and the more visible features of his legacy.

I also want to share a few ideas that I have been working on over the past few years. The first is a model of how management has evolved through the 20th century and where it appears to be headed in the 21st.

This model is based on the work of Rensis Likert. When John and I began working with Likert on survey-guided development, Likert had identified an evolving model of 4 systems of management. He observed that management practices were progressing from System 1-Authoritarian to System 4-Participative. His model is similar to McGregor's famous Theory X, Theory Y model. Likert was more of a scientist than McGregor and so his model is more detailed and precise. I think it was Likert's scientific precision that attracted John.

By systems of management, we mean the whole complex array of inter-acting and inter-related activities and practices of management in an organization. These include values, strategies, structure, policies, goals, standards, controls, communications, decision-making processes, rewards, relationships, responsibilities and authority.

There is a schematic of the evolution of management systems in the 20th century and approximate dates of their emergence.

System 1	System 2	System 3	System 4	System 5
Authoritarian→	Paternalistic→	Consultative→	Participative→	Partnership
1910	1930	1950	1970	1990

System 1, the authoritarian model is characterized by a few leaders who have and exercise all authority because they alone are educated and know all the answers. Authoritarian business management was appropriate in 1900 for an illiterate, inexperienced, immigrant workforce and it still works in emergencies and, of course, in most of the classrooms of the world. System 1, in business, does not always respect people and it led to abusive practices.

As the workforce developed knowledge, skills and experience, they demanded better physical working conditions and forced management to System 2, which we call paternalistic. Workers forced this change by forming unions to bargain with management and by using the political process to enact government regulations more favorable to workers. The Great Depression and Roosevelt's New Deal made great changes in the world of work and made paternalistic management the norm. System 2 is still very authoritarian but it is nicer, hence the term, paternalistic. Paternalism has a pejorative connotation which always bothered John. He would remind me that paternalism wasn't all bad, for instance, the good father in a family and especially God the Father. He wished that Likert would have used a term such as benevolent despotism.

Once that plateau had been reached and, with the economic expansion following WW II, we saw the emergence of System 3. The education and experience level of the workforce had grown substantially and people had ideas which they wanted heard. System 3 is consultative. This is when the manager says: "Before I make my decision on this, I'd like to get your input." The manager agrees to consult with the employees but doesn't really give up much authority. Richard Hackman, who spoke in this series in 1992, calls this transitional management. He sees it as the transition from authoritarian to participative, from Theory X to Theory Y. The problem is that System 3 has not been a transitional system. Most managers today are stuck at System 3: consulting but not really sharing authority. It was System 3 that caused the Quality Circle initiative to fizzle in the United States. It is System 3 that is responsible for most employee discontent and lack of commitment today.

Beyond consultative is System 4 which is participative. In this system real authority is shared with people. Decision making is pushed down to levels where good information is available. To really delegate, management must be sure that everyone knows and is committed to the goals of the organization. That is why John Donnelly turned his attention to the planning process. Setting and communicating direction is essential to significant employee participation. Likert discovered System 4 in small units and departments in larger organizations. He did not find an entire System 4 organization, not even Donnelly Mirrors, although this was John's conscious goal.

Once, John and I and Ren Likert met with the Donnelly production foremen. I think it was Nick Lindsay who said that he liked Likert's idea of System 4, and believed that John truly supported it and that the foremen were trying to make it work on the factory floor. But, Nick said, there didn't seem to be much support for the idea between the President and the foremen. We had a good laugh—but Nick was right. The middle managers at Donnelly were having just as much trouble getting to System 4 as were managers in other companies. It is a struggle to make organizations more human. This is why we can call it a frontier. In the Harvard article I mentioned, John's first observation was that the greatest obstacle on the frontier of participative management was the managers' unwillingness to give up authority.

As I worked with the ideas of System 4, I began to realize that this evolution would continue to System 5 and beyond. We don't know very much yet about System 5. We know enough to say that it will be a progressive step beyond System 4; a system where what is right is more important than who is right; where the operating principle is partnership; partnerships within work groups and partnerships between shifts, between sales and engineering and production, home office and field, and partnerships with customers and suppliers. We see hints of System 5 in certain spikes in organizational performance as when the employees of Delta Airlines took up a collection and bought the company an airplane as an expression of their satisfaction and commitment to the company. Seven thousand employees showed up to christen the plane "The Spirit of Delta." Or, at another Scanlon company, when an entire engineering department postponed their summer vacations to complete a product design and save several hundred production employees from a temporary layoff. We also see evidence of System 5 in volunteer organizations such as the Peace Corps and many service organizations. We saw it in the city of Portland last winter during some serious flooding. People are capable of marvelous acts of cooperation and joint effort. When we learn how to manage in ways that stimulate high levels of consistent cooperation, we will have discovered System 5. Then we can begin to look for System 6.

Another issue I have been working on is the development of participative leaders. We have a program that helps managers and teams learn participative management practices. We don't agree with the popular notion of leaderless work groups. We don't think the solution to poor leadership is the elimination of leaders. We believe that participative management requires a new type of leadership which can be learned. Participative leadership is the responsibility of all members of the work group, not just the boss. The formal leader has certain tasks to perform as do the members. Participative leadership has four major areas of responsibility:

- to develop people as individuals
- to develop work teams and teamwork between teams
- to guide and facilitate the work of the team and individual members
- to focus and coordinate all work on the operating goals of the department and the strategic goals of the company

We have constructed a questionnaire which a team administers to itself. This survey measures the status of team leadership in the four responsibility areas and generates information the team needs to improve its leadership practices and teamwork. It is a process as old as Socrates where we help the team ask itself the right questions, and they are responsible for their answers and any change that might be required.

Remember Lonergan's transcendental imperatives. This leadership program employs all six of them:

- be attentive (the survey)
- be intelligent (analyze and learn from the survey results)
- be reasonable (take appropriate actions)
- be responsible (follow through on planned actions)
- be loving (cooperate and encourage each other)
- develop and, if necessary, change (continuous improvement)

Finally, I want to discuss the planning process. I have always been persuaded, as John was, of the primacy of planning in any system of management. But only recently, as I struggle to understand System 5 and my imagination teases me with thoughts of System 6, have I begun to see a new dimension to business planning. This comes from the essence of System 5 which is partnership. If, as System 5, suggests, a business is a partnership, then it should be operated for the mutual benefit of all partners.

The partners can be conceptualized as a 5-point star-shaped model, involving customers, shareholders, employees, suppliers, and the community. Each of the partners contributes to the success of the company and each has needs they wish to satisfy as their reason for joining in the partnership.

Customers need and are willing to pay for food or TVs or tax advice. For this, they want value. *Shareholders* have a capital surplus which they are willing to invest. For this, they want a return sufficient to cover their risk. *Employees* have knowledge and skills and are willing to work. For this, they want satisfaction of needs that span the whole Maslow hierarchy from survival to service. *Suppliers* have goods and services for sale for which they want payment and a continuing relationship. *Communities* need employment for their citizens and are willing to provide the necessary physical, societal and economic infrastructure. System 5 holds that the business should be managed in a way that *balances* this galaxy of inputs and outputs. So the planning process should include this criteria of balance. If managers would apply themselves diligently to discovering the needs of all five constituents, we would see real meaning begin to surface and guide businesses and the world of work.

For me, this idea has powerful possibilities beyond our imagination. Management must occupy a position in the center of this model and manage the partnership. Management must provide the leadership that will enable all partners to understand and support the full partnership. If management tips the balance to any one partner, all other partners suffer. Currently, we are seeing an imbalance toward shareholders driven by pressures from Wall Street and the big investment firms. Every authority I can find agrees that quarterly financial reports and pressure for short-term performance is hurting business. I think this partnership orientation to planning is a way to restore the system to balance, and the way to put real meaning into the world of work. It would certainly be more just and I believe a very sound long-term business strategy. A partnership planning process would give the business a much healthier strategic perspective: that for the business to grow it must meet the needs of all partners. A business that fails to meet the needs of one partner risks the withdrawal of that partner's contribution and ultimately the survival of the business. For instance, when a business fails to meet the legitimate needs of its workers, we see a decline in performance and customer service, followed by a decline in sales and profit. This then reduces the ability of the business to serve shareholders, suppliers and the community.

A business that satisfies all partners will be able to attract a greater contribution from all partners, which causes the business to grow. A management team that creates a culture where all of the partners are actively looking for ways to serve one another may very well discover the most powerful motivational force ever seen in business. I believe this approach, which John seemed to follow intuitively, to be one of the causes of the 90 year success of the Donnelly Corporation.

These are some of the ideas I have developed from the legacy I received from John Donnelly. I invite you to consider this rich legacy and help expand this important frontier. We must continue to refine the practices and techniques of business leadership just as we must continue to develop new products and technologies. But I am convinced that we won't fully solve the human problem of people at work unless and until we, like John Donnelly, choose servant leadership, servant management, and servant business practices.

A Man of Transactions

Terrence Rafferty

Steven Spielberg's "Schindler's List" is a great movie, and, like all great works, it feels both impossible and inevitable. In the opening pages of the 1982 book (of the same name) on which the film is based, the author, Thomas Keneally, tells the reader, "This is the story of the pragmatic triumph of good over evil, a triumph in eminently measurable, statistical, unsubtle terms," and then confesses to an odd sort of trepidation: "It is a risky enterprise to have to write of virtue." The writer's admission is staggering, because "Schindler's List" is a true story about the Holocaust: you would think that an artist who has taken on the task of portraying that unimaginably monstrous event wouldn't consider the representation of virtue his most daunting challenge. But the story of Oskar Schindler—a dashing and resourceful German Catholic business-man who saved over a thousand Polish Jews from almost certain anni-hilation—is extraordinary even by the standards of Holocaust literature, in which every kind of human behavior *except* the merely ordinary can be found. And, in a sense, Schindler's goodness really is more mysteri-ous—tougher to account for intellectually—than the Nazis' evil, because his actions seem not to have been determined by anything resembling a conscious political, religious, or social principle. He wasn't an idealist (much less an ideologue), but he took the sort of risks that a fanatic or a willful martyr might take, and never troubled to explain himself. According to Keneally, many of the people Schindler rescued still say, "I don't know why he did it."

The triumph of the book is that Keneally's faithful, exhaustively detailed chronicle of Schindler's wartime activities never fully answers the question "Why?" and, besides, persuades us that it would be foolish to try: heroism of this magnitude is, at its heart, inexplicable. Spielberg also respects the mystery of Schindler's personality, and part of what makes the film so moving is that an ambiguous, complex hero is some-thing entirely new in this director's work. The sheer unexpectedness of Spielberg's rigorous refusal to simplify his protagonist's motives seems to connect him, in a minor but distinct way, to Schindler himself; this

458

character is, after all, a man whose dedication and commitment to right-eous action simply could not have been predicted from the evidence of his prewar life. That's the beauty of the story. What Schindler does dur-ing the years of Nazi oppression appears to constitute a kind of self-transcendence, but it's really more like an improbable self-fulfillment: in the unique, deranged circumstances of occupied Poland, his short-comings, and even his vices, somehow turn into instruments of virtue.

Spielberg introduces Schindler with a scene of his preparations for an evening out in Kraków. Before we're shown the hero's face, we see his elegant clothes and the swastika pin that gleams in his lapel. Schindler (Liam Neeson) arrives at a swank night club filled with Nazi officials and expensively dressed women, and looks as if he were right at home. He's handsome, confident, and worldly—the very image of the man of affairs. It doesn't take him long to become the center of attention: he drinks and laughs with the Nazis, and appears to be having the time of his life. The only hint that there might be something unusual about this prosperous-looking backslapper is provided by a handful of closeups of Schindler's watchful face in the moments just before he moves in on the Nazis. He gazes at them coldly, clinically, and it's impossible to tell whether the look in his eyes reflects deep-seated disdain or merely the pragmatic attitude of a businessman plotting his social tactics as he pre-pares to initiate a potentially advantageous contact. The uncertainty about the protagonist's character which Spielberg creates in this superbly directed sequence establishes the tone of the movie's treatment of Schindler, and, precarious as it is, it's precisely the right tone. Schindler, having failed at several businesses in Germany, has come to Kraków with the intention of making some easy money in the wartime economy. Poland, he feels, offers tremendous opportunities for some-one like him—an energetic entrepreneur who knows how to get things done and isn't burdened by an overscrupulous sense of business ethics. The best opportunities, of course, have been created by the Reich's sys-tematic destruction of the Jewish community, and in the film's first hour we see Schindler, apparently without qualms, buying a Jewish-owned factory for next to nothing, staffing it entirely with Jewish workers (because their labor costs far less than that of Polish Gentiles), and tak-ing possession of a large, airy apartment vacated by a family that has been forced to move into the city's ghetto. And in these swift and some-times darkly funny early passages Spielberg gives us glimpses of several other somewhat unsavory aspects of Schindler's character: the movie's hero, we learn, is also an enthusiastic participant in the city's black market and an inveterate philanderer. (His wife has remained in their prewar home, in Moravia, and, prudently, doesn't pay him many visits while he's in Poland.)

Schindler, nestled in a fur-collared coat, strides through this ugly world with a curious air of innocence. He's a war profiteer, but he obviously sees no harm in the way he's making his fortune. He treats the workers at his factory, which makes pots and pans for the German Army, reasonably well, and although they're basically slave labor, their employment provides them some tangible benefit: they can be considered essential to the war effort, and therefore (they hope) a little less likely to be deported to a concentration camp. Schindler is the sort of wheeler-dealer who closes even his most outrageous business propositions with a cheerful "And everybody's happy!"—and seems to actually mean it. The grotesque disparity in the degrees of "happiness" enjoyed by the Nazi occupiers and his Jewish employees doesn't appear to trouble him much; he's not gifted with a keen sense of irony. And, besides, he's just an entrepreneurial capitalist, doing what such men have always done—making money according to the conditions of whatever social system happens to obtain, without passing judgment on the system's fairness.

The hero's evolution from an unreflective profiteer to a conscious and daring rescuer of the Jews is portrayed, both in the book and in the film, with extraordinary subtlety. Keneally provides more detail, but Neeson's quietly brilliant performance makes up for the movie's elisions: this is nuanced and utterly unsentimental acting—exactly what the role requires. Schindler, who is no philosopher, never delivers the sort of high-minded speech that tells us how he made the decision to use his friendly relations with the Nazis for the purpose of resistance rather than of profit. A speech of that sort would violate the nature of Schindler's heroism, which is instinctual, unpremeditated; like a soldier in the heat of battle, he's just responding as quickly and as effectively as he can to the chaotic events around him.

In the movie, however, it's possible to identify a turning point in the hero's consciousness—not because Spielberg crudely signals a change but because he uses the resources of film so powerfully that we, in the audience, feel a profound transformation in our relation to the historical drama we're witnessing. About an hour into the film, Spielberg stages the liquidation of the Kraków ghetto, and in this turbulent and almost unbearably vivid fifteen-minute sequence, the Holocaust, fifty years removed from our contemporary consciousness, suddenly becomes overwhelmingly immediate, undeniable. Spielberg, using his prodigious visual skills with an urgency and an imaginative intensity that he hasn't shown in a long time, creates images that have the force of intimate experience, the terrible clarity of your own most indelible memories. Summary executions are performed, in chillingly objective medium shots, on Kraków's beautiful streets; the narrow corridors of the ghetto's tenements become nightmarishly claustrophobic as the Jewish families rousted out of their apartments try to move quickly enough to satisfy the armed, shooting S.S. men; flashes of machine-gun fire light up the dark stairwells; abandoned suitcases litter the alleys and courtyards; soldiers fire into the walls and ceilings, to dispose of anyone who might be hiding on the other side; thousands of Jews are herded brutally through the old city, and Schindler, watching from a hilltop, tries to track the progress of a little girl in a red coat as she makes her way, alone, through the smoke-filled streets. Sights like these make us feel—viscerally, and in the most concrete terms—the obscenity of the Reich's treatment of the Jews, and the strength of our own reactions tells us that this must be the moment in which amiable Oskar Schindler begins to entertain the idea of subverting the system that has enriched him.

For the rest of the film—which runs better than three hours and doesn't seem a minute too long—Schindler's cunning manipulations of high-level Nazis play out against the background of the increasingly horrific experiences of Kraków's Jews. As the Final Solution gathers momentum, the people who survived the liquidation of the ghetto are sent to the Plaszów labor camp, and there they live under the constant threat of slow death from exhaustion or hunger, and of sudden, violent death at the hands of their captors: the camp's sadistic commandant, Amon Goeth, takes target practice from the balcony of his villa, picking off prisoners at random as they walk across the compound. Schindler puts his disreputable talents to good use, cozying up to the psychotic Goeth and bribing and cajoling him—one man of the world to another—into granting the businessman the most unlikely concessions. Not only is Schindler allowed to continue operating his factory, with the same workforce, but he obtains permission to turn the plant into a sub-camp and move "his" Jews onto its premises. And, late in the war, when deportations to the extermination camps are occurring at an accelerated rate, Schindler contrives to establish a new factory, in Czechoslovakia, and to have eleven hundred Jewish workers who were scheduled for transport to the camps diverted to his facility. He purchases the reprieve of each of the Jews on his list individually, out of his (rapidly dwindling) profits; and then he has to pay yet again, to liberate three hundred women who wind up, mistakenly, at Auschwitz-Birkeneau. "It was Oskar's nature," Keneally writes, "to believe that you could drink with the devil and adjust the balance of evil over a snifter of cognac. It was not that he found more radical methods frightening. It was that they did not occur to him. He'd always been a man of transactions."

The irony of Schindler's methods is that his temperamental indifference to ethical niceties is precisely what makes him an effective champion of the powerless Jews he employs. If he had been a more scrupulous man, he couldn't have done what he did. An idealist would never have dreamed, in the first place, of setting up a business to profit from the misfortune of the Polish Jews; and an idealist would have been sickened to the point of incapacity at having to spend so much time drinking and schmoozing with the likes of Amon Goeth. The people who work for Schindler are lucky to be under the protection of a man who combines the recklessness of a pirate and the oily mendacity of a confidence man; a Gandhi couldn't have served them nearly so well. What's genuinely inspiring about Schindler is that in one crucial respect he did diverge, spontaneously and unquestioningly, from his instincts as "a man of transactions": when his financial interests stopped coinciding with the single, urgent interest of his workers, which was survival, he chose to dedicate himself to *their* interest. By the end of the war, he had spent so much money implementing the ever more elaborate schemes necessary to save the Jews that he was totally wiped out. From the prospective of our own rapacious times, a businessman who values his workers' lives over his own profits seems almost inconceivably noble.

PART VI

Emerging Issues

My job as leader is to keep the five guys who hate me away from the five guys who haven't yet made up their mind.

Casey Stengal

Nice guys finish last.

Leo Durocher

Contrary to the cliche, genuinely nice guys most often finish first, or very near it.

Malcolm Forbes

Be awful nice to 'em goin' up, 'cause you're gonna meet 'em all comin' down.

Jimmy Durante

In our final section, we explore macro-level issues that impact on the process of leadership. The first article, by Geert Hofstede, considers how other cultures have different views of leadership and management. He asks us to consider how our Westernized models may be of limited value in understanding social dynamics in other cultures and offers a model in which cultural dimensions can be categorized in order to explain differences we might observe. The following article, by Clayton Smith and Robert Vecchio, examines the topic of organizational culture and suggests that organizational culture influences the process of organizational strategic management by influencing leader perception, interpretation, and response to the external environment. Mary Zalesny and Robert Vecchio, in the next reading, consider factors that affect technological change in an organization and specifically examine the key role played by supervisors in impeding or facilitating change.

Women and minorities are entering leadership positions in increasing numbers. Ann Morrison of the Center for Creative Leadership and Mary Ann Von Glinow of Florida International University review this trend and examine reasons why women and minorities face a "glass ceiling" that limits their advancement into the highest levels of top management.

The experience of extreme emotion at work is a relatively new and important topic which has been neglected in the past. In the article "It's Not Easy Being Green," Robert Vecchio reviews the sparse information on jealousy and envy in the workplace and offers specific techniques for managing negative emotion at work. While extreme negative emotion is readily recognized as a potential source of problems at work, it is sometimes forgotten that extreme positive emotion at work can also be a source of difficulties.

Cultural Constraints in Management Theories

Geert Hofstede

Lewis Carroll's *Alice in Wonderland* contains the famous story of Alice's croquet game with the Queen of Hearts.

Alice thought she had never seen such a curious croquet-ground in all her life; it was all ridges and furrows; the balls were live hedgehogs, the mallets live flamingoes, and the soldiers had to double themselves up and to stand on their hands and feet, to make the arches.

You probably know how the story goes: Alice's flamingo mallet turns its head whenever she wants to strike with it; her hedgehog ball runs away; and the doubled-up soldier arches walk around all the time. The only rule seems to be that the Queen of Hearts always wins.

Alice's croquet playing problems are good analogies to attempts to build culture-free theories of management. Concepts available for this purpose are themselves alive with culture, having been developed within a particular cultural context. They have a tendency to guide our thinking toward our desired conclusion.

As the same reasoning may also be applied to the arguments in this article, I better tell you my conclusion before I continue—so that the rules of my game are understood. In this article we take a trip around the world to demonstrate that there are no such things as universal management theories.

Diversity in management *practices* as we go around the world has been recognized in U.S. management literature for more than thirty years. The term "comparative management" has been used since the 1960s. However, it has taken much longer for the U.S. academic community to accept that not only practices but also the validity of *theories* may stop at national borders, and I wonder whether even today everybody would agree with this statement.

An article I published in *Organizational Dynamics* in 1980 entitled "Do American Theories Apply Abroad?" created more controversy than I expected. The article argued, with empirical support, that generally accepted U.S. theories like those of Maslow, Herzberg, McClelland, Vroom, McGregor, Likert, Blake and Mouton may not or only very partly apply outside the borders of their country of origin—assuming they do apply within those borders. Among the requests for reprints, a larger number were from Canada than from the United States.

MANAGEMENT THEORISTS ARE HUMAN

Employees and managers are human. Employees as humans was "discovered" in the 1930s, with the Human Relations school. Managers as humans, was introduced in the late 40s by Herbert Simon's "bounded rationality" and elaborated in Richard Cyert and James March's *Behavioral Theory of the Firm* (1963, and recently re-published in a second edition). My argument is that management scientists, theorists, and writers are human too: they grew up in a particular society in a particular period, and their ideas cannot help but reflect the constraints of their environment.

The idea that the validity of a theory is constrained by national borders is more obvious in Europe, with all its borders, than in a huge borderless country like the U.S. Already in the sixteenth century Michel de Montaigne, a Frenchman, wrote a statement which was made famous by Blaise Pascal about a century later: *"Vérite en-deça des Pyrenées, erreur au-delà"* —There are truths on this side of the Pyrenées which are falsehoods on the other.

FROM DON ARMADO'S LOVE TO TAYLOR'S SCIENCE

According to the comprehensive ten-volume Oxford English Dictionary (1971), the words "manage," "management," and "manager" appeared in the English language in the 16th century. The oldest recorded use of the word "manager" is in Shakespeare's "Love's Labour's Lost," dating from 1588, in which Don Adriano de Armado, "a fantastical Spaniard," exclaims (Act I, scene ii, 188):

"Adieu, valour! rust, rapier! be still, drum! for your manager is in love; yea, he loveth".

The linguistic origin of the word is from Latin *manus*, hand, via the Italian *maneggiare*, which is the training of horses in the *manege;* subsequently its meaning was extended to skillful handling in general, like of arms and musical instruments, as Don Armado illustrates. However, the word also became associated with the French *menage,* household, as an equivalent of "husbandry" in its sense of the art of running a household. The theatre of present-day management contains elements of both *manege* and *menage* and different managers and cultures may use different accents.

The founder of the science of economics, the Scot Adam Smith, in his 1776 book *The Wealth of Nations*, used "manage," "management" (even "bad management") and "manager" when dealing with the process and the persons involved in operating joint stock companies (Smith, V., i.e.). British economist John Stuart Mill (1806–1873) followed Smith in this use and clearly expressed his distrust of such hired people who were not driven by ownership. Since the 1880s the word "management" appeared occasionally in writings by American engineers, until it was canonized as a modern science by Frederick W. Taylor in *Shop Management* in 1903 and in *The Principles of Scientific Management* in 1911.

While Smith and Mill used "management" to describe a process and "managers" for the persons involved, "management" in the American sense—which has since been taken back by the British—refers not only to the process but also to the managers as a class of people. This class (1) does not own a business but sells its skills to act on behalf of the owners and (2) does not produce personally but is indispensable for making others produce, through motivation. Members of this class carry a high status and many American boys and girls aspire to the role. In the U.S., the manager is a cultural hero.

Let us now turn to other parts of the world. We will look at management in its context in other successful modern economies: Germany, Japan, France, Holland, and among the Overseas Chinese. Then we will examine management in the much larger part of the world that is still poor, especially South-East Asia and Africa, and in the new political configurations of Eastern Europe, and Russia in particular. We will then return to the U.S. via mainland China.

Germany

The manager is not a cultural hero in Germany. If anybody, it is the engineer who fills the hero role. Frederick Taylor's *Scientific Manage-*

ment was conceived in a society of immigrants—where a large number of workers with diverse backgrounds and skills had to work together. In Germany this heterogeneity never existed.

Elements of the mediaeval guild system have survived in historical continuity in Germany until the present day. In particular, a very effective apprenticeship system exists both on the shop floor and in the office, which alternates practical work and classroom courses. At the end of the apprenticeship the worker receives a certificate, the *Facharbeiterbrief*, which is recognized throughout the country. About two thirds of the German worker population holds such a certificate and a corresponding occupational pride. In fact, quite a few German company presidents have worked their way up from the ranks through an apprenticeship. In comparison, two thirds of the worker population in Britain have no occupational qualification at all.

The highly skilled and responsible German workers do not necessarily need a manager, American-style, to "motivate" them. They expect their boss or *Meister* to assign their tasks and to be the expert in resolving technical problems. Comparisons of similar German, British, and French organizations show the Germans as having the highest rate of personnel in productive roles and the lowest both in leadership and staff roles.

Business schools are virtually unknown in Germany. Native German management theories concentrate on formal systems. The inapplicability of American concepts of management was quite apparent in 1973 when the U.S. consulting firm of Booz, Allen and Hamilton, commissioned by the German Ministry of Economic Affairs, wrote a study of German management from an American view point. The report is highly critical and writes among other things that "Germans simply do not have a very strong concept of management." Since 1973, from my personal experience, the situation has not changed much. However, during this period the German economy has performed in a superior fashion to the U.S. in virtually all respects, so a strong concept of management might have been a liability rather than an asset.

Japan

The American type of manager is also missing in Japan. In the United States, the core of the enterprise is the managerial class. The core of the Japanese enterprise is the permanent worker group; workers who for all practical purposes are tenured and who aspire at life-long employment. They are distinct from the non-permanent employees—most women and subcontracted teams led by gang bosses, to be laid off in slack periods. University graduates in Japan first join the permanent worker group and subsequently fill various positions, moving from line to staff as the need occurs while paid according to seniority rather than position. They take part in Japanese-style group consultation sessions for important decisions, which extend the decision-making period but guarantee fast implementation afterwards. Japanese are to a large extent controlled by their peer group rather than by their manager.

Three researchers from the East-West Center of the University of Hawaii, Joseph Tobin, David Wu, and Dana Danielson, did an observation study of typical preschools in three countries: China, Japan, and the United States. Their results have been published both as a book and as a video. In the Japanese preschool, one teacher handled twenty-eight four-year olds. The video shows one particularly obnoxious boy, Hiroki, who fights with other children and throws teaching materials down from the balcony. When a little girl tries to alarm the teacher, the latter answers "What are you calling me for? Do something about it!" In the U.S. preschool, there is one adult for every nine children. This class has its problem child too, Glen, who refuses to clear away his toys. One of the teachers has a long talk with him and isolates him in a corner, until he changes his mind. It doesn't take much imagination to realize that managing Hiroki thirty years later will be a different process from managing Glen.

American theories of leadership are ill-suited for the Japanese group-controlled situation. During the past two decades, the Japanese have developed their own "PM" theory of leadership, in which P stands for performance and M for maintenance. The latter is less a concern for individual employees than for maintaining social stability. In view of the amazing success of the Japanese economy in the past thirty years, many Americans have sought for the secrets of Japanese management hoping to copy them.

France

The manager, U.S. style, does not exist in France either. In a very enlightening book, unfortunately not yet translated into English, the French researcher Philippe d'Iribarne (1989) describes the results of in-depth observation and interview studies of management methods in three subsidiary plants of the same French multinational: in France, the United States, and Holland. He relates what he finds to information about the three societies in general. Where necessary, he goes back in history to trace the roots of the strikingly different behaviors in the completion of the same tasks. He identifies three kinds of basic principles (*logiques*) of management. In the USA, the principle is the *fair contract* between employer and employee, which gives the manager considerable prerogatives, but within its limits. This is really a labor *market* in which the worker sells his or her labor for a price. In France, the principle is the *honor* of each class in a society which has always been and remains extremely stratified, in which superiors behave as superior beings and subordinates accept and expect this, conscious of their own lower level in the national hierarchy but also of the honor of their own class. The French do not think in terms of managers versus nonmanagers but in terms of *cadres* versus *non-cadres;* one becomes cadre by attending the proper schools and one remains it forever; regardless of their actual task, cadres have the privileges of a higher social class, and it is very rare for a non-cadre to cross the ranks.

The conflict between French and American theories of management became apparent in the beginning of the twentieth century, in a criticism by the great French management pioneer Henri Fayol (1841–1925) on his U.S. colleague and contemporary Frederick W. Taylor (1856–1915). The difference in career paths of the two men is striking. Fayol was a French engineer whose career as a *cadre supérieur* culminated in the position of Président-Directeur-Général of a mining company. After his retirement he formulated his experiences in a pathbreaking text on organization: *Administration industrielle et générale*, in which he focussed on the sources of authority. Taylor was an American engineer who started his career in industry as a worker and attained his academic qualifications through evening studies. From chief engineer in a steel company he became one of the first management consultants. Taylor was not really concerned with the issue of authority at all; his focus was on efficiency. He proposed to split the task of the first-line boss into eight specialisms, each exercised by a different person; an idea which eventually led to the idea of a matrix organization.

Taylor's work appeared in a French translation in 1913, and Fayol read it and showed himself generally impressed but shocked by Taylor's "denial of the principle of the Unity of Command" in the case of the eight-boss-system.

Seventy years later André Laurent, another of Fayol's compatriots, found that French managers in a survey reacted very strongly against a suggestion that one employee could report to two different bosses, while U.S. managers in the same survey showed fewer misgivings. Matrix organization has never become popular in France as it has in the United States.

Holland

In my own country, Holland or as it is officially called, the Netherlands, the study by Philippe d'Iribarne found the management principle to be a need for *consensus* among all parties, neither predetermined by a contractual relationship nor by class distinctions, but based on an open-ended exchange of views and a balancing of interests. In terms of the different origins of the word "manager," the organization in Holland is more *menage* (household), while in the United States it is more *manege* (horse drill).

At my university, the University of Limburg at Maastricht, every semester we receive a class of American business students who take a program in European Studies. We asked both the Americans and a matched group of Dutch students to describe their ideal job after graduation, using a list of twenty-two job characteristics. The Americans attached significantly more importance than the Dutch to earnings, advancement, benefits, a good working relationship with their boss, and security of employment. The Dutch attached more importance to freedom to adopt their own approach to the job, being consulted by their boss in his or her decisions, training opportunities, contributing to the success of their organization, fully using their skills and abilities, and helping others. This list confirms d'Iribarne's findings of a contractual employment relationship in the United States, based on earnings and career opportunities, against a consensual relationship in Holland. The latter has centuries-old roots; the Netherlands were the first republic in Western Europe (1609–1810), and a model for the American republic. The country has been and still is governed by a careful balancing of interests in a multi-party system.

In terms of management theories, both motivation and leadership in Holland are different from what they are in the United States. Leadership in Holland presupposes modesty, as opposed to assertiveness in the United States. No U.S. leadership theory has room for that. Working in Holland is not a constant feast, however. There is a built-in premium on mediocrity and jealousy, as well as time-consuming ritual consultations to maintain the appearance of consensus and the pretense of modesty. There is unfortunately another side to every coin.

The Overseas Chinese

Among the champions of economic development in the past thirty years we find three countries mainly populated by Chinese living outside the Chinese mainland: Taiwan, Hong Kong and Singapore. Moreover, overseas Chinese play a very important role in the economies of Indonesia, Malaysia, the Philippines and Thailand, where they form an ethnic minority. If anything, the little dragons—Taiwan, Hong Kong and Singapore—have been more economically successful than Japan, moving from rags to riches and now counted among the world's wealthy industrial countries. Yet very little attention has been paid to the way in which their enterprises have been managed. *The Spirit of Chinese Capitalism* by Gordon Redding (1990), the British dean of the Hong Kong Business School, is an excellent book about Chinese business. He bases his insights on personal acquaintance and in-depth discussions with a large number of overseas Chinese businesspeople.

Overseas Chinese American enterprises lack almost all characteristics of modern management. They tend to be small, cooperating for essential functions with other small organizations through networks based on personal relations. They are family-owned, without the separation between ownership and management typical in the West, or even in Japan and Korea. They normally focus on one product or market, with growth by opportunistic diversification; in this, they are extremely flexible. Decision making is centralized in the hands of one dominant family member, but other family members may be given new ventures to try their skills on. They are low-profile and extremely cost-conscious, applying Confucian virtues of thrift and persistence. Their size is kept small by the assumed lack of loyalty of non-family employees, who, if they are any good, will just wait and save until they can start their own family business.

Overseas Chinese prefer economic activities in which great gains can be made with little manpower, like commodity trading and real estate.

They employ few professional managers, except their sons and sometimes daughters who have been sent to prestigious business schools abroad, but who upon return continue to run the family business the Chinese way.

The origin of this system, or—in the Western view—this lack of system, is found in the history of Chinese society, in which there were no formal laws, only formal networks of powerful people guided by general principles of Confucian virtue. The favors of the authorities could change daily, so nobody could be trusted except one's kinfolk—of whom, fortunately, there used to be many, in an extended family structure. The overseas Chinese way of doing business is also very well adapted to their position in the countries in which they form ethnic minorities, often envied and threatened by ethnic violence.

Overseas Chinese businesses following this unprofessional approach command a collective gross national product of some 200 to 300 billion US dollars, exceeding the GNP of Australia. There is no denying that it works.

MANAGEMENT TRANSFER TO POOR COUNTRIES

Four-fifths of the world population live in countries that are not rich but poor. After World War II and decolonization, the stated purpose of the United Nations and the World Bank has been to promote the development of all the world's countries in a war on poverty. After forty years it looks very much like we are losing this war. If one thing has become clear, it is that the export of Western—mostly American—management practices *and* theories to poor countries has contributed little to nothing to their development. There has been no lack of effort and money spent for this purpose: students from poor countries have been trained in this country, and teachers and Peace Corps workers have been sent to the poor countries. If nothing else, the general lack of success in economic development of other countries should be sufficient argument to doubt the validity of Western management theories in non-Western environments.

If we examine different parts of the world, the development picture is not equally bleak, and history is often a better predictor than economic factors for what happens today. There is a broad regional pecking order with East Asia leading. The little dragons have passed into the camp of the wealthy; then follow South-East Asia (with its overseas Chinese minorities), Latin America (in spite of the debt crisis), South Asia, and Africa always trails behind. Several African countries have only become poorer since decolonization.

Regions of the world with a history of large-scale political integration and civilization generally have done better than regions in which no large-scale political and cultural infrastructure existed, even if the old civilations had decayed or been suppressed by colonizers. It has become painfully clear that development cannot be pressure-cooked; it presumes a cultural infrastructure that takes time to grow. Local management is part of this infrastructure; it cannot be imported in package form. Assuming that with so-called modern management techniques and theories outsiders can develop a country has proven a deplorable arrogance. At best, one can hope for a dialogue between equals with the locals, in which the Western partner acts as the expert in Western technology and the local partner as the expert in local culture, habits, and feelings.

Russia and China

The crumbling of the former Eastern bloc has left us with a scattering of states and would-be states of which the political and economic future is extremely uncertain. The best predictions are those based on a knowledge of history, because historical trends have taken revenge on the arrogance of the Soviet rulers who believed they could turn them around by brute power. One obvious fact is that the former bloc is extremely heterogeneous, including countries traditionally closely linked with the West by trade and travel, like Czechia, Hungary, Slovenia, and the Baltic states, as well as others with a Byzantine or Turkish past; some having been prosperous, others always extremely poor.

Let me limit myself to the Russian republic, a huge territory with some 140 million inhabitants, mainly Russians. We know quite a bit about the Russians as their country was a world power for several hundreds of years before communism, and in the nineteenth century it has produced some of the greatest writers in world literature. If I want to understand the Russians—including how they could so long support the Soviet regime—I tend to re-read Lev Nikolayevich Tolstoy. In his most famous novel, *Anna Karenina* (1876), one of the main characters is a landowner, Levin, whom Tolstoy uses to express his own views and convictions about his people. Russian peasants used to be serfs; serfdom had been abolished in 1861, but the peasants, now tenants, remained as passive as before. Levin wanted to break this passivity by dividing the land among his peasants in exchange for a share of the crops; but the peasants only let the land deteriorate further. Here follows a quote:

"(Levin) read political economy and socialistic works . . . but, as he had expected, found nothing in them related to his undertaking. In the political economy books—in (John Stuart) Mill, for instance, whom he studied first and with great ardour, hoping every minute to find an answer to the questions that were engrossing him—he found only certain laws deduced from the state of agriculture in Europe; but he could not for the life of him see why these laws, which did not apply to Russia, should be considered universal. . . . Political economy told him that the laws by which Europe had developed and was developing her wealth were universal and absolute. Socialist teaching told him that development along those lines leads to ruin. And neither of them offered the smallest enlightenment as to what he, Levin, and all the Russian peasants and landowners were to do with their millions of hands and millions of acres, to make them as productive as possible for the common good."

In the summer of 1991, the Russian lands yielded a record harvest, but a large share of it rotted in the fields because no people were to be found for harvesting. The passivity is still there, and not only among the peasants. And the heirs of John Stuart Mill (whom we met before as one of the early analysts of "management") again present their universal recipes which simply do not apply.

Citing Tolstoy, I implicitly suggest that management theorists cannot neglect the great literature of the countries they want their ideas to apply to. The greatest novel in the Chinese literature is considered Cao Xueqin's *The Story of the Stone*, also known as *The Dream of the Red Chamber* which appeared around 1760. It describes the rise and fall of two branches of an aristocratic family in Beijing, who live in adjacent plots in the capital. Their plots are joined by a magnificent garden with several pavilions in it, and the young, mostly female members of both families are allowed to live in them. One day the management of the garden is taken over by a young woman, Tan-Chun, who states:

"I think we ought to pick out a few experienced trust-worthy old women from among the ones who work in the Garden—women who

know something about gardening already—and put the upkeep of the Garden into their hands. We needn't ask them to pay us rent, all we need ask them for is an annual share of the produce. There would be four advantages in this arrangement. In the first place, if we have people whose sole occupation is to look after trees and flowers and so on, the condition of the Garden will improve gradually year after year and there will be no more of those long periods of neglect followed by bursts of feverish activity when things have been allowed to get out of hand. Secondly there won't be the spoiling and wastage we get at present. Thirdly the women themselves will gain a little extra to add to their incomes which will compensate them for the hard work they put in throughout the year. And fourthly, there's no reason why we shouldn't use the money we should otherwise have spent on nurserymen, rockery specialists, horticultural cleaners and so on for other purposes."

As the story goes on, the capitalist privatization—because that is what it is—of the Garden is carried through, and it works. When in the 1980s Deng Xiaoping allowed privatization in the Chinese villages, it also worked. It worked so well that its effects started to be felt in politics and threatened the existing political order; hence the knockdown at Tienanmen Square of June 1989. But it seems that the forces of privatization are getting the upper hand again in China. If we remember what Chinese entrepreneurs are able to do once they have become Overseas Chinese, we shouldn't be too surprised. But what works in China—and worked two centuries ago—does not have to work in Russia, not in Tolstoy's days and not today. I am not offering a solution; I only protest against a naive universalism that knows only one recipe for development, the one supposed to have worked in the United States.

A THEORY OF CULTURE IN MANAGEMENT

Our trip around the world is over and we are back in the United States. What have we learned? There is something in all countries called "management," but its meaning differs to a larger or smaller extent from one country to the other, and it takes considerable historical and cultural insight into local conditions to understand its processes, philosophies, and problems. If already the word may mean so many different things, how can we expect one country's theories of management to apply abroad? One should be extremely careful in making this assumption, and test it before considering it proven. Management is not a phenomenon that can be isolated from other processes taking place in a society. During our trip around the world we saw that it interacts with what happens in the family, at school, in politics, and government. It is obviously also related to religion and to beliefs about science. Theories of management always had to be interdisciplinary, but if we cross national borders they should become more interdisciplinary than ever.

Cultural differences between nations can be, to some extent, described using first four, and now five, bipolar *dimensions*. The position of a country on these dimensions allows us to make some predictions on the way their society operates, including their management processes and the kind of theories applicable to their management.

As the word culture plays such an important role in my theory, let me give you my definition, which differs from some other very respectable definitions. Culture to me is *the collective programming of the mind which distinguishes one group or category of people from another.* In the part of my work I am referring to now, the category of people is the nation.

Culture is a *construct*, that means it is "not directly accessible to observation but inferable from verbal statements and other behaviors and useful in predicting still other observable and measurable verbal and nonverbal behavior." It should not be reified; it is an auxiliary concept that should be used as long it proves useful but bypassed where we can predict behaviors without it.

The same applies to the *dimensions* I introduced. They are constructs too that should not be reified. They do not "exist"; they are tools for analysis which may or may not clarify a situation. In my statistical analysis of empirical data the first four dimensions together explain forty-nine percent of the variance in the data. The other fifty-one percent remain specific to individual countries.

The first four dimensions were initially detected through a comparison of the values of similar people (employees and managers) in sixty-four national subsidiaries of the IBM Corporation. People working for the same multinational, but in different countries, represent very well-matched samples from the populations of their countries, similar in all respects except nationality.

The first dimension is labelled *Power Distance*, and it can be defined as the degree of inequality among people which the population of a country considers as normal: from relatively equal (that is, small power distance) to extremely unequal (large power distance). All societies are unequal, but some are more unequal than others.

The second dimension is labelled *Individualism*, and it is the degree to which people in a country prefer to act as individuals rather than as members of groups. The opposite of individualism can be called *Collectivism*, so collectivism is low individualism. The way I use the word it has no political connotations. In collectivist societies a child learns to respect the group to which it belongs, usually the family, and to differentiate between in-group members and out-group members (that is, all other people). When children grow up they remain members of their group, and they expect the group to protect them when they are in trouble. In return, they have to remain loyal to their group throughout life. In individualist societies, a child learns very early to think of itself as "I" instead of as part of "we". It expects one day to have to stand on its own feet and not to get protection from its group any more; and therefore it also does not feel a need for strong loyalty.

The third dimension is called *Masculinity* and its opposite pole *Femininity*. It is the degree to which tough values like assertiveness, performance, success and competition, which in nearly all societies are associated with the role of men, prevail over tender values like the quality of life, maintaining warm personal relationships, service, care for the weak, and solidarity, which in nearly all societies are more associated with women's roles. Women's roles differ from men's roles in all countries; but in tough societies, the differences are larger than in tender ones.

The fourth dimension is labelled *Uncertainty Avoidance*, and it can be defined as the degree to which people in a country prefer structured over unstructured situations. Structured situations are those in which there are clear rules as to how one should behave. These rules can be written down, but they can also be unwritten and imposed by tradition. In countries which score high on uncertainty avoidance, people tend to show more nervous energy, while in countries which score low, people are more easy-going. A (national) society with strong uncertainty avoidance can be called rigid; one with weak uncertainty avoidance, flexible. In countries where uncertainty avoidance is strong a feeling prevails of "what is different, is dangerous." In weak uncertainty avoidance societies, the feeling would rather be "what is different, is curious."

The fifth dimension was added on the basis of a study of the values of students in twenty-three countries carried out by Michael Harris Bond, a

Canadian working in Hong Kong. He and I had cooperated in another study of students' values which had yielded the same four dimensions as the IBM data. However, we wondered to what extent our common findings in two studies could be the effect of a Western bias introduced by the common Western background of the researchers: remember Alice's croquet game. Michael Bond resolved this dilemma by deliberately introducing an Eastern bias. He used a questionnaire prepared at his request by his Chinese colleagues, the *Chinese Value Survey* (CVS), which was translated from Chinese into different languages and answered by fifty male and fifty female students in each of twenty-three countries in all five continents. Analysis of the CVS data produced three dimensions significantly correlated with the three IBM dimensions of power distance, individualism, and masculinity. There was also a fourth dimension, but it did not resemble uncertainty avoidance. It was composed, both on the positive and on the negative side, from items that had not been included in the IBM studies but were present in the Chinese Value Survey because they were rooted in the teachings of Confucius. I labelled this dimension: *Long-term* versus *Short-term Orientation*. On the long-term side one finds values oriented towards the future, like thrift (saving) and persistence. On the short-term side one finds values rather oriented towards the past and present, like respect for tradition and fulfilling social obligations.

Table 1 lists the scores on all five dimensions for the United States and for the other countries we just discussed. The table shows that each country has its own configuration on the four dimensions. Some of the values in the table have been estimated based on imperfect replications or personal impressions. The different dimension scores do not "explain" all the differences in management I described earlier. To understand management in a country, one should have both knowledge of and empathy with the entire local scene. However, the scores should make us aware that people in other countries may think, feel, and act very differently from us when confronted with basic problems of society.

IDIOSYNCRACIES OF AMERICAN MANAGEMENT THEORIES

In comparison to other countries, the U.S. culture profile presents itself as below average on power distance and uncertainty avoidance, highly individualistic, fairly masculine, and short-term oriented. The

Table 1

Culture Dimension Scores for Ten Countries

PD = Power Distance; ID = Individualism; MA = Masculinity; UA = Uncertainty
Avoidance; LT = Long Term Orientation; H = top third, M = medium third,
L = bottom third (among 53 countries and regions for the first four dimensions;
among 23 countries for the fifth)

	PD	ID	MA	UA	LT
USA	40 L	91 H	62 H	46 L	29 L
Germany	35 L	67 H	66 H	65 M	31 M
Japan	54 M	46 M	95 H	92 H	80 H
France	68 H	71 H	43 M	86 H	30*L
Netherlands	38 L	80 H	14 L	53 M	44 M
Hong Kong	68 H	25 L	57 H	29 L	96 H
Indonesia	78 H	14 L	46 M	48 L	25*L
West Africa	77 H	20 L	46 M	54 M	16 L
Russia	95*H	50*M	40*L	90*H	10*L
China	80*H	20*L	50*M	60*M	118 H

* estimated

Germans show a stronger uncertainty avoidance and less extreme individualism; the Japanese are different on all dimensions, least on power distance; the French show larger power distance and uncertainty avoidance, but are less individualistic and somewhat feminine; the Dutch resemble the Americans on the first three dimensions, but score extremely feminine and relatively long-term oriented; Hong Kong Chinese combine large power distance with weak uncertainty avoidance, collectivism, and are very long-term oriented, and so on.

The American culture profile is reflected in American management theories. I will just mention three elements not necessarily present in other countries: the stress on market processes, the stress on the individual, and the focus on managers rather than on workers.

The Stress on Market Processes

During the 1970s and 80s it has become fashionable in the United States to look at organizations from a "transaction costs" viewpoint. Economist Oliver Williamson has opposed "hierarchies" to "markets." The reasoning is that human social life consists of economic transactions between individuals. We found the same in d'Iribarne's description of the U.S. principle of the contract between employer and employee, the labor market in which the worker sells his or her labor for a price. These individuals will form hierarchical organizations when the cost of the economic transactions (such as getting information, finding out whom to trust, etc.) is lower in a hierarchy than when all transactions would take place in a free market.

From a cultural perspective the important point is that *the "market" is the point of departure or base model*, and the organization is explained from market failure. A culture that produces such a theory is likely to prefer organizations that internally resemble markets to organizations that internally resemble more structured models, like those in Germany or France. The ideal principle of control in organizations in the market philosophy is *competition* between individuals. This philosophy fits a society that combines a not-too-large power distance with a not-too-strong uncertainty avoidance and individualism; besides the USA, it will fit all other Anglo countries.

The Stress on the Individual

I find this constantly in the design of research projects and hypotheses; also in the fact that in the U.S. psychology is clearly a more respectable discipline in management circles than sociology. Culture however is a collective phenomenon. Although we may get our information about culture from individuals, we have to interpret it at the level of collectivities. There are snags here known as the "ecological fallacy" and the "reverse ecological fallacy." None of the U.S. college textbooks on methodology I know deals sufficiently with the problem of multi-level analysis.

A striking example is found in the otherwise excellent book *Organizational Culture and Leadership* by Edgar H. Schein (1985). On the basis of his consulting experience he compares two large companies, nicknamed "Action" and "Multi." He explains the differences in culture between these companies by the group dynamics in their respective boardrooms. Nowhere in the book are any conclusions drawn from the fact that the first company is an American-based computer firm, and the second a Swiss-based pharmaceutics firm. This information is not even mentioned. A stress on interactions among individuals obviously fits a culture identified as the most individualistic in the world, but it will not be so well understood by the four-fifths of the world population for whom the group prevails over the individual.

One of the conclusions of my own multilevel research has been that culture at the national level and culture at the organizational level—corporate culture—are two very different phenomena and that the use of a common term for both is confusing. If we do use the common term, we should also pay attention to the occupational and the gender level of culture. National cultures differ primarily in the fundamental, invisible values held by a majority of their members, acquired in early childhood, whereas organizational cultures are a much more superficial phenomenon residing mainly in the visible practices of the organization, acquired by socialization of the new members who join as young adults. National cultures change only very slowly if at all; organizational cultures may be consciously changed, although this isn't necessarily easy. This difference between the two types of culture is the secret of the existence of multinational corporations that employ, as I showed in the IBM case, employees with extremely different national cultural values. What keeps them together is a corporate culture based on common practices.

The Stress on Managers Rather than Workers

The core element of a work organization around the world is the people who do the work. All the rest is superstructure, and I hope to have demonstrated to you that it may take many different shapes. In the U.S. literature on work organization, however, the core element, if not explicitly then implicitly, is considered the manager. This may well be the result of the combination of extreme individualism with fairly strong masculinity, which has turned the manager into a culture hero of almost mythical proportions. For example, he—not really she—is supposed to make decisions all the time. Those of you who are or have been managers must know that this is a fable. Very few management decisions are just "made" as the myth suggests it. Managers are much more involved in maintaining networks; if anything, it is the rank-and-file worker who can really make decisions on his or her own, albeit on a relatively simple level.

An amusing effect of the U.S. focus on managers is that in at least ten American books and articles on management I have been misquoted as having studied IBM *managers* in my research, whereas the book clearly describes that the answers were from IBM *employees*. My observation may be biased, but I get the impression that compared to twenty or thirty years ago less research in this country is done among employees and more on managers. But managers derive their *raison d'être* from the people managed: culturally, they are the followers of the people they lead, and their effectiveness depends on the latter. In other parts of the world, this exclusive focus on the manager is less strong, with Japan as the supreme example.

CONCLUSION

This article started with *Alice in Wonderland*. In fact, the management theorist who ventures outside his or her own country into other parts of the world is like Alice in Wonderland. He or she will meet strange beings, customs, ways of organizing or disorganizing and theories that are clearly stupid, old-fashioned or even immoral—yet they may work, or at least they may not fail more frequently than corresponding theories do at home. Then, after the first culture shock, the traveller to Wonderland will feel enlightened, and may be able to take his or her experiences home and use them advantageously. All great ideas in science, politics and management have travelled from one country to another, and been enriched by foreign influences. The roots of American management theories are mainly in Europe: with Adam Smith, John Stuart Mill, Lev Tolstoy, Max Weber, Henri Fayol, Sigmund Freud, Kurt Lewin and many others. These theories were re-planted here and they developed and bore fruit. The same may happen again. The last thing we need is a Monroe doctrine for management ideas.

Organizational Culture and Strategic Leadership: Issues in the Management of Strategic Change

Clayton G. Smith and Robert P. Vecchio

The concept of organizational culture is certainly not new. The successes of many companies are frequently attributed to their cultures (or to similar terms, such as climate). Likewise, the failure of mergers is often explained in terms of the difficulties of marrying two business organizations with differing cultures (Chatterjee et al., 1992). But while it is generally accepted that organizations may be described in cultural terms, the foundations of organizational culture have proven to be somewhat elusive (Sackmann, 1992). Further, the ways in which organizational culture influences the effectiveness of an organization are not fully understood. As will be discussed below, an organization's culture can greatly influence its strategic management processes—both in terms of the options that are generated in the formation of strategy, and in how effectively a given strategy is implemented.

In this article, we explore the construct of organizational culture and relate it to the process of strategic management. Following an overview of the concept of organizational culture and its significance, a framework is proposed for analyzing the culture of an organization. Six central elements of organizational culture are identified and discussed: (a) critical decisions of founding members, (b) guiding ideas, (c) social structure, (d) norms, values, and premises, (e) remembered history and symbolism, and (f) institutionalized arrangements. The issue of how culture influences the ability of an established company to institute effective strategic change is then considered.

ORGANIZATIONAL CULTURE AND ASSESSMENTS OF "WHAT WORKS"

In the collective literatures of anthropology, sociology, and social psychology, many definitions of the term "culture" can be found. Social psychologists Krech et al. defined culture as:

> . . . the pattern of all those arrangements, material and behavioral, which have been adopted by a society as the traditional ways of solving problems of its members. Culture includes all the institutionalized ways and the implicit cultural beliefs, norms, values, and premises which underlie and govern conduct (1962: 380).

And according to anthropologist C. S. Ford,

> Culture is composed of responses which have been accepted because they have met with success (as quoted in Kroeber and Kluckhohn, 1952: 55).

Similarly, the core of an organization's culture is composed of the norms[1] and the shared values[2] and premises (taken-for-granted assumptions) of its members (Schein, 1984; Smircich, 1983; Wiener, 1988). Norms, values, and premises are reflected in the informal systems that emerge within the company over time—the habits and routines that develop, and the unwritten understandings that people gain about "how business gets done around here," and "what it's like out there." As discussed below, norms, values, and premises are also reflected in the firm's institutionalized arrangements, which include formal management systems (measurement and reward systems, information systems, planning systems, and training systems, etc.), and written policies covering common situations that occur (Peters, 1980). Taken together, these aspects of an organization's culture result from the firm's accumulated experience, experience which gives rise to assessments about "what works" when handling problems concerning the organization and its environment.

Through organizational experience and the emergence of social processes, people develop common ways of interpreting events, and

---

[1] Norms are typically viewed as rules or standards that define what people should or should not do in given situations.

[2] A value is usually defined as a belief concerning what is good, right, wise, or beneficial.

attitudes about what is important and what actions should be taken under given conditions (Wilkins, 1979). This orientation provides members with an ordered approach to routine problems that arise—a way of responding to events according to approved perspectives. Moreover, the company's management systems and policies orient attention and decision making toward "important" issues and information. For example, reward systems gauge performance according to measures that are regarded as important (such as market share at Pepsico). Likewise, formal information systems communicate "valuable" information. In their operation, management systems and policies reinforce norms, values, and premises by directing and constraining the attention of individual members. And the decisions that are made by members "continually reaffirm the corporation's culture and reinforce expected behavior across the organization" (Schwartz and Davis, 1981: 35).

The orientation that develops helps to produce a homogeneous organization, which is a particularly important aid to communication; shared understandings facilitate the flow of information and the making of decisions. However, the cost of these commitments is a loss of creativity, flexibility, and adaptability. They tie the organization to traditional customers; they bind the company to established marketing practices and technologies; and they constrain the firm from altering long-standing patterns of resource allocation. Rooted in the authority of experience and, often, a history of success, organizational culture tends to be inertial (Tushman and Romanelli, 1985). While a company's culture can make the organization more livable, more orderly, and in important respects, stronger, it can also reduce the firm's capacity to adapt and survive under new conditions. Thus, it is important to understand how a firm develops and maintains a "culture," and how an established culture can influence the effectiveness of efforts to institute strategic change. It is to these issues that our focus now turns.

A FRAMEWORK OF ORGANIZATION CULTURE

In this section, a framework is developed for analyzing organizational culture and its foundations. Issues that were briefly introduced in the previous section are examined further, and other aspects of organizational culture are also developed. As shown in Figure 1, an organization's cul-

Figure 1
A Framework for Analyzing Organizational Culture

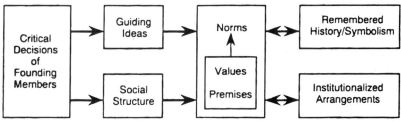

ture can be viewed in terms of a set of six central elements. Through an exploration of these elements, it is possible to gain an understanding of how an organization develops a culture, or in Selznick's (1957) words, a "distinctive identity." The framework also helps to explain the forces that sustain an organization's culture over time.

Critical Decisions of Founding Members

The founder of a company, or a small group of founding members who start a firm, can play a particularly important role in the development of an organization's culture. Such individuals bring their personal goals, values, and dreams to the fledgling organization. Frequently, it is their goals and values, and their conception of the organization's mission, that define the initial commitments of the enterprise. Strategic decisions that are made by the company's founding members concerning the firm's product market scope define the task environment and provide the focus for organizational learning. The nature of that environment—how competitive it is, how rapid the rate of change is, how high the degree of risk is, and so forth—will profoundly shape the organization's experience and its character. Similarly, decisions that are made within this environment to employ certain technologies and methods of manufacturing and marketing shape the organization's experience and character as well (Gordon, 1991).

The recruiting decisions of founding members often fill the organization with individuals who share particular ideas and values, and thereby affect the capacity of the company to control its future behavior. Such decisions help to foster organizational commitment to goals and policies. But at the same time, the values of the new recruits can restrain the firm from making subsequent decisions that would be inconsistent with those values.

In sum, the initial impact of the firm's founding members will be through the making of such decisions, decisions that can be of critical importance in the formation of the organization's culture (Kets de Vries and Miller, 1986). As will be described in the next section, the impact of a company's founding members will also come through the guiding ideas that are conceived and developed as a result of their actions (Clark, 1972). Eventually, their activities will affect other important aspects of the organization's culture, and the character of the company that the founding members build may remain intact long after new leaders and members have assumed their positions.

Guiding Ideas

One of the key functions of an entrepreneur, or any leader, is the creation and maintenance of a system of shared values. A leader performs this function, in part, by articulating a small number of guiding ideas. A guiding idea (referred to as a "superordinate goal" by Waterman et al., 1980) is a statement of purpose or mission that embodies fundamental aspects of the organization's existing character, or the character that a company's leadership seeks to build. A guiding idea is usually set forth by the organization's founder or founding members when the firm is young. However, it is also possible that a subsequent leader or coalition may conceive a guiding idea, or that it may simply evolve. For societies, an example of a guiding idea is "The American Dream." For companies, examples of guiding ideas include "IBM Means Service" and, at 3M, "The 11th commandment is never kill a new product idea." Guiding ideas serve to shape and communicate values and premises; they also serve to foster norms.

Over time, a guiding idea may become a source of direction for thinking and behavior, as members come to share a common experience within the organization, and as the company's efforts meet with success. As a guiding idea is followed, and as it is validated by accomplishments in the marketplace, the firm becomes predictable with respect to that aspect of organizational life. As a result, the company may take on a distinctive identity (Clark, 1972). In most instances, this identity cannot be readily abandoned. An organization's history may be interpreted to show that it has adhered to its guiding ideas, and that they are the basis of the firm's success, thereby giving legitimacy to established practices. Moreover, these commitments may be highly valued by members, and the historical interpretation may take on an emotional loading. Thus, a story of past commitments may influence current conceptions and expectations, and create pressures to continue to fulfill these expectations (Wilkins, 1979).

Social Structure

The social structure that emerges and is sustained within an organization reflects a pattern of interactions that develops among people, between people and their jobs, and among groups. Over time, people develop attitudes about themselves and what they are doing, about others in the company, and about the organization and its environment. The pattern is historical in that it reflects the specific experiences of the organization. It is also dynamic, because it generates social forces, especially internal interest groups made up of people committed to particular aims and policies (Selznick, 1957).

Selznick argues that while the organization begins as a tool, it may subsequently take on added meaning from the psychological and social functions that it performs, and from the unique way in which it comes to fulfill personal and group needs. Because of this, the organization may become valued for itself as members come to see it as a source of personal satisfaction. Some members will value the organization more than others. But the more an organization's social structure develops, the more it is likely to become valued for its own sake. In essence, the organization becomes an institutional fulfillment of group integrity and aspiration.

A measure of the extent to which an organization has become valued for itself is the degree to which it is viewed as being expendable. If an organization is seen as expendable, members will offer little resistance to actions that would alter its character. When value infusion occurs, however, such actions will cause members to feel a sense of personal loss. They may feel that the "identity" of the group has been violated. As a result, members may offer significant resistance, and yield to economic or technological considerations only as a last resort. Their resistance becomes a struggle to preserve the uniqueness of the group in the face of change.

Norms, Values, and Premises

Through organizational experience and the emergence of a social structure, individuals will (within the context of their "location" in the organization) develop norms, or expectations about what the company, its constituent units, and its members should or should not do in particular situations. In essence, norms constitute expectations about what actions are called for under given conditions. People will also develop values, or explicit beliefs concerning what is good, right, or beneficial for the enterprise and its members. And finally, they will develop a set of premises, or taken-for-granted assumptions, that they will use unconsciously when interpreting events that occur in the organization and its environment. In other words, members become sensitized to certain ways of perceiving events that take place, as individuals, as members of parochial groups, and as members of the organization. As with norms, values and premises are shaped by the company's historic experience and the personal involvement of individuals in the organization over time. But it should be noted that values and premises also affect the formation and maintenance of norms as well.

Remembered History and Symbolism

The history of a company, whether informally remembered or officially recorded, is not an integrated flow of events. Rather, certain aspects of history are noted, while others are ignored or forgotten, and still others are exaggerated or distorted. This selective perception of history is tied to the norms, values, and premises of the organization, and can play a very important role in maintaining and enhancing its culture. Clark (1972), Pettigrew (1979), and Wilkins (1979) discuss several social phenomena that are related to the remembered history of an organization, including symbols, sagas, myths, folklore, and rituals. As will become apparent, these phenomena are associated with emotional or attitudinal functions, and information processing functions. They also are important means of organizational control, because they help to shape the understandings people have about what they should do under given conditions.

Symbols

Symbols are objects, acts, concepts, or language that members use to express feelings, images, or values. They may evoke emotions and impel people to action (Dandridge et al., 1980: Pettigrew, 1979). Among the concepts that are important for the remembered history of an organization, "symbols" is the most inclusive category (encompassing myths and rituals for example), and symbols help to express the character of the organization to members and outsiders. Efforts to change the direction of an organization that threaten to erode or destroy important symbols may meet with substantial resistance. However, the effective use of symbols can also be a valuable tool in the successful implementation of fundamental change. The qualities that symbols possess for communicating values and legitimizing practices suggest their importance in the analysis of organizational culture.

Sagas

According to Clark (1972), an organizational saga is a collective understanding of a unique accomplishment of the formal organization. A saga often begins as a strongly stated purpose (a guiding idea), conceived by a single person or a small group. The usual setting is the autonomous, new organization. However, it is also possible that a saga may be initiated in an established organization in the midst of crisis and suffering from years of decay, or sometimes, in an organization that is sound but facing the need for substantial change. A saga typically explores the key events (e.g., the organization's founding, critical incidents, etc.) that helped to shape the character of the organization, and describes how the guiding idea was followed and fulfilled by the actions of its members. In so doing, a saga provides a connection between history and purposes or values, and it serves as an important means of maintaining an image of distinctiveness about the organization.

It may take years (even decades) for a saga to become firmly established. And, while based on historical events, it is often embellished through retelling and rewriting. But a saga that is well-developed will affect the definition of the organization, and will be protected from participants who might wish to relegate it to the past. Usually a saga will prove to be very long-lasting and stable, and will be abandoned only after years of steady organizational decline. By appealing to shared values, sagas serve as a powerful means of producing unity and attachment to the organization and its policies. "It makes links across internal divisions and organizational boundaries as groups share their common beliefs" (Clark, 1972: 183). At the same time, it should be noted that the unique identity that is fostered can suggest differences between the organization and external groups.

Myths, Folklore, and Rituals

Myths are sacred narratives of events that depart from the objective world, and explore (in dramatic form) issues of origin and transformation (Pettigrew, 1979). In so doing, they help to communicate values, and legitimize current organizational practices by offering explanations of past events. Pettigrew briefly discusses the role of myths in supporting stability and unity in the organization. He also argues that myths can be created and used by interest groups to further their causes. It is suggested that myths can be used by individuals and groups to justify their stances "and affirm wavering or aspiring power positions . . . [Myths may] justify and sustain values that underlie political interests, explain, and thereby reconcile the contradictions between professed values and actual behavior, and legitimize established leadership systems faced with threats" (Pettigrew, 1979: 576).

Wilkins notes that studies of folklore indicate that stories are often used to teach the consequences of behavior. "Among the Jicarilla Apache, for example, grandparents or other relatives use stories (isolated episodes) to instruct the young about appropriate behavior" (Wilkins, 1979: 6). Fables and folk tales with morals are also used to instill attitudes and principles into new members of an organization. Rituals are important because of the messages that they contain. They can indicate which are important or marginal values, which goals are most important and which take a lower priority, who the key people of the organization are, and which organizational units have the most power. "It is partially through rituals that social relationships become stylized, conventionalized, and prescribed" (Pettigrew, 1979: 576). And like myths and folklore, rituals help to communicate and reinforce what is valued (Trice and Beyer, 1984).

To summarize what has been said so far, the remembered history of an organization (whether realistic or exaggerated) serves to help maintain and enhance its culture. The concepts that have been discussed can connect history with purposes and shared values, and thereby foster commitment and unity. They can also be used to encourage conformity with social norms, to direct individual action toward common goals, to legitimize established practice and status arrangements, and to reconcile differences between expressed values and actual behavior. By encouraging conformity and serving as a source of shared values and premises, these elements of an organization's culture also guide and limit decision making; the information that they contain about selective aspects of the organization's accumulated experience will often be abstracted and used to handle present situations in an "appropriate" manner. This leads us to consider the social information processing function of sagas and other concepts.

Social Information Processing Function

Because the number of factors that people can consider in decision making is limited, they often make decisions by using what amount to learned "programs" (March and Simon, 1958; Wilkins, 1979). These programs, which are used as though the person is performing a script, will be evoked by stimuli contained in mundane, everyday activities, or in critical situations that have occurred before. Scripts include routines that pertain to the independent actions of individuals, as well as routines that concern the coordinated efforts of members and groups (Stinchcombe, 1990). Since most of the problems that people face pertain to recurring activities, the use of scripts is usually an efficient and effective means of problem solving; it helps individuals to avoid a separate decision process each time a problem occurs. "People simply reduce the problem to one that has been satisfactorily solved in the past and use that program again" (Wilkins, 1979: 7–8).

For example, stories from organizational history may become scriptural and be applied in subsequent situations of a similar nature. Wilkins reported on an organization where there was a story concerning how the firm had avoided a layoff. It was called the "Nine-Day Fortnight" by participants. Wilkins paraphrased the story, which was told to him by company executives:

> In the early 1970s, the entire electronics industry suffered a drop in orders and most companies had begun to lay people off in significant numbers. Our

calculations suggested the need to cut back 10% in our output and our salary level to match the decline in orders. However, an essential part of our company tradition is to avoid layoffs. After considerable discussion, we decided (who actually made the decision and how it was announced are points upon which informants differed) to require everyone from the president to the lowest-paid employee to take a 10% cut in pay and to stay home every other Friday. At first we worried about whether people in the company would go along with us, and there were a few critics, but most people thought it was a great idea. In fact, a good number of our employees got so used to having Friday off every other week that they were reluctant to go back to a full schedule. It took about six months to build up our orders again, but we didn't ever have to lay off our people (Wilkins, 1979: 10).

When a similar situation arose three years later, the scheme was again employed. It was also used at a plant in the Far East which experienced a sharp drop in orders. "Apparently, the nine-day fortnight has become a script in the company, not only because almost everybody remembers the story and thinks it was significant, but also because it continues to be evoked and applied in similar situations" (Wilkins, 1979: 10). In addition to its social information processing and decision-making functions, the story has an emotional appeal in that it helps to communicate the fact that the company cares for the well-being of its members. The story is also used to help indoctrinate new employees, and it is invoked by executives who wish to defend or illustrate existing and proposed personnel policies.

Although only stories have been related to the function of social information processing, the other concepts that have been discussed aid in this regard as well. Each facilitates communication and decision making within the organization. But it should be noted that people who have absorbed a way of perceiving and evaluating experience may apply traditional scripts to non-routine or novel problems where they are not effective. They may do this partly out of habituation and partly out of the desire to conform to established norms. This can make it more difficult for the organization to deal with environmental change.

Institutionalized Arrangements

Beyond the influence of remembered history, the decisions of individuals and groups are also guided by institutionalized arrangements, which encompass formal management systems and written policies.

Management systems include measurement and reward, information, planning, and training systems. Policies are "decision rules that are used in recognizable, repetitive, structured problem-solving situations" (Schendel, 1977: 11). To some degree, an organization's management systems and policies reflect its remembered history. The "nine-day fortnight," for instance, reveals how remembered history can come to be manifested in company policy. But fundamentally, policies and systems reflect the adaptation of the organization to its environment (Stinchcombe, 1990) and the norms, values, and premises that develop in the process.[3] Policies and systems embody suppositions about events that routinely occur, and attitudes about what is important and what actions should be taken under given conditions.

An important point to understand is that an organization's institutionalized arrangements exert a powerful form of control, because they fundamentally influence behavior (Bower, 1970; Peters, 1980). Formal information systems, for instance, orient attention and decision making toward certain issues and types of information, since people tend to respond to what they actually see. Similarly, people will consider how their performance is gauged by the company's reward system as they make decisions and take action. Written policies, of course, provide more explicit control by setting rules for such things as (e.g.) customer service. Because norms, values, and premises are embedded in the reports people read, the incentive systems under which they operate, the training they receive, the forms they fill out, and the policies within which they work, institutionalized arrangements serve to reinforce and thereby perpetuate the culture of an organization.

Studying Organizational Culture

The framework that we have outlined incorporates the central elements of an organization's culture. Each of the identified elements can be ascertained in any formal organization—through personal interviews with members and leaders, through "partial membership" by the researcher in the organization, through self-administered questionnaires, through materials produced by the company pertaining to its his-

[3] For example, if servicing the customer's needs was an important value of an office equipment company, this might be reflected in a policy of providing additional customer training at no extra charge if a customer had trouble learning how to use the equipment.

tory, and through articles and books written about the firm over time (Gregory, 1983; Wilkins, 1983). If the concepts discussed above are utilized as an analytical lens, all of these methods and sources can help to reveal the "makeup" of a company's culture and the dynamics of its cultural development. Indeed, as Duncan (1989) suggests, "triangulation" (the use of multiple approaches) can be a particularly effective means of studying the culture of an organization. While culture is often seen as being a rather nebulous aspect of organizations, it is possible to "get one's arms around it" to a considerable degree.

ORGANIZATIONAL CULTURE AND STRATEGIC RESPONSES TO ENVIRONMENTAL CHANGE

The effectiveness of an organization is substantially influenced by the assessments of members and leaders regarding "what works." These assessments depend to a great extent on the outlook and habits—the patterns of emphasis and judgment—that people develop over time. Such an orientation can be a tremendous source of strength when it is congruent with the firm's traditional strategy. Indeed, a strong culture is sometimes seen as one of the central characteristics of an "excellent" organization (Dennison, 1984; Peters and Waterman, 1982). But where environmental change calls for substantial changes in strategy—as has been true for the major U.S. auto producers for example—an established orientation can become a major liability (Gordon, 1991; Halberstam, 1986; Womack et al., 1990). And even when a firm is not faced with serious environmental threats, the established orientation of the organization may reduce its ability to perceive and take advantage of emerging opportunities.

In 1979, Roy Ash commented about the troubles of AM International, which he then headed. His comments help to illustrate how assessments of "what works," and the orientation on which they are based, can hinder organizational effectiveness.

We have diagnosed our main challenge here at AM International not as sales or manufacturing or cost problems, but rather as cultural problems. Our problems have been mindsets and prejudices. I'm not using these terms in a pejorative sense; it's simply that everyone here knew the decisions that had been made long ago. Those decisions, those prejudgments, guided the organization. Very few questions were being asked. People had stopped raising questions. And any questions that were being asked were answered with responses developed years ago (*Organizational Dynamics*, 1979: 53).

Subsequently, Ash was forced to step down because of the company's poor financial performance under his leadership. This poor performance record was partially due to his failure to build a solid foundation of profits before making acquisitions. Nevertheless, his comments still suggest how the culture of a company can hinder its effectiveness.

Influences on Strategy Formulation

An organization's culture may be viewed as a factor that moderates the reciprocal influence of the environment and strategy formulation. (This "moderating influence" of culture is depicted in Figure 2.) Strategies are built on the beliefs and assumptions that managers make about the enterprise and its environment (Weick, 1985). However, an organization's culture filters the perspective of its members, and affects their ability to *ask the right questions*. Frequently, the questions that are asked and the strategic options that are generated are tied to the organization's general outlook—a tacit image of the company and its mission.

Figure 2
The Reciprocal Influence of Strategy and Environment as
Moderated by Organizational Culture

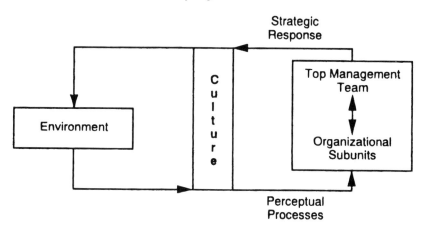

At the same time, the normative element of culture circumscribes the range of options that are acceptable. And when a firm has had a history of success, its success reaffirms the soundness of past practices in the minds of the company's leaders and other members (Argyris and Schon, 1978). The net result is that the options generated are inherently limited and may be inadequate to deal with threats that the company faces or opportunities that it could exploit.

Organizational culture can also influence the politics of strategic decisions. Members of organizational subunits usually hold unit-specific values and, among members of various subunits, there will be different viewpoints of "what works" for the company (Cyert and March, 1963; Van Cauwenbergh and Cool, 1982). Out of these varying perspectives, debates will ensue, and individuals and subunits may engage in bureaucratic maneuvering to defend their interests and steer decisions about strategy in what they believe is the right direction. The top management team will also make assessments regarding what strategies are most likely to succeed. These appraisals will depend not only on their perception of the company's resources and the conditions in the firm's environment, but also on how they believe different individuals and subunits will react to the strategy that is decided upon. In making these assessments, senior managers must consider who will support and who will resist a given alternative, as well as whether their support is vital for that strategy (Quinn, 1980).

Influences on Strategy Implementation

Issues such as the ones described above also raise questions regarding the implementation of strategic change. As individuals and as members of particular subunits, people will decide how organizational choices of strategy will affect them and the well-being of the company as a whole. These judgments will depend on their personal needs, on the norms and values of their units, and on the norms and values of the entire company. Perhaps more importantly, they will depend on the degree to which members personally identify with and are committed to the organization. Based on these judgments, individuals will choose to support the strategic decisions that are made, to remain neutral, or to actively resist them. Generally, when a new strategy threatens to substantially alter the character of an organization, members will offer resistance; the larger the intended change, the greater the resistance is likely to be (Huse, 1975).

There is a less tangible issue involved in the implementation of strategic change as well. Beyond new methods of manufacturing, marketing, and servicing, a new strategy may require an orientation—a way of thinking and processing information—that differs from the one that the organization and its members are geared to. Differing rates of market growth and rates of change, and differing types of uncertainty (e.g., unstable markets or technology) all require different approaches to business management. If a new strategy takes the company into areas that require an approach that is incompatible with the firm's traditional orientation, the organization may be ill-equipped to meet the needs and challenges of that strategy (Prahalad and Bettis, 1986; Stinchcombe, 1990). For this reason, the firm's attempts at implementing a new strategy may meet with limited success, even if little active resistance is met.

REFERENCES

Argyris, C., and D. Schon. 1978. *Organizational Learning*. Reading MA: Addison-Wesley.

Bower, J. L. 1970. *Managing the Resource Allocation Process: A Study of Corporate Planning and Investment*. Boston, MA: Graduate School of Business Administration, Harvard University.

Chatterjee, S., M. H. Lubatkin, D. M. Schweiger, and Y. Weber. 1992. "Cultural Differences and Shareholder Value in Related Mergers: Linking Equity and Human Capital." *Strategic Management Journal* 13: 319–334.

Clark, B. 1972. "The Organizational Saga in Higher Education." *Administrative Science Quarterly* 17: 178–184.

Cyert, R., and J. March. 1963. *A Behavioral Theory of the Firm*. Englewood Cliffs: Prentice-Hall.

Dandridge, T. C., I. Mitroff, and W.F. Joyce. 1980. "Organization Symbolism: A Topic to Expand Organizational Analysis." *Academy of Management Review* 5(1): 77–82.

Dennison, D. 1984. "Bringing Corporate Culture to the Bottom Line." *Organizational Dynamics* 13(2): 5–22.

Duncan, W. J. 1989. "Organizational Culture: 'Getting a Fix' on an Elusive Concept." *Academy of Management Executive* 3(3): 229–236.

Gordon, G. G. 1991. "Industry Determinants of Organizational Culture." *Academy of Management Review* 16(2): 396–415.

Gregory, K. L. 1983. "Native-View Paradigms: Multiple Cultures and Culture Conflicts in Organizations." *Administrative Science Quarterly* 28: 359–376.

Halberstam, D. 1986. *The Reckoning*. New York: William Morrow.

Huse, E.F. 1975. *Organization Development and Change*. St. Paul: West.

Kets de Vries, M. E. R., and D. Miller. 1986. "Personality, Culture, and Organization." *Academy of Management Review* 11(2): 266–279.

Krech, D., R. S. Crutchfield, and E. L. Ballachey. 1962. *Individual in Society*. New York: McGraw-Hill.

Kroeber, A. L., and C. Kluckhohn. 1952. *Culture: A Critical Review of Concepts and Definitions*. Cambridge: Harvard University Printing Office.

March J., and H. Simon. 1958. *Organizations*. New York: Wiley.

Organizational Dynamics. 1979. "Conversation: An Interview with Roy L. Ash." (Autumn): 49–67.

Peters, T. J. 1980. "Management Systems: The Language of Character and Competence." *Organizational Dynamics* (Summer): 3–26.

———, and R. H. Waterman, Jr. 1982. *In Search of Excellence: Lessons from America's Best-Run Companies*. New York: Warner Books.

Pettigrew, A. M. 1979. "On Studying Organizational Cultures." *Administrative Science Quarterly* 24: 570–580.

Prahalad, C. K., and R. A. Bettis. 1986. "The Dominant Logic: A New Linkage between Diversity and Performance." *Strategic Management Journal* 7: 485–501.

Quinn, J.B. 1980. *Strategies for Change: Logical Incrementalism*. Homewood IL: Irwin.

Sackmann, S. A. 1992. "Culture and Subcultures: An Analysis of Organizational Knowledge." *Administrative Science Quarterly* 37: 140–161.

Schein, E. H. 1984. "Coming to a New Awareness of Organizational Culture." *Sloan Management Review* (Winter): 3–16.

Schendel, D. 1977. "Goals, Strategy, and Environment." Unpublished Working Paper. Purdue University.

Schwartz, H., and S. M. Davis. 1981. "Matching Corporate Culture and Business Strategy." *Organizational Dynamics* (Summer): 30–48.

Selznick, P. 1957. *Leadership in Administration: A Sociological Interpretation*. Evanston: Row, Peterson.

Smircich, L. 1983. "Concepts of Culture and Organizational Analysis." *Administrative Science Quarterly* 28: 339–358.

Stinchcombe, A. L. 1990. *Information and Organizations*. Berkeley: University of California Press.

Trice, H. M., and J. M. Beyer. 1984. "Studying Organizational Cultures Through Rites and Ceremonials." *Academy of Management Review* 9(4): 653–669.

Tushman, M. L., and E. Romanelli. 1985. "Organizational Evolution: A Metamorphosis Model of Convergence and Reorientation." In *Research in Organizational Behavior*. Eds. L. L. Cummings and B. M. Staw. Greenwich, CT: JAI Press.

Van Cauwenbergh, A., and K. Cool. 1982. "Strategic Management in a New Framework." *Strategic Management Journal* 3: 245–264.

Waterman, R. H., Jr., T. J. Peters, and J. R. Phillips. 1980. "Structure is Not Organization." *Business Horizons* (June): 14–26.

Weick, K. E. 1985. "The Significance of Corporate Culture." In *Organizational Culture*. Eds. P. J. Frost et al. Beverly Hills: Sage.

Wiener, Y. 1988. "Forms of Value Systems: A Focus on Organizational Effectiveness and Cultural Change and Maintenance." *Academy of Management Review* 13(4): 534–545.

Wilkins, A. L. 1979. "Organizational History, Legends and Control." Unpublished Working Paper. Brigham Young University.

———. 1983. "The Culture Audit: A Tool for Understanding Organizations." *Organizational Dynamics* (Autumn): 24–38.

Womack, J. P., D. T. Jones, and D. Roos. 1990. *The Machine that Changed the World*. New York: Macmillan.

Challenges to Leadership in the Implementation of Technological Change

Mary D. Zalesny and Robert P. Vecchio

This article examines influences on and consequences of the introduction of new technology at the level of the functional work unit and of the organization. In the following sections, the roles of critical variables in technological innovation, spanning both unit and organizational levels of analysis, are described. Also, propositions are offered that tie innovation to culture, and "subordinate acceptance of change" to the neglected topic of leadership influence at the interface of the first-level supervisor with nonsupervisory organizational members. Finally, implications are presented for the management of change in organizations confronted with technological change decisions.

Although the "technological imperative" implies that technology drives structural variation in organizations, changes in structure and modifications in technology frequently are influenced by the actions of first-level supervisors within organizations. The role of supervisors is therefore a critical, but often neglected, element in theorizing about the relation of structure and technology. We argue that leadership can impact on openness to innovation and that the favorability of this impact will be dependent on the nature of or need for supervision, and the extent to which the first-level supervisor's actions are congruent with employees' expectations for the management of change (Lord and Maher, 1990). The structural design features of an organization also are likely to be influenced by higher management's propensity to support change and innovations as a consequence of both inertial and pro-change processes (Gersick, 1994).

LEADERSHIP, TECHNOLOGICAL CHANGE, AND CULTURE

Some individuals, more than others, are likely to play a key role in successful implementation of technological and administrative innovations. In addition, at different stages of the implementation process, specific front-line individuals assume greater importance in achieving successful implementation. In some cultures (most notably in Western countries), first-level supervisors are in critical positions for impacting an innovation as they can directly affect the goal setting, feedback, and performance monitoring that are crucial to successful innovative efforts (Drucker, 1985).

Because these leaders frequently hold key positions with respect to the implementation process, it is important to obtain their commitment to ensure a successful change effort. Overcoming employee resistance to change and increasing employee openness often require the continued attention of immediate supervisors. Supervisors, as well, may understandably resist change as it may threaten their status and, therefore, their political power bases (Staw, Sandelands and Dutton, 1981). Additionally, supervisors may fear that increases in unit efficiency may translate into a reduction in the ranks of supervisors.

Seven factors can be identified that influence the extent to which leaders at the frontline of an organization can influence and maintain change in organizations, such as the changes occurring contemporaneously with attempts to implement a new technology. First, the nature of the work to be performed and the abilities and competencies of the workers will partly determine the *extent to which first-level supervisors are needed to provide feedback, direction, and rewards.* Various views of group leadership have posited roles for task and subordinate attributes in the explanation of supervisory effectiveness (Fiedler and Chemers, 1984; Evans, 1974; House, 1971). For example, if there are standard operating procedures outlined for task completion and task-related indicators for performance feedback, a supervisor's ability to influence workgroup effectiveness may be limited. In their model of substitutes for leadership, Kerr and Jermier (1978) proposed that task, employee, and organizational characteristics can either substitute or neutralize supervisor attempts to influence employees either through support or through initiation of structure. For example, Hofstede (1992) has observed that the expertise of skilled German workers eliminates the need for task direction from supervisors who function, therefore, primarily as task consultants.

Hulin and Roznowski (1985) discussed the effects of advanced technology on tasks that shift some management control and information to technical employees who have the expertise to understand and use both the technology and the information it generates. Through its effects on task characteristics, advanced technology indirectly affects group composition and structure by changing the knowledge and skill requirements of the work. The adage that knowledge is power has particular relevance for supervisors faced with new technologies. To the extent that first-level supervisors lack the technological expertise to make credible pronouncements about the usefulness or appropriateness of a new technology, they may lose some of their credibility and power in their work groups.

Second, the *dominant social culture* surrounding the organization will influence the role and style of leadership that exists in the organization. In discussing three decades of research on leadership in Japan, Misumi and Peterson (1985) identified several cultural factors that may partially account for differences between Japanese and U.S. leaders in the reported effectiveness of performance (or structuring) and maintenance (or consideration) leadership styles. Among these factors are: (a) career patterns in Japan that encourage greater employee reliance on their formal supervisors for career guidance, (b) greater physical proximity of Japanese supervisors to their workgroup members, and (c) greater legitimate, reward, and coercive power of Japanese supervisors compared to their U.S. counterparts (leading to greater employee dependence on their supervisor for valued rewards). These factors, individually or jointly, are likely to contribute to differences between Japanese and U.S. supervisors and subordinates in openness to change and the determination of an optimal change strategy.

Cognitive approaches to group leadership suggest that leadership status is attributed to an individual on the basis of employee perceptions about leadership (Lord and Maher, 1990). Different cultures (and subcultures) are likely to possess differing sets of "criterial attributes" that are associated with ideal leadership. Employees whose definition of ideal leadership includes certain roles, behaviors, or characteristics (e.g., participative, accessible) are unlikely to accept the influence attempts of a supervisor whose perceived attributes do not encompass these criterial attributes, regardless of the formal title assigned to that individual. For example, Hofstede (1992) has observed that in the Netherlands, "modesty" is highly rated as a desired attribute of an ideal supervisor. However, among U.S. respondents, "modesty" is not regarded as an important feature of leadership.

Third, the existence of *formal representation of workers* (and of the government, in certain nations) may constrain a leader's authority and ability to facilitate change engendered by technological innovation. Where management shares responsibility and control with representatives of the employees and society, decisions to implement a new technology are also likely to be shared. Attempts to adopt a new technology that threatens specific jobs or the continued existence of entire organizational units may be seen as a danger to the established management-worker relationships and may result in strong employee or government action to protect the status quo (see, for example, Brett, 1980a, 1980b).

Fourth, *a leader's personal beliefs about employees and the process of leadership* may influence his or her willingness to become involved in the implementation of technological innovation, and to involve his or her subordinates in the implementation process. The Vertical Dyad Linkage model or Leader-member Exchange Theory (LMX) of work unit leadership (Graen and Cashman, 1975; Graen and Uhl-Bien, 1991) describes how leaders at all levels in an organization enter into differential exchange relationships with their subordinates. By their loyalty, effort, and performance, members of one subgroup of subordinates establish close and trusted relationships with the leader (in-group). These individuals function as informal assistants to the leader in accomplishing organizationally relevant tasks, and in return receive special rewards (e.g., greater autonomy, visibility, compensation, personal development opportunities, etc.). Members of the other subgroup of subordinates (the out-group) generally contribute, and receive in return, little more than what their explicit contract with the organization specifies.

Leaders with a broader base of support (i.e., with a comparatively higher percentage of their subordinates being members of their in-group) should be better able to initiate and accomplish successful adoption of a new technology as they have already established a social mechanism through which the acceptance of change by the workgroup may be enhanced. Moreover, leaders who are themselves members of their leader's in-group (i.e., who possess upward influence) will have access to more rewards and inducements for distribution among their own subordinates. Leaders who are in their supervisor's out-group may find it difficult to access and provide sufficient special rewards and benefits to their in-groups so as to succeed in their attempts at implementing new technology. To the extent that exchange transactions described in the LMX model are found to vary in importance across cultures (and there is evidence that LMX exchanges do exist in other cultures, Wakabayashi and Graen, 1984; Wakabayashi, Graen, Graen and Graen, 1988), the quality of exchange relationships may be an especially important avenue for the introduction and acceptance of innovations.

Fifth, supervisors who exhibit *behaviors characteristic of transformational leaders* may also engender greater acceptance of technological innovations among their subordinates than supervisors who do not exhibit such behaviors. Bass (1985) has described transformational leaders as those who can affect their subordinates by (a) increasing their awareness of the importance and value associated with desired outcomes (here, the successful implementation of a new technology), (b) influencing them to consider the greater interests of their workgroup and the organization rather than only their own self-interests, and (c) addressing their needs for personal growth and development. Proposed innovations that have "champions" (i.e., personal sponsors) who display attributes of transformational leadership are more likely to be adopted and effectively implemented. As part of a social process that may be similar in some ways to that used by supervisors to motivate in-group members, transformational leaders rely on special rewards to facilitate their influence attempts (Yukl, 1989). Reliance on transformational leaders for successful innovations may be effective to the extent that the characteristics of transformational leaders are valued within a culture.

Sixth, leaders may differ in the extent to which they are supportive of change in their units as a function of the stage that they occupy in their careers. That is, *more recently appointed first-level supervisors may be more open to innovation* than first-level supervisors with greater seniority. More established supervisors may have greater investments in the status quo, whereas newer supervisors may be less committed to past policies and procedures and are more likely to be seeking ways to distinguish themselves by improving unit performance (Damanpour, 1991; Kimberly and Evanisko, 1981). The primary loyalty of supervisors may also shift over time, such that newly appointed supervisors may be more desirous of implementing change that is apparently mandated by higher management, than supporting subordinates who may be offering resistance to change. This suggests that there may be an "optimal time" for attempting to introduce change that is influenced by a supervisor's willingness to support innovation which, in turn, is based on career stage issues.

In addition, the collectivism-individualism dimension (i.e., the valuing of "working together" versus "working alone") underlies differences in managerial openness to change (Hofstede, 1980). For example, proposing a new idea that does not originate from one's group may be viewed as selfish in a relatively collectivist country, such as Japan (Hornstein, 1986). Similarly, one can hypothesize that the collectivism-individualism dimensions may be associated with employee and supervisor willingness to accept the principles of semi-autonomous (i.e., relatively self-directed) work arrangements, such that team-based approaches to work may be more readily accepted in collectivist cultures.

Seventh, *aversion to risk-taking* (which can play an important role in influencing openness to innovation at a micro level) has also been found to vary by nationality (Bass, Burger, Doktor, and McPherson, 1979). For example, a sample of managers from the United States was found to be the least risk averse in comparison with other nationalities. In a comparison of Far Eastern (Singapore Chinese) and Anglo (North American and British) managers on Cattell's 16 Personal Factors Questionnaire, Gill (1983) reported that Far Eastern managers described themselves as relatively more reserved, conservative, serious, trusting, assertive, expedient, group dependent, and relaxed than did Anglo managers. In addition, the Far Eastern managers viewed themselves as less imaginative and tough-minded. Furthermore, supervisory openness to change and innovation is influenced by the larger culture's endorsement of change. For example, Americans are concerned with a need to control their environment or circumstances, while Hindus are inclined to believe that they cannot drastically alter the nature of personal circumstances (Adler, Doktor, and Redding, 1989). In a related view, the Japanese tend to discourage aspects of competitiveness (Hall and Hall, 1988).[1] Finally, differences may exist between cultures in terms of subordinates' willingness to accept authority as a source of truth versus observation (Solo, 1975).

In summary, we propose that specific leadership and contextual characteristics are expected to be associated with subordinate acceptance of change. Acceptance will be greater with,

(a) tasks that require supervisory feedback, direction, and rewards;
(b) a dominant social culture that espouses employee dependence on supervisors for guidance;

(c) cooperative, versus confrontational, forms of employer-employee sharing of responsibility and control;

(d) supervisors who hold personal beliefs that employees should be involved in the implementation process, thereby increasing their base of support;

(e) supervisors who exhibit behaviors that are characteristic of transformational leaders;

(f) supervisors who are more recently appointed; and

(g) supervisors who are comparatively low on aversion to risk-taking.

STRUCTURE AND TECHNOLOGY

In comparing successful organizations in industrialized and developing countries, Kiggundu (1989) observed that all the organizations followed a rational model of organizing. That is, they accomplished their critical operating tasks (i.e., the basic tasks through which the organization accomplished its objectives) by relying on rational principles of organization and management. However, it appears that highly successful economies (e.g., Japan) adopt, then adapt or modify, a rational model of organizing so as to achieve alignment with the dominant social values within the culture. This process should hold regardless of whether the culture is defined by national boundaries or by the shared history and experiences of a social group.

Societal culture should delimit the extent to which the adoption (and adaptation) of any new technology will alter the existing social systems within an organization to maximize the technology's effectiveness. Highly successful technological innovations developed in one culture may be less successful in another culture if they are simply imported without any modification (Ricks, 1983), and in doing so, may disrupt the established core cultural values among employees (Kiggundu, 1989). Also, it is almost a cliched notion to argue that flexible structures (i.e., structures with greater degrees of decentralization of knowledge and power, less formality or adherence to rules, and little hierarchical communication and authority) are advantageous for enhancing openness to change (Aiken and Hage, 1971; Kimberly and Evanisko, 1981; Pierce and Delbecq, 1977). As the predisposition to create flexible organizational structures is likely to be associated with societal cultural values regarding openness to change, the larger culture can be viewed as having the ability to act as a facilitating or impeding factor.

Hulin and Roznowski (1985) have proposed that technology, in addition to influencing organizational structure, is jointly influenced by the organization's size and developments in the basic industry of which the organization is a member. Larger organizations will certainly have more extensive resources than smaller organizations from which to draw upon when incorporating technological developments (Ford and Slocum, 1977; Dewar and Hage, 1978). Similarly, Barley (1986) and Burkhardt and Brass (1990) have argued that new technologies may actually alter the organizational structure by altering institutionalized roles and patterns of interaction. To be sure, the processes associated with diffusion of innovation within an industry, as well as the capacity of the industry's members to absorb innovation, are central to any complete explanation of technological change (Czepiel, 1975). For example, in centrally planned economies, diffusion of an innovation is more likely when there is ample technical capacity for adopting the innovation and when the necessary labor resources are available (Bornstein, 1985). Also, organizations in industries that are experiencing considerable technological growth will have greater opportunities and pressures to implement new technology than will organizations in declining industries.

THE ROLE OF SOCIETAL CULTURE IN TECHNOLOGICAL CHANGE

Societal Culture, Technology, and Structure

Organizational researchers have come to view technology (i.e., the types and patterns of activity, equipment, material, and knowledge used to perform tasks) as a powerful influence in determining organizational structure (Spacapan and Oskamp, 1990; Gillespie and Mileti, 1977). This view is so widely assumed that it is termed the "technological imperative" (Grimes and Klein, 1973). While accepting the proposed influence of technology on structure, it can be reasonably argued that culture plays a similarly powerful role in determining structure *and* technology. That is to say, societal culture influences the creation and nature of relationships between organizational members and units, as well as the decision to adopt specific forms of technology. In essence, one can argue for the

existence of a "cultural imperative." Although the "technological imperative" and the "cultural imperative" do not necessarily oppose one
another, an area of special interest arises when imperatives are in opposition. Such is the state of affairs when the "technological imperative"
meets opposition from firmly held cultural values. In the West, cultural
values have tended to give ground in many areas of technological
change. However, in parts of the world where traditional values are being
reaffirmed, conflict between the imperatives may be manifest (consider
the confrontation of imperatives that has arisen as a consequence of the
Islamic fundamentalist movement, wherein, e.g., the technology for birth
control and organ transplant is available in certain countries, yet it is out-
lawed because of conservative religious values).[2]

Bamber and Lambury (1989) suggest an even broader view emphasizing a general "contextual imperative." Here, culture and technology
are only two of several factors (e.g., politics, economics) influencing
openness to and decisions regarding organizational change, including
the adoption of new technologies. However, among these context factors, technology and culture appear to be more critical than the other
factors for initiating and sustaining organizational change.

We propose that the "technological imperative" drives structural
change in organizations. However, the "cultural imperative" determines
the openness to change within organizations. The "cultural imperative," therefore, acts as a moderator of the impact of the "technological
imperative."

Temporal Issues

An important factor to consider when conceptualizing technological
change is the temporal element of the innovation process. Neither the
decision to adopt an innovation nor the implementation of the innovation are discrete events (Rogers, 1983). Rather they are "time dependent
processes" (Pennings, 1985) which are characterized by relatively discrete stages that result in innovation adoption (see also, Mohr, 1982).
However, this is not to imply that there is a linear relation between the
amount of time taken to innovate and the acceptance of an innovation.
Each innovation and its context may dictate an "optimal span of time"
required for effective implementation. The time that it takes an innovation to move through various stages of acceptance and implementation

may determine partly its chances for actual acceptance and successful implementation. Administrative innovations that are rushed through the organization without sufficient opportunity for analysis, debate, and consensus-building are less likely to receive the support necessary to maintain them once they are in place. Technological innovations that are similarly installed without due consideration as to how they might affect existing organizational practices and work routines, or without ensuring that required support structures are available (e.g., training in new equipment, expert advice for trouble-shooting problems, etc.), are likely to be similarly handicapped from the start. A complete analysis of successful and unsuccessful innovations, then, necessitates documenting the processes through which an innovation traverses the organization (McGrath and Rotchford, 1983).

Cultural Value Shifts

Cultural change (i.e., shifts in shared values and norms) represents an important process that, depending on the direction and nature of the change, can influence openness to technological innovation. Hofstede (1980) has suggested that affluence may be a major determinant of a culture's shift from collectivism to individualism (e.g., he reported a strong correlation between the individualism score of a country and its per capita gross national product). Also, the mass media may contribute to cultural shifts toward individualism as most media programming (e.g., television, music, and films) originates in individualistic cultures. Cultural change in itself may be the result of societal shifts that reflect continual testing of basic beliefs concerning the nature of reality (Sorokin, 1941).

In order to examine cultural change in a rigorous fashion, longitudinal data are needed (Hofstede, 1980). Shifts in values and norms can be cautiously attributed to several possible causal processes based on the configuration of data across the age of the respondent (individuals or social units) and time. Maturation, generation, and zeitgeist are three possible influences on cultural shifts (Hofstede, 1980). Maturation effects refer to respondent values changing because of an aging process. Across respondents at the same stage of development, no differences are expected. Generation effects are reflected in the maintenance of values that were established during an earlier, formative period. These established values remain unchanged over time for members of a given cohort. Zeitgeist effects refer to dramatic changes in values or norms that occur for everyone regardless of age because of sudden system-wide shifts. Figures 1a, 1b, and 1c portray the patterns of results that reflect maturational, generational, and zeitgeist changes in values or norms.

The three patterns of change can be viewed from organizational and workgroup perspectives, as well as from an individual perspective. That is to say, the age of groups and organizations can be understood as a correlate of change in a manner similar to individuals. The three patterns of results can be taken as suggesting various underlying processes. The maturational effect for an organization is somewhat parallel to the view offered by Greiner (1972; Greiner and Bhambri, 1989) of organizations undergoing changes as they develop. The generational effect in an organizational context may be seen as parallel to cohort differences in organizational commitment of employees that reflect unique experiences, shifts in hiring practices, and changes in work ethic. Organizational zeitgeist effects might be exemplified by shifts in the way in which work is viewed because of dramatic events (e.g., a war-time economy, a severe economic depression, or the emergence of an "economic-bloc warfare" perspective). To complicate matters further, these three patterns can operate simultaneously. To the extent that a particular pattern is of interest as a "main effect," the operation of any additional patterns would be viewed as confounds. Nonetheless, a search for such patterns, especially the possible result that one pattern may be predominant for a given domain, seems worthwhile. Certainly, cross-cultural differences should be expected when one culture experiences a relatively placid environment and another is experiencing tumultuous change. Furthermore, seemingly equivalent employee cohorts in different cultures should not be assumed to exhibit equivalent attitudinal and behavioral responses to a proposed change. For example, flex-time may be a more valued or desirable innovation within a workforce that has a higher proportion of dual-career employees.

To summarize the above points, we offer the following propositions:

(a) An examination of "openness to change" must take account of maturational, generational, and zeitgeist effects;

(b) Degree of "openness to change" will be correlated with certain specific, yet potentially universal, cultural values (e.g., small power distance and low uncertainty avoidance, Hofstede, 1980); and

Figure 1
Patterns of Results Expected for Maturation, Generation and Zeitgeist Effects

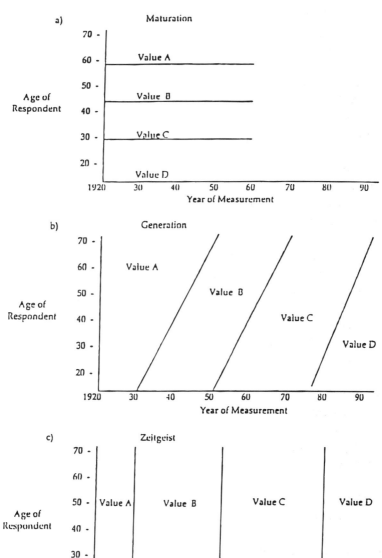

(c) Tracking historical events associated with revolutionary and evolutionary cultural change may aid in predicting shifts in "openness to
change."[3]

INTEGRATING CULTURE, TECHNOLOGY, SUPERVISION, STRUCTURE, AND OPENNESS TO CHANGE

Thus far, we have focused on the influence of societal culture on technology and structure, as well as the influence of culture on the supervisor
via norms for leadership behavior in relations with subordinates. The
successful adoption and implementation of a new technology (especially
when the technology has been developed in one culture and is being considered for adoption into another culture) requires that certain critical
variables be considered: (a) the culture external to the organization, (b)
the nature of the technology being considered, (c) organizational structure, and (d) the role of leaders in affecting openness to change.
Especially during periods of significant change, organizations must
adapt their structures to accommodate the core values that their employees hold most strongly. Persuading employees to accept a new technology will be facilitated if the external social system is integrated with the
organization's internal social system and process. This may mean modifying the new technology or adopting only a portion of it so as to jointly
maximize the integration of the technology with the existing and prevailing social system.

The more advanced and complex the technology, the more it will
impose changes in tasks, in organizational structure, and in role requirements. Technology may cause shifts in the existing status and power
relationships that may be disruptive to organizational functioning. By
taking the existing internal social system into account, cumbersome procedural changes and duplication of effort may result, but these may help
to ensure an alignment of the organizational culture with the values of
the larger external culture. Organizations that are relatively successful
in managing such an alignment may enjoy a comparative advantage
over competitors.

Finally, first-level supervisors may represent an underutilized
resource in the implementation and maintenance of technological innovations. To the extent that leaders are able to make use of relationships
with their subordinates (especially subordinates with critical skills and

expertise), they may be able to influence the acceptance of change through informal means within their workgroups. The role of leaders, however, cannot be fully understood without a consideration of the influences of societal culture and the organization's internal social system.

IMPLICATIONS FOR THE MANAGEMENT OF TECHNOLOGICAL CHANGE

Organizational decisions regarding the implementation of a technological innovation generally begin with an analysis of the feasibility and cost-benefit trade-offs of adopting the innovation. Often, this analysis is largely restricted to economic considerations. We propose that the decision to adopt a technological innovation should be based on a broader assessment that goes beyond the economic utility of the innovation to consider the impact on a wider range of aspects of organizational functioning (Wall, Corbett, Martin, Clegg, and Jackson, 1990; Wall, Clegg, and Kemp, 1987). In addition to the economic impact of an innovation, there are five issues that decision-makers contemplating a technological innovation should consider.

First, is the need for an *extensive analysis of the current state of the organization* (Prasad, 1993). This analysis should accomplish several goals. Initially, it should identify the existing, salient contextual factors likely to facilitate or hinder acceptance and implementation of the innovation. Then, by tracking relevant events, both internal and external to the organization, areas of support and resistance can be determined and appropriate strategies developed. Here, a candid assessment of employee perceptions of the climate and culture of the organization is critical for providing an accurate estimate of the reception the innovation will receive. Also, an organizational analysis should identify and plan for obtaining the material resources necessary to accomplish the technological change. Delays brought about by poor planning and failure to anticipate organizational needs may engender negative attitudes toward the innovation among employees who are tasked with its implementation.

Second, is the need to conduct a *detailed analysis of the proposed technology's consequences*, both intended and potentially unintended, for the organization's formal and informal operating structure. Restructuring of functional areas may result in redundancy of positions, or new skill requirements that will require time and resources to address.

Where workforce reductions are anticipated, decisions must be made about how they should be accomplished. Also, layoffs, early retirement incentives, and attrition due to normal requirements can have a differential impact on the remaining workforce (see, for example, Brockner, Grover, Reed, DeWitt, and O'Malley, 1987). Where new skills will be required, decisions must be made about retraining current employees (or hiring appropriately skilled personnel) and possibly modifying the existing compensation scheme.

Third, *organizational structures should be developed to facilitate the technological change.* One strategy would involve the formation of a change committee consisting of representatives drawn from all relevant constituency groups (e.g., functional area representatives, managerial and nonmanagerial employees, clients/customers, suppliers, etc.). Broad representation on the committee would provide one mechanism for employee participation in the innovation process. The committee would develop recommendations for adapting the innovation to fit the organization's particular configuration of societal norms. Existing lines of communication should be used to ensure unrestricted two-way flow of information between top management and all employee groups. An especially critical link is that between the lowest level of supervision and its workgroups. If necessary, other communication networks, specific to the innovation process, should be established. Assessment of the network of leader-member exchanges across organizational work units should identify the subgroup members most likely to be instrumental in introducing and maintaining change.

Fourth, in addition to the innovation-specific training that will be required, organizations would benefit from *establishing and conducting training programs* that seek to facilitate acceptance and implementation of the technological innovation by influencing the change process. Training strategies that rely on contracting outside trainers, training in-house with Human Resource Development (HRD) staff, or adding training responsibilities to the role of the immediate supervisor, possess inherent relative advantages and disadvantages (Osigweh and Segalla, 1992). At a minimum, training programs should include (a) an orientation to the innovation for all affected employees that delineates the expected benefits to the organization and its employees, and (b) the development of a support group within the work unit that will provide assistance for facilitating changes within the unit. Here again, organizations can rely upon in-group exchanges between leaders and members to establish a core of support within each work unit.

Fifth, the *level of commitment of immediate work unit supervisors* to a proposed technological innovation should be appraised and accounted for in the development of an implementation strategy. Before subordinates are likely to commit themselves to an objective (i.e., an innovation), their immediate supervisors must give unambiguous indications of their own personal commitment to the suggested end-state. As noted previously, there are specific, identifiable supervisory-related factors that are likely to be related to subordinate acceptance of change (e.g., stage of career, supervisor's aversion to risk-taking, etc.).

Although the above implications suggest considerable additional work for organizations, their benefits should significantly outweigh their costs in time and resources. Rather than being unusual or unique approaches to implementing technological innovations, these implications largely reflect the analysis and preplanning that distinguish successful from unsuccessful change attempts.

NOTES

The authors express their appreciation to Peter Dorfman for his comments on an earlier version of this paper.

1. This is illustrated in the Japanese saying that "the nail that sticks up invites hammering down."

2. It is important to recognize that technology is, in a basic sense, value-neutral. However, the parentage of a technology may arouse suspicion and resistance (e.g., a product of Western origin may not be readily adopted in certain cultures because of standing opposition to Western values). Therefore, it is more often the intended use, application, or perceived consequences of a technology that arouses cultural resistance. For example, television and audio-video recording are not inherently opposed in conservative Islamic countries. Rather, it is the content of programs conveyed via these technologies (i.e., Western value-based programming) that may be opposed. As noted by Madu (1992, p. 19), technology also has the complementary capacity to strengthen cultural values.

3. Tracking critical, historical events may also be useful to an organization for determining the impact of various contextual factors and formulating appropriate interventions for the acceptance of change. For example, the end of a collectively bargained agreement may heighten employee concern about issues of job security and changes in job skill requirements that result from a technological innovation, thereby intensifying the stance of an employee union concerning openness versus resistance to change.

REFERENCES

Adler, N. J., Doktor, R., and Redding, S.G. (1989). From the Atlantic to the Pacific century. In C.A.B. Osigweh (Ed.), *Organizational science abroad* (pp. 27–54). New York: Plenum.

Aiken, M. and Hage, J. (1971). The organic organization and innovation, *Sociology, 5*, 63–82.

Bamber, G. and Lambury, R. (1989). *New technology: International perspectives on human resources and industrial relations.* London: Unwin Hyman.

Barley, S.R. (1986). Technology as an occasion for structuring: Evidence from observations of CT scanners and the social order of radiology departments, *Administrative Science Quarterly, 31*, 78–108.

Bass, B. M. (1985). *Leadership and performance beyond expectations.* New York: Free Press.

Bass, B. M., Burger, W. F., Docktor, R., and McPherson, J. W. (1979). *Assessment of managers: An international comparison.* New York: Free Press.

Bornstein, M. (1985). *East-west technology transfer: The transfer of western technology to the USSR* (pp. 91–94). Paris: OECD (Org. for Econ. Cooperation Development).

Brockner, J., Grover, S., Reed, T., DeWitt, R. and O'Malley, M. (1987). Survivors' reactions to layoffs: We got by with a little help from our friends, *Administrative Science Quarterly, 32*, 526–541.

Brett, J.M. (1980a). Behavioral research on unions and union management systems. In B.M. Staw and L. L. Cummings (Eds.), *Research in organizational behavior, 2*, 177–213. Greenwich: JAI Press.

Brett, J. M. (1980b). Why employees want unions, *Organizational Dynamics,* Spring, 847–859.

Burkhardt, M. E. and Brass, D. J. (1990). Changing patterns or patterns of change: The effects of a change in technology on social network structure and power, *Administrative Science Quarterly, 35*, 104–127.

Czepiel, J. A. (1975). Patterns of interorganizational communication and diffusion of a major technological innovation in a competitive industrial community, *Academy of Management Journal, 18*, 6–24.

Damanpour, F. (1991). Organizational innovation: A meta-analysis of effects of determinants and moderators, *Academy of Management Journal, 36*, 555–590.

Dewar, R. and Hage, J. (1978). Size, technology, complexity, and structural differentiation: Toward a theoretical synthesis, *Administrative Science Quarterly, 23*, 111–136.

Drucker, P. F. (1985). *Innovation and entrepreneurship: Practice and principles.* New York: Harper & Row.

Evans, M.G. (1974). Extensions of a Path-Goal theory of motivation, *Journal of Applied Psychology, 59*, 172–178.

Fiedler, F. E. and Chemers, M .M. (1984). *Improving leadership effectiveness: The Leader Match concept* (Rev. ed.). New York: Wiley.

Ford, J.D. and Slocum, J.W. Jr. (1977). Size, technology, environment and the structure of organizations, *Academy of Management Review, 2*, 561–575.

Gersick, C.J.G. (1994). Pacing strategic change: The case of a new venture, *Academy of Management Journal, 37*, 9–45.

Gill, R.W. (1983). Personality profiles of Singapore-Chinese, British, and American managers: A cross-cultural comparison. Paper presented at Third Asian Regional Conference on Cross-Cultural Psychology, Bangi, Malaysia.

Gillespie, D.F. and Mileti, D.S. (1977). Technology and the study of organizations: An overview and appraisal, *Academy of Management Review, 2*, 7–16.

Graen, G. and Cashman, J.F. (1975). A role-making model of leadership in formal organizations: A developmental approach. In J.G. Hunt and L.L. Larson (Eds.), *Leadership frontiers*. Kent, OH: Kent State University Press.

Graen, G.B. and Uhl-Bien, M. (1991). The transformation of professionals into self-managing and partially self-designing contributors: Toward a theory of leadership-making, *Journal of Management Systems, 3*, 25–30.

Greiner, L.E. (1972). Evolution and revolution as organizations grow, *Harvard Business Review, 50*, 37–46.

Greiner, L.E. and Bhambri, A. (1989). New CEO intervention and dynamics of deliberate strategic change, *Strategic Management Journal, 10*, 67–86.

Grimes, A.J. and Klein, S.M. (1973). The technological imperative: The relative impact of task unit, modal technology, and hierarchy on structure, *Academy of Management Journal, 16*, 583–597.

Hall, E.T. and Hall, M. (1988). *Hidden differences: Doing business with the Japanese*. New York: Prentice-Hall.

Hofstede, G. (1980). *Culture's consequences*. New York: Sage Publications.

Hofstede, G. (1992). Cultural constraints on management theories. Distinguished International Scholar Lecture presented at National Meeting of Academy of Management, Las Vegas.

Hornstein, H. (1986). *Managerial courage: Revitalizing your company without sacrificing your job*. New York: Wiley.

House, R.J. (1971). A path-goal theory of leader effectiveness, *Administrative Science Quarterly, 16*, 321–338.

Hulin, C.L. and Roznowski, M. (1985). Organizational technologies: Effects on organizations' characteristics and individuals' responses. In L.L. Cummings and B.M. Staw (Eds.), *Research in Organizational Behavior*, Vol. 7 (pp. 39–85). Greenwich, CT: JAI Press.

Kerr, S. and Jermier, J.M. (1978). Substitutes for leadership: Their meaning and measurement, *Organizational Behavior and Human Performance, 22*, 375–403.

Kiggundu, M.N. (1989). *Managing organizations in developing countries*. West Hartford, CT: Kumarian Press.

Kimberly, J.R. and Evanisko, M. (1981). Organizational innovation: The influence of individual, organizational and contextual factors on hospital adoption of technological and administrative innovations, *Academy of Management Journal, 24*, 689–713.

Lord, R.G. and Maher, K.J. (1990). Alternative information-processing models and their implications for theory, research, and practice, *Academy of Management Review, 15*, 9–28.

Madu, C.N. (1992). *Strategic planning in technology transfer to less developed countries.* New York: Greenwood Publishers.

McGrath, J.E. and Rotchford, N.L. (1983). Time and behavior in organizations. In B. Staw and L. Cummings (Eds.) *Research in Organizational Behavior*, Vol. 5. Greenwich, CT: JAI Press.

Misumi, J. and Peterson, M. F. (1985). The performance-maintenance theory of leadership: Review of a Japanese research program, *Administrative Science Quarterly, 30*, 198–223.

Mohr, L.B. (1982). *Explaining organizational behavior.* San Francisco: Jossey-Bass.

Osigweh, C.A.B. and Segalla, M. (1992). Managing innovative technologies. In C. Madu (Ed.), *The management of new manufacturing technologies for global competitiveness.* New York: Greenwood Press.

Pennings, J.M. (1985). *Organizational strategy and change: New views on formulating and implementing strategic decisions. San Francisco: Jossey-Bass.*

Pierce, J.L. and Delbecq, A.L. (1977). Organizational structure, individual attitudes, and innovation, *Academy of Management Review, 2*, 26–37.

Prasad, P. (1993). Symbolic processes in the implementation of technological change: A symbolic interactionist study of work computerization, *Academy of Management Journal, 36*, 1400–1429.

Ricks, D.A. (1983). *Big business blunders.* Homewood, IL: Dow Jones-Irwin.

Rogers, E.M. (1983). *Diffusion of innovation.* New York: Free Press.

Solo, R.A. (1975). *Organizing science for technology transfer in economic development* (pp. 37–40). Lansing, MI: Michigan State University Press.

Sorokin, P.A. (1941). *The crisis of our age: the social and cultural outlook.* New York: Dutton.

Spacapan, S. and Oskamp, S. (1990). People's reaction to technology. In S. Oskamp and S. Spacapan (Eds.), *People's reaction to technology*, Newbury Park: Sage.

Staw, B.M., Sandelands, L.E., and Dutton, J.E. (1981). Threat-rigidity effects in organizational behavior: A multilevel analysis, *Administrative Science Quarterly, 26*, 501–524.

Wakabayashi, M. and Graen, G.B. (1984). The Japanese career progress study: A 7-year follow-up, *Journal of Applied Psychology, 69*, 603–614.

Wakabayashi, M., Graen, G., Graen, M., and Graen, M. (1988). Japanese management progress: Mobility into middle management, *Journal of Applied Psychology, 73*, 217–227.

Wall, T.D., Corbett, J.M., Martin, R., Clegg, C.W., and Jackson, P.R. (1990). Advanced manufacturing technology, work design, and performance: A change study, *Journal of Applied Psychology, 75*, 691–697.

Wall, T.D., Clegg, C.W., and Kemp, N.J. (1987). *The human side of advanced manufacturing technology.* New York: Wiley.

Yukl, G.A. (1989). *Leadership in organizations*, Second edition. Englewood Cliffs, NJ: Prentice-Hall.

Women and Minorities
in Management

Ann M. Morrison
and Mary Ann Von Glinow

Management and executive positions, along with professional and technical jobs, are among the fastest growing occupations between 1984 and 1995 (U.S. Department of Labor, 1987). However, these occupations include jobs not traditionally held by women and minorities, who comprise the new work force. Therefore, one challenge for American organizations is to assimilate a more diverse labor force into high-status, high-skill management roles.

In this article, we examine the current status of women and minorities in management, including some recent changes. We present theoretical models from psychology and other social sciences, supported by recent data, to explain the progress and the barriers experienced by women and minorities. Finally, we explore potential remedies for the problems that endure, including programs and practices currently being applied in U.S. organizations as well as research directions that may increase our understanding of relevant issues.

We discuss White women and a wide range of minority groups, including Blacks, Hispanics, and Asians, but relevant research varies considerably in its coverage of various groups. The literature on White women is substantial, evidenced in part by the number of literature reviews done (nine reviews within the last 10 years were cited by Dipboye in 1987). In contrast, the research base on other minorities in management is quite small and is dominated by studies of Black men. Even employment statistics are difficult to uncover for minority groups in management (Cox & Nkomo, 1987; Larwood, Szwajkowski, & Rose, 1988a; Leinster, 1988; Thomas & Alderfer, 1989). Reviews of research on White women are cited instead of individual studies whenever possible, and our focus is on U.S. studies published since 1980.

CURRENT DATA ON THE STATUS OF WOMEN
AND MINORITIES IN MANAGEMENT

According to an Equal Employment Opportunity Commission (EEOC) report (cited by Bradsher, 1988), the number of women, Blacks, and Hispanics in management has quadrupled since 1970, and the number of Asians has increased eightfold. However, the rate of upward movement of women and minority managers provides "clear evidence of nothing less than the abiding racism and sexism of the corporation" (Bradsher, 1988, p. 1).

There is considerable evidence that White women and people of color encounter a "glass ceiling" in management. The glass ceiling is a concept popularized in the 1980s to describe a barrier so subtle that it is transparent, yet so strong that it prevents women and minorities from moving up in the management hierarchy. "Today, women fill nearly a third of all management positions (up from 19% in 1972), but most are stuck in jobs with little authority and relatively low pay" (Hymowitz & Schellhardt, 1986, p. 1D). A Korn/Ferry International (1982) survey reported that only 2% of 1,362 senior executives were women. A study of the Fortune 500, the Fortune Service 500, and the 190 largest health care organizations in the United States (Von Glinow & Krzyczkowska-Mercer, 1988) similarly found that only 3.6% of board directorships and 1.7% of corporate officerships in the Fortune 500 were held by women; the Fortune Service 500 and the health industry indicated that 4.4% of board members were women and that 3.8% and 8.5% of their corporate officers, respectively, were women.

Women do not fare any better in management in government or educational institutions. The U.S. government reported only 8.6% women in Senior Executive Service levels (U.S. Office of Personnel Management, 1989), with most female employees clustered in low-paying, nonprestigious GS 5–10 levels (U.S. Department of Labor, 1986). In education, Sandler's 1986 report shows that "on the average, colleges and universities nationwide employ 1.1 senior women (dean and above) per institution" (p. 14).

With regard to the racial composition of management ranks, the statistics show less progress than for women. Only one Black heads a Fortune 1000 company (Leinster, 1988). In the senior ranks, studies by Korn/Ferry International (reported by Jones, 1986) show little change.

Of 1,708 senior executives surveyed in 1979, 3 were Black, 2 were Asian, and 2 were Hispanic; only 8 were women, all of them White. In 1985, the list showed 4 Blacks, 6 Asians, 3 Hispanics, and 29 women. In Jones's (1986) words, "I think it's fair to say that this is almost no progress at all" (p. 84).

Some evidence also exists of a glass ceiling for Asians (Lan, 1988). In 1988, only 2.2% of California's Career Executive Assignment positions were held by Asians despite larger representation at the journey and midmanagement levels "that could be considered as qualifying developmental experience for these assignments" (Lan, 1988, p. 11).

With regard to management, one of the few surveys on minorities in business shows that in 1986 in 400 of the Fortune 1,000 companies, less than 9% of all managers were minorities, including Blacks, Hispanics, and Asians. A 1986 Equal Employment Opportunity Commission survey (cited by Leavitt, 1988) shows that from 1974 to 1984, the percentage of Black women officials and managers grew at 0.7% of the total, to 1.7%. Malveaux and Wallace (1987), Nkomo (1988), and others claimed that minority women are doubly disadvantaged in terms of upward mobility. They also noted that research on certain minority women, particularly Asians and American Indians, has essentially slipped through the cracks.

Those women and minorities who have advanced into management often find reward differentials. There is evidence that at higher occupational levels, women are less satisfied with their pay than are men (Varca, Shaffer, & McCauley, 1983). One study of 2,600 employees found substantial wage differences between men and women in managerial levels (Drazin & Auster, 1987); another reported that "women at the vice presidential levels and above earn 42% less than their male peers" (Nelton & Berney, 1987, p. 17). Earnings of Black men in management come closer to those of White men (Ploski & Williams, 1983).

The exodus of women and Blacks from corporate America is a disturbing trend sometimes attributed to differential treatment in management (Ellis, 1988; James, 1988; Leinster, 1988; Taylor, 1986). Women started their own businesses at six times the rate that men did between 1974 and 1984 (Leavitt, 1988). Of the 100 leading corporate women identified by a *Business Week* survey in 1976, nearly one third had left their corporate jobs for other pursuits 10 years later (DeGeorge, 1987).

A study by Morrison, White, Van Velsor, and the Center for Creative Leadership (1987) concluded that obstacles related to the glass ceiling will impede women's progress toward top management for the next several decades. Others concur, citing little hope for women or minorities in the near future. Dipboye (1987) claimed that even though female managers are progressing faster than their counterparts of decades ago, they still fail in terms of their rate of progress when compared with White males. *Business Week* recently concluded that "except for the true stars, the first generation of Black managers is destined to top out in middle levels" ("Progress Report," 1984, p. 105).

THEORETICAL PERSPECTIVES

A number of theories have been offered as to why sexual and racial differences exist within management. These theories tend to fall into three general groups. First are theories that assume that differences handicap women and minorities; these theories postulate that deficiencies in underrepresented groups are largely responsible for their differential treatment in management. Second are theories that cite discrimination by the majority population as the major cause of inequities. Here, bias and stereotyping on the part of White men in power are held to account for the slow progress of women and minorities. Third are theories that pinpoint structural, systemic discrimination as the root cause of differential treatment rather than actions or characteristics of individuals. These theories claim that widespread policies and practices in the social system perpetuate discriminatory treatment of women and people of color.

Theories Postulating Differences

Riger and Galligan (1980) noted that psychological researchers have emphasized person-centered variables to explain women's low job status. Women's traits, behaviors, attitudes, and socialization are said to make them inappropriate or deficient as managers because of such factors as their alleged fear of success or their unwillingness to take risks. Riger and Galligan noted that investigations of sex differences have yielded mixed results overall but that current field studies have generally refuted this explanation.

Data disputing both sex and race deficiencies come from the AT&T Assessment Center reports (Howard & Bray, 1988), which showed that female and male managers were more similar than different on personality and motivation factors as well as abilities. Race differences were greater than sex differences, but among the high-potential managers assessed, the relative weaknesses among Blacks in intellectual ability were compensated for by superior performance in interpersonal skills and stability of performance. There is considerable other evidence that women and men in management roles have similar aspirations, values, and other personality traits as well as job-related skills and behaviors (Dipboye, 1987; Dobbins & Platz, 1986; Harlan & Weiss, 1981; Liden, 1985; Morrison et al., 1987; Noe, 1988b; Powell, 1988; Riger & Galligan, 1980; Ritchie & Moses, 1983; White, Crino, & DeSanctis, 1981). Donnell and Hall's (1980) unusually large field study of nearly 2,000 matched pairs of female and male managers led them to conclude that "the disproportionately low numbers of women in management can no longer be explained away by the contention that women practice a different brand of management from that practiced by men" (p. 76).

The human capital theory attempts to explain continued sex- and race-related differences in management by suggesting that individuals are rewarded in their current jobs for their past investment in education and job training (Blau & Ferber, 1987). Workers may choose to accept a wage or to invest in acquiring new skills and experiences to qualify for higher-paying jobs. Blau and Ferber (1987) contended that if this explanation is correct, then women should choose the occupational setting they prefer and invest accordingly in their own human capital. Any policy changes that may be called for to correct differential treatment should be directed to the educational process rather than the employment setting because no differences other than those in human capital are seen as operating.

The human capital explanation assumes that investment pays off equally for all groups, but recent studies suggest that investment yields higher returns for White men than for women and minorities. Education level has not fully accounted for discrepancies in level or pay in recent studies of sex and race differences in management (Cabezas, Shinagawa, & Kawaguchi, 1989; Larwood et al., 1988a; Madden, 1985). Results of a survey of Asian Americans in professional and managerial positions indicate that education and work experience yield low returns in promotion or advancement (Cabezas, Tam, Lowe, Wong, & Turner, in press). Thus, person-centered theory cannot adequately explain differential treatment in management; other factors must also be considered.

Discrimination Explanations

The second group of theories targets bias on the part of the dominant group as the cause of differential treatment. The labor market discrimination explanation is an economic theory that assumes that relevant stakeholders—employers, customers, employees, and so forth—have discriminatory tastes even when women or minorities are perfect economic substitutes for White men in the workplace (Becker, 1957). Blau and Ferber (1987) pointed out that employers with discriminatory tastes hire women only at a wage discount large enough to compensate for the loss of utility or level of discomfort associated with employing them.

The rational bias explanation is a psychological theory that suggests that discrimination is influenced by contextual circumstances in which sexual or racial bias results in career rewards or punishments (Larwood, Gutek, & Gattiker, 1984; Larwood et al., 1988a; Larwood, Szwajkowski, & Rose, 1988b). In this case, a manager's decision to discriminate is based on whether such discrimination will be viewed positively or negatively by relevant stakeholders and on the possibility of receiving rewards for discriminating. Rational bias illustrates why discrimination can continue to occur despite substantial regulations against it (Larwood et al., 1988a, 1988b).

Discrimination by the dominant group was also addressed by Wells and Jennings (1983), who argued that Black individuals are not rewarded on the basis of their performance. Organizations that espouse and even mandate racial equality are also characterized by a psychological mind-set of entitlement on the part of the dominant Whites. Blacks' access to resources is limited, Wells and Jennings claimed, and Blacks are systematically excluded from advancement except for a few who are allowed in "threshold" or acceptable positions.

Discrimination occurs in part because of the belief by White men that women and people of color are less suited for management than White men. Comparing actual performance in managerial jobs is difficult, but there is growing concern that differential treatment of women and Blacks is not related to performance alone. Some studies suggest that deficiencies are presumed even when no differences exist because stereotypes based on historical roles persist (Davis & Watson, 1982; Dubno, 1985; Larwood et al., 1984; Leinster, 1988; Powell, 1988; Stevens, 1984; Thomas & Alderfer, 1989). The "good manager" is still described as masculine, rather than androgynous, despite the growing number of female managers (Powell & Butterfield, 1989). Ambiguity or lack of specific information about an individual contributes to bias against women and minorities because judgments are based on negative stereotypes of the group as a whole (Heilman & Martell, 1986; Nieva & Gutek, 1981; Noe, 1988b; Powell, 1988). For example, pay differentials for women may be related more to the salary allocation process than to performance evaluation because salary decisions are made by people less familiar with female managers than are their immediate supervisors (who conduct their performance appraisals), and so bias is more likely (Drazin & Auster, 1987; Freedman & Phillips, 1988). The stereotypes are so strong that contrary data are sometimes ignored in managerial selection and other managerial decisions (Freedman & Phillips, 1988; Heilman & Martell, 1986; Ilgen & Youtz, 1986). This research suggests that individuals, consciously or not, contribute to differential treatment of women and minorities in management.

Systemic Barriers

The third set of theories highlights structural discrimination. Intergroup theory (Alderfer, 1986; Thomas & Alderfer, 1989) suggests that two types of groups exist in organizations—identity groups (based on race, ethnicity, family, gender, or age) and organization groups (based on common work tasks, work experiences, and position in the hierarchy). Tension results because organization group membership changes, whereas identity group membership does not. When the pattern of group relations within an organization mirrors the pattern in society as a whole, such as when Whites predominate in high-status positions and Blacks are concentrated in low-status jobs, then evaluations of Blacks (or members of other low-status groups) are likely to be distorted by prejudice or anxiety as racist assumptions go unquestioned in the organization (Thomas & Alderfer, 1989).

Intergroup theory has elements in common with the dual labor market concept in economics. Dual labor market theory was proposed as an alternative explanation to the human capital theory of the 1960s when education and training of inner-city minority workers did not reduce their unemployment rate as much as was anticipated by policymakers at the time (Thurow, 1969). The dual labor market consists of a set of better, or primary, jobs and a set of worse, or secondary, jobs, with little mobility between the two. Groups most frequently associated with the secondary labor market (including women and minorities) are largely confined there, and discrimination is often justified as economic efficiency (Larwood & Gattiker, 1987; Osajima, 1988). Within management, the secondary jobs may be not only those at lower levels but also those in staff (vs. line) functions, wherein women and minorities are found in disproportionate numbers. Staff positions typically are out of the mainstream of the business and do not lead to top management posts (Jones, 1986; Larwood & Gattiker, 1987; Powell, 1988).

In the field of psychology, structural barriers are included as part of the situation-centered perspective (Riger & Galligan, 1980) and the organization structure perspective (Fagenson, 1988a; Kanter, 1977), which emphasize that women's lack of opportunity and power in organizations and the sex ratio of groups within organizations explain women's lack of managerial success. For example, Kanter's classic research pointed out that if a management cadre is at least 85% men, then the women in the group are "tokens" who very visibly represent women as a category whether they want to or not. These tokens' performances are hindered because of the pressure to which their visibility subjects them and because members of the dominant group exaggerate differences according to stereotypes they believe about women. Because people of color also become tokens in management ranks, the same dynamics may affect them (Ilgen & Youtz, 1986). Women, however, also face sexual harassment, which may be a result of skewed sex ratios favoring men (Gutek, 1985).

The dominance of White men in management poses another structural problem for underrepresented groups. Minorities struggle with fitting into two distinct cultural worlds, a concept called *biculturalism* that has been documented in studies of Black Americans (Thomas & Alderfer, 1989). Bell's (1988) research on bicultural conflict among Black women shows that those from cultures other than that of the dominant work group must choose how to manage the stress of moving physically, cognitively, and emotionally between the two cultural systems. For women of all races, responsibility for home, family, and social activities still accompanies a demanding management job, adding other major sources of pressure (Dipboye, 1987; Morrison et al., 1987; Powell, 1988).

The impact of structural factors is shown by researchers such as Irons and Moore (1985) in their study of the banking industry. They identified the three most significant problems faced by Blacks: (a) not knowing what is going on in the organization or not being in the network (rated as the most serious problem by 75% of survey respondents), (b) racism, and (c) inability to get a mentor. Irons and Moore pointed out that these results concur with those of Fernandez (1981) in showing a strong perception that minorities are excluded from informal work groups. In a study of Asian Americans in professional and management jobs, similar barriers to upward mobility were most often cited: a corporate culture alien to some Asian Americans, management insensitivity, and a lack of networks, mentors, and role models (Cabezas et al., in press). Other research has shown that many female and Black managers feel excluded from informal relationships with their White male colleagues (Rogan, 1984; Rosen, Templeton, & Kichline, 1981; Thomas & Alderfer, 1989).

Mentors and sponsors represent key relationships attributed to career success and, although research results are inconclusive as to whether women and minorities find fewer mentors than do White men, there is some indication that mentor relationships are harder to manage and provide a narrower range of benefits for women and minorities (Dickens & Dickens, 1982; Fagenson, 1988b; Fitt & Newton, 1981; Ford & Wells, 1985; Gooden, 1980; Herbert, 1986; Hunt & Michael, 1983; Kram, 1985; Noe, 1988b; Thomas & Alderfer, 1989). For example, cross-race relationships take longer to initiate, are more likely to end in an unfriendly fashion, and provide less psychosocial support than same-race relationships (Bearden, 1984; Thomas, 1986). Cross-sex mentor relationships are subjected to sexual innuendo, and Black women face taboos across both sex and race (Feinstein, 1987; Kram, 1985; Thomas, 1986). Women and minorities may need more mentors or sponsors than do their White male counterparts—White male superiors in their own area and same-sex or same-race mentors in other areas of the organization who increase their comfort (Thomas & Alderfer, 1989).

Major career development theories do not consider race as a factor, yet evidence from recent studies of Black managers suggests that Black identity development may slow or alter the career development process and affect Blacks' willingness to accept White mentors (Thomas & Alderfer, 1989). Larwood and Gattiker (1987) studied the career development of 215 employees in 17 firms and postulated a dual development model because career patterns differ between women and men as a result of widespread discrimination, competing demands outside work, and other structural barriers. Greenhaus, Parasuraman, and Wormley (1988) studied the career success of 828 managers in three companies. They found differences by sex and race, with Black women having more negative experiences than any other group. To the extent that organizational structures and practices follow models based solely on how White men develop, women and minorities are disadvantaged.

It is possible that elements of all three theoretical approaches described are significantly related to the lack of upward mobility in management for women and minorities. According to some, the interaction of situational factors (in the organization and in society at large) with person-centered characteristics (related to sex and race) accounts for differential treatment (Fagenson, 1988a; Fagenson & Horowitz, 1985; Ilgen & Youtz, 1986; Riger & Galligan, 1980). For example, without opportunities to take challenging assignments, minority managers may fall behind their White cohorts in terms of knowledge and skill development, or they may internalize negative evaluations and stereotypes to the point where they limit themselves and turn down future opportunities for fear they will not succeed (Ilgen & Youtz, 1986). Tests of the interaction between gender and job factors lend some support to this combined approach (Fagenson & Horowitz, 1985; Mainiero, 1986; Yammarino & Dubinsky, 1988) and suggest that remedies and continued research should be directed at all three sets of theories presented here.

REMEDIAL ACTIONS

In 1977, Kanter recommended that adjustments be made in the workplace to better accommodate women. She rejected the notion that women bear sole responsibility for equal opportunity in business. It is no longer uncommon to hear similar sentiment regarding both women and minorities (Larwood et al., 1984, 1988a), although actual implementation of adjustments remains an unmet goal for many organizations.

Some organizations may be able to make adjustments more effectively than others depending on the current status of the diversity in their management. A team at Procter & Gamble recommended that firms go beyond two generations of affirmative action into true "multicultural management" (Merenivitch & Reigle, 1979). Most firms tend to be in what they describe as the first generation of affirmative action, characterized by a focus on numbers that stimulates superficial and crisis-oriented actions, racial or sexual hostility, lack of trust, and a widespread presumption that women and minorities are less capable. Compliance with government regulations is the main goal. Some organizations have evolved to a second generation, where they meet most numerical goals and attempt to provide the necessary critical mass for support and role models. Their concern over retaining high-performing women and minorities means implementing accountability for effectively managing these groups.

Merenivitch and Reigle (1979) proposed that in multicultural organizations, the culture recognizes and appreciates diversity, resources and influence are distributed without regard to race or sex, and policies and practices are responsive to all employees' needs. In effect, the multicultural organization deliberately capitalizes on its diversity. As organizations evolve, different techniques for halting discrimination may be advocated depending on which phase the organization is in.

A variety of techniques are being used to reduce differential treatment and to bring diversity into organizations' cultures. Some techniques appear to be targeted toward the human capital issue, some toward discriminatory treatment, and some toward the structural and contextual barriers. Some techniques cover aspects of more than one theory. Education and training, for example, can be important steps for an organization. Some organizations, such as DuPont and GTE, provide additional classroom-training opportunities to women once they are hired, but the trend is to avoid segregating women or minorities so they are not seen as needing special help to become equally qualified. Many companies, such as IBM and Hewlett-Packard, provide no training at the corporate level for women per se, expecting that the training programs already being offered apply to all equally (Lee, 1986).

A recent development in training is the variety of programs geared to help managers work together within a diverse workforce and reduce discrimination. The value of programs on managing diversity is that issues are brought out into the open, allowing people to discuss their beliefs. One problem this addresses is that women and minorities who have felt pressure to remain silent on issues of sexism and racism now can confront the system rather than have doubts raised about their loyalty or be seen as "too ambitious" ("Blacks in Management," 1983; Jones, 1986; Lee, 1986; Morrison et al., 1987; Rosener, 1986). Eastman Kodak offers such a program to top division managers, and other firms run them for mixed groups, ensuring that at least one third to one half of the underrepresented groups participate in each program. DuPont began running its "Men and Women Working Together" program specifically for managers of saleswomen, but it has since opened it to various employee groups. A spinoff is a program for women only (Lee, 1986).

Despite these attempts to avoid treating women as different, demand for women-only programs is still strong. Because companies have made varying degrees of progress in attacking discrimination, and because some women and minorities rebel against attending segregated programs, the flexibility of organizations in providing different types of training is commendable. Limited research suggests that training may be most useful not in skill-building, but in areas such as career and self-awareness, mentoring, and leadership development (Dipboye, 1987; Lee, 1986; Staley, 1984; White et al., 1981).

Because women and minorities face special situations as tokens, they may need to perfect certain competencies such as conflict resolution. Researchers who have studied Black managers conclude that special skills and, therefore, specialized training may be needed by Blacks. If Blacks do not resolve conflicts that involve themselves or their area, they are likely to be blamed for the conflict (Dickens & Dickens, 1982). Blacks need to be skilled at managing racism and at managing their own rage over the racism they encounter (Cox & Nkomo, 1986; Dickens & Dickens, 1982; Simpson, 1981; Thomas & Alderfer, 1989). Thus, some skill-building programs, as well as awareness and assessment programs, may be appropriate to help women and minorities compete and cope in management.

Some research suggests that bias is most effectively decreased not only by education but also by exposure to and experience with members of the opposite sex and other races (Noe, 1988b; Powell, 1988). Working alongside a woman or a minority group member may be the key to quelling the discriminatory tastes of White men.

Incentives may also be needed to help overcome rational bias and other discrimination that legislation has failed to address and to reduce the effects of tokenism. Some organizations such as Corning Glass Works and Gannett are giving equal employment opportunity accountability to line managers, using bonuses as an incentive. Minority recruitment at Gannett, for example, is monitored by a committee of its publishers and factored into managers' bonus payouts (Roberts, 1988; Schmidt, 1988).

Other organizations use task forces to mandate and even implement changes. The Equitable Financial Company has been using the Women's Business Resource Group to identify and solve women's issues that emerge from the corporation's annual employee survey. According to Nelton and Berney (1987), this task force has been responsible for redesigning the job posting system as well as implementing flextime for working parents and toughening the company stand on sexual harassment. Task forces used in this way—to actually define the problem as well as create the cure—are more unusual than those aimed at problems already targeted, such as those on combining family and career. The task forces most highly praised seem to share several characteristics: direct access to the office of the president, influential members, and the resources required to try out new solutions (Lee, 1986; Nelton & Berney, 1987).

Career management is another key technique for eliminating the glass ceiling for women and people of color. Some research (McCall, Lombardo, & Morrison, 1988; Morrison et al., 1987) has suggested that challenging, successfully completed assignments are important to executives' development. Yet some assignments cited most frequently by the male executives studied were rarely cited by female executives. The indicators are that these assignments are less available to women, including start-ups, troubleshooting, and international experience (Morrison, 1988). The same kind of restrictions on minority managers may also block their advancement. One unusual task force has taken on the challenge of increasing the mobility of women and minorities between "secondary" jobs and primary jobs. Mobil's Committee of Executives targets high-potential women and minorities and places them in key line jobs (Nelton & Berney, 1987).

Senior managers can help move women and minorities out of secondary or threshold management posts by giving them opportunities to take such challenging assignments in the mainstream of the organization and to reinforce their authority in those assignments. A recent study revealed that "only one woman in five found the professional impact of gender to be primarily negative abroad" (Jelinek & Adler, 1988, p. 16). However, confronting superiors' resistance to get the assignment abroad was a major hurdle. Once a woman began the job, her senior male colleagues, particularly from the head office, became important in redirecting early client conversations away from her male colleagues and toward the woman herself to establish smooth, ongoing work relationships (Jelinek & Adler, 1988).

Career development functions such as these are often attributed to mentors; yet, as we noted, women and minorities face special problems with mentoring relationships. Some companies such as Ortho Pharmaceutical Corporation (Zintz, 1988) have tried formally assigning mentors to promising women and minorities, sometimes also including White male protégés in the program as well. However, there is little evidence that assigning mentors is effective (Feinstein, 1987; Noe, 1988a; Zey, 1985). One suggested alternative (or complement) to a formal mentor program is to provide training on how to be a mentor and how to be mentored (Dickens & Dickens, 1982; Feinstein, 1987; Willbur, 1987). Not only may this approach help build awareness of the barriers involved, but it may also allow the element of choice to continue in relationships initiated both by women and minorities seeking a mentor and by more senior managers who want to help.

Support groups may also help. Security Pacific National Bank created a program called Black Officers Support System (BOSS) to help recruit Blacks and reduce their turnover (Irons & Moore, 1985). The Executive Leadership Council in Washington, DC, consists of about 50 Black line managers from major industries who recruit and hire minorities (Leinster, 1988). These groups, along with the many internal women's networks and community groups for women and minorities, may help by providing career guidance and psychological support in managing biculturalism and other tensions.

Despite the existence of these various remedies, the glass ceiling continues to frustrate ambitious women and minorities. Although employers' attitudes appear to be changing, the lack of results can be partly attributed to the lack of employers committed to equal opportunity. A 1983 survey of nearly 800 business opinion leaders (reported by Jones,

1986) showed that of 25 possible human resource priorities, the issue of affirmative action for minorities and women ranked 23rd. Some efforts to attack discrimination in organizations have no doubt been piecemeal, and some may even have been harmful. When women believed they were hired only to meet EEOC guidelines, there was a negative effect on their self-image and development (Heilman, Simon, & Repper, 1987).

Poor results may also be attributed to confusion over which remedies affect which symptoms or causes of differential treatment. As Dipboye (1987) pointed out, few attempts have been made to evaluate training programs, as evidenced by the sparsity of evaluation studies in the literature.

RESEARCH NEEDED

Evaluating potential remedies to sex- and race-based differential treatment in management is no small task. One difficulty is that the organizational context is so complicated that factors external to specific remedies may affect the outcome more than the remedies themselves. Interventions that can and should be made in critical organizational practices such as recruitment and selection, evaluation, career development, and promotion may be greatly influenced by what Merlin Pope called "contextual prejudices," or exclusionary mechanisms that subtly keep women and minorities on the outside (Jaffe, 1985; Lee, 1986; Morrison et al., 1987; Nelton, 1988; Noe, 1988b; Powell, 1988; Sandler, 1986). A major challenge for researchers is to assess specific techniques, taking into account the effects of organizational culture and other contextual factors. Research across organizations to assess techniques would provide useful data that would allow executives to select those techniques shown to be more effective under circumstances matching those in their own organizations. Better links between specific techniques and theoretical constructs such as those reviewed here are also needed.

Many more fundamental research issues are apparent by the questions that remain. These include unraveling the effects of race, sex, and age in studies by separating female subjects by age and race, separating Blacks by sex and age, and so on. Another needed step is separating one minority group from another rather than grouping them as "minorities"; data on Hispanics and Asians are particularly needed. Assumptions are made about how White women experience the same or different treatment as men or women of color, but little research addresses this issue. Studies that separate the various groups would provide useful comparison data, particularly with regard to the impact of various remedial actions within organizations. Further theoretical refinement is also needed so that theories based on one group (such as White men) are not erroneously generalized to all others. Career development is one such area in which models developed on White males' career experiences may be inappropriately applied to women or minorities (Thomas & Alderfer, 1989).

The number of promising research areas is indicated by the number of questions this review has raised. We especially encourage research in organizations using actual managers and multiple methods so that the results reflect realistic situations. However, it is important that research be done on a variety of theoretical and applied issues. Research is needed to answer questions about whether actual or perceived differences are keeping women and minorities below a glass ceiling in management and the extent to which the structures and systems of organizations contribute to limited upward mobility. With the demographic changes already taking place in the U.S. labor force, restricting the pool of potential organizational leaders to White men only is foolhardy. Achieving diversity in management requires action. Continued research will help ensure that effective action is taken.

REFERENCES

Alderfer, C. P. (1986). An intergroup perspective on group dynamics. In J. Lorsch (Ed.), *Handbook of organizational behavior* (pp. 190–222). Englewood Cliffs, NJ: Prentice-Hall.

Bearden, K. W. (1984). *Women proteges' perception of the mentoring process.* Unpublished doctoral dissertation, University of Louisville.

Becker, G. (1957). *The economics of discrimination.* Chicago: University of Chicago Press.

Bell, E. L. (1988). *The bicultural life experience of career oriented black women.* Unpublished manuscript.

Blacks in management: No progress. (1983, January). *Management World.* p. 24.

Blau, F. D., & Ferber, M. A. (1987). Occupations and earnings of women workers. In K. S. Koziara, M. H. Moskow, & L. D. Tanner (Eds.), *Working women: Past, present, future* (pp. 37–68). Washington, DC: BNA Books.

Bradsher, K. (1988, March 17). Women gain numbers, respect in board rooms. *The Los Angeles Times*, pp. 1, 6.

Cabezas, A., Shinagawa, L. H., & Kawaguchi, G. (1989). Income and status differences between White and minority Americans: A persistent inequality. In S. Chan (Ed.), *Persistent inequality in the United States*. Lewiston, New York: Edwin Mellen Press.

Cabezas, A., Tam, T. M., Lowe, B. M., Wong, A., & Turner, K. (in press). Empirical study of barriers to upward mobility of Asian Americans in the San Francisco Bay area. In G. Nomura, R. Endo, R. Leong, & S. Sumida (Eds.), *Frontiers of Asian American studies*. Pullman: Washington State University Press.

Cox, T., Jr., & Nkomo, S. (1986). Differential performance appraisal criteria: A field study of black and white managers. *Group and Organization Studies, 11*, 101–119.

Cox, T., Jr., & Nkomo, S. (1987). *Race as a variable in OB/HRM research: A review and analysis of the literature*. Paper presented at the Symposium on Black Career Research, Drexel University, Philadelphia, PA.

Davis, G., & Watson, G. (1982). *Black life in corporate America*. Garden City, NY: Anchor Press/Doubleday.

DeGeorge, G. (1987, June 22). Where are they now? Business Week's leading corporate women of 1976. *Business Week*, pp. 76–77.

Dickens, F., Jr., & Dickens, J. B. (1982). *The black manager: Making it in the corporate world*. New York: Amacom.

Dipboye, R. L. (1987). Problems and progress of women in management. In K. S. Koziara, M. H. Moskow, & L. D. Tanner (Eds.), *Working women: Past, present, future* (pp. 118–153). Washington, DC: BNA Books.

Dobbins, G. H., & Platz, S. J. (1986). Sex differences in leadership: How real are they? *Academy of Management Review, 11*, 118–127.

Donnell, S. M., & Hall, J. (1980, Spring). Men and women as managers: A significant case of no significant difference. *Organizational Dynamics, 8*, 60–76.

Drazin, R., & Auster, E. R. (1987, Summer). Wage differences between men and women: Performance appraisal ratings vs. salary allocation as the locus of bias. *Human Resource Management, 26*, 157–168.

Dubno, P. (1985). Attitudes toward women executives: A longitudinal approach. *Academy of Management Journal, 28*, 235–239.

Ellis, J. (1988, March 14). The black middle class. *Business Week*, pp. 62–70.

Fagenson, E. A. (1988a). *At the heart of women in management research: Theoretical and methodological approaches and their biases*. Paper presented at the Women in Management (WIM) Conference, Halifax, Nova Scotia.

Fagenson, E. A. (1988b). The power of a mentor. *Group & Organization Studies, 13*, 182–194.

Fagenson, E. A., & Horowitz, S. V. (1985). On moving up: A rest of the person-centered, organization-centered and interactionist perspectives. *Academy of Management Proceedings*, 345–348.

Feinstein, S. (1987, November 10). Women and minority workers in business find a mentor can be a rare commodity. *The Wall Street Journal*, p. 39.

Fernandez, J. P. (1981). *Racism and sexism in corporate life*. Lexington, MA: Lexington Books.

Fitt, L. W., & Newton, D. A. (1981, March–April). When the mentor is a man and the protege a woman. *Harvard Business Review*, pp. 56–60.

Ford, D., & Wells, L., Jr. (1985). Upward mobility factors among black public administrators. *Centerboard: Journal of the Center for Human Relations Studies, 3*(1), 38–48.

Freedman, S. M., & Phillips, J. S. (1988). The changing nature of research on women at work. *Journal of Management, 14*, 231–251.

Gooden, W. (1980). *The adult development of black men.* Unpublished doctoral dissertation, Yale University.

Greenhaus, J. H., Parasuraman, S., & Wormley, W. M. (1988, August). *Organizational experiences and career success of black and white managers.* Paper presented at the Annual Meeting of the Academy of Management, Anaheim, CA.

Gutek, B. A. (1985). *Sex and the workplace.* San Francisco: Jossey-Bass.

Harlan, A., & Weiss, C. (1981, September). *Moving up: Women in managerial careers* (Working Paper No. 86). Wellesley, MA: Wellesley College, Center for Research on Women.

Heilman, M. E., & Martell, R. F. (1986). Exposure to successful women: Antidote to sex discrimination in applicant screening decisions? *Organizational Behavior and Human Decision Processes, 37*, 376–390.

Heilman, M. E., Simon, M. C., & Repper, D. P. (1987). Intentionally favored, unintentionally harmed? Impact of sex-based preferential selection on self-perceptions and self-evaluations. *Journal of Applied Psychology, 72*, 62–68.

Herbert, J. I. (1986). *The adult development of black male entrepreneurs.* Unpublished doctoral dissertation, Yale University.

Howard, A., & Bray, D. W. (1988). *Managerial lives in transition.* New York: Guilford.

Hunt, D. M., & Michael, C. (1983, July). Mentorship: A career training and development tool. *Academy of Management Review, 8*, 475–486.

Hymowitz, C., & Schellhardt, T. D. (1986, March 24). The glass ceiling. *The Wall Street Journal*, pp. 1D, 4D–5D.

Ilgen, D. R., & Youtz, M. A. (1986). Factors affecting the evaluation and development of minorities in organizations. *Personnel and Human Resources Management, 4*, 307–337.

Irons, E. D., & Moore, G. W. (1985). *Black managers: The case of the banking industry.* New York: Praeger.

Jaffe, B. (1985, September). A forced fit. *Training and Development Journal, 39*(9), 82–83.

James, F. E. (1988, June 7). More blacks quitting white-run firms: Many cite bias, desire to help minority firms. *The Wall Street Journal*, p. 37.

Jelinek, M., & Adler, N. J. (1988, February). Women: World-class managers for global competition. *Executive, II*, 11–19.

Jones, E. W., Jr. (1986, May–June). Black managers: The dream deferred. *Harvard Business Review*, pp. 84–93.

Kanter, R. (1977). *Men and women of the corporation.* New York: Basic Books.

Korn/Ferry International. (1982). *Profile of women senior executives.* New York: Author.

Kram, K. E. (1985). *Mentoring at work.* Glenview, IL: Scott, Foresman.

Lan, D. (1988, September 7). *Information hearing on Asian, Filipino, Pacific Islander (AFPI) demographics and employment.* Memo presented to the California State Personnel Board.

Larwood, L., & Gattiker, U. E. (1987). A comparison of the career paths used by successful women and men. In B. A. Gutek & L. Larwood (Eds.), *Women's career development* (pp. 129–156). Newbury Park, CA: Sage.

Larwood, L., Gutek, B., & Gattiker, U. E. (1984). Perspectives on institutional discrimination and resistance to change. *Group and Organization Studies, 9,* 333–352.

Larwood, L., Szwajkowski, E., & Rose, S. (1988a). Sex and race discrimination resulting from manager-client relationships: Applying the rational bias theory of managerial discrimination. *Sex Roles, 18,* 9–29.

Larwood, L., Szwajkowski, E., & Rose, S. (1988b). When discrimination makes "sense"—The rational bias theory of discrimination. In B. A. Gutek, A. H. Stromberg, & L. Larwood (Eds.), *Women and work.* Beverly Hills, CA: Sage.

Leavitt, J. A. (1988). *Women in administration and management: An information sourcebook.* New York: Oryx Press.

Lee, C. (1986, December). Training for women: Where do we go from here? *Training,* pp. 26–40.

Leinster, C. (1988, January 18). Black executives: How they're doing. *Fortune,* pp. 109–120.

Liden, R. C. (1985). Female perceptions of female and male managerial behavior. *Sex Roles, 12,* 421–433.

Madden, J. F. (1985). The persistence of pay differentials: The economics of sex discrimination. In L. Larwood, A. H. Stromberg, & B. A. Gutek (Eds.), *Women and work: An annual review,* (Vol. 1, pp. 76–114). Beverly Hills, CA: Sage.

Mainiero, L. A. (1986). Coping with powerlessness: The relationship of gender and job dependency to empowerment-strategy usage. *Administrative Science Quarterly, 31,* 633–653.

Malveaux, J., & Wallace, P. (1987). Minority women in the work-place. In K. S. Koziara, M. H. Moskow, & L. D. Tanner (Eds.), *Working women: Past, present, future* (pp. 265–298). Washington, DC: BNA Books.

McCall, M. W., Jr., Lombardo, M. M., & Morrison, A. M. (1988). *The lessons of experience.* Lexington, MA: Lexington Books.

Merenivitch, J., & Reigle, D. (1979, January). *Toward a multicultural organization.* (Available from The Proctor & Gamble Company, Personnel Development Department, Cincinnati, OH.)

Morrison, A. M. (1988, May). *Comparing the career paths of men and women.* Paper presented at The Conference Board's conference on *Women in the corporation: The value added,* New York, NY.

Morrison, A. M., White, R. P., Van Velsor, E., & the Center for Creative Leadership (1987). *Breaking the glass ceiling: Can women reach the top of America's largest corporations?* Reading, MA: Addison Wesley.

Nelton, S. (1988, July). Meet your new work force. *Nation's Business*, pp. 14–21.

Nelton, S., & Berney, K. (1987, May). Women: The second wave. *Nation's Business*, pp. 18–27.

Nieva, V. F., & Gutek, B. A. (1981). *Women and work: A psychological perspective*. New York: Praeger.

Nkomo, S. M. (1988). Race and sex: The forgotten case of the black female manager. In S. Rose & L. Larwood (Eds.), *Women's careers: Pathways and pitfalls*. New York: Praeger.

Noe, R. A. (1988a). An investigation of the determinants of successful assigned mentoring relationships. *Personnel Psychology, 41*, 457–479.

Noe, R. A. (1988b). Women and mentoring: A review and research agenda. *Academy of Management Review, 13*, 65–78.

Osajima, K. (1988). Asian Americans as the model minority: An analysis of the popular press image in the 1960s and 1980s. In G. Y. Okihiro, S. Hune, A. A. Hansen, & J. M. Liu (Eds.), *Reflections on shattered windows: Promises and prospects for Asian American studies*. Pullman: Washington State University Press.

Ploski, H. A., & Williams, J. (1983). *The Negro almanac: A reference work on the Afro-American*. New York: Wiley.

Powell, G. N. (1988). *Women and men in management*. Newbury Park, CA: Sage.

Powell, G. N., & Butterfield, D. A. (1989). The "good manager": Did androgyny fare better in the 1980's? *Group and Organization Studies, 14*(2), 216–233.

Progress report on the Black executive: The top spots are still elusive. (1984). *Business Week*, pp. 104–105.

Riger, S., & Galligan, P. (1980). An exploration of competing paradigms. *American Psychologist, 35*, 902–910.

Ritchie, R. J., & Moses, J. L. (1983, May). Assessment center correlates of women's advancement into middle management: A 7-year longitudinal analysis. *Journal of Applied Psychology, 68*, 227–231.

Roberts, J. L. (1988, May 11). Gannett surpasses other newspaper firms in the hiring and promotion of minorities. *The Wall Street Journal*, p. 25.

Rogan, H. (1984, October 26). Young executive women advance farther, faster than predecessors. *The Wall Street Journal*, p. 31.

Rosen, B., Templeton, N. C., & Kichline, K. (1981, December). First few years on the job: Women in management. *Business Horizons, 24*, 26–29.

Rosener, J. B. (1986, December 7). Coping with sexual static. *The New York Times Magazine*, pp. 89, 120–121.

Sandler, B. R. (1986, October). *The campus climate revisited: Chilly for women faculty, administrators, and graduate students*. Washington, DC: The Project on the Status and Education of Women, Association of American Colleges.

Schmidt, P. (1988, October 16). Women and minorities: Is industry ready? *The New York Times*, pp. 25, 27.

Simpson, J. C. (1981, January). The woman boss. *Black Enterprise*, pp. 20–25.

Staley, C. C. (1984, September). Managerial women in mixed groups: Implications of recent research. *Groups and Organization Studies, 9*, 316–332.

Stevens, G. E. (1984, June). Attitudes toward blacks in management are changing. *Personnel Administrator*, pp. 163–171.

Taylor, A., III. (1986). Why women managers are bailing out. *Fortune*, pp. 16–23.

Thomas, D. A. (1986). *An intra-organizational analysis of black and white patterns of sponsorship and the dynamics of cross-racial mentoring*. Unpublished doctoral dissertation, Yale University.

Thomas, D. A., & Alderfer, C. P. (1989). The influence of race on career dynamics: Theory and research on minority career experiences. In M. Arthur, D. Hall, & B. Lawrence (Eds.), *Handbook of career theory*. Cambridge, England: Cambridge University Press.

Thurow, L. (1969). *Poverty and discrimination*. Washington, DC: The Brookings Institute.

U.S. Department of Labor. (1986). *Meeting the challenges of the 1980's*. Washington, DC: Women's Bureau, U.S. Department of Labor.

U.S. Department of Labor. (1987, May). *Work force 2000*. Washington, DC: Employment and Training Administration, U.S. Department of Labor.

U.S. Office of Personnel Management (1989). *Report on minority group and sex by pay plan and appointing authority* (EPMD Report No. 40, March 31, 1989). Washington, DC: U.S. Office of Personnel Management.

Varca, P., Shaffer, G. S., & McCauley, C. D. (1983, June). Sex differences in job satisfaction revisited. *Academy of Management Journal, 26*, 348–353.

Von Glinow, M. A., & Krzyczkowska-Mercer, A. (1988, Summer) Women in corporate America: A caste of thousands. *New management, 6*, pp. 36–42.

Wells, L., & Jennings, C. L. (1983). Black career advances and white reactions: Remnants of Herrenvolk democracy and the scandalous paradox. In D. Vails-Webber & W. N. Potts (Eds.), *Sunrise seminars* (pp. 41–47). Arlington, VA: NTL Institute.

White, M. C., Crino, M. D., & DeSanctis, G. L. (1981). A critical review of female performance, performance training and organizational initiatives designed to aid women in the work-role environment. *Personnel Psychology, 34*, 227–248.

Willbur, J. (1987, November). Does mentoring breed success? *Training and Development Journal*, pp. 38–41.

Yammarino, F. J., & Dubinsky, A. J. (1988). Employee responses: Gender- or job-related differences? *Journal of Vocational Behavior, 32*, 366–383.

Zintz, A. C. (1988, May). *Succession planning, career tracks and mentoring*. Paper presented at The Conference Board, Inc.'s conference on "Women in the Corporation: The Value Added," New York, NY.

Zey, M. (1985, February). Mentor programs: Making the right moves. *Personnel Journal*, pp. 53–57.

It's Not Easy Being Green: Jealousy and Envy in the Workplace

Robert P. Vecchio

Given the inherent competitiveness of a great deal of organizational life, it may be reasonable to claim that the experience of jealousy and envy by employees ranks among the more common emotional experiences in organizational settings. In recent years, I have begun my graduate-level courses by asking students to provide confidential examples of jealousy and/or envy that they have experienced in the workplace, either as an observer or as the person who felt a strong negative reaction. Using this approach as part of an anonymous written exercise, I have found that respondents have no difficulty citing at least several instances of jealousy and/or envy. One confidential survey of the frequency of the experience of employee jealousy (Miner, 1990) revealed that 77% of a sample of 278 employees had observed an instance of jealousy during the prior month, with 58% of the respondents being directly involved in the event. These instances were reported to occur with a mean frequency of 3.6 events per month, and, perhaps more importantly, with a majority of the respondents reporting that managers were not effectively handling these situations.

Despite the fairly commonplace nature of this experience, surprisingly little systematic research on employee affect and behavior has directly addressed these topics (Vecchio, 1993a). Although popular magazines have shown a continuing increase in discussing the topic of jealousy since 1945 (Clanton, 1989), only during the late 1980s and into the 1990s has interest in jealousy and envy begun to receive serious attention from social science researchers (Salovey, 1991; Stearns, 1989; White & Mullen, 1989). The absence of empirically-based attention to these topics may be partly due to the difficulties associated with studying an issue that is inherently distasteful. Many people are simply embarrassed to publicly acknowledge strong, negative emotions. In a study of the likableness ratings of 555 personality-trait words, Norman Anderson (1968) reported that "jealousy" ranked 502nd on "favorableness or desirability," below the traits of "cold" (496th) and "unfair" (498th). "Envious" ranked 425th, comparable to "short-tempered" (422nd) and "weak" (429th). In essence, these emotions are regarded as noxious and unpleasant, as well as potentially inevitable, yet inappropriate for social display. Moreover, there is a tendency on the part of many supervisors to dismiss employee complaints concerning pay allocations, promotions, performance evaluations, and task assignments as "merely" reflecting jealousy and/or envy.

The absence of research on jealousy and envy, particularly in work settings, may stem also from difficulties in measuring these psychological experiences and associated behavioral manifestations. Additionally, the lack of a distinct theoretical framework for defining employee jealousy and envy, and deducing predictions within the organizational domain, may have served to limit work on the topic.

This paper seeks to begin discussion concerning the role of employee jealousy and envy. In the following sections, we consider the definition of jealousy and envy in the workplace, consequences of these emotions, the utility of existing organizational theories for understanding these emotions, their measurement, the generation of specific hypotheses that pertain to these emotional experiences, some preliminary evidence on several of the hypotheses, the management of negative emotions, and further issues associated with the organizational and cross-cultural aspects of these emotions.

DEFINING EMPLOYEE JEALOUSY AND ENVY

Although feelings of jealousy and envy at work are generally denigrated, they have been traditionally recognized in literature and the arts as a powerful influence on behavior. For example, in Shakespeare's *Othello*, Iago is passed over for promotion in favor of Cassio (despite the fact that Iago has a stronger service record than Cassio). Resentment of Cassio's advancement prompts Iago to contrive events so as to lead Othello to suspect his wife of infidelity with Cassio, and ultimately to murder her (Todd & Dewhurst, 1955). A contributing factor to Iago's malice is his prior admiration of Othello. In Shaffer's play *Amadeus* (1981), Mozart's creative genius and personal style spark bitterness and rancor on the part of a colleague, Salieri. The level of resentment is so great that Salieri conspires to limit Mozart's success as a composer and to ensure Mozart's early demise, while simultaneously feigning admiration and friendship.[1] In a number of respects, these literary works highlight some basic elements and processes of jealousy and envy in that the aggrieved adopt courses of action that seek a form of vengeance while concealing their true feelings.

Jealousy

In order to study the phenomenon of jealousy more systematically, social scientists have recently sought to define jealousy. Based on White and Mullen's (1989, p. 9) examination of romantic jealousy, we can more generically define jealousy as a pattern of thoughts, emotions, and behaviors that results from the loss of self-esteem and/or the loss of outcomes associated with a relationship. This perceived loss, or threat, is due to the perception of a real (or potential) attraction between a significant other and a (potentially imagined) rival.[2] This definition suggests that the pattern is a response to an initial perception of the perceived intrusion of a rival, and the likelihood that the rival will reduce one's self-esteem or threaten an existing valued relationship. The definition identifies three essential participants (i.e., the phenomenon is inherently triadic) for whom the relations among the elements form the basis of a "social tension." Also, the definition recognizes that jealousy may be: (1) largely illusory, but that the impact of such illusions for the participants is real, and (2) anticipatory in nature (i.e., a response to expected threats as well as existing threats). Last, the definition recognizes the central role of self-esteem in the experience.

Although the above definition emphasizes cognitive-perceptual processes in the experience, it is nonetheless important to recognize the physiological base of the experience. As is true of other emotions, visceral reactions (a stress "fight or flight" response) serve to define the experience on a personal level (Selye, 1976).[3] In some instances, the initial emotional reaction is quite strong—being referred to as a "flash" of jealousy. This initial strong reaction tends to be recalled vividly and over a long span of time (Clanton & Smith, 1977).

While jealousy may be examined in a fairly generic fashion, it is important to recognize the unique varieties or types of jealousy that exist. Two major types that have received the most attention from researchers are romantic jealousy (White, 1981a) and sibling jealousy

(Banks & Kahn, 1982; Dunn, 1983). In the work setting (a largely unexplored social arena), jealousy may exist for an employee toward a coworker who poses as a rival to a valued relationship with a supervisor or another co-worker. Although probably less commonly observed, a supervisor may also experience jealousy toward a subordinate who poses as a rival to a valued relationship with another subordinate. However, the following discussion primarily focuses on jealousy and envy experienced by employees toward peers.

Although jealousy can be examined in generic terms, aspects of working relationships are sufficiently unique to qualify for a separate discussion. For example, the norms that govern social relations in work settings are distinct from those that operate in family units (i.e., among siblings and parents) and between lovers. The difficulty of terminating relations, and the acceptability of recourse to physical violence are generally lower in work settings versus other contexts, while social pressure to deliberately ignore rivals is greater in work settings (Gayford, 1979; Stets & Pirog-Good, 1987). These differences in norms pose unique constraints on responses to the experience of jealousy. Additionally, the nature of the rewards that are exchanged in working relationships differ from those that are used in other social relations (Foa & Foa, 1980). For example, the ability of a supervisor to confer status via public recognition of a subordinate's efforts and to alter tangible extrinsic outcomes, are rewards that are fairly unique to working relations.

Envy

After stating what employee jealousy is, it is also important to state what it is not. Jealousy is probably most frequently confused with the experience of envy. However, the experiences are, upon scrutiny, recognizable as distinct (Parrott, 1991). Jealousy pertains to the loss of an existing relationship, while envy pertains to another possessing what one desires for oneself. Succinctly stated, envy concerns what we would like to have, but do not have, while jealousy concerns what we have, but fear we may lose (Van Sommers, 1988). Employee jealousy involves a win/lose outcome relative to a rival, while in employee envy, another's gain need not be at one's own personal expense. Moreover, hostility that accompanies employee jealousy is relatively more socially approved than hostility or ill will that may accompany feelings of employee envy.

That is to say, many people believe that it is acceptable to feel anger or resentment in response to the intrusion of a specific rival, more so than to feel resentment of the success of others in general. Furthermore, subjects report that jealousy produces more intense affective response than does envy (Salovey & Rodin, 1986). Individuals also report that envy is more characterized by a sense of inferiority, self-criticism, and a desire to improve, while jealousy is more characterized by suspicion, fear of loss, anger, rejection, and a desire to get even (Parrott & Smith, 1993; Smith, Kim, & Parrott, 1988). One reason that envy may be especially difficult for people to admit to is that in recognizing it in oneself, a person acknowledges inferiority with respect to another (Foster, 1972). In so doing, there is a loss of self-esteem. A further issue that contributes to the confusion of jealousy and envy is the reality that envy can exist without feelings of jealousy, while jealousy may often be accompanied by feelings of envy.

Both envy and jealousy are similar in terms of involving a loss of self-esteem that is derived from social comparison. As a result, both envy and jealousy may coexist in a specific social instance, in that a rival in a jealousy-invoking situation may arouse envy via an unfavorable social comparison. In essence, the experience of jealousy that is derived from an unfavorable comparative appraisal made by a valued or admired other, can lead to a negative self-appraisal or self-dissatisfaction and, hence, envy. Like workplace jealousy, employee envy is a neglected topic in organizational research, despite the unquestioned occurrence of the experience by employees. Envy and jealousy can be viewed as deriving from two fundamental realities of organizational life: competition and hierarchy. It may be said that envy is to competition what jealousy is to hierarchy (Simmel, 1955). Both emotions can be seen as deriving from an inability to control events, in that jealousy reflects an inability to control (or influence) the target member of a valued relationship, while envy reflects an inability to control (or influence) the allocation of outcomes. In a more basic sense, the desire to control events is a component of jealousy and envy (i.e., in order to maintain an extreme form of attachment, and in order to influence the assignment of rewards, respectively). Furthermore, both jealousy and envy can be understood as an emergent concern with the perceived erosion of one's social standing. For purposes of discussion, envy can be formally defined as a pattern of thoughts, emotions, and behaviors that results from the loss of self-esteem in response to another obtaining out-comes that one strongly desires.

A useful distinction of the types of negative emotions that are found in organizational settings lies in the level of threat. Hupka (1984) has offered the terms "*fait accompli*" and "*suspicious*" to define, respec-tively, the incontrovertible and accepted reality that a rival or competi-tor is now receiving the type of attention or rewards that the protagonist values, versus a condition where the threat is only suspected and the nature of the threat is not clear. The condition of "suspiciousness" car-ries a greater sense of anxiety concerning the status of the situation, and offers the prediction that information-gathering behaviors on the part of the protagonist are far more likely (e.g., monitoring the actions of others, and the questioning of others). In some instances, "fait accompli" may lead to cognitive reappraisals of the relationship, and a form of begrudging resignation. The two forms of threat can be viewed as representing two levels of jealousy and envy, with each level predisposing different emo-tional and behavioral responses.

CONSEQUENCES OF WORKPLACE JEALOUSY AND ENVY

As social emotions possessing negative connotations and sources of stress, there is a tendency to view workplace jealousy and envy as neces-sarily dysfunctional. From one perspective, employee jealousy and envy can be, in fact, quite functional in that they can energize behavior and act as discriminative cues for eliciting coping responses. Essentially, employee jealousy and envy can serve the social function of protecting highly valued relationships and circumstances. This is not to argue that jealousy and envy are not potentially pathological. In the extreme, they certainly can be precisely that. Recent reports of increased violence in the work setting (including the murder of co-workers and supervisors) and the more commonplace forms of harassment of rivals indicate that work set-tings are not exempt from pathological reactions (Sprouse, 1992).[4] Short of the range of responses (which includes preoccupation or obsessive thinking) that mark the pathological realm of behavioral response, work-place jealousy and envy can be viewed as sources of "cognitive tension" that activate coping responses (Festinger, 1954). From this perspective, workplace jealousy and envy can serve socially useful purposes for an individual by focusing attention and action on the resolution of a threat.

The available literature on the topic of coping with emotions has some relevance to work settings. White and Mullen (1989) have identified nine major coping strategies, in addition to a variety of minor coping responses (e.g., humor, projection, and fantasy). "Strategy," in this context, means a cognitive structure organized in terms of superordinate goals, and associated representations of the cognitive and behavioral steps that are required to achieve the desired goals. As superordinate goals, the cognitions and actions of the protagonist are directed at either altering the situation (to reduce the threat), managing the associated affect, or both. Tables 1 and 2 list the coping strategies and the superordinate goals of each strategy, and provides organizational examples.

RESEARCH OF POTENTIAL RELEVANCE TO WORKPLACE JEALOUSY AND ENVY: SEARCHING FOR GENERALIZABLE PRINCIPLES

As noted earlier, empirical research on jealousy, per se, among family members is still in an early stage, while research on jealousy in organizational settings is essentially nonexistent. Nonetheless, some of the findings from the existing literature may have relevance for individuals in organizations. Therefore, it can be instructive to review some of these potentially pertinent findings.

One stream of research has begun to examine whether patterns of jealousy in adulthood can be linked to childhood experiences with parental or sibling rivals. A critical argument for studying adult jealousy in this fashion is that work group settings resemble sibling situations as group members vie for the primary attention of the idealized group leader (i.e., the equivalent of a parental figure). Also, it can be reasonably argued that the manner in which people learn to relate to authority figures and peers is influenced by early socialization experiences within the family unit. Interestingly, sibling jealousy has been found to be less common in larger families (Dunn, 1983), suggesting, thereby, that other family unit members can satisfy the needs of an individual beyond the parents. By extension, we might expect to find that employee jealousy is less severe, with respect to relations with a supervisor, in larger work units.

Gender differences have also received study, with the debate focusing on whether one gender is more prone to a jealous response. In a review of research on gender and job values, Nieva and Gutek (1981)

Table 1
Features of Major Coping Strategies: Primary Focus on Jealousy

Strategy	Superordinate Goal(s)	Organizational Examples
Improve relationship with target	Situation	Project image of loyalty or offer praise
		Take on greater work load and responsibility
Interfere with rival's relationship	Situation	Display resentment or hostility
		Arouse guilt
Demand commitment	Situation, affect	Seek assignment to more critical/desirable tasks
Derogation of target	Affect	Come to accept that target is not one's ideal
		Provoke the target to rejection
Develop alternatives	Affect, situation	Seek social rewards in other co-workers
		Become more involved in the work itself
Denial/Avoidance	Affect	Pretend to be unaffected
		Use of alcohol or drugs
Self-assessment	Situation, affect	Alter one's approach to the work setting
Seek support	Affect	Commiserating with a colleague
Appraise challenge	Affect, situation	Renegotiate the relationship
		Use outsider (consultant) to air grievances and manage conflict
Bolstering one's self-image	Affect	Dwelling on one's own positive attributes
		Indulging one's own interests

Source: Adopted from White and Mullen (1989).

argued that women, relative to men, value promotions and salary less, while valuing interpersonal relationships more. Other research suggests that women strive for interpersonal or social success, while men strive for exploitive or competitive success (Buss, Larsen, Westen, & Semmelroth, 1992; Kahn, O'Leary, Krulewitz, & Lamm, 1980; Nadler & Dotan, 1992). Therefore, it seems reasonable to expect differences in response by the genders to threats to relationships and competitive

Table 2
Features of Major Coping Strategies: Primary Focus on Envy

Strategy	Superordinate Goal(s)	Organizational Example
Improve relationship with rival	Situation	Recognizing rival's superior position, but engaging the rival as a friend in hopes of improving one's later rewards.
Diminish rival's outcomes	Situation, Affect	Display resentment or hostility Sabotage rival's work Harassment or ostracism of rival
Demand greater, alternative out comes from superior	Situation, Affect	Seek assignment to more rewarding/desirable tasks
Derogation of rival	Affect	"Back-stabbing" of competitor to supervisor Spreading slanderous gossip, misinformation and disinformation
Develop alternatives	Affect, Situation	Seek alternative rewards in other coworkers, or the work itself
Denial/avoidance	Affect	Pretend to be disinterested in rival Use of alcohol or drugs Compel rival to offer reciprocal compliments
Self-assessment	Situation, Affect	Alter one's approach to the work setting
Seek support	Affect	Commiserating with a colleague
Appraise challenge	Affect, Situation	Renegotiate the relationship Use outsider (consultant) to air grievances and manage conflict
Bolstering one's self-image	Affect	Dwelling on one's own positive attributes Indulging one's own interests
Seek "sop" behavior	Situation, Affect	Encourage rival to offer tokens of symbolic sharing
Seek true sharing	Situation	Encourage rival or rival's superior to genuinely share resources (e.g., rotating tasks, or work schedules)
Seek creation of redistributive mechanism	Situation	Seek imposition of a "taxation" system (e.g., shifting financial resources and adjustments in budgets) Support collective bargaining efforts
Seek encapsulation	Situation	Request separate facilities to reduce social contact

standing. Thus far, the majority of the results of this research has not found reliable gender differences in the level of self-reported jealousy (Bringle & Buunk, 1985; White, 1984). The genders may differ, however, in preferences for coping strategies. Bryson (1976) observed that females predicted they would more likely seek social support, engage in denial, and try to get even, while males predicted they would more likely drink to excess, be sexually aggressive with others, and ask a mutual friend to talk to the target. More recently, Brockner and Adsit (1986) found that satisfaction within a relationship is more strongly related to perceptions of equity among men than women. Kahn (1972) also found that men are more likely than women to distribute income to individuals in direct proportion to their input. Hence, the issue of gender differences remains open to study.

Finally, other research has found that relative dependence is positively related to feelings of jealousy (White, 1981a). Also, a person who is in a more powerful social position is likely to respond to a jealous threat with anger, while a person who is in a more dependent position is likely to respond with depression. This suggests that supervisors are more likely to respond to a threat to a relationship involving a subordinate with anger, while subordinates may experience depression in a reverse of the situation (White, 1985).

IDENTIFIABLE RESEARCH QUESTIONS

Despite its comparative infancy as a topic of scientific inquiry, there are a number of testable hypotheses concerning workplace jealousy and envy that can be generated both deductively (from prior theory in the domain of negative emotional reactions) and intuitively (from experience with social dynamics in the workplace).

The following is a list of questions that forms an agenda for research on workplace jealousy and envy:

1. Do supervisors who display high levels of consideration (i.e., in the Ohio State leadership sense of the term) have units with higher levels of employee jealousy (jealousy among children has been found to be greater in families with intensely affectionate mothers, Stearns, 1989, p. 76)?
2. Are the levels of employee jealousy and envy in smaller work units lower than in larger work units?

3. Are there differences between the genders in reports of jealousy and envy (Kahn et al., 1980) such that females respond more strongly to threats to relationships (jealousy), while males respond more strongly to threats to competitive standing (envy)?

4. Are employee jealousy and envy correlated with such organizational constructs as:

   a. individual in-group/out-group status (Graen & Cashman, 1975)—we should expect to find that out-group members report more jealousy and envy relative to in-group members because they are aware of differences in the quality of supervisor-subordinate working relations, and they are aware of differences in reward allocations;

   b. subscription to the work ethic (Kanungo, 1982; Mathieu & Zajac, 1990)—individuals who value the work ethic may be more attuned to differences in reward allocations and working relationships and hence may report greater feelings of envy and jealousy, relative to others who do not place a high value on the work ethic;

   c. general job satisfaction (Brayfield & Rothe, 1951)—employees who report higher levels of such negative feelings as jealousy and envy could reasonably be expected to report lower levels of overall job satisfaction;

   d. satisfaction with supervision (Smith, Kendall, & Hulin, 1969)—because supervisors play a role in deciding who is in/out in working relationships, and also influence reward allocation decisions, reports of jealousy and envy should be inversely related with satisfaction with one's supervisor; and

   e. predisposition to quit (Dittrich & Carrell, 1979; Spencer & Steers, 1980)—employees who report higher levels of jealousy and envy should also report a relatively stronger predisposition to find alternative employment.

Before the above hypotheses can be tested, measures of employee jealousy and envy are required. As noted previously, people are reluctant to admit to negative social emotions (Sommers, 1984). Jealousy and envy, in particular, are denigrated emotions because they are presumed to reflect insecurity and immaturity. Prior efforts to develop measures of jealousy have produced a number of instruments that require the assumption that self-reports are an accurate reflection of reality, while other instruments rely on "what-if" hypothetical scenarios to obtain individual predispositions. Hypothetical-scenario instruments essentially require a type of role-playing exercise. The construct validity of each of these various scales is far from satisfactorily demonstrated. However, there are some creative illustrations of validation efforts. Specifically, Mathes, Phillips, Skowran, and Dick (1982) investigated the validity of the Interpersonal Jealousy Scale (a paper-and-pencil questionnaire wherein respondents indicate how they would behave in response to various social situations involving a target and a rival) by having dating couples complete the scale, and then having a confederate (of the same sex) call each member of the couple to ask for permission to date the respondent's partner. Tape-recordings of the phone conversations were rated by judges with respect to granting permission. Scores on the Interpersonal Jealousy Scale were significantly negatively correlated with obtained permission for both men and women respondents. Unfortunately, many other instruments in the area do not have comparable validation data, but instead rely largely on evidence of factorial validity and internal consistency. While theoretical definitions of jealousy and envy have viewed it as a complex construct, composed of feelings, cognitions, and behaviors aroused by threat-evoking situations, measures have tended to be fairly simplistic (yielding single, univariate indices). More complex measures might deliberately incorporate separate affective, cognitive, and behavioral dimensions (Bringle & Buunk, 1985).

Studying jealousy and envy in organizational settings may impose other unique problems. For example, one would ideally hope to find agreement in actor (protagonist) and observer's ratings. Yet, impression management of feelings by employees would likely cause observers to have difficulty in making accurate assessments. Also, it seems critical that employees who are experiencing negative emotions be the object of study in order to more accurately determine what protagonists, targets, and rivals actually do, feel, and think (White & Mullen, 1989).

As noted earlier, the emotions of jealousy and envy may be viewed as being related to a feeling that one lacks control over events (i.e., control over valued relationships and reward allocations). Self-esteem is related to one's sense of being able to control events. One of the more frequently studied correlates of jealousy has been the trait of self-esteem. While one would expect that people who are low in self-esteem may feel more vulnerable to threats by rivals, it is also possible that people who are high in self-esteem may be more sensitive to esteem threats (Tetlock & Manstead, 1985). Perhaps not surprisingly, therefore, evidence for an association between measures of jealousy and global self-esteem has been mixed (Bringle, 1981; Buunk, 1982; Hansen, 1982; White, 1981a, 1981b; Melamed, 1991; Salovey & Rodin, 1991), with reported relationships ranging from zero to moderately negative. In one study (Hansen, 1985), low self-esteem was found to be associated with jealousy for females, but not for males. White and Mullen (1989) argue that global self-esteem measures are not sufficiently related to relevant aspects of self to be useful, and that future research employ more focused measures of relevant aspects of self-esteem. In our present concern with organizational extensions of these prior findings, we would anticipate that work-related aspects of self-esteem (i.e., Brockner, 1988; Pierce, Gardner, Cummings, & Dunham, 1989) would likely be more predictive of jealous reactions than global measures of self-esteem. In a study of the effects of co-worker turnover on the attitudes of those who remain (i.e., stayers), Brockner and Kim (1987) found that low self-esteem co-workers (relative to their high self-esteem counterparts) felt more dissatisfied when the departed co-worker took a better job, and less dissatisfied when the co-worker had left for a worse job. Also, low self-esteem employees are more reactive than their counterparts to role conflict, ambiguity, overload, and poor supervisory support (Pierce, Gardner, Dunham, & Cummings, 1993). These findings suggest that employee attitudes, self-esteem, and social comparison processes are intricately linked.

Finally, another stream of work that is worthy of consideration is the search for other personality correlates of jealousy and envy. Some evidence suggests that individuals who are characterizable as external on locus of control, dispositionally dogmatic, or highly insecure tend to be more jealous, while Machiavellianism is not clearly related to jealousy (Bringle & Buunk, 1985; De Moja, 1986; Mathes, Roter, & Joerger, 1982; White, 1984). Evidence on personality correlates of envy is essentially nonexistent. However, highly competitive individuals and highly Machiavellian individuals may experience stronger feelings of envy. Machiavellians, however, may be better able to hide their envious feelings and thereby be better able to maintain effective working relationships. A similar line of reasoning applies to the personality construct of self-monitoring (Snyder, 1974). Individuals who can be characterized as "high" self-monitors, relative to "low" self-monitors, are more attentive to the images that others may form of them through social interactions. Because of their concern with the impression they may convey, they tend to tailor their behavior to fit the constraint of social appropriateness. We would predict, therefore, that self-monitoring would be correlated positively with individual ability to conceal jealous and envious feelings.

MANAGERIAL RESPONSES TO NEGATIVE EMOTIONS

From a practical perspective, it is important to consider how an organization might seek to manage negative social emotions. Deliberate statements by managers of concern for equity and fair treatment may help to create a climate that emphasizes sensitivity to the impact of behaviors (Greenberg, Bies, & Eskew, 1991). Also, providing a forum for discussing how decisions are made, and policies are formulated, may be of value. Additionally, it may be possible to ameliorate feelings of jealousy and envy by boosting an individual's self-esteem. Managers who can foresee that a subordinate may react negatively to an upcoming event, may be in a position to reduce or avert ill will by the administration of praise and recognition. Such a tactic would likely backfire, however, if the subordinate felt that the praise and recognition were deliberately calculated to soothe negative feelings. Esteem-raising tactics may also be effective following the experience of jealousy or envy, perhaps in part because of the distracting quality of esteem-enhancement. Furthermore, the experience of low self-esteem may be qualitatively different for men and women. Research on the relation of self-esteem and ease of persuasability has found that low self-esteem females appear to be alienated from, and rejecting of, attitude-influence attempts, whereas an inverse relationship was found for males (Gergen & Bauer, 1967). This suggests that influence attempts may need to be qualitatively different for males and females.

The assisting of subordinates who may be experiencing jealousy and envy may also be accomplished by giving such subordinates a greater sense of inclusivity in unit activities. As one of the consequences of these negative emotions tends to be brooding and a feeling of being left out, it may be possible to minimize negative consequences by deliberately involving affected subordinates in a broader range of ongoing unit activities.

Subordinates who may be most resistant to feelings of envy and jealousy may be those who are able to engage in self-bolstering and selective ignoring (Salovey & Rodin, 1988). Self-bolstering enables individuals to raise their own esteem by focusing thoughts on personal strengths and positive attributes. Selective ignoring enables individuals to focus thoughts on alternative issues and thereby ignore potentially troubling events. It is questionable, from a human resources development standpoint, as to whether such broad socially adaptive traits can be actively developed in the work setting. Perhaps, from a personnel selection standpoint, it may be possible to identify individuals who display sufficient self-confidence so that they are less likely to be troubled by feelings of jealousy and envy. One can imagine such individuals in terms of being highly mature psychologically, in the sense of being "at peace" with themselves and their surroundings. Attempting to specify the nature of such interpersonally nontroubled individuals brings to mind the prototype of the self-actualized individual who has found personal fulfillment and is not easily troubled by (petty) social conflicts because of having attained a more transcendent view of social dynamics.

The relatively recent approach to fostering employee commitment via self-managed work teams may offer a practical device for minimizing workplace jealousy and envy (Osborn, Moran, Musselwhite, & Zenger, 1990). In self-managed teams, employees have a reduced sense of possessiveness concerning work assignments (as a consequence of mandatory job rotation and limitations on job titles/levels) and working relationships (as a consequence of job rotation, as well as a diminished role for the supervisor as a central authority figure). With shared responsibility for task completion and the deliberate elimination of "turf," self-managed teams provide a model that is distinct from traditional, hierarchical work systems. As a consequence, the magnitude of workplace jealousy and envy that may be found in self-managed or semi-autonomous teams may be significantly lower than in traditional settings. Lessened dependency of the subordinates on their supervisor for information, direction, job assignments, and other job benefits should also aid in the formation of mutual dependency linkages among team members. Jealousy on the part of supervisors toward preferred subordinates could also be lessened because of the diminished attach-

ment/dependency of supervisors on a select subset of dependable subordinates. Because of reduced levels of jealousy, members of self-managed
teams would also engage in less coping-strategy behaviors (cf. Tables 1
and 2). That is to say, one would expect to find less derogation of co-
workers, or projection of resentment and hostility derived from employee
jealousy. Employee envy may also be at lower levels in self-managed
teams as the compensation system is often of a skill-based nature, and job
rotation eliminates the creation of fiefdoms and the holding of "cushy"
jobs by select employees.

It should be noted that the creation of an utopian-type of work environment, where feelings of employee possessiveness toward others are
essentially eliminated, is highly unlikely. As observed by James (1890)
and Kinsey, Pomeroy, Martin, and Gebhard (1953), jealousy and envy
are fairly innate reactions.[5] This view, however, does not negate the
study of employee negative emotion as a socially conditioned phenomenon. Moreover, the results of efforts to create utopian social units
(communes), where nonpossessiveness or openness to sharing includes
sharing spouses, have shown that jealousy and competitiveness are persistent social problems (Stearns, 1989, p. 35).

CONCLUDING COMMENT

Not that many years ago the suggestion that one would seriously
attempt to study jealousy or envy in the workplace would probably have
brought snickers or jeers from an academic audience.[6] The topic was
seen as trivial, perhaps somewhat suggestive of employee infantilism,
and certainly an issue that the proper application of "rational problem-
solving logic" could easily overcome.

Today, jealousy and envy are less likely to be seen as reflective of
infantilism or as inherently abnormal responses, which might be
viewed as indications of a defective personality. Fortunately, most
day-to-day experiences of workplace jealousy and envy are relatively
more "benign" than pathological in nature. However, the cumulative
effects of experiencing such negative emotions would not necessarily
be benign. Therefore, negative emotion at work needs to be better
understood, and not ignored. As the antecedents and consequences of
negative emotion at work are not fully understood, the study of
negative emotion offers a rich ground for original research. For the

near-term, we need to expand our understanding of the immediate reality of felt emotion at work, and its impact on work relations. For the long term, our goals, however, should include the creation of techniques for effectively managing and constructively channeling negative emotion at work.

NOTES

1. It must be noted that the real Salieri's alleged complicity in Mozart's death is, in fact, rejected by historians (Kupferberg, 1986), although there is a substantial amount of written correspondence by members of the Mozart family which attests to rivalry and intrigue between the two composers (Stafford, 1991).

2. Although a number of alternative definitions of jealousy have been offered, they differ from the above by emphasizing either threat to self-esteem (Mead, 1931; Farber, 1973), threat to the valued relationship (Neu, 1980; Vuyk, 1959), or a sense of exclusivity or possessiveness (Ausubel, Sullivan, & Ives, 1980).

3. For the sake of clarity, it is necessary to note that an "emotion," strictly speaking, occurs when sympathetic arousal is noticeable, while "feelings" are evaluative cognitive states that have a low level of arousal. "Affect" is a broader term that encompasses both emotion and feeling (Berscheid, 1983).

4. Somewhat surprisingly, even minimal contact between individuals can result in extreme violence. In an examination of the topic of malicious behavior, Berke (1988) reports a case of a security guard in London who murdered a visiting American banker who was out for a stroll. When arrested by police, the guard responded that he had felt lonely, degraded—an outcast from society—and that he felt cheated upon meeting a man who looked "rich and comfortable."

5. The neurological base of jealousy is suggested by examples of the sudden onset of pathological delusional jealousy (aptly termed, Othello's syndrome) that results from right hemispheric pathology (e.g., a right-middle cerebral artery infarction). Treatment of pathological delusional jealousy is successfully accomplished with the application or withdrawal of certain drugs (pimozide and amantadine, respectively), thereby underscoring the link of neuropharmacology and behavior (McNamar & Durso, 1991).

6. I am not as certain that a candid group of managers would have dismissed the topic as readily, if at all.

REFERENCES

Anderson, N. H. (1968). Likableness ratings of 555 personality-trait words. *Journal of Personality and Social Psychology, 9,* 272–279.

Ausubel, D. P., Sullivan, E. V., Freeman, W. H., & Ives, S. W. (1980). *Theory and problems of child development.* New York: Grune and Stratton.

Banks, S. P., & Kahn, M.D. (1982). *The sibling bond.* New York: Basic Books.

Berscheid, E. (1983). Emotion. In H. H. Kelley, E. Berscheid, A. Christensen, J. H. Harvey, T. L. Huston, G. Levinger, E. McClintock, L. A. Peplan & O. R. Peterson (Eds.), *Close relationships* (pp. 110–168). San Francisco: W. H. Freeman.

Brayfield, A. H., & Rothe, H. F. (1951) An index of job satisfaction. *Journal of Applied Psychology, 35*, 307–311.

Bringle, R. G. (1981). Conceptualizing jealousy as a disposition. *Alternative Lifestyles, 4*, 274–290.

Bringle, R. G., & Buunk, B. (1985). Jealousy and social behavior. *Review of Personality and Social Psychology, 6*, 241–264.

Brockner, J. (1988). *Self-esteem at work: Research, theory, and practice.* Lexington, MA: Lexington.

Brockner, J., & Adsit, L. (1986). The moderating effect of sex on the equity-satisfaction relationship. *Journal of Applied Psychology, 71*, 585–590.

Brockner, J., & Kim, D. (1987). *The effects of turnover on those who stay: A social comparison analysis.* Unpublished manuscript. [Cited in Brockner, J. (1988). *Self-esteem at work: Research theory and practice* (pp. 80–81). Lexington, MA: Lexington.]

Bryson, J. B. (1976). *The nature of sexual jealousy: An exploratory paper.* Paper presented at annual meeting of the American Psychological Association.

Buunk, R. (1982). Anticipated sexual jealousy: Its relationship to self-esteem, dependence and reciprocity. *Personality and Social Psychology Bulletin, 8*, 310–316.

Buss, D., Larsen, R., Westen, D., & Semmelroth, J. (1992). Sex differences in jealousy: Evolution, physiology, and psychology. *Psychological Science, 3*, 251–255.

Clanton, G. (1989). Jealousy in American culture, 1945–1985: Reflections from popular literature. In D.D. Franks & E.D. McCarthy (Eds.), *The sociology of emotions: Original essays and research papers.* Greenwich, CT: JAI Press.

Clanton, G., & Smith, L.G. (1977). *Jealousy.* Englewood Cliffs, NJ: Prentice-Hall.

De Moja, C. A. (1986). Anxiety, self-confidence, jealousy, and romantic attitudes toward love in Italian undergraduates. *Psychological Reports, 58*, 138.

Dittrich, J., & Carrell, M. (1979). Organizational equity perceptions, employee job satisfaction, and departmental absence and turnover rates. *Organizational Behavior and Human Performance, 24*, 29–40.

Dunn, J. (1983). Sibling relationships in early childhood. *Child Development, 54*, 787–811.

Farber, L. H. (1973). On jealousy. *Commentary, 55*, 180–202.

Festinger, L. (1954). A theory of social comparison. *Human Relations, 7*, 117–140.

Foa, E. B., & Foa, U. G. (1980). Resource Theory: Interpersonal behavior as exchange. In M.K. Gergen, M.S. Greenberg, & R.H. Willis (Eds.), *Social exchange* (pp. 77–102). New York: Plenum.

Foster, G. (1972). The anatomy of envy: A study of symbolic behavior. *Current Anthropology, 13*, 165–202.

Gayford, J. J. (1979). Battered wives. *British Journal of Hospital Medicine, 22,* 496–503.

Gergen, K., & Bauer, R. (1967). The interactive effects of self-esteem and task difficulty in social conformity. *Journal of Personality and Social Psychology, 6,* 16–22.

Graen, G., & Cashman, J.F. (1975). A role-making model of leadership in formal organizations: A developmental approach. In J.G. Hunt & L.L. Larson (Eds.), *Leadership frontiers* (pp. 143–165). Kent, OH: Kent State University Press.

Greenberg, J., Bies, R. J., & Eskew, D. E. (1991). Establishing fairness in the eye of the beholder. In R. Giacalone & P. Rosenfeld (Eds.), *Applied impression management* (pp. 111–132). Newbury Park, CA: Sage.

Hansen, G. L. (1982). Reactions to hypothetical jealousy. *Alternative Lifestyles, 4,* 310–356.

Hansen, G. (1985). Perceived threats and marital jealousy. *Social Psychology Quarterly, 48,* 262–268.

Hupka, R. B. (1984). Jealousy: Compound emotion or label for a particular situation? *Motivation and Emotion, 8,* 141–155.

James, W. (1890). *Principles of psychology.* New York: Henry Holt.

Kahn, A. (1972). Reactions to the generosity or stinginess of an intelligent or stupid work partner: A test of equity theory on a direct exchange relationship. *Journal of Personality and Social Psychology, 21,* 116–123.

Kahn, A., O'Leary, V., Krulewitz, J. E., & Lamm, H. (1980). Equity and equality: Men and women means to a just end. *Basic and Applied Social Psychology, 1,* 173–197.

Kanungo, R. (1982). Measurement of job and work involvement. *Journal of Applied Psychology, 67,* 341–349.

Kinsey, A. C., Pomeroy, W.B., Martin, C. E., & Gebhard, P. H. (1953). *Sexual behavior in the human female.* Philadelphia: W.B. Saunders.

Kupferberg, H. (1986). *Amadeus: A Mozart mosaic.* New York: McGraw-Hill.

Mathes, E. W., Phillips, J. T., Skowran, J., & Dick, W. E. (1982). Behavioral correlates of the Interpersonal Jealousy Scale. *Educational and Psychological Measurement, 42,* 1227–1230.

Mathes, E. W., Roter, P. M., & Joerger, S. M. (1982). A convergent validity study of six jealousy scales. *Psychological Reports, 50,* 1143–1147.

Mathieu, J., & Zajac, D. (1990). A review and meta-analysis of the antecedents, correlates, and consequences of organizational commitment. *Psychological Bulletin, 108,* 171–194.

McNamar, P., & Durso, R. (1991). Reversible pathologic jealousy (Othello syndrome) associated with amantadine. *Journal of Geriatric Psychiatry and Neurology, 4,* 157–159.

Mead, M. (1931). Jealousy: Primitive and civilized. In S. D. Schmalhauser & V. F. Calverton (Eds.), *Woman's coming of age* (pp. 35–48). New York: Horace Liverlight.

Melamed, T. (1991). Individual differences in romantic jealousy: The moderating effect of relationship characteristics. *European Journal of Social Psychology, 21,* 455–461.

Miner, F. C. (1990, April). Jealousy on the job. *Personnel,* pp. 89–95.

Nadler, A., & Dotan, I. (1992). Commitment and rival attractiveness: Their effects on male and female reactions to jealousy-arousing situations. *Sex Roles, 26,* 293–310.

Nieva, V. F., & Gutek, B. A. (1981). *Women and work: A psychological perspective.* New York: Praeger.

Osburn, J. D., Moran, L., Musselwhite, E., & Zenger, J. H. (1990). *Self-directed work teams.* Homewood, IL: Irwin.

Parrott, W.G. (1991). The emotional experiences of envy and jealousy. In P. Salovey (Ed.), *The psychology of jealousy and envy* (pp. 3–30). New York: Guilford Press.

Parrott, W. G., & Smith, R. H. (1993). Distinguishing the experiences of envy and jealousy. *Journal of Personality and Social Psychology, 64,* 906–920.

Pierce, J. L., Gardner, D. G., Cummings, L. L., & Dunham, R. B. (1989). Organization-based self-esteem: Construct definition, measurement, and validation. *Academy of Management Journal, 32,* 622–648.

Pierce, J., Gardner, D., Dunham, R., & Cummings, L. (1993). Moderation by organization-based self-esteem of role condition-employee response relationships. *Academy of Management Journal, 36,* 271–288.

Salovey, P. (1991). *The psychology of jealousy and envy.* New York: Guilford Press.

Salovey, P., & Rodin, J. (1986). The differentiation of social-comparison jealousy and romantic jealousy. *Journal of Personality and Social Psychology, 50,* 1100–1112.

Salovey, P., & Rodin, J. (1988). Coping with envy and jealousy. *Journal of Social and Clinical Psychology, 7,* 15–33.

Salovey, P., & Rodin, J. (1991). Provoking jealousy and envy: Domain relevance and self-esteem threat. *Journal of Social and Clinical Psychology, 10,* 395–413.

Selye, H. (1976). *The stress of life.* New York: McGraw-Hill.

Shaffer, P. (1981). *Amadeus: A play.* New York: Harper and Row.

Simmel, G. (1955). *Conflict and the web of group affiliation.* Glencoe, IL: Free Press.

Smith, P. C., Kendall, L. N., & Hulin, C. L. (1969). *The measurement of satisfaction in work and retirement.* Chicago: Rand-McNally.

Smith, R. H., Kim, S. H., & Parrott, W. F. (1988). Envy and jealousy: Semantic problems and experimental distinctions. *Personality and Social Psychology Bulletin, 14,* 401–409.

Snyder, M. (1974). The self-monitoring of expressive behavior. *Journal of Personality and Social Psychology, 30,* 526–537.

Sommers, S. (1984). Adults evaluating their emotions. A cross-cultural perspective. In C. Malatesta & C. Izard (Eds.), *Emotion in adult development* (pp. 161–185). Beverly Hills, CA: Sage.

Spencer, D. G., & Steers, R. M. (1980). The influence of personal factors and perceived work experiences on employee turnover and absenteeism. *Academy of Management Journal, 23,* 567–572.

Sprouse, M. (1992). *Sabotage in the American workplace.* San Francisco: Pressure Drop Press.

Stafford, W. (1991). *The Mozart myths: A critical reassessment.* Stanford, CA: Stanford University Press.

Stearns, P. N. (1989). *Jealousy: The evolution of an emotion in American history.* New York: New York University Press.

Stets, J., & Pirog-Good, M. A. (1987). Violence in dating relationships. *Social Psychology Quarterly, 50,* 237–246.

Tetlock, P. E., & Manstead, A. S. R. (1985). Impression management versus intrapsychic exploration in social psychology: A useful dichotomy? *Psychological Review, 92,* 59–77.

Todd, J., & Dewhurst, K. (1955). The Othello syndrome: A study of the psychopathology of sexual jealousy. *Journal of Nervous and Mental Disease, 112,* 367–374.

Van Sommers, P. (1988). *Jealousy.* London: Penguin Books.

Vecchio, R. P. (1993a). *Employee jealousy: Antecedents, consequences, and testable hypotheses.* Paper presented at 1993 Meeting of the Western Academy of Management, San Jose, CA.

White, G. L. (1981a). A model of romantic jealousy. *Motivation and Emotion, 5,* 295–310.

White, G. L. (1981b). Some correlates of romantic jealousy. *Journal of Personality, 49,* 129–147.

White, G. L. (1984). Comparison of four jealousy scales. *Journal of Research in Personality, 18,* 115–130.

White, G. L. (1985). Gender, power, and romantic jealousy. Unpublished manuscript. University of Auckland, Auckland, New Zealand.

White, G. L., & Mullen, P. E. (1989). *Jealousy: Theory, research, and clinical strategies.* New York: Guilford Press.

NAME INDEX

About the Editor

ROBERT P. VECCHIO (Ph.D. University of Illinois) holds the Franklin D. Schurz Chair in Management at the University of Notre Dame. Since joining the University in 1976, Professor Vecchio has taught and conducted research on organizational behavior and human resources management, with special emphasis on leadership. Currently, Professor Vecchio teaches an undergraduate and MBA class devoted exclusively to the topic of leadership and effective supervision. He has also been an instructor in the University's Supervisory Development Program for over 20 years. From 1983 to 1990, Professor Vecchio served as head of the Department of Management of Administrative Sciences at Notre Dame. He has served on the editorial boards of the *Academy of Management Review*, the *Journal of Management*, the *Journal of Managerial Inquiry, Employee Responsibilities and Rights Journal*, the *International Journal of Applied Quality Management,* and the *International Journal of Organizational Analysis*. In 1995, he assumed the role of Editor-in-Chief of the *Journal of Management*, the first journal to be headquartered in the College of Business Administration at the University of Notre Dame. The *Journal* is a broad-gauge outlet that publishes rigorous empirical research in all aspects of management, with special emphasis on issues surrounding effective management and leadership, as well as social responsibility and research methods. Professor Vecchio was selected as a Fellow of the Center for Creative Leadership in 1974. In 1975, he was awarded a grant from the U.S. Department of Labor to study the leadership process. He has published numerous articles in such journals as the *Journal of Applied Psychology*, the *Academy of Management Journal*, the *Academy of Management Review, Organizational Behavior and Human Performance*, the *Journal of Management*, the *Journal of Organizational Behavior, Leadership Quarterly*, and *Human Relations*. He is also the author of *Organizational Behavior*, a book published by Dryden Press, which is now in its third edition, as well as international editions. Professor Vecchio has served as a consultant to both for-profit and not-for-profit organizations. He is listed in *Who's Who in America* and *Who's Who in the World*.